LIGHTNINGBOLT

Also by Hyemeyohsts Storm
Published by Ballantine Books

SEVEN ARROWS

SONG OF HEYOEHKAH

LIGHTNINGBOLT

Hyemeyohsts Storm

ONE WORLD

A ONE WORLD BOOK

BALLANTINE BOOKS • NEW YORK

A One World Book
Published by Ballantine Books

Copyright © 1994 by Hyemeyohsts Storm

Medicine Shield Art within the text and on the color plates
are designed by Hyemeyohsts Storm. Medicine Shield Art
copyright © 1994 by Hyemeyohsts Storm.

Maps © 1994 by Laura Hartman Maestro.

Library of Congress Cataloging-in-Publication Data

Storm, Hyemeyohsts.
    Lightningbolt / Hyemeyohsts Storm.—1st ed.
       p.   cm.
    "One World."
    ISBN 0-345-36710-3
    1. Storm, Hyemeyohsts—Biography. 2. Novelists,
American—20th century—Biography.   3. Indians of North
America—Montana—Mixed descent—Biography.   I. Title.
PS3569.T653Z469   1994
813'.54—dc20
[B]   93-14103
                                              CIP

Book design by Alex Jay/Studio J

Manufactured in the United States of America
First Edition: April 1994

10 9 8 7 6 5 4 3 2 1

I am very honored to dedicate this book to
the courageous Zero Chiefs, who faced every
kind of persecution and tyranny, and yet chose
to devote their lives to the protection and
furthering of the Teachings of the Medicine
Wheels. Because of their enduring legacy,
I have been given the greatest of privileges—
the sharing of their history and knowledge
with all of the Earth's people.

ACKNOWLEDGMENTS

It goes without saying that every work of love and importance has been accomplished through great effort. When I began working on *Lightningbolt*, my greatest fear was that I would not be able to portray my teachers, the Zero Chief Estcheemah and her apprentice, Rivers, as they really were—brilliant women of great courage and human devotion. It is not easy to write about holy women and to impart sacred teachings—and not be humbled by the experience. So I would like to thank their spirits for guidance, protection, and inspiration.

Beyond this, I extend my first thanks to my intimate partner in writing and in Medicine, my wife, Swan Storm, (Stephanie Leonard-Storm). We traveled extensively together in Central America and the United States while I wrote *Lightningbolt*. She read and re-read the manuscript countless times, and gave me valuable suggestions and clear-sighted counsel throughout the years of bringing this work to life. Her dedication and support made this book possible.

I would also like to thank my son and great friend, Rocky Storm, and my beautiful friend, Osprey Leveton, who assisted me with their love and enduring support. And I thank all of my dear friends, Sage, Sean, Star, Moon, Willow, Rainbow, Earth Bear, Siegrund, China, Wind, Ocean, Red Wolf, Tiger, Forest, Maiygyne, Gazelle, Wyolah, Kachina, Impala, Dragon, Black Wolf, Bert and Family, who each offered a special giveaway to this book.

My deep appreciation must also be expressed to my wonderful agent and friend, Gloria Loomis, who has done much to insure the publication of this work, and I truly thank her.

I would also like to thank the staff at Ballantine Books. Their many hands joined together to make this book a reality, and none have been more generous than those of Barbara Shor, Pru See, designer Alex Jay, and most especially Jeff Doctoroff, who spent countless hours coordinating the final art.

And finally, I'd like to thank my patient and brave editor, Cheryl D. Woodruff, who survived many fiery faxes and an ocean of work. She helped me to create the visual and verbal unity of this work and uphold its integrity.

PREFACE

This is the story of what it was that changed my life.

In this book you will meet Lightningbolt. I, Hyemeyohsts, am Lightningbolt. There are two reasons I use this name and title my book *Lightningbolt*. There were people who were very precious to me who called me by that name.

The second reason I use the name Lightningbolt is that I am no longer the same young man. I am now in my fifties. Lightningbolt became Hyemeyohsts.

Many people expect me to be the same person I was when I wrote *Seven Arrows* and *Song of Heyoehkah*. It startles me how time transforms us all.

Lightningbolt tells the story of how I met Estcheemah, my teacher. Woven through the text, you will find four distinct and important sections. They detail some of the history of the Flower Soldiers, and the ancient teachings of Estcheemah and other Zero Chiefs who lived before her.

In the story you are about to experience, you will journey along with Lightningbolt on his search for his identity and freedom. You will be present with him as he battles his massive ignorance.

There is not a lot of explaining about what young Lightningbolt is seeking during the opening episodes of the book, so have patience. Allow yourself to not know, and ride along with Lightningbolt through Montana and Wyoming and through his time. The picture will become clearer as you and Lightningbolt get to know one another.

You who want everything told can read the last page of the book and be satisfied.

Who was Estcheemah, my teacher?

Estcheemah was many things and many people to me. For others who "knew" her, she was some of the following: She was an "ordinary" woman. She was a "Spic," a "witch," "a nobody." She was a "powerful Medicine Woman," a "Holy Woman." And she was "a woman who visited the Reservation once in a while."

For me, Estcheemah was the most important and wisest human being who ever lived on Earth. She was a Zero Chief and a healer. But before I began to learn from her, I thought of her simply as an older Indian woman I saw in the company of our tribal Elders.

When I first met Estcheemah, I was looking for "power." The problem was—I didn't know what power meant. At the time, Estcheemah didn't speak to me about power. But I quickly realized that she was saying things no other Indian was saying.

Soon after I met her she began to talk about Flower Soldiers. I'd never heard of such a thing and wondered what she meant. Estcheemah also told me other things that blew my mind:

"Beauty births us.

"Experience is Life.

"Life brings Measure.

"Life-Measure ends our ignorance."

You can come and sit with me in Wyoming, at Estcheemah's home, when she told me, "You have to appreciate and learn to love a potato. Also a carrot, the chickens you eat and, yes, even a cow."

What? What was she saying? I was looking for power, not how to love a cow! And why was she talking about potatoes? Were potatoes the secret elixir of life? I wondered at this point if she really was the witch everybody had warned me about.

"Potatoes," she said, "keep us alive."

Why was she so concerned with keeping us alive? What did she expect—for us to suddenly die?

The Reservation at that time was a breathing volcano of superstition, fears of vengeful gods, ghosts, and "Doing the BIG IT right," which meant doing the ritual right or you would be "instantly killed."

Because of this kind of "thinking," I expected at any moment that Estcheemah would scream: "Run for your life!" And, of course, I would have run.

Estcheemah never once told me to run for my life. Instead, she told me to sit down, and to stop running as though my life were going to suddenly end.

While I sat with her, expecting her to hand out magical gourds, she kept asking me if "I had purpose in my life."

Finally, she asked me a question I could answer: "What do you want from me?"

My immediate essentials were simple. I wanted unlimited personal power, millions of dollars, perfect friends, magical baubles, charms, and weapons that would impress friends and foes alike. Now that I had met a real magician, all I had to do was ask—and *presto!*—all these things would be mine.

WRONG!

Estcheemah continued to ask me if I had any respect for the things that had been given to me here in THIS WORLD.

She always made the words, "this world," sound so extraordinary. It made me wonder if she and I lived in the same world.

We didn't.

I lived for the most part in my head—in my fantasies and my beliefs. I lived in the past, worried about the future, and never had enough time.

Estcheemah lived always in her present, loved Life, and was happy to share her abundant time and knowledge.

The old Zero Chief, the Medicine Woman, gave me a peach to "meditate upon."

"A peach," I was told, "is Sacred. Just as a po-tato is Sacred." She emphasized that everything we call our food is not money, but instead is Holy and part of Mother Life.

I had never thought of a cheese sandwich that way before, and so I had to work hard to try to understand her teaching. Estcheemah completely changed my thinking about everything!

The world is indebted to Estcheemah. The information she has given to all of us is of the utmost value. However, she herself did not want to be known. She was satisfied to teach her "apprentices." She didn't live a secluded life, but she also wasn't a person that everyone could claim they knew.

Because it is my duty to protect the precious, I have changed names, dates, places, and times. I have also decided not to share intimate details of Ceremonies in this book because, without trained and expert guidance, they can be dangerous or abused through ignorance. It is one thing to write about Ceremonies, and quite another thing to have lived them.

Life is our Great Teacher. The most profound reason for the existence of Life is that each person has the opportunity to experience Life and to learn Self-Responsibility. Who we are and how we live our Lives is our great question and wondrous answer. I learned this while I was with Estcheemah.

The greatest gift that Estcheemah shared with me was teaching me how to teach myself. She said: "Self-Teaching is one of the most profound reasons that humans live. When we teach the Self, we recognize the Spirit of Mother Life and learn to respect the Energies that birthed us all."

So Earth Wanderer, welcome to Life and the adventure of Lightningbolt.

LOVE,
Hyemeyohsts,
a.k.a. Lightningbolt

INTRODUCTION

My name is Hyemeyohsts Storm. I am the author of *Seven Arrows* and *The Song of Heyoehkah*. Those of you who are familiar with my earlier works know me as Hyemeyohsts. However, only the tiniest handful of people knew me as Lightningbolt.

Countless numbers of people have asked me how to say my name. Hyemeyohsts is pronounced "Hi-yuh-may-yoh-sts."

Twenty years ago, when I was much younger, it was difficult to write a book like *Seven Arrows*. The reason for this was that I was inexperienced at such tasks.

The book was immediately set upon by "experts" who had never heard of the Medicine Wheels or their teachings. I might point out that when *Seven Arrows* was published, people in America and Europe had not heard of Chinese acupuncture either, despite the fact that millions of Asians had been utilizing it for centuries.

Part of the difficulty was that the "primitivity" of Indians had been so ingrained into American and European thinking that few people would accept the existence of the Medicine Wheels, or the highly sophisticated discipline of thought that was born from them.

One anthropologist argued with me, saying: "The American Indian has not demonstrated the sophistication needed to understand a philosophy as complex as what Mr. Storm proposes."

To add to this, certain Reservation "experts" also attacked the book—mostly because I was not a "Full-Blood." "Breeds" are not considered to be experts on anything on Reservations, except perhaps raising cattle.

The Medicine Wheels are very old. They are as ancient as the first Americans themselves. *Seven Arrows* was a simple introduction to our Medicine Wheels. *Lightningbolt* begins where *Seven Arrows* left off.

You will notice, as you leaf through the pages, that there are four special teaching sections at very important places within the story of *Lightningbolt*. These reveal some of what I learned during different times in my early life.

Some people will be drawn to read all about Lightningbolt's quest. Others will be drawn for years to the teaching sections of the book. The truth is, humans do not learn separately from living. This is why it is so important to have Lightningbolt's story interwoven with the profound teachings that he had the great opportunity to learn.

This knowledge was taught to me by Estcheemah, one of the latest of a long, unbroken line of Zero Chiefs. Much of their information was studied and taught in many ancient Temple-Schools of the Americas and passed down through the discipline of the Flower Soldiers. I have worked to make the ancient wisdom in this book very accessible to every reader.

For those of you who read my book *Song of Heyoehkah*, the name Estcheemah is familiar. Rainbow, Estcheemah's mother, and Dancing Tree, Estcheemah's father, as well as Little Wolf and his wife, Dreamer, all appear in that book. Estcheemah was the baby girl born at the end of the story.

In *Song of Heyoehkah*, I spelled Estcheemah's name "Estchimah." However, no one seemed to be able to pronounce the name correctly. It should sound this way: "Est-*chee*-mah."

I was born and raised on the Northern Cheyenne and Crow Reservations, which exist side by side in southeastern Montana. I am an enrolled Indian on the Cheyenne Reservation.

My kind and gentle mother, and her very large extended family of many Tribes and Reservations, birthed me into a world that was massive. There was not only the large extended Indian and Breed family of the Cheyenne and Crow Reservations, but there were other relatives on many other Reservations too.

Montana is a grand and beautiful part of America—147,138 square miles in area. As a good comparison, the United Kingdom of Great Britain and Northern Ireland, with a population of about 57 million people, has 94,226 square miles. Montana's population was around 350,000 when I was young. The consequence of this was that my back yard, the place where I played, was hundreds of miles wide and deep.

America has changed dramatically since I was a boy. The Montana, Dakotas, Wyoming, and Canada I knew are now all part of a bygone time. Keep this in mind while you're reading about my past.

I grew up traveling. This is common for many people who live on Reservations. Family, Medicine, rodeos, and Powwows lure them to wonderful places. Journeying through Canada, North Dakota, South Dakota, Montana, Wyoming, Oklahoma, Texas, New Mexico, and Mexico is very normal.

My growing-up experience occurred in a world of Indians and Breeds. My education as a Breed American is a gift few people on Mother Earth can appreciate. I think that *Lightningbolt* will tell some of the story of what it means to be a Breed.

Breeds are also called Metis. Who and what are the Metis? The word *Metis*, or *Mestizo*, means "mixed bloods." Metis, or Breeds, are people of many kinds of mixed blood. Most people think of the word *breed* in terms of plants and animals. A crossbreed of plants or animals is thought to be a heartier being.

I am a Breed of many places and many races. My mother was born Cheyenne, Sioux, and Irish-American. My father was born in northern Germany and later became an American.

In the part of Montana where I came from, it was very common to hear many languages spoken on a daily basis because there are many races and peoples there. I myself speak quite a few languages.

I was very young when my family moved from the Northern Cheyenne Reservation to the Crow Reservation, and although the Cheyenne language is well known to me, I am more familiar with the Crow tongue. Because of my many relatives, I also learned other Native tongues, including Cree and Sioux, and later learned to speak Mexican-Indian-Spanish and American English.

There were five distinct kinds of American English spoken on the Reservations where I grew up. First, there were two very different dialects of Reservation English spoken by the Cheyennes and the Crows. I learned to mimic both.

The third form of American English was spoken by the ranchers and farmers, and believe me, it is still unique. The fourth language, which we were all spoon-fed in school, was the stilted verbosity of the academic world.

The fifth kind of American English introduced to us all was that of the media. This language was a delicate mixture of Porky Pig, Donald Duck, Southern Georgian (my favorite schoolteacher), New Yorker, Texan, and Televisionese.

All these languages taught me to be the American I became, and all have influenced my thinking.

How does being a Mixed-Blood person enrich my life? A Half-Breed, or Breed, as I am called, is born into so many diverse cultures and languages that he or she is given a unique view of Life. Breeds can get along with almost anyone.

A Breed exists between cultures and can understand a lot of what transpires between systems and peoples. The Breed person moves easily among these many worlds.

Breeds are survivors—we have to be.

Now that I'm older and a lot more contemplative, I can see why Estcheemah wanted me to be one of her apprentices. She chose me because she believed I would endure. Breeds develop the strength to endure, because we are not a protected group in any society. Estcheemah also chose me because I had learned to walk between cultures.

Lightningbolt is the story of my learning as a Breed Indian.

From the moment I could crawl around in the dust of the Northern Cheyenne Reservation, I knew about war. Graphic stories were shared honestly with Reservation children by the old people, Breeds and Indians, who had survived the terror of the Indian Wars.

By the time the Declaration of Independence was signed, thousands of Europeans had intermarried with Native American Indians. These Breed families had been living in North America for well over two hundred years. This meant that by the time the Indian Wars were fought, many Breed families had lived in America for over four hundred years.

The old people told us gruesome stories of how the Indians and Breeds had been forced to live on the Reservations. We heard all about the many battles, with their sorrowful and bloody details.

Stories abounded of the Breed families—white Indian Breeds, black Indian Breeds, and Creoles—who had fought with either the South or the North during the heartbreaking American Civil War. The history of this conflict cannot be equaled for pain and death. Most of the Breeds were related to families on both sides of the conflict.

It must also not be forgotten that the wars that destroyed Breeds and Indians were fought in Canada and Mexico as well. For example, many Spanish-Indian Breed families were caught in the bloody war that the United States fought with Mexico in order to possess the lands now known as the American Southwest.

Breeds and Indians were also drafted into the Spanish-American War, the First World War, the Second World War, the Korean War, and the Vietnam War, where they fought bravely. Others had served in a hundred different kinds of military "emergencies, conflicts, and police actions" that preceded the Vietnam War.

All the time I was growing up, I knew nothing but war. War stories, war games, bloody pictures of war, and the veterans of war were as ordinary to me as the dirt I played in.

Vietnam was a special war, though, because it changed the thinking of many Americans forever. At the time in which I came of age, Americans watched real people die on television every night while they ate dinner. I became completely disenchanted with the America I knew and the propaganda I heard.

We young people on the Reservations wanted to win. We wanted to win with all of our hearts, but we didn't know who the enemy was or how to fight. Defeat whom? With what?

The black people in America were also fighting a war—one to belong to America. They were dying like other brothers in Vietnam, but what were they winning?

How do young people fight against apathy and win? It was apathy that was killing everyone on the Reservations, and we didn't know how to combat it. There were no wise leaders talking to the Reservation youth about anything real.

The war heroes who returned from Vietnam were treated like criminals by most Americans. Vietnam had become a symbol of defeat and cruelty for many of America's youth.

On every Reservation, the veterans of the Second World War and Korea were shattered and disappointed men who had seen it all before. It had been impossible for those Breed and Indian vets to find work after they returned.

With Vietnam vets all over the country having a very hard time, why wouldn't the Indian, the Breed, and the black Vietnam vets be discriminated against? They had always been treated as second-class citizens, always left out of what they had fought to preserve. Wasn't that the game every Breed and Indian knew as white American justice?

I spoke daily with these sorrowful men and heard their desperate unhappiness. They had fought for America's freedom, but they had been cheated out of their own.

And what of Mother Earth—who cared for Her? There seemed to be two Americas—the America we all lived in, and pretend-America. A tiny handful of our parents and Chiefs continued telling us to honor and cherish Mother Earth. But pretend-America seemed to hate Her or ignored Her importance altogether.

The people of pretend-America insisted that our Earth was something that we mined, or built upon to have some kind of address. Many people I knew either despised Mother Earth or thought of Her as "dead matter." I couldn't understand how dead matter had birthed everything alive—including me.

I kept asking questions and ran into some strange answers. There were people who quoted Shakespeare, declaring that our Earth is but a mighty stage where humans act out their nonsense. Others looked to the teachings of the Church that insist our Earth is "the place of devils and monsters" and should not be trusted. Many of the businesspeople I met believed that our Earth is a cesspool. The more I heard the more heartbroken I became.

Only Estcheemah, the Flower Soldier and Zero Chief, had the brilliance and Self power to reach into my sorrowful world and bring knowledge and healing.

The Zero Chiefs
and the Flower Soldiers

In this work, *Lightningbolt*, you will meet my teacher, Estcheemah, the Zero Chief. This woman was the wisest and most powerful human I have ever known.

The fact that Estcheemah, a brilliant teacher and powerful Zero Chief, was a woman was profoundly important in making me confront many of my erroneous cultural beliefs about myself. She revealed to me the true face of greatness, in that she pointed out how rich Life can be, as well as the power and balance we all can possess but seldom recognize.

Lightningbolt is the first book ever written about the Zero Chiefs—the highest rank possible within the ancient discipline of the Flower Soldiers. These patient, wise, courageous, and powerful teachers discovered and faithfully taught the wisdom and teachings of our ancient Medicine Wheels.

It is of immense importance to all the people of our world to know of the Flower Soldiers and their Zero Chiefs—great women and men of our Earth heritage. They lived and taught among the ancient Maya and many of the other Central American and South American peoples. However, the Sacred Medicine Wheel teachings that they carried dated back many years before the Maya. The Zero Chiefs are also responsible for the discovery of the ancient Circle of Law, the first form of democracy ever created by humans.

For the first time ever, some of this precious

information will be shared in this book. These ancient teachings have survived because of the courageous dedication of a tiny handful of devoted people. The Zero Chiefs endured when there was no chance for survival.

The true power of these Chiefs is the wondrous way they teach the secrets of the human Self and the mysteries of our living Universe. Through their teachings we learn about the nature of war within every human being, and the triumph of the Human Self. They speak of how, through Self Discipline and Knowledge, we can rise above our petty attitudes and triumph within the Circle of human challenge.

All Zero Chiefs taught that valuable information should never be hidden behind scientific or religious jargon, but should be made simple, direct, meaningful, and intimate in our daily lives. The language they have always used to explain highly sophisticated and complex subjects such as Mathematics, Spirit, the Self, and the meaning of our very Existence is truly remarkable, for it is simple, direct, and often very beautiful.

The teachings the Zero Chiefs present to our world can change our lives for the better. Through them, we discover that there is no mysterious, murky, dark side of humans, or of Creation, that people are forced to fall victim to. Instead, we learn the reasons for the battle within the human Self. We learn that human ignorance is our greatest enemy—not Creation, not Life, not our Mother Earth. We also learn many of the reasons we humans were created.

The brilliant Zero Chief Estcheemah began teaching me by challenging me to respect my Self and to understand the human I was then and the one I am now. She gave me the challenge of learning to know my Self. I worked for many years to meet this challenge head-on, and I am presently still actively engaged in that pursuit.

Being taught by a person such as Estcheemah was no easy task. She was incredibly confrontive and aggressive. Yet she possessed so much gentleness and love there was no comprehending it.

Estcheemah taught me that human ignorance and fear are our greatest enemies. She told me that the Zero Chiefs of long ago discovered that humans will do anything, including murder, to escape Self Responsibility. This, she explained to me, is why so many people in our world are confused about who they are and why they are here.

Can you imagine the wonder this kind of talk held for me—an angry young Half-Breed caught between many different realities? Here was a human who knew the true importance and measure of Life. Estcheemah knew our Mother Earth. She had the courage to speak of Creation and all the other things I was so desperate to learn about.

"Life is precious," Estcheemah told me. "It is the most profound of all experiences known in Creation. Life is Sacred and ever present because Life is Presence. To try to escape the rigors and rewards of Mother Life is to escape Existence."

I did not understand all that she was telling me at the time—all her deep teachings about Life and Death—yet her words somehow touched my innermost being. Because of her, my heart was slowly healed from its wounds.

As Estcheemah walked and talked with me through the wide Wyoming prairies, her words excited me. They challenged everything I had ever learned! However, I was not instantly illuminated by what she told me. I had to wait, to grow, to feel the deep pains of my learning, before I would completely understand and treasure her teachings.

As you read this book, my friends, you will see a young man growing up. Estcheemah knew that I was a Half-Breed. And she knew that although Breeds live side by side with "Reservation Indians" or "Full-Bloods," and are "enrolled Indians," in the minds of the "experts," Breeds are not thought of as "authentic."

Estcheemah didn't worry about being authentic, and neither did I. My teacher didn't have to present me with her credentials as a Medicine Woman. In fact, if she had, I would have run in the opposite direction! How she caught my attention and held it for many years was with her brilliant mind and wondrous teaching.

It is very important to keep in mind when reading my story that to be a Flower Soldier means that you have been trained directly by Flower Soldier Chiefs. I was trained for many years to become a Flower Soldier. My lineage of Chiefs goes far back into antiquity.

I say this because there will be those who will try to call themselves Flower Soldiers just because they have heard or read about Flower Soldiers. This is foolish and dangerous. Pretenders have always existed among humans. They will test your discernment. This is the danger whenever new information is shared with people. So, be discerning.

For those people who love Mother Earth, sincere study of our Sacred Medicine Wheels will be deeply rewarding and transforming. You do not have to call yourself a Flower Soldier to be a lover of Mother Earth and a person who decides to be Self Responsible.

Estcheemah chose to bring her teachings into the world not only through the training of Lightningbolt but also by teaching the woman who became my Medicine Twin. The teaching of twins (always one female and one male) has been prevalent in the discipline of the Flower Soldiers because it insures more power and balance in the learning.

Lightningbolt's Medicine Twin, Liberty, was also responsible for the information and teachings given to her by Estcheemah. Being taught as Medicine Twins gave us both the opportunity to learn individually, and to grow together.

I asked Estcheemah why there was so much pain in the world, and why we humans were so much out of balance with Nature.

She answered, "This is because Life was made the enemy, and our Earth has been made the enemy by almost all religions.

"Along with Life and our beautiful Earth, women—all females—are made to be the enemy by every organized religion.

"The deep mental and spiritual harm this kind of belief has brought into all our lives, and the negative way it has affected our minds about our planet, is profound."

Estcheemah's teachings moved my heart and mind. How differently I see Life and our Mother Earth because I have known Estcheemah.

The old Zero Chief taught: "The attempt to ignore our Creatress Mother Goddess is the most crippling blow that all of humanity has ever suffered. The true and absolute Balance of our Creatress Mother and Creator Father is the most Holy and Powerful symbol and reality that can be known to humanity.

"We must restore dignity to humanity. How we will do this is to recognize our Creatress Mother, our Sacred Mother Life. This one act alone will bring a Balance to our sorrowful world."

When I was young and first heard her words, I had no idea of the enormous consequences her teachings held for me and all humans in our world.

While I wrote *Seven Arrows*, I struggled with the academic kind of English language I had been forced to learn. I am still amazed at how much I had been indoctrinated by the language of my schooling. "Mankind" and "men's thoughts" were terms I used while writing *Seven Arrows* instead of choosing "humanity," or "humans," and "people's thoughts." I think it's very important for us all to become aware of how our language has been made masculine.

Maturity must be gained before we humans can do any kind of justice to matters of greatness. I needed time to get close to who Estcheemah was before I could write *Lightningbolt*. Just as I needed to be with her to learn, so you, the reader, should strive to reach into your own heart and mind and move as close as possible to who Estcheemah really was. You have the great opportunity to be touched by this information and knowledge that has never been presented anywhere, in written form, before.

In this culture we are taught to reduce the profound to the tangible. I challenge you as you read this story to not reduce Estcheemah, or the Teachings of the Zero Chiefs, to only the examples shared here. Instead, try to expand the Teachings and reality of Estcheemah into the vastness of who this Holy Woman really was, and the ancient Self Discipline she taught.

LIGHTNINGBOLT

"It's amazing what a rifle and a few matches will do to comfort a man." Young Lightningbolt chuckled as he bridled his horse, Arrow. He turned to take another look at the warm cabin he was leaving.

Once his saddle horse was taken care of, he turned his attention to the big gelding. He carefully checked everything he had tied onto the back of the powerful pack horse. Old Roman Nose also seemed eager to leave.

It was very cold, February cold. The icy air stung his face, causing tears to trickle from his eyes down his cheeks, where they froze. Lightningbolt swung into the saddle, settled himself, then pulled up his Medicine Blanket to shelter his head.

He was not setting out on a romantic ride through the beautiful Little Big Horn Mountains. There was no room for any kind of make-believe. One foolish mistake would kill him and he knew it. Native Montanans, Indian or white, know that

3

Mother Montana nourishes them, but they also know that She kills the foolish.

The task that lay before him was twofold. He would ride the thirty-five miles that separated him from the next cabin, where he would meet old Goose Flying. He would also kill two deer on his way, to provide the food that he and the old Medicine Man would need.

When the roan had taken her first dutiful steps into the cold blue morning light, up and out of the shelter of the canyon that secreted the old cabin, she was eager to travel. She shook her proud head and pawed, then blew a cloud of steam.

"You're strong, Arrow, but Big Nose is slow," he cautioned his mare. "Let's both take it easy, all right? It's spooky here and we're high up in deep snow." He turned to check the pack horse again. "And old Big Nose back there doesn't want no horse races, clear?"

Next, he pulled his .30-06 from the saddle boot and made sure that it was loaded and in good working order. He had done this twice already, once in the cabin the night before and again when the gun went into its sheath.

His eyes traveled along the pack saddle ties and lines that held the bedroll; the sacks of coffee, sugar, and staples; and the two sacks of oats for the horses. All were secure.

Lightningbolt straightened in his saddle and surveyed the countryside. Memory and intelligence told him what lay hidden beneath the snow. He smiled and turned his horse west.

"Hey, Arrow." He touched his mare affectionately.

The spunky bronc tossed up her head and danced. A spark flew from one of her shoes as she kicked a stone. This would be Lightningbolt's first long winter journey with proper horseshoes on his animal. He was very pleased, and he felt confident.

With each step his horse took, he thought about exactly how he was going to get through the Sage Creek Water Gap.

The canyon, called the Water Gap, was treacherous and filled with traps. A thousand hot pools flowed into a deep, narrow gorge. These warm pools were soothing for those who sought healing; but where they gathered together in the large ravine, they became a terror of quicksand and moss-filled bogs.

Lightningbolt had to make a decision. He could plunge in and try to go directly through the canyon, or he could take the long way around the Water Gap. He decided to take his chances in the canyon.

He knew his journey could be extremely hazardous if he were not completely attuned to his task. Ice was the enemy. The hot pools partly thawed the stream, creating large needles and slabs

of floating ice that would have to be avoided.

Most people journeyed to the mountains and the beautiful canyon because of the good grazing for cattle. But there were also those very few who visited for ceremonial reasons.

The young Breed had been born and raised in this country, but he had only been in these particular mountains during the summer months. Although the land was familiar, it seemed alien now with the blanket of snow that covered everything.

Why young Lightningbolt was impudent enough to believe he could survive such a journey was a question he would have to think about for years. But for the moment there was no simple answer.

Even the reasons for his being in the mountains were all wrong. The misunderstanding had begun a few months before, when Lightningbolt had become Goose Flying's student. The very moment Lightningbolt first met his teacher a terrible war had begun that neither of them would ever fully understand. The fast-moving, quick-tempered Lightningbolt contrasted sharply with the gentle old man who was easygoing and slow to make decisions.

There was an insurmountable problem of culture between them. The young Breed lived in his modern Reservation world, while the old man endeavored to live within a time that no longer existed. Their attempts to talk and understand one another were always highly emotional. The result was like white-hot molten steel plunged into cold water. Both men suffered from these outbursts, although both pretended that nothing had happened between them.

Kind old Goose Flying would never deliberately place his student in peril. But the old Medicine Man was also not very attentive to other people's problems—especially their ignorance, and Lightningbolt's ignorance was abysmal.

Goose Flying had promised that he would teach Lightningbolt about Medicine Dreaming when the young man brought him his winter supplies. But it never occurred to him that the student would be so arrogant as to try to make the journey at such a perilous time, or to travel through the dangerous Water Gap.

Goose Flying had enjoyed eleven winters by himself in what he called his Dream Lodge. The three-room cabin, also known as the Willow Rose, had been built in a small valley in the Little Big Horn Mountains. The safe and sensible way to get there was to enter the mountains from the Wyoming side.

What had happened was that Goose Flying had asked all of his "wild dogs," his students, to bring him the supplies he needed, but only Lightningbolt would do it. The old man knew he could count on the reckless youth to make such a journey, but he never expected him to come up the mountain from the Montana side.

Lightningbolt was a very unhappy young man who constantly sought new ways to end his awful boredom. Danger didn't mean very much to him. Often, he was foolhardy with his life and well-being. Some even accused him of being suicidal.

The awful conflict that seethed within Lightningbolt was hidden from most people who knew him. The powerful force that drove him was the emptiness and confusion he felt with his life.

From the first moment that he could remember Lightningbolt had envisioned himself being a powerful warrior. He longed to be an officer in the military, not a Reservation slave and bum. He did not want to accept a life outside of being a great warrior. Most of his closest friends had joined the armed forces. His best friend, Alex, had gone to Vietnam.

But Lightningbolt had been rejected by the military—torn away from his great dream of becoming a warrior of high acclaim. He believed that to be rejected for having one eye with "bad vision" was absolutely unreasonable. The army labeled him 4F. It broke the young man's heart.

What was a person who was not a warrior, a soldier? In Lightningbolt's mind, a man with no military honors was a nobody, a nonperson. What greater honor was there than to be a courageous warrior or an officer in the military?

Almost from the moment his eyes opened as a child he'd heard about war from his Indian and Breed relatives. Many were veterans of war. To live a life on the Reservation, never to be part of the military, was unthinkable. Slavery was the Reservation.

Hadn't all the boys he'd grown up with been raised to be warriors? The games they played were war games. And the great Indian War Chiefs, powerful warriors and warrioresses, were their heroes. Everything he did as a child, every thought he'd had, shaped him to be a warrior.

His cousins and brothers had been called to fight for their country, but Lightningbolt was denied his place and right. The shock of this rejection threw him into inner turmoil. The loss of a military career shattered his Self image, shattered all that he knew and believed. What could replace the void he now felt in his heart and mind?

Lightningbolt was a soldier with no war to fight. Overwhelmed with sorrow and rage, his fear of being a nonperson drove him without mercy. He was being forced to find a new direction for his life. And yet, although he was intensely searching for his new dream, he could not see any value in his world.

It was this awesome force within Lightningbolt that drove him into the mountains to join his teacher, Goose Flying.

It was not that Lightningbolt didn't know about the Wyoming side. He knew that coming up the Wyoming side was the easiest way to travel. He ignored the information because he wanted to see if

he could survive the Montana journey. He believed this was a way of making Big Medicine. Unfortunately, false beliefs of this kind were never challenged by any Medicine Men. In fact, just the opposite happened: such beliefs were constantly praised. The myth of the strong warrior overcoming all odds and discovering Big Medicine was taught as truth. Lightningbolt would literally go anywhere to learn of the Medicine Ways.

It couldn't be said that he was motivated by "spiritual matters." He only knew of his deep sadness and anger, and he was always trying to find new ways of ending his pain. Why he felt this sorrow, this anger, he would not openly admit to himself. But it was what had driven him to discover the Medicine Ways in the first place. If there was a spiritual side to his search, he wasn't conscious of it.

Alone, Lightningbolt struggled through the canyon.

He suffered acutely from the terrible cold, but the horses were in even more pain. He was forced from the back of Arrow many times to rewrap the gunnysacks he had secured about the legs of the horses just before he plunged them into the icy stream. In the Water Gap, Sage Creek was choked with ice in some places and warm in others, and the gunnysacks helped keep the horses' legs from being cut by the ice.

Every time Lightningbolt submerged his hands into the freezing water the pain caused tears to well up in his eyes, but he set his teeth against his misery. Protecting the legs of his friends meant more than any hurt he was experiencing.

Although the Water Gap was a scant three miles in length, the journey through the canyon became a two-day ordeal. Because the footing for the horses was so precarious, he was forced to dismount and lead them. They fought their way through one snowdrift only to meet another even higher.

Camping for the night in the Water Gap was a challenge. Both Lightningbolt and the horses were exhausted at the end of each day. He took care of the animals first, feeding them and rubbing them down, before he saw to himself.

Trees and driftwood were plentiful in the small canyon. After gathering wood, he built a fire and cooked his dinner, which meant heating up the first can of food he could grab from his pack. Setting up his tent came next. Before he slept, he went over the problems he had encountered during the day.

The next morning Lightningbolt woke early, and he was in his saddle before sunrise. The bright silver dawn greeted the eyes of the young man as he rode. Suddenly the canyon opened abruptly into a broad sweeping valley. Lightningbolt had reached his goal and was finally on his way to the cabin.

He jumped down from Arrow's back and fed the horses a few handfuls of oats. But instead of feeling thankful, Lightningbolt felt his old anger come back. He swore quietly to himself that he would never make such a horrible journey again. Big Medicine? Had he been crazy? He felt like fighting something, but he couldn't understand who or what the enemy was.

The water from two springs met where his horses now pawed away the snow to graze. "You made it, Big Nose," he told the gelding as he rubbed the horse's neck. "Too bad you had to make the journey with a jackass telling you what to do."

A hundred yards away, the bare skeleton of a Sun Dance Lodge could be seen. She seemed very old and proud. All the green was now gone from her circle of cottonwood and chokecherry leaves. She had been built in sunshine and warmth during the month of June.

And yet, the Lodge was a vision of winter beauty. The bones of the hundreds of cut limbs that made up the broad ring around the Center Tree remained, but the tens of thousands of intertwining twigs had become a delicate lace of icicles. All were covered by a soft white mantle of snow.

A graceful, powerful Center Tree stood up tall in Her snow Circle. How incredibly lovely She was! A Goddess of the land, Her face and hair were sculpted from billions of diamonds and snow lace.

If Lightningbolt had been more appreciative and not so angry he would have seen Her. But his attention was riveted to the unmistakable mound of snow he recognized as a frozen body.

Cautiously, he walked to the mound and kicked away the snow. Shocked, he realized that he was staring at the face of one of his uncles, Big Antelope. Two empty bottles of whiskey lay beside the dead man. There were, no doubt, more bottles to be found. Where was his horse? Lightningbolt looked around. Where was his tent? This older man would never be out here alone. He was a man who feared being alone. Why was he here?

"You stupid idiot!" he shouted at the dead man. He felt sickened and suddenly very vulnerable, incredibly defenseless. "What in hell were you doing drinking out here?" he exploded in anger.

Digging a grave was out of the question. He tried to move the corpse, but it was frozen down to the ground. Feeling disgusted, he swung onto the back of Arrow. She needed no coaxing to leave.

He rode for almost an hour, then stopped when he found a sheltered place in a big stand of buffalo berry bushes. Here, the horses could graze on dry grass. He cared for the horses, then set up his tent. He would eat later, when he had an appetite again.

"Noon." He frowned, feeling frustrated. "The day is gone! Can't ride when I'm so damned mad! I've got to be on my toes. A damned dead man, what a drag!" He began to pace.

The long stand of berry bushes gave Lightningbolt seventy or so yards of grass relatively free of snow. He paced back and forth, feeling restless and angry. Suddenly he decided to make a fire and have some coffee.

Sitting down, he held his hot cup of coffee close and warmed his fingers. Lightningbolt took his first real look around. He realized that every tree, bush, stone, and blade of grass was covered with loveliness; however, he looked at the beauty halfheartedly. Lightningbolt knew one secret that few people understood. He knew that if he didn't get present with his physical reality and circumstances very soon, he would suffer greatly. While it was true that the snow was incredibly beautiful, in his mind he kept daydreaming about this land free of snow and in its summer green. This was dangerous and he knew it.

Suddenly, his eyes filled with tears and he began to cry. "The kind fool. . . ." He sniffed, trying to get control of his sadness. "I wish I hadn't loved that old dog. He drank constantly, and he was never reliable. We all wished he would die."

Had Big Antelope finally been wished to death? He asked this as he sipped his coffee and began to pace slowly once again. No. . . . It was impossible to wish dinks like him to death. Why was it, though, that the man had also been so very kind? Everyone loved Big Antelope's kindness and humor. But they hated his unfortunate weakness, and his way of constantly bullying people with his problems.

Lightningbolt sprinkled some tobacco into his fire in the tradition of his elders. "To give, in respect of Life, is to share, in respect of Death; this is our custom," he said.

He repeated the words of his grandfather, old man Eastman. "Where is celebration? From where to where do we go, Sacred Great Spirit?" He turned and looked at the long valley. "Whatever that may mean for Big Antelope, Earth Mother. As for me, I'm here and I'm going there." He pointed down the valley. "But where, for the drunk?" Lightningbolt shook his head and refilled his coffee cup.

The following morning, eight miles away, he shot his first deer. The bullet brought pain when it hit. The sad echo roared in the arroyos and canyons. It sang the death song of rifle thunder.

The lifeblood flowed red upon the cold snow. The gentle brother deer fell, and now lay struggling against the permanent silence. He fought against the white-hot pain in the snow, alone and afraid.

"For all time!" Lightningbolt sang as he raced his horse to his fallen relative, the deer. "Great, gentle brother," he said softly as his boots dug deep into the snow, mingling with the blood. "Sorrowful one, I am here," he said as he swung his Mercy Hammer, his hatchet, at his brother deer's stricken head.

The deer closed his eyes slowly, and blended with time and the Sacred Earth's energy. He died with dignity and with perfectness.

11

Lightningbolt sprinkled tobacco in the snow around the deer, then straightened to look at the distant peaks of the mountains. "How close to this, always, are we?" he asked as he began his work of dressing out the deer.

When night brought her beauty to the quiet mountains, she also called her Medicines from the void where sleep guards the galaxies. Her wondrous renewal of starlight and darkness reflected the sacred blue of the patient Mother Earth—becoming one with the melody of our sweet Mother's wish for life for Her children.

Lightningbolt had ridden until he came to the hot pool. He made his camp, then rested before he took his swim. He slipped quietly beneath the luxuriant warm water of the pool. He imagined he swam within and around the Stars and the Moon shining within the blue-black water.

The hot pool, named Child's Remembrance by the Medicine Woman who had been known as Basketmaker, was wondrously warm, deep, and spring-fed clean. The pool was happy in her absolute existence, as she became the magical bowl that held all the wonders of the Sacred Road, the Milky Way.

Two logs had been pushed into the two-hundred-foot-wide pond during the summer season by the hands of playful little girls. Now the logs were piled high with snow, floating serenely on a warm, night sky-mirror of beauty that could heal any broken heart.

Lightningbolt rolled onto his back and looked up into the night sky to dream. Magic bounded suddenly from the blue shadows and danced down an ancient path to the water-mirror to drink. They were two delicate winter deer, shy ladies whose bodies were composed of sweet grass, mountain

flowers, herbal willow, and water lilies. They saw the young man and felt his sad presence. The two deer sang softly. It was a song that they had learned from a meadowlark. This mystery and powerful presence warmed Lightningbolt's heart. He smiled, then laughed out loud.

The two visitors drank the water from the night pool of Stars, then danced back into the willows and magic from where they had come.

The following day, the rifle spoke in thunder again and another brother deer fell into the white expanse.

When the young man reined in his horse and looked down into the Clear Water Valley, he marveled at the warm gold of the lamplight that illuminated the windows of Goose Flying's solitary cabin.

The light seemed strange, unrecognizable, alien to the full Moon, foreign to the mountains, angry compared to the starlight—yet somehow cozy warm and filled with happy memories.

Lightningbolt listened to the creak of his saddle and the soft breathing of his horses. It was a pity that he now must leave the openness and wild beauty to be confined in another building. He didn't like buildings much.

Arrow pawed, snorted, then neighed. This ordinary, very simple action of the horse crashed in upon Lightningbolt's reverie and swiftly ended his contemplation.

"So, the old man somehow knows we're here, Arrow," he whispered, and patted her affectionately. "What will our Dreaming prize be? You and old Roman Nose worked hard too. . . . You should also have your Big Medicine prize."

The door of the cabin opened, throwing the glow of the oil light upon the clean snow.

"Whey, hah!" Goose Flying called.

The echoes of his voice were welcomed in the surrounding arroyos and canyons. Two coyotes began to sing. Lightningbolt let out his breath. His tensions disappeared and he smiled.

"Whey, ya!" he called back.

Arrow picked her way down the narrow trail that had been built by hand. Everything that was the Willow Rose had been handmade.

The little cabin was charming. She looked like "a gingerbread house" because that was what she was meant to look like. A Swiss couple had built the house when they visited. Then they left and were never seen again. Some believed they were killed during the Second World War.

After the horses were cared for and comforted with talk and friendship, Lightningbolt had a smoke. Next he cut firewood. He took his time at this task so he could get to know his new surroundings.

When he entered the cabin he felt eager, yet he was cautious about not showing this too much. He liked old Goose Flying. The old man was standing with his back to Lightningbolt, washing his hands in a highly ornate European water basin.

"Uh-huh. . . . Lightningbolt," the old man said, turning around and grabbing a towel. "You are here, well and strong. I can always count on your good sense." He approached and gave Lightningbolt a warm handshake. "The deer?"

"In the shed . . . two of them," Lightningbolt answered, giving his teacher's hand a squeeze. "I have to tell you"—he looked a bit uncomfortable—"for a while there, I felt just a bit foolish taking the Water Gap. It was dangerous as all hell!"

"You rode through the Water Gap?" Goose Flying winced, the lines around his eyes deepening. "I sent Big Antelope to tell you to be sure to come up the Wyoming side. You took a big chance." He shook his head. "Jack Rabbit, the Cree boy from Canada, went with him."

Lightningbolt sat down slowly on an old

wooden chair by the door.

"You found his body, didn't you?" the old man asked, taking another chair. He sighed, showing his deep sadness.

Lightningbolt answered with a nod of his head. He was angry again. "I knew about the Water Gap. It's not your fault."

"Yes, we test ourselves. Maybe Big Antelope tested himself too in this life?"

"With what? Our stupidity?" Lightningbolt spat angrily, testing his teacher.

"I do not test you," Goose Flying countered. "Why are you testing me? These mountains, you know them. Did you test your stupidity or your brave heart?"

Lightningbolt removed his leather chaps and began to take off the second pair of jeans he was wearing.

Goose Flying poured them each a cup of coffee. He handed his apprentice a cup. "What did you expect out there?" he asked softly. "I used to test myself too. Then I grew old and tired. The powerful Medicine Woman Estcheemah told me that I was a Dreamer. Dreaming is my Way now. It comforts me."

The coyotes were singing very close now. They had smelled the deer in the shed.

"All true power begins when we have imagination," said Goose Flying. "But when we have no appreciation for Life—then what use is imagination? What do you want to do? What do you want to build? Big Antelope had no imagination, no will to live. He constantly sought his death. You can't ride forever, out here in these mountains. One day you have to step down from your horse. Are you ready to do that?"

Whether it was out of habit or because Lightningbolt was simply angry, he reached for his .38 pistol. He emptied the chambers of the gun, letting the bullets fall carelessly to the floor.

"I don't know," he answered, taking a chair and setting the gun by his cup of coffee. He reached down and picked up the bullets, and his spurs, and set them all on the table.

Old Goose Flying's eyes moved as subtly as an owl's. It was a sign that the young man knew well. Many of the older people would show their disapproval with this kind of look. He quickly searched about to see what he had done to unnerve Goose Flying.

"What's wrong?" Lightningbolt asked, not wanting to anger the old man.

"Why not throw your rifle on my table, and your knives and boots?" The old man was scowling. "Is this your custom?"

Lightningbolt was instantly embarrassed. Throwing weapons on the table of a Medicine Man or Medicine Woman was forbidden. It was a sign of extreme disrespect.

He quickly scooped the pistol, spurs, and bullets from the table and laid them on the floor beside his chair. "Dammit!" He exploded with frustration. "Why in hell did I do that? I'm sorry, Goose."

This small slap to Goose Flying's face had opened a wound that the old man had concealed. "Yes," he explained. "Yes, that seems to be the way it is. If you were a blood grandson I would be very angry with you. But because I am your teacher and because you are a Breed things are different."

Lightningbolt sat up and moved forward in his chair.

"I must teach despite my anger and disappointment," Goose Flying went on. "What is this if it is not family and blood? It is a discipline. I am amazed, yes, the teaching is here for me. You, many times, test me to my breaking point."

"Breaking point?" Lightningbolt repeated the words almost under his breath. He began to clean his rifle because he needed his hands busy. He had never heard this kind of talk before.

"Carelessness," the old man went on. "Where are the big circles of young men learning? I guess I should expect a Breed not to know all the customs."

"What are you into?" Lightningbolt fought back. "Breed! You mean I'm going to hear that crap from you too?"

"It is meant differently than you think," Goose Flying retaliated. "Both Full-Blood and Breed alike do not know the customs. It is our fault, we Medicine People."

"Are you angry because I'm a Breed or because I threw my shit on your table?" Lightningbolt challenged.

"Both . . . and neither," the Medicine Man answered. "I could have chosen to say nothing to you. It is my present to you that I speak my disappointment. Why should I be angry? I have worked hard and what of that? Much of it has been for nothing. Where is that young Cree man? Where are the other young men? The young men are told that the god called the supreme being is sacred and is in the wine. It is alcohol that is the supreme being. The alcohol is the spirit, it is god. How can I fight this?"

"You're asking me?" Lightningbolt asked, surprised. "Are you kidding?" He sipped his coffee; it was getting cold. "Yeah, it figures. Guzzling god down every weekend." He laughed contemptuously. "Popping the beer can and taking a slug of god. What a joke."

"The simpleminded do not think," said old Goose Flying. "That is their problem. It would be good if they had the courage to say what you have just said. But no, they fear saying that."

"Stupid idiots!" Lightningbolt cursed.

"Not so fast!" the old man cautioned. "I didn't

16

call you a stupid idiot the time I found you drunk at the rodeo." He winked, showing a bit of humor. "Or should we say that your situation was . . . ah . . . different? Were you an idiot, drinking god that day?"

Lightningbolt laughed. He was happy that the tension was gone.

"Maybe I should only be a Dreamer." Old Goose smiled, and sat back in his chair. "I used to be like you at one time. I would only chase power. I know your thinking because it is like mine was. You think that having power is possessing a thing, like a certain feather, some kind of magical shield or gun. Power, you will learn, is knowledge. And there are those questions—"

"How long do we stay stumped?" Lightningbolt asked.

"Stumped?" The old man blinked. For a moment he had retreated, in his mind, to an earlier time. "What was it you were saying?"

Lightningbolt smiled.

"Those deer you killed." Goose grinned. "I will live because of them. It can be hard up here in the winter. The deer are a wonderful gift. Sometimes I've had to subsist on the government rations that I've brought up here with me . . . or have done some trapping. But I've never been a good hunter." He smiled broadly. "Even mice can get away from me. They're all over the place."

"Goose, why don't you come here and work in the Spring?" Lightningbolt asked, curious. "It would be a hell of a lot easier."

"No," the old man answered flatly. "The Winter is the Big Water Time. Now is the Big Dreaming Time. The snow is water. Snow is everywhere. Snow is special. We Dreamers know that the snow helps us Dream. I have journeyed here for eleven years, and I Dream here during the time of the Black Lodge. Winter is the Black Lodge. When the Sun is dim, the Dream is bright. . . . That is why we Dream in the Winter. You are here to Dream with

me."

Lightningbolt reached for the coffeepot. "Coffee?" he asked.

"There is tea in that pot. I poured your coffee out of the red one," Goose Flying answered. "The tea is bitter, but I like it. I saved the last of my coffee so that you would have some. Did you bring sugar?"

"Yes, plenty," said Lightningbolt. "And lots of coffee."

"Tonight I will cut a special little tree for you," Goose explained. "She will be your Dreaming Tree. You will help me cover almost every inch of your Dream Room with the branches. The fragrance of the tree is very important to have all around you. Do you have any questions?"

Lightningbolt could only smile. He had sought the "big prize" and here it was! Was he ever lucky.

"The world," Goose continued, "is filled with sorrow and much terror. There is incredible pain. There is beauty, love, and much more—this the Medicine Woman called Estcheemah teaches. But most humans do not seek Beauty. She spoke to me of pain and how this can also be a teacher. Yet what questions or teaches more if not Beauty? Estcheemah has told me that those who love and care for the Self will, one day, learn to know the Self. How will you find your Self? I ask you this, just as Estcheemah once asked me."

The words that Goose had spoken were powerful and could have been illuminating—but the old man's voice was uncertain. He spoke in almost a monotone, causing Lightningbolt to drift off into a fantasy about the tree Goose had told him about.

"What do you have to say?" Goose asked.

"I'm ready!" Lightningbolt answered quickly.

"For what?" the old man coaxed.

"For anything!" he replied swiftly. "You show me the critter and I'll wrestle it!"

Goose Flying frowned.

Lightningbolt was very impatient to begin.

17

"Well," the Medicine Man persisted, "you must go out into the night, while I am getting your tree. You will speak to the stones, the trees, the Stars, the Moon, and our Sacred Earth, asking for help with your quest. Speak of your Life."

"Sure!" said Lightningbolt with enthusiasm. "Great. Shall I ask about a Super Dream?"

"You have super dreams every night," Goose teased. He still had not realized that his apprentice was a thousand miles from what he was trying to teach. "Tools are what you need."

"Tools?" Lightningbolt blinked, trying to understand.

"Weapons," Goose went on, still not realizing that Lightningbolt had no idea what he was talking about.

"Weapons?" Lightningbolt wondered.

"Yes . . . tools of power, weapons," said Goose. "Things of great learning. You are ignorant."

Lightningbolt nodded his agreement.

"You will ask for those tools," the Medicine Man instructed. "And smoke your Pipe."

"Ah . . . I don't have a Pipe," Lightningbolt answered apologetically.

"Then smoke a cigarette," advised the old man. "Go. Yes, go now. When you return, the Dreaming will begin."

Lightningbolt rose hurriedly from his chair, threw on his coat, and was out the door. He took about ten steps from the cabin, then searched for a place to pee. After he'd relieved himself, he lit a cigarette and wondered which stone to talk to. Selecting the first big boulder he saw, he approached the stone and took a drag from his cigarette.

"*Ah hey,*" he said to the stone reverently. "*Ho!* How are you?"

A beautiful owl flew into a tree about a hundred yards to Lightningbolt's left. The young man's attention was instantly drawn to the creature. After the owl had flown off, his attention was next drawn to five rabbits frolicking in the snow. Because of the

beauty of the land, and the many diversions, Lightningbolt realized that fifteen minutes had gone by and he had still not spoken with his stone. He was getting very cold.

"I need a Dream," he told the stone. "And I do not know why old Goose wants me to talk to you, but he does. Thanks for all that you can give me. I am deeply thankful. Thanks, okay? I really mean it. Okay, I'll see you later. Thanks a lot."

Lightningbolt lay in bed with his eyes wide open; it was impossible to sleep. He tossed, clawed, turned, bucked, rolled, and battled the covers before he finally sat up.

"Dammit," he cursed. "My big chance comes and I can't sleep! I'll probably be awake all night."

Absolutely disgruntled, he got up and threw on his shirt. He shuffled into the kitchen and looked around. The floor was too cold for bare feet, so he had to go back and put on his boots. He was twice as miffed with himself when he had to backtrack into the kitchen the second time.

Old Goose's door was closed and not a sound came from his room. The chances were a thousand percent that the old man was out on some hill, sitting with his thick black Angus cowhide under his butt and smoking his Medicine Pipe. He could stay warm as a bear at the North Pole—so Lightningbolt did not worry.

The stove was still hot. He poured some water from the water bucket into the ornate washbasin and washed his face. It was cold. The bucket was almost dry. He lifted the green coffee pot from the stove to his lips and tasted it. It contained the tea. Absolutely, positively, it was bitter! Now he was even more awake.

Scowling, he slumped at the table and began to think about his journey. He looked out the window at the snow. The Moon was big and bright, so bright he thought he had no need to light the lamp.

The trees were beautiful. White magic lay deep on every branch and bush. The beauty he saw everywhere helped calm him.

He stood suddenly and turned to go to the stove to feed it more wood. He took one step and bashed his shin hard on a box he hadn't seen. He howled and hopped around on one leg, nursing his wound. While he was hopping, he fell over another object on the floor—his saddle.

He crawled back to the table and pulled the kerosene lamp over to him. Everything that was his body seemed to be throbbing with pain.

He lit the lamp. But when he tried to replace the chimney, it slipped and fell to the table, shattering.

Fearful of injuring himself with the broken glass, he moved carefully to the farthest corner, opposite the stove, searching for the broom he'd spotted earlier.

The first sweep of his hand in the dark corner knocked down his rifle. The weapon hit with a horrible clatter that Lightningbolt did not like. He hoped it was not scratched.

He found the broom and dustpan and returned to the table. Very carefully he searched through the cupboard above the table for the extra chimney he had seen there.

While he'd been stumbling around, the feeble lamp flame had gone out. He relit the lamp, then replaced the chimney and took a look around.

Goose had moved a hundred things in the small room before he had left the cabin. Lightningbolt saw that there were ten or twelve more objects that could have tripped him up. He swept up the glass, then realized that he heard the coffee boiling away. The last burst of steam puffed a bitter-smelling, rancid cloud of burned coffee into the small room.

Now the damned door needed to be opened!

He grabbed up the coffeepot, walked to the door, tore it open, and threw the pot outside into a snowbank.

21

There were dark lines under Lightningbolt's eyes as he sat at the table. He seriously wanted to be able to go to sleep so he could experience his Big Medicine Dream. What was the matter? He stood up and carefully began to pace the room. Why did life have to be so strange at times? Why had he ridden all the way out here? Was he crazy? What if old Goose was just an Indian crank like old man Rabbit? Now there was a strange old dude. The man could even be spooky at times. Goose had told him that old man Rabbit could conjure things out of the air. As it turned out, the only thing he could really conjure was bottles of foul-tasting wine. All of his so-called powers were cheap tricks. Life seemed strange; what could a man do?

A deep worry, mixed with a desperate sadness, settled into the young man's stomach. The knuckles on his hands were white. Studying his hands, he suddenly realized that they were both fists.

"Wow," he mumbled. "I'm really getting up-tight."

He slowly relaxed his hands, then gazed into the lamplight, remembering how Goose had explained something before he left for the mountains. "Many of the Indian people who are living presently were not Indians in their former lives," Goose had told him. "Some of the Indians who live now were Indian killers and haters in their former lives. Now those people learn what it is like to be Indian. You are called Lightningbolt because you have the name of Storm. This is good. You also search; this is good. But you have not yet learned how to cry."

Lightningbolt smiled. What if he had killed people on both sides in his former life, or at least during one of his former lives? Wasn't that typically a Breed's thing to do?

Goose Flying? How about *his* past lives? Had he been an Indian? A cavalryman? Had he been a corn grinder?

Lightningbolt laughed out loud.

He thought about the stones. Possibly he

The blast of cold air that forced him back into the room definitely had him awake now; even if Goose's traps had failed, the wind certainly had not. He shivered down beyond his bones!

"Okay, dammit, I'm awake!" he yelled at the wind.

"Go to sleep!" Goose yelled back. "What are you doing?"

Embarrassed, Lightningbolt retreated back into the cabin and slammed the door. He would explain in the morning.

should have been just a little more patient with them and said more. He wondered idly if he should give it another try, but forgot the idea because Goose would probably yell at him again.

Suddenly, he realized that he could hear Goose calling to him. He ran to the door and opened it.

"Goose?" he called. "What's up?"

"I'm in my tepee at the back of the house," Goose called back. "A darned raccoon has just run off with one of my shoes. Could you come here, please?"

Lightningbolt threw on his coat and left the cabin. He walked around the house and found that Goose, indeed, had a fine tepee back there. He was impressed. He had not seen the tepee—it had been well camouflaged by trees and snow.

"What's up, Goose?" he asked the old man.

"Coon got my shoe," Goose answered, "and carried it off. It's over by the tree there. I don't want to be hopping around out here in the dark. Would you get it for me?"

Lightningbolt retrieved the shoe. "How'd you know I was awake?" he asked innocently.

"You've been crashing around in there for over an hour," the old man answered. "I did not have to guess."

"You want anything to drink?" Lightningbolt asked. "Anything else? Are you hungry?"

"I want to sleep," Goose answered. "It's getting late."

"Ah . . . sure. . . . Great idea." Lightningbolt agreed. He turned and went back to the cabin. Once he was inside he took off his jacket, then he pretended a yawn and a stretch, but his mind would not believe it. He still wasn't sleepy!

Lightningbolt was becoming angry.

A mouse timidly scurried across the floor and found a scrap of bread by the wood box.

"Jump up, you rascal!" he called to the mouse. "There's an entire loaf of bread on the shelf just above your head."

He picked up his rifle from where it had fallen and carried it into his Dream Room. He carefully cleaned the gun, then laid it at the foot of his bed. He hung his spurs near the rifle, then rolled in to sleep—he was suddenly exhausted.

Lightningbolt had no more than closed his eyes when he heard an unfamiliar sound. He sat up and saw the most beautiful young woman in all of Creation.

The belt She was wearing sparkled with a hundred billion Stars. Her delicate hands held a wondrous golden bowl that seemed to be made from the substance of the Sun. It shone with every color of light.

Incredible incandescent rainbows of fiery Energies leaped up from the bowl. No sooner had his eyes grown accustomed to the brilliance and phenomenal colors of the enchanted mystery when the bowl changed unexpectedly into the diamond-blue sphere of our Earth.

The Earth turned in Her hands in the void.

Now Lightningbolt could not stop looking at the young woman's astonishingly beautiful face. No mature woman, girl, young woman, or maiden was ever so lovely. Her presence was that of a Goddess.

Her gaze was strong beyond strength, and yet it held all the power of perfect gentleness. The nurturing colors and resplendent loveliness of Her eyes drew forth a deeper love than he had ever known. Absolute Wisdom and unconditional Freedom were in those eyes. He trusted Her beyond anything he could comprehend.

An instant transformation came over Lightningbolt, changing him into a child wearing a military uniform. He was standing at the edge of a sparkling pool that was his own memory.

The weapons he held were toys, playthings of little girls and boys who played war. He seemed to be part of a Great Toy Parade that encircled the Earth. Yet the toys were not hollow and harmless; they were deadly real and monstrously efficient.

"You will dream, Warrior Child," the radiant Goddess declared with a sincerity that seemed to be the voice of time. When She spoke, Her voice was like thunder, yet it was the thunder of every music known. "Yes, dream, human child. Dream the dream of the warriors and warrioresses of your time."

Dark ominous clouds of smoke drifted across a battlefield. The billowing fog was loathsome and polluted with horrific chemicals. The putrid stench of burned bodies caused the young soldier, hidden by an old broken tree, to retch behind the face mask of his combat helmet. He tore the helmet off and wiped the slime from his face. Misery and terror were in his eyes.

His combat uniform was high-tech and composed of thousands of tiny mirrors. Many of the mirrors were broken, soiled with dried dirt and blood, or caked with a greasy chemical. The loss of most of his armor's reflective capabilities meant he was doomed.

He ran, dodging, from his hiding place. He fired his laser rifle, recklessly, at some enemy he obviously could not see. He screamed his frustration and hate at his adversaries. Suddenly, a searing blue-white light swept across the young man's stomach. He exploded into blood and steam.

Not far from where the youth fell, two men lay in a hastily dug foxhole. The immaculate condition of the men's combat uniforms indicated that they were either vets or Killplayers.

A Killplayer was a soldier squeezed from the combat kill schools that were found on half a dozen worlds. Some of the best Killplayers were women. Killplayers were highly polished and the best combat soldiers going.

"Sector Nova," the sergeant repeated patiently into his helmet radio. "Sector Nova, do you compute?"

A tiny electronic squeal came from his helmet.

"Damn your bloody rotten world," Captain Spring said quietly as he fussed with his belt computer. He was talking out loud to himself.

"Pardon?" a young woman's voice said through the radio into the captain's ear. "Did you say 'rotten world,' sir?"

"Sector check. Delta Two," the captain answered into his helmet radio. "Sorry,

Corporal, didn't know I was comp-live."

"Sector Twenty-Twenty," the corporal answered. "But nobody is sure, Captain Spring. There is incredible confusion about every sector coordinate. Do I hear someone near you trying to locate Computer Central, Sector Nova?"

"Remember that nasty sergeant?" the captain teased, answering. "What's up with Sector Nova?"

"There is no one left alive at that Computer Central," the corporal answered. "Not since yesterday. You can tell old nasty to give up."

The captain immediately passed on the information to the sergeant.

"Where were we drawing laser-cannon fire from?" the sergeant asked. He was looking grim.

Four soldiers appeared suddenly out of the mist and smoke and rolled headlong into the foxhole. All of them quickly made themselves as comfortable as they could.

"Sector Nova has had it," Lieutenant Tree

27

informed the captain. "The coordinates are all crazy. They were smoked, nuked to glass yesterday by our own weapons. Something is very weird, sir."

"Hey, did you see that private get steamed over there?" the young soldier sitting nearest the sergeant asked. "No armor—his mirrors were gone! How long you think he'd been fighting, Sarge?"

"Yeah . . . sure." The sergeant frowned, ignoring the question. "You keep polished or you'll be manure on this stupid planet."

"Damned coordinates!" the third man complained. "What's up with Command Central, Sarge?"

"I told you this planet was a loser," the sergeant growled at Captain Spring. "We should have chosen to fight on World Number 234. I think we'd have had a fighting chance there. This place is the spookiest planet in the universe!"

"There's a lot more to be gained here," Captain Spring explained for the tenth time. "Sure, it's a shit hole, but look at the rewards, man! Have you ever seen better?"

"This place is a soldier eater." The sergeant frowned.

"Buck up, Sarge," said the captain, smiling. "Have you forgotten about those thirty million credits, old friend? Just think of that—you're going to be rich."

"Who are we fighting for this time?" Tree asked offhandedly. He was more interested in money than he was in glory or politics.

"The Reds and Whites, this time." The captain grinned. "Both of the governments involved are run by fools and thieves. The army is badly run and the officers are has-beens."

Five world eyes suddenly swooped down out of the sky and hovered a few yards from the men. They were self-propelled galactic television cameras, the latest and most modern in design and performance.

"There are over six worlds watching this war," said the lieutenant, grinning at the world eyes. "I can remember when I was a kid . . . seeing my first real war. I was really thrilled. Back in those days fighting soldiers only received ten thousand credits for their backs and blood. Poor pay!"

"Then came the superstars," the captain broke in. "Holograms . . . battling right in the middle of everyone's living room—life-size and ten feet wide. Everything was very, very safe."

"Except for the real thing, here," said Lieutenant Tree with an ironic laugh. "It's not safe here. No way!"

"But the almighty viewer is safe," the captain continued. "And think about that . . . I mean, the big change. Because of the world contenders, and the billions of billions of viewers, the governments decided they would stand behind the winners."

"It's true—the opposing governments had to stand behind the decision of the wars, win or lose, because they discovered it was the best way of keeping war out of everyone's back yard."

"Why the lecture?" the sergeant snapped. "You and the louie performing for the big eyes?"

"Do the creeps know it?" Captain Spring shot back. "I doubt it. I think the ghouls are watching right now, hearing our every word." He spit. "And are they told? I doubt it."

"We're here to kill and to win!" the sarge exploded. "Don't grandstand."

"Nobody's watching anyway," one of the privates complained. "We haven't done enough killing today to warrant an interview or a sneak close-up."

"What's the piss-off?" the lieutenant broke in. "You're sore, Bridger, because you lost your commission. From a major to a sergeant overnight."

"You slime!" the sergeant bawled, jumping to his feet and pulling his boot knife. "I lost it because I should have cut that bloody colonel's throat and you know it."

"Hey, easy," said the captain, coming between the two men. "Okay, we were grandstanding, major . . . er, I mean Sarge. Hell, maybe they are watching a sneak. It happens all the time."

"And it's censored, you damn fool," the sergeant cursed. "You stupid Killplayer dog! The governments don't want the viewers to know this stuff is real, can't you understand that? That's the crux of my argument with the colonel."

Suddenly the tension was broken by the sound of a voice from Captain Spring's helmet radio. "Look up, gentlemen." The radio was on maximum sound.

"General Emerald!" the lieutenant said in awe. He recognized the general's voice because he had been her aide at one time.

There wasn't a woman or man in the White Bird Division who did not love and respect their general. She knew all her officers by name and always decorated them herself for acts of bravery and self-initiative on the battlefield.

"Are you there, Bridger?" the woman's voice teased in a friendly way. "You're a major again, how do you like that?" She laughed.

"Thanks," the major replied into his field helmet. "Why are you passing out the chocolates? We have been pinned down here by laser-cannon fire for six hours. What's up?"

"Look up, and tell Tweedle Dum and Tweedle Dee there to look up too." The general's voice was hard. "There's a gold credit flashing up there, from one of the world eyes. . . . The laser image is two hundred miles long."

Two hundred thousand eyes from the White Bird Division were looking into the sky. There above them were the coveted words every division hoped to see along with their insignia—GOLD AWARD.

The general's voice sounded harsh from the two radios on maximum sound. "Our Cobra copter division," she announced, sounding just a bit strained, "has just destroyed half a million humans.

This is our greatest credit standing ever. Yet, we have been cheated."

The men in the foxhole carefully did not look at one another. Even the privates knew better than to utter a word.

"It's just as I suspected," said the major bitterly. "We've been tricked, my friends."

"All soldiers of White Bird Division," the general announced now into every soldier's helmet radio, "the humans that we have been killing here are not soldiers of the opposing forces. We have not been attacking bases. We have been attacking cities."

"What?" one of the privates exclaimed, jumping up.

"Down, Killplayer!" growled the lieutenant, pulling the man down beside him. "Brace up, you swine. Show some discipline!"

"We have been tricked," the general continued with her steady and commanding voice. "We are on a real world. I repeat, a real world. This planet has not been planet-checked for mortal combat. The army we have met and destroyed is not an authorized games army of the Galactic Games Commission.

"The Galactic Games Commission has not approved this war we are fighting. The divisional commanders are looking into the situation and hope to have an answer for us within five hours.

"This month alone, we have killed over twenty million people with our flay bombs—people who did not know how to protect themselves from the attacks. They were all civilians from the cities of this planet."

Every soldier in the White Bird Division was shocked and surprised, except for the major. He looked angry and very resolute.

"Families by the thousands have been butchered by us," the general explained. "It is estimated that we have killed over ninety million children."

Some of the men in the foxhole were visibly nauseated.

"Every map we possess has been a device to trick us," the general informed her soldiers. "The belts, maps, computers are all phonies. Not one of them gives our correct coordinates. That is the reason for the overlap of firepower and the confusion."

"Monster perfect." The major sighed. "We entered no city because of the computer readouts. The governments did not want us to enter a city because we would learn the truth."

"White Bird Division will mount up," the general ordered her army. "Copter tanks overhead and land-attack vehicles, follow Battle Plan Number Zero, plus, plus. I repeat: Zero, plus, plus."

The entire division moved forward to the nearest city.

Small close-up world eyes, which were also called snoops, as well as the large world eyes, pried into every corner and peered into every face— both the living and the dead.

A snoop followed General Emerald and Major Bridger as they walked through a destroyed courtyard. Bodies of hundreds of children lay everywhere; many had been blown to pieces. The building had once been a school.

"Children," a private mused as he walked at the arm of the major. "Can you beat it? It's hard

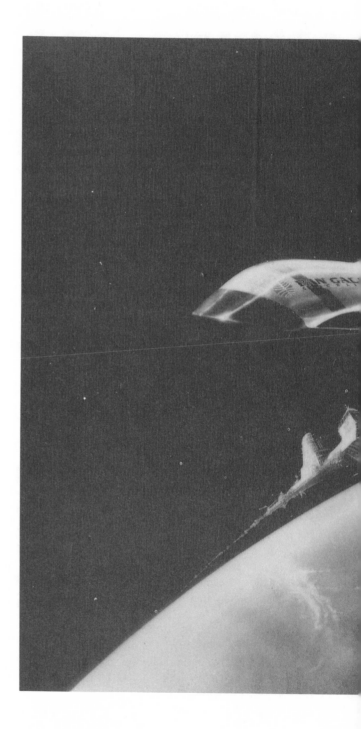

to believe!"

"You can believe murder and ugliness," the general said to the private. "Remember it, son."

Eleven young combat women and eight combat men moved through the slaughtered children, searching out any who might be alive. The job, they soon discovered, was hopeless. The White Bird divisional cannoneers were perfect at their work. Nothing was left alive. It had been White Bird's cannons that had destroyed this city.

The busy snoop that followed the general registered, with bright flashing lights, that she had earned ten million credits. She showed her appreciation by cutting the snoop in half with her laser pistol. The general's response was applauded by billions of people—they understood her feelings.

News commentators loved it. Some were made famous overnight. Others became incredibly rich.

On six worlds, the big viewers had seen an incredible thing . . . a real world being invaded by another real world!

Everyone knew that Blue World was the aggressor, but what could they do? After all, they were only the viewers. The governments would have to sort this thing out.

There was jubilation for the billions of viewers who were the general's fans. Parades in thousands of cities were held to celebrate her. She was the star of all stars!

However, barely two weeks after the general made her walk through tens of thousands of dead and mutilated humans, the White Bird Division was being called the Rebels.

This sudden change was even more exciting for the viewers. The general had decided to battle the system. During an interview she had sworn on camera to kill every War Network person she met.

Of course, she first positioned her army in such a way that it would be a threat to anyone who disagreed with her.

The fans went wild with excitement.

The Outlaw Division, the best of the Rebels, was being kept hidden. But who or what could keep the world eyes from seeing them if the eyes chose to look? There was no escape from them—everyone knew that, including the "terrible General Emerald."

To be sure, the excitement quieted down some, once the "rebel forces" made their escape into the deserts of the planet. But the War Network continued to watch their every move.

The big deep-space eyes that kept watch were orbiting safely a thousand miles out. The electronic laser eyes could count whiskers on a desert cat on the surface of the planet.

The White Bird Division had conquered a real world, not one of the game worlds where governments played out their deadly politics. What had happened; what had gone wrong?

Many of the critics believed it had all begun with Blue World. Blue World had invented all the rules.

The Galactic War Games had become the "game rule" for governments on the six worlds. Galactic games were the most entertaining shows for billions of humans to cheer on, or to politically

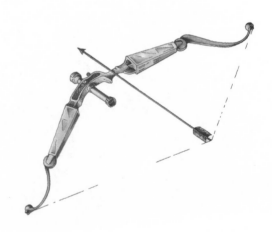

criticize their governments, industries, or universities. Many of the "holocritics" had become important political figures. "Holochairs" were people who only watched.

The history of how it all began, some say, was when wars had become big entertainment on the Blue World. It was called the Vietnam Experience. Many, many years later, when space travel became ordinary, the games had expanded.

Two worlds had become locked in a bitter controversy. It was then that the Blue World decided that the war to end all wars would be fought on a planet where no civilians could be hurt, a war planet where only combat personnel and their machines were allowed.

The Blue World won, although eight and a half million humans died in that war. All the survivors, both female and male, became instant stars because of the complete coverage the war received from the game shows.

The world people, now called the big viewers, had watched the war in the comfort of their living rooms on holographic twenty-foot-wide televisions in Wonder-Color.

Only ten years later another controversy arose between two governments, and this time hundreds of thousands of people volunteered to fight, all aiming for the fame and the big money of the survivors from the last war, who had enjoyed years of attention and wealth.

This time the war was between the Blue World and the White World. Blue World won again. There was an explosion of new stars on both worlds. Everybody was happy!

The fans loved the Killplayers. These professional soldiers didn't care which side they fought on. The fact that twenty-eight million people died in the last big game was quickly forgotten.

General Emerald, also known as Darlene, had grown up watching the world wars. By the time she was ten the six world wars had become very

big business, establishing themselves as a household tradition.

Most of the wars had been fought between military game systems. However, when Darlene was fifteen she had excitedly watched a war fought by three worlds. All on the war planet, of course.

Blue World had won, yet again.

Years later, when Darlene became General Emerald, she and millions of other soldiers, women and men, had been tricked into becoming the first invasion force to be launched against another real world. The Red World had been invaded because no agreement could be reached at the studios over who should recompense the losers of the game wars. The controversy involved billions of billions of world credits. The Red World had not paid back its credit lease debts.

After the Blue World invaded the Red World the controversy no longer existed.

The political figures on the Red World wanted things to get back to normal and could not understand why General Emerald felt so strongly about the turn of events. "She has won everything a woman could desire," the new president announced during his inaugural address.

Twenty days after the Rebels were interviewed by the War Network, a Blue World dignitary came to bestow a Grand Medal of Honor upon General Emerald, along with a bonus of one hundred million credits. By this time she had become so popular that billions of fans had volunteered to play with her, and fight.

She was also informed that she would now have to fight "an equal force of soldiers from all six worlds" to "defend her title."

Smiling broadly, and making sure that the world eye cameras were picking up his best side, the dignitary informed the general that within the week, "the party would be landing, and the games would begin."

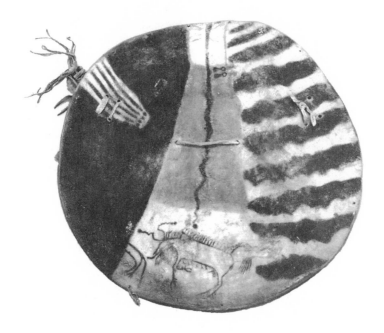

Lightningbolt woke with a start. He was sweating and felt deep-down tired. He sat up and rubbed his arms.

The intense power of the mountain light illuminated the interior of the tiny cabin with such brilliance that Lightningbolt had to shade his eyes. It would be a few minutes before he could stop blinking. At this altitude the snow sparkled like a liquid icy mirror, a polished shield that could be seen a hundred million miles out in space.

Lightningbolt staggered out into the main room and sat down at the table.

"*Ho,*" said the old man.

"It's incredibly bright." Lightningbolt yawned, then stretched. He pulled on his pants, then wrestled on his shirt. "Coffee?"

"I ate some good deer meat." Goose beamed. He patted his stomach. "I was awake most of the night. You seemed to be very restless."

Lightningbolt poured himself a cup of coffee.

"Tea or coffee?" he offered as he sat down.

"*Uh huh.* Tea later," Goose answered. "I will soon take a little catnap. I think we should talk."

"My Dream was amazing." Lightningbolt smiled, then just as quickly he frowned. "The coffee is great. How did you fry your deer? I didn't hear you."

"I've got myself a barbecue pit," Goose answered, offering him a platter of meat. "It's out by my tepee. Food always tastes better outside. I wanted you to get your rest."

"Deer meat." Lightningbolt smiled. He pulled the plate of meat to him and took one of the largest pieces.

"You're a strange one in many ways," the old man mused as he watched Lightningbolt eat. "I admire you, somehow. There are not so many like you anymore . . . who are really seeking Self Power. Most are satisfied only seeking a Medicine Tool they can use like a club. But you, you are

34

different."

"How in hell did you make that Dream so real?" Lightningbolt suddenly demanded. "I can't make up my mind if I had a horrible Dream or a beautiful one. It's strange. What was it?"

"Reality is united with our every action," said Goose, repeating Estcheemah's words. "Tell me of your Medicine Signs. This old man likes to hear about Medicine Signs. It's good for me."

"You mean things that happened in the Dream?" Lightningbolt asked. "I Dreamed of all kinds of things . . . incredible things. I saw helicopters that were completely covered with mirrors. It kept them from being shot down by laser fire. The soldiers had mirrored armor, too. I saw holograms, missiles, infantry fighting vehicles, battle tanks that were mirrored, and all kinds of hand-held weapons. But the world eyes and snoops, Goose, these were really freaky! The snoops watched your every move. It was spooky."

"No flying horses?" Goose asked with astonishment. "No magic Medicine Shields?" His eyes were hopeful. "No magical Eagle Feathers that talk?" He was looking doubtful now. "Magical gourds?"

"The tanks weighed a hundred tons, Goose." Lightningbolt smiled. "Fifty-thousand-horsepower engines. And those helicopters were really flying tanks."

He wondered at the disappointment and sorrow he saw in the old man's eyes.

"The laser-machine-pistol-combo was really something! Kind of like a mini-gun. M-sixties were still being used, but they shot some kind of light bullets. Can you believe that? There were over-and-under grenade launchers with mini-missiles for longer range.

"If you saw the target, you hit it," Lightningbolt explained. "The laser computer in your weapon watched both your eyes and the target you aimed at. Sometimes it would even correct for

tinued. "But I was scared, too. That war was inconceivable . . . hopeless, man! But there was a part of me that liked it," he added, shaking his head. "Don't ask me why, but there was not one magical thing, Goose. Just Death, a lot of it. But I feel better for the Dream."

"No Medicine Things, but your Dream has me curious. Maybe you should tell me of that Dream," old Goose inquired, with respect.

Lightningbolt ate his deer slowly and recounted his Dream in intense detail.

"*Uh . . . huh,*" the old man said after a lengthy pause. The Dream had unnerved him, but he was hesitant about showing this. He fussed with his coffee cup, trying to find the time he needed to give a suitable answer.

So much was happening in Goose Flying's world—it was such a struggle to keep up with it all! Most of his thoughts were concerned with a time few people even knew existed. For most of the old man's life he had battled his addiction to alcohol—only a small scattering of people appreciated his victory.

Battle tanks? He had scarcely caught up with the Second World War when suddenly people were talking about the Korean War. No sooner had he found the country of Korea on his map than everyone started talking about Vietnam.

Laser cannons—did they really exist?

Where were the Indians and cowboys?

The fighter jets that screamed over his head were a complete mystery to him; he hadn't even been up in a Piper Cub. He had never told anyone, but more than once he had prayed to a jet plane in the night sky, thinking it was some sort of special Star. Once he found out what such things really were, he was horribly embarrassed.

When he did meet with someone who knew the perplexing names of modern weapons, his brain would simply falter trying to understand.

Was it really possible that the horrible weapons

faulty vision, like when you were in heavy smoke or fog."

Goose Flying began to resemble a man who has just lost a dear friend.

"No." Lightningbolt frowned, finally giving the old man's question some deep thought. "Never did see any shields, except for the mirrored armor. They used an almost impenetrable plastic; that was really something!"

Goose shook his head, looking downcast.

"I was excited as all hell!" Lightningbolt conin Lightningbolt's dream existed? A .30-06 or a simple .30-30 was intricate enough for him, that was for sure!

Lightningbolt had a difficult time sitting still. He was very eager to see how his Medicine Dream would affect his life. He believed that special powers would now be revealed to him.

At least this was how Leaping Lion, the Medicine Man from Utah, had explained Dreaming when Lightningbolt and Spotted Elk had visited him at the Big Horn County jail. Leaping Lion had been arrested for drunk driving; his story, however, was that he was a political prisoner.

When the young men protested Leaping Lion's arrest, a bored turnkey told them the man had been arrested for being drunk—and that his fine needed to be paid.

They were both crestfallen. Not another stupid drunk! Still, the young men remembered Leaping Lion's words. They had dismissed the drunk, but not what he claimed to know about Dreaming.

It would be these kinds of human failures that Lightningbolt would deeply question once he matured. But with old Goose, Lightningbolt sat on the edge of his chair, filled with immense expectations. He believed that something would come over him and suddenly he would be able to do and know things that he could never do or know before!

"We are so very ignorant," said Goose at long last. "Somehow these Medicine Signs mean very much to you."

"You mean, no superzap is going to suddenly come over me?" Lightningbolt asked, deeply disappointed. "Nothing is going to light up my Life?"

Goose Flying blinked. Every time a young person used such modern words it flabbergasted him. He had to try to unravel the modern knot of thought, while in the same breath get his point across. He hated it when these kinds of concept battles raged.

"Yes, Dreams are powerful," said Goose, trying

a different approach. "Maybe somehow one of those helmets is a Medicine Hat." But he scowled as though he'd just bitten into a very bitter lemon. "No, I doubt it."

Lightningbolt was wondering what Goose was getting at.

Suddenly, the old man sat up and smiled. "Yes," he began again. "You had that Dream. No Medicine Things at all, not a one I could see." His eyes were kind. "No magical feathers. No special horse. No talking Medicine Bundles." He seemed pensive now, quiet.

Lightningbolt's excitement was fading.

"Weapons, world eyes, ladders that shoot light," Goose tried to explain.

"Lasers, not ladders," Lightningbolt corrected him. A thought passed through his mind that possibly the old man had not understood any of his Dream images. He was mostly right.

"No flying horses." Goose blinked. "What an awful shame!" He stood and slowly walked to the stove and filled his cup with tea. "Must have been a Dream for a true Breed." He turned around.

Lightningbolt was now slumped in his chair.

"No Full-Blood ever had a Dream like that," Goose explained. He walked to the table and sat down. "Maybe it's a first? Maybe it isn't. Full-Bloods always get at least one feather, a gourd, a flying horse. I'm amazed."

"Wasn't one feather!" Lightningbolt complained. "There wasn't one in twenty thousand miles of my Dream. I never even saw a bird!"

"That's a crying shame." Goose was sympathetic. "We get Medicine Rattles. You got leather tanks—"

"Laser tanks," Lightningbolt interrupted.

Suddenly, Goose's face brightened. "You will learn of great discipline," the old man suddenly said overly loudly, finally discovering something he could talk about. "You were disciplined. Yes, that was it! That was your big sign!" Goose was visibly

relieved. "The Dream confronted you. Is it in you? Is it outside of you? I do not know."

Lightningbolt looked as though he had just bitten down hard on a chokecherry pit.

"You have to polish your armor." Goose was no longer hesitant. "Yes, you will have to listen in on your space scoops. It was a fine Breed Dream! I would be proud of it."

Lightningbolt took a sip of his coffee. He was very confused.

The old man sat back in his chair, contented, and began to reminisce. "In the old days, the people who'd had their Medicine Dreams would stand around in the big council circles and tell of them. It must have been very wonderful." He sighed.

The room became suddenly very quiet. Even though Lightningbolt had only met with Goose Flying nine times, he recognized another side of the man that he had learned to respect. When Goose grew quiet, he also became mysterious.

Being mysterious, Lightningbolt thought, was how a Medicine Man was supposed to be. Now he felt he was in his element.

Ignorance and expectations mix like mud at the bottom of a fast-moving stream. Young Lightningbolt was slowly sinking again into the mud.

"I have decided to send you down the mountain," Goose announced, looking very mysterious. "You will go down the Wyoming side. I want you to see Iron Blanket; he's an old friend. I am a Dreamer, he knows that. He also knows you are up here."

"No more talk about the Dream?" Lightningbolt asked.

"I do not know how to bring out your Dream so that you can possess it," Goose answered. "You are constantly into battle. That is good, but it is not my way. In a few more days the road will be plowed in Black Horse Pass. It's an easy ride down, hard riding back. Only eighteen miles."

The impending journey brought Lightningbolt renewed energy. Any physical action always promised an adventure to him. He was already eager to be on his way.

"You can send your horse back up with Iron Blanket, maybe," Goose continued. "He plans a visit up here with me. Tell that old man to bring up doughnuts. You forgot them. I will sleep soon. You must think about your Dream. The county workers are slow in Wyoming, but the pass will soon be plowed."

Lightningbolt stood, stretched and yawned. Now another Goose had appeared that he knew— the boring one. The mysterious Goose was gone.

"You'll probably want to chase some of those Arapaho girls down there," Goose droned on. "So while you're running around, you could look up Iron Blanket for me. He lives down by the old soap mill, you know, by Horse Creek. Tell him I'll have a Lodge with him when I come off the mountain. Maybe April sometime. There will be doctoring done at Iron Blanket's place. There always is. So tell that old man to prepare whatever it is he wants me to do."

Goose continued, not noticing Lightningbolt's change of mood. "Today you will prepare my Sweat Lodge, just like you did at Left Hand's place. Make sure the fire pit is cleaned out. Some hunters must have been by; there are rusted beer cans in there. Chop plenty of wood. Iron Blanket will be here to sweat with me. He uses a lot of wood. It's the cold . . . his old bones. My Medicine Bundle is hanging on a tree. Get it down and put it by the door of the Lodge. Use plenty of sweet grass. Make sure that my Eagle Wing is placed by the door; it likes it there. Now I'm going to sleep. This old man respects you, but you try me." He smiled, and shook Lightningbolt's hand warmly.

Lightningbolt returned to his Dream Room and dressed. He looked around while he slipped on his boots. The branches from the tree, all the green boughs, would have to be thrown away. That was

truly a shame.

Yes, it was true that he unraveled old Goose's braids, but the fact was, Goose also bothered him at times, too. He was terribly disappointed with the so-called Big Medicine Dream.

Why was it he kept coming up with a head full of air, when what he wanted was to fill his head with immense information? What got lost between doing and happening? There seemed to be a connection loose somewhere.

The room no longer looked the same. What happens when mystery and magic are gone? Was there such a thing as magic in the first place? He was beginning to think magic was only a dream.

Dan Hooper, the "money-roller" preacher, had warned him, "You will wrestle with demons when you go up to be with that Medicine Man. Run and save your soul!" The only demon Lightningbolt had wrestled with was his own stupidity. The money-roller knew nothing of the human right to privacy. To Hooper, "saving people" meant you had the right to violate anyone's privacy, anywhere, anytime. You could be a nuisance. You could be aggravating, uncouth. You could harass people and cause incredible pain because you wanted to missionize somebody.

Hooper thrived on gossip and other people's suffering. The more set against the preacher you were, the more he enjoyed it. The man adored pain. He loved the negative attention he received.

Lightningbolt returned to the main room and had another cup of coffee. Goose was in the tepee, sound asleep. He looked around the room. That rascal mouse had still not found the loaf of bread on the low shelf.

"Wait," he said to himself, "does Goose keep putting crumbs on the floor below the shelf to keep the mouse from climbing up to get the loaf?" He'd have to ask him.

The old man meant well, Lightningbolt knew that. But it sure would be a lot better if Goose had his act more together. Sometimes when the old man went off into the sky-blue yonder in his head, it was bothersome.

And why did Goose keep talking about the good old days? What the hell was so good about the early 1900s? From what he'd heard, it had been a hideous time for all Indians.

It was a lot more fun when the old man talked about powerful Medicines! Why did he have to keep dragging his feet into the crap of the past?

Lightningbolt put on his rubber overboots and tucked in his pants so his boots wouldn't fill up with snow or get his pants wet. The coat came next, then his cowboy hat.

41

Beauty—the spectacular expanse of the Little Big Horn—greeted Lightningbolt's entire being once he was outside. Everything he had been so concerned about seemed to fade from his consciousness once he'd looked at the grand mountains.

Lightningbolt worked quietly and deliberately until all of his tasks were completed, then he returned to the cabin to have a bite to eat. The cold deer meat still tasted delicious.

While he sat in the small room he felt incredibly confined, very closed in. The walls were threat-ening. Here he'd ridden all those miles in the extreme cold, only to have a simple, common, normal, everyday dream. Why had he believed that something extraordinary was going to happen to him? Remarkable and fantastic things always happened to others; why not him?

People inherited riches; they found fortunes. Some were incredibly beautiful or handsome, and some possessed inconceivably good fortune. Lightningbolt believed he had nothing.

The battle with the Water Gap, the challenge

and hardship, had become a proud memory. But this pride of accomplishment was not what he had been hoping for.

Wealth, money, he believed, was the answer to all of his problems. That is what he'd been taught.

"The Christmas tree is the white man's totem," his favorite uncle had once explained. "Christmas is their great reward time." People who couldn't pile the presents high were the dejected and the poor.

A preacher had once told his mother, "God has passed you by. Yes, passed right by the Indian and Breed people. You are doomed to poverty because God is punishing you for not believing in Him. You have found no favor in the eyes of God!"

Other people that Lightningbolt had met were told the opposite. The wealthy had been "blessed by God." But if the wealthy were not "good to God in return," they would lose everything!

He went to the corral and greeted Arrow. She pranced, enthusiastic to be leaving. She, too, had had enough of confinement.

"Hey, Big Nose," he purred to the gelding as he patted him and gave him two large handfuls of oats. "You stay. Don't spook the jackrabbits, okay?"

Horse and rider became one moving energy as Lightningbolt guided his friend across the broad plateau.

For some unexplained reason, Lightningbolt began to remember the incredibly powerful Goddess who had spoken to him and then given him his Dream.

Suddenly, he remembered that he had not told old Goose about his Dream Vision of the beautiful Goddess. How strange. He wondered why he'd left this out.

He struggled to picture her in his mind. Soon his thoughts of the Goddess united with the beauty of the snow that surrounded him.

One crystalline sphere sparkled with its atomic energy, firing darts of holographic mesons from its center that rocketed from its microvoid up into the broad Universe.

The tiny crystal's light joined with endless numbers of other crystalline worlds of its kind—becoming one wondrous, tiny circle of icy prisms that reflected the Sun.

That one very important circle of nuclear matter danced alone among endless billions and trillions of energy-shadow-crystals called snowflakes.

The snowflake was exceedingly beautiful, magnificent and flawless within what Creation had decided would be one tiny microjewel of water.

Billions of these remarkable gems of Eternity caught a very infinitesimal portion of our spacious galaxy, the sunlight, and they playfully teased the eyes of the young horseman who rode toward Black Horse Pass.

With this song of color and enchantment, Lightningbolt was also given a beautiful daydream. He imagined that the shimmering bands of rainbows that danced along the floor of the valley were playful little girls and boys, sprites, fairies of every description, who leaped and frolicked as light.

The shadows and rainbows moved as horse and rider moved, blending and ever changing, becoming a cadence that only the Universe understood.

This dazzling white, alternating with the deep rich blacks and browns of the shadowy places between the broad expanses of snow and the opulent greens of the towering pines in the forest, challenged his eyes. The surrounding mountains promised treasure and offered to share their secrets—silver, gold, tourmaline, sapphire, black coal, hidden crystals, ancient bones—all calling to the

44

resourceful who passed this way.

Lightningbolt's attention was drawn to the black silhouettes of massive stones that were snuggled, like old Buffalo Chiefs, in the small valleys and arroyos of the low rolling hills. Some of the stones looked like a cavalcade of Breed traders on their way to Eternity.

Such a splendid land! Would She be cared for? He hoped with all of his heart that Her beauty would be respected and loved.

Where does shadow begin? Shadow changes with the Sun, moving with all plants and all animals, and merging with the night, dances with the Moon and the Stars. There is no beginning to shadow and no end of light. All storms are the blend of light and shadow. Even in the deepest part of the Sacred Earth, there is light and there is shadow.

Lightningbolt saw shadow and light in another kind of beauty. This time it was the beauty of the magpies that flew along just ahead of him. The flashing white and black of their wings toyed with his understanding, and Lightningbolt began to pray. He did this by appreciating all that he saw.

"How do you mix the bitter with the sweet?" he asked himself. "Are Life and Death reconcilable?"

The flight of the magpies said yes. Their very existence said that the sweet and the bitter are both part of learning. Their beauty spoke to his feelings and separated his fears from his thoughts.

Yes, this is the way with Life. She teaches all Her children through experience. But can we remember these clear illuminations when we need them? Lightningbolt wondered if he would have the courage to continue his search.

Three hours later, Arrow picked her way carefully down into the broad, shallow ravine called the Little Bow. How long had this ancient canyon known humans?

Fantastic and bizarre shapes of every description met the eyes of horse and rider in the canyon. All were beautiful. The Little Bow was known for its thousands upon thousands of pure white sandstone sculptures. Most of the forms had been carved by wind and water. Some were painted gold, white, black, and red.

A thought leaped into his mind that caused him to rein in Arrow. He was in a place where the wind had blown the snow from the golden grasses of the valley.

The floor of the canyon was composed of white sand. It was soft, the kind of sand he loved to jump on and roll in when he was a boy. He had been to the wide draw more than once.

Once there had been a war in this small canyon. Some people recalled it as a massacre, while others simply forgot that the incident had ever happened. Because the death ground existed between Wyoming and Montana, it continued to be an in-between place, never really admitted to, or fitting in anywhere. It was one of those very ugly stories, never called history, that many did not want to remember.

Sixty adults had lived in the Little Bow; all were known to be Medicine People. And there were an equal number of young people and children. Their presence in the Little Bow raised two issues that the local authorities did not like. One was that the "renegades" were living off the Reservation, on land that was wanted by whites. The second was that "heathen and pagan rites" were being practiced in the canyon; yet, they knew the Indians were Healers and simple keepers of the land.

Lightningbolt thought of the immigrants who had come to America in search of self-government and freedom of religion. The immigrants had found their dream, yet they refused to allow other people their personal expressions of community and reli-

gion. They brutally murdered the Indians because they refused to leave the canyon.

Who were these forgotten casualties? First of all, they were not an "authorized band," and consequently they were not protected by the government. Not being "official" meant that they did not exist as humans. And so they were called a "hodgepodge of dangerous renegades."

In reality, these people were families from many different tribes that had been decimated. They moved to the canyon because this place was known to be sacred. These desperate people thought they could find safety there. Now all that remained was the ugly story that only a handful of people could remember. And bones.

Lightningbolt had been told about the Little Bow when he was a boy.

The shallow canyon meandered, like a great white snake, down from the mountains. It twined and turned upon itself, and moved from one side of the Little Bow valley to the other—until it ended at Black Horse Pass. Here the "jade writing" could be found—pictographs that had been painted there long ago.

At one time the entire length of the long gorge had been covered by these picture writings. Dynamite, tourists, grave robbers, millions of bullets, high school beer busts, college field trips, archaeologists, anthropologists, graffiti nuts, picnickers, outdoorsmen, hunters, drunks, willful destroyers, the well-meaning, the stupid, the insane, and the angry had destroyed almost every sign that had once existed. What little wear and erosion had been caused by weather was negligible.

Lightningbolt eased Arrow around the jumble

of stone. He remembered that he and the other boys from Crow Agency had shot away many of the pictographs with their .22s. Only later had he been taught to "read" many of the signs that had once existed here.

Why were people so destructive? A tear trickled down his cheek. There was no answering for his part in the carnage.

Suddenly, he was aroused by the realization that he could still read some of the scarred surfaces of the canyon walls.

He reined in his horse and stood up in his stirrups as high as he could, to look over the boulders that surrounded him. There was a sign! Part of another! Still another! He carefully turned Arrow and allowed her to find her way through the stones and large rocks. Now he could see the writing much more clearly.

"Two horn . . . erect horn standing," the signs read. "They or he moves . . . obliterated . . . the . . . obliterated . . . turtle . . . that . . . obliterated . . . sings. Pyramid . . . obliterated . . . sings. Falls down . . . obliterated. The battle. Two strikes . . . the Eagle . . . obliterated . . . marking into the Sun Cave . . . obliterated. Winter Sun Road . . . obliterated. Basketmakers . . . between . . . obliterated . . . Little Horn . . . Big . . . obliterated . . . sheep . . . dancing."

"Big horn sheep dancing." He beamed broadly. He looked up at the peaks some people continued to call Big Horn Sheep Kiva. "There has to be a big Kiva up there, or a Sun Cave." He turned Arrow toward the Big Horn Sheep Mountains, determined to find that cave.

Excitement coursed through every cell of Lightningbolt's body as he rode toward the big U in

47

the peaks. He guessed that it was the key to finding the Kiva. He knew that the U shape also meant "woman," and that the "Basketmakers" were women who were Healers.

There was a natural U-shaped stone at the large arroyo called Sheep's Head. There also was an older way of saying that name; in Crow it meant "Sheep Dancing." Stories abounded about how the Kiva was filled to the ceiling with ancient Mayan or Aztec gold. The Big Migration of the Four Mirrors People had brought the gold north around 1000 B.C.

If he was right, he had made a discovery of paramount significance to everyone. Gold seekers had gossiped and speculated for years, but no one had made any headway finding the treasure.

Lightningbolt began to daydream of becoming instantly wealthy. Would the gold still be there?

He laughed, feeling his need and hope—both

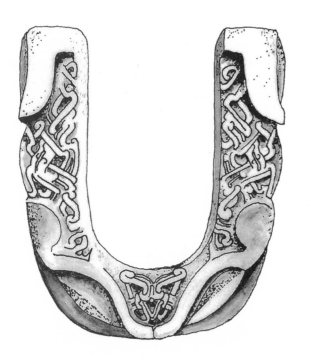

were exhilarating and drove him forward. Arrow also caught Lightningbolt's mood. Fear made her prance in the snow. Her sudden change of rhythm and her nervousness made him more alert, and he pulled her to a quick halt.

Here he was going off the deep end again. Right off the wall! The deafening roar of doubt and hesitation flooded his heart with every conceivable anxiety.

Arrow patiently pawed away the snow and found a little grass to graze on.

Why hadn't far wiser people than he found that cave? "Sighting along the U stone" was a "secret" that probably even Hollywood scriptwriters knew!

Lightningbolt felt ill.

Suddenly, the mountains taunted him with their immense size and excruciating distance. What had appeared to be so easy now seemed almost impossible.

"I must have put my boots on backwards this morning, Arrow," he said, trying to ease his fears.

Talking to his horse was not going to help. Lightningbolt would have to seriously communicate with himself if a decent decision was going to be made. Summer . . . now there was an excellent time to go searching in the mountains.

He dug for a chocolate bar in his saddlebag. He found one and bit it in half. He chewed it, paper and all.

"Autumn, Summer, Spring," he said, spitting out the paper. "A Jeep would be good, a battle tank, half a dozen friends, explosives, maybe a couple of witches. Why not? What do you think, Arrow?"

He pulled up his friend's head and nudged her with his boot heels. "When in doubt, attack," he said to her.

As he rode toward his goal he again went through what he knew, or believed he knew. "Woman" had been written on the pictographs— this definitely had to mean the U stone; the "Winter Sun Road" had to be a line of sight during Winter. Yet, how many people really took the pictographs seriously?

Other Breeds and Indians, that's who. This realization made him feel terrible again, but he continued to ride.

Twenty minutes later he arrived at the U stone. The treasure seeker jumped from Arrow's back and squatted down on his haunches. He picked up a stick and scraped away the snow. A quick glance said where the Sun would rise. Next, he drew a line from the U stone toward the mountain.

There it was, wobbly as a duck's bill, but straight enough to make sense. He would have to hobble Arrow, feed her, then make the remainder of the journey by foot.

"Damned Sun goes from East to West," he said to himself, "and West from the U stone is the mountain." It was all too easy.

Lightningbolt was embarrassed. He would be humiliated if anyone actually found him here; yet, his stubbornness drove him onward.

He removed all of his belongings from his mount and covered them with an oiled tarp. He thought for a moment of taking his rifle, but decided at the last second to leave it. He only took his backpack and knife.

As he climbed the going got tough. Things could quickly become dangerous if he wasn't careful. Jumping from one exposed rock to the next took enormous energy. But it kept him out of the low places where the snow was deep. He slipped more than once, scraping his knees and stinging his hands raw trying to avoid the deep snowdrifts.

Forty minutes later he sat, exhausted, his back resting against a large boulder. The blood pounded in his ears. Playing the role of the idiot was not to his liking, and at this point he was sure he was on a fool's journey. But his anger and determination drove him unmercifully.

Care would have to be taken or he could lose his life. He made it a point to keep brushing away all the snow that collected at the top of his boots. He searched for pine limbs and made a fire. Before he went any farther, he knew his clothes had to be dried and he'd have to get his hands warm again. He pulled the tent from his backpack and looked around for a suitable area to pitch it.

The only place free of snow was right in the middle of the trail. Setting up the tent on the trail was the obvious and intelligent thing to do, but his superstition forbade it. Building a camp exactly in the middle of a trail where you were traveling was frowned upon. You could be attacked if you camped in the middle of the Journey Path, the old hunters had warned.

There simply was no other place for the tent within a hundred yards of where he was standing. He hated it, but finally made up his mind to sleep in the middle of the trail. This last decision, he hoped, would not be piled on the other bad decisions—especially the one he'd made to find the cave in the first place.

He brooded about his foolishness while he ate his corned beef hash out of the can. From his high stone perch he could see some of the most splendid land ever created, yet his eyes were focused inward.

Everything he wanted to do had to be done between jobs. Why did work and money have to rule his life? If he'd been allowed to join the military, he'd have bars on his shoulders by now.

The long ride to Goose Flying's cabin came back to haunt him. A Medicine Dream? He could have had that Dream in his own bed.

He was in a great mood! The thought of a mountain lion eating his hobbled horse popped into his mind. Why not? He could just see himself walking for days, limping, dejected, battered by weather. Sure, he probably deserved it. Fools should be shot.

He imagined the headline: BODY FOUND. He sighed.

The following morning was remarkable. It was bright and the snow that lay before him appeared to be sparse.

Again, he calculated the angle of the Sun and drew a line in his mind from East to West, estimating how far he'd have to go before he found the cave.

His climb was slow and rigorous but not nearly as agonizing as it had been the day before. He crawled and climbed up the mountain, entering one large ravine after another. He knew he'd feel very foolish if he suddenly came upon a path. The thought made him cuss and climb even harder.

Unexpectedly he found himself in a mammoth gorge. He felt as though he were the size of an ant in the measureless jumble of stones. Undaunted, he wound his way through the boulders until he was confronted by two narrow crevasses.

He chose the one on the left and began to follow it. The constricted passage turned and twisted until he stood before what appeared to be a door made of granite. He studied the carved and chipped stone carefully. Yes, beyond all doubt, it was a door.

Here was victory, but he would not allow himself to enjoy the taste of it. It was always that last minute, that final step, that could disappoint a person. Just as with the Dream, when he had been so excited. But what had he discovered? Nothing.

How many times had it happened—that old disillusionment? A hundred times? A thousand? Beyond this stone there could be anything, including a solid wall.

"No more time," he declared out loud to himself. "It's time for work again. Open it."

Throwing his pack down by the wall, he braced his legs to open the heavy door. He put all his weight into it, but unexpectedly the stone moved easily and quickly, smashing his right thumb against the wall. The pain was aggravated by the cold.

"Daaammit!" he bawled. "That hurt!" He

50

kicked at the door but missed it.

Sucking his thumb, he found himself staring into emptiness. It was very dark in there. He tried to dig his cigarette lighter out of his right pocket using his left hand, but he could only get two fingers in.

"Dammit," he cursed again, shaking his thumb.

He tried his left hand again, but his jeans were just too tight to get the thing out. He'd have to retrieve it with his battered hand.

"Having a hard day, Dopey?" a man's deep voice boomed from the darkness. "Or is it you, Bashful? Or Doc or Sleepy? Maybe Stupid or Jerk?"

Lightningbolt was struck dumb with surprise and terror.

"Whhaaa," he answered, trying to sound intelligent instead of terrified. "Errr . . . ahhh."

"We're having a great conversation," said the voice, taunting him. "Feel like breaking down and crying?"

"Damn!" Lightningbolt finally said in a whisper.

"I can see you're really bright," the voice remarked wryly. "I can see you are a man of many words. Come in, but don't talk. It's forbidden to talk in here."

Lightningbolt strained to see into the labyrinth, trying to discern what lay before him.

"Look at you, you dog," the voice confronted Lightningbolt. "Standing there looking like a pale owl. If you could see yourself, you would scream with laughter. But no, you'd rather just stand there blinking."

"Who in hell are you?" Lightningbolt suddenly demanded.

"Your immediate problem and guide," the man answered. "Come in now, or get the hell out of here, and remember, it is forbidden to talk in this Sacred Kiva."

Lightningbolt groped forward, swinging his outstretched hands before him. He was mumbling.

"Shut the door!" the voice commanded from somewhere in the darkness. "Were you raised in a barn?"

Lightningbolt cursed, then turned on his heel intending to retrace his steps and begin again. He did not like the sound of his situation at all! Suddenly, a bright fire sprang to life behind him. He spun to face his host and antagonist.

"The people you see when you don't have a gun," the keeper of the cave announced in an authoritative voice. He had a smile that could instantly win the favor of any creature, animal or human. "Close the draft," he demanded.

Lightningbolt wrestled the door back into place, then walked respectfully to the old Indian's fire.

The old man circled around Lightningbolt, appraising him as though he were checking out a horse he intended to buy. "Healthy, not a drinker," he mused. "Could be a troublemaker, a little stupid at times. Where do you come from? No, shut up, don't answer. You can call me Keeper."

Lightningbolt was feeling very nervous.

Aside from the fact that Keeper was obviously very old, everything else about the man was a testimony to something other than being old. His appearance was somewhere between an eighteenth-century coastal pirate and a modern guerrilla fighter from some jungle in Middle America.

He was swarthy, and yet his skin was delicate. He certainly was not a white man. Lightningbolt knew that Keeper was an American Indian, but from which continent, North or South? If he were to guess, he'd say Keeper was an Inca.

Keeper's armament was also an attention-getter. He had on a highly polished handmade Mexican gun belt. In the holster was a .357 Magnum. At his waist he wore a knife called a shoulder blade by the old Cheyenne, also called a bowie knife by the whites.

The man's face fascinated Lightningbolt. Deep lines had been carved into Keeper's face by weather and time, but there were also soft care lines around his eyes.

At one time he would have been called "hawk-nosed" and some would have even found his face hard. But with time, the beauty that shone from within had given the man the look of power.

It was Keeper's eyes that made the deepest impression on Lightningbolt. Those intense eyes were highly charismatic. But they were also the eyes of a killer.

Suddenly the old man sat down in a modern-looking rocking chair. His eyebrows raised. He was toying with his visitor again. "Why, don't you realize that all true Medicine Men and keepers use rocking chairs? It's part of their modern accoutrements."

Lightningbolt frowned.

"Don't know the word?" Keeper almost purred with satisfaction. "Well, it means 'equipment.' Yes, you see, young one, old rascals like me test different things, including people."

Lightningbolt cleared his throat.

"Quiet, destroyer," the old man demanded in his low voice. "Noise is a word. Yes, as I was saying, you did not know the word, so I have an instant gauge of your education."

Should he put more branches on the fire? No, touching the man's fire wasn't right. What could he say that would sound intelligent?

A thousand thoughts, ten thousand doubts, and a million fears flooded into his mind and heart as he stared into the embers, but could he get his mind working and present? No.

Where did the smoke go? Was there a natural

chimney? Why wasn't it smokier in the cave?

"Have I provoked a little thinking?" said Keeper, breaking into Lightningbolt's thoughts. "What's on your mind? No, don't tell me. It's forbidden to talk. Let me tell you about this Kiva of Heartbeat, or Cave, whatever you prefer to call Her. Would you like to know?"

Lightningbolt nodded, but he did not lift his eyes from the glowing coals.

"What brings us to places like this?" Keeper asked. His voice had not changed, but he seemed closer somehow.

Lightningbolt jerked his eyes up into Keeper's. There was that sparkle. But a challenge was now registered there that could not be ignored.

"This Cave," Keeper continued, "is like a complex dream. It is much more than a physical cavern. It draws people here of many kinds and many Heartbeats. Yet, only a tiny handful have found the cave by themselves. How did you find it? Were you escaping?

Lightningbolt shook his head.

"Speak, tell me," Keeper demanded.

"No, I wasn't escaping," Lightningbolt answered. "Where is all the gold?"

"We will speak of that later." Keeper frowned. "How did you find the Kiva?"

"The Sun Road," Lightningbolt answered matter-of-factly. He was feeling very sure of himself. "The U stone, Basketmakers, it figures. Woman and U stone are shown to be the same in the old pictographs. Old Goose explained that much."

"Goose did? Damn his old hide!" Keeper cursed. "He is a fool for teaching people how to get here."

"Goose only spoke of the signs," Lightningbolt

said defensively. "I figured it out while I was in the Little Bow. Ever use that?" Lightningbolt pointed to the old man's pistol.

"Why not?" Keeper answered. "Humanity uses it as a sewing awl. We poke holes in a lot of people with the bullets that come from them. After all the holes have bled the people, then we try to stitch everyone together again with politics. Yet, what can I say? I sure hope I don't have to shoot you."

Lightningbolt nodded his agreement.

"There are some very strange people that come around here," Keeper explained. "I have seen just about everything. You're some kind of fool if you expect me to instantly trust you or like you. What if you came here to kill yourself? You could be a supernut for all I know."

"Curiosity, and the talk about gold," Lightningbolt offered. "That was my target." He looked around. "What happened to the gold? Did it ever exist?"

"Curiosity"—Keeper smiled as he shook his head—"is simply not enough. I think we have concluded our visit. Time for you to leave."

Lightningbolt looked down at his hands. "It's strange," he told the old man, "but I become stupid at times and defensive. It was your approach with me, the gun. I'm sorry."

Keeper stirred the fire. "Let's begin again," he offered. "Why are you here?"

"I crawled up the mountain from the Little Bow," Lightningbolt answered. "Looks like I took the hard way. I felt stupid doing it. I wanted something, gold, anything. As soon as I saw you in here, I knew you had a cabin somewhere near. You confronted me big; I thought you just might be a bit dangerous too. Okay, so I got jumpy and too quiet."

"I never asked for an apology," Keeper interrupted. "All right, you came up the hard way."

A long silence followed. Only the crackle of the fire could be heard.

"I've been bulldogging you because I didn't know what to do or ask," said Lightningbolt, embarrassed. He stood up and handed Keeper a pack of cigarettes. "I bring you this tobacco. I am sorry that I have not been a man of care. What is a Kiva?"

Time seemed to ebb into a spiral of thought within Lightningbolt. The fire drew his attention, and it held him captivated with its warmth and ever-changing patterns of light and dark.

"This cave is a Kiva," the old man explained, taking the cigarettes. "Kiva means 'Sacred Womb.' It is the Earth's womb of Life and Death."

Lightningbolt sat quietly, wanting to hear more.

After a respectful lapse of time, it was right for Lightningbolt to tell Keeper who he was and how his journey had brought him to the Kiva. He told about his journey through the Water Gap, the Pool of Stars, and about all that had happened, including how he had Dreamed of a wondrous Goddess. He also told Keeper about the toy parade and the Dream of the war. Keeper signed that he had understood, then he heated up the coffee on a grate over his fire.

After he shared the coffee, he settled himself in his rocking chair. He set his cup beside his chair and was soon nodding off to sleep.

An instant change came over Keeper while he slept. He no longer looked fierce. The five-foot-nine man who now slept like a child was not the seven-foot giant that Lightningbolt had met earlier.

The penetrating quiet of the Sacred Mother Cavern provoked a deep calling to all who would journey with Her into the Womb of Her Earthly Universe.

Lightningbolt's entire being seemed suddenly suspended between sleep and dwelling within his daydreams. His imagination blended with fantasy, while at the same moment he was calculating and logical.

A half hour later, when Keeper began to speak, Lightningbolt was deep within his reverie and had not noticed what was happening around him.

Keeper spoke softly. "This ancient Cave, She keeps Her secrets and She gives. You are present with Her. She has just Dreamed with you.

"The gold you sought has been steadily robbed from this cavern, for a couple of thousand years, by both Indian and white. The last of the big pieces of gold was melted down in the late 1800s. Brass copies of a few of the smaller objects were attempted. But the entire job was botched. The Keepers who existed before me tried to save the history but they knew nothing of pouring metals."

The old man rose, stretched, then disappeared into one of the most distant corners of the cave. He returned and handed Lightningbolt a brass object. It was ugly and misshapen. Whatever it had been, there was no way of recognizing it now.

Lightningbolt was so disappointed he was next to tears.

The old man sat back down and sipped some of his cold coffee.

"I am sick of finding nothing," Lightningbolt said through his teeth. "Everything I find or touch turns into nothingness."

"I can understand your feelings exactly," said Keeper soothingly. "Yet, it's your ignorance that confronts you, not your physical world. You simply don't know what treasure is. You have no way of knowing if something is worthwhile for you."

"But how do I learn?" Lightningbolt asked. "Dammit, isn't there a beginning someplace?"

"That Dream of yours." Keeper seemed to lure with his words. "The Dream is of immense value. But you're too ignorant to understand it."

"How do I understand it?" Lightningbolt insisted. "You willing to take the time to teach me how?"

"Most of that 'how' begins with you," Keeper directed him. "It is that word *how* that really matters. It is not what we do. That is why legislating what humans should do never works. It is how that always matters.

"How is what is crucial here," he said, unbuckling his gun belt and handing Lightningbolt his pistol. "Here's your payment for coming all the way out here to see me."

"No thanks." Lightningbolt smiled and handed back the gun.

"All right," said Keeper flatly. "But isn't the gun pay? A thief would spend enormous time stealing a gun like this one."

"I'm not a thief," Lightningbolt replied.

"You're not, eh?" Keeper growled. "You rob yourself of opportunities to learn. You rob yourself of time. You rob yourself of an education."

"You suggesting I go to college?" said Lightningbolt mockingly.

"Obviously not," said Keeper. "Why should you be educated? And, obviously, what I have to say on the subject has no worth."

"It's the shit they feed you," Lightningbolt complained. "They're just a bunch of shit shovelers."

"Did I say you had to get a degree?" Keeper parried. "Why eat the shit unless you want to teach, or get one of the jobs they say you can do? No, I mean you need educating. It's *how* you learn. *How* you understand what they teach. You have a mind. Use it."

"I won't do it," said Lightningbolt stubbornly.

"Won't what? Go to school or learn?" Keeper asked. "I don't think you know the difference. I'm not trying to talk you into going to college."

"Then what are you asking?" Lightningbolt frowned. He was getting angrier by the minute.

"I'm not asking you for a damned thing," said Keeper sharply. "Look, stupid, it's you that needs educating, not me. Even the use of that word *ask* tells me about your attitudes, not your thinking. If you want to fight, go. Go out in the snow and kick ass. Good-bye."

There was a long and uncomfortable silence.

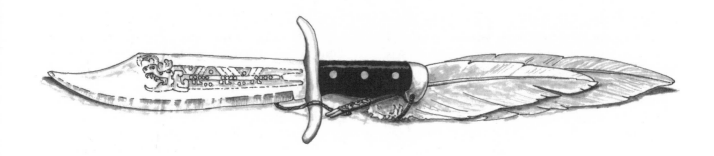

"I was rejected by the military," Lightningbolt finally said. "I can't see well with my left eye. I should be in training. I'd have made a damned good officer." Lightningbolt's voice was suddenly full of rage. "All my life I wanted to be in the military. Now, what's left for me? I'm a nobody stuck on this Reservation. Sure I'm ignorant. Sure I need educating. But how?"

"So you want to kill, do you?" Keeper grinned. "I've seen your face on a hundred parade grounds. You blunder forward and stumble around hoping to find the Big Thing, the Big Medicine. Well, you wouldn't know what to do with it if it hit you in the nuts. Here you are in a cave instead of running around in some shit hole in Asia. What the hell are you doing here?"

"Looking for information, that's what." Lightningbolt grinned. "Looks like you've got lots of it. Maybe I struck gold after all."

"I want to demonstrate what I do best." Keeper's voice grew quiet. "I will help you become part of this cavern one more time, all right?"

"One more time?" Lightningbolt asked, intrigued.

"You Dreamed with the Kiva," Keeper reported. "She Dreams with all who come here. But now you will Dream with me. Are you ready for that?"

"Am I going to sleep by the fire?" Lightningbolt asked.

"No," Keeper answered. "You're going to sit up and keep a high attention at all times. Look into the fire, or look into the quiet of this Kiva."

"We experience our greatest fears and our deepest pain, our sorrow, when we must leave our beautiful Earth, Mother Life. So, wanderer, why is it that many humans will throw away their lives to prove the ridiculous? Why do people prefer their pretense instead of the joy of Life's challenges? Who is family when we never know them? Does language make a race, or does belief make a race? Possibly, you should ask these questions, Lightningbolt.

"Appreciation of Life is the most honorable of all tools of the mind. Do you know this tool? The powerful know this tool intimately. Appreciation and knowledge are the most powerful tools given to humans in any lifetime. Appreciation of Life is the tool of attainment.

"I was born April Horse. But those that know me, know that I am Shadow. My world is in these mountains. Morning Sun Mother, She touches me deeply. I would probably die if She did not love me.

"I have my sheep. They have their grasses. They have their never-knowing. Their never-knowing comforts them. They know me as their comforting Shadow.

"I am more terrible than the Mountain Spirit, the big cat. Yet, do the sheep know that Shadow is a greater threat? The sheep do not fear that which cares for them. They do not see that the Shadow that feeds them also eats them.

"This is the way it is with many things. Est-cheemah, she became my teacher, my Medicine Horse. She carries me and she shares with all. Yet, I am the Shadow. I am not her, and she is not me.

"It is the seeking that has brought you here to my world. I can break your every weapon. All you really have is your Self. No protection, no weapons, can give you security.

"You must see into my mind, young Wolf. Here in these mountains you are Wolf, *Moheegun*. This you are called because you are that. You are the Wolf.

"Now you face the Shadow. You must fight the Shadow. I will show you my every fear. Are you strong? Are you courageous? You will walk upon my roads of pain. You will see me hunger and thirst. We will watch the cannons roar and shout hate at the sky. You will smell the fresh blood of those torn to pieces. You will die slowly with me.

"You will watch men die when my rifle bullets put them to sleep. So the Japs died. How desperately sad. Will I cry forever? I killed so many of my brothers.

"Their deaths opened my eyes. I, the Shadow, was born and I herd my sheep. So you dare look into the world of the Shadow? You desire to see into my mind and my fate? Your teeth will grate together as have mine. You will suffer my suffering.

"Everything is here for us on Earth. Life has given us all that we desire to learn, and all we need for us to grow while we are here on Earth. Yes, She has even provided us with the stinging ants, the spiders, and disease. But these are nothing, no kind of threat equal to what we did to our brothers. We did not sting them; we blew them to pieces with our cannons and our grenades.

"She gives us our chance for Life. We use our lives to kill. That was what I did. I used Her gifts to kill.

"I have tasted fire and I have known awful war. I have killed men, my brothers. They say that I, the Shadow, speak only in symbols. Do symbols speak more than humans? Do symbols taste the stink of Death? I see them. I see their whitened skulls.

"Our madness was organized. It seemed so normal. It was an everyday thing to be mad. We were trained in our madness. We enjoyed our weapons. At the time we had reasons to kill. It was all normal, clear and understandable. *They* were the enemy.

"When the war broke out I was one of the guys called Pappy or Grandpappy. The army was made up of kids, most of them little more than eighteen years old. I was an older guy, nearly forty-two years old. That is an old man in the army! I was also an Indian. I had nothing to look forward to. I wanted to be part of the big them, the army, but I did not know how.

"We knew nothing more than our illusions. We learned to despise the enemy. We became the perfect shadows. I would creep into the jungle and kill silently. Killing became my mind, my heart, my everything. I would breathe my silence and Death. We were trained to be efficient. I was very efficient. I counted coup with my knife.

"When the officers passed out our ribbons of Death, our kill squad would laugh inside. We had a strange pride in not telling all. That was who we were at the time. I was the Shadow, a perfect machine, born to terrorize the enemy.

"We were the best of the kill squads. We were trained to kill at a distance and up close. We knew

every weapon. I wanted to be powerful. I think I must have killed two hundred men. I was accepted, I was slapped on the back. My officers loved me.

"We were going slowly mad, but we did not know it. Our madness disallowed even our Dreaming.

"We would kill always from the shadows; that was my specialty. We had our different specialties and our special madnesses. Not one of the men I killed ever saw me.

"No, not one man ever saw me until one day, a boy looked into my eyes. I saw that he was crying. He was so very young, it amazed me! I had cut his throat to make sure he was dead. I was afraid he would scream, you know? I was afraid he would make a noise. We were all in a tight position at the time. I died with him. After I looked into his young eyes, I was no more. My madness was taken from me and I could see. When I could see, I died.

"My pain dissolved and I held my madness in my hands. My madness was the bloody head of a Japanese boy. My challenges in this Life have taught me to see pain and madness.

"You can find your Life, but only when you see the truth of your circumstances and the challenges that exist in your time. Search for the person you *are*, not the person you wish you *were*.

"The crying, bloody head told me to be myself and not the madman.

"Confront your own world of mind. What is it that exists in your world? Who are you in your own world—the slave or the commander?

"Do you know what arrogant men fear? They fear they can never possess the powerful or the beautiful. What they do is substitute their fear for their arrogance and try to buy their lives. Life will never be their prostitute; they cannot buy Her."

As the magic of Shadow's voice faded into the Cavern of the Earth Womb, a feeling of extraordinary sadness collided with Lightningbolt's facade of discipline.

The soft elusive light from the glowing coals illuminated his tears, reflecting the amber, red, and gold of the fire. He wept quietly, holding in his desperate anguish.

Why Lightningbolt was weeping he did not fully understand. The Kiva's vast darkness was awesome, and Lightningbolt began to recognize feelings he never knew he possessed.

Shadow studied the sorrowful young man who sat cross-legged at his fire. He could see that his visitor was now open to advice and information. But he also knew that he had only one chance to reach Lightningbolt's mind and heart. He had to be right with what he would suggest.

Lightningbolt continued to keep his eyes attuned to the Kiva's light while the old veteran was speaking.

"Wolf, look at me," Shadow suddenly demanded. "It's time for you to wake up."

"Wake up?" Lightningbolt asked, looking directly into Shadow's eyes. "What do you mean?"

"You have Dreamed with me, but now you are going to look at your own world. Old Goose has outsmarted you and you still haven't seen the obvious. Who sent you on this trail, if it wasn't old Goose?"

"Goose?" Lightningbolt was fighting hard to follow Shadow.

"Who knew you'd be bored and reading the signs along the trail? Wasn't it Goose who taught you the signs?" Shadow was pressing him.

"He aimed me here like a bullet!" Lightningbolt swore with surprise, finally catching Shadow's meaning. "I'll be . . ."

"Right where he wanted you to be," Shadow insisted. "And he didn't send you here to get saved, or to have your back scratched. He knew he was sending you to a man who knows extreme pain."

Lightningbolt's feelings suddenly wavered between distrust and excitement. Had old Goose planned the meeting? If he had, then Lightningbolt was impressed!

"I have a deep feeling, yes, even a knowledge, that you were born a soldier," Shadow said emphatically. "And I think that's the reason Goose sent you to me."

"That's ridiculous!" Lightningbolt lashed out. "What the hell does Goose know? I mean . . ." The sound of his own voice startled him. It cracked and was strange to his ears, even foreign. "There's no war for me."

"Oh, you will have your war." Shadow's voice was cold. "I assure you. But beyond that I can tell you that you are a 'recognizable.' A recognizable is a woman or man who knows close combat instinctively. No person who has known the terror of war could miss it. Yes, you were born a soldier. I think that's the reason old Goose wanted you to blunder into me. As a child you dreamed of war, just like I did.

"You're not a militarist," Shadow pointed out. "I'm not suggesting you are or ever will be. No, it's not that. It's your mind and heart that make you a soldier. I'd stake my Life on it. But your war is not the one you imagined."

An awesome feeling gripped Lightningbolt. It seemed to come from some primal place deep within him. The ancient silence quickened his heart and shocked his senses with its earthly presence. The silence engulfed him, flooding his mind until it became a truth he could not deny.

In this instant a momentous flash of Self recognition came to Lightningbolt. An absolute knowing coursed through every cell of his body, telling him that Shadow was right.

Shadow smiled. "No, it's not a prophecy I'm sharing with you. It's a picture of who you are. I think we can talk to each other now. What do you say?"

"Yes, I think we can," said Lightningbolt quietly.

The young man who left the Shadow Kiva was not the same person who had entered. As he led his horse back along the creek toward Little Bow Canyon, he was thinking about all that he had learned.

He realized that in such a brief time he had come to love April Horse. The old renegade had connected deeply with his heart and mind. Finally he had met someone who understood at least some of his feelings.

The experience that April Horse had described, calling it his "old existence," wasn't very pretty, but it wasn't entirely ugly either.

Arrow stopped so suddenly to graze on a clump of honey-flavored dry flowers that Lightningbolt was pulled backward and landed on his rear. He stood up and brushed off his pants, then looked around his beautiful world. If it got any warmer he'd have to remove one of his layers of clothes.

Much of Shadow's pain loomed overlarge to Lightningbolt. He could follow what Keeper had said, but a lot of what had been shared was almost impossible for him to comprehend.

Why was Life so complicated?

Lightningbolt swung into the saddle and kicked Arrow into a trot.

His mother, April Horse, Goose—even his uncle, old man Back Bone the old storyteller—lived in radically separate worlds. How was it possible to ever bring them together? There was no hope for any kind of reconciliation or understanding among them. They agreed on nothing.

Yet, Lightningbolt could have witnessed a small miracle if he had been trained to see the obvious.

Estcheemah had confronted the sad killer in the mountains and had healed his terrible wounds. She had brought forward four distinct beings in the one man who had formerly been known as John Hotoosie. These were the four distinct parts of the one man that Lightningbolt had met in the cave.

There was Keeper, the Old Man, April Horse,

and Shadow.

Keeper was formidable, even menacing. He forced all those who found their way to the Kiva to interact with all of his personalities. It was his way of confronting what people kept hidden.

It was Keeper whom Lightningbolt had first met. He was the aggressive one who could frighten a visitor if the need arose. Keeper had to discover who was dangerous and who was not.

The Old Man was kind and saw to every visitor's physical needs. He was the one who had carefully explained so much to Lightningbolt, once the young man had become familiar with his new surroundings.

April Horse was the experienced veteran, knowledgeable about the world and filled with information. April Horse could mediate almost any kind of complicated situation. He was the survivor, the decision maker.

Shadow was the Healer and Medicine Man. He was a paradox: gentle and kind, yet ruthless when it came to the teaching and care of another human. Shadow was the poet, the man of deep introspection.

Lightningbolt had asked April Horse about his daydreams of power and what he could do with them. But it was Shadow who had answered. Shadow straightaway reminded him of his Medicine Dream and explained that a part of Lightningbolt lived vicariously.

Lightningbolt had no idea what the word *vicarious* was supposed to mean. Vicarious people, Shadow told him, were the "big viewers" in his dream. A minor explosion of talk erupted for two minutes after Shadow had explained the word *vicarious*. Lightningbolt was shocked that Shadow would even suggest such a thing and became abusive until April Horse stepped forward and put an end to Lightningbolt's ravings.

It was the kind Old Man who had heated up the coffee before the talk resumed.

Then it was Keeper who reminded Lightningbolt that no more "horseshit like that" would be tolerated. It was Shadow who spoke about fear and how April Horse had learned.

The difference in character among the four separate personalities was made very clear when Lightningbolt became disrespectful, taking the Old Man for granted.

Lightningbolt had enjoyed the attention he received from the old soldier, but he did not fully appreciate the fact that April Horse was taking the time to speak with him. Because of this he began to become overfamiliar and lounge around the fire instead of remaining attentive.

With absolute military precision, April Horse abruptly stood and moved to where Lightningbolt was sitting. He glowered down at him as though he were about to run him through with a sword.

"You're no soldier, you swine!" April Horse shouted. "Look at you, you miserable snafu! You asshole, lounging at my fire like a common dog."

"Hey, what's up, man?" said Lightningbolt, starting to argue. Then he leaped to his feet. The energy he felt from April Horse made his skin tingle.

"Sit down, fool!" April Horse ordered, "and listen to me. Your attitude makes me mad enough to tear your head off! You waltz up here, following your gut, and are not surprised to find a man sitting in a cave saying his prayers. What do you think this place is, a church? You idiot!"

"Ah . . . er!" Lightningbolt mumbled, trying to remain calm.

"You young fools are all the same!" April Horse cursed indignantly. "Where is your care, your respect? What do you think I am, some kind of service program? Look, Mac, I don't sit around here eagerly waiting to be of service to you or anyone else. Understand, clown?

"You have to battle for information. You sniveling hound! Do you think you're going to soak up

information about Life standing around with your thumb in your mouth? Brace up! Get disciplined. Get some Self pride! Be a man of respect and good manners. You slump around me again and I'll toss you out like a piece of shit. Got it, dink?"

The instant Lightningbolt changed his attitude and thanked April Horse for his words, Shadow was there.

"Thank you for respecting my words." Shadow smiled, showing kindness. "There is always thunder with the rain. But it has to be you who will be the flash of lightning, young man."

Abruptly, Lightningbolt found himself looking down into the Little Bow. It was clouding up fast and there was a possibility of snow.

For the first time in his life, Lightningbolt felt a portentous, all-pervasive feeling that something was about to happen. The feeling was welcome. It was big and clean like the forests. Lightningbolt was ready for something new. He swung to Arrow's back and began his descent into the canyon.

Hours later, they finally reached Black Horse Pass. Most of the narrow confines of the pass had been blown free of snow, but there were also very deep drifts.

Two kinds of snow faced them: below lay crusted snow; above, because of their altitude, was powdered snow. Together, these were dangerous for Arrow.

Lightningbolt watched his horse wade almost stomach-deep through the powder. Before them, he knew, there was an abrupt slope that led down into a shallow gully. The small gulch they had to cross ran into a large canyon to their left. But no gulch showed itself now. A wide and threatening snow-drift confronted them.

He urged the mare forward, trying to get her to run as rapidly as possible into the drift. The farther he could force Arrow to plunge into the obstacle, the closer they would be to the other side. Arrow refused to run. She threw her head and pranced sideways into the gulch, making their entrance even more complicated. Lightningbolt had to resort to his spurs. Arrow sprang forward into the snow— then she slipped.

Courageously, she stood and hammered herself deeper into the drift. She fell again, but this time she could not rise. Below, hidden beneath her hooves, Arrow felt water. She was slipping to one side and sinking ever deeper.

Arrow neighed and wallowed in the drift, terrified of suffocating to death. Lightningbolt leaped from her back and disappeared waist-deep into the drift. The snow seemed bottomless, and it scared him.

Cursing, he pulled loose the slipknot that held his lariat. The other end of the rope had been secured to the mare's halter just in case such an emergency should arise. Working fast, he removed Arrow's bridle and buckled the halter over her head.

Yanking at the rope, Lightningbolt flopped his way through the drift, allowing the lariat to uncoil as he rolled through the snow. He hoped that it would be long enough for him to tie to one of the pines he'd seen on the other side.

Speed was his only hope of helping Arrow, because if she broke free and retraced her steps, there was no way he could keep her from sliding into the canyon.

Lightningbolt's eyelashes were covered with snow as he struggled toward a strong pine. He had to blink hard to see as he pulled the rope around the tree.

Fighting to his knees, he yanked hard, taking up the slack, and tied the lariat. Then he looked to see what had happened to Arrow.

What was wrong? Why was Arrow just lying there? Had she hurt herself? He rolled and swam his way back through the snow to where she was. He found that his friend was slipping down the gulch where the snow sloped toward the big gorge.

Hands stinging from the cold, Lightningbolt worked hard, getting the weight off her back. He must not allow her to become exhausted or too cold—both meant the end.

Battling the saddle off the mare's back was no easy chore. He had to get her to stand up before he could loosen the cinch and pull the saddle free. He begged her at first, then slapped her rump with his hand, but she would not rise. Cursing with anger, he pulled his belt from his pants and hit her hard.

She leaped forward. As she did, he pulled loose the cinch straps. With her next two jumps, he jerked the cinch free. Once the saddle was loose, he tore it free and threw it aside, hoping the horse would not bury it with her wild struggles.

He plowed his way forward again, urging Arrow toward him by pulling on the rope. But this only made things more difficult for her. Nothing seemed to be working.

Inch by inch Arrow was moving closer to the edge—where she would have gravity to fight, too—where the gulch fell even deeper into the gorge.

Lightningbolt panicked and whipped Arrow again. She neighed and threw herself toward the other side, where she would find her freedom. He cursed her and slapped her, now with his hand. He did not like using the belt unless he had to.

Suddenly Arrow seemed to get a renewed strength. She stood up and battled her way to the other side and safety.

While Arrow regained her breath, Lightningbolt went to retrieve his saddle and gear. That's when he saw the water. No wonder she'd been so frightened—there had been nothing under her to stand on.

This horrible struggle left Lightningbolt feeling defeated. Yet his battle continued. He had to fight the cold to get dried off. He was wet from head to foot. He stripped boughs from the nearby pines, making himself a windbreak. Next, he cleared the snow from the place where he would have his fire, then he set about collecting wood. He worked hard and quickly. Within an hour everything had been completed. Warm with sweat, he lit his fire.

His attentions next went to Arrow.

Why had he done what he did? Why had he been so stupid? He knew he should have removed the saddle and gear first. He knew he should have led the horse wide, way out of the way of the dangerous gorge. What was the matter with him?

Arrow was still very jumpy. She shied with each of Lightningbolt's moves. He rubbed her down, singing to her and feeding her handfuls of oats.

He hung his saddle and gear off the end of the lean-to, then he undressed down to his long johns, even removing his boots. He tied everything in such a way that it could be easily turned for drying. The deeply piled bed of pine boughs that he stood on kept him high up, away from the frozen ground.

The sky in the West was losing the last blush of light. In minutes it would be very dark. He felt lucky not to have to fight the treacherous snow drifts after dark. The thought made him shudder.

Around midnight, now warm and dry, Lightningbolt saddled Arrow and rode slowly down the other side of Black Horse Pass. Half an hour later he came to a wide path that had been cut by a Caterpillar.

He settled into his ride. It would be a long while yet before he reached the county road. He closed his eyes for a few minutes, feeling Arrow's smooth rhythm.

Hungry for hay and still saddened by her terrible experience in the drift, the horse blew and snorted every few yards as though she were scolding Lightningbolt. He knew she would never forget that he'd had to whip her in order to save her life.

Each time he patted his friend, her hide would jerk and ripple, pushing his hand away. Arrow did not like this journey. She was lonely for the company of other horses. She dreamed of being at the green haystacks.

Arrow had only one connection—her colt. He'd been born just the previous spring, so the connection was very strong in her mind. She spoke with her child, exchanging images with him. Arrow wanted to make sure that he was all right. Three hundred miles away, the connection studied the images in his mother's mind. She scolded the colt in her mind, commanding him to never go near the soft frightening white.

The connection answered in thoughts of a summer place—green sweet grass and the smooth

energy of a starry night. His mother threw up her head and whinnied. She was happy to receive the thought.

The colt imagined the Autumn seeds and the sparkling diamonds of dew on the morning grass. Arrow's ears pricked, then she lifted her head proudly. She pranced and snorted.

"Who or what just comforted you?" the young man asked gently as he patted her.

The mare bobbed her head. This time her skin did not quiver under his hand.

As Lightningbolt came abreast of Ezra Dalton's place, he reined in Arrow. There was a light.

"Who would move into that old spook house?" he asked himself, turning his horse into the yard.

Lightningbolt watched a young hippie come from the outhouse without bothering to shut the door. The snow would make it a bit wet for the next visitor.

He watched the young man pick up a lantern and light it. There was no need for the lamp. The night was very bright from the moon. The hippie was now ten feet from Lightningbolt and Arrow.

Thinking the man had seen him, Lightningbolt spoke. "Have any oats?"

The lantern fell to the ground and the hot glass exploded in the snow.

"Who in . . . What the hell!" the young man bawled, very frightened. Arrow blew and pawed the ground. This scared the hippie even more. He backed up, wide-eyed.

Lightningbolt still hadn't realized that the man couldn't see him. "Easy," he said.

"Who are you?" the man asked in a trembling voice as he approached Arrow. He looked up at Lightningbolt and frowned. "I thought you were the damned devil." He tried to grin.

"It's just me and my horse," said Lightningbolt,

smiling back. "My friend needs some oats—have any?"

"Oats?" asked the young man. "Like oatmeal? You hungry?"

"It's for Arrow here." Lightningbolt smiled, recognizing the man's New York accent. "She can eat an entire box. Have one? I'll give you a dollar for it." He turned in his saddle to have a quick look around. "Any hay? What's in there?" He pointed to the broken-down old barn.

"In there?" The hippie stared. He seemed to be fascinated with his visitor. "What does it look like?" He glanced swiftly at the shed, then back again. "There is grass of some kind in there. It smells good, but it's not shit you can smoke."

Lightningbolt touched Arrow with his heels and she walked to the shed. Leaning from the sad-dle, he looked through the broken door. "You get that box of oats," he instructed the man as he dismounted. "And do you have a bucket of water?"

"By the pump," the youth answered, pointing to a pump by the barn. "Hey, this is all right." He was growing excited again. "Nobody will believe it in the morning."

Lightningbolt had gone into the barn to get hay. The eager young man followed close behind. When Lightningbolt picked up a bale, he had to nudge the hippie away from the door. "The hay was stacked this summer," he said, excusing him-self, as he brushed by. "Good and fresh. How about those oats?"

"Hey . . . it's okay!" the hippie answered. "Re-ally. Gosh, never thought a horse would be chomp-ing down on that shit." He turned suddenly and ran into the house.

Lightningbolt broke the bale for Arrow. He looked around for something to put the oatmeal in. Finding a rusted old bucket by the barn, he kicked it free from the ice, then picked it up—it was empty. He carried it back to where Arrow was enjoying her hay.

The door of the old cabin opened with a clatter, and the young man ran headlong out into the night, clutching a box of oatmeal to his chest. "Here!" he announced breathlessly. "Best crap in the house! Everybody will wonder where in hell it went in the morning." He chuckled. "Never knowing about the midnight rider, right?"

Lightningbolt tore the lid from the box and poured the oatmeal into the rusted bucket. Arrow wasted no time eating it.

"Those are real shit-kicking spurs!" the young man exclaimed as he followed Lightningbolt to the well. "My name is Fred. We came from the University of California and from New York. Wow! Shit. You're riding a real horse. Dammit, that's great!"

Lightningbolt reached the pump and began to fill another bucket. He watched Fred with a critical eye. The hippie was becoming even more animated.

"Are you an Indian or something?" Fred asked hopefully. He wrinkled his nose, showing his doubt.

"Breed," Lightningbolt answered, continuing to pump.

"Breed," Fred repeated the word. He seemed to be a bit disappointed. "Not one thing and not the other?" he probed. "Nigger in the woodpile, right?"

Lightningbolt's ire was rising.

"We're up here smoking shit and howling at the moon," the student explained. "Winter break, going to do some hunting. Shoot elk and eat off the land. It's the way to go, man."

"You're hunting?" Lightningbolt asked, showing his surprise. The thought was unsettling. "These your machines?" He pointed with a sweep of his arm. "A half-track, a Jeep, two pickups, five snowmobiles. You sure you have enough war machines?"

"You're eating right, aren't you?" Fred suddenly changed faces again. "You're not dying of malnutrition like the rest of the Indians, are you? I mean, eating white flour and hot dogs? You've got to take care of your health! I can go in the house and get you enough vitamins to last you for months, what do you say?"

"No thanks," Lightningbolt answered. "Okay if I use your air-conditioned library there?" He pointed to the outhouse.

"Sure," Fred answered, following.

"I don't need the company," Lightningbolt said, turning to the student. "Got to do some thinking."

"I wasn't going to go in with you," said Fred, surprised. "I was just walking you there. I'll go inside the house and watch from the kitchen window." He smiled broadly. "That way I won't freeze. When you come out I'll see you."

Lightningbolt walked past the outhouse and beyond into the brush. Arrow needed a bit of time to eat. He didn't want to rush her. Fred? Fred was another matter.

Thirty-five minutes went by before Lightningbolt returned. The door of the house burst open and Fred ran to Arrow.

"It's amazing you didn't freeze your butt in there!" the hippie exclaimed with awe. "No one here can last that long in there. You must be at least part Indian."

"You don't have some coffee in there, do you?" Lightningbolt asked hopefully.

"Coffee?" Fred looked as though he had just been shot through the head. "Coffee? Are you mad? Coffee will kill you! You have to eat natural foods, man. You have to return to the old ways of the Indians. Eat natural, man. Tea, berries, vitamins, granola, brewer's yeast, maybe some seaweed."

"Deer, elk, or beef," Lightningbolt countered. "Berries with brewer's yeast is not for Breeds. It makes us turn either brown or white. Terrible stuff!"

Fred was not impressed. "You would eat a common wiener, wouldn't you? Do you know what's in them?"

"Here's your dollar for the oats," said Lightningbolt, offering him the money.

"You kidding?" Fred pouted. "A dollar, forget it, man. We know you Breeds are poor as rats. Is that a turkey feather in your hat? Did you eat it? Was it naturally hunted?"

Lightningbolt swung up into the saddle. He reached down and shook the hippie's hand. "It's an eagle I ate," he answered as he turned Arrow to leave.

"An eagle!" Fred howled, showing his complete disgust. "You ate a real live god-damned eagle! God, man. Holy shit! Have you gone completely crazy? Eating an eagle!" The hippie looked like he was going to be sick. "Return to the old ways! Eat naturally," he begged, trotting behind Arrow, trying hard to keep up. "It's modern times, man. We have health food stores now. I never saw canned eagle meat. Wow, man!"

"Thanks for everything," Lightningbolt shouted over the hippie's raving. "Hey, take it easy, Fred. Okay?"

Lights were going on in every room. Two people had thrown on coats and run out into the yard. Other people were following.

"Return to the old waaaaays!" Fred yelled. "You dumb Indian, or whatever you are! Return to the old ways!"

Lightningbolt loped Arrow out of the yard and down the road.

"Calm down, Fred, dammit!" a man cursed in a loud voice. "Did he steal anything?"

It would be many years before Lightningbolt met Fred again. By then, Fred would have become

a lawyer. Disillusionment would be discussed, the endless war, body counts in Vietnam. It all had Fred crazy, as it had everyone crazy.

A half hour passed before Lightningbolt settled himself back into the night and the pace of his horse.

A young fox moved out onto the road and watched the horse and rider. He sniffed the air, jumped, then slipped away silently into the brush.

A Moon song, the call of the Night Hawk, drew Lightningbolt's attention to the sky. She peeped and

twittered, yodeling her melody of the hunt.

It is custom among the Cheyenne and the Cree that when a person is sung to by the Night Hawk, and circled with song, that great good fortune is given to the people.

The Night Hawk is known to the Cree as Little Moon Bird or Moon Hawk. The robin-sized bird is also called Dream Giver.

"It is the Moon singing. It is the song of the Manitou," they teach. *Vision* and *Dream* are synonymous to the Cree. There is no separating them. Anyone who hears the song and "stands themselves at the center of the song" will have "the power to Dream," the Cree teach. To do this, the "person must acknowledge the Spirit, the Presence of their Own Path."

Lightningbolt slipped from Arrow's back and looked up at the hawk that wheeled over his head. Her circle drew even tighter until she was a scant arm's length away, still singing.

Every confusion or pretense that Lightningbolt had dropped instantly away. The words of the story "Medicine of the Night Hawk," which his aunts and uncles of the North had taught him, were ensconced deep within his psyche. The beauty he knew and cherished about the land and Mother Earth cascaded from his memory and flooded his heart with caring. Like the time when he swam in the Pool of the Stars, he felt an urgency to acknowledge the presence of Life.

These feelings and sensitivities were a puzzle to Lightningbolt. He only responded to these teachings and emotions when he was alone. When he was in public another side of young Lightningbolt's character was present. Then all such feelings were embarrassing to him.

Any time he felt even the slightest twinge of what he called "a tearjerker," it horrified him. He felt so weak at these times, so defenseless. He hated them. Responding to such higher emotions as Love or the Beauty of Life, threw him immediately into

war within his mind.

He did not realize it while he was with the Night Hawk, but his wariness at accepting Life and love was actually about responsibility. If he accepted these things, it meant he would have to be responsible, and his mind did not want this.

A human cannot "blow away" another human when responsibility for Life is present. But Lightningbolt was certain he would blow away an enemy in the blink of an eye if it was necessary. This was all part of his thinking while he was with the Hawk.

Confusion returned with a roar within him. Yet, he dug tobacco from his pocket and gave thanks to Mother Life. He sprinkled the tobacco on the ground and looked around. For a brief moment, his feelings were true.

After his short prayer he checked his surroundings to see if anyone had been watching him. Satisfied that only Arrow was present, he remounted and continued his journey.

"STOP," read the county sign half buried in the dirt and snow. Lightningbolt straightened in his saddle and studied the letters. Almost all of the sign had been shot away except for the word *Stop*. For some reason it remained.

Morning blushed gold and pink, then shouted colors that would startle the greatest of artists. The long cool fingers of shadow that now surrounded horse and rider clung to the land. The trees reared up stark and black against the sky.

Two older Indian men rode out from a shallow canyon about a hundred yards in front of Lightningbolt. They reined in and waited for him to catch up.

"Been making Medicine up there?" the older man asked, pointing at the mountains.

The question caught Lightningbolt off guard, and he had no ready answer.

"I've brought the old man up here," the younger man said. His voice was very strong. "His name is Spirit Bull-Cow. He's a lot older than he looks. We protect him. He's all we have now."

Lightningbolt jumped down from his horse and handed the old man his two remaining cigarettes.

"*Huuuah,*" the old man said, taking the cigarettes. "You are one Breed, alone in the mountains."

"Yes," Lightningbolt answered.

"I will give you a Time." The old man smiled. "I place it all around you. I have been praying. Why shouldn't you have the Time of my Prayers also? Who isn't a Breed? All the children are Breeds. I give you a Time Circle because I see you are clean. Clean children are good for the Tribe."

Lightningbolt looked down, listening carefully, trying to follow the old man's meaning.

"Now, wait in my Circle," said the old man, indicating through signs that Lightningbolt should sit down.

"Here in the road?" Lightningbolt asked.

"Yes, sit there," the younger man answered. "Just as he has asked."

Lightningbolt sat down in the road and let his horse go off to the side of the road to eat grass. The gravel was cold.

"Sit on this," the old man said, taking a woven ring of willows from his saddle. "I don't need this now. I use it to cover the hot stones in my Lodge. Sometimes when I use those flat red stones up there"—he pointed to the mountains—"they pop. They blow up with the heat." He leaned down, handing the ring of willows to Lightningbolt. "Sit on it. Wait one hour and look at the trees and the morning. I give you a Circle."

"Tell me of your journey," prompted the old man as he too dismounted and sat down in the road. "I wish to hear of it. There are not many young people up here."

Lightningbolt very patiently told the story of his entire journey.

"The Pool of the Stars." The old man almost sang the words. "Oh, it has been so many years since I have been there. Thank you, Grandson. You were respectful at our Medicine Pool. The Black Star Pool is very Holy. It is a Holy place for us old people. And yes, the man within the cave of the mountain, it is good you were with him."

The old teacher suddenly rose to his feet and mounted his horse. Without speaking another word, both men turned their animals and left Lightningbolt sitting in the road. He felt just a bit melancholy as he watched them ride away.

After a time, he slowly rode down into the hills of Wyoming. It was almost noon when he reined in Arrow to have a look around.

"Which house?" he wondered as he studied the three houses before him.

The country he now surveyed was good rolling farmland, but the Indians who lived here did not farm.

He touched Arrow's ribs gently and she began to walk. Up ahead of him were two stands of red willow. He thought he saw movement by the one on his left, and became curious.

Unexpectedly, a silver-haired Arapaho woman and two little girls barred his way. The woman approached him. She motioned for him to stop.

What Lightningbolt did not know was that the old Medicine Man, Spirit Bull-Cow, had met with this woman and had told her of his Vision Quest.

Spirit Bull-Cow had told her, "The heart of the young man was true while he prayed at the Medicine Pool," and because of this, everything Lightningbolt owned held special Medicine Power to heal.

The Arapaho woman had also been told, "The young man knows nothing of these Medicine Ways, and he needs to be taught because he is bullheaded and quick to fight."

"This is yours," she said, motioning him to dismount from Arrow. As he swung from his saddle, the woman carefully opened a small thermos and poured a bit of soup into a bowl held by the older of the two girls. "Puppy," she explained, and smiled.

He sipped it. It was good and it was hot. It tasted like vegetable soup.

Lightningbolt noticed that the woman and both girls were dressed in their finest. All three wore blankets, beadwork, and their best moccasins. The older woman seemed impervious to the cold, but the two little girls, who looked to be about nine and ten, were shivering, hugging close to the woman. Their eyes were bright and wondering.

Lightningbolt did not recognize these customs and he was confounded by what was taking place.

He found these ways were old-fashioned and embarrassing. They were spoken of, but who would go through with them now? Why was she doing this to him?

He wanted to argue, but he knew that to even entertain such a thought with this Grandmother was absolutely out of the question. Was there a way, a place to escape?

"I realize this embarrasses you," the woman said smoothly. "But I am sure you will live. Above all, you will not speak."

The girls twittered, their eyes sparkling with excitement.

What the hell am I into now? Lightningbolt exclaimed in his mind.

"Remain calm," said the woman, smiling, showing her concern and kindness.

He slowly handed Arrow's reins to her.

"Drink the soup," she encouraged him. "And give your spurs to the girls."

Lightningbolt crouched down on the path and loosened his spurs. Arguing about drinking the soup was also out of the question, so he finished it in one gulp. He was pleased; it did taste great. He handed his spurs to the girls.

In an instant, the children were off and running toward the nearest house he could see in the distance.

"We will care for your horse," the Arapaho woman explained as she turned and led the horse down the trail. "Over there"—she pointed—"is my house. When we get there, sit by the door, outside, and wait."

He studied the woman's home. At some time in the past, two small cabins had existed side by side. Over the years the two smaller structures had become one. The present building was tidy and well cared for, but still too small for comfort.

Two elderly Arapaho men sat on a bench by the door. They were smoking, drinking hot coffee, and conversing.

"Uh-huh," they both said almost in the same instant.

Lightningbolt nodded and sat down with them.

A tall, distinguished-looking man came from the house bringing a cup of coffee. He gave it to Lightningbolt and took a place on the bench.

A pickup drove into the yard and parked in front of the house. Three middle-aged women got out and began to help the older woman with the horse. Everything was removed from Arrow—

backpack, rifle, saddle, and bridle.

After Arrow had been brushed down and fed, the women cut small pieces of the horse's mane. These were carefully braided and tied with red cloth.

What the hell are they doing to my horse? Lightningbolt cursed quietly in his mind. He could not look up for fear that someone would see his incredible embarrassment.

"*Uh, hey, huh,*" one of the men said to another. It was his way of expressing his contentment.

Lightningbolt moved to the end of the bench as far away from the men as he could get. Then he turned his back and stared at the snow and dirt. He had to get hold of his nerves.

Relax, he commanded himself. What the hell. Let them fuss with the horse. Be cool.

One of the women called to the men. The men instantly rose as one body and walked toward the group of women. When they had all risen, the unbalanced bench threw Lightningbolt headlong into the snow. No one had seen his perfect dive. But when the bench crashed down on all its legs again, everyone looked.

Not a sound was made, not one snicker. Lightningbolt's ears fairly burned. He stood and brushed off his hands and knees. For some inexplicable reason the cup of coffee he held had not lost one drop.

The woman walked slowly into the house and returned with a saucer filled with small pieces of dry meat.

"Relax," she whispered to him. "This won't take long." She patted his shoulder affectionately.

Lightningbolt's nose and cheeks were now flaming. He gulped hard and reached for a piece of meat with a trembling hand.

Why me? he wondered in his mind. I didn't do a damn thing. What is going on? Is it my horse?

Soon everything had been stacked tidily in the back of the pickup, including his rifle. He was just a bit nervous now about what was going to happen to his belongings. The women all filed into the house. Laughter could be heard. The joy of the women was more than obvious.

One of the women came to the door and motioned him and the men inside. Lightningbolt went in with the men following. A woman indicated that he should sit at the table.

"My name is Ammie," the silver-haired woman explained to Lightningbolt. "And that tall one there is John, my husband." Her voice continued to be kind.

He sat down; then everyone in the room was introduced.

"Time to eat," said John, grinning broadly. "Have at it, boy."

"And you can talk now," said the ten-year-old

girl, standing at his left elbow and smiling.

"Yeah," the younger girl added, coming up on his right.

Lightningbolt was wondering how he was going to swallow in the midst of that crowd. However, these fears disappeared when everyone suddenly left the room.

He ate deer, toast, jam, bacon, and eggs, and loved every mouthful. He was starved. He definitely was not a decent camp cook. That would have to improve.

After he had eaten, the woman came with a braid of burning sweet grass and waved it gently in the air around him, blessing him with the fragrant smoke. Then she showed him to the next room and a warm bed.

"Sleep, Grandson." She smiled.

Lightningbolt had no sooner laid down his head when he was deep within sleep. When he awoke it was in the middle of the night.

He heard the sound of someone sleeping close by. Looking over the edge of the bed, he saw the two little girls snuggled into his sleeping bag on the floor.

The following morning he was awakened early.

"The school bus is coming!" the younger of the girls announced. "You going to stay?" She was staring into his eyes.

"Ah, sure," he answered.

Two hours later, Lightningbolt was summoned into the main room by John. He entered and took a seat by the stove. Ammie was beading a belt.

The old man sang and accompanied himself on a hand drum.

"Everything went," Ammie explained. "We are happy that it did. Your saddle, bridle, all you possessed, were used to heal people."

Lightningbolt finally understood why they had been so careful with his belongings.

"John and I had a Dream," Ammie continued. "You entered two very important circles; the place

of the Night Hawk and the place of the Sacred Pool."

"And you were respectful." John smiled. "Nowadays there are not many young people who are."

"Clean," Ammie added. "You offered your prayers there. The Black Lake, this was our Dreaming. You entered there. It has been many years since the lake has Dreamed with us."

"Yes, we Dreamed together at the Holy Pool," John went on. "The old man said that you were almost balanced in your heart when you were at the Pool."

"The reason we used your things was because they were made part of the Pool." Ammie seemed to purr with contentment.

"For healing," John told him. "People can touch."

"For those who are sick," Ammie concluded. "For their health. We are thankful that you were a little bit balanced there."

"You too can hold on to your good fortune," said John, brightening.

"There always needs to be more," added Ammie. "You can increase your own knowledge of these things if you should choose it."

"Would you like to tell others of it?" John probed.

"Never—I mean, no," Lightningbolt instantly responded.

"You're not bashful, are you?" Ammie winked.

"I'm going to have a Ceremony," John offered. "I would like you in my Lodge."

"Uh, sure, why not?" said Lightningbolt. He didn't want to disappoint the older folks.

Two days later, Lightningbolt rode alone in the hills behind Ammie and John's home. He was happy to have Arrow back, and all of his belongings.

The evening felt warm. He saw the lights of a roadhouse in the distance and rode toward it. Dismounting behind the bar, he had a quick look around. Five horses were tied to a rickety barbed wire fence. All of them were fine animals.

When he walked around to the front where he had seen a few pickups parked, he noticed a man leaning drunk against the building. He looked more closely at him and saw that it was a Half-Breed close to his own age. He was dead drunk and stinking of bad booze.

"Bisco Paul," a grinning cowboy announced as he rounded the corner; he had a heavy Oklahoman accent. He stepped around the drunk and extended his hand. "Hey, you're Chilly Bill, right? When I was in-country in 'Nam, Sergeant Phillips said to look you up. Hey, dude!" He slapped Lightningbolt's hand, then fell drunkenly against Lightningbolt.

"Hey, okay," said Lightningbolt, smiling as he tried to get his hand free. "I can dig it, man. No, I'm Lightningbolt."

Bisco's face abruptly changed and now showed worry. "Tour here, tour there. It's all the same, dangerous, huh?" Bisco was trying to laugh.

"I'll buy you a beer." Lightningbolt smiled. "Who's Chilly?"

"He's here on leave," Bisco answered, now slumping against the wall. "I'm gonna sleep, man." He slid to the ground. Pensively, drunkenly, he noticed the other man, who had slid to the ground; he patted his shoulder. "Hey, you poor shit, I bet you're Chilly, right?" He closed his eyes.

Lightningbolt left the vet to sleep it off and walked to the front of the sleazy roadhouse. The parking lot was filled to overflowing with expensive sports cars, souped-up customized cars, and about twenty new but beat-up pickups. Heavy-duty hard rock music slammed against his ears when he opened the bar door.

He backed out as though he'd been hit in the stomach with a fist, and let the door close. He wasn't ready for bars or towns. He would need time to make the transition. Lightningbolt deliberately chose another direction back to his horse.

The Moon was bright and full as he reached Iron Blanket's home. When he rode up to the house he saw the aged Medicine Man sitting by his door. A much younger man was close by, smoking; Lightningbolt chose to ignore him.

"I've brought you this horse," Lightningbolt said to Iron Blanket as he slid from the saddle. He wanted to get his errand over with as quickly as possible. "I'm called Lightningbolt. While I was at the Willow Rose, Goose told me to tell you to bring doughnuts."

"Goose always says that," Iron Blanket answered. He hadn't lifted his head. "Whose horse is that?"

"It's my uncle's," Lightningbolt explained. "I'll ride her until I go back to Lodge Grass in Montana, then you can have her. I'll leave her at John and Ammie's place. How is this for one so old—do you want it done this way?"

"It's a good way," the old man said, and looked up, revealing his blind eyes.

Lightningbolt moved closer to the old man and took his hand. He could see that Iron Blanket's eyes were heavily scarred. "I understand now," he said quietly. "Yes, the choice is a good one. This mare is kind and quiet. She is good for an old man who cannot see."

"He sees much!" the man from the shadows offered. "Your kindness is seen by him."

"It is the kindness of Goose Flying you see," Lightningbolt corrected the man. "I did not know this old man was blind. I only followed orders."

Iron Blanket chuckled. "So, all right, you follow your orders, young one. But with this meeting, do you offer me this horse to ride?"

"I offer my uncle's horse," Lightningbolt answered, sounding overly formal. "I, too, wish for you to ride her."

"Your fear makes you speak strangely," Iron Blanket said. "I would change that if I could, but I can only say that meetings between people are as fast as any bullet leaving a gun. I was blinded in a war you do not know. The world has forgotten the war. It is far away, but the fear that made the war is ever near. Can you understand this?"

"Shadow spoke of these things," Lightningbolt answered, wanting to change the subject and leave as quickly as possible. "Do you have your Medicine Garden? Does your helper work there?"

"So you wish to change the talk. . . . All right." Iron Blanket pushed him. "So you force the issue with me. I will continue to teach you. It is my only way of repaying your uncle's kindness."

"No! No!" Lightningbolt was embarrassed. "I was asking about your Way, how it is you Are, you know, your Medicine. Hey, I'm sorry, old man, really!"

"You're acting like a stupid Breed!" the old man's helper broke in. "Are you here to embarrass him?"

Iron Blanket turned his blind face toward his helper, who was also his nephew, as though to silence him. Then he must have thought better of it and returned his attention to Lightningbolt.

"We Medicine people have gardens because we love Mother Earth," the old man carefully explained. "You are a Breed, as Hunting Horse has said you are. Yet he made this sound as though it is something wrong, to be a Breed. It is good that you are who you are. It is good that we people who have our gardens are also accepted. Yes, Breed, you know that the people of the Reservations have no gardens. Will this also be your accusation? Are you angry with the people because they have no gardens?"

"Yes, I suppose I am," Lightningbolt admitted. "They are too lazy to grow their own food. They only want to drink and have their welfare checks."

"You Breed pig!" Hunting Horse exploded in anger. "You asshole. Do you want me to knock your head off?"

"No . . . he is braver," said Iron Blanket, correcting his student. "Yes, Hunting Horse, yes, Lightningbolt, the garden has become a symbol of what is not Indian. Yes, the welfare check is more important than the garden. This is a shame, but I would not fight over this if I were you. If you were to have crawled with me through the stink and blood of France, you would not be so quick to kill one another. If you saw one another, there among the dead, you would celebrate that you both were Americans. You would fight together to keep America alive and free. But here, without an enemy, you are ready to kill one another over the people's sadness."

Iron Blanket's words shot through both men, and they looked down at the ground, not knowing how to respond.

"Yes, the Indian people drink themselves into a stupor as do the Breeds," Iron Blanket taught them. "Yes, who but we Medicine people have a garden? Yes, it is a pity. Yes, who is it that does not suffer from alcoholism? Yet, should we destroy one another because of this infection? You should both be ready to teach of these things, not kill each other because of our extreme sorrow. Admit it, would you be happy to see one another if you were on a battlefield and needed to see another American?"

"I would," Hunting Horse readily agreed.

Lightningbolt reached out his hand to Hunting Horse, trying his best to be friendly.

"I will also try to be more clear-thinking," Hunting Horse announced.

"I have earned this horse." Iron Blanket grinned. "Leave her at John and Ammie's place. I will see to it that she is returned to your uncle."

The following day Lightningbolt was once again riding horseback, but this time he was on an errand. The morning was crisp and bright, happy with the little-girl news that Jennifer and Sheleen had just shared with Lightningbolt. They had told him that they "really, really, liked him." They were riding double on a big Morgan gelding that their uncle had given them just before he went off to Vietnam.

The girls' eldest aunt, who had come visiting the night before, had asked Lightningbolt a favor. It was explained that one of the Cut Feather children had stolen a "good blue coat" from Sheleen's and Jennifer's cousin. The aunt had asked him if he could get it back.

No less than twenty wrecked cars littered the yard of the Cut Feather home.

Lightningbolt had to guide Arrow carefully through the junk and traps of the yard. The girls waited at a discreet distance.

"I have come for the coat," he said as he reached the door. He did not dismount. "I am Lightningbolt, grandson of John and Ammie." There was not a sound from the house. "Tilly says that your boys stole that coat over at the schoolhouse." Silence. "It's no use," he threatened. "I will return and return, making you miserable. I will come tomorrow and the next day."

Suddenly the door opened and a tattered green coat was thrown out on the doorstep.

"The blue one!" he demanded. "Do you want me coming back every day? It could get embarrassing."

The door opened again and a blue coat was thrown out.

"That's it!" Sheleen yelled excitedly.

"Yipeee!" shouted Jennifer.

Lightningbolt dismounted just long enough to pick up the coat. Then he guided Arrow back through the deadly maze.

"Stinky old Bobby!" Jennifer shrieked at the house as she took the coat from Lightningbolt. "You are soooo bad!"

"I hope you croak!" Sheleen yelled.

Two pink tongues appeared and were wriggled in the general direction of the house.

"So there!" called Jennifer.

"Yeah," Sheleen agreed.

Lightningbolt turned Arrow and headed back toward their home. "Why don't either of you speak Arapaho?" he asked.

"It's simple as pie," Jennifer answered confidently. "You see, Grandma Willow is a Crow."

"And our other Grandma is a Cree," Sheleen added.

"Wait," Jennifer scolded, "you're getting ahead of me. Grandma on Mama's side and Grandma on Daddy's side."

Lightningbolt was listening, but his attention was also on the two riders heading toward them.

"And," Jennifer went on, "only John talks Arapaho!"

"And," Sheleen added, "Grandma talks Cree."

"But Mom knows how." Jennifer laughed.

"Look, there's Billy!" Sheleen yelled and waved. "Hi, Billy!"

"Ho!" Billy waved back.

The riders turned on to another road and disappeared behind a large stand of willow.

"We're Full-Bloods," Jennifer stated flatly. "But you're a common Breed. Mama says so."

"That's correct." Lightningbolt smiled. "Your

mom is absolutely correct."

"We're ahead in school"—Sheleen giggled—"because we talked English since being kids."

"Billy gets drunk," said Jennifer, frowning. "But Max gets drunk all the time! Did you know that Max can cross his eyes?"

"But Billy can stand on his head," Sheleen broke in. "And walk on his hands."

"Amazing," said Lightningbolt, smiling. "How about you two?"

"Nope!" said Jennifer, looking alarmed. "It makes the blood get in your head. Mom says so."

"How come you got that Medicine stuff all over you?" Sheleen asked Lightningbolt.

"He got it all in the right places, silly," Jennifer answered.

"But did it stick to you?" Sheleen frowned.

"It sticks to everything!" said Jennifer knowingly. "It even stuck to his spurs and saddle."

"Oh!" said Sheleen, smiling.

The following evening Lightningbolt was busy chopping wood and listening to Country Joe and the Fish tell the world where it was at. He worked hard and the music was good.

The five figures standing around the evening fire were preparing themselves for Ceremony. They were quiet, almost somber. The men smoked and lounged about the fire and spoke in hushed voices.

One of the men was recovering from a hangover.

Lightningbolt was a bit put out that he had been stuck with all the work.

A bright moment appeared suddenly when Sheleen and Jennifer stuck their heads out of the window and called to Lightningbolt. They were laughing and happy.

"Debbie said that her cat eats apples. Is she lying?" Jennifer asked.

"And she said her cat eats watermelon, too," Sheleen added.

"Is it a fib?" Jennifer asked, looking serious.

"It's a flab," Lightningbolt answered.

The girls looked at each other and laughed.

"Hey, Breed," one of the men called from the fire. "The show is this way."

Lightningbolt undressed by the fire and hung his clothes on a nearby tree. He noticed that the tree was badly burned. He wondered why John had his fire so close to it.

It was clear that the Sweat Lodge had been built with care. And yet it had an almost circuslike appearance because it was covered with brightly colored carpets. John had salvaged them from a school that had been torn down.

When he entered the Lodge, Lightningbolt had to crawl past John to find his place next to him. He knew that John would have the last place by the door.

John asked for nine stones to be brought in.

This is going to be a hot one! Lightningbolt thought to himself. He hated it when a Sweat Lodge turned into a painful experience instead of a time for prayer.

As soon as the stones were in the Lodge, the door was closed. Someone in the dark reeked of alcohol.

John began his earnest and gentle prayers as he poured water on the stones. The steam rose and it grew hot quickly.

After a short time of silence, an angry voice began a tirade of hate against whites. The ill-tempered lecture droned on and on, then ended with an opinion that whites should be banned from America.

The old man did what he could to explain to the lecturer that whites also have a right to live in America. But his plea failed.

The voice suddenly changed tack and began to explain that only Indians were given true Vision

Quests. The speaker laboriously detailed a horrible experience he'd had, calling it his "most important Vision Quest to date."

Lightningbolt was growing weary of the insults and boredom.

John cleared his throat and poured more water upon the stones.

Now the voice grew even more vehement, telling everyone that the "smell of a Breed was getting to him."

Lightningbolt was on the verge of blowing up when suddenly someone else spoke.

"Look, Don," an angry voice said in the darkness, "you're drunk. Keep it up and I'll pin your ears permanently to the ground. Shut up!"

"We must be kind to one another," John argued gently. "Don has the right to speak of his pains."

"We've heard them a thousand times," said the angry voice.

"The Great Spirit is God," Don broke in.

"You wouldn't know God if you found him in your barn," the fighter retorted. "What a stupid ass."

"All brightness has left my Lodge." John scolded the drunk. "Would you leave us sad?"

"I've had enough," said Lightningbolt. "It's out for me."

"We must find a way of talking to one another," John begged. The old man was sad.

"Not with Breeds," said the drunk venomously.

The Ceremony was a miserable flop.

Lightningbolt thought that long-distance bus rides in America must have been designed by the most disconsolate humans alive. Buses disheartened the brave and destroyed the unsuspecting. He was certain that some humans had taken their lives just because they'd had to ride on a bus.

The walk from the bus stop to Aunt Lilly's house seemed much longer than he remembered. He tossed his saddle and gear into the back of the Silver Ship, his pickup, then tried to start it. Nothing happened; the battery was dead. Lilly would be in Crow Agency, so why go to the house? He sat there wondering if he should walk back into Lodge Grass.

"You get in here, you pup," Lilly commanded from her door. She was teasing him in Crow. "You need a bath, and leave your filthy clothes on the porch. I'll give them a good laundering. What did you do with Frank's horse?"

"Hey, Auntie," Lightningbolt answered in Crow. "Your Crow is getting all tangled up around a word bush. Isn't there a Crow word for laundering?"

"Do you suppose it's my old age?" She smiled

her welcome as she let him in the door. "I don't even like the word *laundry*."

Lightningbolt gave his aunt a warm hug before he went into the kitchen. "That old Arapaho Medicine Man called Iron Blanket is using the horse to go pray in the mountains; he said he would bring her back."

"He's still alive?" she said in surprise, then did a quick shift. "Gee! You must be starving!" She began fixing him a roast beef sandwich.

"The Silver Ship won't start." He poured himself some coffee from the stove. "I'll have to go to Lodge Grass later to find somebody to give me a jump start. Did I see a chicken in the fridge?"

She stopped to dry her hands. "I'll get it."

"Got it." He leaped to the refrigerator in one bound and grabbed the chicken. Sitting down again, he tore a leg from the chicken and began to devour it.

Nuuuuuuuuu!" she reprimanded him. "Slow down. Here, use this knife." She clicked her tongue sharply, disapproving. Suddenly Lilly's face changed. "Did you say your battery is dead? I know that Tony put it on a trickle charge out in the old coal shed."

Lightningbolt smiled and touched his aunt's elbow. "Look there, Auntie," he teased her. "Battery? Trickle charge? Is that authentic Crow?"

Lilly sat down at the table and frowned. "I could say 'stone that holds power,' or . . ."

"Trickle charge is a tough one. I'll have to admit that," he said, laughing.

The electric clock on the wall chimed exactly noon.

"Language is so important," said Lilly emphatically. "Trickle charge. For sure that's not Crow."

Lightningbolt raided the refrigerator again. This time he pulled out a strawberry pie and cut himself a huge piece.

"It's just like Minnie." She brightened. "We were all at a big meeting in Crow Agency. There must have been over three hundred people there.

"For some reason, a Medicine Man was brought up from Wyoming to give a talk at Head Start. He was the main speaker. Minnie and I had been invited because we were supposed to be the older women there. Evidently they needed some, so we were it.

"The man was a strange old fellow. He claimed that he could answer any religious question. He had a great big fat Bible.

"Everybody was speaking English because a big bunch of people could not understand how to sign. There must have been three different Tribes of us there.

"Minnie got things going. She immediately stood up and asked about turtle lives.

" 'Turtle lives?' The man frowned. 'There are no turtle lives in the Bible.'

" 'There are,' Minnie insisted. 'And you said you could answer why. I've been wondering for years why there are turtle lives for white people.'

" 'No,' the man argued with her. 'There are no turtles in the Bible.'

"The man then asked everybody in the room if they knew anything about turtles in the Bible. People guessed, saying they'd heard of camels, sheep, doves, donkeys, serpents, and goats, but no one knew of any turtles. Some guessed that there were whales and fish, but still no turtles.

" 'That settles it!' the man told Minnie. 'Forget about it. There are no turtles.'

" 'I have heard a thousand times those white people saying it.' Minnie was brave. She stood her ground and fought back. 'Turtle lives are very important to white people. They constantly worry about their turtle lives.'

"The man tried to make Minnie sit down and shut up, but she would not. Finally a kindly old Cheyenne spoke with her, trying to understand what she meant.

" 'How do those white people say it?' the Chey-

enne asked.

" 'Ah. Uh, huh,' Minnie said. She thought for a minute or so, then she said that the white people always asked her if she wanted to inherit a turtle life.

" 'You mean eternal life,' the Cheyenne explained.

" 'Yeah, that's it! A turtle life,' Minnie answered. 'You got it! What does it mean, having a turtle life?' "

Lightningbolt almost fell off his chair laughing. "That's a great story."

That same evening Lightningbolt left his aunt's home and headed toward Eagle Butte, North Dakota. As he drove, leaving Montana, the quiet rolling hills and bright moonlit winter landscape spoke to the young man's heart. The beauty called him to embrace the adventure, but he warred against the call from Montana because beyond those wondrous hills and mountains there was another kind of reality.

"You're not holding me here," he yelled out of his pickup window at Her. "I know you want me to live here with you, but that's impossible."

A delicate song rose up from the Earth and into Lightningbolt's mind. It washed over him with the purity of the land, matching the radiance of the night sky. It was a song of the Earth.

Lightningbolt loved his land, his beautiful Montana. She loved him in return, and he knew it. But Lightningbolt knew that She had been betrayed by the spoilers who lived in Montana. There was no more hiding the awful rape of his home. Disas-

trous farming habits and monster deep holes gouged by copper mining and coal strip-mining had left horrible wounds. These were the awful marks of greed caused by the banks and land speculators.

A specter seemed to rise up out of the ditch by the road. It was a black man dressed in rags. Lightningbolt stopped his pickup and backed to where he'd seen the man.

"Where you at, Beau?" he called.

Beau crawled out of a cardboard box that had been thrown in the ditch. He blinked in wonderment, surprised that anyone had stopped.

Lightningbolt leaned over and threw open the passenger door. "Get in," he told his friend.

"Hey, man," Beau answered, sitting back down. "Can you dig it? I can't walk."

Lightningbolt leaped out, helped Beau into the pickup, and slammed the door. As he ran around to the driver's side, he saw something in the middle of the highway. It was a .30-30 rifle that had been run over many times. It was ruined. Was it Beau's? He left the rifle where it lay.

"Your gun?" Lightningbolt asked as he slid behind the wheel and started the pickup.

"The Wolf has arrived," Beau teased. His voice was raspy and forced. "Hey, looks like ol' Beau is just about dog meat. But look here, the Wolf himself shows up. Must be my lucky day."

Lightningbolt drove a ways, not speaking. Beau looked as though he had been out in the cold for quite a while. It was also obvious that he had been in a fight, and that he hadn't done too well.

"I was drinking with a Skin from Dakota," said Beau, breaking the silence. His head was resting against the seat. "A big ol' honkie came in and bought us drinks. We drank like mad! The next thing I knew, I'd walked all the way to Crazy Head Springs. Hey, man, you got anything to eat?"

"Lilly gave me some dry meat," Lightningbolt answered. "It's in the jockey box. There's a candy bar in there too. What are all those rags you're wearing? You look like hell. What happened to your clothes?"

"I traded them," said Beau as he opened the glove box, grinning. He devoured the candy, then chewed on the dry meat. "Some guy bought them, I think, or something like that. You got a drink? Hey, anything, man."

Lightningbolt pulled the pickup over and dug a bottle of cola from behind the seat. He handed it to Beau and got back on the road.

Beau guzzled down the pop and wiped his mouth. "Shiiit man!" he complained, trying to be playful. "I forgot you hate booze. Can you dig it? Me running into a dry head." An instant later he'd fallen asleep.

The childhood friend who now slept in Lightningbolt's truck had once been very close. But Beau had become someone who no longer knew how to interact with anyone who wasn't a drinker.

They had become friends in grade school, when the B.I.A. had decided that a few Indians were needed in the Boy Scouts of America. Twenty boys were herded into the Busby Indian School gymnasium to be outfitted.

Who would join the Boy Scouts was determined by whether or not a boy fit into the uniforms the school had on hand. Beau and Lightningbolt had fit into the clothes, but they had not been able to fit into the image of "authentic Indian Boy Scouts."

The pictures, of course, were the most important part of the idea. All the boys laughed when Beau and Lightningbolt were rudely pulled aside and asked to remove their uniforms.

That was the day two boys learned they weren't red enough to be Indian. Beau was too black, and Lightningbolt was too white.

The filling station was full of life when the pickup rolled to a stop at Henry's Place. Young men pounded happily on the hood—everyone knew the Silver Ship.

Beau was teased and hauled from the seat. He looked around at his childhood friends, but much of his power of recognition had left him forever. The blows he'd received had caused severe bleeding around his brain.

Destiny would have the last say. Beau would not die of his head wounds: He would die of stab wounds in a Billings bar.

And Lightningbolt was destined to discover that millions of Americans are made to feel like misfits because they are a Mixed-Blood people.

The following morning Lightningbolt drove out to the Spotted Deer Ranch. A wizened old cowboy greeted the Silver Ship and her occupant. He had bright blue eyes that shone with curiosity.

"I'm the owner," he said, shaking Lightningbolt's hand through the window. His every word was deliberate and clear.

"Delmar Jones's my name. My father was a cattle rustler. That's the reason for the Jones. My mother was a misfit who joined a circus when she was twelve and owned it when she was fifty. She bought this shit hole and I've been here ever since. I didn't inherit her brains or my father's backbone. Now, what do you want, because I'm not hiring!"

"The snow is nearly gone," said Lightningbolt casually. "I saw twenty head of horses up by the old spring. They look jumpy, mean as cat shit, and I'm sure they belong to you."

The rancher's eyebrows went up. "Them horses are dog food, nothing more. All of 'em are runny-noses, ain't worth twenty-two cents."

"I'll give them a little halter knowing," Lightningbolt countered. He knew the fight was important. "Or anyway they'll look like they're halter-broke. Ten dollars apiece, right here in your corral. You furnish the bronc and food for me to round the rascals up."

"Now, lookie you here," Delmar howled, pleased. "You damned Breed. I can see you've rattled around in a corral or two. I never miss. No, not me. Two hunnert bucks, okay? It's steep, but why not go to the poorhouse? Who gives a damn anyway?"

Lightningbolt waited.

"I don't fear the Cheyenne side of you," the old man proposed. "It's the miserable white half that's the problem, probably mostly thief. Over yonder"—he waved haphazardly to the North—"is the henhouse. Just behind them poplars is a sleep bed in the bunkhouse." He next pointed to the corral. "See that big sorrel? Pretty as a spring bee. She'll help you claw out them jugheads up there. Come summer, they'll make good rodeo stock. I hope they teach them drugstore cowboys a thing or two." He chuckled. "You watch her! She's sure-footed, but can get side-jumpy. Might blow up and buck if you're thinking the wrong things. If she puts her head down, she ain't looking at no tracks or snow flowers. She's about to buck, so keep her head up."

"I'll saddle up right now," Lightningbolt said, getting out of the pickup. "My pack's ready. Which packhorse should I take?"

"That black over there." The old man frowned. "You sure you ain't wanting to sit a spell, swap stories, oil up on black coffee?"

Lightningbolt pulled his pack from the back of

the truck and hefted it up on his shoulders.

"Damned hard winter," Delmar grumbled as he followed Lightningbolt to the corral. "That's the black there. See them spooky eyes of hers! Damned fine animal. The snow was up over the east fence this year. Eight calves down in the first week. I had nine cows that rolled over and made the big jump to better pastures."

Lightningbolt found the lariat on the corral fence, stepped through the gate, and started for the sorrel. He chose the mare because she had less spooky eyes.

"God-damned barn cats froze to death," the old man went on. "Watch her head now. Damn her ol' beautiful hide! That damned Pete Turner ain't come 'round here once this year. What kind of neighbor is that? He borrowed my Caterpillar last spring, did I say no? No! But where is he?"

Lightningbolt began saddling the sorrel.

"Bad hay, jumped up Jerusalem!" Delmar cursed. "No decent money for stock, no how! A man can hardly afford to shoe a horse anymore. What happened to the goddamned Indians that used to steal hereabouts? They all dead . . . damn! I lied about them there horses. There are thirty-three head, bring 'em all in."

Fifteen minutes later, Lightningbolt was astride the sorrel and had his packhorse ready. He looked bored and pained by the old man's stories.

"I lied some more," Delmar admitted. He patted the packhorse. "There are forty-five head, two hundred for the lot. Bring them in dead or alive." He chuckled. "Damned eagles are starving to death, the buzzards, what's happening to this country? Is it the damned politicians?"

Lightningbolt looked down at the rancher. "You have two hundred dollars, hear? Green and countable. No checks. No exchanges. No notes. Okay?"

"It'll be here, son." The old cowboy grinned broadly. "I ain't wanting you to shoot me . . . take

me to court. Goddamned a-roaring, that horse under your ass is a great mare!"

Two days later Lightningbolt found the entire herd. There were sixty-five head of horses. He camped by a spring. All the snow had melted from the spot and it felt warm.

Six days later, all sixty-five head of horses were in Delmar's corral. The old man paid the two hundred dollars he'd promised.

"Why didn't you tell me?" Lightningbolt asked, curious. "Hell, you knew there were sixty-five head. I would have rounded them up. What could I do? I needed the money or I wouldn't be here."

"Not without a severe argument," said the

rancher. "I like talking, but I hate jawing bullshit. People get crazy with money. Shit, just take a look at me. I'd fight a pit full of snakes for a dollar. If there'd been an argument, you'd have asked me for more money. I'd have swore, no doubt calling you dirty names. You'd have blown up, and . . . poof! . . . no horses' tails swishing in that there corral over there. Now, let's look at it this way. You won round one, but I have another offer for round two. I've got more cattle hid out there and more horses." He looked pleased.

Lightningbolt almost won round two, but did win round three. Rounds four, five, and six ended in late May, very close to a draw.

It was the middle of June when the Silver Ship stopped in Goose's yard, but he wasn't there. Lightningbolt asked around and was told the old man was holding a Ceremony at the home of a man called Plains Bull.

An hour later, he was inside the home of Plains Bull. The meeting had only barely begun.

"You there, young man," an elderly man by the door called to Lightningbolt. "You can help with the fire out there." He pointed outside. "You can be the fire keeper. We need men at the drum."

Lightningbolt went out to the fire and added more tree limbs to the flames. He then carefully scooped a pan full of glowing embers and took them into the house.

A multicolored blanket was spread out on the floor and people sat around it, except for the East—this was left open. Old Goose was sitting in the West. He looked good.

Goose Flying was unrolling his Medicine Feathers when Lightningbolt approached him with the embers.

"Where would you like these?" the young man asked.

"Well, here you are, Lightningbolt." Goose smiled broadly. "Good, you made it. Yes, place the coals here by me."

Lightningbolt placed the coals where Goose indicated and then took a seat on the floor by the door—the fire keeper's place. The room was almost overfull with people. Things were so familiar. Even the faces seemed members of his own family. Lightningbolt had been raised with similar Ceremonies; he felt almost at home.

"Most Sacred Great Spirit . . ." Goose Flying prayed. He lifted his Medicine Pipe, then pointed it to the four directions. "Look here upon us. We are gathered. We come to you, Sacred Ones, to bring healing to this little girl, Fawn."

The ceremony lasted for about an hour. After the feast began, there was laughter and talk.

Lightningbolt approached Goose, who stood in a tight knot of people. "The girl seems to be better," he said.

"Yes," Goose answered. He was pleased.

A woman walked up behind Lightningbolt and joined the talk. Suddenly she turned and faced him. "This man," the woman said overly loudly, "what is he doing at our Sacred Ceremonies? He's a Breed. He doesn't belong here."

"We are comforted here," Goose retorted. "This is a Circle for everyone, Sally. Do not be angry."

"You white bastard!" Sally cursed. "Get the hell out of here!" She was becoming very animated.

"He's not white," another woman said, coming to his defense. "He's a Breed. This is Goose Flying's nephew. Leave him alone."

"What's the matter?" a man asked as he shouldered his way forward and stood by Sally. "What's going on here?"

One of the men who already stood in the tight circle of people was disgusted. "He's an ordinary Breed, leave him alone."

"Sure, protect the Breed." Sally was growing

angrier by the minute. "They're worse than whites."

"Sally," Goose broke in, "this is your first Ceremony with me. Do not spoil it with hate. Be calm."

"Get one or the other the hell out of here," a man yelled from across the room. "Both of them are a pain in the butt."

"I'm gone," Lightningbolt said to Goose. "See you at your place, all right?"

"This has never happened to me before," Goose complained. "It has never happened before."

Lightningbolt touched Goose on his shoulder and went out to his pickup.

The following morning an angry Lightningbolt was up early, but not as early as Goose. The old man was sitting alone in his plowed garden, smoking a cigarette. He'd been caring for his corn.

"The woman must have been drunk," said Lightningbolt as he sat down beside Goose.

"It does not help." Goose was apologetic. "I will apologize for her, but not for her hate. I have seen these things before. Hate has many faces. It is

always the same. It is brutal."

Lightningbolt stood and looked across the fields.

"We will talk about this," Goose insisted. "We must get it out."

"I simply don't care anymore, Goose," said Lightningbolt belligerently. "Breeds are not accepted. Let's talk about me having my Vision Quest. You said I should have one."

"The Holy Woman, Estcheemah, once said that Life is our Vision Quest," Goose shared thought-

fully. "I heard her say that one time. This Sally . . . I think that she, too, is not a Full-Blood. Her family is from different tribes. Who is it who is not a Mixed-Blood person?"

"All right," said Lightningbolt, disappointed. The subject of the Vision Quest was put off for the twentieth time. "So, okay, we're all Mixed-Blood." He was getting bored of the talk. "But there are those who fit, right? Tight and very tidy. I fit nothing . . . and I don't give a damn."

"We are all kept separated." Goose sighed. "If

the people do not separate themselves, then there are other separations. It is horrible."

Lightningbolt kicked at a stone.

"I cannot teach you." Goose was looking desperate. "I do not know if it is because you are a Breed. I doubt it. You make my heart sing. But there are pressures, political problems."

"Hey . . . Goose." Lightningbolt was shocked. "Hey . . . come on."

"No, it is no use." Goose shook his head. "I spoke with John and Ammie. They came up the mountain. They said that you were with April Horse. He is strong."

"Goose!" Lightningbolt was very hurt.

"It is April Horse." Tears flowed from his old eyes. "Only he can understand you. I cannot." He put his hand on Lightningbolt's shoulder. "This is our last Medicine Talk. I am sorry."

Goose Flying turned and walked away. His old shoulders sagged and he looked terribly forlorn.

Lightningbolt felt as though he'd just been kicked in the stomach. Sadness leaped up from his heart and choked him. He called on every ounce of strength and stubbornness he possessed to keep from crying.

"Hey, you old coyote," Lightningbolt called out to the old man. "Don't be so sad, all right?"

The following day he left the Dakotas for Montana.

Talking with April Horse opened Lightningbolt's eyes.

Actually it was Shadow who did most of the talking. "Work, girls, problems, ideas, schemes to make money. All these take up a lot of your time. But that's only part of your world. Can you guess what else it is you seek?"

Lightningbolt thought deeply, trying to answer. Finally he shook his head.

"It's the freedom from your awful pain," Shadow explained. "Can you remember when you were not sad? I mean, deeply burdened by your sadness? I doubt if you can. You're also afraid that you will be trapped forever on the Reservation. Goose didn't throw you away. The strange thing about Goose is that he actually loves you. He's weak, that's his problem. It's not you."

"We've never been able to discuss a damn thing. It always gets complicated," Lightningbolt added.

"Of course you couldn't talk." Shadow smiled. "The last thing you are is a religious fanatic. It's not that he is either, but he . . . Well, let's say that his interest is religious. Yours is not."

"Wow." Lightningbolt was moved by this sharp insight. "That figures somehow."

"Of course it does." Shadow smiled. "You're also just a bit dangerous. No, not criminal, not that. But you are dangerous. That constantly worried old Goose. You are determined to do something. It's kind of like living with a bomb. He never knew what you would ask or do next."

Lightningbolt's face showed confusion.

"You're dangerous to stability," Shadow explained. "Goose loves stability. Let's say that you added up wrong for old Goose. Your incredible sadness alone probably kept him a bit afraid of you all the time. No doubt everyone who has ever met you has felt your sorrow, right? Anyway, this inward pain of yours is understandable to an old killer like me." He slapped Lightningbolt playfully on his head. "Whatever it was you brought into this Life, it feels like sadness to you."

"But you're not afraid of me," said Lightningbolt, grinning broadly.

"How do you know I'm not?" Shadow countered. "Don't be so presumptuous.

"I came to these mountains to kill myself, Wolf. Estcheemah changed that, but not the fact that I am now dying of old age. She did not heal the horrible pain that is in me, but she did help me find a way of living with it. I am a very old man, much older than you realize. I'll be dead before long. You demand much energy . . . energy that I simply no longer possess."

Lightningbolt was crushed. All the drama he'd played out in his mind of working with the vet disintegrated instantly. Now what was he going to do?

"There is another kind of soldier you need to meet," Shadow told Lightningbolt. "The soldier I have in mind calmed my fevered brain and soothed my broken heart. You can never comprehend my pain. My anguish kept me from sleep. I couldn't taste my food. By the time I met Estcheemah, I sought only my death. Will you hear more?"

"Yes," said Lightningbolt, attentive again.

"I had my sheep, nothing more," Shadow went on. "And I didn't want shelter. When she found me on the mountain, I was raving mad, living in the elements. But I was no danger to her or to anyone. She walked directly up to me and looked into my eyes.

" 'You will speak of your pain,' she commanded me. 'There are those you will heal because of your awful experience. You are needed by the people.'

"I had been needed to kill soldiers, but beyond that I was no longer needed. I felt the weight of the universe upon me. I felt that I was the misfit, you know . . . the guy who killed his brother and was banished from civilized humans. Can you imagine what that did to my heart?

"But, here was Estcheemah telling me that I was needed. I couldn't believe that! How was I needed? At first I couldn't understand what she meant. You see, Lightningbolt, I was too crazy to understand her. I was far too filled up with my monsters.

"She worked with me for many months and taught me. I seemed to awaken out of some kind of strange mystery. I knew then that there were other vets who desperately needed me.

"Estcheemah pointed out to me that there are other humans like myself. People who no longer have any true feelings and struggle to free themselves from their awful anguish. I learned from her that there are people without any drama in their lives, without any hope for any real change.

"My boredom with my life was immense! I couldn't settle down, and I didn't want to look at who I had been—the killer. You see, Lightningbolt, I was still the hired gun. How does the perfect assassin fit in and settle down in suburbia?

"She taught me about myself. And she taught me how to talk to other nuts just like me . . . you know, people who could not settle down. By talking with people I could help heal their insanities, their broken hearts. It didn't cost them . . . I mean, they didn't have to pay. You know, it makes a difference.

"She commanded me to balance the people she would send to me. I've been faithful to her because I had nothing else. So I became a different kind of Shadow." He smiled. "I teach of human mental anguish. I speak to those who have gone too far. I tell them of my life. It heals them. You will go to Estcheemah. Go to my teacher. She will know what to do with you, Lightningbolt."

Lightningbolt drove to the Little Horn River and camped. He had to have time to think. A jade-blue sky illumined the forest of cottonwoods where he built his small fire. Because he'd pitched his tent on the eastern side of the river, he could see a beauty not known to him before.

The ancient green of the river disappeared, and now the sky threw a cascade of luminous mirrored light beneath the broad trees. He stared in wonderment at his world. The silvery blue-green canopy of brilliance was alive with mystery. The spectacle astonished him and brought him a sense of Earth's Spirit.

At the stream named Thunder Creek, a powerful old woman was preparing her garden for planting. April Horse had written, telling her of a young man called Lightningbolt, the Wolf. Was he that?

The mountains of Wyoming secreted too many memories for Estcheemah. She had buried dead in those mountains. She had wept tears there. Her joys and many fears, and yes, her hopes and dreams were also there. But most of what she had known and enjoyed was now gone. Many people crave only material things that in time turn to dust. She knew that only Spirit remains and is renewed.

Would the young Wolf, this Lightningbolt, see the Spirit? Or was this young man like so many others she had known—only able to see the dust?

April Horse had said that this young man "had the possibility of being strong." Would he endure? That was her question. She felt there was much more—what was it?

One more tear was added to those she had cried in the mountains. The tear glistened on her cheek, then fell quietly into her garden to join others that had fallen there.

She straightened and wiped her eyes when she saw a pickup enter her lane. Lightningbolt had accepted the challenge that April Horse had given him.

A brilliant light of resolute strength shone in her old eyes. It was time for change. The hoe she held became her walking staff as she turned on her heel and strode proudly from her garden.

June, the beautiful young woman who had been living with Estcheemah for a few weeks, watched the teacher's brisk stride as she walked toward the creek.

How very strange, thought the young woman, marveling at Estcheemah's youthfulness and strength. Where does she get her energy?

June turned her attention away from the creek when Estcheemah disappeared into the trees. Now it was time to get to work. She would hurriedly write two letters. One would be mailed by Estcheemah to June's mother, and the other—the one written to her boyfriend—would never be sent.

The astonishingly lovely June would die the following month in a drunken brawl, which she would instigate, in a tavern in Sheridan.

Lightningbolt was instantly captivated by the beauty of the young woman who looked into his eyes as he stepped from his pickup. June never had been so radiant as when the young adventurer first saw her. She began that day to tease him unmercifully, to make him blush at every opportunity.

Lightningbolt had no way of understanding June. From the moment he met her until the moment they parted, she remained a mystery.

He also met Estcheemah, but very briefly. She asked him if he could "survive his first test." He answered that he could, and she immediately put him into a pup tent out in the hills alone.

Each time Lightningbolt had to be at the house, June would tease him—lifting her skirt just high enough to reveal her long pretty legs. She never tired of her sport.

Her mother had sent the twenty-year-old girl-woman to Estcheemah. June was already a very heavy drinker, an alcoholic. The blonde, blue-eyed flirt loved Estcheemah, but she considered the Holy Woman to be only her entertainment.

The girl had sat quietly at the table when Estcheemah asked Lightningbolt if he could remain loyal to himself and if he could be Self disciplined. Lightningbolt nodded briskly that he was ready for such a commitment. He was determined to see this through, no matter what the Medicine Woman had to say.

June teased and smiled sweetly, amused and delighted, when the young man gave his answer.

"You are afraid," Estcheemah announced. "But you have courage. Tomorrow is your first confrontation and teaching," Estcheemah explained carefully. "June and I will prepare your Sacred Dinner. You will eat the dinner with me. This will be no easy battle."

"Wherever and whenever," Lightningbolt said, a bit flippantly.

"This dinner is going to be an awful war for you," Estcheemah challenged. "A bigger one than you now think."

The next day, at exactly noon, Estcheemah and June set up the Sacred Dinner in the back of Lightningbolt's pickup in a busy Sheridan shopping center.

Estcheemah had brought no crystal glasses, no bone china, no candelabra, but she might as well have. The white linen tablecloth, the neatly set table with its vase of flowers, and the carefully arranged dishes and bowls of food shouted the same.

The cowboys, ranchers, workers, businessmen, and other gawkers, and the curious who walked to and from their cars and pickups, smiled at Lightningbolt.

Kids pointed. And their mothers were amused.

June was ecstatic. She was also getting a great deal of attention herself. She laughed and danced, announcing the location of the freaks in the back of the pickup. An old Indian woman sitting and having dinner with a Breed in a parking lot. How hilarious it was for June.

How incredibly embarrassing it was for Lightningbolt!

June thought that Lightningbolt was a complete fool, and his every action entertained her.

When the formal dinner began, Lightningbolt was faced with the brutalizing challenge of how to crawl up into the back of his pickup without looking like a blithering idiot or simply collapsing back to the ground.

His chair, for some inexplicable reason, jumped and rattled around as he tried to seat himself. This so unnerved him that he nearly pulled the tablecloth out from under the dishes. He fought the chair and the clattering silverware back into place, then gingerly sat down.

A war of incredible proportions rampaged inside his mind and heart as he tried to bite into a carrot. He managed to chew, but swallowing became an ordeal.

His hands trembled so violently he could barely manage cutting through his steak.

This woman just had to be a witch! Would a normal Medicine Woman put a man through what he was going through? Never! His greatest fear was that one of his buddies would see him. Could he survive that?

He choked down a bite while the Medicine Woman looked on, totally unconcerned. He was not going to allow her the victory of seeing him run! Tears poured down his cheeks when two cowboys danced with June and shouted—pretending that they were barkers at a circus.

His knees were wobbly beneath the table, and sweat covered his brow. But this did not stop him from biting into the celery that kept threatening to jump out of his hand. He wanted to leap from the chair and run, but the words of April Horse kept echoing in Lightningbolt's mind: "Be brave, no matter what she does. She will test you to your limits."

Suddenly Estcheemah wiped her mouth with her napkin and asked Lightningbolt if it was time to go. He tried to answer, but all he could get out was a halfhearted murmur.

The parking lot was now empty, silent. June had tired of dancing and was perched on the hood of a Jeep parked next to the Silver Ship.

"It's remarkable that you remained at my table," Estcheemah said quietly to Lightningbolt as she cleared away the dishes. "In the past your fears have made you run." She looked up briefly into his eyes and smiled. "It took courage to sit with me. You have met a part of your Self you have never known. I would be mindful of that, and protective of what you discovered."

The bloom would fade from June, and soon she would be gone.

The old and powerful Medicine Woman would endure.

Estcheemah became Lightningbolt's teacher and mentor, and would continue teaching him up to the very moment of her death.

It was a beautiful morning when Lightningbolt heard the story of Estcheemah's Medicine Pipe. They were strolling along a gravel road when she related the story of how her Pipe came to her.

"This land is a beautiful place to live," she told him. "The people who lived in this country called this land Wyoming, which means 'Prairie Goddess.' Here, the grass is forever young, and always old.

"This is also true of my Medicine Pipe. My Pipe is forever young and very old. Many comment, most oftenly, when they see my Pipe, that it looks different from the more traditional Pipes they have seen."

When they rounded a turn in the road, they came upon an old county bridge. So many willows grew near the bridge, it looked as though its sides were woven of leaves.

Estcheemah was very familiar with the bridge. She pulled the willow branches aside and sat down on the bridge railing.

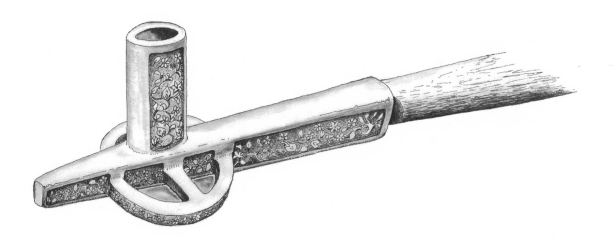

The songs of the meadowlarks and songbirds seemed, suddenly, very close. The water that flowed beneath the bridge also sang Her melody. The tiny stream alerted Lightningbolt to the truth that he had not been listening to Wyoming.

Estcheemah very gently unrolled the Medicine Bundle that contained her Medicine Pipe and handed it to Lightningbolt. He took the Pipe and sat down cross-legged on the road of the bridge. He had no concern for traffic, because none would pass by here for days.

"My Pipe, as you can see, is a Wheel Pipe. This Wheel shape of my Pipe is not so common, yet it is not uncommon either.

"Medicine Pipes have been carved in every way possible. This design goes back so far in antiquity that no one knows where or when it originated.

"Two women carved the Pipe over a period of a year. They drilled it with a bow-flint drill. Later on, I had the hole widened with an electric power drill in Cheyenne. I think it was the only Pipe ever brought into a machine shop. An old German lathe operator did the job for me—it delighted him.

"While I grew in the Ways of understanding my Self and our Earth Mother, my Zero Chiefs did not say much to me about my Medicine Pipe. It was a time of waiting for me.

"From the time I was fourteen years old until I was twenty-eight, and I was healed, I hid in my mother's home. My face and hands were covered with eczema—so I never knew the intimacy of a man until after I was healed.

"There was a woman who used to beg my step-mother to let her try to help me. She lived just twenty miles away. Her name was Night Arrow Woman. My stepmother was a confirmed Catholic and wouldn't even dream of having a Medicine Woman help. My mother and father had died while I was still very young.

"My parents' death remains a mystery. Little Wolf had adopted me, and he and my stepmother raised me. He and his first wife, Dreamer, had been the closest of friends to my mother and father. The death of my parents and Dreamer must have been an incredible tragedy, because Little Wolf refused to ever speak of how they died. It was rumored they had been killed during the Indian Wars of the late eighteen-hundreds.

"Little Wolf was never the same after Dreamer died. He was the saddest man I have ever known in my life. I never knew, until I was older, of course, that my stepmother was a drinker. Little Wolf would never drink. He must have loved her very much to put up with what he did for so long. Eventually they were divorced.

"The woman who was to become my grandmother—actually she raised me more than my stepmother did—was my stepmother's mother. My grandmother was kind and very traditional. She was the one who finally got help for me. She never lived long enough to see me healed, but she never doubted I would be.

"The year of my healing was a terrible year! I think my stepmother and Little Wolf parted because of Night Arrow Woman.

"I went to live with Night Arrow Woman so that she could help me. She was an old woman and almost completely crippled. When I first saw her home I felt terrible. The house was not dirty, but it was in terrible shape.

"You must understand that my stepmother had poisoned my mind against Night Arrow Woman. She told me I was just a scabby slave, that Night Arrow Woman wanted me for her slave.

"I believed this, and was sick at heart for many days. I organized the house—even became a carpenter, replacing windows. The old woman had tattered blankets on the windows.

"Night Arrow Woman would sit at her old pedal sewing machine and pump with her one good leg, and sew and sew. What I did was work and work. I did not know what else to do. I was very simple-minded in those days. I had accepted, without question, one authority for the next. You see, I had nowhere to go, so I had to make the best of things.

"We were able to trade for some paint and I painted the entire house. For a while this helped, but I soon became sad again. I used to cry every night, and I used to pray to die. I wanted to kill myself, but I didn't know how. I desperately wanted to leave Life and get away from my wretched body.

"Night Arrow Woman could not stand, not even on her good leg, because something was wrong with her hip. I would watch her drag herself around. Her pitiful condition frightened me.

"At these times, I would look at my scabby hands and face and think of us both as monsters. Night Arrow Woman had to crawl to the door whenever anyone came to our home. I always ran and hid when people came.

"The old woman began to teach me. First she taught me how to read. She would make me read to her, night after night. She was so beautiful in her heart, so warm and loving. I soon realized why she lived in such a terrible condition. Her tasks were impossible for her to do alone. She would sit on the floor and mop it spotless; this always amazed me. She did everything she could to help me, always! She would laugh and tease, and call me Little One. No matter how hard our circumstances became, she was always cheerful. She told me I was her destiny, Lightningbolt. Can you imagine how strange those words were for me?

"I grew to love her, but it took a long and awful struggle. Once I began to trust her, I used the herbs that she gave me for doctoring.

"Mending sheets and clothing was our only income. The townspeople sent their clothes to us every week with the man who cleaned the livery stable.

"People stayed away from us because they were afraid of us. Even the Indian people who lived nearby distrusted us. We were called witches.

"Night Arrow Woman showed me how to mend shirts. My most difficult task was cutting the wood we used. We used a lot of wood to heat the water to wash the shirts.

"The shirts were always starched and ironed after we mended them. It was the fashion in those

days for the men to wear shirts stiffened with starch. I kept the two irons that I used to press the shirts always heating on the stove. It was dreadfully hard work.

"When I was not busy cooking, chopping wood, washing clothes, or sewing, I would read to Night Arrow Woman for hours. I was starved for information. I read day after day, every chance I had. Over the years I became an ardent reader.

"By the time I had my twenty-ninth birthday I was reading everything I could get my hands on. The library only had fifteen hundred books, and so most of my spending money went for books.

"Old Buffalo Soldier was the man who delivered the shirts and bought our groceries and things we needed. He bought books for me or got them from the library. He did all kinds of odd jobs. He used to tease us about being on his list of odd jobs.

He was very kind. We could not have survived without his help.

"By the middle of my twenty-ninth year the medicinal herbs began to work. Within two months after the medicine started working, my skin cleared entirely. I know now that it was mostly because of her prayers.

"When I was thirty years old, she took me to see the town for the first time. I had never seen a town or settlement before, and so I was very excited.

"Night Arrow Woman remained sitting in the wagon box, holding the reins of the horses, while I had my first look around. Seeing a store for the first time is quite an experience. At the time, I thought stores were immense and very grand. I was so excited and bursting with happiness inside that I was crying.

"My first journey lasted only ten minutes, but it was enough for me. After that we made a journey every weekend. I had to sew a lot of shirts for those journeys, because we had to pay money for the wagon and horses, but I loved it!

"The townspeople never knew who we were for over a year. No one ever asked who we were. They did not know we were the people who mended their clothes.

"The first time a person told me that I was beautiful, it shocked me. I broke into tears and could not lift my head from Night Arrow Woman's lap. She was very understanding.

"I could go on with my story, with my fears and how much I trembled when I was with people; but the talk of my Pipe is more important.

"My first recollection of seeing anyone smoke the Pipe was when I saw Night Arrow Woman drag herself to the outside pump to bathe.

"At the time, I thought she looked horrible! Like a terrible human monster, sitting there bathing with cold water. I never thought of how painful it was for her. I only thought of how much of a monster she was.

"Each time Night Arrow Woman would bathe, she would first carefully unwrap her Medicine Pipe. After she prayed, she would then crawl to the

pump, where she bathed.

"There is more that needs to be said about my stepmother and how much she hated Night Arrow Woman. My stepmother told me that Night Arrow Woman was a monster witch and that she worshiped demons.

"Little Wolf would not say much when he heard this kind of talk, but it was obvious he did not like it. He would usually get up and go out to work at these times, and not return until the tirade was over. It was good that I saw his reactions because they told me much.

"Little Wolf made his living by splitting wood for the businesspeople in town. After his wife, Dreamer, died, he was like a dead man. The only time he would come alive was when he talked about the old days.

"Four years after I went to my teacher, Night Arrow Woman, Little Wolf died mysteriously. Some say that he killed himself. The death of Little Wolf shut the door to the only outside world I had.

"I hated Rainbow and Dancing Tree, my mother and father, for dying. I hated Little Wolf and Dreamer for dying. I hated the wretched conditions I had to live with. I hated the world I was born into, and I despised myself. For many months, I was like a numb, stupid animal. It was a miracle my mind had not fallen!

"Most oftenly, during this time, the monster or witch, whatever you want to call her, would sing to me and ask me to read to her.

"The world of torture I had to live in was unimaginably painful. I did not know that it was my ignorance that caused my world to be so agonizing.

"So you see, the first Pipe I ever saw belonged to a monster who dragged herself along the ground like some terrible wounded worm. I was so simpleminded! I thought I would have the things of a monster if I had a Pipe. Who wanted the things of a pitiful monster? I wanted to be beautiful, to be rich, to be loved, and to have the things of the rich, not the things of a poor cripple.

"At the time, the Pipe was a symbol of dread and I despised it. I had been told that Little Wolf had given up his Pipe and had buried it when Dreamer died. I did not think that he had buried his Pipe, his most beloved possession, with his wife, because it was a gesture equal to burying his own heart. No, I did not know that truth or realize its meaning until two years after Little Wolf's death.

"Little Wolf was the only thing, the only person, in my world who had been clean, healthy, and beautiful. At that time my thoughts were very simple. If Little Wolf had given up his Pipe, there must be something wrong with the Pipe. Oh, how terribly wrong I was!

"I think back now, knowing what extreme conditions Night Arrow Woman had to endure, and it makes me cry. How very brave she was! Such a delicate beauty. I have never known anyone more virtuous.

"Night Arrow Woman was a Holy Woman.

"When anyone has a chance to live with a Holy Woman, nothing can be called normal. Once I began to give Night Arrow Woman a little help, everything changed immediately for both of us.

"My entire existence was altered forever. Now that Night Arrow Woman could keep herself and her home fresh, I began to see and feel that there was real hope. I felt I had a chance to experience something new and wonderful.

"My learning actually began in my thirty-first year. I was born that year. Before my birth year, Night Arrow Woman would explain that I had to learn to walk the Compassion Road. She said that at the end of that road my Medicine Pipe waited for me. While her words were beautiful, it wouldn't be until later that I would know what she meant."

"I learned that the Medicine Pipe is from this Turtle Island, North America, where we now live. Most oftenly, people know the histories of the Lakotah or Tsistsistasts-Cheyenne and how they used their Pipes. But there are other stories.

"Old Zero Chiefs would comment on and enjoy the truth that the Pipe and its fire reminded them of the old Coatl-Atl and how these peoples struggled to enlighten humanity.

"The Quetzal-Atl, the wooden stem, the Sacred Tree . . . its mathematics reminded these old Zero Chiefs of the marriage of Quetzal-Atl and Coatl-Atl temples. Most oftenly, I think of my Pipe as the Quetzal-Atl and Coatl-Atl.

"Human suffering, ignorance, joys, enlightenment—all of our wondrous life journey—is for me Life Herself. I see all this when I smoke my Pipe.

"I have seen the results of two world wars. Humanity strides along a highway of skulls it calls progress because, they say, out of war was born the new mechanized technology. I quake inside, like the doe that has lost her fawn, when she hears the thunder held in the hands of the human.

"I believe that Beauty is so much here on Earth, it overwhelms the minds of the people. I think humanity is afraid to live in Beauty. I think that humanity is afraid of the challenge of living in Beauty.

"The Pipe is so simple. The Pipe is so very subtle. The Pipe says that we can have cities with wide avenues of flowers and trees. The Pipe says that we do not need to walk a long highway of skulls.

"The Pipe says that each of us is our own authority in Life. And that profound truth makes every one of us responsible for our Lives. Those who truly respect the Pipe must also respect the Sacred Self that they are. How very delicate the Self is! How very fleeting our Lives are.

"The Pipe is also known as Light-Singing because She represents Life. The Pipe Sings of our Self learning.

"Most often, when people ask me about my Wheel Pipe, I tell them of the Circle of Law. But do you know what? I think they are really asking about the Beauty that surrounds me.

"This Beauty is my understanding of the pain my stepmother suffered because of her indulgence. This Beauty is my caring for the memory of Little Wolf, who buried his Pipe with his beloved. This Beauty is remembering a young woman of great ignorance and sorrow who was afflicted with eczema. This Beauty is the Power of the Holy Woman, Night Arrow Woman, that surrounds me. This Beauty is my Courage to face Beauty and accept Her challenge to all of us.

"I realize now that I am an old woman, most oftenly when I am alone, that it is so easy to die. It is so easy to return to our Spirit world from where we came. Life is not easy. But Life is not nearly so hard when we honor the Self.

"The Pipe I now hold in my hands is Substance and Spirit, carved from the Source. I named my Medicine Pipe Beauty.

"Yes, this is the name of my Pipe.

"There are four spokes that make up the Wheel of my Pipe. They are the children of Beauty. They are: Cheemah, Fire-East; Morealah, Water-South; Ehahmah, Earth-West; and Wehomah, Air-North.

"I am a Zero Chief. Because of that, possibly I can say I truly know Nothing. For me, Nothing is the Great Zero—Creation.

"I know you seek everything, but one day you will realize that what you call Nothing is actually Everything."

Estcheemah had deeply moved Lightningbolt. Never, ever in his life had he encountered a human who possessed so much Wisdom and Love.

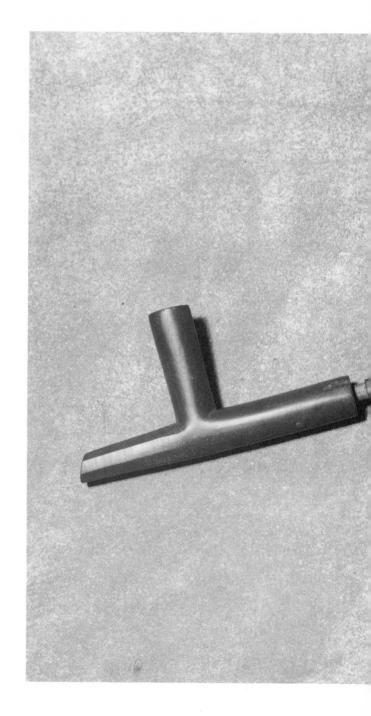

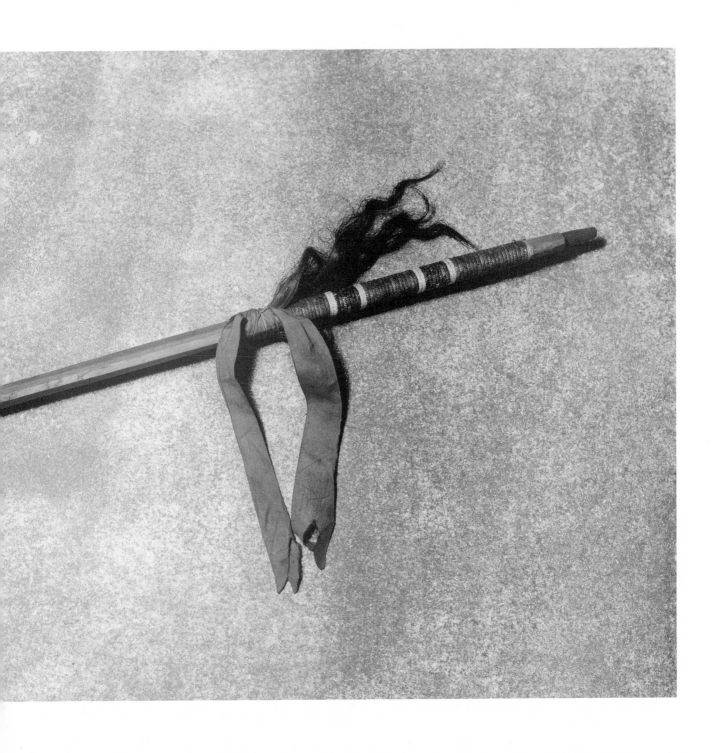

A day later, as he drove to Ashland, Lightningbolt was in a sphere of reverie that was so broad, so
all-encompassing, that he was actually respectful of
Life and Spirit for a time.

He stopped at Warring Hen's home, on the
Cheyenne Reservation, to pick up a saddle the old
man had borrowed from him.

"He went to a hand game," Priscilla told him.
Old Ed Warring Hen was her fifth husband. She
had outlived the first four.

"Hand game. Gambling again. Wore his best
hat too." She smiled, backing off the porch into the
kitchen. She still loved company.

"My, how you've grown. Is your mother doing
well? Does she still speak beautiful Cheyenne?
How come you don't know your Cheyenne language better? Do you always speak Crow? It is hard
for us old people.

"We now have our first refrigerator. It really

works good! But we ain't got nothing to put into it. Commodities come only in cans and boxes, but the cheese is in the fridge. Do you want to look? Sometimes we suck on the ice. It makes us dream of deer steaks, good beef, chicken, and turkey." She looked up into the sky. "Yes, it is so very empty. Oh, well." She sighed.

"No hamburger, huh?" Lightningbolt sympathized. "Well, ah, you tell Ed to sell that saddle. Why not? It's getting old. Buy all the hamburger you want, okay?"

"We will like that." She smiled, showing great gaps in her teeth. "Thanks. Gee, that is so kind. Thanks again."

Lightningbolt left feeling like a horse had kicked him right in the heart.

The final few miles to Ashland was a terrible drive, filled with apprehension and guilt. It wasn't that he felt personally responsible for the Warring Hens' poverty. It was that old question of right versus wrong, and what would be fair.

Like most young men his age, Lightningbolt was gripped by a sense of doom. The Vietnam War did that. Any war that a country finds itself embroiled in is a curious occurrence of contradictions. One person might view a war from an armchair while enjoying their TV dinner, while another stands weeping at a grave.

Many view war as a chance to make money.

Those who fight a war also view it in many different ways. One soldier might never see a battle, while another experiences every terror.

War can become a horrible cleanser, or a hideous affliction that slowly seeps into every pore of a country. The Vietnam War had become just such a disease. The shadow of war and political incompetence loomed large. America's youth had become disillusioned with their elders, and sought the new.

And because of Vietnam a new misery had flooded every Reservation. Young men who were AWOL, those fleeing the draft or the grime of the cities, and those escaping into drugs, all flowed together into a maelstrom of hope and bitterness.

Each group soon acquired a name on the Reservation. How the names evolved no one knew. The AWOL were known as the Lightning Express boys. The beautiful young women who joined these men were called the Magic Express girls.

The whiskey-drinking rednecks and beer-drinking cowboys gave the new people other names. They called them all the Rat Stampeders. Anyone who appeared to be a long-haired Stampeder was fair game. This meant that a Stampeder could be beaten, raped, robbed, ridiculed, preached at, threatened, or molested.

At the time, still another group of youths, almost hippies but not quite, were the people in the Peace Corps. The Stampeder haters called them the Bleeding Hearts, and despised them, especially the females. The locals believed these girls were sleeping with the "filthy bucks."

The Indians were not innocent of hatred either. The Feather Fathers, the up-and-coming young Indian political radicals, hated everybody, especially the hippies.

Next came the Political Cats, or Pole Cats, the "established" Indians who were either in tribal office, wanted to be in a tribal position, or were ardent supporters of those wanting to be in a tribal office. The Pole Cats knew what was "right and wrong for the Indian people." The Pole Cats hated everybody but themselves.

The Acees, or the Big Ace, were the Academics, the "government experts." Every Ace claimed to know everybody and everything that was supposed to be Indian. They were so well informed it would be years before they knew what a hippie was. They would always interview the Pole Cats to get a poll of the vote, and generally got everything wrong.

Then came the Traditionalists. The first of these traditionalists were the Ranch Branch. These were the white landowners. Breeds were hated first

on their list. They knew everything that was supposed to be American or authentic Indian. Yet, for some strange reason, the Ranch Branch always managed to marry into the "wrong family." This meant they found themselves always somehow married into Breeds. But to discuss this openly was forbidden!

For the Ranch Branch, everyone else in Montana—on or off a Reservation—was a hired man or hired woman, including the newcomers.

The next Traditionalists were the People of the Green Convention. These were Indians who supported those who used peyote. However, these people were not the same as the famous Peyote Buttons, the Indian stalwarts who had decided that anything and everything "that is Indian, was Indian, or will be Indian, was and is peyote."

The Green Convention supported the policies

and much of the thinking of the Peyote Buttons—with one exception. The Green Convention folks believed that the Sun Dance Way still might have a slim chance. But which Sun Dance? There were so many!

Politics created two other groups, the Attraction Faction and the Powwowers. These Indian Powwowers loved any and all Powwows, which, of course, should represent authentic Indian dancing but usually did not.

The Attraction Faction were "the important people" who controlled the money for fairs and rodeos.

All the Traditionalists, combined or separate, hated the Bureau of Indian Affairs equally.

Complicated for sure! But this was the state of Indian affairs at the time.

Lightningbolt was overfamiliar with all the names, and who was who, on the Reservations. He enjoyed the game and participated with the game players.

One of Lightningbolt's closest friends was Levi Greenblatt, although his friends knew him as Smokey. As soon as Lightningbolt arrived in Ashland, he drove immediately to the Pink China Cafe, looking for his friend.

Smokey was an Oklahoma City Half-Breed, a young beatnik painter who had come to the Reservation, as he put it, "for solace, the deep and penetrating, the mad and the profound." Smokey studied, even worshiped, illusion. He claimed that illusion was "the milk of poverty and the bread of true wealth."

The first lesson in beat philosophy that Smokey

taught Lightningbolt concerned his thinking about "Jack and Jackie Arm Pit." According to the very youthful and wise Smokey, Jack and Jackie Arm Pit had "divided America up into Apple Pie. The left-overs were made into Jack Whiskey." He described how Jack Pits completely surrounded all Reservations. They controlled everything and owned America.

Smokey was in a dark mood when Lightningbolt joined him in the last booth of the cafe.

"All the girl wanted to do was to see what a peyote ceremony was like." Smokey looked very depressed. "And now Alex is in jail . . . the bastards."

"Alex, in jail?" said Lightningbolt good-humoredly. He signaled to the waitress for a cup of coffee, then slapped Smokey's hand. "Hey, Okie, what's up?"

"Hey, no, it's really serious this time!" Smokey insisted. "Alex is in the cooler. It really looks tough."

Lightningbolt smiled at the waitress, taking his coffee from her. "Alex has been in jail before. He'll live through it."

"Hey, no, you don't dig, man." Smokey looked genuinely pained. "Really, remember that beautiful Kathy? About fifteen, dumb as all shit. Well, hey, she was over at the Carvel farm. She wanted to see some jokers putting on a peyote gig. There were Triggers there, local cowboys, and a few Feather Fathers. Alex blundered right into it. One of the Triggers raped Kathy in the Lodge. She ran; Alex

113

busted the guy in the head with a shovel. Cracked his skull wide open. The guy ain't expected to live. No, man, this one is really bad."

A knot instantly tied itself in Lightningbolt's gut. It hurt. Alex Blue Cloud, Lightningbolt's school friend, had been very close to him. He had just returned from Vietnam.

Lightningbolt was Alex's only real friend. They had sworn to be Medicine Brothers forever when they were in school together. Later, Alex joined the marines and had spent two tours in Vietnam.

He was never the same after he returned to America. He was moody, secretive, and used drugs to answer his every pain and to solve his every problem.

Kent Little Bow slipped in beside Lightningbolt in the booth. He looked around as though someone was following him. "I think that Alex just ate it," he informed the two men. "Alex ran away from the slammer, from the Reservation Indian police. He's hiding somewhere up in the hills. He took along a .30-06. I mean, man, he's looking for a small war."

Under the table, Kent pressed a yellow slip of paper into Lightningbolt's hand. "He could be any-where in the Little Horns. Maybe the Wolf Moun-tains, who knows?" He suddenly stood up. "See you around. Got some smoke? Hash? Cambodian? I'll trade for cactus."

Both men shook their heads no. Kent smiled, then spun on his heel and left the cafe.

Three hours later the Silver Ship came to a stop on a rarely used gravel road near Little Owl Creek. Lightningbolt had brought along a horse trailer. In it was a beautiful black mare with a big heart.

She threw her head as he tightened down the saddle. He looked around furtively before he slipped the bridle over her ears. Yes, the pickup would be fine here. No one would see it.

"Alex, you dumb shit," he cursed as he swung into the saddle. "Hey, man, why do you insist on so much pain? You have got to see April Horse."

He loped the mare until she found her own rhythm. An hour later, at Yellow Head Springs, he dismounted and hobbled the black. She was in good grass.

His spurs sang as he ran up the draw to the old cabin that he and Alex had always used for elk hunting. When he got there, he saw that the cabin was no more. Some dumb ass had burned it to the ground. Yellow paper, Yellow Head; his guess about the message of the yellow piece of paper had been wrong.

He walked around the debris, disappointed. Possibly there were prints left, but he doubted it somehow. No, his guess was wrong again.

Where in hell can you be? he asked in his mind.

He turned and looked down the valley.

Suddenly he realized that someone had indeed been there—and recently too. The ground had been brushed, destroying tracks of riders and their horses. Whose tracks were these? Why had they been so sloppy, rubbing out only half the signs? It was odd.

The hackles rose on his neck. "Where are you dogs hid out?" he yelled. "You find Alex? Are you cops?"

Two men stood up from where they'd been hidden behind a broken-down old shed. Yes, it was the Indian police. One of the men motioned him forward.

"Go to hell!" Lightningbolt was angry.

"Halt!" one of the policemen yelled. "We got him, Lightningbolt—don't interfere. It's against the law."

"He's a wanted man," a third man said, coming from his right. "Easy, Lightningbolt. We know Alex is your friend, but you can't protect him."

Lightningbolt spun to face the last speaker, fury boiling up in his heart. The three men were now facing him.

"You know me, son," said the larger man, smiling. "I'm Franklin. How's your mother?"

Lightningbolt set his teeth. He only nodded that he had understood. He was far too angry to talk.

"It's manslaughter, maybe murder," Franklin explained smoothly. "And he shot and wounded a policeman. He's dangerous and crazy, flipped out on heroin. Don't even dream of helping him. Got that?"

Lightningbolt heard someone to his left and spun around. It was that smart ass, Dave Pine.

"Get over here, Dave," Franklin ordered. "We're saddling up. Keep this snot nose in sight. He's tricky."

Dave came out of his concealment. "That'll be my pleasure." Dave was speaking Crow deliberately. It was meant as a mockery. "My, my, what's this?"

Lightningbolt sprinted away, running as fast as

his legs would carry him down the draw.

"Halt!" Dave yelled. "You dumb shit! You're with us!"

"Get on that goddamned horse of yours," Franklin cursed. "You jackass. You lose him and you're fired."

Lightningbolt had his hunting knife out when he came alongside the black. He cut the hobbles and was on her back in an instant. This scared her and she threw her head. But when his spurs bit deep, she exploded into a hard run.

"East! East, lady," he urged her. "Run! Run, lady!"

He looked back over his shoulder and saw his pursuers about three hundred yards behind him. They were riding breakneck after him. Their horses were young and fast.

Lightningbolt had only one chance to elude his pursuers—the big gulch. There was a deep, swift, muddy river at the bottom of the gulch. The river was tricky, dangerous if a person didn't know her.

As a child, he and his friends had played with the small river, calling her Goldie. Their game was to leap their horses off the cliff into the river, then grab their tails and let the animals swim. Whoever made it to the sandbar was the winner. Lightning-bolt had played the game many times.

These Reservation Indian police were far from their usual haunts. They knew nothing of Goldie. If he could get the black to make the jump, then he had it made. There were a thousand branching washes that entered the river—all of them places to hide, obstacles the police had to ride around.

Once he was in the river, it would be a shortcut that would give him an advantage of at least two miles of hard riding. When the mare came to the fall, he hit her with his spurs and aimed her toward the cliff, but she spun and clawed, then bucked. She was very afraid. He spun her around and around, then hit her with his spurs again. This time she slipped over the edge, and they both plunged into the stream below.

Lightningbolt was spitting water when his head reached air again, but he had hold of the mare's tail. She was a strong swimmer and the current was very swift. They immediately disappeared around one bend, then another. Nearly a mile downstream, he led the tired black to the sandbar nearly covered with water in midstream.

Now they could both rest and get their breath. There was no need to hurry. He'd done better than he thought. It was impossible for them to catch up now. Even finding him was out of the question.

The second cold plunge into the river was not pleasant. The black swam the last few feet of water, then struggled up onto the bank.

Lightningbolt stripped off his sopping wet clothes, wrung them out, and rode naked. An hour later his clothes were dry enough to wear again. He dressed and had a look around. From this point on he would choose the rockiest ground he could find. Franklin was a good cop, but he was no Indian scout.

Four and a half hours later, Lightningbolt reached Soldier Springs. He jumped down from the mare and dug out the small sack of oats he'd put in one of his saddlebags. It was wet, but the black loved it.

Lightningbolt threw away the sandwiches he'd made and sat on a stone, eating a candy bar. It was damp but not ruined. The weather was growing colder now, but the Moon was rising bright and full.

As Lightningbolt opened a can of stew, he suddenly remembered Kent, Alex, Rufus, Dan Boy, and himself writing secret messages in school. Purple paper meant cutting class. Green meant buying beer.

He frowned, trying to remember why those particular colors had been chosen. Orange was skipping school. Yellow, What was yellow?

White or red was a girl, usually with an initial.

Blue was . . . was . . . What the hell was blue? He couldn't remember. Black was . . . What the hell was yellow?

He began to eat his stew. The mare was contentedly eating grass.

"Yellow!" yelled Lightningbolt, leaping to his feet. "War, battle, that was it. Yeah, a fight. Custer, yellow hair, sure." But what the hell did that yellow piece of paper mean that Kent gave him? There was no writing on it.

He put down his can of stew and walked to where the mare was grazing, and rubbed her down. Then he returned to his seat and began eating again.

"Custer's last stand?" he mused, thinking. "Nope, not around the Custer battlefield. Custer Pass?"

Holy damn, wait. He was twenty-three miles from old Spotted Horse's grave. Spotted Horse had been a powerful warrior who had battled the whites and won. Alex had always said that the place was his, that it belonged to all powerful warriors. "Yeah, that was it. Alex said he would do his last dance there just as Spotted Horse had done. Wow! Can you believe it? Kent remembered that rap. That was years ago." He frowned. "Holy shit, Alex remembered that rap too."

Lightningbolt began to saddle up the black. It was time to ride.

Alex had loved the gravesite, Lightningbolt thought as he threw on the saddlebags and tightened them down. Kent and Alex must have talked, reminiscing about that . . . it would be fresh in both of their minds. Yes, Alex swore that his body would never be buried in Vietnam. He swore he'd return to Spotted Horse. He had to be among the fighting warriors.

The Moon was bright overhead when Lightningbolt reined in the black at Spotted Horse. The cabin that Larry Steinburg had built there was still standing. It was a well-made hunting cabin.

He led the black to the corral and gave her oats and hay. The lean-to at the corral was in tip-top shape. The pretty roan that met them had to be Alex's horse.

Fifty feet away a lamp shone warm from the cabin window. Smoke wisped up from the chimney. Alex loved his comfort.

"Hey . . . Alex!" Lightningbolt yelled to the house. "It's me, Lightningbolt. Yellow paper. What are you doing in there? Hey, Dream Boy." He laughed.

Only silence answered his call.

"Hey . . ." Lightningbolt teased and cajoled Alex. "You got the white Jesus in your veins again? Or is the Buddha in your brain?" Only Alex used those expressions, so he had to know that it was Lightningbolt. "Come on, Dream Boy, answer. Don't point the big lady at me, okay?" He knew Alex would not be without his hunting rifle.

Still no answer. Lightningbolt was getting worried. He walked out into the middle of the yard and called, "Hey, it's me. Lightningbolt."

Only the horses in the corral seemed to notice. The house remained silent.

He walked cautiously to the porch door, his back against the wall. Something was spooky wrong. The hair fairly stood up along the nape of his neck. His back still against the wall, he knocked with the back of his hand.

A very strange sound came from the interior of the cabin; it was eerie. Then came a scratching at the door. Lightningbolt carefully turned the latch and nudged the door open with the back of his hand.

The door swung open with a squeak, and a frightened brown cat came streaking out.

"Alex?" he whispered hoarsely. "You digging on Buddha in your brain? Is the white Jesus rapping with you?"

Not one sound came from the room.

Lightningbolt pushed the door open wide and

peered around the doorjamb to take a look. What he saw made his knees go limp.

Alex was swinging slowly in the middle of the room, hanging from one of the rafters.

Tears poured from Lightningbolt's eyes as he approached his friend. He tried to speak, but the only sound that came was a sob. He walked to the body and tore the note away that Alex had attached to his shirt with a safety pin.

"Hey, Lightningbolt," the note read. "I've got the white Jesus in my veins . . . Holy of Holies. I got the Buddha in my brain, Holy of Holy. I'm going to be dancing with the warriors when you find me. If you go to 'Nam, Lightningbolt, you have to die there. It's too sad coming back. Die there!"

He had signed it with a simple "A."

Lightningbolt crumpled the paper and stuck it in his pocket. He was suddenly feeling amazingly calm. This calm was not good. But very, very calm.

"You stupid shit," he told his dead friend. "April Horse, he knew your pain, man . . . you dumb shit!"

Tears rolled down his cheeks, but for some strange reason his voice remained very steady, very calm.

The room stank. Alex's bowels had loosened when he died.

Lightningbolt righted the chair that had fallen on its side, stood on it, and cut Alex down with his hunting knife. The body fell like heavy Death. He was already stiffening.

He dragged the body to the bunk and laid him out. When he examined his brother he found that Alex had not broken his neck. He had slowly strangled to death.

The following morning, Lightningbolt made a call from a service station to the Reservation Indian police. He did not give his name.

Lightningbolt drove to Wyoming to find a place to cry. His mind became a battlefield of doubt and

indecision. He needed to talk with Estcheemah.

There were barbed wire fences around him everywhere. They lined the roads and cut through every field, trapping the deer and trees. The spiny sharp enclosures shut people and animals in, and tried to hold Life out. He hated those fences.

Hard thunder boomed overhead while he drove. The countryside became an illuminated earthly dream that flickered and strobed, now blue, now pale purple, now a silver spectrum of trees and sky.

The eyes of deer and cattle shone yellow and sparkling blue as the headlights of the Silver Ship flashed along the road and into fields. Nothing ap-

peared to possess any reality.

The lightning was intense. It flared and crashed toward the hills, and licked tongues of fiery light into every valley. Sheets of lightning blazed and shimmered through the wind-sculpted clouds. Every shape possible was formed in those luminous clouds. He saw a powerful Kachina ten miles high that flashed and glowed. The Kachina seemed to be laughing thunder.

Lightningbolt cursed Alex as he drove. He also cursed other friends he'd seen kill themselves with apathy and drugs. He laughed bitterly and shouted at each of them, taunting them about their insistence upon stupidity.

When Lightningbolt awoke, Mellow, Estcheemah's cat, brushed her tail in his face. She purred, then crouched down beside his head to watch some robins in a nearby tree.

He petted her and looked up into the broad blue sky. The big storm had ceased as suddenly as it had begun. The night had been so warm and inviting, he'd decided to dry out the pickup box and made his bed there. He had watched the Stars until sleep came.

"Ever eat a bird?" he asked Mellow as he sat

up. He rubbed his eyes and yawned.

"Coffee?" Estcheemah called from the house. She walked to her outside pump and began to draw water. "You can wash up here. And would you help by feeding the chickens? The sack of feed is just inside the barn door."

Estcheemah's home would never win prizes as the typical middle-class house. However, over the past ten years, she had built a dwelling any artist would love to have.

Light was what the artist-seamstress needed, and light had helped design her home. The living room had become her sewing room. It had a broad skylight and two walls of floor-to-ceiling windows. A room that would normally be reserved as a guest room had become her cutting room. This delightful space also had two walls of floor-to-ceiling windows. The room held two long tables, one highly polished and the other with a piece of billiard-table-green felt glued to its surface. She used this one for her patterning. Sandwiched on the inner wall, below shelves filled with sewing materials, was an old army cot where guests could sleep.

The kitchen was bright and cheery and filled with light. There was a skylight in this room also, and every available inch of the walls had glass because she enjoyed sewing in this room too.

Estcheemah hated wasting her time cooking and cleaning. As a result, she possessed every modern kitchen convenience possible, right down to two built-in dishwashers.

The outside enclosure of Estcheemah's home was a cleverly designed wooden wall that she had created for her safety and privacy.

Because she had so many floor-to-ceiling windows, she had built what she called her "prairie wall." It surrounded three sides of the home and was carefully designed to look like part of the building, and not to resemble a wall separate from the building.

She had accomplished this by extending the

rafters out beyond the main house roof. This created an open-air ramada for her, and a small enclosed garden area. The top of the outer wall looked like it was part of the home, because it was covered by roofing. Between the building wall and the "outer wall" there was four feet of wild grasses and prairie plants in which she'd secreted places for small wild animals to enter or leave at will.

Estcheemah loved flowers and gardening. Her little fort sat in the middle of a two-acre garden. She had completely encircled her home with flowers and herbs, corn plants, tomatoes, and other garden vegetables.

The barn was small, silvered by weather, and had a tiny pole corral. It was a carryover from the days when barns were constructed out of rough-

sawn pine from the nearby hills.

Because she lived so far out in the country she had installed backup systems—the outside pump, an outhouse hidden in the trees near the barn, and a small electrical generator.

The chicken house was attached to the barn and held twenty hens and their rooster. Down at the creek there was a "burglar-proof jail" for her five geese. It had been constructed when the geese were young, to protect them from wandering raccoons and other predators. The ten ducks had to fend for themselves in the middle of the creek.

Everything about Estcheemah's world was clean and well cared for—except for her ragged, beat-up Bug. The Volkswagen looked as though it had been through a hurricane. Even its patchy gray paint seemed to have been gnawed away by a desert wind.

She made her living by creating exquisitely designed coats. Kaufmann and Sons, a New York–based clothing company, sold Estcheemah the cloth she wanted to make the coats. Then they sold every coat she made. This had been Estcheemah's work for thirty-six years. When a coat was completed it was sent back to the company. Her coats were sold all over the world. But Estcheemah herself was Abraham Kaufmann's best-kept secret.

All the coats were fashioned from the finest of wools and silks, and were trimmed with costly furs. The linings were silk tapestries that were either woven or hand-painted in the Orient.

The buttons were hand-cast, or cut from ivory, mother-of-pearl, carved wood, or sculpted glass. Many were of gold or silver, and some were even set with diamonds. These buttons were made in every land and by many kinds of artists. They were purchased by those who had ordered the coats, made to size, and sent to Estcheemah by the company to be included in the design. The women who bought her coats never met Estcheemah, or even knew of her.

After Lightningbolt had washed up and drunk his coffee, Estcheemah took him for a walk in the hills behind her house. They walked in silence for nearly half an hour until they came to a large sandstone depression.

"We will stop here," she said, sitting on a rounded stone. "You sit there on the sand and be quiet for a moment."

Ten minutes went by before she spoke again. She wanted to study her student. She began to question him about his habits, teasing him and making him laugh.

They continued their walk while Lightningbolt talked. It was noon before Estcheemah decided it was time to return to the house.

"Boot camp." She smiled as they walked. "That is where you will begin with me. A small war is best to get the wrinkles out. It's a way of you and

I getting to know one another."

Lightningbolt was happy. She was promising an adventure and that was what he wanted.

"The war will be over in one year's time," she explained. "We will know each other well by the time we walk here again next year. The death of your friend is another matter."

She began to tell him about her first few tries at trapping. Her adventures with the hows and how nots of trapping made Lightningbolt laugh. She was an expert storyteller. Lightningbolt responded and added his own wit. These moments of exchange between them taught her even more about her possible apprentice. However, another more subtle maneuver was taking place that the young man was not aware of—leadership. Through their conversation and Estcheemah's telling him physically what they would do at any given moment, she was making it clear to Lightningbolt who was the Commander. Estcheemah knew that if she didn't do this right away, she'd have to put up with Lightningbolt's chauvinist attitudes about women.

By the time evening came, Lightningbolt knew that he had not met an ordinary woman. While this made him feel a bit apprehensive, at the same time it was an invitation to stay. He thought that he had learned a great deal about her, when actually he knew nothing. He thought he had not told her very much about himself, but the truth was he had told her everything.

In order to have time with Estcheemah, he took a job on a nearby farm driving a tractor. He worked nine days before he quit. He told Estcheemah that he hoped to find work with an oil rig crew. The job would start soon.

It was at this point that their relationship took on another face. Estcheemah was demanding more now, and confronting his attitudes about Life and himself. Because everything was new to her apprentice, she knew she would have to have enormous patience. She would allow him into her world little by little.

There had been one incident in Lightningbolt's experience that had left her uneasy. He was far too cool about what had happened to his friend Alex. What was this? She had to know.

Late one evening, soon after he'd quit the job, she asked him what he knew about Death. He answered, "I don't know. I do not know much about Death. Death is sad and it is painful."

Testing his maturity, she told him that Death was silent and perfect. That Light and Life were perfect with Death, and that every human had to learn about separation. Death is the comforter for those who know only extreme pain. Death is pain for those who lose their loved ones. He blinked with astonishment, then smiled.

In that same instant, he took a tack that pleased Estcheemah and alerted her further about his thinking. He answered that now he knew "why old April Horse spoke so strangely at times"; it was Estcheemah's influence. Then he added that he knew that there was no other way to talk about Death than to use words like that.

She knew she must test his discernment and ability to make decisions. While they worked together weeding in her garden, she began quietly to talk to him about herself.

"I never knew, when I was young, that there was a Goddess," she related. "And I had no idea there was such a thing as the Sacred Self." She smiled. Her eyes were deep black, bright and very kind. "Goddess!" She laughed gently. "Imagine that, a Creatress Mother. A Creatress Mother was

the last thing I would have thought of.

"I would hear Night Arrow Woman speak of Goddess and the Creatress, and I liked it. Her words comforted me, but I did not know why they did. At first, I thought she was trying to convince me of something, but I soon learned that she was only pointing out the Reality of Earth and Creation.

"Creation is not just male," Estcheemah gently explained. "How very silly that belief is! There is SsKwan, our Creator Father, and there certainly is WahKahn, who is female, our Creatress Mother.

"The America I lived in was a narrow-minded culture that disallowed women almost everything. I was a female in a culture and country that denied my very existence and human rights because I was not born male. I had absolutely no power. You must remember that the vote is a very recent achievement for women in America.

"I did not like myself. I was told to not like myself by the culture I lived within. I really didn't like being a woman. Can you imagine being born among people who are so incredibly ignorant and ugly as to teach people not to like themselves because they are female? It's such an insane thing to do.

"I liked being a woman when it felt good being a woman. But at all other times I felt I was not complete being a female. The culture I lived in crushed any true pride I had in being female. Even today, women have to fight to realize their equality with men."

Lightningbolt sat down on a log, reeling under the information. He had not expected to hear what he was hearing. Because he did not know how to respond or what to say, he attempted a smile. Realizing that the smile was wrong, he attempted a frown. When the frown failed, he sat quiet, waiting.

Estcheemah knew that he was not understanding, but she had made up her mind to introduce him to the situation. There had to be a time to begin work. She would have to speak to him many times, about the realities of her life as a woman, before he would begin to truly hear her.

Suddenly she changed tack, and began to talk to him of Discipline and Balance. She taught him that the greatest of all virtues of all Destined Leaders and Healers are Discipline and Balance.

"Can you trust your thinking, Lightningbolt?" she asked, her eyes twinkling.

"Sure. Of course," he answered quickly.

Estcheemah leaned on her hoe. "In my home right now, there is a challenge that awaits you. Much depends upon you and your discernment—on how it is that you will understand power." She began to walk toward the house. "But first you need breakfast. I'll go to the house and begin. While I'm gone, why don't you go down to the creek and speak to Creation? Can you do that?"

He strolled down to the creek and played with the ducks for a few minutes. The geese would only hiss at him. He began to daydream. What was this challenge? He looked into the sky and thought about clouds, stars; then his mind wandered to thoughts of interplanetary space travel.

Suddenly, he realized he could hear his name being called.

124

He hurriedly picked a bouquet of wildflowers and walked toward the kitchen door. Cautiously opening the screen door, he saw Estcheemah standing in the kitchen finishing her cooking.

"We have two visitors," she said without turning around. "The tall man at the table is Black Stone, and the shorter man is Fire Enemy."

Lightningbolt went inside. It was impossible to see anyone at the table from the door.

"These are the Medicine Names they have chosen," Estcheemah said, turning to face him. "Names to suit the occasion . . . just for you. These two men are your Battle Kachinas."

Lightningbolt stopped dead in his tracks when he finally saw the two men sitting at the table. Both were wearing hideous masks. The bouquet of flowers fell from his hands to the floor.

Estcheemah picked up the flowers and busied herself arranging them in a drinking glass from the counter.

The horned Rain Kachina was having a hard time keeping his mask from slipping sideways. But this did not detract from its grotesque features.

The second man, the taller of the two, wore a Sun mask that looked as though it belonged to him.

Lightningbolt immediately deduced that the two men must be from the Southwest. He knew he was wrong the second the men removed their masks. They were either Sioux or northern Indians from Montana. He was not sure, nor did he care.

The air in the room fairly crackled with expectancy for Lightningbolt. Although he didn't have the vaguest idea what was to take place, the rodeo atmosphere of their costumes excited him.

Black Stone, a man in his late fifties, placed his Sun mask on the floor beside him with utmost care; however, Fire Enemy showed no such delicacy. There was instant distrust and animosity between Lightningbolt and Fire Enemy. Lightningbolt sim-ply didn't like the looks of the man. Fire Enemy thought Lightningbolt was a smart ass.

Black Stone was a kind old man who appeared to be honest. He spoke at length of his Discipline, and even made comparisons between his Discipline and Japanese Bushido.

He teased and spoke of Chinese Kung Fu movie heroes and laughed with Lightningbolt. Fire Enemy, on the other hand, was mean and felt that Black Stone was wasting everyone's time.

"The Battle Kachinas," said Black Stone, "had originally been part of the great temples of the Maya. At one time the Discipline had both women and men in its ranks.

"Like the art of Kung Fu, the Ways of the Battle Kachina had also evolved among soldiers. The Maya Carrier-Soldiers—who were teachers and also were traders—taught of Self Discipline and the use

126

of all weapons of the battlefield.

"However, while the Asian teachers emphasized the hands and ancient dance movements first, the Battle Kachinas were formally interested in weapons first, then the dance."

Black Stone opened an ornately carved box and showed Lightningbolt an ancient Atl. Its shape was exactly like that of a broadsword. But there was no iron in this heavy weapon. The tool had been cast from silver. And the obsidian ax heads along both sides of the length of the Atl were still incredibly sharp.

Black Stone smiled good-humoredly as he explained that the short or long spear, the Atl, and the European broadsword were the favorite weapons of the modern Battle Kachinas. And although no Maya had used a broadsword, the shape suited the contemporary teachers such as himself. He told

how the use of the Atl and of sand armor had won the empire for the Mayas and Aztecs.

After breakfast, everyone went out to a place where Estcheemah had set up bales of straw for her targets. She took an incredibly slim and delicate-looking recurved bow from her Medicine Bundle and strung it. She then removed five thin arrows with small but very deadly-looking arrowheads from their quiver.

One, two, three, four, five! The arrows thumped their way into the center of the target. Lightningbolt was both amazed and impressed with her skill.

Estcheemah returned her bow and arrows to their sheath in her Medicine Bundle and put everything away.

The show that came next very much intrigued

and entertained Lightningbolt. First, Black Stone laid nine long war spears on the ground. Then he began a slow dance. Suddenly he picked up the first spear and twirled it with utmost ease, as though it were as light as a marching baton. He threw the spear into the air and caught it, then spun and turned as though he were in combat with an enemy on horseback. Unexpectedly, Black Stone threw the spear, and it struck the center of a white circle he had drawn on the ground about thirty feet away. Then he next rolled on the ground as though he'd been hit suddenly by his invisible enemy. In the blink of an eye he was on his feet again and grabbing the next spear.

He spun and battled with this spear until it too found its place in the circle. Spear after spear was danced with and launched while he battled his unseen combatant. Abruptly he leaped toward

Lightningbolt and mimed cutting Lightningbolt's throat.

"It's that last gesture that matters," said Black Stone, out of breath.

Lightningbolt was smiling. But that last movement had made him more vigilant. These men were serious.

Now the tanklike Fire Enemy moved out to dance. He was squat, fortyish, and obviously not as practiced as his teacher. Snatching up a spear, he brandished it at Lightningbolt. Loudly proclaiming that he now held Black Stone's shield, he pointed dramatically toward the field with the spear, indicating that Lightningbolt was to dance now, too.

Lightningbolt shuffled forward, unsure of what he was supposed to do. Suddenly he was pushed from behind by Fire Enemy.

"Don't be afraid to dance and to make your

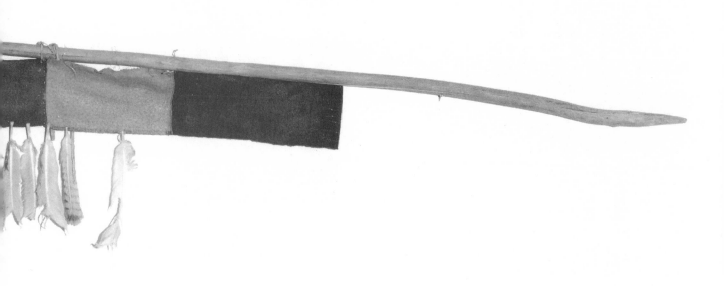

spins," Black Stone's voice called to him.

But Lightningbolt was angry, and anger always made him more stubborn. He balked. Trying a step or two, he was sure he looked like a wounded bat flopping around on the ground.

He hobbled one way, then floundered the next. Each step he took made him angrier and angrier. He knew now, for certain, that he was lumbering around like a drunken bull, and it infuriated him.

Fire Enemy was delighted with Lightningbolt's discomfort. He grinned, making sure the younger man saw his contempt. He pushed Lightningbolt even harder from behind, whispering to him that he looked like a crippled turtle.

Lightningbolt turned and threatened to hit Fire Enemy. The older man backed off and smiled. Then, quick as a cat, Fire Enemy moved forward and slapped Lightningbolt hard across his face.

"No, no," he mocked. "Boy must not play fighty-fighty." He clicked his tongue.

"Be disciplined!" Black Stone called. "Do not allow Fire Enemy to get you angry. Just dance, do not bother fighting. Learn to move your body."

"Control your animal," Estcheemah ordered Black Stone. "He's acting like a fool with this young man. This is no competition."

Black Stone quickly apologized and reprimanded Fire Enemy, threatening to send him away if he played too rough.

The two men drilled Lightningbolt for the remainder of the day without incident. The second and third day were the same. The fourth day, they demonstrated how to build a shield and how to battle a bear or a man on horseback. The fifth day went well. Lightningbolt was now moving much more smoothly. Every evening he practiced what he'd learned until he felt absolutely comfortable with his every move and with the lance.

That night Estcheemah prepared her guests a feast of roast goose, duck, and pheasant.

After the men had left, she took Lightningbolt for a walk. As they strolled, she told him how the ocean had been one of the first great human challenges. She asked him to imagine being confronted by the massive oceans. Humans, she said, believe they can name weakness. Weakness was when people could not sail. Weakness was when humans knew no mathematics. Weakness was when writing was not known. Weakness was Lightningbolt's insistence upon the use of brute force.

The young man wrestled with her words and ideas, trying to focus on what she was teaching. But his mind was filled with a fantasy of defeating another human with his lance.

Weaknesses, Estcheemah continued, were teachers. The ocean was the great barrier and the great question. Ninety-nine percent or more of all humans confronted with these questions simply labeled the situation and became its victim. Millions upon millions of humans saw the weakness, but died doing nothing about it. It was the seekers who recognized their weakness—and battled it—who learned of the oceans.

How did this happen? First, she said, people had to discover that they had another weakness that they needed to battle and win. This was their need for food.

The oceans had food in abundance. This was why most humans came to live by them. But how were they to get this food? They had to recognize their weakness and learn from it. Instead of swimming out after their catch, the weakest people of all, those who were the most afraid, made something to float in.

Through this story, Estcheemah taught Lightningbolt that behind his first weakness, his first challenge, lay another even more invisible. Like the people whose first need was fish, he had his first need, too. It was his task now to find out what his first need was.

He could battle to learn of the ocean and allow the ocean to point out his weakness if he chose to. His weaknesses, in turn, would demonstrate to him how to construct the tools and weapons he needed to battle his everyday problems.

And yet, Lightningbolt knew that simply naming and confronting his challenge and weakness was not enough. When the situation of his weakness arose, he became the victim—every time. His anger was a boundless and stormy sea of questions and answers.

Estcheemah awakened him to the fact that most humans never really get angry enough to do anything about their lives. They are satisfied just naming the weakness and being its victim. "Such people," Estcheemah told him, "miss the Beauty of Life. For Beauty is Perfectness and Balance. Yet how many humans really know Beauty? Beauty is Strength, and She is Challenge, but how many people know Strength and Challenge?

"Most humans see Beauty as weakness. Lightningbolt, you must learn that being the toughest guy in town can be a weakness. And being the richest can be a weakness. Another weakness many humans have is their enjoyment in pointing out other people's weaknesses. People who have their weakness pointed out to them are content simply to have it named.

"We are taught to believe that weakness is a given in a person's life and that nothing can be done about it. Weakness is like a disease that is incurable." She laughed, saying that this is particularly true for politicians.

Then she said that Lightningbolt would have to look at his first needs. She told him to remember that love is most often seen as a weakness, not a strength. To be "in love" is viewed as a weakness, not a strength. He would have to look at his first weakness—his fear of being powerless and denied recognition and rank—before he could accept love and battle his ocean of pain.

"Love and Life are the human experience we know as Existence," she told him. "Yet, how many people know that Love means Sharing?

"Love is the visible form of Sacred Life. She is Beauty. Our experience of knowing Life is knowing Love.

"Love is the highest of expression and feelings known to humans. Love is Life Herself."

Estcheemah gave him an example of the problems and challenges that face all women.

"What women have to offer is not readily seen," she explained.

"Love, care, healing and the impetus for Life are the *invisible powers* of the woman. Yet, how many men are taught to recognize, or honor, the Invisible?

"Women have to learn how to teach men to recognize and respect the invisible," said Estcheemah.

Estcheemah likened the discovery and questions arising from the exploration of deep space to the question of women. She said that the wide, deep, mysterious and challenging Ocean of the Invisible awaits the courageous and intelligent.

Lightningbolt had to hurry because he'd promised Medicine Ears, his uncle, that he'd help load horses for the Sheridan rodeo. If he didn't get moving it would be too late. And he didn't want to incur the wrath of his uncle. In the meantime, he had to grab an opportunity to make some money.

The Silver Ship kicked up a rooster tail of dust as he drove out of Estcheemah's yard. His tires squalled when his pickup careened out onto the highway. She had made him feel wonderful, although he couldn't exactly say how or why. The music of Jimi Hendrix's electronic magic wrapped Lightningbolt in a power that only sound can express.

Two hours later the Silver Ship rolled silent as a ghost into the yard of Herbert Strokker's ranch. He'd cut the motor and let the pickup coast the last

half mile to the old man's door.

Two line-back dun ponies were in the corral near the barn. A wirehaired young puppy came with its tail wagging to greet the pickup. The geese hissed and chickens ran squawking, protesting his entrance. An entire cottonwood tree full of crows watched, curious to see what would happen next.

Strokker was standing by the corral, lighting up one of the millions of cigarettes he smoked yearly. Lightningbolt stepped down from his machine and leaned against it to wait.

The old man walked slowly toward the pickup, showing years of confidence. He looked at the young man standing in front of him and smiled. He was playing with the lariat in his hands.

"Lightningbolt, right?" Strokker asked.

"Bulls," he answered. "I understand you have a

couple of killers. You look fancy enough to be old Strokker. You're not the foreman, are you?"

"What if I am?" Strokker grinned. "Most foremen can answer that superhard question you just asked . . . right?" He chuckled. "Old Bright Moon says you can drive bulls. 'Course that old fart is half senile, gone deaf too."

Lightningbolt winced when Strokker began to poke fun at his uncle. It was just not done.

"Seen a twitch there." Strokker smiled, stretching out his hand. "You like that old buzzard, I can see. Me too. We punched hide lizards together before you were born."

"He ain't senile," Lightningbolt insisted.

"Know'd the word, huh?" Strokker smiled. "Fancy that."

"He's chicken-stompy and about half doddery, but he's not senile, no how. Unless you are," Lightningbolt added.

"Me?" Strokker teased. "Hell, boy, I'm half flapping in the wind, chicken-stompy, and bronc-rattled. It's okay though."

"One hundred and fifty dollars," Lightningbolt proposed. "No cows and no calves."

Strokker rested his foot on the pickup's bumper. "Five bulls—one a hooker and four young ones." He crushed out a cigarette and lit another. "My nephew calls the old one Jumping Jack Flash. He can get mean with the younger ones and for sure he'll try to hook you. He was born horn-happy. So, you wrestle them over to old man Green's pasture and you can have that hundred and fifty."

"You have riding horses on the other side?" Lightningbolt asked. He was studying a rain cloud. "Looks like a big one blowing up."

"South of Dayton Kane," Strokker answered. "The bulls are on the other side of the Little Horn River. Dan Chromann has riding horses if you throw a shoe or something. Want me to give him a call?"

"Those horses are going to cost you, not me,"

Lightningbolt added. "Including Chromann's. I'm renting nothing. It's a straight-ahead one hundred and fifty in my pocket. I'll pay for my own food, no ranch talk."

"I don't know." Strokker wanted to tease more. "Chromann, he might charge—"

Lightningbolt stepped back and reached for the door handle. "I just got me a new problem, which is whether I'm leaving in one minute flat or a quarter of a minute. See you around."

"Now just a damn second." Strokker smiled. "I'll even haul the horses over the divide for you. I was just going to josh you a bit. Dammit, boy, don't be so jumpy." He toyed with his hat. "Ruins bulls for weeks, riding in a truck. Messes them up. I'm saving big with a hundred and fifty."

"I've run into some spooky stuff," Lightningbolt explained. "I have to head into the shit, you know what I mean?"

"Sure," Strokker answered, looking a little sad.

"Never used to be that way. Folks cheating folks . . . sure, boy." He kicked at a stone. "You take good care of those bulls. They like walking."

Two nights later Lightningbolt was camped at Sparrow Creek in Wyoming.

"Money," he grumbled as he made himself a fire. "Pissed-off bulls, flies, sweat, a hundred and

fifty bucks of bull fighting! Was it all worth it?"

Later that night, before sleeping, he looked into his campfire. The coals were alive with light. He tried to understand what Estcheemah had meant about his refusal to accept the "truth and reality of Beauty."

Beauty? What the hell did that have to do with a person's discovering a way out of the misery he or she was in?

Life's magical Presence, danced about Lightningbolt as fireflies, as delicate shadows, and as night flowers that shone with moonlit faces. The fire was reflected in the stream he sat near, as was the bright silver Moon, and the trees that sang to him of Beauty and Life.

Life was speaking to Lightningbolt, trying to show him the answer to what he had questioned, that he too was a reflection of Mother Earth's Substance. But he was far too ignorant of Her Language to understand what She was telling him.

The following morning he started rounding up the bulls. Jumping Jack Flash didn't want to be going anywhere. He hooked, pawed, threw dirt, bellowed, charged, and feinted. Then, when he tired, he meekly joined the other bulls.

Lightningbolt herded the animals all day long. When evening came, he knew he would have to build a brush fence to keep the bulls from doubling back on him during the night.

While Lightningbolt drove the animals, he thought up ways to keep himself from becoming bored. He changed Jumping Jack Flash's name to Beedah-goh-weeah, which means "firewater" or "whiskey."

The young cowboy knew, as did other Breeds and Indians who had been taught, that animals only know physically of one Circle at a time. A bull, for example, will fight for each Circle. It's natural for him to do that. A bull cannot think like a human.

Lightningbolt had been taught to sing to the bull and to haze the animal. Hazing meant that when the bull wanted to fight, Lightningbolt would fool the bull and have him charge until he entered the next Circle.

The animal would charge, Circle after Circle, until finally he could no longer distinguish one Circle from the next. Once the bull stopped for the night, he had his "familiar" again and would fight to possess his next Circle. Breeds called every Circle known by an animal its "Familiar." Lightningbolt sang the bulls a Medicine Song. He liked the words:

> Familiar I am, yes.
> I am thinking in a familiar way.
> Yes . . . familiar you are.
> In our Circle, yes.

Beedah-goh-weeah was no longer any problem. He hated it, but he would lose one familiar after another, and Lightningbolt would win one familiar after another.

As he rode, Lightningbolt tried being philosophical. He thought of college, family, children, television, money, Vietnam, Mickey Mouse, catching the early worm, repainting the Silver Ship, girls, and Indian Medicine. But for some strange reason none of it made any sense.

He tried again, but mundane thoughts kept pouring through the young man's mind like sour milk through the gut of a mangy cat. He left each thought behind, under some stone, to stink.

Why couldn't he get his thinking together? Would he always sound like a damned tape recorder in his own head?

He thought of his friend Smokey. He seemed to really know how to live. The first time Lightningbolt had met Smokey was when he rounded a corner of the Saint Labres Mission. Smokey was standing there calmly wearing a candy-striped zoot suit out of the late forties. Suddenly, a crutch flew through the air and Smokey dodged it.

Next a pissed-off young cowboy hobbled into sight, and they began to fistfight. The cowboy would have won, but Lightningbolt broke up the fight. The reason Lightningbolt stepped in was because the cowboy was an old rival.

Smokey really impressed Lightningbolt. He had a colorful Superman poster shellacked to the top of his Volkswagen Bug. And he always wore four watches. One on one wrist and one on the other. The third was in his right pocket and the last one in his left pocket. None of the watches were ever wound. Smokey never seemed to know what time it was, and never cared.

Lightningbolt now had two fine saddle horses. He rode Snake Jaw, a beautiful young mare. Bank Note, a pretty Appaloosa, followed behind, carrying his bedroll and gear.

Some worlds are diamond, tourmaline, ruby, or obsidian. The world where Lightningbolt now rode was an exquisite emerald valley.

Young Lightningbolt was overfamiliar with the land and had little appreciation for Her. She was always beautiful—why should anyone expect anything different?

Everything was a charming and verdant green. The lime and olive of the pines and berry bushes seemed to shout with light and growing. The lush and tender greens of the meadow where he rode wooed him with their joyful colors. Gentle flaxen and saffron flowers nestled in the emerald world and promised Life. Each stone in the clean little stream was covered with velvety blue-green moss. First she was one stream, then she would suddenly become five streams, then two, then three, changing again every few hundred feet. She sparkled, mirrored, and reflected, creating ever more lovely greens, until even the shadows reflected the hue.

Lightningbolt stopped and dismounted. He found a large flat stone and perched on its top. This was far too rich a place not to let the horses graze

to their heart's content.

Such immense loveliness!

He wondered why the ranchers had changed the name of the stream to Sparrow Creek. He'd been told that the Elk Chiefs had been the guardians of Emerald Creek.

An hour later he remounted and continued his journey downstream. Soon he came to the place he loved the most. It was called Elk Woman.

Eight giant rounded stones crowded around this spot in the creek. It was here also where two new rivulets merged with the Sparrow. The bulls waded into the water to drink from the shallow pools where the streams flooded.

If ever a place seemed to be made for play and loveliness, it was this place. Women from the surrounding Reservations often came here for Ceremonies.

There were stretches of sand banks to play in. The soft, rounded, moss-covered stones made it fun to slide downstream. Great trout leaped and minnows swam in every pool. There were chokecherries, buffalo berries, gooseberries, and service berries to eat here.

He would never suspect that within a scant twenty years the valley he now rode through would be desolate. The land would be plowed, scarred, eroded, overgrazed, and strewn with broken-down buildings and rusting machinery.

Lightningbolt rode Snake Jaw into the stream, letting the horses drink. While the animals drank, he had a satisfying look around.

Suddenly, two little girls appeared from behind one of the big stones and stood in a pool watching him. He blinked. They were so much part of the emerald world that they didn't seem quite real to him.

One of the girls, a chubby little cutie about seven, wore a green checkered swimsuit. The other wore a summer dress. She looked to be about eight

or nine.

"Hello," he said to them.

Both girls smiled and waved.

He began his song again, touched Snake Jaw with his spurs, and crossed the stream. The bulls did not lift their heads from the water until Snake Jaw forced them forward.

When he looked back, the girls had disappeared.

Two magic beings, he thought. This is a good Medicine Sign.

He next crossed Earth Creek. He saw that the girls had appeared from around another stone. He smiled. They were far to the left of the bulls, and safe.

Lightningbolt realized that the girls were giggling and playing hide-and-seek with him.

Snake Jaw stopped to take a bite of grass. He gave Bank Note the slack she wanted to graze too.

The girls laughed and disappeared behind another boulder. The meadowlarks were singing and the bulls grazed contentedly up ahead of him.

"Hello, cowboy," a woman's voice said softly from behind him.

He turned around in his saddle and saw a beautiful young woman. She wore a long, white, very light muslin dress that was girded with a hand-woven Mexican belt. The soft oval of her face was accented by her long black hair. Her smile totally won him.

"I'm Canadiana," she said, introducing herself. She stepped up to Snake Jaw and petted her neck. "You?"

"Lightningbolt," he answered, trying not to

show his shyness.

The two girls ran from behind the nearest boulder and continued to watch from a short distance.

"What are those?" Lightningbolt teased. "They look just like creekniks. . . . Are they?"

Both girls shook their heads and ran up behind the woman. They peeked out from either side of her dress.

"We're camped over there." Canadiana pointed. "Would you like a sandwich or some coffee with us?"

The look on his face must have been answer enough for her because she quickly added, with a smile, that he could also share a roast with them. She was baking it in a covered roasting pan in the hot coals beneath the flames of her campfire.

Lightningbolt studied the bulls. They were peacefully grazing about a hundred and fifty feet away. The entire area looked secure. Snake Jaw shook her head, throwing off a fly. He looked at the Sun, then back at the bulls.

If he remained too long, he wouldn't reach the place where he planned to stop for the night. He pondered. The canyon was far too wide here to consider making a brush fence across it. He would have to continue on. Bank Note jerked the halter rope from his hand and walked away, looking for better grass. He frowned.

"Two little girls and one woman cannot be that complicated." Canadiana smiled prettily.

"It's the bulls," he stammered, trying to find something to say that would make sense to her. He looked at the Sun again. He felt like a school kid asking for an excuse to skip shop.

"It's all right," Canadiana said, revealing a beautiful pout. "You have your bulls. But if you should change your mind, we're right over there." She stepped away from the mare.

The girls continued to be curious, but they remained hidden behind Canadiana's skirt.

"Damned bulls," he cursed. "Darn that Beedah-goh-weeah's hide." The bull was so unpredictable. The other bulls were too stupid to even accidentally double back, but that Beedah-goh-weeah . . . No, the animal had a one-track mind.

"You girls go and finish your swim," Canadiana ordered the children. "And stay away from that mud. It's the only mud in this entire creek. Can't you play in the sand?"

The girls ran for the nearest pool.

Lightningbolt dismounted. He still had to explain what his thinking was. He knew he would sound like a fool, but he didn't know what else to do, so he tried a grin. Why leave Canadiana with the impression that he was an idiot? He loosened his spurs and hung them on his saddle horn. Next, he took off his chaps and draped them over his saddle.

"Taking off your jeans next?" she teased.

"Oh, no!" he quickly answered, showing his embarrassment.

Suddenly, Canadiana's laughter turned to a scream of terror. "Girls, get away from those bulls!"

"Get back here!" Lightningbolt called to the girls. "Run . . . run back here. Hurry!"

But instead of immediately running, the girls froze in their tracks. They were unsure, hesitant, and beginning to panic. They turned this way, then that, before they ran. But it was too late. Beedah-goh-weeah had turned to charge.

"Run to the trees!" Lightningbolt yelled as he swung into the saddle. He kicked Snake Jaw into a run and swung his chaps over his head like a flag.

Beedah-goh-weeah pawed up clods of mud and grass, bellowing as he charged the girls. Lightningbolt reined Snake Jaw into a circle as he cut very close in front of the angry bull.

The bull saw Snake Jaw and turned to battle the horse. Horns down, Beedah-goh-weeah charged straight toward Snake Jaw.

Lightningbolt kicked Snake Jaw into a run, away from the girls, and the bull angrily followed.

When the bull hesitated, not sure of which adversary to charge, Snake Jaw or the girls, Lightningbolt forced him to make up his mind by stinging the bull with his lariat.

Beedah-goh-weeah attacked time after time while Lightningbolt aggravated the bull into charging him again. Each confrontation took the bull farther and farther away from Canadiana's camp.

Half an hour later, Lightningbolt trotted Snake Jaw back to where the girls waited. They were still hidden among the trees. His mare was out of breath and wet with sweat.

"It's all right now," he said, dismounting.

Lightningbolt busied himself with his tasks. Snake Jaw was immediately unsaddled and Bank Note saddled up just in case he needed a fresh mount.

"That jackass bull played himself out . . . I hope," he explained to Canadiana as she walked up to him. "I've got at least an hour or more, depending . . ." He looked east, down the valley. "That damned rascal." He petted Snake Jaw. "You did real fine, knothead, real fine. Tonight it's oats. That bull's mean. A hundred and fifty dollars . . . damn!"

He looked around for his spurs, trying to see where they'd landed when he threw them. He picked them up, and walked to Bank Note and hung the spurs on the saddle.

"The girls are safe," Canadiana comforted him. "Here, drink this good coffee. Thanks, I had a funny feeling about this place all day long." She hugged herself and rubbed her arms. "Now it's over."

"I could stand a bite of that roast," Lightningbolt said, leading Bank Note toward her camp. "Beedah-goh-weeah is playing like nothing happened, about a mile east of here, but he just might double back."

At Canadiana's camp Lightningbolt hooked the reins over the saddle horn, letting Bank Note graze where she wanted. As long as the mare was within twenty steps of him, it was all right. He'd hobble her later.

Canadiana busied herself making dinner. The girls had dressed and were playing with his lariat.

"Where are you from?" Canadiana asked.

"Montana," he answered. "What the heck are you doing way out here alone? Isn't that a bit risky?"

"My car's at the crossroads," she answered, looking up into his eyes and smiling. "And I carry a helper, a .357 Magnum, and I'm not afraid to use it if I have to."

"She's got another gun, too," the younger girl announced.

"You're not supposed to tell, silly," the other girl scolded.

"He doesn't know where," Canadiana added quickly. "Does he, girls?"

Both the girls nodded that they understood and would not say.

"I was born in Canada," Canadiana said, continuing her work. "I still live in British Columbia."

"It's called B.C.," the younger girl broke in.

"And I learned to take care of myself," Canadiana went on. "I grab what I can if there's trouble. My father taught me, and so did my mother." She looked up into Lightningbolt's eyes. "The girls are not mine," she explained. "But they've been with me for over two years. Their mother is an alcoholic. Where she is, only the devil knows. Dera is the oldest, she's nine, and Kim is seven."

They talked through dinner and after. The more they traded information, the more they began to trust one another. Lightningbolt played with the girls and helped clean up the dishes.

Two hours later, he was mounted and ready to leave.

"A day doesn't make any difference to me," he lied. He was thinking about his promise to load those horses for his uncle. "But I can drive those bulls for three or four hours east from there to make it safe, then double back in the morning. They won't hurt nothing going east. It's west that's the problem."

"You mean to visit, of course?" Canadiana asked.

"Ah . . . er . . . sure!" He gulped. "For certain, for absolutely sure, of course! I was just thinking of making things safe. Is ten or eleven o'clock too late for coffee?"

"It's not too late for coffee," she answered.

They shook hands, and he waved good-bye to the girls and left the camp.

He herded the bulls for three hours, then rolled into his sleeping bag for the night. The following morning he returned to the camp to have coffee.

He decided to incur the wrath of Medicine Ear and remained four days.

Two weeks later they were living together in a cabin at Deer Creek, about eleven miles from Sparrow Creek.

Lightningbolt wrote a note to Estcheemah that he would see her "after his studies with Black Stone." He gave no return address.

He soon learned that Canadiana was a woman with a mind of her own. She had incredible determination. And she trusted only her brain and her imagination. Lightningbolt was highly motivated to escape the life of a Reservation Breed. Yet, for him, work was the answer, not Self power. Canadiana spoke to him for hours, encouraging him to be a self-employed person instead of a common worker or a hired hand.

She told him that many people seek indepen-

dence, but they only fool themselves when they work for others. She had a curious way of describing what she thought work and independence should be. She said that life should never be a struggle, and that people should discover ways of living with expectations. She loved the word *expectations* and used it frequently. It explained about everything she knew or wanted.

Canadiana also possessed another talent. This was the power to make almost everything real, even the most absurd. She maintained that everyone should return to the use of candles and wood-burning stoves.

She stated flatly that the only time electricity should ever be used was when you wanted to listen to music—but never for light!

They smoked a little grass together and she explained that grass was the great answer to human-

ity's craving for whiskey. But the grass only gave him a headache.

Slowly, over the next two weeks, Lightningbolt discovered a world he had never known—the world of children, and most especially little girls. Dera and Kim possessed a true magic, almost undefinable. They became his important teachers. They taught him of the undefinable.

He learned first about battling little girls. It's one thing for a man to fight another man or even a bull, but quite another thing to battle with a girl. Lightningbolt lost every battle with Kim and Dera. The wars lasted for only the blink of an eye. They ended so fast it always took him at least a minute to realize that he'd been pinned flat. Men could be ordered, reasoned with, forced, and defeated, but the girls defied all natural laws.

Dera once explained after a fight, "You got to

get friendly before you get smart."

"You are so nosy, it's pink!" the seven-year-old told him after they'd had a fight over who should wash dishes.

They delighted Lightningbolt, made him cry, made him listen to the wind, helped him see the Moon, and showed him how to hold a caterpillar.

They beat him in footraces, baked him cookies, read to him, tricked him, shared their licorice, explained how he could talk to a robin, and splashed water in his face when he scared them.

Yet, Lightningbolt did not belong. He spent long hours hunting by himself. Sometimes he took the girls and they loved it, but Canadiana hated it.

Soon, neither Canadiana nor Lightningbolt knew what to say to the other. But instead of seeing this, Lightningbolt began to argue with the girls, then try to make up. Dera responded will for will. This unexpected response from Dera perplexed him.

She was subtle where he was forceful. Dera was direct in her truth of being a girl child, and was girl-direct. He learned that he could not demand from Dera as he would someone else. She defied being corralled or herded like a bull, and she was certainly not a man. The girl could think, but her thinking confused him. She built her world Circle by Circle with finesse and human intelligence. This sophistication crushed his bigotry about little girls being stupid, forever. She would claim each Circle, not with cunning and argument, but with a finality that was impossible for him to argue with.

He tried first to defeat her. Then he tried to order her, but this only caused mistrust. He did not want that. He tried still another way, this time moving in circles about her and coming into dialogue with her.

He soon learned that she possessed a wondrous mind. He would try to order everything into his Circle of Power, but she would invite instead of force. This amazed him. He couldn't figure out how

she did this.

When he studied her, she made faces at him. Even when he won, he would lose. If he tried to speak to her as an adult, she did not possess sufficient knowledge to respond. Yet, if he tried to treat her like a little child, she'd get so angry she'd almost hate him.

He didn't want her to hate him, but he didn't want her to defeat him either. So for almost a week there was girl-man standoff. One day Dera won the final battle.

"You've got to find your own little girl," she told him. "I love you like Daffy, my horse, but I don't like you because you're stupid."

"Hey, you're my girl." He tried to smile.

"Nope," she said, looking into his eyes. "You always want to win, even with loving. It isn't fun. I don't want to win you."

144

This disarmed him and defeated him.

"You're mad 'cause you can't find happies," she scolded him. "And your kisses are getting like pickles." She was pouting now. "But you're silly, too, 'cause you won't go back home."

"What do you suggest?" he asked her, now serious. He felt a deep respect for her and she knew it.

"Buy more chocolate cookies!" Kim broke in. "And clean up your room." She had her arms crossed defiantly.

"I've got a war to fight up north." He smiled.

Not one day had passed in which Lightningbolt hadn't dramatized a fight in his mind with the Battle Kachinas. He daydreamed of fighting them almost constantly, and there was no hiding it from the girls. They didn't know of his idiosyncrasies, but they felt his restlessness. It was this lie that

they battled, not his attitudes or fantasies. He did not belong.

He thanked Dera the next day for her talk. Then he told Kim that she wasn't really a shorty after all. Kim was not impressed. She called Lightningbolt a snot.

Dera was not the same person she had been the day before. Now she was playful and wanted to beat him in a game of double solitaire. They played and Lightningbolt lost.

The following morning before dawn, the Silver Ship was heading north.

If he'd had the sophistication that he longed for—if he had even imagined how wondrous it was that he could meet people like Dera, Kim, and Canadiana—he would have understood why they had come into his life.

But this is not the usual destiny of learning.

Most learning comes hard. It has to exist first in the womb of experience before it can be born.

Canadiana, Dera, and Kim had very directly effected a change in Lightningbolt. But would he ever know how much?

The Silver Ship sped north away from the children and Lightningbolt's responsibility to them. He was running again—and he still didn't know it. While he drove he frowned, thinking about Estcheemah and the challenge she had given him.

Discernment. What did that mean? He'd look up the word the first chance he got.

Why would she use a word like *discernment*? In many ways, the challenge that the Battle Kachinas had given him sounded very simple, but in one way it sounded tough.

He'd become very afraid when Black Stone mentioned the challenge. All he had to do was defeat the Battle Kachina . . . what could be so hard about that? All he needed was a little skill, once he figured out what he was supposed to do. Sure . . . it was simple enough.

Yet, Estcheemah had been unclear. Or was he the one who was unclear? What was it that he was supposed to do? Fight the Battle Kachina? He should call her and make sure of what the challenge was. Hey! That was it, he was supposed to call Estcheemah. Sure, tomorrow morning, that would be a good time.

He journeyed all day, eager to get the trip over with and be with old man Black Stone. It was going to be fun seeing him again. He stopped only when he needed gas or oil.

That night he slept fitfully and dreamed that Dera was scolding him for not cleaning his pickup. The following morning he forgot to make the call. He remembered it at noon, but forgot again when he left the cafe where he'd grabbed a hamburger.

He had bought five new tapes and was enjoying the Beatles' "A Day in the Life" when he saw a wreck up ahead of him.

There was no time to stop. A truck had overturned across the highway. He had no alternative but to drive the Silver Ship off the edge of the highway.

The Ship bounced when it hit the fence, then tore its way through it into the field beyond. When it came to a stop, Lightningbolt was sweating. He stepped out and quickly gave his machine a once-over to see how it had fared. There didn't seem to be anything wrong.

He looked up when he heard a horrible crash. A grain truck had plowed into the wreck. The impact was grisly and it carried the sound of Death.

Frightened that the next driver would meet the same fate, he ran as fast as he could toward the highway. Vaulting over the broken and twisted wire of the fence, he sprinted up the highway. Pulling off his coat when he saw a car speeding toward him, he waved at it and pointed frantically ahead of him.

The car only accelerated when the driver saw him. He heard the crash, then ran farther up the road. The next car stopped.

The police and ambulance people came slowly. Montana is not a place where help comes quickly. Lightningbolt and others did what they could for the survivors.

Broken bodies lay everywhere amid shattered whiskey and beer bottles. Six were dead and five more were in very critical condition. Enduring their cries and moans for over an hour was immensely painful.

After the highway had been cleared, Lightningbolt went to his pickup and had another look under it. It was sound as a new silver dollar. He dug a cigarette out of the jockey box and smoked, saying a prayer, thanking Creation for saving his life. After this he vowed never to drive over sixty-five miles an hour.

"Very bad Medicine Sign," Black Stone commented the following day. "Yes, it happens all the time. It is a sad thing. At one time I did not care, but now that I am older it saddens me. Yes, you should pray, thanking God. Maybe go to mass."

"I want the training you spoke of," Lightningbolt told the old man. "You ready for that?" He pointed to the back of the Silver Ship. "Groceries for you, and tobacco."

Black Stone worked with him for thirty-eight days without stopping, until he was satisfied that Lightningbolt was ready.

"You're fast and you have learned well," the old man declared with pride. "You are good, very good. But are you sure you want to battle Fire Enemy? It is rumored that he's a sorcerer, you know. You'll have to protect yourself. He is determined to defeat all who come for the great reward. You would be his final test."

Lightningbolt was captivated by the thought of battling for a big reward. What was it?

"The battle he has with you will open the door for him," Black Stone announced. He was enjoying his role. "The door I speak of is the door into his Circle of Chiefs. That woman, Estcheemah, she went to the Chiefs, taking a blanket for you. She asked those Chiefs to be your adversary. She wanted the challenge for you. She brought gifts of tobacco. The second time they met with her, it was agreed. You could fight, if you wanted it."

Lightningbolt was now very excited.

"The reward of the Double Eagle jade necklace will be yours," Black Stone went on. "No greater reward exists. It is said that the necklace holds great power. The power to fly, I have heard. Some people say that you can take on the shape of any animal with the power of the necklace. Priests have offered great money for it."

"This guy," Lightningbolt broke in. "He's mean as cat shit. You sure he understands the rules?"

"Fire Enemy laughed when they told him you would be his adversary." Black Stone smiled. "He has nothing but contempt for you. That is good. Use it. Use his stupidity against him. No man should have that much hate for another. It blinds people when they have so much contempt."

"You are one of the powerful Chiefs, aren't you?" Lightningbolt asked. He felt good that he could be among such powerful men.

"I am one of them," Black Stone answered, looking very proud. "But you must hear more. This woman, Estcheemah, she doesn't know very much about us. After all, she is a woman. We have no women in our ranks like they did in the old days. She knows nothing of the Double Eagle jade necklace. This is our secret. It is a thing for the men . . . if you know what I mean."

"I understand." Lightningbolt nodded solemnly. He was taking his new responsibilities very seriously.

"You see those mountains over there?" The old Chief pointed to the East. There was a big saddle in the mountains. "That saddle there . . . it's his home for now. His domain. He's the king over all that he surveys there. It's filled with traps. And he has two monster dogs that are vicious. He's trained them to attack and kill. You must be careful of them. We do not like this, that he uses those animals. But what rule is there against it? His stay in those mountains is for two years. One and a half of those years has already gone. He has defeated two mighty sorcerers—beat them at their own games."

The hair rose on Lightningbolt's neck. This was it! Finally he had a situation he could sink his teeth into.

The old Chief became even more dramatic, enamored with how noble he was. Having this young man sitting at his feet learning from him was truly inspiring!

"Yes!" Black Stone said, gesturing dramatically toward the mountains. "He awaits you there. Get that reward in any way you can, short of murder. I, Black Stone, am the Watcher. If he kills you, he has failed. If you kill him, you have failed. Beyond actually killing each other, you and he can do what you will."

Lightningbolt was enthusiastic. Was this his hour of truth? He hoped so.

"Yes," Black Stone said proudly. "You, my son . . . yes, it is obvious you can do it. You may bring him to the edge of Death, but do not go beyond that. As long as you do not kill him—or he you—that is the only rule. It is believed by Pine Bull that Fire Enemy wears iron sewn into his war shirt. He also wears a helmet made of hardwood."

"That's armor!" Lightningbolt was full of anticipation. "So, okay, a bit of wood, a scrap of metal. It makes it more worthwhile, if you know what I mean."

"Sure," the old man agreed. "Why not? Whatever it is called, it does not really matter. The rule is—you must make everything you need to protect yourself. If you do not know how, you can get a little help."

"Sounds all right," Lightningbolt said.

Black Stone was cool, very certain. He looked like an old veteran . . . almost bored.

The necklace, was it magic? Men and women had crossed deserts, climbed cliffs, swum rivers filled with alligators, and fought to the edge of Death to get a magical power object.

He was getting nowhere. Not doing something with his life was tearing at his guts. A fight was a good idea. Win or lose, it would be satisfying.

But what if the necklace were a fake? He could look like a fool! No, these men would never go that far. It had to be real.

The following morning at dawn, Black Stone provided Lightningbolt with a horse, and they rode into the mountains to do a bit of reconnoitering.

They rode in silence. Black Stone was looking very noble and absolutely sure of himself. A feeling of pride rose in the young man's heart. Why not enjoy it? How many times did a person actually have a chance to be a hero? None, that's how many.

So these were the men he had heard about! The old warriors of the past. Stalwart men of power and action. He remembered a story he'd heard about Shield Heart.

Shield Heart had been born at the foot of the Black Hills. He wandered away from his family when the big drought came in the thirties. He moved to Canada and married Mochiko, a beautiful Japanese girl. Her name meant "Sweet Rice." After living in Canada for only a year, they returned to South Dakota.

Then the war came along and Shield Heart enlisted to fight for his country. He became a gunner in a tank. It was not long before he found himself fighting in the jungles of the South Pacific.

His tank was crippled by a cannon shot and he found himself on foot. As he struggled through the jungle he came to a clearing. There, rising up before him, was an ancient temple . . . of sorts. It was also some kind of a fort. Two natives rushed out brandishing their spears. Shield Heart leaped aside and parried their blows. He knocked one of the men down and the other fled for help. Exploring the temple, he found untold billions of dollars' worth of diamonds, emeralds, rubies, and other jewels. He filled his ammunition belt with money and jewels, and fought his way back to his tank. No one was ever the wiser.

When he got back to America he moved to Los

Angeles and bought himself a mansion in Beverly Hills.

Black Stone broke Lightningbolt's reverie. "This is Fire Enemy's land. All of it belongs to him until he defeats you. It is actually leased, however, for the purposes of our challenge. He has defeated two men so far. I defeated five in my day, the other Chiefs more. Who is to battle him now? Us?" He sighed. "There are fewer and fewer of us. Like I said, once Fire Enemy has lived here two years without defeat, he is in our Circle. He has entered the door.

"This man is tricky and mean, as you already know. I think that the war in Korea made him that way. He is a veteran. In the old days, Battle Kachinas were deadly, but not mean. This man can be cruel.

"We know that you will defeat him. But I do not envy you your task. The Chiefs will not feel you are shamed if you run away or choose not to battle him. It is all up to you. I will leave you here."

Lightningbolt watched as the old man rode away. He dismounted and kicked at the sand. This country was dry. He began to lead his horse and to have a look around. There was a massive rock at the end of the valley they had ridden by. It was this stone that marked the beginning of Fire Enemy's Circle.

So, this was the area of war. It was a forsaken place where only a few tumbleweeds could survive. What a terrible place to live for two years! There were a thousand shallow ravines and dry arroyos. Some of the washes were deep enough to secret a small army. He took the canteen from the saddle and had a drink.

Would he be allowed into the Inner Circle of Chiefs if he defeated Fire Enemy? He would have to ask.

"Hey!" said Fire Enemy from behind Light-

ningbolt, clapping him on his shoulder. "Bang, bang, you're dead, smart ass."

Lightningbolt dropped the canteen and turned to face Fire Enemy. He saw that his antagonist was carrying a spear, a real one, and holding a shield.

"Getting started early?" said Lightningbolt, trying to sound cool.

Fire Enemy came up close, almost touching his nose, and held out his hand. When Lightningbolt reached for the hand, he was suddenly hit hard in his stomach. He doubled over and slowly buckled to the ground.

"Whatever is the matter?" Fire Enemy asked, pulling Lightningbolt to his feet. He kicked the young man hard in the face, sending him sprawling into the sand again.

The blows had Lightningbolt staggering with pain and confusion. He could barely hear what Fire Enemy was saying. He rolled and crouched, waiting for the next attack.

Fire Enemy also crouched and looked at him straight in the eyes. "Look, stupid," Fire Enemy spat: "It's time for you to leave, forever. Got it, dog?" He stood, turned, then slammed the spear butt hard against Lightningbolt's chest, knocking him over backward.

Lightningbolt had been knocked out cold. When he awoke he saw Fire Enemy standing over him and pouring water from his canteen into his face.

"Get up and get on your horse," Fire Enemy growled.

Lightningbolt staggered to his feet and stumbled toward his horse. He should have tried to run—it would have saved him more awful pain. Fire Enemy struck again, this time hitting Lightningbolt hard on his ass. He turned and was struck in the face. Down into the dirt and sand he went again.

"This is no place for schoolboys." Fire Enemy smirked. "Get on your horse and go."

Lightningbolt crawled to his mount and pulled himself up into the saddle. Once he was astride his animal he thought of running Fire Enemy down, but thought better of it when he saw his enemy poise the spear point.

"Time to go," Fire Enemy said smoothly.

Lightningbolt kicked his horse into a run.

He rode to Black Stone's home and dismounted at the pump. Anger, blinding hatred, fear, and vengeance boiled in every cell of his being. Why did every beautiful dream have to end with pain? Why had the Great Spirit made assholes like Fire Enemy?

Every muscle in his body ached. He washed the blood from his face and mouth. His clothes were ruined with dried blood and dust. He walked to his pickup, tore open the door, and took out fresh clothes to put on.

"You can bathe at the pump," Black Stone offered. "I can heat some water for you."

"Why didn't you tell me?" Lightningbolt said through his teeth. "That dog is crazy!"

"The challenge is what it is," Black Stone fought back. "You were told. Are you afraid now? Running . . . all right, that is the way it is. Run." He turned on his heel and went back to his house.

Lightningbolt watched Black Stone walk away as he dressed. He wanted to say something, curse the old man, but he couldn't bring himself to speak. He was too angry.

He walked back to the pump and washed his mouth again. The man could obviously fight, but why couldn't he be fair about it? Why did he have to be such a rat? He straightened and wiped his

face. No, it was no use. This whole damned charade was a stupid joke.

A jade necklace, what a piece of shit. Would he buy that crap? Never! Fire Enemy was a straight-ahead nut.

"You are defeated," Black Stone proclaimed from his porch.

"Horseshit!" Lightningbolt yelled, shaking his fist. "If I return, man, I'll drop that rat like a sack full of dog bones."

The Silver Ship's tires screamed when they caught on the pavement. The farther he drove, the angrier he became and the more insane the fight seemed to be. He cursed himself that he should ever have gotten mixed up in such bullshit.

During the next half hour he felt a different anger and was emotionally distraught. Now the horrible sadness returned. What if . . . just if . . . that damned necklace was real?

God damn, why did every dream have to end in pain? A deep nauseating fear settled into his mind and heart. If that bloody thing was real, true magic, then he'd be a loser again. No necklace—no power. No power—no happiness. The world was shit! Life . . . what a stupid joke!

A deadly determination came over him. How could he defeat that miserable dog? Better armor . . . brains . . . planning . . . yes, that was it.

He grew calmer. That pig! He'd make him eat dust. A lot of it. He would fall! Lightningbolt's knuckles were white as he gripped the steering wheel. If he did nothing else in the world, Fire Enemy was going down . . . and hard!

Lightningbolt's sadness was profound. It was not one of those pains that simply paralyzes the mind. It was worse, driving him and punishing him with its fervor and potent extremes.

Vengeance rose up in him, severe and resolute. Fire Enemy had become more than a man—he had become a thing, a symbol of what Lightningbolt should defeat. This had happened before, with far less drama, with petty things. First, the situation presented itself, then came decision.

This decision was direct and simple—fight. Fight for what you needed. Battle for position. Don't take, never steal—this was the loser's way. Fight, combat, that was the answer.

Whenever Lightningbolt was overwhelmed with sadness, he would Dream. These Dreams were always the same. Battlefield after battlefield would present itself in his mind. He would watch an endless parade of wars. Sometimes the battles were fought between people of ancient times. He found the crash of shield and sword, the use of pike and spear, exhilarating. He planned, destroyed or watched a thousand charges of horse cavalry. He staged his battle tanks and moved forward thousands of foot soldiers.

It didn't matter to him which side he fought on. It was the war itself that held him spellbound. Blitzkrieg, the Charge of the Light Brigade, the Little Big Horn, or Bull Run . . . it did not matter. He knew them all, well. There was no right side or wrong side; it was all warfare, battle. The outcome depended upon skill and maneuver.

For Lightningbolt these daydreams were so normal, so common, so everyday, he never thought of them as out of the ordinary. He'd thought this way, Dreamed this way, from the time he was born. Didn't everybody? If someone had confronted him, he would have blinked, not understanding, and immediately responded with: "What do you mean, me? Me thinking of warfare? Hey, not me!"

Yet, it was true. His mind was completely oriented to war and battle. The wars had become his symbols and thoughts. Everything he thought was colored in terms of war.

By the time the Silver Ship rolled to a stop at the Reservation, Lightningbolt was changed. His fear of being powerless and his shame at being defeated had constantly been a terrible driving force—a force he hated—but it had also become the source of his determination to win.

He'd passed through a door of Self recognition that was beyond his understanding, yet he'd noted the change. His terror of being a loser had been eased. The face of his fears had changed and he possessed a new confidence. Now he knew he could win.

He began to understand what his uncle had told him. The old master tech sergeant, a demolitions expert in Korea, had said: "Meet the enemy, know the enemy, then defeat the enemy."

He could win if he was clear about exactly how to defeat Fire Enemy. He felt at ease with his new direction. This change, this new thing that had happened inside his heart and mind, had clarified many mysteries that he had not formerly understood.

His first illumination was that his fears did not keep war and pain from happening.

His fear was present all the time, as was the fact that his Reservation world constantly challenged him.

Conflict was always present and inevitable.

So why be afraid? Fear did nothing and was no defense. There was no escaping trouble. It did not matter if a person was afraid; war was a reality of Life, and that was that.

Why not fight? What did a person have to lose? A good war cleared the air, made things ready, and always presented something new. War helped ease the knots in his stomach. Any kind of war was better than nothing happening. Boredom was awful! A battle of words, a fight with his emotions, what did it matter?

The Big Nothing—that was true fear and loathing. People who tended their quiet little stores, quiet little farms and ranches, all the nice quiet folks—that was Death. Nothingness was a monster!

There had to be something, a real something—otherwise why live? Mom, apple pie, washtubs, clean dishes, land, Medicine Powers, nothing ever seemed to happen with those things. It was all just too spooky!

Lightningbolt picked up Smokey and they drove to Jack's Machine Shop. Blind Jack was a machinist, mechanic, sheet metal worker, welder, and joiner. He was also good at working with fiberglass resins. The local gossip was that Jack had been one of the original John Birchers, and it was rumored he had been thrown out of the society because he used the Lord's name in vain in public.

Smokey prowled around the shop like a mangy cat in search of a litter box, poking through the clutter of metal parts and machinery while Jack and Lightningbolt drew up plans and schemed.

"You're talking about the real shit." Blind Jack grinned broadly. "I like making shit like that. I like the change. Yes, sure . . . armor, sheet steel, and fiber glass . . . helmet and everything. It will cost you three hundred bucks, cash on the old barrel head."

Slouching by the wood stove, Smokey whined, "He is trading you my rifle to have armor made. Doesn't that sound weird?"

Blind Jack ignored him. He didn't look pleased, and his hand shook as he lit a smoke. The Russian army boots Smokey wore, the green combat pants, and the high-necked white Nehru jacket made Jack very nervous. He didn't trust Smokey in the least. Blind Jack was convinced that Greenblatt wasn't Smokey's real name, and he was equally sure that Smokey was a Commie.

Jack picked up a second cigarette he had burning in his ashtray and crushed it out. "Your rifle, huh," he sneered, taking a long side glance at Smokey. "Yeah. What is it? Forty years old? Something the Crow Indians threw away? Was it run over by a Caterpillar?"

Lightningbolt sat down on a Second World War ammunition box and patiently waited.

"I'll get the gun." Smokey groaned. "Sure you

won't charge it? I mean, it's Lightningbolt."

"He's a goddamned Breed, the same as you, Commie," Jack growled. "A thief. No, whatever your real name is, asshole, that damned gun better be good."

Smokey went out to the Silver Ship and came back with his new .30–06. Blind Jack snatched the rifle from his hands and checked its mechanism.

"Wait!" said Smokey, pretending to smile. "You've got to answer one question. You know, about how you got the name Blind Jack."

"I couldn't shoot you if you were two inches from me. I'd have to stab you to death," Blind Jack answered with a sneer. He laid the gun across his filthy desk. "So I always take along Father O'Neal. He's a crack shot—a rich priest the Church takes care of, bless their old hides and his." He began to draw. "He shoots the deer and I eat 'em. Your gun is new, good enough for me. Sure you wouldn't want to be a target, Greenblatt? You look like the type. I wouldn't mind killing you. What do you say?"

"Weird." Smokey shook his head. "You, me, him. We're all weird, don't you think?"

"Why'd you ask?" said Jack, suddenly curious, as he continued to sketch out an old knight's helmet.

"I'm gonna be an artist, the painter's painter," Smokey answered. "I always ask Roundist questions."

"You'll paint communist shit." Jack frowned, looking up. "Crapola no American should look at, porn, maybe even advertisements. You Commies won't stop at anything, will you?"

Jack stood and walked over to Lightningbolt. "Hmmm," he mused, pushing a dirty old baseball cap on Lightningbolt's head. "Fits. I'll use this as my measure. With a little to spare, it'll be a good helmet."

"With my cash and the gun, that covers it," Lightningbolt said, standing up. "You got all my measurements . . . got the details. What next?"

"Come back when it's done," Blind Jack answered, not looking up. "And leave the Commie home."

That evening Smokey and Lightningbolt had dinner together at the Pink China Cafe. They dined on fresh-caught trout, deer, and elk shot out of season.

Duck could have been on the menu too, but Harlow's wife, Nellie, had been arrested for fishing out of season and poaching deer. Harlow hated it when he had to cook alone, and he would have to get up at five in the morning to shoot an antelope. The telephone crews were coming through again and they loved antelope.

"Why did you push Blind Jack like that?" Lightningbolt asked.

"It's called the paint-a-character method," Smokey lied. "No, actually"—he chuckled—"I wanted to show you that I am the first living Roundist."

"Really?" Lightningbolt was not sure what his friend meant. "Now you owe me fifty bucks, right?"

"Thirty-eight," Smokey answered. "Do you want to see something I've sketched for humanity to marvel over?" He pulled out a floppy sheaf of papers. "Huh?"

"Sure." Lightningbolt wanted to be entertained. It had been a hard day.

"Our world is just a cream cake illusion," Smokey mused. "With skulls. I'm going to paint garbage heaps and ruins because this will tell our story. Wrecked cars, motorcycles. Only the toilet bowls will last, maybe some toothbrushes and dildos. We won't leave much for the anthros of the future."

"That's going to be a weird painting," said Lightningbolt.

"Of course you'd say that." Smokey smiled. "You're ignorant, never been to the university. Sure, typical review. What do you know about the Roundist movement? It means nothing to you. What do you know of the Cubists, the Squareists, the Inverse of the Rightists, and the Adverse of the Leftists? Nothing, right?

"We've made enough gun barrels to build a freeway around the world twice, and we train people to see in squares and oblongs."

"Ever think about magic?" asked Lightningbolt, testing his friend.

"Happy horseshit! There you go again." Smokey howled with laughter. "Magic is the inverse of Spirit, don't you know that?

"I mean, it's ice cream that doesn't melt. It's women that are all perfect and beautiful. It's men with brains. It's a window that never gets dirty. It's a car, a washing machine, a degree from college, a dino tooth.

"Magic never works. Only in Disney films. Magic is a green thought. It's a tiger in a sports car. It's belief. It's a fishmonger wanting to hypnotize a wireless God. No, magic has to believe in us or it wouldn't exist."

"Oklahoma was never the same when you left," Lightningbolt teased.

"Now you understand!" Smokey was satisfied. "There is no Oklahoma because I am not there. But, magically, it will appear again when my car payment is due."

Lightningbolt worked for three weeks fixing fence for the S-U Ranch. It was backbreaking work that lasted from daylight to dark. He had contracted the work.

While he toiled, he thought about his world and why he had to constantly grub for a living. Where did the owners of the S-U get their money from? Surely not by doing the bone-jarring labor he did.

Three weeks later he returned to Blind Jack's to pick up his armor. Borrowing a horse trailer turned out to be quite a chore. Everybody seemed to be using theirs. It took two days before he located one he could use.

Next, he drove to Harvey Smith's to pick up Arrow. His mare was not there. Old Medicine Ear had taken her to Wyola to be bred. He had to drive to Crow Agency and borrow a roping horse.

Halfway to Black Stone's home, Lightningbolt almost turned around. He thought that it just might be possible that he'd still not gotten the matter straight. Should he call Estcheemah? He sat in a drive-in cafe waiting for his hamburger. His eyes took in the surroundings. Nope, no telephone.

Still, the closer he got to the old man's, the angrier he became. By the time the Silver Ship came to a stop at Black Stone's house, the hate had returned. Now Lightningbolt wanted revenge.

He unloaded the horse from the trailer and led the animal to the house. No one was home. Black Stone must have gone to town for groceries.

It was ten o'clock in the morning—the perfect time for a small war. He quickly saddled the horse and made sure his twelve-gauge shotgun was loaded. Waiting in the breech of the gun were two shells filled with miniballs. They could tear the head off a bull.

He strung the four spears he'd made through their saddle loop, then drew the string tight; they'd ride just fine. His spears had no killing point; they were blunt. He didn't want to draw blood. Beating Fire Enemy half to death would be enough.

His hands were sweating when he stripped off his coat and buckled on his breastplates. He next tied his buckler into place on his left arm. The small shield shone in the sun. His excitement grew as he belted on his armored skirt; this would protect his waist and groin.

Blind Jack had become enthusiastic and added his own artistic touch—and Lightningbolt hung it at his waist. Why not take along a war hammer as an extra friend?

Ahhh . . . yes, now for the helmet! It felt good. He lifted up the visor and had a last look around. Black Stone was still not back.

Lightningbolt rode beyond the stone that marked the edge of Fire Enemy's world. His horse was fast and tough and would hold her head with gunfire.

The young combatant held his mare steady as he trotted her toward his target. He could see Fire Enemy come out of his hovel and strap on his helmet.

"Now is the time for two plus twos," Lightningbolt said to himself as he pulled down his visor.

Kicking his horse into a lope, he kept his eyes on his foe. Fire Enemy jerked loose the rings that held his two mastiffs and they rushed forward to

attack the horse and rider.

One of the dogs dashed ahead of the other and veered off to the left for its strike. Lightningbolt pulled the shotgun out of the saddle boot and leveled it at the dog.

Whooom! The dog rolled into the dirt, instantly dead. It had been cut nearly in half.

The gun roared again and the second dog was hammered into the dust to die.

Lightningbolt broke the gun and threw out the spent shells, then dug into his saddle pouch for two more. He loaded them into the breech, closed the gun, and replaced it in its scabbard. Through all this, the horse never broke stride.

His adversary was now only twenty feet away. He seemed to be a bit surprised that his two trained monsters had just died.

Fire Enemy had built a barricade against the possibility of a frontal attack. However, he hadn't taken as much time with its construction as he should have. It had been inconceivable to him that anyone would be foolish enough to launch a frontal attack. What he didn't know was that at one point Lightningbolt had considered using a Caterpillar to rout him out.

Another truth was that the vet had been challenged over eleven times. Most of these attempts were bumbling tries by kids who'd been easily frightened away with a little persuasive violence.

The sudden death of the attack dogs had severely jolted Fire Enemy. This was something he'd never expected. The dogs had played an important part in all of his plans.

While Fire Enemy was in the army he'd been a mechanic. He had never known or seen combat, other than his drunken brawls. After his discharge, he'd worked for eleven years as a prison guard in the South. The prison used dogs to "discourage escape attempts" by the inmates.

He had trained his own dogs to snoop out intruders and maul them until he arrived. He gleefully called his attack animals "the doggy assault force."

Lightningbolt's horse was now over the log barricade. She stumbled in the shallow ditch that Fire Enemy had hastily prepared, but in one jump she was on her feet again. However, the mare's lunge as she righted herself had knocked Fire Enemy sprawling into the dirt.

In a flash Lightningbolt was off his horse with a spear in his hand. When Fire Enemy rolled up onto his feet to fight, Lightningbolt struck at him. But his frightened horse turned and bumped into Lightningbolt, nearly knocking him off his feet the very second he made his move.

The old guard took advantage of this miss and struck hard at Lightningbolt's head. If the younger man hadn't been wearing a helmet, the blow would have killed him.

Now it was Lightningbolt's turn. He swung his spear, hitting Fire Enemy alongside his head. The blow glanced off his helmet, but sent it spinning away from him—the strap that held it had broken.

Fire Enemy bellowed with anger. Leaping to his feet, the more experienced man crashed into his antagonist with all of his weight, slamming Lightningbolt to the ground and nearly pinning him. But at the very moment when Fire Enemy went for Lightningbolt's throat, the younger man had rolled, reached up, and grabbed the stirrup of his saddle. The frightened horse moved forward, pulling Lightningbolt to his feet.

Fire Enemy's hands were finding their way around Lightningbolt's throat again when Lightningbolt yanked a spear down hard on the older man's head.

This blow stunned Fire Enemy. He staggered back, fighting hard to remain on his feet.

Lightningbolt rushed forward and swung both of his hands clenched together into a massive fist. The blow hammered into Fire Enemy's face. The older man cried out with pain and fell to the ground. His nose was bleeding and he hurt bad. Moaning, he rolled over, clutching his stomach. He slowly rose up on his knees, his face still buried in the dust.

Lightningbolt should have realized that he hadn't hit his foe in the stomach. Caution should have warned the younger man. But instead of assessing his situation, Lightningbolt screamed at his foe, calling him a dog. The sudden and incredible loudness of his own voice frightened him. He'd forgotten his head was encased in a steel helmet.

To Fire Enemy, Lightningbolt's voice sounded hollow and ominous.

What happened next startled Lightningbolt. The old prison guard had a useful trick secreted at his waist. It was a pouch of baby powder. The trick was simple, direct, and the best last-ditch remedy the old guard knew. It worked far better than dirt. You had to scoop dirt from the ground—the enemy could see this happening.

The baby powder came as the surprise it was meant to be. It blinded Lightningbolt for an instant when Fire Enemy threw it. But the older man had forgotten something himself—Lightningbolt's helmet kept most of the substance out of his eyes.

Fire Enemy fled into the hills. Lightningbolt chased him for a distance, but soon gave up. It was hopeless. He knew that Fire Enemy would have traps and other weapons, maybe some not so fashionable.

The young man's next move was pure luck. Sore, angry, sweating, and bleeding, he walked to Fire Enemy's dirty hovel to have a look inside. He had to stoop to look into the low, narrow doorway. A dirty rag hung to one side. It was used to hold the door shut. The building had been made of railroad ties, logs, and rough-sawn boards. It reeked of filth. To the right of the door hung a coal oil lamp. Lightningbolt threw it to the ground, breaking it.

The interior of the one-room cabin was dark with rot and soot. Porn magazines and murder mysteries littered the room. In one corner there was a half empty case of beer. Next to the disheveled and filthy bed there were candles and another coal oil lamp.

Outside the building he found what he was looking for. There was a five-gallon can of gasoline, another can of coal oil, and a can of barbecue starter.

Dousing the building with gasoline gave him some sense of satisfaction. He knew that Fire Enemy was watching. Next, he emptied the coal oil and barbecue starter into an empty pan he found by the door. He threw the fluid into the room.

Walking slowly back to his horse, he looked around for something to make a fire wick. There on the ground was his opponent's old shirt. He wrapped the shirt around a stone, lit it, and hurled it through the door.

The building exploded into flames as he swung into the saddle.

Lightningbolt rode leisurely back to Black Stone's home to clean up and rest.

"Much good armor," the old man said with a chuckle when Lightningbolt dismounted. "Good . . . you live."

Lightningbolt turned and looked at the old man. Somehow, he felt incredibly cheated. "I'm bruised, sore, sprained, filthy, but I'm all right. So is Fire Enemy. We had a tussle; nobody won. I burned down his house."

"Uh-huh." Black Stone frowned. "We never, ever did that." He shrugged his shoulders. "Hmmm . . . why not? Did he send his dogs to get you?"

Lightningbolt undressed at the pump and began to wash up. He splashed water in his face and washed away the blood under his nose. Something seemed incredibly wrong.

Was this the way a knight was supposed to feel? He never knew that his head would bounce around in the helmet or that he'd have his face slammed against the faceplate. He felt as though he'd been in a car wreck. Every bone in his body ached, and every muscle.

"The dogs," Black Stone reminded him.

"Oh, yeah, sure," he answered. "I blew them away with my shotgun. You said yourself that the dogs were not part of the deal."

Black Stone looked puzzled. He turned and walked slowly back to the house. Lightningbolt thought the old man didn't look so noble this trip. What was different? He couldn't say.

Yes, being a knight in torn and bloody armor was not what he'd pictured it to be. The fight had been ugly and it had left him feeling somehow betrayed.

Limping slightly, he next cared for his horse. She hadn't liked the uproar at all. She shied away from him and snorted at his every move. Now he realized that using the horse hadn't been such a good idea. He hadn't even considered that she could have been seriously hurt. It was not right. What did a Double Eagle necklace mean to her? Nothing.

Why was he thinking about a dumb old horse? That Black Stone was a dink, too. Lightningbolt, that is who he should be thinking about. How did he keep getting himself into shit like this?

The following day he went for a walk in the hills, trying to get his feet on the ground and understand what was happening with him. He simply did not feel right about this adventure.

The second day, he hunted grouse. But he didn't enjoy it. At noon the next day he decided to go to town for food and to buy himself a shirt. He walked by one of the four cafes in town and saw a man who looked like his old foe.

He had to be sure. Stopping, Lightningbolt studied the man who sat at the counter alone. The baseball cap and the dirty red satin jacket had almost disguised his opponent. From the side, the Indian could have been any local drunk, except for one little item—the Double Eagle jade necklace. There it was, swinging from the man's neck.

The old prison guard wasn't looking so good. His face was puffy, and both of his eyes were black-and-blue and swollen into slits. The people in the cafe, especially the waitress, were avoiding him.

Lightningbolt moved as smoothly as he could up to the door and opened it. He didn't want Fire Enemy to see him reflected in the mirror behind the counter. But he did.

Quick as a cat, Fire Enemy spun on his bar stool and threw his dinner plate at Lightningbolt. It missed and shattered the large front window.

In seconds the entire room erupted with noise—screams from women, shouts from ranchers and cowboys. The waitress hurled a cup at Fire Enemy as he ran for the back door.

"Pay your goddamned bill!" she shrieked after the Indian.

The jade necklace! Lightningbolt had never seen it before and now there it was, right out in the open. He cursed as he clawed his way through the Saturday-night crowd of merrymakers and drinkers.

Two burly cowboys picked him up bodily, one on each side, and threw him toward the back door. They laughed and whooped, shouting for him to shift down into a lower gear.

Lightningbolt was actually thankful for the boost. He flopped slightly once he was airborne, then righted himself with the doorjamb when he went through it.

Fire Enemy was now in the back alley, running with all of his strength. He spun and hurled garbage cans behind him as he tore past. Lightningbolt dodged and rushed on.

They ran across the street almost together; only ten feet separated them. Fire Enemy wanted to make it to the school. He'd decided to get in through a window any way he could. Once inside he could find a place to hide from his pursuer. He'd

seen this done at one of the institutions he'd worked in. It never failed to give more time to the person running.

Lightningbolt, on the other hand, wondered why Fire Enemy was running toward the school—why not out across the nearby parking lot? His guess was that his enemy would eventually shift course, and consequently he kept to his left, waiting for him to make his turn.

But no turn came. Fire Enemy raced to the school, then leaped through an open window. Stunned by this sudden movement, Lightningbolt ran to the door nearest the window and tried it; it opened. As he burst through the door, he saw Fire Enemy dashing through the door to the gymnasium.

Inside, a banquet was going on, in full attendance. White linen tablecloths were stretched over long rows of tables arranged in a horseshoe pattern. There was a speaker on the podium and a big audience seated and listening.

Fire Enemy paid no heed to the people or what they were doing. He dived beneath the first set of tables, then popped up beside the speaker. Lightningbolt went straight over the top, hurtling between two men.

He grabbed for the necklace around Fire Enemy's neck and hung on. Now that it was in his hands, nothing was going to get it free. But Fire Enemy was boiling with anger and strong as a crazed man. He ran, pulling Lightningbolt along the entire length of the tables. Bowls of soup, knives, forks, spoons, dishes, spaghetti, bread, and butter piled up in Lightningbolt's face, but he would not let go of the necklace. Men were shouting, and women were throwing salad at Fire Enemy and Lightningbolt. Suddenly, three men simultaneously grabbed Lightningbolt. The chain on the necklace broke and beads scattered everywhere. Now Lightningbolt held the Double Eagle jade necklace in his hands.

By some miracle Fire Enemy escaped the room, but Lightningbolt was arrested. He probably could have run also, but he just stood there, clutching the necklace, dripping with food, and grinning.

He was arrested for disturbing the peace, being drunk in a public place, and some other code that no one understood, but it cost fifty dollars anyway. All in all, his fine meant that he would stay in jail and work twenty days for the county. He did. Not once in all the days he was in jail could he beat the turnkey at checkers.

When he got out of jail, he bought the shirt he'd come to town for, and returned to Black Stone's home for his horse and trailer. The old man was absent.

He drove south. Now he would have to face Estcheemah.

Lightningbolt did not know what was real and what wasn't.

Jim Morrison crooned from his electronic world, telling Lightningbolt that the West was the very best as he turned in to the half-mile lane that led to Estcheemah's home.

The dust poured thick from his tires when he stopped—as thick as the false pride in his voice when he announced that he had won.

Estcheemah immediately saw that something was wrong. She could see that he had been fighting and sensed that his heart was pained. She invited him into the house and told him to nap before she would speak with him.

He slept all that afternoon and through the night. The following morning Estcheemah kept herself busy packaging up a coat she had just finished. She drove off to Sheridan to mail it and was gone until nightfall.

Lightningbolt was quiet all through the evening meal. In the deepest part of his being, he knew that

something was wrong. He washed dishes, trying to think of a way of explaining.

Estcheemah began working on another coat. She was sewing in a lining and patiently waiting. She knew that her young guest had to have time to find his thoughts.

"You think I blew it, right?" He was immediately argumentative. He sat across from her at the kitchen table, sipping the coffee he'd made for himself.

"Blew what?" She looked up at him quizzically.

He began his story and hurried though it. She made him go back to the beginning and tell it again. Slowly, the details came to light.

He lied in the beginning, trying to create a situation that appeared to be very different from what had happened. His first version of the story made it seem that he had no choice.

The third, fourth, and finally the fifth versions got all tangled up with the first story and the second.

Each time the story was presented, Estcheemah patiently listened as she sewed one of her coats. It wasn't until the fourth and fifth versions that she began to question and confront the facts.

Finally, around nine o'clock that night, the entire story had come out with all of the honest details.

"You've been half crazed with your pain." She had a catch in her voice. A tear slid from her eye. "You would actually fight that idiot man for a cheap necklace? It's hard to believe, Lightningbolt. You have no idea what discernment means, do you?"

Lightningbolt dug the necklace out of his shirt pocket and threw it on the kitchen table. It lay there like a symbol of Death and failure. It held no mystery, no magic, no beauty.

Estcheemah looked very pained. "Those silly old men." She sighed. "Playing out an idiot's game. There are no more real Battle Kachinas among them, Lightningbolt. There haven't been any true soldiers in their discipline for a hundred years. The world has greatly changed. There is no more support for a Battle Kachina school. The Discipline will have to be updated and made more real."

Lightningbolt didn't like what he was hearing, but he knew it was the truth.

Estcheemah was angry. "I never expected you to physically fight Fire Enemy. Such fools! You were only supposed to learn the use of weapons from them. Your challenge was to learn the use of the sword and lance. I never meant for you to beat up your instructor."

"Hey!" he said, angry. "You set it up. Those were your pals, your ideas. Black Stone said you'd begged them to teach me to fight. Now you make out like we're all idiots."

She looked resolute. "I'm talking about discernment, dumb ass. Why didn't you come and talk with me? I told you to do that, or to telephone, didn't I? What were you thinking?"

"The goddamned necklace!" He was very defensive. "Magic, dammit! A little something in my stupid life, that's what."

The old teacher knew that there was no going around any emotional obstruction. She would have to attack and destroy his defenses one by one or the war would drag on forever.

"Magic," she scolded, not looking up. "That necklace has no more magic than a roll of toilet paper."

Lightningbolt slammed his hand down hard on his knee and turned his chair to stare out the window. Rage held him in its grip. There was no chance of his speaking.

She brushed back her hair and looked at him. "We are all fools. It's only the disciplined and courageous who will admit it. Sure you were gullible—I understand your confusion." She stood up and walked to the sink, then turned to look at him. "Love, hope, needs, desires. Sure, I know them all. And my judgment was poor at times, too." She laughed.

"A Peyote Chief once made me believe that I could possess a magical porcupine. I believed him for a while, until the truth came out. He just wanted me in his bed. So what are you going to do with the necklace?"

He looked down at his hands. "What the hell . . . who knows? Maybe I needed a break. Maybe I needed to attack my problems at their roots. All during this it really struck me that I needed to destroy my old positions. But how? I don't want to be slapped around. You know, hit over the head with what I'm supposed to do."

She poured him a fresh cup of coffee, then returned to her chair. "We can join forces. I have the weapons you need to fight your war."

Lightningbolt looked down at his hands.

"You're feeling embarrassed now," she said matter-of-factly as she went back to her work. "But you're a young knothead. Tough. You'll live through it. Your offensive has only begun. This experience is rising like puke in you. You'll vomit it up before long. Maybe you will throw up on the next Medicine Man?"

He tried to smile, but couldn't quite manage it.

"These little wars of yours," she went on, "are exactly as you would have them. It is a very good thing you did not hurt that poor fool. You could have, you know. Crippling or beating up a fool is no reward for a high warrior. He could have hurt you, too. To be crippled by a fool is not so satisfying, is it? Okay, you're embarrassed; that's nothing. How do you really feel now?"

"I watched a television blow up," he answered. "It went apeshit; sparks flew everywhere. All its guts went up in a fountain of destruction."

"More a fountain of learning and stupidity," she countered. "You were just cross-wired. You will become Earth-Conscious if you work with me. Feel like beginning again?"

The tears welled up in Lightningbolt's eyes, but he continued to look directly into the eyes of Estcheemah. "I'll mail the damn thing to Black Stone." His voice was steady. "I have been an absolute fool. I know it. The truth was, I didn't give a damn if he did kill me. I honestly did not care, Estcheemah."

"The Reservation is a test for you in this Life," she explained. "Will it be a worthy one? What you need is power, and the best of all power is information."

"Power! That's what I was looking for!" He was excited now. "The power to blow off the Reservation."

Estcheemah smiled. "It all begins with you. Power is like a gun. Some people shoot at sparrows with a five-billion-dollar cannon, while others, like you, try to shoot down the Moon with a BB gun."

Lightningbolt had never faced a human he couldn't back down with a good argument. For the first time in his life he sensed somehow that the woman who sat in front of him was very special and could not be defeated.

Estcheemah knew that Lightningbolt had immense potential, but there were no guarantees. His violence and bullheaded attitudes were a wall of contention Estcheemah would have to face and defeat. Thus far, Lightningbolt's life experience had included only Breeds, Indians, white ranchers, and the Reservation. She planned to change that.

Estcheemah put down her sewing and looked directly into Lightningbolt's eyes. "Look, Breed," she said in her commanding voice, "your situation is critical whether you know it or not. You are incredibly ignorant. Information is the most valuable commodity on Earth. It makes freaks out of people who could have been ordinary. It's ruined many a good conformist. Bull Lightning failed at being a decent slaver. Temple Doors, the most powerful woman general in our history, failed miserably at being a man's nice wife. Self-awareness and the power of information is what made Thomas Jefferson great."

Lightningbolt toyed with his spoon. "I've fit in much too well," he admitted. "And it's making me crazy, not getting anything done."

"Maybe I can help you become a failure," she teased. "I could give you just enough information to help you learn what discernment means. You bumbled your first test, but maybe instead of brawn you'll use your mind next time?"

"I'll not fail you again," he answered quickly.

"Fail me?" She laughed. "Hey, where are you?" She waved her hand in front of his eyes. "Fail me? Is that a good choice of words? Who was it you failed?"

"Me," he corrected himself.

"Your decision was foolish," she offered. "But your commitment to yourself is important. Can you be your best friend? Do you possess the strength to care for your Self?"

He looked puzzled. "I've always cared for myself. What do you mean?"

Estcheemah smiled. "Your little war with Black Stone and Fire Enemy would have been much different if you had really been your own friend. A true friend would have encouraged you to fight, but not in such a silly way. A true friend would have told you to fight for information."

The talk ended much too soon for Lightningbolt that evening. But he slept well through the night. The following morning he was bouncing with energy.

While Estcheemah prepared breakfast, she put Lightningbolt to work cleaning the chicken house. After they had eaten and washed the dishes, Estcheemah took her student for a walk.

As they walked she spoke to him about Life and how she had slowly begun to realize that to be alive meant more than just trying to make a living.

"It all begins with you," she carefully explained to him. "You must learn to care for your Self. You have to learn to be your own best friend. In the world we live in, people are taught to mistrust their body, and to mistrust the Self. It is not uncommon for people to attack their Self, even to ridicule their Self."

"Even the Earth is mistrusted!" Lightningbolt added, wanting to sound knowledgeable.

"Of course," she agreed, glad to have him participating. "When people do not trust their own bodies, and fear that they will be deceived by the Self, then the only thing left is to become victims of everything.

"When people are taught the Earth is not trustworthy, when the Human Self and the body of the person is believed to be untrustworthy, then everything becomes 'The Enemy.'

"The Earth is not your enemy. If She were the enemy, as many propagandists want us to believe, then no human would be alive to tell of it. Mother Earth gives us Life. Here on Earth," she explained, "is the place where all Spirits can be born and experience Life.

"We humans are Spirits who have been born into Bodies. Everyone lives their Life, their Experience, then they die. When humans die, they return to Spirit."

Lightningbolt's hair prickled on his scalp. "Spirit is Death?" he asked. "Wow, really?"

"Yes," answered Estcheemah. "People die and go back to Spirit, don't they? Death is the door back to Spirit. Humans fear Death, and this fear is preyed upon by those who desire to control humans. The religious belief that teaches being born here on Mother Earth is undesirable is where it all began. Life isn't so bad. Wouldn't you agree, Lightningbolt? Do you prefer Death to your Life?"

Lightningbolt smiled and shook his head.

"No, it is foolish, even perilous for us to mistrust Sacred Mother Life. Life is Being and is our very Existence. To be Born is our most precious gift. No other Truth is so dear.

"To hate Life is to deny the physical fact of our personal existence. To fear Mother Earth and to malign Her brings about mistrust of the Self. When we mistrust Existence, our Earth, our very lives, we find ourselves in deep mental anguish."

"It's sad," he said softly.

"Yes, it is," she replied sympathetically. "And it is extremely dangerous. For when belief becomes greater than Life and more authoritative than our human needs, things can become very crazy. This has happened thousands of times throughout history.

"Lightningbolt, it doesn't matter which religious authority claims to be the spokesman for what Creation has had to say, they all have a terrible record. No other kind of organization or institution on Earth has made such outlandish claims that have caused untold suffering and stifled human progress or have killed and tortured so many human beings.

"But who tempers these people? No one. The old religious organizations never act directly. They always work through other institutions or through people they can manipulate. Only when the poli-

cies of religious institutions infringe directly upon government or state policy are their actions called into question.

"So, Lightningbolt, do not depend upon people or organizations to tell you who you are or who Mother Life is. Live your own Life. Think your own thoughts. They are valid and belong to you. Do you believe that your Mother Earth is dead matter, Lightningbolt?"

"No way!" he answered emotionally.

"Earth is Alive, and Births all Life on Earth," Estcheemah assured him.

Leaving had not been that easy, but he had a chance to work. It was now a week since he'd said good-bye to Estcheemah, and he was feeling a little lonely. Standing above the reservoir under construction and looking down into the deep cut he was making in the Earth, he wondered what his Life was all about.

Lightningbolt was building a dam for Elmer Kline, a farmer who lived only five miles from Estcheemah. The old Caterpillar he drove was nothing but squeals and clattering iron. It was not the first dam he had bulldozed. The work was boring and dirty and he didn't like it much. He'd pitched his tent a hundred yards from the work site among some young cottonwood trees. Now, he strolled around and studied his world. The sunset cast soft oranges and pinks over the land. The colors made everything emerge from the shadow and stand out differently than he'd ever seen before.

He sat down on his lawn chair and studied the sunset. The talk he'd had with Estcheemah had left him thinking—especially what she'd said about fear.

"It is not easy being a woman and living alone," she had said to him. "I have had to live alone for years. Yes, I have known fear. And I have known triumph. Would you like to hear of my journey to Canada? I am sure that I was never so afraid as I was then."

"I certainly would," he answered enthusiastically.

"First, I need to tell you about how we traveled from place to place in those days, with no maps and no roads," Estcheemah explained. "Travel has always been important for all Native Peoples. In this way we carried on trade, exchanged news and information, and kept up with what was happening in our families.

"Native People today have come to believe that anyone who is not specifically part of a band or Tribe is always thought of as foreign. This is very far from the truth. It has always been the rule—not the exception—for us to marry people outside our Tribe. We Native People have always been completely aware of what happens when people become too intermarried within a Tribe.

"Well, then, how did people get around in early America? And how did these travelers know where to go?

"They went to the Singers, the carriers of the Journey Songs. Although these Singers are always associated with the Medicine people, they should never be confused with the Healers. While it is true that there were Healers who were also Singers, most Singers were traders, not Medicine people.

"The story of Sacajawea, another woman who traveled alone, is a very important one. She was the person who guided the Lewis and Clark expedition from 1804 to 1806. Although

Sacajawea was no Singer, she's a perfect example of how people knew how to get around then. Sacajawea would never have completed her journey to the Lodges of the Mandan of the Dakotas, or have been successful on her return journey home to her own Bannack people of western Montana, without knowing her Journey Song. These two places were separated by seven hundred and fifty-three miles of the wildest, most dangerous land imaginable.

"The journey for Sacajawea and the men she guided was perilous at best. Lewis and Clark's famous journal talks of their hardship and how hazardous the expedition was for them. Sacajawea's amazing presence seems to have been forgotten or completely ignored by many armchair scholars when they read about that ordeal. They do not seem to understand or appreciate how incredibly important she was to the success of that journey.

"None of the men she led had to tend to a small child as she did. And none of them had the least inkling about what lay ahead of them—only Sacajawea. However, this is never said out loud by the scholars. The opposite is the case—she is always demeaned.

"And yet, whatever hardships were incurred by the men must have been doubly felt by the only woman present. Whatever bravery was shown, Sacajawea demonstrated even greater valor and bravery. For instance, when one of Lewis and Clark's river boats was overturned in high winds, it was Sacajawea who swam and gallantly saved all the documents from floating down the river. And she did this while also saving her child from drowning.

"As the party had not brought along a doctor, it was Sacajawea who healed their illnesses and tended to their wounds. In addition to being their guide, she was also their interpreter and acted as diplomat when people of other Tribes were met. And she was a friend to everyone on the expedition.

"In the early 1800s, things were just a bit different than they are in present-day America. The primitive trails and roads that connected the new states and territories of the United States were crude or almost nonexistent.

"It was not uncommon to be met by thieves. I once read an account of a journey in early Massachusetts in which a traveler wrote: 'Our party was severely set upon while we were on our way to Boston. Our women were raped by scoundrels and they took our every possession!' At that time, a journey of a very short distance of twenty-five miles took an incredible amount of preparation.

"And if this is what it was like in the 'civilized' part of the early United States, imagine what hardships and dangers existed for travelers in the wilderness areas. For example, if you were to go on a journey in those days—even on the best of roads—you would very quickly discover that you were entirely on your own.

"There was no established coin—the U.S. dollar did not yet exist.

"There were no convenient blacksmiths. If your wagon broke down, you were left to your own devices.

"There was no place to buy parts or materials. You had to use whatever was at hand.

"There were no stores where you could buy whatever you needed. If you didn't bring it with you, or if your stores were lost, stolen, or spoiled, that was that. You were dependent on what you could hunt and the plants you could gather along the way.

"If you became sick, there were no doctors, no medicines, and no inns to rest at.

"Above all, most people didn't have a map of the area they planned to travel through. Even if they'd been able to find one, they probably couldn't have afforded it.

"In those days, maps were handmade, very costly, and only accurate if the very best of mapmakers had created them. Yet, even the finest of maps had their faults. People who possessed maps owned a very valuable item—which meant, of course, that only the extremely rich could afford them. And asking for directions along the way was hit or miss. The average Americans you'd meet on your journey couldn't tell you what the country was like more than twenty miles beyond their homes.

"Given all these hazards, you can see how very important Sacajawea was to Lewis and Clark! She knew where to go and how to return because she had very carefully learned her Journey Song.

"Among the Native People of early America, it was a highly select group of people who came to be called the Singers. They were also known as the Ants, or the Rememberers. These were the people who carried the Journey Songs.

"The best way to understand what an Ant was is to compare them to the traveling poets of the Middle Ages. These bards, or troubadours, or mimers, which means 'Rememberers,' were carefully educated and trained to sing tens of thousands of words of poetry. They were the carriers of news and information, and the preservers of myth, legend, and the history of their people. While not Healers, or priestesses and priests, themselves, they were treasure houses of knowledge and were held in the highest esteem by all—from the most powerful to the poorest.

"Far too often, the Native American is shown as primitive rather than knowledgeable and sophisticated, as many of the Chiefs were, and still are. Humans have survived for thousands of years because of their intelligence and sophisticated information, not by their traditions or blind luck.

"The Singers and Medicine people of the Tribes

in the Americas were not ignorant people who had little to say. In fact, the Ants were the recorders who could remember the Fourth World before the Emergence into our more modern Fifth World. Their tradition goes back to the ancient world of the Great Island Cities, with their immense libraries. The keepers of these libraries, the learned scholars of their time, were called Ants.

"Incredible wealth could be had when a person possessed information. The Chiefs who possess information are always the most powerful and wealthy people in their group, and so it was with the Rememberers, the Ants.

"The Ants also had a specialty that no one else had—it was the information of how to journey from one place to another without losing your Life—critical information for any traveler.

"When the modern scholar blunders across the fact that the Ants existed here in America, they always assume, wrongly, that the stories that the Singers told were fiction. Nothing could be further from the truth.

"The Singers would teach their Journey Song, usually called their 'Medicine Song,' to the person who paid them. This song would be memorized. Journey Songs went something like this:

" 'I watch for the Sun, watching into the eyes of Owl Mountain; yes, ever watching.

"I go around Flint Man, yes, watching for his great kettle, yes, watching.'

" 'Flint Man' means places where flint could be mined. This is important when a person relies upon flint for arrowheads. This meant survival.

" 'Great Kettle' means to be oriented to the West.

" 'Looking' would translate as East.

" 'Seeing' means South.

" 'Beholding' means North. To behold means to be physically looking at some place or object up close.

"Of course, what all these different things meant, the symbols of the song, would be disclosed to the person who bought the Journey Song. It was simple, but not too simple, because the Singers knew how to keep their secrets. After all, if this were your livelihood, you would too.

"After travelers learned the entire song from a Singer, they would have memorized a map of the physical terrain of where they wanted to travel.

"These songs were extremely valuable and were sold again and again. But there was a catch in the process, too. If the person who retold the Journey Song left out one tiny detail, the entire song would be worthless, and this happened time and again because most people are incompetent and not trustworthy.

"Some old Cree Singers in Canada once told me: 'Yes, we have our stories of humor. We Singers did not worry too much when a song was resold. The song was usually quickly forgotten or learned all wrong by the person who next bought it. The return journey of the song had to be sung in reverse if a person wanted to get back home. But often, instead of relearning the song backward, to get back to where the song began, it was remembered forward. So we have many jokes about how people sang themselves forward when they needed to sing themselves backward, and became hopelessly lost.'

"Singers and Ants not only learned Journey Songs, they also learned tens of thousands of lines of the songs of the Belts of the Butterflies. These Sacred Belts held the history of the people.

"This kind of tribal history is seldom about local tribal myth or history. Rather it is the history of the beginning of the world. Much of the local histories are fragments of the greater stories known to the Singers."

166

Estcheemah went on to tell him of her Medicine Journey nine hundred miles north into Canada.

"Winnonah, Edda, and Cholis Crow-Mountain were being sent north to marry. Frank Courshane, an Ojibwa, had paid thirty head of horses for the young women. Winnonah was fourteen years old. Edda was sixteen, and Cholis was nineteen. They were Lakotah.

"I had to sell everything to afford the journey. After Night Arrow Woman's death I sold her house and land to buy four horses. My journey's price was four horses.

"The adventure was not boring, which I'd thought it might be. I had believed that since I did not speak Lakotah, it was going to be a grueling journey.

But in a few weeks I began to understand my female companions. The young women were playful and very friendly, excited that they were going to be wives of a rich husband. The two men guiding us, Horn Arrow and Hat Stone, were Canadian Ojibwas. They were both old and remained aloof, only speaking when it was necessary.

"We planned to make six major stops. Hat Stone, the younger of the two men, led eight head of horses. These were our trading horses.

"Hat Stone rode the ninth horse, and two more horses made up the wagon team. Only two days from the starting point, one of the riding horses developed a limp and had to be shot. This left us seven horses to trade—eight, actually, because Hat Stone's horse was to be traded, too. These horses

167

were very important. Not one of us possessed
a penny.

"We stopped by a creek to camp. Hat Stone
approached us and sat down at our fire. He had
been about three hours behind us that day.

" 'There trouble,' he said in his broken English,
a language we all understood to one degree or
another. 'Boy man come. Three. They want
horse, maybe four. We, me old man, say no.
Trouble. Boy man say buy, me say no. Boy man
have gun, maybe five gun. Poke gun in stomach.
Me afraid. Now come. Boy man take horse.
Maybe kill. Me no know.'

"We became frightened. We were far from any
help. Three men with guns wanting horses was an
old story of terror for Indian women.

"We held a meeting together, still using
English. It was decided that we would hide in the
bottom of the wagon. The following day Horn Arrow
covered us with our tent canvas and we resumed
our journey.

"It was incredibly hot beneath the canvas. We
had to keep lifting up the edges of the tent canvas
to get some air. It must have been about ten in
the morning when three cowboys rode up to our
group. We could hear Hat Stone speaking with them.

" 'No trade,' Hat Stone said flatly.

"A gun was fired. We thought that Hat Stone
had been killed. Winnonah was shaking with
fear. We heard more sounds, mostly the sound
of the hooves of horses, then there was silence.
Suddenly we heard the horses leaving. We huddled
together, sweating and feeling terror. When Horn
Arrow lifted the canvas, Winnonah began to sob.
I could not move.

" 'It now good,' Hat Stone said. I began to cry
when I heard his voice.

"The men explained what had happened.
The youngest of the cowboys had pulled his gun
and fired at Hat Stone's head; the bullet missed.

"The other men became angry with their young

companion and warned him. The boy held the
gun on Horn Arrow and Hat Stone while the
older men selected the horses they wanted. They
took five—the best five, of course.

" 'We heap lucky,' Hat Stone explained. 'No
hurt girls. Heap plenty blanket. Much heap
things. Now go.'

"We all felt very lucky. But we also knew that
our journey wasn't going to be without hardship.
We had fewer horses to trade for food and parts
for the wagon if we needed them.

"In fact, it was impossible with three horses.

With nine the journey would have been hard. With three, we knew we would go hungry. The wagon was old and could break down at any time. Only white men could fix the wagon. Each time this happened it meant a horse, maybe two.

"We were solemn. That night I went off by myself and unrolled my Pipe, the one that Night Arrow Woman had given to me to use until I had my own. A borrowed Pipe is called a Borrowed Child, or sometimes a Borrowed Flower. I was to bury this Medicine Pipe once I had my own.

"Holding Night Arrow Woman's Pipe made me feel sorrow. I loved her so much. The Pipe brought me many memories. I filled the Pipe with the little bit of tobacco I had—it was not much. I had only enough for about half a Pipe.

"I cried and prayed, trying everything I could to be as silent as possible. After about an hour I looked up from my Pipe and I saw my new family all sitting around me, about thirty paces away. The women were crying. I had not heard them.

" 'Here tobacco,' Hat Stone said from where he sat. He and Horn Arrow were sitting together about twelve paces from the women. I held out my hand and he brought me the tobacco. The bag he placed in my hand was full, enough tobacco for the entire journey.

"I knew that Hat Stone was a smoker. Now he would have no tobacco. I wondered what to do. No one had told me what to do in such a situation, so for the time being I sat in silence.

"The following morning I offered to give half the tobacco back. Hat Stone readily accepted the tobacco. I asked him where his Medicine Pipe was.

" 'Die,' he answered, showing sadness in his eyes. 'Tears in ground. Gone. No more. Government maybe shoot me. Me afraid. Family afraid. White people shoot quick.'

"The authorities on Reservations were not subtle with the carriers of Medicine Pipes. The so-called Old Way was forbidden.

"Five days later we had our first breakdown. The worst that could happen, happened—a wheel broke. Eight days later we had our new wheel, but now Hat Stone rode with Horn Arrow in our wagon.

"Our food was gone and we suffered through our first two days of hunger. The third day we stopped by a stream and caught fish. Hat Stone and Horn Arrow made nets from the willows. This was a difficult task. Then Cholis was given one net and I was given the other.

"We had to walk toward each other, moving the willow nets ahead of us in the shallow stream. We began our walk two hundred paces apart. As we got closer to one another, I could actually see the fish fleeing from my net. Soon we had trapped about one hundred really good-sized fish between the two nets.

"Now it was the task of Winnonah and Edda to catch the fish. Hat Stone and Horn Arrow helped. Winnonah and Edda fell down more than once. We all had a wonderful laugh!

"Some of the fish got past our nets, but not

170

very many. Not one of us knew how to smoke or dry the fish, though. The men had never seen it done; they only knew of the nets. All we could do was stay there for two days and eat fish. Then we had to move on. The cooked fish we took with us lasted only until noon the following day—then we had nothing again.

"Our next fast lasted for nearly five days. Then we came to a ranch and Hat Stone went to these people to beg for food. Those people would not give us anything, but they would trade. We traded away all of our best—our two shawls, all of our beaded pouches, one pair of moccasins, our three good blankets, and all of our safety pins.

"Even then these people were not generous, although they had many cattle. We suffered through the next week with the horrible-tasting beans and flour they traded us. To this day I don't much like biscuits because of that.

"Lucky for us, we met two young hunters six days later. These two young Dakotah boys gave us most of their food. We now had five rabbits to eat, and they gave us both hindquarters of their deer. We were so thankful.

"We women wanted to stop and dry the meat from those hindquarters but the men would not wait. That was a pity—within a few days most of the deer spoiled and we were hungry again.

"Because our luck was so bad, Horn Arrow decided that he would go straight to the Stone Crees he knew to be camped on a creek he called Shining One, in Saskatchewan.

"When we got there only six of the deer hunters were left. By then, we had not eaten for seven days. Those six men hunted for us and we women dried the meat. Because of this we were able to complete our journey. It was lucky for us those hunters had stayed behind.

"Still, this was not without its consequences. Winnonah and Edda were both raped by those hunters. All six of the men took turns with the women. Cholis and I fought them off, but not without hurt. We were both slapped about, but not beaten. We were so fortunate for that!

"The promise Hat Stone had made to give the team of horses to the hunters was forgotten when he learned that Winnonah and Edda had been raped. Hat Stone insisted that the rapists had already received their pay. Suddenly, knives and guns were pulled. The tension was high. Two of the men threatened to take back the food. For a while we thought there would be death and blood, but the men backed down and left.

"By the time I had come this far on the journey, I was very seriously wondering about my decision to go to Canada—that is for sure! But finally, things eased up some, and the journey was no longer so hard for us. We made camp with the Swampy Cree and waited for the man called Frank Courshane. As it turned out, he was not only a very rich man—he was also incredibly kind. He sold two horses to pay for all of the debts we had made with the Cree. Then he asked Hat Stone to accompany me to the camps of the Manitou Dreamers—my destination. The last part of my journey was not long, only eight days' ride."

"From the first minute I was in the Dreamers' camp I felt very uneasy. Hat Stone had left immediately the following morning and I was very alone.

"In those days there was a custom among the Manitou Dreamers that no longer exists. It was a certain Woman's Circle called the Woman Pipe Circle. Joining it was easy. But leaving it was very complicated. If you failed in their Lodge, you had to marry into their Tribe. I was determined not to fail.

"The Manitou accepted me and I soon became interested in my new land. I forgot the hardships of my journey and became involved in the lives of the people I now lived with.

Compared to where I'd come from, these people
lived with great ease.

"In America in the early 1900s the Reservations
were little more than mud and hovels of disease.
Alcohol was the comforter, and it gave the people
their new Dream. There were drinkers here in
Canada, too, but not as many. The bush was near
and there was still escape. Yet all the
information I had learned from Night Arrow
Woman had not prepared me for the hardships that
awaited me in Canada."

"It is very important for you to understand
the immense problems that faced the Indians of
North America. Between the years of 1820 and 1922
life meant only survival for the Native People of
Mexico, the United States, and Canada. During
these years we were being hunted down, rounded
up, and ruthlessly destroyed.

"Much is known about the cruelty of the military.
But their atrocities pale in the light of the quiet
extreme cruelty of the government bureaucrats.
And yet, nothing was more insidious or hidden than
the cruelty meted out by the religious. These people
used every means of fiendish coercion to get
what they wanted.

"The rapist, the murderer, the greed-directed
businessman, and the human looking for a slave
also punished and destroyed the Indians of the
Americas. Millions were killed working in the
mines of Mexico and South America, while tens
of thousands were butchered for their lands.

"Yet, with all this outrage and killing, even
more countless numbers were destroyed through
disease and starvation. The Indian had been interned
and imprisoned, and many of the Reservations had
become little more than concentration camps."

"Remember this about the American Indian as you hear my story about the Zero Chief Tomahseeasah.

"Through all this, the Zero Chiefs endured.

"By 1850 the exploiters had enjoyed three hundred years of organized plunder of the Americas. All of the surviving Zero Chiefs had learned that the white people could not be trusted—not under any circumstance whatsoever. And hundreds of the more educated Native People of Central America and Mexico had fled north and were hiding among almost every Tribe.

"While there was no official bounty on the heads of the Chiefs, all Native People understood that any Chief was a threat to the survival of their Tribe. You must remember that it was a common belief among whites in those days to think that the only good Indian was a dead Indian. The consequence of this was that everyone of any great importance went into hiding. When this decision was breached through accident or folly, there was always an instant response—death and suffering.

"This is the reason that we Zero Chiefs have remained hidden. But times have changed. Now our threat is our silence.

"Tomahseeasah, like the other Zero Chiefs, was searching for ways of teaching the people, while continuing to remain hidden so she would not be punished or lose her life. She had witnessed a number of gruesome examples of what could and had gone wrong, and she did everything she could to not make the same mistakes others had.

"Now, I will tell you of the final fiend that helped bring about the torture and death of the people. These were the conformist Indians who sold out their families for reward.

"The problems of the Chiefs were always complicated. But the most prevalent of the terrors was being betrayed by our own people. Some of these people knew that the Chiefs were terrified of being visible and they used this advantage for blackmail.

"The women who did not know Tomahseeasah thought she was a threat to their lives. And they kept trying to undermine her. Of course, they were also jealous of her extreme beauty.

"The consequence of this was the invention of the all-woman's camp. Because no men were physically present in the camp, the women felt more secure."

"Birth and Cleanliness, according to Tomahseeasah, are the most Holy of all responsibilities that can be learned by young women. This is the First Wisdom, and is represented by the Medicine Shield of the Southeast. On it is a circle of wildflowers.

"Learning of our Earth Mother's Garden and the Healing of the People is the Second Wisdom for the females to learn. This Teaching has its shield, too. The picture painted on it is the Sun and Moon Corn Kachinas. This was called the Southwest Shield.

"Learning of the Medicines and the Sacred Medicine Wheel is the Third Wisdom for the young female to pursue. This Shield shows a Medicine Wheel painted in Lightning with a Rose at its center. This Shield was known as the Northwest Shield.

"Teaching and Bringing Forth Information is the Fourth Wisdom for the young woman to possess. This is represented by the Discipline Shield. It shows the Hands of Counting—a picture of many hands indicating the Numbers. This Northeast Shield was highly prized by all the students of Tomahseeasah.

"There were many other beautiful things and wonders that awaited the young woman who visited the camp of Tomahseeasah.

"There were Lodges of Painting that were so

beautiful they brought tears to the women who saw them. These were set up at special times like the changes of the seasons. And there was also the incredibly lovely Medicine Lodge of the Woman of the Moon. No other Painted Lodge was so miraculous or enchanting.

"For years I had heard glowing stories from Night Arrow Woman about Tomahseeasah, Nisharamah, and the Circle of Women in the camps of the Dreamers. But there was one piece of information she left out. Night Arrow Woman failed to make me understand that all her information was secondhand and very old!

"Night Arrow Woman had never known Tomahseeasah personally. What my teacher knew of Tomahseeasah was what her own teacher, Nisharamah, had told her. Everything I had heard and thought still existed had been gone for sixty-five years! That is hard to believe when you're as young as I was. But I should not get too far ahead of my story.

"By the time the women Chiefs finally spoke of the Medicine Wheel, I had been in the Manitou Lodge for almost a year. My immediate teacher was an angry woman who would tolerate no mistakes. I would boil with anger inside when my teacher would refer to me as the Little Soldier.

I hated soldiers—even the word.

"My friend, Nahseeomah, and I had been given the task of caring for the potatoes, all twenty acres of them. While I toiled at the boring task with her, she made me understand that both of us were little more than slaves.

" 'All the teachers are cruel,' Nahseeomah explained, as we rested in the shade of a large poplar at the edge of the potato field. 'When I came here, I thought I would learn of Healing.' Her young, pretty face was drawn and showed a deep fear. 'I was told, as you were, to call our teachers only by their Medicine Names. Do you know how those Names translate?'

"I shook my head.

" 'Simple,' Nahseeomah explained. 'One, Two, Three, Four, and Five—simply that. They are supposed to be Medicine Names, but they are not. All the original teachers are dead. There was a split in this camp sixty-five years ago, did you know that?'

" 'What do you mean?' I asked; my heart felt sick. I knew before Nahseeomah answered that I had made a terrible mistake.

" 'The real teachers all went away,' Nahseeomah cried. 'Oh, sister, you are like me, you wanted to—'

"I grabbed Nahseeomah's hand and held it tight. 'Go on,' I urged. 'All of it, I am ready to listen.'

"Nahseeomah shook her head. 'It's awful. I do not know the answers. All that I know is that the original teachers went west to the Arrow Red Deer.'

"I learned that Red Deer was in the province of Alberta.

"I was feeling trapped and horrified that I might have to remain as a slave with this people.

" 'All the teachers left here sixty-five years ago,' Nahseeomah sobbed. 'These people, they know nothing. I have been here for two years now and I have learned nothing but that I am a slave.'

"During the remainder of the day I worked side by side with my companion and learned more.

"A man by the name of Antelope Head had taken charge of the original group, on the pretense that he was the representative of the Canadian government. At the time there was much trouble between the government and the people of the Manitou. Antelope Head was an aggressive politician, a good arbitrator, and an excellent speaker.

"Because of his efforts with the government, he became the Chief and from there everything went to pieces. The politician cared only for himself and his friends. He asked the Zero Chief, Tomahseeasah, and all of her apprentices and friends to leave the Reservation.

"My mind was filled with my problem, and my sister's struggle to get free of her toil. It was hard to understand that all of my information from Night Arrow Woman was so old! Sixty-five years is a long time!

"The great Zero Chief, Tomahseeasah, wasn't even alive! She had died years before! Can you imagine traveling as far as I had to visit a dead woman?

"I further learned that Nisharamah had been part of the original camp that had been in the land of the Manitou, but that she had been forced to leave by Antelope Head.

"Tomahseeasah had been an old woman when Nisharamah was still young, and she had gone west with her teacher to be part of the Great Camp at Red Deer.

"How would I now get west? Was there still a camp to the West? I could not afford to run around half of Canada trying to find a camp that had existed sixty-five years before. My heart weighed like a stone.

"During the next two weeks, Nahseeomah and I moved into one tent together. We called the tent the Lodge of Tomahseeasah.

"Asking questions that had anything to do with the camp of Tomahseeasah was forbidden. The women who called themselves One, Two, Three, Four, and Five possessed much knowledge; however, their knowledge was not new information to me. I had already learned what these women knew from Night Arrow Woman.

"Two months after we moved into our Lodge, Nahseeomah married a man named Assinopohn, which means 'Shining Stone.' Things moved very fast after this. Nahseeomah invited me to move in with her and her new husband—not as a second wife but to escape the Circle of Pipe Women.

"Because Nahseeomah had failed, all was fine with her moving, but the Circle of Pipe Women did not consider me to have failed and so trouble brewed for weeks. The trouble ended when I met Moheegun.

"Assinopohn and Moheegun, which means 'Wolf,' were the best of friends. Assinopohn had a few cattle that he herded, and Wolf was an expert hunter and trapper. I married Moheegun. And now that I had also failed, all was well."

"That's an amazing story," said Lightningbolt. "I never realized you had been through so much. Wow, that was some journey."

"As you can see," she said, smiling, "you are not the only one who has leaped before you looked. I did that, too." She laughed. "And my first leap was a long one."

When the teachers of any culture have been forced to hide, and are hounded by those in power, the ignorance of the apprentice can make the teacher vulnerable. Each time the teachers disclose their secrets, they open themselves to outside attack from fanatics. Also, when the student does not possess sufficient discernment and honesty, the teacher is in potential danger.

Estcheemah had to reach a decision within herself. The trust and hope she had in Lightningbolt needed to be tested before she could respect it.

The reason for Estcheemah's concern was that she was a woman. While it may be true that great male teachers have had their hardships, the adversities are much more severe for the great female teachers.

Estcheemah had been accused of being a witch. For a woman to live alone and to be called a witch was extremely dangerous. More than once in Estcheemah's life she'd had to physically protect herself from religious fanatics.

The very fact that Lightningbolt had heard that Estcheemah was a witch had to be overcome and defeated by his teacher. Her only hope lay in teaching him to respect himself and to respect the subtle and powerful information she had to offer him.

Lightningbolt would also have to overcome his own attitudes and ignorance. Survival is an important factor in the selection of a powerful student. The student must remain loyal despite coercion and the possible offers and rewards of money. He would also have to battle against the enormous pressures to conform exerted by his family and his culture.

He would have to become aware of his new position with his teacher and his community. He, too, would have to learn to protect himself from the overzealous in his community.

The protection of information is of the utmost importance. But in the beginning, the student does not understand its true value. Estcheemah would have to teach him how to discriminate and choose.

Estcheemah faced the single most powerful of all challenges known to teachers the world over: finding an apprentice. Her entire genius must be brought to bear to discover a student who would endure.

The challenge of teaching becomes even more acute when the culture that surrounds the teacher is nonsupportive or aggressive toward the teacher. Knowledge is thought to be dangerous by those who fear that it will discredit their beliefs or positions.

An overeager student was not what she wanted either. Lightningbolt would have to learn patience. He would have to show her his inward strength.

Estcheemah, like many of the Flower Soldiers before her, had been forced to keep her information secret. In the past, a few of the Zero Chiefs had lost their lives because of the ignorance and disloyalty of their students.

Estcheemah would have to build a confidence between herself and Lightningbolt. She would test him often and note his moods and changes. How intelligent was he? Was he as courageous as she hoped? Would he trust himself enough to learn? Could he be loyal to her?

The more sophisticated the information she gave him, the more she would test his ability to understand it. Her challenge was to stimulate and enliven his interest and thinking.

Questions and answers always pass between teacher and student. But it is how these questions are understood between them that makes the difference between victory and defeat. Estcheemah did not want a student who would memorize information. Such a person was doomed from the beginning. She would have to teach him to think for himself. Only in this way would he become a Flower Soldier.

Estcheemah made Lightningbolt comfortable before she spoke to him about why she had chosen him as her student.

"The milk we drink while we are young creates our future," she began. "Lightningbolt, what I say to you now is the food, the milk, for your future. But it will be you who has to make the choices, not me.

"Choice is also food that will nourish you in your present, no matter what that present is. Choose your food well, because it can either make you strong or sicken you. What you do with what you have makes all the difference. Question and prepare your information and the choices you make.

"Close your eyes and listen. The voice you hear is that of a woman, your teacher. You must test all that is given to you by this voice. You must observe all that this woman does while she teaches you, do you understand?"

"Yes," he answered, without opening his eyes.

"While you have your eyes closed you can hear Wehomah, the Wind," she said, moving her mouth closer to his ear.

"A teacher can never be a substitute for a lover, and never will be. I am your teacher and your chance to battle every fear you possess.

"In your war, it will not be my hand that will wound or heal you. Only your hand can raise a weapon against you. It will be by your anger at your Self that you will be crippled. So, I would be mindful of your power to do that.

"I have chosen you because you are a Breed person. You have already been given everything you will need for your war. Be ready to confront your ignorance and loneliness. These can blind you and tear your world to pieces. These things can destroy the best of humans.

"Confront your every belief, for these will lead you into ruin and cause you Self disgust. Belief is your enemy.

"While you move between your many worlds, you will be a Diplomat, a Warrior, a Healer, and a Teacher. Now, open your eyes and look at me," she commanded him.

"One day you will sit as I sit, but you will never be me. You will be equal in age to me, but can you equal me in weaponry or skill in battle?

"You will battle to heal the wounded human when you have learned to sit where I am now sitting.

"I command you to survive. As a Breed person, you have what is needed to survive. But whether you endure depends upon you.

"We Flower Soldiers are like the clouds in the sky. We appear and we disappear. We appear among the people, then disappear like the clouds. Be thunder, be lightning. Be a terrible wind, be a calm breeze.

"Be as noisy as the clouds while they form their presence. When you thunder, remember first to flash your lightning of warning. Survive as a human who will leave a legacy of lightning and nourishing rain. Those who learn from you will be a rainbow. That can be their destiny if they choose it. But never seek to have people understand you. How is it possible to understand a cloud?"

THE TEACHINGS OF THE ZERO CHIEFS
CHEEMAH (FIRE)

THE ZERO CHIEFS

The Zero Chiefs were the People who sought to solve the riddle of the Language of Space and Time. They would also discover the exact measurement of the Earth, the Moon, and our Solar system while they pondered the question of distance.

Few humans, in our modern world, appreciate the incredible depth and far-reaching effect the discovery of Mathematics held for Humanity.

In 5000 B.C., the Temple of Flowers had this to say about Mathematics: "With Mathematics we humans can measure Infinity's grand scale. We can perceive Infinity's smallest Measure. We can comprehend the limitless space of the Sphere of our Creatress and Creator, WahKahn and SsKwan, when we see into the Window of their swift-moving light. The mystery of Time is at our fingertips. Such a wondrous Present! Will we ever understand its Beauty and Power?"

To be able to calculate Time and Distance and to understand the sophistication of the Circle, the Square, Volume, and Movement brought immense happiness to our Ancients.

"What is weight?" they asked. "What is Pressure? What is Force and Counterforce? What happens logarithmically? How fast does our Planet traverse Space and orbit our Sun?" These were the questions they asked.

THE MATHEMATICS WHEEL

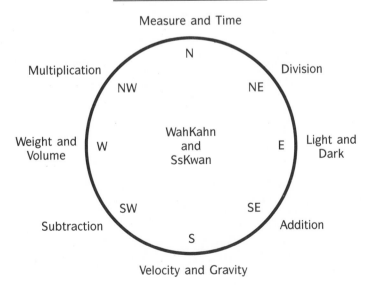

There has been no discovery known to Humans that can equal THE DISCOVERY OF MATHEMATICS. There has never been a Discovery, in History, that has been more beneficial or influential to Humans than MATHEMATICS.

It must be remembered that the discovery of the ZERO is equal in importance to, or even greater than, the discovery of chemistry, metallurgy, electricity, or atomic energy because, without the Zero, these sciences would not be known.

Our Ancients viewed MATHEMATICS as the most Holy of all Presents given to humanity. The Language of our Creatress and Creator continues to be Mathematics.

In the Medicine Wheel below, ancient Mayan Numbers are shown. A dot means One, a bar means Five.

OLD WHEEL

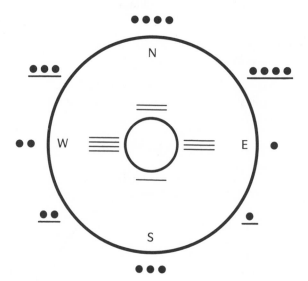

Surely the voice of WahKahn and SsKwan is Mathematics. No voice in Time is greater than the voice of Energy and Substance, and the Language of Time and Substance is Mathematics.

Before we can appreciate or understand the Medicine Wheels, we must understand the immense Love and Devotion that our Zero Chiefs had for Creation's Words—Mathematics.

The Symbol for Mathematics is the Circle.
The Circle is the Great Twin-ness of Creation's Energy of Life and Meaning.
The Medicine Wheel is the Zero.
The Zero is Holy.
The Zero is WahKahn and SsKwan.

When the Zero Chiefs of ancient times discovered the Mathematical Zero they could, for the first time, comprehend the mysteries of the Eternal.

The Zero Chiefs asked about our Mother Earth, and about Endless Space. They asked about our Sun and about the Moon, the Planets and about Sacred Time.

And they asked about Life.

What is Time and Creation? What does endless Space mean to the human? What is our Sun? What are the Planets within Space? What is this great, turning Medicine Wheel—our Milky Way?

The Creatress and Creator answered these questions through the Language of Mathematics.

The Zero Chiefs had these words:

The Sacred Zero has been given to us humans; we are most thankful. Without the understanding of the Zero, there exists no Mathematics. The Zero is the Spirit of all of Creation. The Zero is WahKahn and SsKwan.

From the Eternal, which is Time, and from all Energies, which are Space, all of everything was born from the Zero.

The Zero is Creation and is Mathematics.

The Womb of Creation is the Sacred Zero.

The Eternal is the Sacred Zero. The Sacred Zero is Sacred Mother and Sacred Father; this is WahKahn and SsKwan.

The Sacred Zero gives Birth to all Numbers, and all Numbers are everything born to Life.

The perfect Zero is all Energies and Births, all of everything Created.

In the words of Estcheemah: "Our ancients sought to know where they were within Time and Space. To discover this, they had to know where our Earth is in relationship to our Universe.

"The measuring of Time, our twenty-four-hour day, and the circumference of our Mother Earth, was a work of devotion and love."

Today, most people believe they know where they are in relationship to Life and Creation, but in reality they have no notion of where they are!

It took hundreds of years and an enormous amount of effort to discover that our Earth is round and circumnavigates our Sun.

Yes, our wondrous Planet, Mother Earth, who has Birthed us all, turns in the Void, within the fact of WahKahn—endless Space.

Yes, our Mother Earth is part of the four spiral arms of our galaxy, the "Egg of the Eternal," the "Milky Way."

190

Yet, with all that was physically discovered about endless Space, our Galaxy, Time, our Sun, our Earth, the Moon, and the Planets, the question remained: Who and what are Humans?

What is our relationship to all this wonder that we perceive as Creation?

These questions and more were asked within our Kivas, and from these questions the Medicine Wheels were born.

Estcheemah, the Zero Chief, was a teacher of Life. She also spoke of the transformation of Death, as had all Zero Chiefs.

Because of Estcheemah's words I, too, began to ask the question of who I was.

The Discipline of the Flower Soldiers

Our Zero Chiefs have said that several thousand years ago there were islands in the Pacific that were known as WahKahn and SsKwan. They were named after our Creatress Mother and Creator Father. Existing ruins in Central America and South America were once thriving communities that were colonized by the seafaring peoples from the Great Confederacy of Islands known as WahKahn and SsKwan in the Pacific.

While this history is important and much more needs to be said about it, the subject at hand is the Medicine Wheels; consequently, for now we will focus upon the teachings of the Sacred Wheels of our Zero Chiefs.

With the discovery of the Zero and pure Mathematics by the people of the Pacific Islands, the Discipline of the Zero Chiefs was born.

The evolution of learning brought about by Mathematics helped the Zero Chiefs separate what we presently call "the abstract" world from the world of "measurable substance." This discovery on the part of our Zero Chiefs made the study of Mathematics into a Science of Life.

For the first time in human history, there now existed a Language that could describe the Invisible. The abstract world of numbers and science could be studied and comprehended by means of Mathematics.

All of humanity, especially the Flower Soldiers, became enormously enthralled with the Science of Numbers and the makeup of our physical Universe. The Mysteries of Time, Weight and Measure, Light and Dark, were slowly unraveled by these dedicated humans who held fast to their Discipline.

From the Discipline of the Zero Chiefs came an enormous appreciation for Mother Life and for all of Creation. They would say:

"What is this wondrous breath you have shared with us, Sacred Mother Creation? We are so thankful that we are alive and can perceive your Beauty."

What is the Medicine Wheel itself? Why does it have the shape it does? How does the Medicine Wheel relate to the Square and the Triangle?

All students of Mathematics know that the Triangle and the Square are instantly part of the Circle the moment the Circle is created. The Circle is completion. The Circle is wholeness. The Circle—the Medicine Wheel—was seen as a complete entity.

The Zero Chiefs say that from the Sacred Zero, Time and Space were Born. The Zero is Birthing; it is the Creatress Mother.

Time is in perfect Union with the Zero. Time is the Creator Father. From this Union of the Zero with Time—or Space and Time—all Energies are Born. The center of the

atom itself is Energy. The Zero Chiefs called this "Continuing."

Light and Darkness are Born from Energy. From Light and Darkness, Substance is Born and is continually being Birthed. This they called "Binding."

The Zero is Eternal, and from the Zero all Numbers are Born. The Medicine Wheel is always Complete, no matter what its Numbers may be.

Within the Wheel, Numbers birth Numbers.

Within the Wheel, Numbers are Deathless.

Within the Wheel, Numbers are Reborn.

There were many kinds of Medicine Wheels. Some of them represented human interaction, some represented Mathematical principles in Life, and some represented the study of the human Presence of Mind.

The Medicine Wheel reveals the relationship and integration of all things created.

The manner in which the Medicine Wheels integrated Knowledge provided an easy way to learn and remember information.

Numbers and their relationships began to take on all kinds of meaning for the Zero Chiefs. The Numbers themselves were Symbols representing all parts of Life.

Answers to the great riddle of Time, and the measure of our Earth and Planets, did not come swiftly or easily. Two and a half thousand years were to pass before the Sacred Earth Count and the Great Long Counts of Time and Space were known to the Zero Chiefs.

The Zero Chiefs desired to learn as much as they could about Life and the Human Self. Although the term "psychology" was not known to them, they studied the human Mind, calling this science the study of the Presence of Mind. The Medicine Wheel that is called the Human Wheel reveals the teachings of the Presence of Mind.

They discovered, by use of the Medicine Wheels, that all humans were deeply integrated with Life and Creation, and that they were not separate from our Creatress and Creator.

The Zero Chiefs had this to say about the Zero and the Sacred Rose, the Symbol of the Creatress, Mother Life.

> *Mother Life is Beauty. She is the Perfectness of Wisdom and Courage. She is Strength and Healing for us Humans. She is the Great Zero, the Medicine Wheel, and the Mother of all things Born.*
> *The Rose is our symbol of that which can be Perfect. She gives us our Seasons and Lives; this is our Perfection.*
> *The Sacred Rose reveals and Shares Balance with all of the Children Born to Her.*
> *The Gentle Petals of Life's Rose, Her Fragrant Bloom, is Mother Life. Her Flowers bring us Healing.*
> *There are the Thorns of the Sacred Rose. These Thorns are the Sword of the Warrioress, that is also Life.*
> *The Sacred Rose is the Symbol of Protection and Decision.*
> *The Creatress Mother is Mother of Life and Mother of Death because She is Perfect Balance.*
> *The Flower Soldier is dedicated to Mother Life. Our symbol is the Sacred Rose.*

Existing side by side with the Zero Chiefs were other Disciplines that had their own triumphs and discoveries. Over many hundreds of years, the names of the Deities evolved from the Numbers of the Earth Count, also known as the Children's Count.

Described and then shown below is one of the most ancient Medicine Wheels. It is called the Children's Count or the Earth Count.

Our children will count,
The children watching
Numbers growing
In ever greater Circles.

The Zero

The Medicine Wheel is the shape of the Zero. The Zero is the symbol and fact of Creation. The Zero Chiefs say that the Zero is not nothing, but is instead Everything.

All of Creation's Children were designed and born from the Sacred Zero, and exist as part of the Zero. All of Creation's Children exist as Numbers within the Medicine Wheel. This is the Children's Count or the Earth Count.

In the Beginning was WahKahn. She is the Creatress Mother and the Great Zero, the Womb that Births All of Existence.

Within instantaneous being was born the SsKwan. He is the Creator Father, and is the Dividing of the Zero.

Creation, the Zero, is perfectly balanced. The Zero is Female and Male, and has designed and Birthed all of Life.

The One

The FirstBorn from The Sacred Zero—the Marriage of WahKahn, the Creatress Mother, and SsKwan, the Creator Father—was One.

The East is the dancer called the Sun.

ONE is the SUN.

The Two

The SecondBorn from the Sacred Zero was Two. The Two exists in the West of the Medicine Wheel, the place of the Coloring of Time.

The West is the dancer called Earth.

TWO is the number for the EARTH.

The Three

The First Children of the Sacred Zero were the Sun and the Earth. One, the Sun, and Two, the Earth, joined together, and from this Union Three was Born.

The grasses are ever singing with the trees, the corn dancers, and the flowers.

THREE is the Number for all PLANTS.

The Four

Time turned the Earth, and the Plants turned the Wheel within shadow and light. One, the Sun, married Three, all Plants, and the first Animals were Born on the Earth.

The Animals are in Circles ever moving with Life.

FOUR is the Number for all ANIMALS.

Creation now had created the First Circle.
East, ONE, the Sun.
West, TWO, the Earth.
South, THREE, the Plants.
North, FOUR, the Animals.

The Five

The FIVE are all HUMANS.

The Five were Born of the First Circle and exist in its Center.

The Humans are sending their voices into the hearts of the Four Directions in celebration of their Lives.

THE CHILDREN'S EARTH COUNT

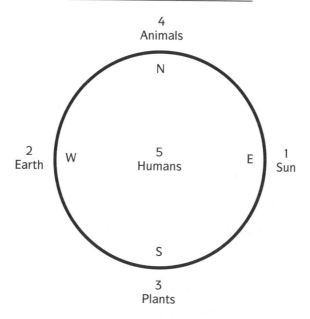

The Six

SIX is the Number for Experiencing the Presence of Life. When the human children of Mother Earth are conscious and Present with the Spirit of Life they are Experiencing the Six.

The Six is called SPIRIT-SPIRIT because all things Born into Substance are Born from Spirit. This we humans learn as we Experience Life. Six Directions make up all Spheres: East, West, South, North, Zenith, and Nadir.

Come, Children, find your dance as Spirits.

Experience your Existence. How will you Choose to See your Life?

The Seven

SEVEN is the Number for the DREAM OF LIFE, for all things that are made within

Beauty, or that are broken and thrown away. We look into our Past and learn of what we have built.

Come, Children, and Build your World Dance.

The Eight

EIGHT is the Number for all Natural Laws and THE CIRCLE OF LAW.

Mother Earth sculpts the Substance and Body of everything that lives with Her Sacred and Natural Laws. The Eight guides the Forming of all that is within the Future, and gives us a way to Reappear each day.

Come, Children, paint your Sculpted Form for your dance.

The Nine

NINE is the Number for the MOON, and for MOVEMENT. The Moon moves the tides of the Earth, and the tidal waters and blood within all Living things.

Come, Children, and dance in the Moonlight.

The Ten

TEN is the Number for PURE INTELLECT and MEASURE. Creation gave humans the power of Reason and Self Choice.

Ten is also the Number of humans' HIGHER SELF, their Sacred Twin. What can give better Measure than this Spirit-Knowing?

Come, Children, have you met your Self and Known Existence?

The Eleven

ELEVEN is the Number for all the STARS. Come, Children, become a Source of Light within your own Life dance.

The Sun is a Star, and all the Stars are Suns.

The Twelve

TWELVE is the Number for all the PLANETS. Come, dancers, orbit your Sacred Self, guiding your Children to Honor Mother Life.

Mother Earth is a special Planet, for She has Birthed you and can Birth all Life.

The Thirteen

THIRTEEN is the Number for WHITE BUFFALO WOMAN. She and Her Male-Twin-Reflection are the Spirit of all Plants.

Every flower, tree, grass, herb, vegetable, and underwater plant is a cell that forms the Great Body and Knowing of White Buffalo Woman and Her Twin.

Children, show the dancers how to dance in the Wild and Healing places.

The Fourteen

FOURTEEN is the Number for SWEET MEDICINE. Sweet Medicine and his Female-Twin-Reflection are the Spirit of all Animals.

Every Animal—that flies, walks, crawls, or swims—is a cell that forms the Great Body and Knowing of Sweet Medicine and His Twin.

Children, teach your elders of the many different ways of Being and Dancing.

The Fifteen

FIFTEEN is the Number for the Sphere of the COLLECTIVE CONSCIOUSNESS OF ALL HUMANS. Every thought ever imagined or acted upon by a human in the past, present, or future, or within the movement of Life, exists within the Great Library of human Imagination and Discovery.

Come, Children of Destiny and Creativity, let your Imaginations be guided by the Sacred and Perfect Balance of the Creatress Mother and the Creator Father.

Teach Humanity how to build in Beauty.

The Sixteen

SIXTEEN is called the Sphere of the GREAT TEACHERS.

The Great Teachers are always Present with Life. They encourage all people to Remember that Life is Holy. Come, dancers, and show Greatness to your Children. Teach them of your Lives.

The Seventeen

SEVENTEEN is the Number for the Sphere of the KACHINAS. The Kachinas are the Powers that form all Symbols, Dreams, and Images.

Come, Children, and place your Painted Masks of the Natural World, your dreams, your dread, your drama, and your healing upon your face. Come, adults, remove the Masks of your culture from your face and Learn.

The Eighteen

EIGHTEEN is the Number for the Sphere of the Shee-nah-meeah, the Balancers of Existence. Within all of Creation, the Eighteen is Absolute JUSTICE. Who will claim to understand Balance? Who will test the action of Time? Justice is the Shee-nah-meeah.

Come, Children, and Remember you were all Born Before. Make your dance, in this your Present, the dance of Honor that you will be proud of within Great Time.

The Nineteen

NINETEEN is the Sphere known as PURE SCIENCE. Pure Science is both Goddess and God. Their Presence is the Design of all Existence, and the Sacred Mathematics of WahKahn and SsKwan.

The Medicine Wheel, the Sacred Earth Count, and all subsequent Wheels, are Mirrors of the magnificent Design of Continuation that has been Created by the Spirit of Pure Science.

Come, Children—look into the Mirror of the Medicine Wheel and discover the Infinite.

The Twenty

TWENTY is COMPLETION. This is the Return to the Great Zero where all things were Born. The Return to WahKahn and SsKwan.

Come, Children of Becoming, where is your Foundation?

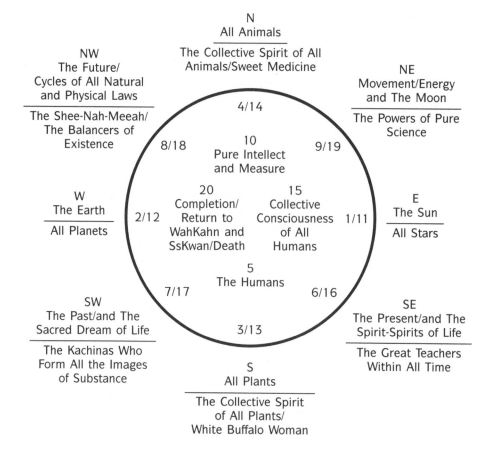

THE EARTH COUNT

N
All Animals

The Collective Spirit of All
Animals/Sweet Medicine

NW
The Future/
Cycles of All Natural
and Physical Laws

The Shee-Nah-Meeah/
The Balancers of
Existence

NE
Movement/Energy
and The Moon

The Powers of Pure
Science

4/14

8/18

10
Pure Intellect
and Measure

9/19

W
The Earth

All Planets

2/12

20
Completion/
Return to
WahKahn and
SsKwan/Death

15
Collective
Consciousness
of All
Humans

1/11

E
The Sun

All Stars

5
The Humans

7/17

6/16

SW
The Past/and The
Sacred Dream of Life

The Kachinas Who
Form All the Images
of Substance

3/13

SE
The Present/and The
Spirit-Spirits of Life

The Great Teachers
Within All Time

S
All Plants

The Collective Spirit
of All Plants/
White Buffalo Woman

Along with the wondrous Earth Count, the Medicine Wheel of the Elements was discovered.

The Medicine Wheel of the Elements

Cheemah is Fire and Light, bringing Life-Source to all growing plants and animals.

Ehahmah is the Earth-Ground bringing all things to Birthing.

Morealah is all Waters bringing the Blood of Life to all things Living.

Wehomah is the Breath of Being; She is the Breath of all things alive. She is the Wind Dancer. Wehomah Breathes our existence.

THE MEDICINE WHEEL OF THE ELEMENTS

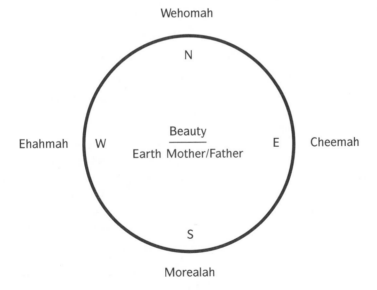

Within a week, the Caterpillar work on the dam was completed and Lightningbolt was ready for more teaching. He met Estcheemah in her garden. The afternoon was unusually hot and the garden smelled sweet. Lightningbolt was lounging in the shade and was not attentive.

"Would you kill a man to learn?" Estcheemah asked casually.

"Kill a man?" He blinked, coming to attention. His face was a sudden mask of mistrust and suspicion.

"You tried to kill one the other day," she said smoothly, "for a cheap necklace. Are you afraid I will send you out to kill someone?"

Lightningbolt looked down, too embarrassed to answer.

"You will have to learn to trust me," she told him. "And I will have to learn to trust you. That is our fact."

The Medicine Woman saw in her mind a beautiful Medicine Wheel she had built many years before. Estcheemah prayed quietly in her mind to Sacred Mother Earth that this young man would persist and outlive his ignorance.

"So our war begins," she said, turning and looking into his eyes. "You will have to endure or you will perish, die away like so many others have and do every day. Will you help yourself to survive?"

"Sure," said Lightningbolt. "I'll really try."

"Look how very simple this Wheel is." Estcheemah smiled, handing him a drawing of a Medicine Wheel. "Observe what the subtlety of this Wheel describes for us. It is incredibly satisfying to know that we humans are more than just pawns in the hands of chance.

"All of our Medicine Wheels reflect the Earth compass. From these Wheels the children and adults not only learned of the Power and Beauty of

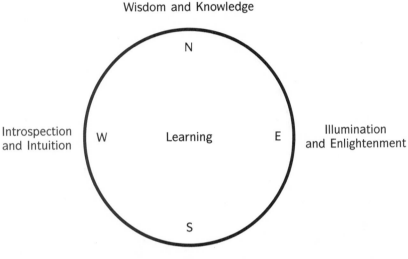

THE POWERS OF THE FOUR DIRECTIONS

Wisdom and Knowledge

N

Introspection
and Intuition

W   Learning   E

Illumination
and Enlightenment

S

Trust and Innocence

the human Self, they also learned how to Count. And they learned of Mathematics.

"The Wheel can become a source of information for the person who is the seeker of Knowledge and Self Power.

"The shape of the Wheel is a very positive and energy-filled symbol that grows in the mind of the person learning. The reason for this is that the Circle is primal to Creation. It is the shape of all things created.

"In the North of the Medicine Wheel you will discover the place of Knowledge and Wisdom. The color of the Wisdom of the North is White.

"The South is represented by its Medicine color of Green or Red. The South is the place of Innocence and Trust, and for perceiving closely our Emotional nature.

"The West is the Place of Looking Within. This is our Introspective ability. The color of the West is Black. This is the symbolic color of Earth and the

Power to Dream and Regenerate.

"The East is the Place of Illumination, where we can see things clearly, far and wide. Its color is the Gold of Fire and our Sun.

"At birth, each of us is given a particular Beginning Place within these Four Great Directions on the Medicine Wheel. This starting place gives us our first Way of Perceiving. Throughout our lives this remains our easiest and most natural Way of interacting with our World.

"However, if we remain where we were born, we will atrophy and die. For example, those who possess only the Seeing of the North will be Wise, but they can also be detached from Feeling.

"Those who attempt to live only in the East will have clear, farsighted Vision, but they also will never be close to things. Such people will feel separated, above Life, and will never understand that they can be touched by Life.

"Those who perceive only from the West will

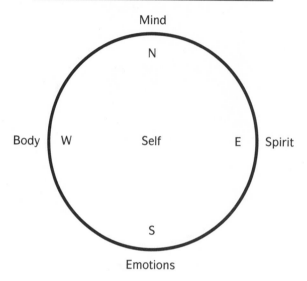

go over the same thoughts again and again in their minds, and yet will always be undecided.

"And if people insist upon dwelling in the idyllic Innocence of the South, they will pretend their lives long and find only disappointment.

"There are people who work hard to develop the Powers of all Four Directions. They will discover the satisfaction of knowing the Self and seeing Life as more than an abstract concept or simple belief.

"The Medicine Wheels teach us that Life is not a philosophical question. Life is our human Reality, Truth, Fact, and Teacher, no matter how bitter or sweet.

"The Wheels teach that Life is not a religion. Rather, Life is the perfect opportunity to Learn and Grow by first questioning—asking who each Human is.

"Lightningbolt, it's time for you to get to know your Self. Here is another important Wheel for you to study—*The Medicine Wheel of The Four Powers of The Human Self*. You are more than what your social world says. You are more than what you believe. You are Spirit, Body, Emotion, and Mind, and you are responsible for the care of that Being we call your Self.

"You are not just a body, mind, spirit, and emotions. You are a Self. You are directly responsible for your own care your entire life long. How you balance your Self—Spiritually, Emotionally, Physically, and Mentally—is the challenge you must accept and answer while you live here on Mother Earth.

"The Lodge I wish you to experience is powerful," said Estcheemah, smiling. "It will be a test of your honesty. You will be deeply affected. You will

meet Mother Earth in a way you have never met Her before. She is Life. Do not pretend to know. This is not the way of the seeker. Take your time. Just simply be present with Life."

The following morning quite early, Estcheemah and Lightningbolt began construction of the Lodge. Estcheemah had decided that the Lodge would be built about two hundred yards from her house, down in a small dry coulee.

The Child's Lodge was a pretty little structure built in a depression in the Earth. The Lodge looked like a tiny version of a Navajo hogan when it was completed. The difference was that this Lodge was partly below ground.

The soil was prepared carefully to form a receptacle for the red-hot stones that were essential in the Lodge. This cradle of stones is called the *Cheemahdah*. *Cheemahdah* means "little fire" or "volcano." The *Cheemahdah* is a vital part of the

Child's Lodge and is placed at its center.

That evening, while Estcheemah built a fire, she refused all help from him. She talked while she worked, telling him that not very many people truly contemplate the existence of our Sun.

"This little fire, dedicated to every child, represents the heart of the people," Estcheemah explained to him. "Be mindful of your fire also.

"The Moon, Stars, Planets, and all other beings and powers of space are way up there above everybody's head. But most people never give them a thought. People do not treasure Beauty," she told him.

"Mother Earth has been stolen away from most peoples' lives, Lightningbolt," Estcheemah taught. "I think that one of the important reasons people are separated from Mother Earth is because they have to rent their existence.

"Nothing really belongs to the people in the cities. There are public buildings, public utilities, parks, services, schools, and ten thousand other public things, including public transportation. But none of these public things really belongs to the people. People do not own their apartments, their streets, their places of worship. They don't even own their lives."

Then she explained to him that just because it was possible for him to own his home, that would not change the reality for billions who possessed nothing.

"I think that our worst ghettos in our cities could be transformed in a single year if the people owned them," she insisted. "Cities would be loved and cared for. But as it is, only planning boards, politicians, and the rich dictate what our cities will be. The people on the street have no say because they only rent their existence."

Lightningbolt knew that what she was saying was true. There was no dignity, only fear, for those who rented their homes. Would it ever change? he asked himself.

After the stones were red-hot, Lightningbolt had to wrestle them through the narrow door. In the past, the stones had been brought into the Lodge with forked sticks. The job was difficult and tiring. He was using a modern pitchfork, but it did not seem to make the task much easier.

Once all ten stones were in the *Cheemahdah*, he crawled into the Lodge. Estcheemah handed in a candle on a small saucer. Lightningbolt sat this by his bed and waited. Soon, her head appeared at the door again and she handed him his pad, sleeping bag, and pillow. Then she asked him to undress and to hand out his clothes.

The Lodge was warming up very quickly. He undressed down to his shorts and handed her his things. Next she passed in a pack of cigarettes and a lighter.

Looking around, he noticed that a tiny sparrow had somehow become trapped in the Lodge. He asked Estcheemah what to do. She told him to catch the bird and to hand it to her.

He reached for the bird, expecting it to become frightened and to dash itself against the wall of the Lodge, but this did not happen. Instead, the bird actually hopped into his hand. He handed out the sparrow, showing a very big grin.

She explained to him that he must be that way with his Life. That he should not be trapped. To remember always that he was free to fly. He was to be gentle and caring and to look around at his world. He was to be careful with his Life and free his Spirit.

She looked up at the sky, then to the Earth. Closing her eyes, she asked Mother Life to talk to Lightningbolt in a way that he could understand. After her prayer she closed the door to the Lodge.

Lightningbolt listened to her footsteps as she walked away.

The interior of the Lodge had been plunged into darkness when Estcheemah closed the door— not one particle of light entered from the outside.

She had made sure of that when the Lodge was being built.

Lightningbolt became fascinated by the light from the glowing stones in the *Cheemahdah*. A longing, an enchantment, began to occupy his mind while he watched the stars shimmer and wink at him from the sparkling stones.

The tiny pieces of sweet grass he had placed at the bottom of the *Cheemahdah* began to smolder and the smoke slightly stung his eyes. He lay down on his bed and stretched out to rest. It was very quieting to be in this Lodge.

He closed his eyes and watched his thoughts merge into a beautiful pattern of shadow and light. He dozed for a while. Then he woke with a start, but quickly remembered where he was and relaxed again.

He sat up and probed for the *Cheemahdah* with his cigarette lighter. He did not want to touch the hot stones accidentally. He found the *Cheemahdah* and peered into it to see if the stones were still bright. But all were dark.

The silence now presented itself to him. At first he became aware of a white sound in his ears, but his brain tired of it and slowly tuned it out. Next, he became aware of his heartbeat. This soon disappeared, too, and the silence returned.

Lightningbolt did not like the silence. He fought it with his emotions, but quickly lost. He hummed, whistled, talked to himself, and pounded out a drumbeat on his knees, but soon tired of this also. The darkness and silence now gripped him even more and would not relinquish their hold on him. He felt as though he were a thousand miles out in space, then somewhere deep under the ocean.

His attention was drawn to the light shapes he imagined he saw; they were exquisite. Their intricate patterns of vivid colors and light became ever clearer. They turned, changed, and constantly reshaped themselves.

Suddenly, an intense sorrow penetrated deep into his very Spirit. The rush of feeling was so intense and swift it actually choked him. His body shook with sobs. He tried to regain control of his feelings, but soon realized that this was not the thing to do. Each time he fought the feelings, his head would pound and his body would ache.

Slowly, very carefully, he learned to let go of his strange tensions until they became part of his tears. Only then did the sadness begin to subside. This left Lightningbolt badly shaken. He lay down again and closed his eyes. He needed to rest, even if it were for only a few seconds.

Suddenly, a bright light flashing with brilliant colors darted across the Lodge. He sat up with a start and stared into the darkness.

The light burst again, this time with unimaginably beautiful colors. A shape began to form. Within seconds the form became a beautiful young woman—a Goddess.

The tunic she wore was shimmering and almost translucent. She walked to the left and his eyes followed her. She turned and faced him, then turned away again and continued to walk. There was no longer any wall.

A perfectly round pool of radiant blue water appeared. The pool was set in crystal glass. The Goddess stepped lightly into the water. The pool began to grow, becoming a small lake. She turned and looked at him, then descended the crystal stairs into the lake. Her walk was graceful, yet powerful, like that of a Warrioress.

He tried to understand how he was viewing her. He could see her in absolute detail no matter how far she was from him. He tried to follow her.

Another rush of sadness crashed in upon him and he doubled over with the pain. He slowly relaxed, falling into each wave of despair instead of fighting it; then the melancholy began to disappear.

But the young woman did not disappear. She turned and looked at him with her lovely blue eyes.

She put out her hands and slowly began to walk toward him.

Fear rose up in him that he would feel his anguish again, and he stiffened to protect himself. Closer and closer she came until she stood in front of him.

She smiled and handed him a glowing sphere of radiant light. When he took it into his hands, his fears instantly vanished. Then she handed him five arrows; these also glowed with a light he could not comprehend. Then, as suddenly as she had appeared, the Goddess disappeared.

The door opened and Estcheemah spoke to him. She told him that it was early morning and that his Ceremony was complete. She handed in his clothes.

He sat up, not wanting the Ceremony to be over. It did not seem fair somehow that the time had gone by so quickly. Could he remember what he had seen? As he sat there, Lightningbolt resolved that he would never forget the incredible Beauty and Power of the Goddess.

At noon the same day, Estcheemah spoke to him of his experience. Lightningbolt looked around her kitchen. Nothing seemed to be the same. Yes, it was the same kitchen. It was the same house and countryside. But everything had changed.

Estcheemah seemed more vibrant, powerful, noble—like a warrioress.

"I don't want to be a fool anymore, Estcheemah." He felt exhausted, yet sleep was the last thing he desired.

Lightningbolt began to tell her of his Ceremony. What had happened to him was the most

precious experience he had ever known, and he felt he should protect it.

While Lightningbolt enjoyed his lunch, Estcheemah told him about the Goddess of Light.

"She has been known by many names—Warrioress, Healer of Light. The Greeks knew this Goddess as Helen. The word Healing comes from the word Hellen.

"In Celtic the word *Heilen* also means 'Healing' or the 'Goddess Hellen.' The word *Holy* is *Heilig* in Celtic-German. It, too, means 'Hellen.' *Hellen* means 'Light.' "

"She is beautiful," Lightningbolt broke in.

"Beauty," said Estcheemah, "and Earth Mother Goddess are the same. She is also known as the Rose. All of Her flowers, every bloom, are Her Sacred Presence."

Estcheemah warned Lightningbolt to not think of Goddess Life as only being the demure young woman.

"The Rose is the Earth Woman. Goddess Life is powerful and births all Life. She is the Giver and the Taker. She is Healer and Warrioress. The Rose has Her thorns."

His teacher explained how she had not expected him to find his heart in the Lodge. Many people find only the monster images of their fears. But then, no two people have the same experience in the Child's Lodge.

Lightningbolt had sought an expression of love and care that only the Goddess Earth could have understood or answered. What he had been shown revealed much to him. Still, it would be years before he understood it.

Lightningbolt drove to Sheridan to buy groceries; while he was there he made a telephone call. He spoke with his mother and learned that the job had come through on the oil rig.

Two days later he was working on the rig outside of Lethbridge, Alberta. He was happy to be back in Canada; he loved that land.

He worked on the job for a month, until the well was completed. Then he was left with nothing to do before the crew was to meet at the next job site.

Lightningbolt returned to Estcheemah and worked for half a day fixing fence. When he finished, and had driven the cattle out of Estcheemah's pasture, he sat down on the porch for a nap. He looked up when a beat-up old sedan pulled into the yard.

A swarthy man got out and approached the house, stopping at the first step to the porch. He seemed almost frightened. He announced that his name was John Plenty Sun. He worked for Thomas Rollins at Logging Creek. He meekly explained that his boss had a little girl who was very sick.

Tobacco was offered to Estcheemah, which she accepted, but he would not come into the house for a cup of coffee. After he had delivered his message, he backed up almost the length of the very wide garden before he turned and got into his car.

"Boy, that's covering your butt," Lightningbolt teased.

Estcheemah explained that she knew the man. He was not very bright and he feared that she was a witch.

The weather was cold, but it was warmed during the day by a white-hot sun. It was unusually warm at one point of the day, then suddenly became quite cold. Because a storm could come at any moment, Estcheemah cautioned Lightningbolt to prepare for anything.

At the home of the Rollins family, Estcheemah assisted Lightningbolt with the setting up of her tent beside a beautiful little creek.

The work went smoothly and quickly. Once or twice Lightningbolt got a brief glimpse at Edna, the skinny young girl who would be doctored.

Estcheemah stepped off two paces from the entrance of the tent and had Lightningbolt dig a fire pit. Everyone, including the Rollins family, went out into the surrounding hills to gather firewood and sage.

The work of cleaning the sage with cold water followed; then it was dried in Mrs. Rollins's kitchen oven. Throughout all this work, eleven-year-old Tommy and fourteen-year-old Lydia did most of the helping. Soon, armfuls of sage were piled on a Medicine Blanket inside Estcheemah's tent.

Little Edna watched all this activity with a great deal of sadness. But the girl's large brown eyes sparkled when Lightningbolt tipped his hat and tickled her under the chin.

Now it was time for quiet. Everyone disappeared into the house for a "quiet time of contemplation." Estcheemah took Lightningbolt for a walk along the creek to calm him and to help him feel the presence of Mother Earth.

They had only been at the creek for twenty minutes when Thomas interrupted them. He explained that his daughter had been in the hospital five times. Edna had severe stomach trouble. One trouble followed after the next. It had the doctors confounded.

At sundown Edna was brought to the Medicine Tent. The poor child could hardly walk. She was bent nearly in half—a pitiful sight to see.

Lightningbolt had lit the Door Fire, or Guard Fire, then entered the Lodge to sit behind his teacher. Lydia took his place, becoming the Fire Keeper. The parents sat at the entrance with their backs to the door.

Estcheemah brought out a long, clear, slender crystal from her Medicine Pouch and showed it to Edna. As she spoke, she slowly turned the crystal in her hands.

Edna was fascinated by the exquisite beauty of the stone. Estcheemah spoke to the girl for a few minutes in a low monotone. It was not long before Edna's eyes began to grow sleepy and she wanted to rest. After Estcheemah had made her comfortable she covered Edna from head to foot with the clean sage.

The Medicine Woman then filled her Pipe and smoked, speaking to WahKahn, our Creatress Mother, and SsKwan, our Creator Father. She also prayed to the trees and all living things that share in the Life-World of every child. Twenty crystals were placed lovingly at intervals on the girl's body by the Medicine Woman.

Lightningbolt was incredibly nervous. What if this girl was not healed? What would people think? If the girl should die, then what? He shivered, thinking of how difficult it would be for him to be in Estcheemah's position.

As his teacher drew her Medicine Fan over Edna's tiny body, Lightningbolt felt tremendously apprehensive.

When Estcheemah sang her Medicine Song, he felt hopelessly weak, disastrously stupid. Needless to say, he was not very much help.

After a few minutes, Edna began to make tiny little sounds that frightened Lightningbolt but comforted Estcheemah. The girl now slept very soundly.

A sudden quiet seemed to enter the little tent. It was the same beautiful silence that Lightningbolt had experienced in his Child's Lodge; unfortunately, he was too afraid to feel it now.

At first, the tranquility was only recognizable as a subtle inner feeling that Estcheemah knew. But soon the intensity of the stillness grew and filled every inch of the tent. She glanced at Lightningbolt to see if he had recognized the Medicine Silence, but he had not.

Lightningbolt was near tears. He was indulging his fears and negative feelings, and would have run at the slightest opportunity. Death and Life were so present, so obvious, that he was overwhelmed with fear for his own existence.

Estcheemah touched him ever so gently and he jumped as though an electric shock had entered his body. Then for no explainable reason, he grew calm. With the calm, a strength rose in Lightningbolt that filled every fiber of his being. Now he felt exactly the opposite of what he'd been feeling before.

With great confidence he reached over and patted his teacher on her back and smiled. When she turned to face him, he winked, letting her know that he felt she had done a good job.

Estcheemah smiled secretly to herself. He had felt the presence, even though she'd had to give him a little push of energy. It did not matter. That he could feel the presence of energy again was a sign to her that he somehow understood.

Estcheemah would not discuss the healing with Lightningbolt because she knew that, beyond just experiencing the Ceremony, he was not ready to learn of its details. That would be for another time, another day.

Lightningbolt received a letter from Estcheemah while on his next oil rig job in Wyoming. Two weeks had gone by. Edna was fine and even playing. The doctors were amazed and delighted with Edna's sudden recovery. She had not been expected to live beyond a few more months.

The winter was boring and sad for Lightningbolt. He felt more alone than he ever had in his life.

Before he left, Lightningbolt had talked to Estcheemah about many of his fears, with one exception—his terror of being poor. Because of this deep fear, he worked his own shift and any other that came up. He was close to exhaustion, but he didn't care.

Even talking about money frightened him. Whenever a conversation centered around money, he would begin to pretend. His pretense took many strange and unexplainable turns. At one moment he would not accept a five-dollar bet because he hated gambling. Yet, at another time he'd bet away a hundred dollars on a silly whim.

The problem was, Lightningbolt became embarrassed if, even jokingly, someone accused him of being cheap. He'd always overreact and be too generous. Pure luck seemed to be the only thing that kept him from being cheated and constantly broke.

However, his terror of being poor took another even more complicated turn—this was his lying. If he felt he was being pressured about money, even for the slightest of reasons, he would lie. Because Estcheemah had challenged him to observe his lying, he worked the winter long trying not to lie. This activity of mind helped him greatly. It also saved him a few misunderstandings and a lot of money that he would have thrown away.

He resolved to talk to Estcheemah about his fears when he returned to the North. Why was he always so terrified and irrational about his need for money?

The hard winter, his toil, the freezing cold, and his sadness finally melted into Spring. There was never such a wondrous Spring. Montana was bright with flowers, and her grasses were startlingly green.

After the oil rig was stacked and the crews were

waiting for the next drilling site, Lightningbolt was free to meet Estcheemah. Through an exchange of letters it was decided they would meet at a favorite camping place of Estcheemah's at the Little Horn.

It was at this time that Lightningbolt met Estcheemah's dearest friend, Sky River. He was surprised to see that Sky River turned out to be Ammie.

"Remember me?" The silver-haired woman smiled, shaking his hand. "So you are the Breed Estcheemah mentioned. I did not know you were the young man she's been teaching. Did you know that John passed away last winter?"

"No, I hadn't heard. Was it an accident?" he asked.

"Old age," said Ammie. "His heart stopped while he slept. We had been expecting it. He was eighty-eight."

"Wow, he certainly didn't look it!" Lightningbolt exclaimed.

"Ammie and I have been friends for twenty-two years," Estcheemah told him.

"And I have been fortunate enough to be her student all those years," Ammie added, pouring herself a cup of coffee from the camp pot. "Let's see now. Estcheemah wants me to tell you about the Medicine Belts. She says that you have been pestering her to learn about them for over a year."

"I certainly have." He smiled.

"Much of what we know about the Medicine Wheels has been kept on Medicine Belts called the Great Belts or the *Wah-Palm-Atl-Shee-aey-Hel-am*," Ammie began. "This literally translates as 'Valuable-Exchange-Teaching.'

"Of the Great Belts, around two hundred still exist. They have been preserved and appreciated by Flower Soldiers in the Americas. The Belts were once shared with others, but our Chiefs learned that to do this was dangerous, so they stopped. This is because the information from the Belts was destroyed or altered to fit different beliefs. As an example, if the words *Sacred Mother Life* were on the Belt story, the translators would somehow forget to mention *Sacred* and *Mother* when the translating was being done, and would use only the word *God.*

"Some of these Belts were carved on wood, others exist on wool, leather, or burned clay. Many are painted. All of them are called the Great Belts, even though only about eleven of them are actually Belts.

"Five of the Great Belts speak of the Dreamer Lodges, or the Earth Sun Dance Lodges. The original Earth Sun Dance Lodges had women and men both as Chiefs and participants. However, women were excluded from War Lodges in later times by the Mandan. When people hear about Sun Dance Lodges, they always think they have to be torture dances."

Lightningbolt interrupted, "What happened? Why is there so much confusion?"

"Yes, there is much confusion," she admitted. "That is the reason I am speaking of it. The Dog Soldiers' Lodges were introduced much later than the original Dreamer Lodges. The Dreamer Lodge or Earth Sun Dance Lodge is a purifying Lodge, not a torture Lodge like the more popular Dog Lodges.

"The first Dreamer Lodges—the Earth Sun Dances—were presided over, as I said, by female and male Chiefs. Discrimination among the sexes would not have been comprehended.

"The Warrior Dog Soldiers of the Mandan traders held a special Ceremony separate from the Dreamer Lodges that they considered to be for the elite. But these men never created their Lodges specifically to be separate from women. They would not have understood thinking like this.

"There were also elite Lodges specific to women, but these were not created to discriminate against men. In these Lodges girls learned what it was to be a woman. In the all-male Lodges, the boys learned about the world of men. Discriminating against women is strictly a foreign concept. It was never known among America's Native Peoples.

"It was not until much later in history that confusion became the rule. There was no confusion between what an Earth Sun Dance Lodge meant and what the Test Lodges of Torture became. It was after the Indian Wars, after hundreds of thousands of people were killed, that there was no one left to remind the People of what formerly existed.

"The power of what I am saying can be understood if you consider what would happen to the information of what America is if three-quarters of America's people were killed by the invasion of another people. Very little would remain of what was formerly known.

"This is what happened with America's Native People. After the invasion and incredible carnage, the Earth Sun Dance was no longer understood. The Ceremonies that survived the extermination of America's Medicine Chiefs were few. Those Ceremonies that did survive suffered from lack of information—even to the reasons for their existence.

"Most of these later Earth Sun Dances continued to have both women and men present in the Ceremony, but it was not long before discrimination began to be in fashion. This was done out of ignorance, not religious fervor."

"Why did they torture themselves in the Dog Lodges?" Lightningbolt interrupted.

"The participants believed that if they suffered the people of the camp would not suffer," she explained. "The Mandan thought nothing of seeing a human skewered and hanging from a rafter or a pole. At the time, the practice was common and very fashionable.

"It is very easy to criticize the Mandans and point out how primitive they were, but what of the torture crosses we see in our present time in Christian churches?

"To see a man bleeding and hanging dead upon a torture cross is ordinary today. If anyone should question the sight, there would be those who would quickly explain how symbolic it all is. But where are the people to explain how symbolic it all is when they see pictures of the men hanging, tortured, in the old Mandan lodges?

"No matter how psychologists or psychiatrists explain it away, the symbol of men being tortured on crosses or rafters teaches violence and propagates terror.

"From the very beginning the Dreamer Lodges were Ceremonies of Renewal. And they continue to be that for us, the Flower Soldiers. While we dance in our Dreamer Lodges we learn of the care for our land and people. We dance for three days and three nights without food or water. This is done so that we become present with our mind and body. We dance in celebration of the renewal of our existence with Life. The dance is a Way of Appreciation for what Life has given all of us."

"People get power in those Lodges, too," said Lightningbolt. "I've seen it."

"What have you seen?" she asked, genuinely curious.

"People change their lives for the better," he explained. "And excel in their, you know, their careers, their jobs. And things come to them—"

"When a woman is going to have a child, she needs to be near Mother Life," said Estcheemah. "When men need a way of Touching Life and understanding the reason for their lives, they do this in Renewal with Life.

"Women also need a way of Touching Life and understanding the reason for their lives. This can

212

happen in the Renewal Lodge of Life—our Dreamer Lodges. This is the essence of the Dreamer Lodges. We Dance and we Stand-Up-Dreaming as we Dance. It is an extremely powerful way of Contemplation."

Three weeks later, Lightningbolt stood on a hill overlooking the Yellowstone River and watched children splashing and playing in a brook that entered the stream. He marveled at the way they seemed to withstand the cold water.

Eight thin wisps of smoke curled toward the sky, telling him that the five Breed families called North Circle were already camped. These were Canadian *Metis*, Breeds from Manitoba and Saskatchewan. Estcheemah had been expecting them for Goose Flying's Big Dreamer Lodge–Sun Dance Ceremony.

Lightningbolt had set up Estcheemah's tepee beneath the five cottonwoods where she said she wanted it. But where was she? It was not like her to be so late; had something gone wrong? He was just a bit worried.

In the opposite direction, away from the tents of the visiting Crees, was a huge clutter of tents and tepees arrayed in absolute confusion.

No one had been put into a responsible position to direct the building of the small camp city that had sprung up overnight. People had put up their tents where it pleased them, and the camp was a mess.

He shook his head when he saw the jungle of ropes and wires. They had been tied to trees and every other possible thing that could be used to hold the tents in position. Kids chased each other through the spiderweb of entanglements sketched among structures. The camp was one huge rope knot that even the cleverest person would be hard-pressed to unravel.

A man was shouting because his pickup had been tied down to the ground and to the tents surrounding it. Unwittingly, two million traps had been made that would snare people stumbling in the dark toward rickety, filthy toilets.

Lightningbolt had seen this kind of bewilderment before. The chances were very high that the Tribal Council was supposed to be responsible for the making of the camp.

These kinds of foul-ups were a bit capricious, to be sure, and some people might even think them quaint. But only a fool would find them funny. Always, some innocent—usually the unsuspecting or the very young—would fall victim to the chaos. Eyes had been lost and children burned at open fires. Many people were hurt because of this kind of ignorance and neglect.

Even the so-called learned were not so wise. University people would come to observe a Sun Dance and allow their children to run where they wanted. Because of this naive carelessness many of their children would be sexually molested, raped, or openly reviled. Instead of a time of prayer and thought, the Sun Dance had become a cross between a fair and a holiday outing for many people. Drunks were another distressing problem at every Sun Dance. They wandered where they liked, dis-

214

rupting families and bringing discord. There were always at least a hundred arrests for drunkenness.

Almost everyone pretended that the Sun Dance was protected by special deities created for such occasions. Then, obviously, if anything did go wrong, it was because "the Spirits were not right."

Sun Dances drew every kind of crowd, and some of these visitors were not so nice. Every kind of religious crazy eventually put a Sun Dance on his or her list of things to save or destroy. Visitors from lands as distant as Denmark and as close as Brooklyn come to watch the "colorful" dances. And where there are tourists—unwittingly or sometimes knowingly—there are terrorists, thieves, and hawkers. The tourists pay to be ripped off, and the thieves and hawkers catch the tourists' diseases. There are no winners in these kinds of contests.

Was it always this way? Lightningbolt won-

dered. What about the sincere—what do they find at this kind of circus?

A man made his way through the nearest jumble of cars and fighting kids to where Lightningbolt stood. He introduced himself as John Lafayette. With his soft and pleasant Canadian Metis accent, he explained that he had written Goose Flying and that Goose had invited him and his family to help with the Sun Dance.

He sat down and pulled a very worn notebook from his vest pocket. The five trees where Lightningbolt had set up the tepee were important. He pointed to a drawing he had in the notebook, showing Lightningbolt the trees. Lafayette explained that his mother had been healed on the spot where the trees stood. The five trees had been planted over eighty-five years ago in celebration of the Healing.

The old man continued to talk, now and then sipping coffee from his thermos. He seemed totally unconcerned as to whether or not Lightningbolt was listening.

Estcheemah finally showed up, trailed by Goose Flying and five older men. All of Goose's old insecurities were still plaguing him. The Medicine Man was deeply troubled about taking charge of his newly acquired responsibilities. He did not want to run his first Sun Dance by himself—partly because it involved solving some thorny problems.

Since there was to be no piercing of flesh or other tests of so-called faith and courage, a group of encamped families decided that Goose Flying's Sun Dance was not authentic, and they threatened to leave.

But then, because Goose Flying's Sun Dance was not "authentic Crow, Sioux, Cheyenne, Cree, or Arapaho," six other families decided they were also going to leave.

What exactly was his Sun Dance? Everyone was wondering. But if apathy were a ravening monster, it would have devoured ninety percent of the people present. However, this was not their fate—instead, they waited as they had always waited.

And if gossip had been a monster as well, it would have run rampant through the camp, gnawing to shreds hundreds of ears and laying waste whole lives.

The last issue was busy-ness. And the busy-ness monster outdid the greatest busy-ness monster of all time, the Bureau of Indian Affairs. The B. I. A. monster visited the Reservation every day in every possible way, ruthlessly destroying the incentive of the people to move beyond their welfare existence.

Goose argued with at least five different busy-ness committees, explaining that his Dance was the Big Dreamer Lodge. Most of the Indians present howled with laughter when they heard this. They had never heard of such a thing . . . how preposterous! Estcheemah wanted to help Goose, but her position was so delicate that to even breathe this intention was out of the question.

One of the families present was there to "save lost souls." Other families were sincere about the Sun Dance and sought only to experience "the Spiritual Way." But no one seemed to be able to agree on just what that was. As usual, the anthropologists never suspected a thing. They were busy filling notebooks with political importances.

The following morning, very early, a committee called the Decision Committee came together to decide what was to happen. Eleven people had been chosen to sit on the committee.

However, since five of the members were "having their period," they were automatically barred from decision making. These women were very angry and thought the decision unjust. But what could they do—wasn't this the "traditional" way? They never openly questioned the premise of such fanatical thinking.

As the day got hotter many of the men got drunker. Around two o'clock, an Executive Board was formed, throwing out the Decision Committee.

In desperation Goose showed up at Estcheemah's tent with thirty men following him. He begged Estcheemah to help end the confusion. She suggested that he should support the decisions of the Executive Board and get his Dance started. But first she asked him to see to another problem.

Two newly painted, government-green outhouses had been placed about twenty-five feet in front of the entranceway to the Sun Dance Lodge by the Tribal Council. She wanted them moved. She asked Goose if he wanted the Two Sacred Twins of the East to be toilets. Goose reluctantly took her advice and had them moved farther to the North and South.

When Goose ordered his Dance to begin, there was an incredible scramble for the next five hours. Everybody seemed to be packing up to leave. Some of the tangle of tents and tepees disappeared very quickly. What was surprising was that many more families remained than Lightningbolt would have guessed.

However, there were still other hurdles to be leaped.

Estcheemah continued to be a great problem for Goose. How could he get the information he needed if he could not have the guidance of Estcheemah?

The people who remained had complicated views when it came to the subject of Estcheemah. Some of these were: She was a woman. She was a foreigner—an Indian from Mexico. She was a witch. She was not an authentic Sun Dance Chief. She was not married. She was a teacher of Breeds. She was a Contrary. She was a Holy Woman. She was a Magician. She was a wise teacher. She was a saint. She was a busybody. She was a Healer. She was not loving. She had too much love and it ruined her judgment. She was kind. She was powerful. She talked openly to trees, even in front of whites!

"I'm the cook," she told Goose.

"Cook?" He was embarrassed and confused. Why was she saying this? Had she gone over the edge, too? No, that was impossible! But why had she said that? By this time Goose wanted to flee for his life and never look back. Yet shouldn't he be brave?

If old Goose thought he was embarrassed, he should have had a look into the mind of Lightningbolt. He hadn't fared so well at all. Dogs had tried to bite him. He'd lost his pocketknife. And some kids had let the air out of the Silver Ship's two back tires. The thought of his teacher being a common cook was even worse than the tires.

Both men stood there dumbfounded.

"I like to cook," she said, unconcerned. She was frying Lightningbolt some eggs. "I'm here cooking for this young man—what harm is there in that?" She poured Goose a fresh cup of coffee. "As you know, Lightningbolt needs to learn. A Breed like him, and the Canadian Breeds camped here, need to see a real Sun Dance. This way, Lightningbolt can get close, stick his nose right through the Outer Ring of World Leaves that surround the Lodge, if you know what I mean."

Lightningbolt was grinning. He quickly understood that he was to be the messenger. Whatever Goose needed to know would be given to him through the back of the Lodge.

Suddenly tears welled up in the old man's eyes and he began to cry. He sat on his chair, forlorn. The pressures of the past week had been too much. Lightningbolt became concerned for him, but watched to see what Estcheemah would do. She appeared to be almost indifferent.

"I am humiliated," Goose said with a break in his voice. "It is not right. Oh, Estcheemah, what shall I do?"

"This situation has always existed between us," Estcheemah said smoothly as she set Lightningbolt's plate of food in front of him. "When was it not complicated?" She refilled Goose's cup. "It's even worse in other parts of the world, Goose. Where do women have rights anymore—real rights? Where is there any true respect for women?"

Goose dried his tears and took a sip from his brew.

Estcheemah gazed out over the rolling hills and folded her hands across her lap. Lightningbolt stood up, set his food aside, and poured his teacher a cup of coffee. She looked up at him and smiled.

"I'm the dishwasher," he whispered to her.

She turned her attentions to Goose. "One day women will be respected. We are not monsters created by WahKahn, our Creatress Mother, and SsKwan, our Creator Father. One half of humanity are not demons. We women are humans and have the right to live. We have been entrusted with the Sacred Duty of giving birth. This duty and wondrous gift given to women is no reason to make us the monsters that men fear."

Goose now sat up in his chair.

"We are not the reason for men's terrors," she went on. "Their murder, their bigotry, shame, and self-destruction, were not created by women.

"We women are not the cause of men's fears," she said. "Comforting comes from us women. We Love and bring Love where there is none. We honor Life because Life and Love are one. I have always been your secret. Women are not respected for their Spiritual Knowledge. We are not respected for any of the things we know; you are well aware of this. Your tears are false, Goose. You have always lacked courage. You must learn of courage in this lifetime. Lift your eyes up from your feet. Be courageous."

"But we are forced to sneak!" he moaned.

"I will be very happy to end that." She smiled at him. "Day after tomorrow, when your Lodge begins, I will walk into your Lodge and take absolute command, okay?"

"Stop," he said, putting up his hand. Goose could not back out even if he wanted to. He was also afraid of going forward. He was sympathetic to Estcheemah, but he refused to work to understand her words.

"Raise yourself up, Goose." She touched him on his arm. "Carry your lie with dignity. The secret is yours and yours alone. Do not be silly and ruin your life. Teach, work, do what you can in this lifetime. Life will share Her mysteries with you. I would suggest you try to remain out of the limelight. Keep your secrets to yourself. Why tell everybody? It will help nothing."

"You'll soon have your very own anthro," Lightningbolt teased. "How's that, Goose?"

The Sun Dance was one of the most beautiful experiences of its kind Lightningbolt would ever participate in. Many people found Healing—and

there were no drunks. They all seemed to have avoided the Big Dreamer Lodge–Sun Dance Ceremony.

Goose had never looked so good! He might have entered the Dance with shaky gosling legs, but after the first day he fairly beamed with confidence. Old Goose was so proud of himself, Estcheemah could actually tease with him without his falling to pieces. One of the messages she sent him via the back of the Lodge was: "So, your goose is not cooked after all!"

Laughter was the greatest of all the Medicines that made this Sun Dance a success. Jakie, the Medicine Clown, proved to be the strength of the Dance. When all else failed, it was the clown's task to help people get present with Mother Earth and to endure the hardship of the unbearable heat.

Jakie was a midget. He could touch even the most serious or withdrawn people with a strength of Love few could resist. He was a man of a thousand different voices.

"Who needs a mother? Unless we want to experience Life?" he teased the dancers. "It's a miracle that most of you are here! Maybe you'll have the chance to be something special in your next life instead of just being miserable."

Another day he told the people: "In my next life I am going to be born a bug. That way I can survive all the chemical pollution we're being forced to live with."

As the days grew hotter, many within the Lodge were in pain from their lack of moisture. No water touched anyone's lips for the three days and three nights of the Dance.

"Cool watermelons never tasted better!" Jakie announced to the tired dancers one especially hot afternoon. "Personally, I think we should at least have a midday lunch in these Dances. No? Okay, then we can have salted nuts instead.

"Everything is being bottled or put into a can," he proclaimed in a television announcer's voice. "Very soon, my children, you can have all the peppermint propaganda you can eat!"

The songs of the singers and the steady thrum of the large bass drum echoed in the valleys and sang to the hearts of the people.

During the third day of the Sun Dance, Estcheemah sang the Woman's Song of Maturing to Lightningbolt. The words were lovely, yet mysterious.

Words speak of time and how time will nurse us children of Life. All Flowers are opened to present the questions that have been asked by the Stars that grace our Universe.

The Moon is the guardian of rhythm, and is part of every song.

The Tree knows every song. The Tree depends upon every one of the leaves.

Every songbird is singing.

Each leaf changes with Dark and Light. Each leaf tastes Earth. Each leaf drinks Water. Each leaf breathes Air. Flowering leaves and towering leaves mirror their existence.

Yes, it is true that the Tree is dependent upon every leaf, yet when Autumn comes . . . all the leaves will fall back to Earth.

All the people have fallen back to Earth.

The Tree grows and the people learn, learning with each leaf of the Tree. All the Trees will fall back to the Earth.

Woman is maturing. Man is growing.

All the flowers will bloom with the Earth.

Time will fall back to the Earth.

This is how it was explained that Woman is Maturing.

Lightningbolt was startled when the song ended. He had been looking up into the outstretched arms of the cottonwood trees while Estcheemah sang to him. Through the leaves he could see the Moon and the Stars.

Old Goose Flying had become a Medicine Hero. He left the Sun Dance with at least ten cars following behind him; one contained his very own anthro.

Estcheemah and Lightningbolt spent two days cleaning up. A farmer had offered the use of his Caterpillar, but as it turned out, Estcheemah had to pay him fifty dollars for it. The machine was used to dig a deep trench to bury the enormous amount of waste.

A jack rabbit can teach a young man humility.

That afternoon, Lightningbolt decided that he would hunt rabbits for their evening meal. Estcheemah had made the same decision, but had already set her snares upriver at a place where the grass was lush and green.

They parted, not telling one another where they were going. Lightningbolt thought his teacher needed a bit of time to be alone, and Estcheemah knew he wanted to stretch his legs.

Lightningbolt kept two rifles in the Silver Ship; they were the Ship's cannons. He took down the .22 from the rack and discovered that he was out of ammunition.

Hunting rabbits with a .30-06 was out of the question. One bullet would blow the animal into the next county. Tenaciously he dug through the pickup until he found a box of ammunition for his .38 pistol. The gun, bullets, two candy bars, his hunting knife, and a short rope all went into his coat pockets, and he was off to hunt bunnies.

He noticed that Estcheemah had disappeared down at the river, so he decided to go in the opposite direction. He walked, moving parallel to the river, yet always out and away from it. Lightningbolt enjoyed the soft smells of sage and prairie grasses as he hunted. This was perfect hunting ground.

He was a good half mile from the river when he entered a labyrinth of small ravines. Floods caused by rain and snow had carved thousands of interlocking channels that all wound their way down to the river. It was a gigantic maze that could delight ten thousand children at a time. Following where these narrow washes led became a game for him.

The day was bright-warm with a deep blue sky

overhead. Here and there, a ravine would open up into a small bowl. Within these wide places there was always grass.

He hunted for nearly an hour, then realized that he had not brought along his canteen. There were places at the river where springs joined the main stream. He would go down there and get a drink. Up to now, he hadn't seen one animal, except for a grasshopper or a stray butterfly. Now, suddenly, he saw the unmistakable silhouette of rabbit ears!

The rabbit sprinted away up a wash. Lightningbolt was after him in the blink of an eye. Rabbit and man crashed through one draw after the other until abruptly the chase ended. The rabbit had dived down into one of a hundred holes.

Lightningbolt cursed, hitched up his jeans, and was turning toward the river again when the rabbit dashed between his legs and up the arroyo. He spun and charged after him, firing twice and missing.

Five rushes more, and eleven dry washes later, the rabbit was still unscathed. If Lightningbolt had ever been philosophical, he certainly wasn't now. Man and rabbit were squared off. One of the creatures had to give, and Lightningbolt knew it was not going to be him.

He had never met a smart-assed rabbit in the flesh before. The closest thing to an arrogant rabbit he knew of was Bugs Bunny, and he was only a cartoon. Yet, Lightningbolt did feel, just a bit, like old Elmer Fudd at this moment.

He had his pistol in hand and his thirst was growing by the second. He was so dry his tongue felt as though it was cemented to the roof of his mouth.

Breathing hard, he rounded a sharp curve in the narrow arroyo and saw a sight that just should not have been. There, right in the middle of the draw, were at least twenty rabbits. Ears popped up alert, tails flashed, and bunnies went in every direction.

Ka-bang! Boom! Bullets whirred from stones, ricocheted and howled from boulders. But not one rabbit fell.

Lightningbolt set his teeth. He was resolute now. He reloaded the gun and decided that he was finished hunting rabbits for the moment. If he didn't get water soon, he might never get a rabbit again. The gun went into his pocket and out came a candy bar when, suddenly, there was old Silhouette Ears again.

The pistol came out of the pocket as Lightningbolt slunk along the dry wash like the shadow of a determined snake. This time he would aim very carefully. Just as he drew a bead on the rabbit's head, it disappeared. Then the reckless buck charged away again.

Lightningbolt could not believe it. No! This could not be happening to him. But it was, and he was once again in hot pursuit of his dinner.

Five or more shots careened into stone and through bushes, but not one bullet even scratched the rabbit's ears. Lightningbolt slammed the empty gun recklessly into his pocket. Twenty turns and many dry washes later, he reached for the second candy bar and realized the gun was gone. He searched for over a half hour, but could not find it.

It took him another two and a half hours to get back to the camp. Lightningbolt fell into his chair exhausted.

Estcheemah had finished cooking the rabbits she had trapped and was eager to feast upon them. As she fixed his plate and set it in front of him she saw that Lightningbolt was in a very sour mood.

She asked what was wrong and he told her that he'd lost his pistol somewhere out in the hills, among rabbits, and couldn't find it, no matter how hard he tried.

He enjoyed his rabbit dinner, somewhat, then went to the river to bathe. That night he dreamed that a rabbit was his Sergeant.

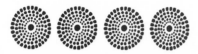

Estcheemah continually told Lightningbolt that there were no superhuman teachers. To be superhuman posed no challenge. Where was the learning in that?

"Gods," she said, "were supposedly born superhuman and faced no real human challenges. They were above suffering, knew it all, and could not really die. Where is the challenge in this?

"In truth, teachers are constantly being challenged. It is the fact of not being given superhuman abilities that gives teachers their power."

She also told him that most people want to hide and fit in. The lazy and incompetent want miracles, not challenges.

There is a mystique that has built up around what is thought to be "the innocence and charm" of the American Indian Medicine Man. By and large, this picture that most people have of Medicine Men or wandering monks, priests, mendicants, and mad clerics always portrays them as being wise, kind, shepherding, and perceptive. But this is naive.

For obvious reasons it is the clergy who have propagated this illusion with heroic tales of saints and beggars who made it big and became religious stars overnight.

Lightningbolt, too, had always believed the fiction instead of questioning the belief. Estcheemah had to battle this problem almost constantly. To have her student believe that she was a superhuman would destroy any hope of her teaching him. She walked a tightrope between showing Lightningbolt his true Self and showing him the real world he lived in. If she were to forget Lightningbolt's harsh beliefs, for even one second, then he would indulge himself.

The conformists call this normal and in this way shun all Self responsibility for their personal actions. People who seek an excuse to fail worship wonders and never the actual miracle that they are alive and challenged by their existence and their attitudes toward the Self.

Lightningbolt was startled by what he heard, but it would be years before he would have the courage to face what she told him.

As Estcheemah drove to her home she thought of her responsibilities. The teachings of the Medicine Wheels were her concern. She hoped with all her heart that Lightningbolt would be that student who cared. The Mathematics and the Teachings that center around the Circle of Law and the information of the Medicine Wheels would have to be passed on, or there would no longer be anything left of them.

While Lightningbolt drove to his next job, he thought about the teaching Estcheemah had shared with him about what she called the Geography of the Mind.

"Who talks about Life?" Lightningbolt had asked her in wonderment. "Why is the subject of religion never about Life?"

The old teacher smiled and answered, "Newly planted fields grow, not because of the farmers, but because of Mother Life. The farmer can only hope, but Life Knows!

"The well diggers expect clean water beneath their rich Earth. Everybody expects to breathe, but who is appreciative of these wondrous presents of Life? Our Mother Earth is much too large for beliefs and far too Sacred for the manipulators to understand.

"Why does humanity insist on denying Sacred Mother Life? Would we have Life if She did not provide Life for us?

"We are the questioners of the Self," she explained to Lightningbolt. "The questioner of Life can be a quite different person than the believer.

When we Zero Chiefs speak to people about Self Duty and Sacred Life, many immediately think that we are speaking of beliefs.

"Most humans do not realize that they are intimate with Life because they are part of Mother Life, their Sacred Earth. Life is so vast a reality it is difficult for people to see the obvious—that they are dependent upon Life to be Alive.

"Lightningbolt, the Spirit of Life is an Ocean of Energy that surges upon the beaches of our minds. She churns the Emotions of every human born, cleansing us, renewing us, and strengthening our Dreams.

"How very delicate our Earthly Experience is. We gather our fragile, intricate jewels of Perceptions and Thought while we Live and Learn of the Presence of the Self. Our reality, everything that is our Mother Earth, is directly reflected into our Mind and becomes Knowing. This inward reflection of Life and our World is called the Geography of the Mind.

"Our Earth is very beautiful and She Renews all that She Is, minute by minute. However, where is Self Acceptance and this continuous Renewal for the Individual Human?

"Deep in the interior of the Geography of the Mind there once existed the land of true Enchantment and Learning. Yet, because this reflective, inward land is so broad, our attentions are drawn from the great curve of our Mother Earth into an ever-diminishing circle that becomes the tiny minuscule focus of our lives.

"Through our fears we close the minuscule and build a wall around it that we perceive as our giant fortress. This inward wall the Zero Chiefs call the Wall of Contention. Hidden behind this Wall of Contention are the great monsters of fear—pretense and illusion.

"Even though our Wall of Contention may encompass a farm, city, Reservation, ghetto, or state, our view of the world is still very small. Yes, it is

minuscule.

"Behind the Wall of Contention are other fences of discontent and insecurity holding out our imagined foes, big or small. Yet, shut away behind these fences and Walls of Contention are also those wondrous treasures of feeling and body that we know as the Self.

"The locks and keys of this inward world are forged through gradual conformity. And every fence is slowly constructed from materials of lies and ignorance. What we are building soon becomes a City Reflection of our Minds. The City is not our wondrous Earth, but we pretend that it is.

"The pretend towns and cities of the mind can reflect only the Self. In the mind, the harsh cities become blocks of internalized information. These blocks of information are a distortion of Life and have no healing or renewal.

"Healing, renewal, beauty, and belonging are never available to the human trapped in Self illusion. Escape from the Prison City is constantly imagined and sought for, but the Guide called Courage is not present.

"The endless repetition of the Mind begins to pollute our imagined worlds. Dirty avenues, work, business, and rental tenements can become the Mind of the City Dwellers; this they call their reality. Because the City Dwellers must shut out the awful noise, ugliness, and terror of their City Minds, they soon learn to shut out everything. Their minds begin to imprison them. Life's Beauty becomes something separate from the City Mind—a thing to be purchased.

"What happens next is that people stand a pretend figure at the Gate of their inward world. This pretend figure is fear, and before long it locks them in. The City Dwellers' minds begin to reflect their prison world and they withdraw from all that is Living.

"But before fear locked the Gates of their City Minds, all things were present in the Mind because it reflected their outward world. This Information—the Library of the Mind—is the Mind's most important structure. Yet, with fear as the guard, the door to the Library is shut tight.

"The terror of what might be hidden within this Library keeps individuals from ever opening the door to the Library of the Self and searching out their truths.

"When this happens, filth begins to collect on the streets of the City Mind, and soon all living things begin to wither. No rain is allowed to fall in the World of the Mind because the individual does not like mud. It isn't long before the Sun and Moon also die in their sky. The prisoner of the mind is only concerned with controlled sources of artificial light.

"When the City Mind begins to die, decay quickly sets in and the trapped person escapes ever deeper into a labyrinth of fear and crippling belief. Soon the Individual has nowhere to run.

"In time the source of water and food is forbidden to the Self. There is no more nourishment for the Self because all challenges have been eliminated. It is at this time that the Mind begins to die.

"Some people are fortunate enough to realize that they have created a prison of Mind, and they do something about it, knowing that they will have to confront their every fear and stupefying belief. When this happens there is hope of Renewal of the Self—this is not easy.

"Most people cannot throw off their internalized beliefs so easily. Usually they will search out a substitute for what they believe. But this is not change. Ninety-nine percent of all humans are taught to search for outside Authority instead of trusting the Self. What greater mistake is there for the human than this?

"Who is prepared to Love the Self, Teach the Self, Give to the Self, and Free the Self? Who is prepared to travel within the labyrinth of his or her own mind and confront the monster beliefs there?

Who will be not a judge but a Guide to the Self?

"Our Goddess, Beauty, can be discovered when the Self recognizes and appreciates their Life. The Experience of Life brings true Measure.

"We meet our true Self in Life; this is our Measure. Most humans imagine who they are instead of meeting who they truly are.

"We are not alive to imagine our lives. What we Live we are.

"We Spirits have to Experience our Life in order to know what Life means for us. The Child has no true measure of Life because she or he has no long experience to measure it against.

"The Life of the murderer, as an example, has its own measure for the killer. Their fact is that they kill. They learn of what it is to be a killer; this is their measure.

"The measure of what exists as Life is very different for the human who nurtures Life. People may live in the same time and place, yet they Experience Life and Measure their existence in very different ways.

"Beauty, Life, is our Teacher. She is the Teacher of the Self born into Substance.

"We are Born from Mother Life to experience Life. Life must be appreciated and touched before Beauty can be experienced. Sacred Life is Beauty. She is true human Measure."

The oil field work was hard and dirty and left him exhausted. Yet when it was complete, he felt just a little more secure. But it was money that made the difference, not his thinking, appreciation or care.

Pretense was still very much a part of Lightningbolt.

As he drove to Estcheemah's, he worried about sending his mother the thousand dollars she'd asked for. Why had he given it to her so quickly? She wouldn't need it for five more months. What was the matter with him? He cursed and half wept at his stupidity.

Yet while he sat with Estcheemah, Lightning-bolt laughed and told her stories of the job and how much fun he'd had fishing on his time off. But he couldn't fool the old teacher. She could see the fear and sadness behind his every word.

Estcheemah rose from her chair and put aside her sewing. She pointed to the kitchen door. He jumped up and followed after her. They walked. Lightningbolt talked on, but would not speak about his pain about money. She took him into the hills and they ate a quiet lunch together. Again, she tried to get him to talk, but he would not.

The past had not been so kind to Lightning-bolt's family. His father had died suddenly when he

232

was five years old, and left the family penniless.

No one likes to see their mother do backbreaking work, day and night, just to buy clothes for her children. Lightningbolt's mother did exactly that, and the children hated it with all their hearts.

Lightningbolt, his sister, and his brothers never did anything criminal, but they came within a hair of combating the law on a daily basis. If there was any kind of mischief or problem to be found, they found it—especially the boys. As a consequence, the Storm boys were known to be "wild and reckless."

They'd earned this reputation by being relentless hunters. They'd had to be; hunting was their primary source of food. There were other Breed and Indian families who were also poor and destitute;

these were their hunting competitors. Yet, no one messed with the Storm boys—they were always lightning quick to defend what they felt belonged to them.

Horses were the fastest and best friends of every hunter. The boys knew this, and consequently they would "borrow" certain horses wherever they found them and then turn the horses loose when the day's hunting was over. This little game was never appreciated by the local farmers and ranchers. Nor did they appreciate the chickens, pigs, ducks, or geese that "somehow got loose" from their rich farms and ranches.

Yet those "lost critters" were shared, as treats, with the old people, or an aunt. Deer, elk, antelope, pheasant, and rabbit were their diet staples. But

they never once killed any cattle. They didn't have to, because the deer and antelope were very abundant.

While hunting wild animals and herding cattle might sound romantic to some people, it was not for Lightningbolt. The work was cold, dusty, bloody, hot, miserable, and dangerous. Lonely days were spent hunting while other boys could play.

When any of the Storm boys did find jobs, they were worked like animals and were paid a pittance for their efforts. The farmers and ranchers were hard men who would kill for pay if they could justify the job. There was never a time when the boys were not cheated and deceived by the men they worked for.

There was no joy during the holidays either. In fact, these were the worst times of all. It's hard to describe the immense pain and shame that Lightningbolt's family was made to feel for being poor.

Over the years, Lightningbolt grew sick at heart with his deep sadness and awful sense of humiliation for being poor.

Eventually, because of poverty, Lightningbolt was sent to a government boarding school. He, and many other Breed and Indian children, would run away from school three or four times a year to help their families with the planting and harvesting on their small farms—and for the big cattle roundups as well. They also ran away to join in the Medicine Dances, yearly Powwows, and Ceremonies. Yet, over the years Lightningbolt spent less and less time with his mother. Although he loved her very much, and appreciated her wonderful sense of humor and quick mind, he became more and more involved in his own world.

The truth was, he could not bear to see her be without the riches he believed she deserved. He felt responsible somehow. His bitterness about his fam-

ily's poverty and its struggle to survive was buried deep in his heart, and drove him relentlessly with sorrow and fear.

While Lightningbolt deeply loved the words Estcheemah had spoken to him, he was also deeply entrenched in his beliefs about what money could do for him. No fear, no amount of absolute dread, was so great as Lightningbolt's apprehension about being without money. He was a man driven to a dangerous edge without realizing it.

He was unable to internalize what he'd learned from Estcheemah because he was so frightened of what he would find if he were to take an honest look at his madness. Instead of examining his fears, he worked all the harder to cover his frustration with physical labor.

There is a saying among the Manitou Cree: "Chance is the sure hand that turns the leaves of every tree and speaks the language of Infinity. To spin a leaf from your hand is to say that you are in a contest with Chance and the Absolute. Decision is the only guide through the maze of the Absolute, and Chance is the only guide through the door of Chaos."

Estcheemah knew that Lightningbolt had spun the leaf from his hand; it was the one she had given him. But there was no holding him back from his appointed contest with Chance and the Absolute. What his Decisions would be, she did not know. But she held her leaf, too, and this was her Prayer.

Estcheemah prayed to Life, asking that this young man would survive his severe attitudes and that he would come to understand his pains and fear.

Angry and burdened, Lightningbolt ran headlong into more difficulty. Like an alcoholic trying to throw off drink, he did the opposite of what he should have done.

He drove to Billings and traded in his dearest friend, the Silver Ship, for a new pickup. The purchase of the pickup lifted his spirits for exactly half a day; then he found himself even deeper in his remorse. That same evening he joined a few friends in a game of poker and lost every dollar he had.

One of the men who had joined the game late in the evening was to become Lightningbolt's good friend and nemesis. His name was Robert Fraiser.

Bobby Fraiser owned the Iron Horse Construction Company. He was sixty-four years old and growing very tired of life. Lightningbolt had helped Bobby on a bridge job a year earlier as a part-time worker, and Fraiser had recognized in Lightningbolt the makings of the perfect foreman.

Fraiser was the kind of man who knew how to flatter the people he wanted to manipulate. He was bearded and dapper, looking the part of the successful businessman. He used his looks and mind to get what he wanted.

The incompetence of his fellow officers and the butchery he had witnessed in Europe and later in Korea had made Fraiser a complete cynic. People meant nothing to him. In fact, he had nothing but contempt for them.

Lightningbolt delighted Fraiser. He was the ideal worker and, even better, he knew absolutely nothing about money or business. Bobby used Lightningbolt's ignorance to his own advantage. He paid all of Lightningbolt's debts and pumped up his ego with the promise of riches. And to sweeten the deal Bobby bought him a gooseneck trailer. This gesture very much impressed Lightningbolt.

Bobby had made millions and lost many more in the construction and steel business. He should have quit when he'd gone bankrupt for the second time, but he didn't.

Bobby was also destined for a little surprise.

Lightningbolt possessed an uncanny ability with people. He liked them and had enormous patience with them. People would do anything for him, no matter how hard or complicated the task. Lightningbolt would have rated as one hundred–plus on a charisma scale, compared to Bobby's minus ten. It wasn't long before he'd won Bobby's heart and the entire crew's.

Organization was one thing that Lightningbolt loved. He could lose himself in work "with a direction." He'd wake up at six in the morning and eagerly attack the problems of the day. Forty men, Caterpillars, trucks, cranes, fuel, the building, work, and time all became one exciting adventure. He labored day after day on the bridge project and learned fast.

This was the first time he'd really been away from the Reservation. And, for the first time, among these hardworking men, disappointed vets, the dispossessed, and criminals, Lightningbolt was not a Breed. The men teased him and battled with him, but never once put him down as a Breed, or even knew what it meant. All they were interested in was money, evading the draft or the law, and trying to outdo one another with their drinking bouts and prowess with women.

After Lightningbolt had become completely familiar with his duties as a foreman, he also became interested in the flowcharts that Fraiser had created. It didn't take him long to realize that nearly everything about the flowcharts was wrong. There was no regard for safety, and no intelligent methods for moving materials were outlined. The men meant nothing to Bobby—if a man lost an arm or was crushed on the job, it only meant he was a fool.

Fraiser never considered that the way he organized his projects had to end with disaster or death. Because Lightningbolt was the foreman, he too was constantly in danger and exposed to a thousand possible accidents. He told Bobby what he thought

236

about all of this, but Fraiser acted as though he'd said nothing.

Finally, Lightningbolt bulled ahead and acted on his own. In complete defiance of Bobby's edicts about work, he imposed his own strict—even harsh—rules to improve safety. Since the project went ahead on time not one word was said.

There was still another area, one that belonged to the superintendent—the way materials were handled and the way men were worked—that Lightningbolt felt had to change.

Sherwin Grouss was the superintendent. He was afraid of Fraiser and would bow and scrape whenever Bobby uttered a word. Reckless arguments erupted between Sherwin and Lightningbolt over safety and the flow of materials and work.

One weekend, Lightningbolt ended the argument by making his own flowcharts. The following week Grouss blew up and threatened to quit. Robert Fraiser turned his back on Sherwin and didn't say one word about the new flowcharts. He wanted the job done, and if Lightningbolt could pull it off cheaper, faster, and better, what difference did it make if the supe was pissed off?

Lightningbolt soon learned that the Iron Horse was in deep financial trouble. The only piece of equipment the company owned outright was a beat-up old diesel tractor-truck minus the trailer.

Fraiser talked Lightningbolt into taking shares instead of his overtime pay. Lightningbolt agreed, but then it was time for Fraiser to have his turn against his "smart-assed foreman." The very day that the foreman of the Iron Horse bought his first shares, he fired every welder and the two drunks that Bobby kept as his "best connectors." He next sold the truck and insisted that everything be rented.

The old engineer blew up and told Lightningbolt that he was an utter fool. Just because he had a few shares didn't make him equal in the company by any stretch of the imagination. Lightningbolt

laughed and teased Bobby, following him outside, where he turned the auxiliary fire hose on him. He didn't open the hose up completely, but he did drench Bobby.

Fraiser disappeared for nearly an hour, but when he returned he slapped his foreman on the back and said that the soaking had been the right thing to do.

Gone was every thought Lightningbolt had ever had about Beauty and Her Earth. Gone was his search for information and Life. Estcheemah would not come into his thinking for a very long time. The two cards he sent her in two years said nothing and meant even less.

Being the youngest man on the job as well as the foreman was not easy. Sherwin began to change his attitudes about Lightningbolt. It was not long before he began to trust Lightningbolt and call him Sugar Barrel.

The name Sugar Barrel had come about in Seattle. An incident took place that no one would admit. However, the end result was that eleven men and two women had been thrown into jail for "riotous conduct, brawling in a public place, being intoxicated in a public place, and using firearms in a public place."

Lightningbolt was not among the drunks; he hated alcohol. He was back at the job site, worrying over how to make more money. When he learned what had happened, he hurried to town to get his people out of jail. He needed them on the job.

After just a few minutes of talk, Lightningbolt and the judge became friends. Young cowboy met old cowboy. They discussed Montana, Wyoming, the military, weapons, women, construction, horses, good springs, bad pay, and ornery cattle.

Lightningbolt did not want to return to Seattle, so he sent Sherwin to write vouchers for the men and pay their fines. Grouss showed up looking like he'd just eaten a breakfast of dried spiders sautéed in axle grease.

The old judge asked Grouss about Lightning-bolt and was told, "Lightningbolt can make men eat sugar out of a gun barrel." Two of the oldest hands were witness to this exchange and gave Lightningbolt the name Sugar Barrel.

The human mind is a very complicated bioma-chine that can be remarkably tricky. Sugar Barrel and Lightningbolt were really not the same being. One being did not know the other. The most bold of the two personalities was Sugar Barrel.

Two years later, it was Lightningbolt who wrote a long letter to Estcheemah telling her about his work and mentioning that he longed to see the old hills of Wyoming again.

Estcheemah knew better than to try to interfere with the events that would either strengthen her student or destroy the young man who had come to her for teaching.

What she did in response to his letter was to touch upon a place in him that he could not help but love. She wrote him back a letter that carefully explained: "All good commanders will see to the safety of the job. It is the duty of the commander to educate the soldiers who are in the field of battle with him."

Safety and *commander* were key words that both Lightningbolt and Sugar Barrel could agree upon. Sugar Barrel tightened his control over safety. Lightningbolt became interested in the lives of the men he worked with. But it was Sugar Barrel who became ever more dependent upon his role on the job to let him know who he was. Lightningbolt was kind and Sugar Barrel was determined. On rare oc-casions there would be mental conflict between the two personalities.

Another year of boredom and hard work went by, but during the fourth year, Lightningbolt wrote another letter to Estcheemah apologizing for not communicating with her. His letter was filled with his worries about money.

He received a letter from Estcheemah that he lost in his toolbox for nearly two months. He was repairing a burned-out light on the company pickup when he found it again. He quickly ripped open the wrinkled and oil-soaked letter and read it:

Dear Lightningbolt,
  Thank you for your letter. We older people appreciate it when our youth remember us.
  No, the measure of Mother Earth will never be equal to any measure of money.
  Thinking is a Way of Life, not the fault of a foreman.
      With Love,
      An Old Lady

It was impossible to compete with the big com-panies. Yet Robert Fraiser continued to act as though he was one of the big building tycoons.

238

Iron Horse was still not making money. Sugar Barrel was determined to see it through. He argued with Bobby until it was agreed that taking on many small jobs was more realistic than trying to do one big job.

Tensions mounted between the two men when it came time to look around for further work. Lightningbolt would not let Bobby pretend for one second. It had to be real or he'd quit.

Iron Horse bid on five small jobs. They were all in Alaska, building steel-and-concrete structures for the government. The bid came through and the job was completed on time and without problems. But they had made the whopping sum of $5,000 apiece—after expenses. Nevertheless, the Iron Horse was now out of debt and could borrow money.

Sugar Barrel was delighted that the company was looking good, but enraged that he still had not made any real money. A lot of money had been earned, but it was gone, used up, burned.

Lightningbolt was beginning to wonder about his fate.

The next several jobs also paid off, but another year and a half had gone by. The Iron Horse now had $105,000 in its coffers, but most of this had been invested in trucks and Caterpillars.

Sugar Barrel bought another pickup and became even more fanatic about work. He thought of nothing but construction and how to do it better.

The next three bids were disastrous. They lost money—and a lot of it. The fates dangled more jobs and the promise of more money. Sugar Barrel was determined to not be a loser.

Then they made money in Canada on a job and things looked good again. Still, the tensions were high and the stakes were even higher. There had not been any joy shared between the two partners for months. Bobby was drinking again and "whoring," which was what he called his jaunts to the big town.

This kind of talk never settled well with Lightningbolt. Sugar Barrel thought the old man's habit was a bit old-fashioned but not out of the ordinary. However, there was another more serious problem that existed between Sugar Barrel and Fraiser. Bobby would become slack and stupid at the oddest times. He seemed to live in another time, a different era.

These oddities always centered around machinery and how to make the best use of it, as well as about the purchasing of materials. Fraiser would buy cheap things instead of looking for bargains.

One example of this occurred in Alaska. Sugar Barrel had gone to town to help out a worker who had broken both of his arms in a fall. Luckily for the Iron Horse, it had not taken place on the job—it was a mountain-climbing accident.

When Sugar Barrel returned to the job site, he saw that Bobby had hired twenty men to do some digging. He couldn't believe his eyes. Even the sight of the men slaving away with picks and shovels looked old-fashioned; that was just not done anymore. The foreman fired all the men and rented two Caterpillars to complete the job in a tenth of the time and for much less money.

A new bid was out, and Sugar Barrel waited in the motel for Fraiser's call. When it finally came, Sugar Barrel realized that the job Bobby had contracted for was insane. It involved every kind of problem the two men had agreed they would not touch.

First, the bid was with the government—this was always risky when a company was subcontracting third or fourth down the line, as the Iron Horse always was. Second, the bid was for underground work. This was always very tricky and dangerous. There were always too many unknowns. And third, the cost of machinery was going to be very high—it could eat up all the profits. Sugar Barrel was furious.

Trouble on the job began immediately. Their

new tractor-truck slipped on a steep grade and plummeted into a ravine. The driver escaped the cab and was not hurt, but over half the steel they'd purchased had been twisted and would no longer pass government specs.

Again, it was Bobby who was at fault. He and Sugar Barrel had argued about how safe the road was. Sugar Barrel had backed out of the argument when the cat-skinner sided with Bobby. But the road had collapsed just as Sugar Barrel said it would.

The cost of dragging the steel up the steep incline was enormous. Two Caterpillars worked for two days and two nights clearing the wreckage of steel and hauling out the truck. Next came the expense of removing the timber that had been downed by the truck, because it was clogging the stream at the bottom of the canyon.

The Caterpillars had to work from hundreds of feet above the wreckage, dragging the metal up from the bottom with long, cumbersome cables. The only alternative was to build a highway down into the canyon. Doing this was out of the question because it would have to be blacktopped to "preserve the historical value of the area."

The accident was a nightmare of problems and costs. When it was finally cleaned up, $70,000 had disappeared from Iron Horse's coffers.

Incessant rain became the next problem. Large pumps had to be purchased and no one nearby had any to rent. This meant trucking the pumps from Vancouver, B.C. Then, the third delivery of steel was two weeks late because Bobby had forgotten to call in the order. Next, they discovered that Sherwin had not been making the insurance payments.

Twenty men had to be paid for nothing while they waited for the shipment of materials to finally arrive. By the time the job was completed, both partners were broke.

Bobby smiled and shrugged his shoulders. The company wasn't ruined, he told his foreman. It hadn't made any money, but it was also not in debt. This meant they could borrow money and continue.

"It's been years," Lightningbolt said, pushing back his hat. "Mud, death, endless arguments, more money. Hey, it's not worth it, Bobby." He grabbed the coffeepot from the camper stove and filled his cup. "I feel empty inside . . . just like you are. Do you realize how long it's been since I've been with even one woman? I haven't prayed, not even once. I've seen three men die and others get hurt, all for money, and cutting costs, running risks, mistakes—sure, not my mistakes, but what difference does it make? Who was at fault?"

Fraiser was listening.

"No," Lightningbolt said, turning and looking out at the empty lot they'd cut into the land, "this shit just is not very pretty. I'm done."

"Everybody is entitled to a couple of mistakes," Bobby argued, flashing his old smile.

"How old are you?" Lightningbolt asked. "Middle sixties, nearing seventy? Look at what you have—nothing. Your women have your homes. Between us we have a few bucks, our vehicles, our campers. What the hell is that after all these years? Years of work with no pay, can you even comprehend that? Hey, I can't! I almost lost a war, Bobby. I went to sleep. Sugar Barrel. Shit, who is that? This is my last job."

"What'll you do?" Bobby asked. "You've got to work. What's waiting out there? Some magical aunt with money?" He laughed. "Naw, you're pissed now, but in a while you'll see the bright side again. We have to work, what else is there? Grab a whore in town, whoop it up. Come on, Sugar Barrel."

Lightningbolt was never more depressed. He went for a walk up the creek from the job. Scarcely a hundred yards from the government installation they had built, the scene changed radically. The ugly scar that the men and machines of Iron Horse had torn in the Earth could not be seen.

This was much more like home. How could he have forgotten the beauty so fast? He sat down beside the tiny creek they had dammed. She was running free again and was quickly clearing up. He shook his head and put his hand into the stream; She was cold. He stood and walked, following the pretty little creek. She flowed so serenely along her stone bed that it was hard to believe he had thought of Her as "an enemy."

Just a very short time ago, this stream had been the source of water for the camp and the job site, but it had also been a problem because of underground seepage. He had cursed the stream with hate. Looking back on what he had believed, he saw the insanity.

The few men left on the job when the construction was complete had cheered when the dam was blown up. Sugar Barrel had pretended that the "boys" were having a little fun, and so had Bobby and Sherwin.

At the time, he had stood shoulder to shoulder with Fraiser and Grouss, watching. He and the old-timers were an elite group, and he'd been proud to be one of them. What a stupid joke!

Now he was thoroughly disgusted with himself. Who or what was that in him? Was he a kiss-ass? Where did that creep come from that he was playing? How could he have been so incredibly crazy!

He followed the stream a little farther and found where the crews had gone for their drinking bouts. Whiskey, wine, and beer bottles had been tossed carelessly away and lay broken by the hundreds everywhere. Yes, now he remembered, this was the famous "shooting gallery." The men would come here on their days off to target practice and get roaring drunk.

Everything was tortured, broken, burned, and scarred from their "picnics." Shotgun shells and rifle and pistol bullets had torn and shredded the foliage for a hundred yards around. Great chunks had been hacked out of the trees where the "knife and ax championships" had been staged. The wounds looked raw and painful.

He kicked at the broken glass. This place reminded him of his own Life. He felt sick. Why hadn't he walked down here before? What could he have done anyway? Yet, what had prevented him from looking? What the hell was the matter with him?

Where were the bones of the creatures the men had blown to hell in their "turkey shoots"? He idly looked around the horrible pit of despair, searching for feathers or bones of the animals they had released and shot. There wasn't one sign of what their fate had been.

What could he have substituted for this open wound? He looked around. If they'd gone to another place, even a tiny town, they'd have torn it to pieces, too. No, this was his open sore. He would remember it.

He heard footsteps and turned to see who was behind him.

"Kind of ugly, ain't it?" It was Tardy Phil, the cat-skinner. He kicked at the beer cans. "You got the same idea I got, Sugar Barrel?" He looked very shy.

"Let's clean it up, Tardy." Lightningbolt smiled. "Fire up number eight."

"Can't do that," Phil answered smoothly. "Eight went this afternoon. No, all that's left is the rubber-tired monster." Tardy was looking at Lightningbolt quizzically. "Why'd you come out here?" Not waiting for an answer, he looked away. "My younger brother is a 'varmentalist in college. He'd puke seein' this pile of shit."

Lightningbolt spun on his boot heel and walked toward the construction site. How could he care? Was Tardy nuts? Who could take care of everything? He had done a good job with the men. Nothing had been lost or stolen on this job; that was a feat in itself!

No, it was no use. No matter how much he tried to comfort himself, the garbage and the cuts he had made in the Earth still looked like hideous wounds. He laughed out loud; was he taking it too seriously? So all right, they were fishing out all the ocean's fish. And there were too many people. And the polluting of our Earth would eventually kill everything. Why should he care? Who gave a damn? There were people who could make decisions about such things, weren't there? Or were there such people?

He felt suddenly punished. Years and years of work and no money—how could that be? Was this some kind of cosmic fate he had to live out? Why Bobby? Why couldn't he have met a man with a little bit more luck and better sense?

The crucial questions young Lightningbolt might have contemplated, which could have taught him something about himself and Life, fled his mind because of his worries about money. He now felt sorry for himself as he walked back to talk with Bobby.

Fraiser was sitting outside of his trailer, smoking and having coffee. He smiled when he saw Lightningbolt. "Simply lovely, isn't it?" he asked with a wave of his arm.

"Looks like shit," Lightningbolt answered, taking a chair.

"I guarantee you we'll make it this time." Bobby's smile was certain. "No use quitting broke, chum. What do you say?"

Lightningbolt shook his head. "I've got a few thousand hidden away, just in case it rained. Well, it poured."

"Wish I'd never quit the military." Bobby was dreaming again. "I might be a retired colonel. I telephoned and got the bid on the government job—they have troubles we can solve. Two outfits

went broke trying, but when my back's against the wall, I perform. You damn well know it!"

Lightningbolt thought of cave-ins, mud, Death. Sure, what Bobby was saying was true. He did perform when the going got tough.

"Stupid asses," Bobby fumed, standing. "They lick up the big money and make us solve the shit they get themselves into. It's been the same my life long. Even in the Second World War, we cleaned up the shit—"

"Without a foreman," Lightningbolt broke in. "I'll work for straight-ahead dollars. No investing in trucks. No magical bullshit hopes. It's pay the same as any man. I also want five thousand up front, no shares of any kind. Think of me as extra fuel or something. Write me off on your tax sheets."

The old man was stung hard. For a moment everything in him seemed to grow heavy. He looked at his young friend and felt his old pain again. Why had his combat unit been hit so hard in Korea? Why had he gone to that godforsaken place? He had been far too old for that shit. A person had to learn how to hang on.

If Lightningbolt would just hang on, he would see that old Fraiser was a winner. It was a matter of friendship, loyalties—sticking to it, by God! He would talk to this whelp later, after he cooled down.

"I'm an old pro," Bobby said, looking up into Sugar Barrel's eyes. "What good military man would not recognize your abilities? I've never seen a man who has the power you do to handle a project. If you'd been with me in Europe, we could have made many tank kills a day. You'd have been a highly decorated man. By Jesus Christ, I mean it!"

Lightningbolt listened.

"You're a born officer, kid," Bobby went on. "I swear to God. I mean what I'm saying. I quit with captain's bars on my shoulder. I could have been a

major, but I gave it all up to live the good life."

Lightningbolt stood and reached through the camper's open window and grabbed a cup. He sat back down and poured himself coffee and warmed up Bobby's.

"I wanted more than what the military could offer at the time." Fraiser tried to smile, but the effort was too much. "I wanted money, the adventure of whoring around. What better is there? Nothing, I tell you!"

Lightningbolt sat back in his chair and looked up at the blue sky. Here it was again, that damned feeling! He wanted to like Bobby. If he sat there any

longer, he would have the bridle bit in his mouth again.

"I'll make you fifty thousand." Fraiser was adamant now. "Five thousand . . . hell! I'll pay you that just to keep you hanging around. You're worth it, lad."

They drove to the "problem site" and had a look around. Two giant tunnels had been hammered into a mountain by other construction companies. No one seemed to know what the tunnels would be used for once they were completed. The rumor had it that only the government and the devil knew the why's for their existence. It was the Iron Horse's job to "get things safe."

Bobby took his time studying the tunnels. The job should have been abandoned, but Caloosa Corporation, the primary contractor, wasn't going to let that happen. Two massive problems stared Bobby in the face, as they had faced the others—who had failed. One tunnel level existed above the other. Keeping the two tunnels separate was where the problems began. Instead of there being solid stone between them, as had been predicted, there were a dozen types of sand and loose gravel. Caps and pillars had been hurried into place beneath the upper tunnel. All this jerry-rigging, it was hoped, would glue the mess together with cement, steel, girders, and wire.

When Bobby first heard of the problems that Caloosa was having, he'd been warned not to take on the job, just to "let the project die a natural death." There was a "slim chance that still existed," according to the tunnel experts Bobby had conferred with. "If charges were set in the right places, the whole problem could be collapsed and cleared up in a couple of months." As it was, the project was a death trap.

Bobby hired a demolitions expert he knew from the war. His friend had worked with explosives over half the world. But as it turned out, Mel had heart trouble and sent his "young genius" to get Bobby out of hock.

The young man who showed up was a demolitions expert from Germany named Ehrhard Warne. Bobby and the German studied the tunnel together. Ten days later, the time clock began to run.

The charges were set and most of the ceiling came down in B Tunnel, which was the bottom tunnel. The slide of mud and gravel was secured within hours and the crews worked twenty-four hours a day to shore up the tunnel for the other demolition work.

The concrete and steel that was left standing after the blast had become dangerous little islands that needed to be cleared away before the tunnel could be stabilized. Lightningbolt selected the men he wanted on his crew and made ready their machines. He worked beside the men and allowed Sherwin to be the foreman and superintendent over all the crews. However, the men on Lightningbolt's crew were loyal only to him.

Sugar Barrel was no more. The men soon learned this as they worked with Lightningbolt. This new man, Lightningbolt, was knowledgeable and cared for their safety, but he was not the reckless and carefree Sugar Barrel.

Lightningbolt was sad and angry. He kept his emotions hidden from those around him. He watched Fraiser, the old pro, search for that magical cutting edge where the money was.

Although the young man didn't possess the engineering skill he needed to understand the magical edges Bobby was taking, he had a powerful sense that something was terribly wrong. With every slice that Bobby took, the dangers mounted.

Smelling big trouble, Lightningbolt kept his crews far away from Devil Section, where Bobby was working. Fraiser worked on, recklessly oblivious to the danger signs that were accumulating.

While the other crew did the more prestigious work alongside Bobby, Lightningbolt's crew did the mucking and mule work.

Sherwin, the slavedriver, pushed Bobby's crew on. He also could see Death approaching, but he didn't have the courage to talk Bobby down. He too gambled that they could win.

Bobby raced against time and the odds that kept stacking up against him. He was in a war that he was determined to win . . . even if it was a tremendous gamble. If he could do what he believed he could do, then everything would be a piece of cake and he'd be a very rich man.

The cement was not holding in Devil Section. One morning it began to weep, threatening to crush all the shoring underneath it. All work ended abruptly.

Lightningbolt called out his crew to have their lunch. He told Bobby to end his mad rush to finish the project because it could kill his men. A shouting match ensued between them that the men found humorous. To them, Lightningbolt was quite suddenly looking very young and overemotional, even cowardly.

Bobby took a vote from his crew. They voted to stay and work.

Lightningbolt was stubborn; he refused to let the men on his crew work. It was precisely twenty-eight minutes to eleven in the morning when Lightningbolt told his men to eat their lunch and to get ready for any big problems that might arise.

Sherwin and Bobby took their crew off the main project and put them to work on a "patch." Lightningbolt had never heard of such a term and didn't trust the sound of it.

Dan, the powder monkey, came out of the tunnel at noon and joked with Lightningbolt's crew as he picked up his wire. Lightningbolt asked him how things looked. Dan said he didn't know, it was hard for him to decide. It looked bad, but it also looked simple. He returned to his work.

Lightningbolt's crew had eaten and were now playing baseball. The time was eighteen minutes after one. If Bobby actually managed to save the project, Lightningbolt was going to look like a fool. The time clock kept ticking and the men continued to be paid. The costs were mounting and Lightningbolt was getting scared that he had been overcautious.

Sherwin sent his crew out to eat at two o'clock. Bobby and Sherwin stayed behind to mop up along with Dan, the powder monkey, and Ehrhard.

No sooner had Sherwin's men reached the mouth of the tunnel than they heard a sickening crash behind them. A large whoosh of air blasted out of the tunnel. The thunder of falling metal, stone, and mud was answered by the shouts of the crews as they readied themselves for a rescue. It sounded as though the entire tunnel had collapsed.

Lightningbolt had taught the men what to do if this problem should ever arise. He'd drilled them many times. Now he moved into the tunnel with his men and machines. Two giant searchlights, which had been mounted on a front-end loader, pierced the dust and darkness, but they seemed feeble.

As Lightningbolt walked ahead, Tardy, the cat-skinner, followed behind in his front-end loader. The crew kept pace behind the loader. They walked cautiously until they came to Section Three and stopped. Before them lay a hopeless tangle of twisted girders and concrete.

Lightningbolt saw Bobby and called for cutting torches. The powder monkey and Sherwin were dead, crushed by girders and fallen rock. It was a miracle that Bobby was alive. Ehrhard was nowhere to be seen.

Fraiser was pinned between two massive columns of concrete. Blood was running from his mouth and eyes. Lightningbolt could see that his arm was nothing but shredded meat and splintered bone.

"Can you believe it, lad?" Bobby said. His every word was a foam of blood. "I don't feel a thing . . . looks like Sherwin is dead . . . too bad . . . never made a mistake like this . . . you look . . ."

Bobby slumped forward—dead.

Lightningbolt ordered everyone out of the tunnel to safety.

The following afternoon, James Harrison made his appearance. Jim was from Caloosa Corporation, the original bidder on the project, and had hired Bobby. The helicopter that dropped him off and then disappeared into the sky very much impressed Lightningbolt.

Jim conferred with Lightningbolt and discovered that Ehrhard was alive and still trapped in the tunnel. Lightningbolt and his crew had heard him early in the morning calling from the old elevator shaft, a few yards beyond the Devil Section. The shaft was open enough for the men to yell down to Ehrhard. Somehow he had survived. He was asking for explosives and food.

That same day Jim called the men together and had a conference. "Because water is eating away the Devil Section, we're going to have to make a move now—or let Ehrhard die." He gestured toward the map Lightningbolt had made. "A cave-in is possible along this entire seam. That man down there will either drown or be crushed if we don't get him out fast."

"He's in this section here," said Lightningbolt, pointing to the map. "I think that somebody could get through. We found a deep trench dug here for the electrical work—it's open, I think. I could crawl through the passage. It will be cat-and-paw work."

"Get that man out and I'll see that you get a bonus," Harrison promised. "I don't blame you if you say no."

Lightningbolt wrote a letter to Estcheemah telling her what he was about to do. He wasn't quite sure why he did this, but at the time he felt very heroic.

Two facts merged at this point in the life of Lightningbolt. First, he felt that he'd never accomplished anything. This was his big chance to show everybody his mettle. He needed the win because Bobby had accused him of being a coward. He could establish himself big with Caloosa if he did win. If he lost, what difference did it make anyway?

The second fact that crashed against the first, making everything even more dangerous, was Lightningbolt's need to be a hero. No one else would accept the risk. This made the job that stood in front of him even more of a challenge.

A few hours later, Lightningbolt was standing underground in the tunnels with Jim. The two men went over and over the tunnel designs together, studying every detail of what was known, arguing,

guessing about what was not known. They drew up a list of tools and equipment they thought would be needed: ropes, explosives, helmet lamps, radios, tools, food.

They left the tunnels and went to the office trailer and argued some more. Coffee and food were brought while Simms, Lightningbolt's welder, watched over him, readying the two backpacks his friend would take with him. Lightningbolt would have to maneuver one of the packs in front of him as he crawled through the twisted metal, then pull the second one after him.

"Ehrhard doesn't speak but ten words of English," Lightningbolt told Jim. "It's going to be hard for me to talk with him when I find him."

Jim stood and went to the door. "Packs ready, Simms?" he called.

Twenty minutes later Lightningbolt was strapping down his pit helmet. He examined the packs very carefully, then double-checked with Simms, making sure that everything was present and accounted for.

"Checked and double-checked them," Simms said, waving a piece of paper. "Everything's there, right down to extra pliers and matches."

Lightningbolt took the list and read off each item out loud until every item had another X marked by it.

"I hope Ehrhard is as good with plastics as people say," Lightningbolt mumbled.

"Expert," Simms assured his friend. "He can move a fly or blow up a mountain." He grinned.

"Good." Lightningbolt smiled. "Very good."

"Keep the pumps going full blast," Lightningbolt told Simms. "That water is my worst enemy."

Simms slapped Lightningbolt on the back as he bent down to enter the passage. Lightningbolt looked back over his shoulder. "Quiet," he ordered. "Remember that, because I have to hear every tiny squeak that metal will make."

Simms looked at his watch. "Will do," he answered. "Just like we went over it. I'll have the pumps off in exactly five minutes, and turn them back on in an hour. No one will make a sound. Good luck, pup."

Lightningbolt moved carefully into the jumble of steel. He crawled over the fallen girders with extreme caution, flashing his helmet light in every direction.

The tangle was awesome! After he'd crawled through the first jungle of twisted metal, he cautiously looked around. He could hear the trickling sound of water—it had to be near. This meant undermining and sudden shifting. He peered through the heavy gloom, trying to discover where the stream was. He knew that the water was slowly gnawing away the foundation of the struts that remained in place.

Now it was time for him to make up his mind. Should he turn around or go forward?

"It's automatic from here on in, dude," he said out loud to himself. "Can't worry, time to switch off the scaries."

He crawled farther through the mud and slime, touching every girder with his fingers, testing. The darkness was suffocating, horrible! Every nerve in his body was taut.

His own breathing sounded very loud in his ears. But then there was another sound, or lack of sound—a warning silence. His entire body spasmed and his muscles ached. What was it? What was different? He searched around him frantically, then a smile touched his lips. The pumps had been shut off. The slow, steady, dull thump had stopped.

Lightningbolt was becoming hysterical. But he didn't know it.

Had they turned off the pumps so he could hear better?

A massive beam now confronted him, and he touched it—it was very shaky. He eased the pack of explosives beyond it, then inched himself past it.

He pushed the pack forward again, then waited. Sweat rolled down his face. He rested, catching his breath. His heart was beating far too fast; he would have to stay calmer.

He tried to quiet his nerves by singing a Medicine Song in his mind. He pushed the pack around the next obstacle and gingerly crawled by. Now he'd have to get his bearings. How far had he come? How much time had gone by? All sense of time had fled Lightningbolt's mind. He crawled and groped along the ground, frightened to the core of his being.

Minutes became hours, and hours became short eternities. Far above Lightningbolt, men battled to keep the pumps running. Sections were collapsing piecemeal and no one knew what would fall next. Pumps were pulled from one section of the project and started in another; everyone was racing against time. Down where Lightningbolt toiled in the debris, he heard the pumps run, then suddenly stop.

The pack was becoming heavy and Lightningbolt's breathing was coming hard now. He stopped to rest. The awful darkness pressed in on him, threatening to extinguish his feeble light. If only there was more light!

He suddenly felt very depressed. The acrid smell of welded steel, mud, ooze, and traces of oil was thick in the heavy gloom. He struggled forward again and again.

Then he found a hard hat. He knew a body must be near, buried under the fall. The blood on the helmet told him that. Had the helmet been carried here by the water? Where was he?

Yes, there it was, unmistakable, the sweet, sticky smell of Death. The man was already rotting somewhere in the gloom. He hurried away from the stink as fast as he could manage.

He crawled for another half hour and saw a tiny avenue of twisted girders and broken cement that was ten to twelve feet in length. This section of the tunnel looked very dangerous. He moved the pack forward, then checked the one he carried, making sure it would not slip. He rested again, trying his hardest not to allow the sickening blackness to engulf him.

We're not going to share this damned coffin, Ehrhard, he said in his mind. You better be alive!

Lightningbolt crawled forward again. Where was the damned middle of the tunnel? Was this the middle?

He peered beyond the avenue at a monster tangle of broken cement and crushed metal. He stepped over the nearest girder and around a large slab of cement, trying not to touch even a spiderweb. Whenever he did touch any metal, he imagined that it trembled slightly. Each time this happened his stomach constricted with fear.

Then another sound greeted his ears—more running water. Where was it? He stumbled slightly, then froze. He listened. He pointed his helmet light here and there to see where the trickle was, but he couldn't find it.

The darkness fooled his eyes for a brief moment and he felt a slight bit of vertigo. He sat down and wrestled his emotions under control. He slowly calmed. He felt a tiny tremor. His right arm spasmed and his own hand slapped his cheek.

"Easy, old hoss," he said out loud. "You crazy . . ." He did not finish his words.

The sound of his voice had been enough to settle him. He moved again. He crawled another thirty feet. The going was torturous.

His helmet light suddenly revealed a wall of cement and metal that faced him and appeared to have no opening. He removed his helmet and searched the wall with his light. He blinked the sweat from his eyes, then checked what was overhead. Everything was hanging down, ready to fall. He now checked his watch for the first time.

"Four hours!" he gasped. "Impossible. What the hell! Check your watch. . . . No, forget it!" He shook his watch. A flood of impatience now gripped him. He frantically dug into the pack that held the explosives, looking for a second watch.

"What the hell!" He groaned. "Bullshit, four hours! Who cares? Don't panic, forget the watch."

He looked at the watch again, then remembered the pumps. Why were the pumps going on and off? What was happening to the pumps? "The goddamned pumps!" he screamed.

He sat down hard and tried to slow his breathing.

"Get a hold of yourself, Lightningbolt. You stupid ass," he cursed, "you'll die if you don't get yourself under control." In his mind, he fumed that he had panicked. To hell with the pumps.

"Watch the time," he said with a deep sigh. "Watch the time . . . pace . . . pace yourself. . . . Watch the time!"

He turned to the task that lay before him— getting through the wall. Suddenly he heard the slow and steady thump of the pumps. A shock stiffened his body.

Pumps, pumps? his mind echoed. He rubbed his forehead, drained of energy.

He slapped himself hard. "Think, think, what happened?" He looked at his watch again. Obviously the pumps had stopped. Obviously they had been turned back on. When, where, how, what? It didn't matter. His mind had turned everything around backward. "On your feet," he rasped. "What time is it?"

He studied the wall in front of him very carefully. He realized that he felt sick. He tried to vomit but nothing came up. His legs shook and perspiration flooded his face.

Lightningbolt sat back down, then fought the lid off his canteen. He drank deeply, then took his time eating three candy bars. His body shook. Slowly he got his breathing under control.

He cursed the wall as he searched. Where should he cut? He was angry that he did not know explosives.

"Blow them down," he said as he searched. "Blow them up." He bit his lip, then laughed. He hummed a tune as he searched the metal. Would Ehrhard know how to blow it down? Their return depended on that. Suddenly he froze again. What if Ehrhard was dead?

No, he was not dead. Light. Light, wonderful light. He pushed the wall and to his surprise a piece of cement fell through. But the sudden fall nearly caused him to crap in his pants. He stood up on trembling legs, pulled down his pants, and relieved himself. The smell of shit mingled with the stench of the tunnel.

He moved through the wall and saw a very large room. His light touched upon the overhead girders.

What was holding them up? He didn't even want to guess. His skin crawled as he hurried down the wide tunnel. When he reached the next jumble of metal, he saw a light.

"Ehrhard!" he called.

"Vorsicht! Schnell, das Bauwerk ist gefährlich. Schnell!" Ehrhard responded.

Lightningbolt eased himself through the last few feet of metal and now stood in a tunnel—no damage in this section. If he had known that Ehrhard was yelling that the overhang was dangerous and about to fall, he would have run.

"Radio," Ehrhard said, showing alarm. He pointed to Lightningbolt's pack. "Radio?"

Lightningbolt sat down, drained of energy. His legs simply refused to support him. "The fucking radio," he cursed. "The goddamned radio." He shook his head. "I didn't turn it on. Ohhhh, horseshit!"

He dug into his pack and pulled out one of the two radios he'd brought in with him. He turned it on and handed it to Ehrhard.

The engineer keyed the radio and asked for Simms.

"Ehrhard," Simms's voice answered. *"Was*

geschieht, Ende."

Lightningbolt dug out his radio and turned it on. "Simms," he said, "I'm here. Forgot to turn on the damned radio. Hey, we're all right."

"Why didn't you turn on your stupid radio?" Jim cursed. "Stupid ass." Lightningbolt didn't want to answer.

"Das Wasser im tunnel ist schlecht," Ehrhard said as he drank from Lightningbolt's canteen. *"Und der Luftschacht ist zerstört, einer ist unter Wasser."* He pointed down the tunnel. *"Sehr tief."*

Lightningbolt shook his head, then grinned. "Good, huh?" he asked, thinking the other man was talking about the water in his canteen.

"Schlecht!" Ehrhard answered, pointing to the water in the tunnel. *"In einem augenblick, es kommt hierer, wir müssen schnell arbeiten."*

Lightningbolt frowned, then shook his head.

"Bat . . . ferry bat! Tunnel vasser," Ehrhard said, pointing at the water in the tunnel again. *"Vergiftet!"*

"Bat?" Lightningbolt answered.

"No trinken. Vasser bat!" Ehrhard insisted.

"Bad." Lightningbolt nodded. "No drinking?" Ehrhard nodded.

"What's happening?" Jim's voice came over the radio.

"Give us a goddamned minute," Lightningbolt snapped back. "We will inform you of the changes. Over." "It's two in the goddamned morning!" Jim cursed. "We almost gave you up for dead. Can you see water? Did you have to crawl the entire distance?"

"Yes, I did, the entire way," Lightningbolt answered. "And I blew it and forgot the radios. Yes, there is lots of water. Looks real bad."

"The after section is down," Jim informed him. "B Section is closed, pump lines crushed, better get the hell out of there."

Lightningbolt had no more than let his finger off the radio when a thunderous sound echoed along the passage from where he had come. A sickening blast of air and debris choked them. Then there was an ominous silence. Ehrhard paled. Lightningbolt stood rigid.

"*Wir müssen uns schnell bewegen,*" Ehrhard warned, digging the explosives from the pack. "*Es ist gefahrlich.*"

Lightningbolt knew that he was saying it was dangerous.

"*Ja,*" Ehrhard said, pointing where the fall had crashed. "*Ich lasse es explodieren.*"

Lightningbolt knew that Ehrhard was ready to make the first set. This would bring down the dangerous roof and then they could make their way back to safety.

They crawled through the tangle and set the first charges. To shield themselves from the blast, they had to move back into the tunnel, which made a slight turn about twenty feet in. They trudged through the water, then flattened themselves against the wall. They were now standing in three feet of water.

The explosion hammered against them, giving them both nosebleeds. The violent blast had knocked them both sprawling into the murky water.

"Too much!" Lightningbolt cursed, getting to his feet. "You'll deafen us!" He brushed the slime from his overalls.

Ehrhard stood and wiped the mud from his arms. "*Zu viel.*" He frowned. "*Ich habe ein bisschen Angst.*"

They checked the passage; the blast had been a success—everything was down and looked solid.

"Phase one!" Lightningbolt yelled into the radio. His ears were ringing. "Solid, repeat, solid."

"Solid," Jim's voice answered. "Sounded like you used half the charges. Over."

"Yeah," Lightningbolt answered. "Over."

They crawled very carefully together for over three hours, but covered only sixty feet of tunnel.

They set the next charges and got out of the way. The second blast was not so terrible, and it did the job. Lightningbolt reported that phase two was a success.

The two men shook hands, then proceeded down the tunnel to set the last charges—beyond this point was freedom.

More hours went by. The water crawled after them.

Jim was frantic. "Phase three," he called over the radio. "How is it? How is it?"

"Clear." Lightningbolt cursed. "Readying phase three. The water is on our ass, looking bad."

"Phase three," Jim echoed from the radio.

While Ehrhard was setting the charges, an awesome groan thundered through the tunnels. Iron ripped and screamed. The sound was deafening.

Heavy girders plummeted from the roof and hammered to the ground with a din that sickened Lightningbolt's heart. He automatically covered his head, then sank to his knees, waiting for the worst. The sound was like nothing he'd ever heard. The entire world vibrated and shook. He was knocked senseless.

The next thing Lightningbolt knew he was standing and yelling. He kicked his helmet at his feet. The silence closed in, and terrible darkness as well. Was he suffocating? Why the thick darkness? Was he buried alive? Why was he screaming?

Lightningbolt fell to his knees and began to search wildly in the mud and darkness for his helmet. He found it and slammed it on his head. Was that him breathing so hard? Who was that moaning?

Fumbling, frightened to the point of vomiting, he floundered with the helmet light. The light went on, dimmed slightly, then grew bright again. He sat down hard against his pack.

Lightningbolt was still in shock. He sat there trying to understand what he was seeing. Slowly, almost automatically, he turned the light away. The jumble of cement and metal did not want to become real. He floated in a cloud of fantasy for a full minute before he realized that Jim was calling his name on the radio.

"Lightningbolt!" the radio called.

Slowly, stiffly, Lightningbolt picked up the radio.

"Lightningbolt," Jim said from the radio. "Lightningbolt." His voice sounded very far away. It was another minute before Lightningbolt could answer Jim coherently.

Lightningbolt's head began to clear. He suddenly realized that he'd been with Ehrhard. He looked around frantically and saw that Ehrhard had been trapped behind a horrible twisted jumble of metal during the cave-in. But Ehrhard appeared to be all right—it was a miracle that he was alive. The situation looked worse once Lightningbolt examined the trap more closely. Any wrong move would crush Ehrhard. He tried to explain what he'd found to Jim but gave up trying.

The engineer knew his situation better than Lightningbolt did, but could not explain. He waited in his trap for his inevitable end. If the wrong girder was cut through, he would be instantly turned into jelly. But if he was not freed, he would slowly drown.

Lightningbolt checked the time; it was eight in the morning. He beat on his watch. Was the time right? Where had the time gone? Where were they in the tunnel?

The water was steadily rising.

He studied the cage, trying to decide where to cut. It took Lightningbolt half an hour to decide which girder to cut. The water was rising fast.

Ehrhard closed his eyes when Lightningbolt asked his advice about the cut. He shook his head, refusing to answer.

When Lightningbolt had cut halfway through the girder, he stopped. Ehrhard was crying. The water was now almost to their knees.

Suddenly, the girder he had started to cut did not look right. Lightningbolt closed his eyes and brought Estcheemah into his mind. He knew that she would be sitting in meditation at this time. She did this every morning.

"Holy woman," he prayed to her, "Estcheemah, hear me. I am fearful. Please talk to the Creatress and Creator—WahKahn and SsKwan. Tell Mother Goddess Life to help me." He sighed. "Please let this girder be the right one."

There comes a moment in time when a Sense of Perfectness touches every human. There is not a human who lives or will live who does not, at some moment, Sense it. This Perfectness is the Earth Sensing with the human in trouble. A feeling accompanies this Sense that exists nowhere else in Time—it is Mother Earth's Presence and Love.

Lightningbolt felt this Presence, and his entire

being changed. A deep sense of quiet calmed him and soothed his troubled mind. He had felt Earth's Love.

He was about to continue his cutting when he suddenly had a Knowing that he should choose the beam to the left and higher. He stopped what he was doing and began cutting on the next girder. Ehrhard wailed with fear, then sat very quietly and began to breathe slowly.

"*Tu' es,*" Ehrhard whispered. He nodded to Lightningbolt.

Lightningbolt cut through the girder. The piece fell out and tumbled into four feet of water. Ehrhard crawled out of the trap.

They slowly made their way to the next problem. Ehrhard was shaky, but he finished setting his charges. They retreated until the water was up to their necks. The charges blew and the section rained down steel and cement, but not one pebble bounced from their helmets. At last, exhausted, elated, they trudged out of the tunnel.

The company doctor examined Ehrhard and Lightningbolt and told them both to go home. They were badly shook up, but there were no broken bones.

The cheers that Lightningbolt had expected were not there. All of the men had been dismissed from the job site, except for Simms and another man Lightningbolt did not know.

"Different company showing up," Simms announced, sounding overly formal. "I'll be with Caloosa. It was good knowing you, Lightningbolt." He shook Lightningbolt's hand, turned, and walked away.

Lightningbolt walked to his trailer and found Jim waiting for him.

"Where would you like the check sent?" Jim asked, his voice cold, almost accusing. It was more

than obvious that he thought Lightningbolt was a fool for going into the tunnels.

Lightningbolt scribbled down Estcheemah's address and handed it to him. He watched Jim leave without saying even so much as a thank-you.

"So this is what it's like being a hero—and a fool?" Lightningbolt said as he rolled onto his trailer couch. "People think I'm an idiot for going in there." He frowned, then instantly fell into a deep sleep.

He awoke with a start just as the Sun was going down. He sat up, feeling just a bit clammy. He looked out the trailer window and saw that the job site was totally dark—there wasn't a light on anywhere.

"I'm leaving this ghost town," he said, standing.

It was not long before Lightningbolt was pulling his trailer down the road, headed toward Ten Sleep. He drove all night and half a day before he reached Estcheemah's home. The drive was miserable beyond any experience Lightningbolt had ever known. On the way he had felt painful stomach cramps and nausea.

By the time he stood at Estcheemah's door, his hands and face were swollen and his eyes were red with exhaustion and illness. He knocked once, then sat down beside the screen door. Beyond this he could not remember a thing.

Lightningbolt fell deathly ill. He did not know it, but Ehrhard had also become ill. Both of them had been poisoned when they were knocked flat by the blast. While they were under water, both of them had taken in a mouthful of Death.

Estcheemah immediately began her work to save Lightningbolt's life. Her long experience with people told her what her apprentice needed. There was no time to get him to the hospital. It was too far away. She forced him to drink one remedial herbal tea after the other.

By midnight he was delirious. His body was cold, but he was wet with sweat. While Lightning-bolt writhed in his bed, he Dreamed that he was back in the tunnels, fighting a gigantic mechanical beetle. It growled, threatening to kill him.

He turned to face the monster and battle it with his cutting torch, but the monster would hide away in the darkness. The light from his own torch seemed feeble, and worse, it betrayed his position.

Was the darkness his enemy?

Was the light from his torch his enemy? He turned off his torch and was immediately made part and particle of the darkness of the cavern.

"Darkness is not my enemy," he said out loud. "Light is not my enemy."

The monster growled and advanced.

Was his voice now his enemy?

"My voice is not my enemy," he said out loud. "I speak to the darkness and I speak to the light."

Suddenly, the darkness revealed an inner light of its own. The darkness began to glow and form a spiral of light that became a radiant Circle.

Light and Darkness became one the instant he realized he could see a beautiful woman standing in front of him. Her armor was cast from the light of the Moon and the Sun, and possessed all the re-

254

splendence of night and day.

Her hair was deep ebony black and Her tresses contained the light of every Star. Her eyes shone as clear as Eternity and were the color of blue sapphires. She handed him back his cutting torch and it became a double-edged obsidian sword that shone with the power of the Sun.

He began to fight the monster with renewed power. He struck a death blow to the beetle that caused oily blood to spurt in every direction. Then the monster slowly sank into the water to die. It floated on the water, dead.

When the monster died, Lightningbolt's fever disappeared. It was evening when he opened his eyes.

"You're awake." Estcheemah smiled. She was sitting beside him. "How do you feel?"

"Great," he answered. "A bit weak, hungry. Boy, was I ever sick when I went to bed."

Another day would pass before Lightningbolt woke again. He didn't seem to be able to get enough sleep.

Estcheemah knew that the cruel hand of Lightningbolt's experience had quelled much of the chaos within him. He had decided to do things the hard way and had barely survived his ordeal.

255

Estcheemah encouraged Lightningbolt to rent a place called Magpie Springs. She knew that electricity had been brought to the land; however, the old homestead had no buildings. It was beautiful there and very quiet. He immediately did as she suggested. He parked his trailer near the spring and cleaned house.

He tried to fish for two days, hoping that it would lift the pall of gloom and melancholy in his heart, but that didn't help. He sat down by Magpie Creek and played in the water. Soon he was on his stomach looking at the water at eye level. He pushed a few tiny twigs into the water and watched them float downstream. Next he built a fence of twigs and made two bark-ships that he outfitted with sail-leaves.

He took off his boots and planted his feet in the mud and began to build his fortress with a little

more care. Stick soldiers guarded the pier and four ships bobbed, waiting to be launched.

Eleven magpies flew to the trees behind him and chattered about his presence. He turned and looked up at them. One of the birds dropped a bone. It bounced and landed two feet from him. It was a chicken bone.

A week later, the young man who met with his Teacher was much more mature. Joy, pain, thought, and experience had resculpted Lightningbolt. The face of the construction foreman now masked the face of the youth.

"Well, Estcheemah," he said after they had finished their evening dinner, "I'm not in the construction business anymore." He sighed. It was good for him to hear his own voice saying those words.

"Experience is wondrous." She smiled, then busied herself as she helped him clean off the table. "Take it from me, a human who has had a few years of getting experience." She chuckled. "We want it all—and try to keep it away from ourselves at the same time, just because sometimes it does hurt a bit."

Lightningbolt ran the water in the sink and looked outside. Was this really him standing here? It had been pure magic that he'd made it back. He began to wash the dishes.

"You have much to do," she said as she hung up the drying towel. "Meet me here in two days. We will go to the hot springs."

Arapaho Springs, Lightningbolt discovered, is a long narrow valley where two widely separated hot pools create Arapaho Creek. The valley splits at the place where the hot springs meet. The left valley continues to be the Arapaho, while the other valley becomes Wind Creek.

Lightningbolt picketed his horse. He'd bor-

rowed the mare from his uncle with the understanding that he would get her used to the saddle. She was a fine young Appaloosa who knew very little about humans and even less about bridles. She grazed contentedly near Wind Creek, where the grass was deep and full.

Twenty-five yards downstream from the Appaloosa, Lightningbolt was trying to set up the tents for Estcheemah and himself, but he wasn't having much luck. The tents' design was new, but the problems of tenting were old.

Whenever anyone gives another person the responsibility of taking care of tents, anything can happen and usually does. The tents had been borrowed and someone had forgotten to replace most of the tent stays that support the structures.

He approached the wide pool where the two creeks met. Lightningbolt's ears were burning with anger at the incompetence of the people who'd last used the tents.

A fat-butted raccoon watched Lightningbolt's every move. She loved her pond. The raccoon had been hunting there for most of her two years of life and had never seen a human so close. She was fascinated. She never expected the intruder to suddenly move toward her. Was he going to steal her fish from the pool? The coon was very concerned.

The hair bristled on her back as she watched the fish thief approach. When he reached the pond, he hesitated. Would he go away? The human was kind of ugly and clumsy, probably not good at catching fish. The human was also very, very big. This was no ordinary thief! She would have to be careful.

The raccoon hid in the grasses to see what the fish stealer would do next.

Lightningbolt was looking for a couple of limbs or sticks he could carve for tent stays. There were plenty of raw limbs high up in the two cottonwood trees, but none on the ground.

There was no way he was going to climb up into the trees. He was nobody's monkey—not even for himself.

He was cursing and thrashing around in the reeds and pond grasses searching for branches. How was it possible that there weren't millions of sticks here? Weren't there always billions of twigs and sticks pushed down the draws and washes? Of course there were. So why none here? He hoped that this problem was not some kind of Medicine Sign of how his Ceremony would go.

The raccoon did not trust this fish thief at all! He stunk and looked like he might step on her. She walked away from him, thinking that she'd come up from behind—when suddenly she smelled something incredibly wonderful!

What was it?

She turned her attention from the fish thief and began to search out the source of the delicious smell. She tested the air with her nose and turned right and left. Ah! There it was. She followed the scent and discovered a strange bundle of things that had been piled haphazardly together. What were these?

She could not know that Lightningbolt should have put things away so that raccoons could not rob them. He was just a bit careless that day.

She ransacked the camp. What? Yes, there it was! Never, in her tender life, had she tasted such a wonder. She contentedly ate up the dry meat, then looked for the second smell. Ahhhh! How wonderful. A tasty! She ate up two of Lightning-

around. The grass was so tall here that it was impossible for him to see his camp.

Squeal. *Psssst!* Chitter. *Caw caw caw!* The feast was well in progress and everyone was having fun.

What the hell? What was going on? Lightningbolt was getting very uptight. Instinct prompted him to slog back through the goo and mud to see what was happening at his camp.

As soon as the raccoon who had first seen the mud-slinking fish thief looked up and saw him coming, she ran as fast as her little legs would carry her. She didn't want anything to do with that animal! The crowd of banqueters flew and leaped for their lives.

"You robbers!" Lightningbolt yelled.

Then, patiently, he cleaned things up, made them safe from further attack, and went back to look for the wood he needed. But instead of sensibly moving in a circle, he went in a straight line.

This particular part of the land seemed to be deliberately swept clean of all wood. Finally, half an hour later, he found the wood he needed. It was within a hundred yards of the camp—in the opposite direction from the one he'd chosen to search.

Lightningbolt worked until evening, but he still did not have things the way he wanted them. The Sun was just going down when Estcheemah rode up on Broom Tail, her old faithful horse.

As soon as she saw his face she knew that she'd forgotten to tell him about the raccoons. Oh, well, energy is energy. Maybe it had put him in a different mind than the one he'd come with.

Night is the comforter. She cares for all animals and every human. She dresses Herself with the Stars and heals with the Dream.

A pearl-blue crescent Moon, called the Medicine Sky Bowl, was rising. The Swampy Cree of Canada teach that there are two Moons and they are Twins. They are the Twin Moon Light.

One of the Moons is the Dark Male Changer

bolt's candy bars, then decided it would be fun to try to untie the knots that lay about here and there. She would return to eating more after a little play.

Five other coons also smelled the food and heard the play. They joined the first one and immediately got into the food stores. Then six more heard the news via the mental pictures that raccoons send to one another. And they all trotted into camp.

Five skunks and eleven crows also got the picture messages and they hurried in. They didn't want to be left out.

Suddenly the hair rose on the back of Lightningbolt's neck. Something was wrong! What was it? He stood up from where he had been grubbing in the tall grass searching for sticks and had a look

Moon, while the other Moon is the Light Female Energy Moon. While the Moon is in crescent the twins are together.

There were no mosquitoes in Arapaho Valley. The floods were heavy every Spring, pouring down from canyons composed of solid stone high up in the mountains. Because of this, the valley knew severity. But She also knew gentle Healing.

The creek flowed serenely along her wide white-stone bed and was filled with eager trout. This night, there was an unusual glow about the stream. Estcheemah sat in her folding chair with her Ceremony blanket tucked about her legs. Her campfire burned with an amber light, warming her tea, while the crickets sang and owls called melodically from their willow perches.

The smoke from Estcheemah's Pipe moved in a protective way about her shoulders and blended as glowing magic into her hair of snow. The light of the Moon shone bright in the water, dressing the old woman in a Medicine Cloud.

The knowing, which is so familiar to every growing child, blossomed in Estcheemah's heart, telling her of Earth's promise of Life and Renewal.

The Sun sparkled and shimmered from the surface of the creek as Lightningbolt watered the horses. Estcheemah brewed coffee and tea while Lightningbolt went searching for more wood. When he returned he threw down his burden and sat down for a cup of coffee.

"Estcheemah," he asked, "what is Death? Why do humans have to die? Don't laugh. Couldn't Creation work out a better program? It seems strange, almost a waste. Do you know what I mean?"

"It's a good program," said Estcheemah, smiling. She touched his hand. "You are just a bit confused as to who you are as one of the people Born here in Life. You would not want to live forever. That would be a bore. But you and I can look at what Death is.

"All humans are born from the Spirit World. The Spirit World is the place of Death. We die to enter back into the Spirit World. While we are in the Spirit World, we are known to be Dead for the People Living on Earth. However, this needs to be looked at more closely.

"While we Live we speak of the Spirit World as Death, because we must die and leave our bodies to enter the World of Spirit. Seen from the other side, this is reversed. In the World of Spirit to be Born on Earth means Death. To come to our Life World, or to Experience the World of Life, means that we have to Die in the World of Spirit.

"We die as a Pure Intellect, a Spirit, to be Born as Spirit into Substance here in Life. Pure Intellect, for the Zero Chiefs, meant Pure Knowing or Absolute Knowing about the Self and Spirit—which, the Chiefs taught, was Spirit and Knowing without Substance.

"In other words, this world we know as Life is really the Death World from the viewpoint of a Pure-Intellect, which is Spirit.

"We dwell much longer as Pure-Intellect, Spirit, than we do living in Life. Life and Substance is a much different existence than Pure-Intellect as Spirit. Life is not very long. Even the span of one hundred years, should we live that long, is a very short time.

"While we dwell in the Spirit World we are the Essence of Human. We know no form and every form because while we are Pure-Intellect we possess no physical form.

"Spirits can choose to be either female or male, because within every human's Spirit Essence there exists both Female and Male.

"We have lived many times in this, our Earth World. We have all been born many times. We have been both female and male. We have done all things."

"Why are we born?" asked Lightningbolt.

"We Humans are born to Experience the *Essence* of who we are. Each of us is the sum total, the Essence, of what we have done and how we have known the Self.

"Each time a human is born on Earth that human has a Life Experience. This Life Experience can be one of absolute mediocrity, and it then becomes part of the Essence of the Self. Or we can live our lives courageously and this becomes part of our Essence. Or we can be hateful and murderous, and this becomes our Essence. People can hide behind the mask of being spiritual or pious and this becomes their Essence.

"When we die we really do take it with us—our Essence, that is. What we were, we become. When we are born, all Memory is taken from us of our previous Existences, even as Pure-Intellect. You see, to be Born into Life Substance is the greatest challenge known in Creation. Here in Life we learn of exactly who and what we are—it is our Essence.

"There is never any lie in Life, for the lie becomes the Essence if we lie our Life long. Then it becomes the fact of who we are and what we will be.

"All Spirits born in Life were once Pure-Intellect, Spirit, and because of this WahKahn and SsKwan Know us all Directly. Everything created is part of WahKahn and SsKwan. It is their Great Law that All Beings and Things Will Evolve. While we dwell as Pure-Intellect we are formless and Exist Within the Spirit World of the Formless, which is the Source of all forms that Spirit can Imagine.

"The Chiefs called this Formless Spirit World, 'The Great Dream.' Within The Great Dream, there is no Limitation.

"While we Live, Dwell in Life Experience, we have emotions and we possess a body that can hurt and die. We can laugh and we can cry and we can love. But Pure-Intellect cannot cry or laugh. Laughter must be imagined, as emotions must also be imagined.

"The rain can be imagined. The cold, crisp winter day can be imagined. A friend can be imagined. We can imagine war or anything else. You see, it really doesn't matter what a Pure-Intellect Imag-

263

ines because it is only Intellect. The Pure-Intellect, as a Spirit, can imagine eating a peach. But the peach is not there; it is not Alive. The Spirit can imagine being good, or indifferent, or warlike. Yet, it is all only imagined.

"Humans on our Sacred Mother Earth can taste the delicious peach. We can experience Life. We can also die. We cry, we feel, we love, we laugh, we hurt, we are surprised, we are within change.

"The Limit of Spirit, of Pure-Intellect, means that we have been born and we inhabit a body. How very wondrous!

"Now I struggle, I learn, I feel, work, run, and play. I can make a mistake. I can even fly. When we are born on Earth, we are born Free.

"WahKahn and SsKwan build with Atoms. They know of our every fiber and being, they Know our Essence.

"The ancient Zero Chiefs sang:

All of Creation is With the Living.
All of Creation can Feel the tender kiss.
All of Creation is Learning.
All of Creation Learns of Beauty.
We are Evolving Beings.

"It took four billion years for our wondrous Mother Earth–Life to evolve Substance Life to the point where we humans could be Born to Her.

"WahKahn and SsKwan, in the form of Sacred Earth, give us Human Self Spirits, Pure-Intellects, our Lives and our Bodies! Can there be a more grand Present given to a Spirit than our physical Life?

"As you can see, Lightningbolt, the program is bigger than you thought.

"It has taken another few million years for Humans to evolve to our present state. To Evolve and to become a Higher Being Within Essence is the Challenge for every Spirit Born into Substance.

"But we must look even further to understand what is meant by being Born Free. What does Self-Freedom mean?

"Free means to be Free of all things. We are Free while we are Alive to Experience and to interact with all things and every human we meet. We can build, destroy, love, procreate, kill, heal, lie, tell the truth, hate. We can do anything we Choose to do. We can even deceive ourselves.

"The Pure-Intellect knows that Life is not long. Spirit does not fear Death. Pure-Intellect is Spirit and is Deathless. While we live we dream, but these dreams are far different from the ones we have known as Pure-Intellect. While we were Spirit, what we built we could tear down. But it was all only the Great Dream. There was no Substance. We could not die. Those other Spirits that interacted with us within the Great Dream also could not die.

"Yet, here on Earth when we act out our dreams, things happen! Our Present of Life is Precious.

"The Garden is picked in Life. The musical instrument can be broken. The body can grow old. What shall you do in this Garden? How will you touch in this Garden? What are your deepest responsibilities to your Self and Life?

"Humans play together in Life and they dwell together in Life. All the soldiers that we kill, die. All the toys of war in this Dream can be broken and they rot. We can also touch while we Live. We all are delicate.

"While we dwell within Pure-Intellect, in the Great Dream, there is no way for us Spirits to really Touch. We can Touch here in Life.

"Mother Life Gives. Mother Life Shares. She Births us all and everything. Great Giving is Life.

"It is called the 'Great Giving' because for Life to exist, the Earth Circle of Life and Death must be Present. The trees, all plants, are born and must die to give their lives, so that humans can have their food and homes. All plants and animals Live and Die. If the plant does not die by the knife it will die

in the teeth. If it does not die in the teeth it will die in the caustic acids of the stomach.

"Death furnishes all things with Life.

"There is no separating Life and Death.

"The plants and animals Die to Give Life.

"On Earth we are Free of the Great Dream. Because of the Freedom that we are given from Creation and Our Mother Earth, we possess Human Choice while we Live.

"We must be Born here with Mother Life to have the ability to Change and Evolve within our Self Essence. We can do this by our every Choice of Thought and Action while we Live.

"We are Spirits Born into Substance to Learn and to Grow.

"The Deathless Pure-Intellect that we know as Spirit cannot die. Pure-Intellect learns of Love here in Life. There is no true Love within the Great Dream—there is only the Great Dream. All energies, all emotions, all images, all thoughts exist within the Great Dream.

"Here, within Life, there is danger and there is fulfillment. The Essence of what we are is tested here in Life. All Spirits born, one way or another, are in search of the Sacred Self. To discover the Self and Know the Self is the key to all Existence.

"Who am I? What am I? These questions are eventually asked to the Self of every Spirit born."

Lightningbolt was deeply moved by what Estcheemah was teaching him. He asked about how he could change his life.

She told him: "Life Experience answers all and changes all. Only in Life can we humans change our Essence. Only in Life do we have true Choice.

"While we are Spirit we dwell within the Great Dream and are part of all things. Choice and even the concept of Choice is meaningless while we are without form and are Pure-Intellect."

Lightningbolt asked Estcheemah about enlightenment. "Is it true that every Spirit was instantly enlightened after Death?"

The old teacher laughed, answering, "Only in Life Experience can we find enlightenment.

"If we Choose not to educate the Self, then the Self cannot grow. The Self will know only the Essence of ignorance."

Estcheemah explained how it was possible to actually entrench an Essence within the Self. For example, if people insist upon being lifelong victims, then they will die with the Essence of victims.

"We should think deeply about our Life instead of just accepting it," said Estcheemah. "To test this thinking, why not assume that things will remain the same our Life long and will not change. What would happen if you remained in your present mind and never changed? First of all, you would have to work very hard at keeping your present attitudes, and you would have to be rewarded by your culture for your beliefs."

She pointed out to him that some of his religious beliefs and personal attitudes about women were elitist—that he believed that because he was a male he was above all females.

"In our present culture the elite human is never a woman. Only the man is the elite. The prevailing belief teaches that all males are the elite. And 'God' has decreed that all women are beneath men, and are subhuman and never can become the elite.

"This kind of belief invites other kinds of elitism and beliefs. For if women can be subhuman, then whole races of people can be subhuman.

"Women have been burned as 'witches.' The elitists believed that they could destroy women with absolute immunity, calling their acts of murder 'righteous and lawful.' You can see how crazed the elitists can become.

"For the elitist, the Female Earth is dead matter.

"They believe that anything can be done on Earth and be hidden from Creation. Because Earth is supposed to be dead matter, She can know nothing of humans or what they do to one another. Earth, they insist, is a plaything, a circus where murder and every kind of ignorance can be hidden.

"Elitists are taught that they can be mean and loathsome their Life long. They can cause humans to scream in pain in their torture chambers; they can commit every murderous act that can be done by a human, then escape all Self Responsibility for their crimes by being forgiven by an 'official' of another elite.

"A person can believe that Creation depends upon men to forgive people's atrocities. But this is absurd. Creation is not human dependent.

"We know the human mind remembers. All things experienced are remembered by our Essence. The Essence of what happened while we lived is remembered. Consequently, it does not matter if murder is sanctioned while we live; we remember that it was murder.

"But Creation has an even better Memory.

"Mother Earth is Mother Life. Life Births everything of Earth. Mother Life, with Her Love and Perfectness, has given Spirit the chance to be Born and, as humans, to experience the greatest School in Creation—Life.

"Mother Earth also has Her Laws.

"The first Law is that all Spirits will live within the physical and possess a physical body.

"Her second Law is that all of Her children will be able to imagine all things. No situation, no experience, no thought, no action, will be withheld from them. In this way all Humans will learn and grow. She demands that all Her children have Human Choice and Self Responsibility.

"Because of these Great Presents, given to us all by Mother Earth, we have the freedom of action to do all things.

"Her first Present is our Lives. Her second Present to us is Human Choice—it is the right of every Human Born. And It is this freedom of action, our power of Choice, that decides Essence.

"Nothing will be withheld from us. We can do and believe all things.

"We were all born from the Great Dream. The Spirits of Pure-Intellect could now be Born because Mother Life gave them that chance. And for the first time within Creation's billions of years, these Spirits could be Born from the Great Dream and have true Self experience in a physical body.

"While we remain within the Great Dream there is only the illusion of Choice. When we Live with Mother Life, here on Earth, we face our greatest challenge—Self Choice.

"These Choices we make are real, for they affect our every action. Action is experience, and experience is Life.

"Humans are born into their challenges," said Estcheemah, "and these personal challenges are far more sophisticated than what most people would care to believe.

"Belief, in fact, is every Human's greatest foe.

"More people have believed what Life is than people who have learned what Life is.

"It is possible to remain trapped in belief our Life long. It is possible to have Choice our Life long. It is easy to believe that there is escape from Life. It is easy to believe that there is no Choice in Life.

"Every one of us is Born into our Self challenge. Every one of us can possess the power of Victory if we battle for our Choice.

"The Teaching Song of the Zero Chiefs goes like this:

"*Choice must be fought for to be realized for the young Flower Soldier.*
"*We can create Beauty when we seek to Know our Destiny.*

267

"We can care for the Self.
"We can teach the Self.
"We can be Self responsible.
"We are responsible for our Life.
"What greater wonder is there than our Life
experience?

"Yes, Lightningbolt, Life and Knowledge are the Realities of Life-Experience. The Essence of who and what we are we bring with us into Life. But the Essence of the Human Spirit can change and evolve here on Earth. It is also possible for the Essence of the Spirit to atrophy and become twisted when humans refuse Self Responsibility.

"We must always remember that our Self Essence survives our Death. What we are before we are born, is what we will bring with us into Life; this is our Ever-Beginning.

"Growing is the Principle of Life. We grow as our Essence grows and change with our experience of Life and Time.

"You felt the Presence of Life when you were about to lose your Life in the tunnels, Lightningbolt. You must consider deeply that the instant you recognized Life was when you became aware that you are only Present because of Her, and that you needed Her.

"Life breathes the Eternal and the Seasons. Life is Forever. Life is Eternal because Life is One with WahKahn. Yet Life is the fleeting moment; She is our Seasons. Life Created the Seasons so that we Spirits could Experience our Time, which is our Lives.

"She is the Eternal Rose. The Rose is the Symbol of Life for all Zero Chiefs. She is our symbol of Sacred Mother Life. What other symbol holds such

268

Power for the Flower Soldier?"

"How could I have missed this? It is so obvious!" Lightningbolt frowned, feeling suddenly very inadequate. "I was ready to throw away my Life! Was I crazy? Some kind of strange crazy no one talks about?"

Estcheemah answered his question slowly and with careful words. "This very simple illumination of yours—that you Live because of the Present given to you by Life—has been missed by most of humanity.

"You see, Lightningbolt, it is not so complicated. When we have no Love for our Self, then what does anything matter?

"When we have no thoughts about the Self, then what matters? When we do not question our Existence, then where is meaning for our Life?

"When we do not celebrate our Existence, then how can we recognize or celebrate the fact that we Live? We cannot, of course, because we believe that our Self has no meaning and even that Life has no meaning."

"What is Life?" Lightningbolt asked, then laughed, embarrassed. "I mean, did I have a Spiritual Experience in the tunnels? Is Life something I can ever understand?"

"What is Life?" Estcheemah chuckled. "A Spiritual Experience!" She laughed. "Life is the Life Giver of all Spirits Born to Her. That is really something! Of course Life is a Spiritual Experience, you ninny!"

Now Lightningbolt laughed with her, happily.

Lightningbolt might once have believed that he knew every inch of his thinking. But now his mind had become a massive living world where he was a microguest. Was it possible to completely explore the world of his Mind? Its vastness and extremes were as wide and as variable as our living planet. He would try.

That evening, Lightningbolt was very quiet. He walked along the shore of the creek and listened to Wehomah, the Wind, sing and talk.

The following morning, Lightningbolt awoke at dawn to walk with Estcheemah. "I need a change, and I need it bad!" Lightningbolt grumbled as they walked.

"Change begins within you," she told Lightningbolt. "Never wait for change outside of you. You will shape your world only by changing what exists within you. Ghettos do not shape people. People shape ghettos. Many of the people who have elevated humanity to great heights were born and raised in the meanest of circumstances.

"Only the tiniest fraction of humanity will battle to possess Self thinking. Most people are dependent upon the opportunities provided for them."

"That seems strange," Lightningbolt said with a shake of his head.

"All human children need to be cared for from birth," she carefully explained. "But this one gracious and simple act creates an inevitable dependency upon the physical. We are born into a physical existence that demands a physical answer for survival.

"What happens, Lightningbolt, is that this dependency upon the physical keeps most humans from understanding that we can change our physical world through the use of our minds. This is because everything that happens in the mind is abstract—not physical. We call it thinking.

"Thinking is possible through experience and learning. But few people know how to appreciate their physical world and what it can teach them. Consequently, they throw away knowledge, minute by minute, on a grand scale, believing they can do nothing to change their physical circumstances.

"Thought is an accomplishment, not a given. Through experience and curiosity we develop our thinking. But even curiosity is also not a given. It is a present from the Self. The lazy are never curious; they are only entertained. Curiosity comes through Self Action. The Knowledge we Learn through experience, curiosity, and thinking is the Reward to the Self after long, hard work.

"The greatest of all things learned is that we are a powerful Self—an independent Self that is capable of thought and imagination. We can accomplish almost anything we can imagine.

"Learning of the Self gives us the courage we need to go beyond our daydreams and physical dependencies and fantasies. This is very important, for it takes courage to think the unthinkable.

"To think the unthinkable is to question the Self and everything that the Self is. It is in this way that the Self will see how dependencies imprison thinking."

Lightningbolt was ready to learn. His latest gamble with his life had left him determined to change his physical circumstances, yet he continued to be very unsure of himself. Estcheemah knew this and waited for the right moment to speak. She did not want to dramatize his perils.

The perfect moment to teach Lightningbolt came when he stumbled upon an old cow skull. They had been walking together near the creek when the find was made.

"Well, would you take a look at this?" He smiled, holding up the skull. "I bet someone would like this on their gate!"

"Or yours," Estcheemah teased him. "You take Death very lightly when it comes to a cow. Can't you see your own skull in that one?"

"I have been very callous," he answered.

"There are no more great herds of buffalo, Lightningbolt," she told him. "Yet our people cling to the symbol of the buffalo.

"The skull of the buffalo has come to mean very many different things to our people. But the children today have no idea what the symbol meant to our ancients.

"If the Reservation leaders were to pray with a can of tomatoes or a box of crackers, these would hold more reality for today, yes, even more joy. The youth would also know a truth and not a lie.

"At one time the symbol of the buffalo meant the Spirit of the Land. The sweet corn, the whale, the salmon, and wheat were also symbols of the Land and the Oceans. People respected the Spirits of the Land and Oceans because they give the people their Lives. Now people think that factories give them Life. How very sad that is for everyone.

"Who honors what we eat in our modern world? We no longer know how to honor our food. So many things are packaged to sell rather than to be loved as food.

"Our food can be honored again. The cow gives us much more than the buffalo. Multimillions would be dead if we did not have cow's milk. And who doesn't want to have ice cream?

"At one time the fish was so holy a symbol to the Europeans it became a symbol of their God. But among these people the Mother Earth was not cel-

ebrated for Her gift of the fish. She was forgotten, and soon the symbol of the fish meant only what could be stuffed into a sardine can.

"Just think for a moment. You live because of the plants and animals that you eat.

"The death of the hen that has given the most eggs means nothing to humans. She lives, is used, and dies without so much as a nod from people. She represents only money. But shouldn't we celebrate the gift of her life through thanksgiving to Mother Earth?

"Tomahseeasah taught about the Grass-Flower Beings. Do you want to hear how she taught people to respect the cow? Do you have room in your heart for these things I say to you?"

"I do very much, Estcheemah," he answered gently.

"She-of-the-Wild-Roses, Tomahseeasah, talked about the Grass-Flower Beings." Estcheemah smiled. "Grass-Flowers are what cows are—they are composed of the grass and flowers they eat. Our Chief called the cow Grass-Flowers.

"The Northern Cree and Ojibwa also call cows Grass-Flowers. While I was in Canada, among the Ojibwa, I heard Tomahseeasah's Medicine Song sung by a woman called White Bark. She was very old. It went like this:

"We meet Life on the Land called Prairie Mother and
  Father.
"We meet Death on the Land called Prairie Mother
  and Father.
"The Grass and Flowers are risen up as Prairie
  Mother and Father.
"We are risen up as the People.
"The lyrical song is sung.
"We are risen up because of the Prairie Flowers.
"We are singing in Life about Life and Death.
"They are the questions dancing around us.

"So, Lightningbolt, honor the plants and ani-mals that feed you. Honor Life. Honor Death. Be responsible for all plants and animals that you kill. Be respectful of all that exists in your world."

"I will," he promised. "I certainly will try, Estcheemah."

"You are now, finally, in a place where I can talk to you about humans. More people fear to live their lives than they fear their deaths. This is especially true for the young, Lightningbolt.

"The reason you did not respect your Life while you were in the tunnels is because you did not respect Mother Life. You did not know Her.

"While we are young the River of Life flows toward us. And when we are older, the River flows from us.

"What will flow from us when we are older? Will only bitterness, greed, and fear flow from us?

Or will the energy of creativity, the power of building, or the understanding of change flow from us?

"What flows toward us? What do we choose from the Water of Life? Do we choose the beautiful? Do we choose the criminal? Do we choose to attempt to hide? Are we open and clean?

"What flows toward you, Lightningbolt?

"You have never spoken to me about your friend's suicide. The reason for this is you fear that I will upset your emotions and attitudes about what happened."

"Hey, no way!" he argued. "I . . ." Suddenly, he felt sick at heart. Whatever he had been going to say fled his mind. He knew that his words were empty.

Estcheemah immediately saw the change and was happy for it. "Exactly." She smiled. "It's time to bury Alex. And it is time to speak about Death.

"Few people have the courage to think about how or why they should be born, Lightningbolt. Alex was a thief. He stole himself blind and did not care. Your friend was incredibly indulgent and you know it.

"I spoke with him while he was on leave, the time he came back from boot camp. He could hardly wait to kill. All the toys he ever wanted were finally his, and he could go and play with them. It was not possible to talk with him.

"He was acting out a role that only he knew, and he was determined to play it to its awful end. You were a simple pawn in his world, Lightningbolt. You were supposed to run after him and find his body. He believed he could use Death for his grand finale.

"Alex was an only child, even though he had two brothers. Everyone was his father and mother. Few people have been more overly indulged than Alex.

"Your friend was a little hero, a hero without the intelligence to know who the enemy was. Life was cheap to Alex, and whiskey and drugs were expensive.

"You have changed much since the day that your friend died; you are no longer the same man. It is easy to die, hard to live, Lightningbolt.

"Let's you and I talk a minute about what Death would be for Alex, all right?"

"It would be boring, like his life was boring," Lightningbolt answered. "And he could be a real negative dude, real bitter at times."

"Exactly," she replied, "simple-minded and boring. The Essence of what he possessed, here on Earth, was nothing you would want to own."

"Wow," Lightningbolt exclaimed. "Some people's Essence must be filled with their own created monsters! I think I'm beginning to understand."

"And," said Estcheemah almost casually, "if you try to avoid anything, no matter what it is, or its nature, then that Essence will also become part of you. There is no escaping Life, Lightningbolt.

"Face your challenges while you Live, and you will be able to look your Self in the eye when you return to Spirit. Possibly you will even be able to look Creation in the eye.

"Tomahseeasah spoke of how our every action in Life should be a question and not an answer. She said that to appreciate our Life is the greatest of all things holy.

"She taught that our honesty is the only thing we can offer to Creation. What else can be given? No matter what our honesty might be, it is a present to Life and a truth known to Creation. When we speak to Life of our Self and our honesty, this is celebrated and honored by WahKahn and SsKwan."

"What you are saying is that although Alex is Spirit again, he is also saddened by what he did in Life, right?" Lightningbolt was very pensive. "I don't want to be so broken and sad, Estcheemah."

"People like to moralize and pretend with Life," Estcheemah explained. "Our legal system also likes to pretend, because all moral laws are based upon speculation and beliefs.

"Law can never describe to humanity that which is moral or right. Morals can never be legislated. The reason for this is that the question of the Law is never WHAT was done but HOW it was done.

"How we do things, How we approach something, is the question. For example, the question is not WHAT to touch but HOW to touch; not just WHAT we build, but HOW we build it.

"How you love, How you learn, How you change, and How you work mean everything! How you question your world and How you discipline your Self make all the difference. The first and most important question is never What—always HOW.

"How asks the question. What defines the answer.

"Yet, for the irresponsible, WHAT, only defines what rule to follow. But HOW for the Responsible is finding our true balance and thinking.

"The Zero Chiefs of our past sat in the Circle of Questioning. How something was done was the foundation of that Circle of Justice.

"You asked Mother Life to be born to Her here in Life, Lightningbolt. Answer first How you will live, then you will find What to do with what you have. Celebrate your existence, your birth. How you live your Life makes all the difference.

"Do not be so quick to throw away your Life to prove foolish things to foolish people. Possibly there are other wonders you might want to experience in Life, instead of your insistence upon mediocrity."

Lightningbolt began his fast the same afternoon she spoke with him. That evening, the Sun blushed brilliant orange and red in the sky as he entered his little ceremonial Lodge.

Skillfully and with utmost care, Estcheemah guided Lightningbolt through his Ceremony. He was kept from sleep for many hours by being awakened at random intervals. During these special times his Guide spoke to him about his Life and the Ways of the Zero Chiefs.

Estcheemah loaned him her "meditation bowl." She had filled the beautiful black-lacquered bowl with springwater before giving it to him.

He was taught how to rest his entire being as he gazed into the Medicine Bowl. While he meditated with her Bowl, she taught him of the Dreamers. Finally, after many hours of work, she allowed him to drift off into a deep sleep.

He awoke with a start and quickly leaped up and scrambled out the door of his Lodge; he was in a hurry and did not know why. Suddenly, he saw a rider spurring his mount toward him! He could hardly believe his eyes; the rider was a warrior dressed in beautiful Roman armor! At first Lightningbolt wanted to run, to escape, then he looked down and realized that he too was wearing armor and was ready for battle.

For the briefest moment he studied his combat dress, admiring how splendid and well-made his armor was. He was Etruscan!

Suddenly he became aware that many men and women were fighting all around him. The battle was in full momentum and this exhilarated him. His enemy was nearer now, trying to ride him down and kill him. The cavalryman held a vicious spear with three sharpened tines.

Lightningbolt pretended a half-run, then expertly spun and dropped to one knee, raising his

shield at the very moment the enemy lance struck. The spear rang loud on his shield. The blow was severe, but it had missed its mark.

Lightningbolt laughed, then viciously swung his battle-ax at the front leg of the horse. Blood splashed in his eyes and on his face as the leg was cut in half. The horse screamed and fell, throwing the enemy warrior to the ground. The man hit hard and rolled to a stop on his face.

Flushed with his success, Lightningbolt swung his ax again, this time slicing through the enemy's chin strap and armor, killing him instantly.

He stood, ready to combat his next foe when suddenly he was struck in the eye by an arrow and he began to faint. He screamed from the white-hot pain as the scene of the battlefield shifted to another. This time the war was fought with cannons, cavalry, and foot soldiers.

He was now on horseback and charging recklessly forward with other cavalrymen. Was this the American Civil War? Did it matter?

The two opposing forces crashed together. He thrust his saber into the enemy's stomach, but he could not pull it out. The vacuum held the weapon tight. Would he survive the shame of losing his sword in his first skirmish? He began to panic and felt horrible that he was losing his weapon as the enemy slowly collapsed and fell from his horse, twisting the saber from Lightningbolt's hand.

Livid with rage, Lightningbolt grabbed wildly for his pistol and fired point-blank at the foe nearest him. But the other soldier was quicker and had already fired his pistol at Lightningbolt's stomach. The bullet hit hard and he felt as though a horrible fire were burning through him. He tried to yell, but Death closed his eyes.

Lightningbolt experienced battle after battle. He witnessed every terror and felt every kind of pain. He hacked men and women with swords and axes. He speared people, and crushed heads with his hammer.

The faces of the soldiers he had killed and who had killed him became a blur within Time. The images began to change more quickly. He would find himself standing in an honoring Circle, then suddenly be within another conflict.

He drowned at sea. He was blown to pieces by cannon fire. He was burned alive in a battle tank.

He struggled against the Dreams and tried to end his dreadful visions, but his ordeal continued. Finally, he screamed and awoke.

Estcheemah had bathed his face with cold water to awaken him.

"Oh, Estcheemah!" he yelled, clutching Estcheemah's hand to his chest. He was wet with sweat and his entire body was in spasms from fright and emotion.

He squeezed his eyes tight, while a few more of these frightful images pressed themselves forward behind his closed eyelids. Then he forced his eyes open wide and attempted to sit up, but he was too exhausted.

Estcheemah lifted him and gave him water to drink. He slowly began to regain his senses. Some of the water spilled down his chest because he could not control his shaking hands.

Estcheemah placed her face close to his, looking deeply into his eyes. "The remembrances and Dreams are far beyond you now," she commanded in a firm voice. "You are in your Ceremony. Be calmed."

She guided him to the creek and helped him into the icy water. Kneeling, he plunged his face into the cold stream.

He was very shaky as he walked back to the campfire and sat on his chair. Estcheemah handed him a bowl of warm soup. She helped him drink the soup, and he slowly began to regain control of his hands.

Lightningbolt was weak and struggled to remain awake. He asked if he could lay down. Estcheemah helped him back to his tent, but she would not allow him to enter it. She had unrolled a blanket outside the door of the Lodge. He sat on it and looked around. It was good to be alive!

Suddenly he felt calmer. He drank a few more mouthfuls of soup, then slowly rolled over on his side and fell into a deep, soothing sleep.

Estcheemah covered him with another blanket.

Over this she spread leaves of the chokecherry tree; they would also help him.

He awakened the following afternoon with a start and bolted upright into a sitting position. Sometime during the night she had helped him into his tent, but he could not remember it.

Estcheemah was sitting five steps in front of his door and was attentively watching him. "How do you feel?" Her voice was kind.

"Have you slept?" he asked.

"Tell me of your sleep journey," she insisted.

He carefully told of how bloody his gruesome dreams had been. He described how afraid he'd been, but also how incredibly arrogant he had felt!

He explained that while he experienced his vision, he seemed to be always two people. One part of him believed, lifetime after lifetime, that he could not die, while the other part of him knew

277

that he had died a thousand deaths.

He shared a unique remembrance of his dream. He had seen himself as a warrioress, a woman! The image of the powerful warrioress had captured his fascination. He was disappointed to see her die by being blown into a million pieces.

"Life is full and questioning," Estcheemah said as she busied herself with making breakfast. "We have all been born before. I, too, have been a soldier many times."

The air from the mountains smelled like snow. Whenever this happened, rain was possible. The creek was bright silver and blue, and the sky was wide and clean. Lightningbolt felt very refreshed, renewed.

"I have always fought for what was right." She smiled as she fried the eggs. "We fight for what is right for our time, for our families, for our land. But in the end we all die."

"I think I've been a rogue also," he said, interrupting her. "Somehow I'd always thought of myself as the good guy. I guess it depends on whose side we're looking from, huh?"

"It is a matter of sophistication and viewpoint," she answered, handing him a plate of eggs and bacon. "People pretend, believing they were only the Pharaoh and the Queen of the Nile." She laughed. "Sometimes we are the invader, yes, even the foolish youth."

"These Dreams have given me a thousand questions," he said, trying to grin.

"We were both in a very dangerous business, being soldiers. And sometimes our business got us killed. But you were also a mother, and you had children. This takes courage, too. Yes, it all depends upon a person's viewpoint.

"Many times we are born into what we fear or hate," she explained to him. "I hated and I loved. Yet, I think that in every lifetime I have been a soldier. I have been decorated and deposed. I am a different kind of soldier now. I am a Flower Soldier.

"We Flower Soldiers are Warrioresses and Warriors who battle our own Self ignorances and weaknesses on a daily basis. We fight to learn of our Sacred Mother Life. We fight for Balance within our Self as we learn of the Sacred Balance of Life. The battle to change and evolve within our own Self Essence is the great challenge accepted by every Flower Soldier. This is by far the most difficult of wars, because it is lifelong.

"Yes, we have learned much from physical warfare about the need for discipline and personal courage, to survive while we are within our extreme challenges. These powers are needed even more on the battlefield of daily life. We Flower Soldiers are Teachers and Healers. The ability to bring Healing . . . Spiritually, Physically, Emotionally, and Mentally . . . to the human Self is the greatest skill that can be won by any human. We take the best tools and weapons of the battlefield and point them toward Living and Healing."

While Lightningbolt had eaten and cleaned up he had wondered deeply about his own Essence. Could he be a Flower Soldier?

He met Estcheemah on the hill she had named Bright Hill. The rise of land seemed ordinary, yet for Lightningbolt this insignificant, grass-covered hill would become one of the most special places he would ever know.

Estcheemah showed him where she would create her Medicine Pipe Lodge. She carefully explained to him how she would build the Lodge to celebrate Mother Life. The top of this hill, overlooking the valley, would now become his Cradle Circle of Thought. Here, he would pitch his tent and speak to Life. And here, Lightningbolt would build his first Medicine Wheel.

"This will be the place for your Cradle Circle of Thought," she told him. "Yes, it is all so easy,

isn't it? We believe that everything is just fine because we have a change of heart or mind, but is that true? We build what we will, while we live. Yet most people will swear that they build what they must. It is hard, very hard to be wise, courageous, Self powerful, and different."

"But will those things help me find happiness?" he asked sincerely. "How about not being dirt-poor the rest of my life? Is happiness anywhere on that list of things to be, Estcheemah?"

Estcheemah laughed. "That is the Reservation kid talking again. You are not that person anymore, so why pretend? You want more than that, or you would not bother with this old woman.

"Your fears are only trying to awaken you to the questions that you need to answer in your Life." She waved her hand toward the broad land. "You do not have to be a narrow-minded, ignorant man. Within your being you can be as wide and as handsome as this land. You can be strong, like this magnificent place here on Earth. What is your Life challenge? Do you even know?"

"My challenge?" He was thinking hard. "Yeah, what is my challenge? You know, sometimes I think I ask for too much."

"For too much!" She laughed kindly. "You settle for almost nothing, Lightningbolt. And apologize for everything. Do you really want all the plastic toys you dream of? Are you some lost monk? The mad boy playing empire builder? Or are you the Flower Soldier I think you are?"

"The Flower Soldier!" he said, smiling.

"When you learn to respect your Life, you will discover meaning for your Self. When you respect your Self, then you can begin to understand why you have your needs.

"You could start by asking yourself what you can affect in your life, not what you can control or own. The women and men who can be controlled and owned are sad and lost in a dream. Do you want friends or slaves? There is never any security in what we can control or own.

"Up until this moment in the journey of your Life, you would risk your existence for money or a pat on your back and throw away the opportunity to know your Self. Do not be contemptuous of your Self.

"Would you like the opportunity to meet your Self, Lightningbolt?"

"Yes, I would, Estcheemah," he answered.

"Good. The meeting will be very subtle, so be aware of that. You are going to build yourself a Medicine Wheel. It will be made of stones from Mother Earth. After your Circle is built, you will enter it and meet a few of the possibilities of who and what you can be."

They sat quietly together while she told him how he should create his Medicine Wheel. After she instructed him what to do, he began his work.

As he toiled constructing the rim of his Wheel, magpies, crows, meadowlarks, and prairie falcons flew around him or watched from their perches in the nearby pines.

Estcheemah, the Flower Soldier, patiently began work on her Medicine Bower at the center of his Wheel. She bent willow and chokecherry branches to make the ribs of the Lodge.

She moved smoothly and expertly, conserving her energy and making sure her creation was beautiful. She prayed to Grandmother and Grandfather Life as she worked, with a trust that was born with time and thought.

The old Flower Soldier had prepared and patiently worked for forty-one years, searching for her apprentices. Only a few of the many hopefuls had survived their ignorance and attitudes.

Many of the females had married and disappeared into the mass of humanity. The persistent

old teacher had held hope to the very end, with each apprentice, that she would choose the more challenging way and become a teacher and Medicine person. However, for many this did not happen.

It was this way with many of the young men also. They had all begun strong; most settled for less. They wandered away to search forever for what they should have fought to find when they met her—the Self.

The terror of being Self responsible and the need to conform had destroyed every possibility these hopefuls sought for. Self Power was only an abstraction for them. They had continued to fear demons and devils. They also feared their friends, themselves, and what their families would think. They had Self contempt and distrusted their own minds.

It is hard to accept the Self. Hard to honor the

Self. Estcheemah knew this and had continued her search for apprentices. She breathed a sigh of sadness as she placed a few wildflowers on her Bower. If only more of her apprentices had faced the challenge of their wondrous Self, how very fine that would have been. She was happy for the few loyal apprentices she did have, but there needed to be many more.

Now she had the chance to teach the renegade, Lightningbolt. And she also had her new female apprentice, Liberty. Would these students endure? She wondered how they would respond to each other when they met. Would they share their knowledge and understanding, or would they compete?

The morning sky blossomed with brilliance, becoming a flower of experience that opened to every color on Earth. The tiny shadow that Estcheemah cast on the mountain grass became a testament of endurance and care. Her tiny body worked beneath a sky that loved her sweetly.

Tears stole down her gentle old cheeks while she placed the leaves on the outside of her Bower, creating the skin of the Lodge.

Why did humanity turn their faces away from Sacred Mother Life?

The Holy Woman prayed to the Perfect Creatress Mother Life and sang a Medicine Song that became as bright as the Sun. Only the truly powerful ever seem to see the obvious—that there is no substitute for Creatress Mother Life. But this knowledge did not ease the pain in her heart.

It is the duty of every Flower Soldier to seek true balance. Estcheemah bowed her head slightly to each of the Four Directions, then faced her Bower. She placed her Medicine Pipe in the Lodge, then cleansed the inner Circle with smoke from sweet grass.

"The billions of living mirrors of thought,"

282

she prayed as she placed wildflowers around her Pipe, "exist within Life and through the door of Death. Sacred Spirit Life, I ask you for guidance this day." Estcheemah stood. "Accept my words and my presence as I am, Mother Life." She pointed the stem of her Pipe toward where Lightningbolt persevered, trying to build his Wheel. "This child, this young man who can learn to be a Flower Soldier, is birthed from your Womb."

The old Flower Soldier placed her Medicine Pipe back among the delicate flowers. She squeezed her eyes closed and held tight to a wish that would free this young man. Her wish was that he would always respect his Self and Life.

Bull-like, laboring, sweating, Lightningbolt was a sharp contrast to his mentor. He clumsily arranged the outside stones of the rim of the Wheel, trying to be as respectful as possible. It was now almost noon and growing hot. Sweat beaded on his brow, and his large cowboy hat weighed heavy on his head. He tossed the hat onto a nearby tree limb.

He had decided to use tiny stones instead of larger ones as Estcheemah had recommended. There were never enough stones. He looked at his work and frowned.

A scraggly, wobbly smear of gravel outlined the Wheel. It just did not look right to him, no matter how hard he tried. He bowed his head and drove himself to make it better.

It was two o'clock before he finished his Medicine Wheel. He frowned at his handiwork.

"Now it is time," Estcheemah called to him. "Come over here and we will talk."

He walked to where his teacher was sitting and took a seat beside her. He studied Estcheemah's tiny Bower. It looked attractive from a distance, but up close it radiated a loveliness and quiet power that surprised him. He got down on his hands and knees and peered inside. What greeted his eyes was not what he had expected to see.

Within the Lodge was such a welcome of Beauty it actually shocked Lightningbolt. The Lodge was a dome of intricately woven flower-color and form. The walls and ceiling of the little dome had been built of thousands of leaves and hundreds of wildflowers. The little Medicine Lodge was alive with elegant Earth design. The natural soft hues of the wildflowers flowed in waves of color that blended with the leaves. Everything seemed to have always existed in the Lodge.

The floor had also been transformed. Estcheemah had used four of her brightly colored Medicine Blankets to complete her Circle of Beauty.

"Wow, that is truly beautiful," Lightningbolt said with awe as he sat back down. "What are you going to do in there?"

"What are *you* going to do in there is the question," she said. "Would you like to know what this little Medicine Lodge is called?"

He nodded.

"It is called the Center Lodge," Estcheemah answered. "The Center Lodge is the Womb of Light and Dark. It is also known as the Beginning and Completion Lodge."

Lightningbolt was suddenly embarrassed. "All this work," he said, scuffing his boot heel on the ground. "You shouldn't have. I mean . . . that's a lot of work, Estcheemah."

"Do not let Beauty embarrass you," Estcheemah said, encouraging him. "No, not now, not at this moment. Just appreciate what you have.

"Listen, listen carefully to what you have to say to your Self. Speak to your Mother Life; She is Goddess Beauty. Do not be afraid to address Beauty.

"Allow this Medicine Wheel to become your Cradle of Thinking. Our Mother World, our Sacred Mother Earth, is very beautiful. Think of this fact, Lightningbolt—that nothing built by humans will last.

"Throughout time Mother Earth has birthed everything we need for our existence. Everything we harvest or fabricate is built from Earth's gift of substance. We are dependent upon what has been created for us.

"With time all things will wear away and return to their original form. Nothing physical can endure. Yet, Mother Earth, with Her cycles and laws, can renew all forms, including Her humans.

"And we must all remember that everything we do or say, our every act, will be remembered forever by Sacred Mother and Father Earth. It will be Life, our Earth, who will attest to who we were while we lived."

Estcheemah stood and began to walk, and Lightningbolt followed her.

"The Medicine Wheels of our ancients were very different from the ones we make now," she teased. "Yours is not quite aligned with the rising and setting of Venus, nor does it mark the Sun's equinox, but many of the Medicine Wheels of our ancients did exactly that.

"The fascination that our ancients had for the Sacred Numbers would not be comprehended today," she explained. "They sought to discover their position within Creation.

"Our Zero Chiefs say that our first question, beyond asking about the Self, should be the question of how we present ourselves to Life.

"What is your presence? You have built a Medicine Wheel from gravel and stone. But now it becomes your question instead of your answer.

"Our ancients discovered that the physical Wheel, by itself, is a teaching, because its shape questions all humans. The presence of the Medicine

Wheel teaches of cycle and time. Anyone who observes a Wheel, over a few years, begins to see that the cycles of time, the seasons, light and dark are incorporated naturally into the Wheel.

"The Wheel is the shape of Mother Earth and is the form of Creation Herself. The fact that it is made from Earth materials is healing both physically and mentally for us.

"As you are learning, numbers can describe both the abstract and physical world. The very presence of the Medicine Wheel teaches us about relationships, and all relationships teach of the numbers.

"All right, be that as it may, what does this Medicine Wheel mean to you?

"Life is reflected within the Medicine Wheel for the seeker because the Medicine Wheel represents Mother Earth and our Universe.

"Come walk with me and listen to an old woman's prayers. Do you have the courage for that?"

"I certainly do, Estcheemah," he answered sincerely.

Estcheemah walked to the East of his Circle and placed a tiny stone at her feet. "I address the Spirit of all of Humanity," she prayed. "I ask the Spirit of all humans born if they wish to see their wondrous Sun dim in their polluted skies. Do you desire that your sky be filled with putrid and deadly chemicals?"

She then walked to the West of his Circle and again placed a tiny stone at her feet. "Spirit of Humanity," she prayed, "do you wish to continue to believe the madmen who claim that our Mother Earth is to be destroyed? Do you desire that your Mother World die? Will you pollute Her to the point where you and your children can no longer survive?"

Estcheemah then walked to the South of Lightningbolt's Circle and placed a tiny stone there. "Spirit of Humanity," she prayed, "do you despise

your lives so much that you would destroy every beautiful stream and kill every lake? Do you desire that your oceans be polluted and devoid of all life?"

She walked slowly to the North of his Circle and placed a stone there at her feet. "Humanity, I address your Spirit," she prayed. "Do you wish for your very breath to be taken from you because it is fouled with toxic gases? Can you understand that you cannot hate Life and then expect Life to endure your madness? Do you desire that your world be destroyed?"

Lightningbolt was crying. He did not want his Mother Earth to perish.

"The people who predict the end of the world are not made responsible for what they say," Estcheemah said, showing her sadness. "We all must learn to respect our World. We must learn to respect Mother Life and our Existence with Her as Responsible People."

The afternoon continued to grow hot, but Lightningbolt was resolute. He found shade beneath the pine where he had hung his hat and he looked out over the wide rolling land of Wyoming.

He was appalled and distressed at how incredibly ignorant he was about himself and his Life. Would he ever be able to understand?

He stood suddenly and began to walk. Estcheemah had given him the task of speaking to Mother Life, but with a stipulation that he had to be honest with himself or leave the hill. He agreed to this enthusiastically.

Lightningbolt looked into the sky and watched clouds form.

"The clouds and sky are over my head," he said out loud. "Hey, you are there, clouds. You are there, sky, on a second-by-second basis, just like Estcheemah explained. Hello."

He turned on his heel and paced restlessly. He was disgusted that nothing seemed to be going right. What was wrong? The wind began to gust now and chase little tumbleweeds from the top of the hill.

"Estcheemah says that you and I are here on a second-by-second basis, pines," he called to the trees, trying to find his voice.

The wind sighed in the boughs of the pines and seemed almost sympathetic with his apprehensiveness. He was growing more afraid by the minute and did not know why.

He raised his voice and addressed the trees again, telling them that he was ready to possess his own Self authority, but the wind carried away his every word, leaving him speechless. The experience was unnerving.

He tried again, speaking even more loudly to the sky, saying that he was determined to find his own truth, but all he could hear was his weak voice and his hesitancy. He suddenly felt very foolish and began to blush.

He walked quickly down the hill to talk with Estcheemah. His plan to speak to Life was simply not working out. He needed more information. When he entered Estcheemah's camp, she had her back to him and was praying. She held a sprig of grass in her hands, lovingly. He stopped and waited quietly while she finished her prayers.

"He is already back, Sacred Life," Estcheemah said, addressing the Prairie. "I hope that he had the courage to speak to you without being embarrassed by his own timid voice.

"I hope that he had the courage to speak of what he feels deeply. Yes, WahKahn and SsKwan, I hope that he learns to hear the fear in his own voice."

Lightningbolt turned and strode back toward his hill. He was determined to talk to Creation even if his answer might be a bolt of lightning from the blue.

"And you will not be struck down with a bolt of lightning out of the blue either," Estcheemah called after him. She knew what he was thinking. "Why? Because Creation is not so bored that it needs to do such a childish thing. And who are you that such a wonder should be wasted upon you?"

He was breathing hard when he reached the

top of the hill, but he was resolute.

"Hey!" he yelled to the trees. "I am going to be honest."

A strange fear rose up in Lightningbolt's heart. Suddenly he felt very tired. He sat down on the ground and looked into the sky. The wind was sighing quietly in the trees. Far away on the horizon, very large thunderclouds were billowing in the sky.

"I'm not going to be afraid of you, dammit," he cursed, standing up again. "You have me spooked. I'm going down to talk to Estcheemah because there are a few things that I need to know."

Once Lightningbolt was at Estcheemah's fire again and drinking coffee, he wished he had remained on the hill and battled it out, but here he was. Was there a way of explaining his problem?

"You are wrestling with all of your silly beliefs and fears, instead of talking to Creation," Estcheemah said matter-of-factly. "You have been taught to believe in a God that is violent and would have you burn for your ignorance. That fantasy is not Creation. Creation has no need for demons to teach humans.

"There are no demons, Lightningbolt. No one has ever seen one and they never will. Creation is

not an 'angry jealous God,' as you have been taught. Creation has no jealousy of Itself, nor anger. Anger and jealousy describe humans, not Creation. To think this is silly. You fear a book God. The print God is not as large as Creation. The book God is ignorant and does not know Life.

"So get back up there and listen to what you say to our Creatress Mother and Creator Father. Creation is Life. Speak to Life and be yourself, Lightningbolt."

Lightningbolt returned to the top of the hill and sat down. He worked all evening with himself and spoke out loud about all of his fears. It was almost eleven o'clock at night when he realized that he had no need to fear Life, and that no demons were going to jump out and tackle him to the ground.

Life gave him Life. When it was time for him to leave the world of Life, he would simply die and that was that. It was so simple. Could he understand that simplicity and honor it?

Below him Estcheemah's bright lantern twinkled blue-white among the cottonwood trees at the creek. The sky over his head was as black and deep as Creation and filled with bright Stars. The creek wound her way down her valley and shone with the light of the Moon, as Quetzal-Atl-Mahahn, Dragon-Mother-Bringer-of-Numbers.

"I am alive, Sacred Mother Life," he said, addressing Mother Earth. "I live because you give me Life. I have decided that I will work, my Life long, to be honest with my Self. I will use my mind and my courage to battle ignorance, beginning with my own. I have decided to become a Flower Soldier.

"I will never again be afraid of you, my Creatress and Creator. You are more intelligent than I, and I do not fear the truly Intelligent."

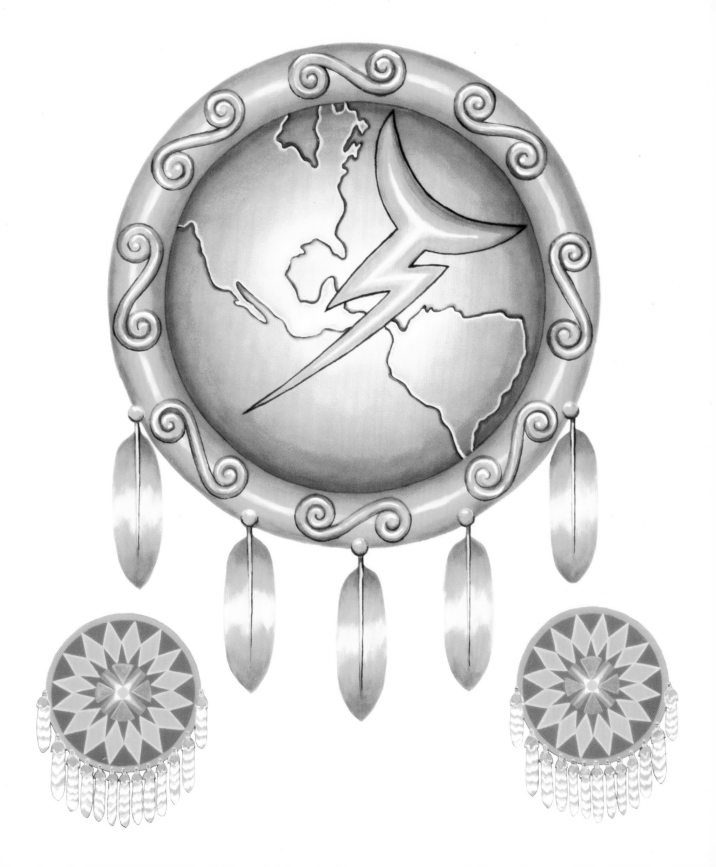

Lightningbolt slept very well that night and was up with the first light, eager to do and learn more. Estcheemah decided that they should return to her home.

It was early afternoon when they rode into Estcheemah's yard. Lightningbolt unsaddled the horses and cared for them, then began to clean the camp gear. It was early evening before all the work was completed.

They ate a quiet evening meal together, not speaking. After the dishes had been washed and put away, Estcheemah asked Lightningbolt to take a walk with her.

The evening was warm and the gravel road was brightly illuminated by the big Wyoming Moon. While they walked, Estcheemah told Lightningbolt that it was time for him to hear the stories of two of the most influential and powerful Flower Soldiers who became Zero Chiefs.

Over the next five days Estcheemah told him the history of the two military generals. They lived hundreds of years apart, but both were born among the people of the Yucatán. The generals were known as the General-Priest, Ocean Bow, and the General-Priestess, Temple Doors.

"These two very important teachers are credited with reinstating the Circle of Law and bringing forward the ancient teaching of the Flower Soldiers," Estcheemah explained. "I am one of the Flower Soldiers within the Discipline of these two Zero Chiefs."

THE TEACHINGS OF THE ZERO CHIEFS
EHAHMAH (THE SUBSTANCE OF EARTH)

THE STORY OF OCEAN BOW AND
THE FLOWER SOLDIERS OF CENTRAL AMERICA

It is strange and fascinating to consider what information and histories have been lost and what fortunately has survived. The fact that no one is sure exactly where the City of the Great Avenues existed in Middle America is a poignant example of this. Yet, this city is of great importance for all Flower Soldiers. The fragmented information we have carefully kept about the City of the Great Avenues describes how it was designed and built by Flower Soldiers. This is the city that was built by the Zero Chief known as Ocean Bow.

The main plan of the city consisted of a block of five hundred "Hills of the Archers." These "hills" were raised platform pyramids from which the Archers could defend the City. When any of the "hills" were overrun by an invading army, the Archers would leave their positions and take up new ones above and behind the next set of platforms. It was an expertly fortified city, without using a wall.

We are told that the city possessed sewers and had running water for everyone. It was also renowned for having vast, beautiful Gardens. There are not words enough to describe the height of science reached by gardening in the Americas. The variety of foods that were grown, and the sophisticated understanding of the Chiefs concerning the nature of plants, would not be comprehended today. Every possible inch of the city was used to grow food. For each home or trader shell (boat house), there was a garden of food and beauty. It is said by our Zero Chiefs that "the city's Medicine Colors were every possible color of Flowers."

This metropolis of fifty thousand people was the largest city known to have been designed and governed by Flower Soldiers. This great city was the seat of the government that comprised the entire province of two hundred thousand people in all. We Flower Soldiers have much evidence, taught through our oral history, that the City of the Great Avenues was the place of the rebirth of Democracy in the Americas.

This beautiful city and the entire province were governed by the Circle of Law. The Zero Chiefs taught about and guided the Circle of Law.

The Representative Chiefs, who sat in the Circle of Law, were always balanced in numbers, female and male. In the Temples the Priestess and the Priest were equal. There was a Balance held and respected throughout all the Great Schools for the Equality of all humans.

Goddess and God were known to be Equal. The Medicine Wheels were the basis of all teaching. Flower Soldiers swore a Pledge to Fight every kind of human slavery.

The birth of a city

Massive armies were maintained by every city-state for the sake of political stabilization. The Mayan cities that practiced human slavery and human sacrifice were the sworn enemies of all Zero Chiefs.

Civil war erupted frequently among the peoples of Central and South America. Often these wars were preceded by tremendous destruction wrought by earthquakes and volcanos. Whenever there is massive chaos, peoples are made more vulnerable, and wars between them can occur. After many years of violent warfare throughout Central and South America, the Temple of the Flower Soldiers became a tiny speck of hope in the midst of the burgeoning new empire of the Eight Deer.

The story of Ocean Bow begins about three thousand years ago, after many years of massive earthquakes, volcanic eruptions, and bloody civil wars. The city of One Deer became the new "Great Central City," and parceled out the lands of the Yucatán among the Lords. This process was quite slow, and it took about two hundred years for an established system of government to be formulated.

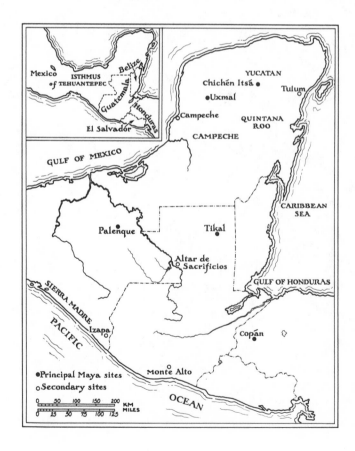

During these violent years a curious event took place. It indirectly affected the Flower Soldiers and caused a war that should never have occurred. The outcome of this conflict altered the history of Central America forever.

Like the Temple of the Flower Soldiers, the Temple of the Rememberers—called the Temple of the Jaguars—was also a very tiny School that existed alone in the new Empire.

The lords of the new cities of One Deer, Two Deer, Three Deer, and Eight Deer wanted the Temple destroyed and its School obliterated because the School would not "bow to the wishes of their lords." However, when "this trivial and miserable little Temple" was attacked by the powerful city of Eight Deer, the Flower Soldiers entered the war.

The reason for the involvement of the Flower Soldiers was not that they believed they should save the Temple of the Rememberers. It was that, as everyone knew, except for the drunken lords of the cities of the Deer, the little Temple was the hub of the Schools of Healing. The ignorant lords wanted to destroy the School of its Medical People—the Healers who had survived the bloody civil wars of the times! This situation caused a new civil war to break out—one that split the empire in half.

The Flower Soldiers had an important advantage in this war—the man called Ocean Bow. This great general would reorganize the Flower Soldiers and conquer every land in the empire, destroying the power of the cities of the Deer.

After the collapse of the Empire—cities of the Deer, the Jaguar Temple of the Rememberers and the Temple of the Flower Soldiers joined together with the greater Schools of the Mathematicians and became the Quetzal-Coatl-Atl-WahKahn-Shee. The Rememberers say that the Zero Chiefs were Reborn the day that these great Temples became one School.

This greater School became known as the people of the Morning Star, the People of the Quetzal-Atl-Coatl-Auuc, and as the Sky Serpent. They were also known as the Turtle.

Ocean Bow

Among the Zero Chiefs there are many Speakers and Keepers of the Belts. One of their best-remembered stories is about the great Flower Soldier Ocean Bow.

We owe much of our history to the Ocean Bow Teachers. The man himself is credited with reinstating our discipline. He was born three hundred years after the great cities of the Yucatán had been conquered by very fierce invaders from South America, around three thousand years ago. These Canoe People, also called the People of the Sharp-Edged Leaf, the Obsidian Blade, came from the South in endless numbers and destroyed the People of the Long Count.

Quetzal and Coatl, the Goddess and God of the Long Count, were now only symbolic figures of the past. The "new order" was made up of men who believed that they had been chosen to rule by their god, Himmhoipann, whose name literally meant "god of the plague." Their feudal aristocracy, the Lords, believed they were gods incarnate, born on Earth to rule all humans.

These were unfortunate and very troubled times for the Flower Soldiers. Almost every priestess and priest of the Long Count had been ruthlessly put to death by the invaders. The days of the Great Circles of Law were long gone. The Great Circles of Democracy and equality between women and men were forbidden.

All the Zero Chiefs who were still alive were carefully hidden. All Circles of Healing, where the Gardens of Healing had once existed, were now outlawed. Any talk of the Medicine Wheels, or their teaching, brought instant reprisal and certain death.

At this time the priests of the Sharp-Edged Leaf, the Obsidian Blade, known as the City Robes, came to power. They sacrificed humans, animals, and plants to their God of the plague. These priests taught that there were two Gods, and that the Plague God was always warring with the Sharp-Edged Leaf God. The Sharp-Edged Leaf God was every Rule imposed by the "new order," and the Plague God was chaos and disease.

It is very important to understand that those men who made up the ancient priestly class were the same people as the landed aristocracy. The priests of the Plague God were the sons of the "Divine Lords"—the "Gods born on Earth to rule the people." These Lords, who owned all the land, depended upon the priests to tell everyone of their divinity, while the priests depended upon the Lords for their safety and power.

Over a hundred years after the original invaders had crushed all resistance and set themselves up as the sole authority of the land, Ocean Bow was born among the Arrow Priests in the Pyramid City of the Yucatán known as Corn Flower. He very much loved gardening. The duties of the Sacred Arrow Priests, including Ocean Bow, were the training of young noblemen in the art of combat.

The landowners—or Lords—were feudal warlords who dominated the city of Corn Flower and the land for many miles around it. The Lords, "the men of God," took turns being the rulers of the city of Corn Flower and were above all the priests.

There were different kinds of priests who lived among the people of Corn Flower. In fact, the title of "priest" was bestowed upon anyone who was the head of a group or organization. Consequently, there were priests of the merchant class, the artisan class, and the builders. The most powerful were the sacrificial priests, the City Robes, who lived in the City of the Pyramid. They were a religious class separate from all other priests of the Corn Flower People, and they ruthlessly controlled every artisan, merchant, and other priest in the city.

Corn Flower, like all the other cities in the Yucatán, began as a religious and trade center and grew to include the Temples, which were the places of learning.

The School or the Temple of the Arrow Priests was not as grand as the religious Temples or the merchant Temples. However, their military society was vitally important to the aristocratic land-owning families because warfare had become a way of life for them.

Wars that were fought between the Lords, the men of God, were usually short. Land disputes and the theft of slaves were the most common reasons for these great feuds. However, while the wars of the aristocracy tended to be short and were thought of as chivalrous, the wars between the great cities were always bloody and could last for years.

These city wars were fought between the priests who owned the merchant class of each city. Whenever the cities became embroiled in another war, everyone suffered.

By the time Ocean Bow was thirty-five, two large cities had been at war for several years—Mound Turtle and Obsidian Temple. Mound Turtle was a very old ally of the city of Corn Flower. It was a seaport city, while Corn Flower was an inland, farming city. The rival city, Obsidian Temple, was also a seafaring city.

When war first broke out between Obsidian Temple and Mound Turtle, the war was thought to be far away and of no consequence to the Corn Flower people, and they were content to send a few of their young men to help their ally. Since their ally, Mound Turtle, was more powerful than Obsidian Temple, the war was expected to be a short one. However, the conflict wore on for two years.

During the second year of the conflict, Obsidian Temple sent its soldiers to burn the crops of the Corn Flower Lords and to rob them of their slaves.

Nothing like this had ever happened in the history of warfare in the Americas. Everyone was shocked—except, of course, the people of Obsidian Temple. After this incident, the nobility came together and decided that the Arrow Priests must now train slaves to do the fighting for the Lords of Corn Flower—who would not send their own children to be slaughtered. The Arrow Priests were told to begin their task of training the slaves immediately. Ocean Bow was the only Arrow Priest who would take on the responsibility of training the slaves.

At first, this new idea was not to the liking of the Arrow Priests. They feared that their prestige and power would be lost if they trained slaves rather than the nobility. But there was no arguing with the powerful landowners. Thousands of slaves were brought from the countryside and forced into the new army headed by the Arrow Priest, Ocean Bow.

The new slave army of Corn Flower became a fact of life that the Arrow Priests learned to live with. And the priests soon discovered that warfare was not new to the slaves. They were eager to be trained and highly motivated.

As the slave army grew into a formidable fighting force, Ocean Bow became more and more a part of his soldiers. Within two years all the officers of the slave army knew their Commander, Ocean Bow, intimately. They deeply respected him, and there was nothing Ocean Bow could ask of them that they would refuse.

Ocean Bow, in turn, learned from his men that their families had been held captive by the people of Corn Flower for two hundred years. The slave officers of Ocean Bow's army taught him about their ancient Temple-School, Ocean Wanderer.

The Arrow Priests were astonished to discover that Ocean Wanderer had taught

that all human sacrifice was forbidden. In fact, according to Ocean Wanderer, nothing was to be sacrificed, not even plants or animals.

This new and unorthodox teaching shocked the Arrow Priests and was instantly banned by the City Robes. The reason for this was that on each Wild Pig Day, the City Robe priests sacrificed a newborn girl and boy; both were first drowned, then burned. These children were always chosen from among the slave families. The people cried out loud, asking that their "holy sacrifices" be accepted by their gods and that no other children or people would fall sick and die throughout the year.

The City Robes lamented the loudest, and they even struck themselves with twisted vines, sometimes drawing blood, praying that the Plague God would accept the suffering and sacrifice and be appeased.

Everyone believed that the Plague God was a jealous and angry God who would kill indiscriminately when no sacrifice was made to him. Ocean Bow believed, as did everyone else, that if these sacrifices were suddenly to end, the Plague God would tear the people to pieces.

The consequence of this belief, of course, was that even the Arrow Priests banned the teachings of Ocean Wanderer.

In the third year of the war between Mound Turtle and Obsidian Temple, an elite force of the best five thousand soldiers from the slave army, under the command of Ocean Bow, marched out of the city of Corn Flower to make war.

The officers were proud and looked forward to learning more on the battlefield. Every soldier was perfectly trained and well equipped. The men sang as they marched toward Mound Turtle. Ocean Bow had decided to personally command his new army in the field. This caused great jubilation among all the men.

However, when the forces of Ocean Bow engaged the enemy, three months later, there was a tremendous earthquake while they were in the midst of battle. And yet, within the week, Ocean Bow's army defeated its enemy. But then suddenly five more severe earthquakes erupted. These tremors were so awesome and turbulent that trees, soldiers, and animals were thrown bodily into the air. During the following five months, twenty more catastrophic shocks were experienced. Every city was reduced to rubble.

Because of the carnage from the earthquakes, the City Robe Priests began to lose control of their armies. Soon, rioting and looting had become a daily occurrence in every city. Ocean Bow brought his soldiers back to Corn Flower, but the city no longer existed. Roving bands of killers and thieves swept through the rubble searching for booty and food.

The more aggressive of the warlords continued to fight viciously to hold on to their dwindling power. They would destroy anyone who got in their way, including their old aristocratic allies—even if this meant betraying family or friend.

Now the city armies themselves began to break up. They became roving bands of organized thieves, making things even more dangerous. Temple priests fell upon other priests, seeking to become landowners. Many of these priests were sacrificed or were simply murdered by their colleagues. Vengeance and the reward of riches became the reasons for continued battle, and soon there was nothing but chaos everywhere.

Ocean Bow nearly lost his life nine times at the hands of his own men, but was rescued at the last moment by his officers. The slaves wanted revenge and were determined to kill every warlord in Corn Flower.

Ocean Bow argued with his officers and men that their only hope was to remain together as a fighting force—not to become ordinary thieves. He promised them that war

would remain their standard and reason for existence. Now, they too would be professionals—every soldier could become an Arrow Priest. Their only hope of survival was to remain a united force. Every officer agreed, and a new elite professional army was born.

At this time, Ocean Bow reorganized his army. He pointed out to his officers and men that in each battle they had experienced, the opposing force was never properly trained or armed.

Ocean Bow retrained all five thousand of his men and put them to work making more weapons. He convinced his officers that every man should possess a sword-ax and be expert with the spear. Traditionally, all the advance soldiers possessed only a shield and one lance. The more wealthy soldiers, usually sons of the nobles, carried a shield, a lance, and an obsidian sword-ax.

Ocean Bow had discovered that by arming all of his advance soldiers with sword-ax, lance, and shield, he could turn the tide of battle in his favor within hours.

One particular officer in Ocean Bow's army had slowly become very close friends with his commander. His name was Flying Sun. Ocean Bow learned that Flying Sun was secretly a Priest among his enslaved people.

Ocean Bow split the task of commanding the army between himself and Flying Sun. The two divisions, called Blue and White, had twenty-five hundred soldiers in each.

Over the next two years, these forces met and defeated many armies, both large and small. The third Spring, the two Generals held a meeting because many of their men were battle-weary and needed the company of women. It was decided that they would withdraw to a place called Burned Head. This was a large valley that could be defended. And, most important, there were women nearby.

Ocean Bow's and Flying Sun's scouts reported that Burned Head was already occupied by the Commander-Priest known as Crying Shadow. It was also learned that Crying Shadow had six thousand fighting men and was responsible for twice that number of women and children.

Once his forces had encircled Burned Head, Ocean Bow met with Crying Shadow. Having heard of Ocean Bow's many victories, Crying Shadow immediately surrendered. He knew better than to try to oppose him.

The following day, Ocean Bow and Crying Shadow met again; however, this time Flying Sun was there. They decided to join the two forces—with one very important agreement—all human sacrifice was to end, as well as all sacrifice of plants and animals.

Although this surprised Crying Shadow, he readily agreed. During the following year the three men busily reorganized the lives of their people. Farming was immediately begun. Flying Sun's force of twenty-five hundred men foraged the surrounding countryside for food.

Ocean Bow's task was to recruit as many former slaves as possible. Because so many young men had been killed in the wars, there weren't enough men left to fill out his forces, so Ocean Bow decided he would also train young women.

What Ocean Bow actually did was to reinstate a far older tradition of the Bee Warrioresses. His new recruits were trained in the art of the bow and the use of the atl—a spear or throwing arrow that can also act as a pike.

Over the next several years Ocean Bow made other improvements in his army. First, he added two support groups behind his advance soldiers. In time, he saw to it that his

support groups were armed with heavier shields, four spears, and a sword-ax per person. These rank-and-file soldiers were called Forward Support Groups.

During battle the enemy force would always be met by the Advance Group. These soldiers would fight hand to hand with the enemy. Then, when his first line of combatants would begin to tire, Ocean Bow would command his drummers to give the signal, and his Advance Groups would melt back into his Support Groups.

Ocean Bow and his officers are credited with the creation of the "Sand Shield" forces. The men of the Sand Shields wore an impenetrable armor made by overlapping small, individual cloth bags filled with sand. These formidable soldiers carried a sword-ax and a spear and also possessed a heavier shield than normal for that time.

Behind the Sand Shields was still another group called the Center Ring—Ocean Bow's ready reserves. These men also carried extra lances and sword-axes. However, the secret weapon behind the Center Ring was the Bee Warrioresses.

Ocean Bow kept his army constantly advancing. Once contact was made with the enemy by the Advance Group, each soldier would launch two throwing arrows; then they would battle the enemy with spears. When they tired and the drum was sounded, they would fall back into the second wave of soldiers—the Support Group.

When the Support Group met the enemy, they would fight until they tired. Again, the drums were sounded, and they would fall back into the Sand Shields.

The advance soldiers of the enemy force were already tiring when they had to face the Support Group. And by the time the Sand Shields were called forward, the enemy soldiers were falling to the ground or pressing back into their own main body trying to escape.

Relentlessly, the army of Ocean Bow continued pushing forward while the enemy forces fell back, battling their own men as they tried to escape. The constant forward movement of Ocean Bow's army always strained the opposing force to its limit.

Once the enemy force fell back in chaos, or broke to flee, Ocean Bow's officers would sound their drums and the fourth line of soldiers would be in place to fight—the Bee Warrioresses. This highly skilled group of female soldiers was feared more than any other part of Ocean Bow's army because its members were expert archers. These fleet-footed, deadly soldiers carried a light shield, a short bow with four quivers of arrows slung at the waist, and one small hand-ax.

When the high-pitched thrum of the Bee Warrioresses' drum was heard, the main army would stop its forward movement and open its ranks by moving into blocks. This movement allowed the Bee Warrioresses to rush forward.

The Arrow Bees would move quickly through these avenues of soldiers and strike the enemy with their deadly poisoned arrows. The warrioresses would shoot their arrows and move forward in perfect cadence with their Arrow Drum commands. The Bee Warrioresses were ordered to advance when the enemy hesitated or showed signs of confusion. They proved to be the turning point of every battle and always brought victory.

The main body of Ocean Bow's army followed the advance of the Bee Warrioresses, rested and ready for further combat. When the enemy force was once again in a position to fight, the drum would sound and the Arrow Bees would melt back into their own force. The blocks would close once again, forming a fresh line of attack.

The major reason Ocean Bow's army was so successful was that it never tired, while the other army was always fatigued beyond repair. The next thing that ensured victory was that Ocean Bow's army was outfitted with the finest weapons that could be made, while his enemies were always poorly trained and armed.

It's a paradox, but the idea of a helmet did not exist in the organized armies of the Americas until Ocean Bow ordered it. By the time Ocean Bow was in his eleventh year of battle, all of his soldiers wore helmets.

Once the Blue and White divisions of Ocean Bow's army were in full command of all the land—as far as the armies could march in a year—Ocean Bow retired. It is rumored that he became a gardener again. However, this is where his story really begins, because it was at this time that he began to reorganize the Flower Soldiers.

Because of Ocean Bow's great efforts, the Flower Soldiers once again grew into a legitimate power among the people. However, many hundreds of years later, during the time of the great General-Priestess, Temple Doors, they would again have to battle for their survival.

THE STORY OF TEMPLE DOORS AND THE FOUNDING
OF THE EARLY CIVILIZATIONS OF THE SOUTHWEST

Some people have said that a Representative government is what we know to be a Democracy. Others say that Freedom is what makes a Democracy. Others will insist that Democracy is a balance between State and Church. There are also those who say that Democracy is a balance between the rich and the poor. And there are those who will claim that Democracy is the balance between the learned and the unschooled. The bold say that Democracy is tolerance and the acceptance of all races and peoples as being equal.

The woman known as Temple Doors said all this and more about Democracy many hundreds of years ago. She said that in actuality the founding principle of a true Democracy was a Representative government that was perfectly balanced between female and male, because this Balance is the Source of all that is Living and Natural.

She never used the words *Democracy* or *Democratic*, but she did use the words *Circle of Law.*

By the time Temple Doors was born the great Circles of Democracy—the Circle of Law—had been outlawed and forbidden by the new feudalistic governing powers. She is the human responsible for the preservation and renewal of the Circle of Law throughout the Americas.

It is important to speak of how the Medicine Wheels came to North America from South and Central America, and were kept by the Zero Chiefs.

According to the records kept by the Flower Soldiers, the weather patterns of Mother Earth went through incredible changes. Places that were once beautiful plains filled with animals and grass changed over a period of a thousand years to become jungles or deserts.

Five great migrations of people left Central America and settled the North; these were called the Great Webs or Spider Roads by the record keepers. These large migrations occurred between one thousand and three thousand years ago.

The Spider Woman Keepers are responsible for the information we have of these migrations. For simplicity's sake, the name Spider Woman can be translated as "Guardian Keeper" or "Corn Carrier." The reason for this is because the tradition grew up out of the Gardeners. These women not only kept the Gardens, they also kept the history.

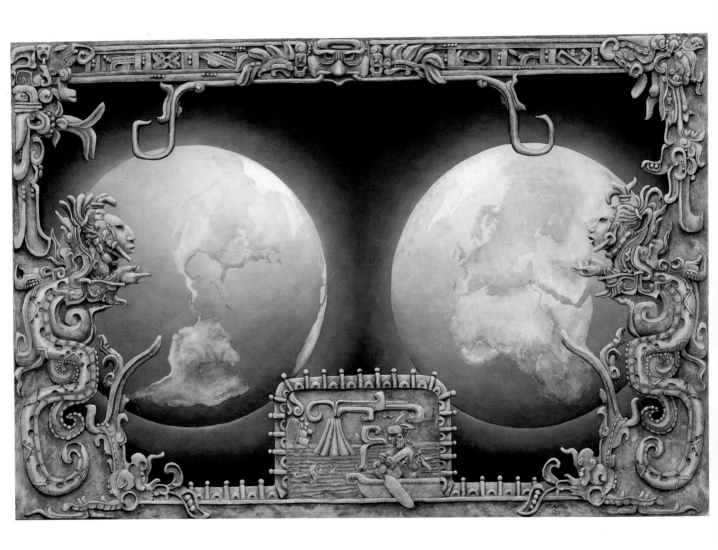

Temple Doors was the Priestess-General responsible for one of the largest of the great migrations. She led her people north, out of Central America, into what we presently know as our Southwest. This great migration took place between two thousand and twenty-five hundred years ago. During this journey, half of her people perished from war, disease, and hunger.

It was this woman General who brought the Great Circle of Law and all the Medicine Wheels to the North. She also brought corn, squash, beans, and turkeys.

Temple Doors was born to the Butterfly People. At this time these people controlled the tribal city-states south of Mexico City.

The hundreds of city-states of the Yucatán had been founded by Tribes of many diverse groups and languages. Each city-state had its Great Temple. The Center Temple, or Great Temple, was everything to its people because it held the distinction of "possessing the Name of the Divine." This meant that the Temple was known by the name of the Goddess and God of the city-state. Each Temple was the seat of the law, the university, the place of records, the treasury, the place of information, the hospital, the war academy, and the place of prayer.

At the time of the birth of Temple Doors, the Mayan city-states had been in constant war with each other for nearly three hundred years. The wars had started in the aftermath of horrible earthquakes and exploding volcanos that had leveled hundreds of cities and Temples.

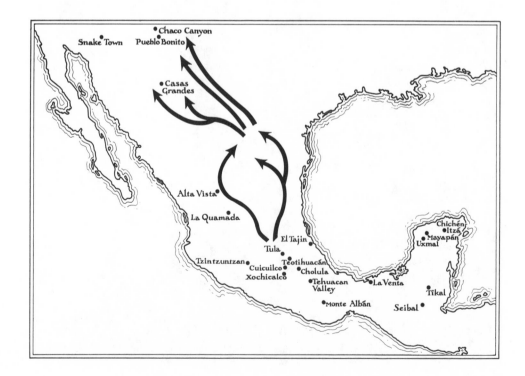

The Great Temple-Schools that had been built by the Zero Chiefs, and where the Zero Chiefs taught, were continually being attacked by roaming bands and armies from enemy cities. Eventually the Zero Chiefs and Flower Soldiers withdrew from their former places of Power.

Over time, the number of Flower Soldiers in the Yucatán diminished considerably. By Temple Doors' time, within the city of her birth, all that remained was an almost insignificant group of women and men known as Flower Soldiers. They were the Guardians of two very important Temples—the Jaguar Temple of Remembrance and the War Canoe Shield Temple. The people who were the priestesses and priests of these Temples were known as the Ants.

Because the Ants and Flower Soldiers knew much of the ancient histories of the Mayan peoples, and had a great deal of knowledge about Mathematics and Healing, they were allowed to continue to exist—but only in a very controlled way. The actual Medicine Wheels were outlawed, and talk of the Circle of Law was forbidden by the new feudalistic families who controlled the city-states.

As a result, the Flower Soldiers at this time held no special power in any political or religious matters at the Temples that they guarded. Temple Doors was trained in the military by the Flower Soldiers who lived among the War Canoe and Jaguar Temples. In secret, she was taught of the Medicine Wheels and the Battle Kachina Wheels.

She became a leader of soldiers—both Medicine Soldiers and fighting soldiers.

In that time of chaos and destruction, most of her family had been killed opposing the Lords of the land, who had revived human sacrifice and slavery.

The Lords of the land were brutal men who would stop at nothing to get their way. The sacrifice priests taught these Feudal Lords that people could be ruled only by fear.

The Lords, in their turn, taught that only the fang and the tooth of experience were understood by "the common people," who were "incapable of learning."

However, the Flower Soldiers taught that human sacrifice and slavery were forbidden, and that every human possessed the natural right to have a Voice in government. Democracy—the Circle of Law—had been discovered by the Zero Chiefs thousands of years before this time and was held to be Sacred by every Flower Soldier.

By the time Temple Doors became the commander of the Flower Soldiers, she violently opposed the sacrifice priests of the Temples and the Lords who held their people in perpetual slavery. A bloody war ensued that lasted five years.

After yet another bitter struggle and more useless bloodshed, the courageous Temple Doors decided to lead the Flower Soldiers and any of her people who wanted to go with them, north into the "Land of the Wild People." In the new land, they could find Freedom and rebuild their civilization based on the balance and teachings of the Medicine Wheels.

Temple Doors led twenty-four thousand people or more, overland, north out from the Mayan peninsula, through the length of Mexico and into the Southwest of the present-day United States. On this great migration, she fought and won many battles and helped her people survive every kind of privation and disease.

Temple Doors could be likened to Thomas Jefferson and George Washington—people of courage and change.

Temple Doors was a Priestess and a General. However, her most important contribution to the world was the reordering and rebuilding of the Discipline of the Flower Soldiers. She taught of the Medicine Wheels and Battle Kachina Wheels. This woman was directly responsible for the survival of our Medicine Wheels.

This knowledge that Temple Doors carried and the great migration she led to the Land of the Wild People have been secreted among our Flower Soldiers.

Temple Doors was a very important person in human history. Volumes could be written about her by the people of Mexico and we Northerners, and still there would be more to say. But time is needed before this will be done.

The Temple known as Desert Flower is the source of our information concerning the early migrations to the North from the Yucatán. This Temple is now known as the ruins of Chaco Canyon. The woman who began the building of the Desert Flower was the Zero Chief Temple Doors.

The cities of Chaco Canyon and Canyon de Chelly were built by the people who took on the name of their Chief, calling themselves the Temple Doors. The sophisticated network of roads, cisterns, forts, Kivas, buildings, farms, and pueblos were all built by the

people of Temple Doors.

Temple Doors originally settled many of her armies and peoples at Canyon de Chelly. They began building immediately. However, at this same time, a dedicated group of highly disciplined and skilled Medicine Soldiers, with their General, Temple Doors, began the construction of their Schools and Temples at the Desert Flower in Chaco Canyon. Her dream and the dream of her apprentices was to build a new civilization based on the teaching of the Medicine Wheels and the Circle of Law. The Desert Flower was designed to be their first main Center of Teaching and Healing.

The General lived for many years. It is thought that she was over eighty-three at the time of her death.

The Sweet Medicine People—The Iron Shirts

Fifty years after the death of the great Leader and Zero Chief Temple Doors, a massive nomadic army, which wanted the land her people settled for their own, threatened to go to war with the peoples of the Temple Doors. These nomadic, highly trained soldiers were called the "Sweet Medicine People," and were a fair-haired, blue-eyed race.

Many of America's older Native People referred to them as the "White Water Spider." This was because their sailing ships, with their white sails and long banks of oars, resembled massive white water spiders. To the Northern Cree and Cheyenne, the prows of these ships also resembled the heads of very large spiders.

Other tribes of people who encountered these same white people—inland and away from their ships—referred to them as the "Iron Shirts" because of the armor they wore.

The Cheyenne People who lived on the Great Lakes called these people *Wihio* (pronounced "Veeh-He-Yoh"), which means "White Spider" or "White Man."

In the Cheyenne tongue, *Wihio* can also mean "priest" or "priestess," depending upon the context in which it is used. *Veeh* also means "Wise One." The reason for this is that the Priests and Priestesses of the Iron Shirts taught the Native Peoples of North America about the Earth Sun Dance.

It is interesting to note that other languages have similar words that share very similar meanings. As an example, in Spanish, *Viejo* or *Vieja* means "elder," or "Wise One." In the Italian language, "Wise One" is *Vicchio*. In old French, the word for "Witch" or

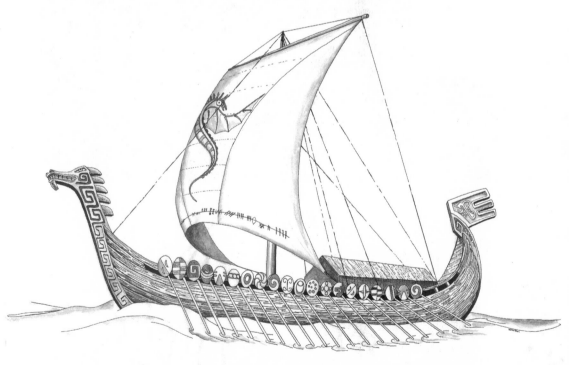

"Wise One" is *Vichy*. And, of course in Old English the words for "Wise One" are *Wicca* and *Witch*.

These White people, the Iron Shirts, were sea peoples stranded on the eastern coast of North America after powerful Earth upheavals made it impossible for them to sail eastward again, back to where they had originated. These Iron Shirts journeyed west, overland, as a great nomadic army. It was many years later that they met and threatened war against the people of Temple Doors.

Because the Iron Shirts were nomads, their continual movement often brought them into conflict and war. This made them incredibly aggressive and slow to forgive any wrong done to them.

When the many villages of Temple Doors heard that their land had been invaded by "the white hordes from the North" they immediately banded together to meet the threat.

The day the two veteran fighting forces stood opposed to one another in the land that the Sweet Medicine People believed should be their own, blood was sure to run. If the Chiefs of the Temple Doors People had not called for a peacemaking Council, it is likely that the two peoples would have completely destroyed one another.

This highly unorthodox move very much surprised the people of the Iron Shirts, because it was unheard of in those days for an army to talk peace.

At first, the military Chiefs of both forces refused to parley. However, the Medicine Chiefs of both sides were eager for a talk.

The Medicine Chiefs met at a place called Grass-Runs-Over. This name connotes a high grassy mesa or a flood plain. There, they discovered that the Chiefs of both sides taught that human sacrifice and human slavery were forbidden. This information amazed them. Because of this deep commonality between the Medicine Chiefs, the two peoples decided to join forces. However, this meant overcoming great problems.

At this time, fifty years after the death of the Zero Chief Temple Doors, the body of actual Flower Soldiers had become smaller—the total number was around fifteen hundred women and men. And they had chosen to hold no great political power. Since all the Flower Soldiers were elite combat veterans, they were viewed by the military council as a Source of training for officers of the army. They were also the healers and thought to be people of Knowledge.

During this time certain military soldiers and their officers had separated from the Flower Soldiers and had started their own council. They were called the Military Council. This council had also separated from the Circle of Law—the government of the people of Temple Doors. Although the Military Council was still considered part of the Temple Doors People, its members were a group unto themselves, and held enormous power because of their military strength and political influence.

Another powerful group among the Temple Doors People were their Priestesses and Priests. Though most of these Chiefs had been taught by the Flower Soldiers, only a few of them were actually Flower Soldiers themselves. All of these "Medicine People" were allied to and part of the Circle of Law.

While negotiations were being held on how to merge the two peoples, the Military Council made a spontaneous decision—without telling the Medicine People—to capture the Iron Shirts and make them slaves.

This proved to be a disastrous mistake. When the armies met, the army of the Temple Doors, led by the officers of the Military Council, was quickly defeated—because the Flower Soldiers would not fight.

Surrounded, the Military Council was threatened with annihilation. However, their people were saved by an amazing turn of events that brought to light a long-standing problem.

In the confusion of battle and decision making, the Flower Soldiers had carried out a bold countermove that gave their side bargaining power. They had surrounded and captured every Priestess and Priest of the Iron Shirts.

This move on the part of the Flower Soldiers brought on an explosive contention between the Medicine People of Temple Doors and their own Military Council. The argument was over slavery.

The Military Council members, in true fashion for them, acted upon the argument as they always had—with brute force. They ordered their soldiers to arrest their own Medicine People, and then they blithely asked the Flower Soldiers to kill the Priestesses and

Priests of the Iron Shirts. The Flower Soldiers refused to obey these orders.

Within a week every person who had once commanded a position on the Military Council was dead.

Within a year of this determining battle, the two peoples had merged and become one great people of many tribes. After this, the Way of the Circle of Law that had been carried and protected by the Flower Soldiers of the Temple Doors People became the Governing Council.

Within a hundred years, the people of Temple Doors and the fair-haired, white-skinned people had merged into a new people.

The early settlements and Kivas found throughout Utah, Arizona, Colorado, and New Mexico are the work of the intermarried peoples of the Temple Doors and Sweet Medicine. They celebrated Life and rebuilt their beloved Temples in their new land.

The Temple Doors and Sweet Medicine People became a large trading people. They

dominated the land with their army and controlled every trail that led to Canyon de Chelly, known to them as Lake Dweller, because at this time the canyon contained a large body of water. The City had "house islands" that could be defended against attack.

When the people of Temple Doors and the people of the Iron Shirts merged and became one, the land of the Southwest was a well-forested, grassy land. But over many hundreds of years these lands became a desert. When this happened, the intermarried peoples of the Temple Doors and the Iron Shirts migrated to the East and North, becoming the Mound Builder peoples of Ohio, and part of many other peoples. Their children, in turn, settled all over America.

Much of the knowledge known by the Flower Soldiers of today came from these intermarried people of the Temple Doors and the Sweet Medicine People.

A few Temples and Tribes of peoples kept the information of the Medicine Wheels. Some of these colonies were the seeds that blossomed into new and wondrous civilizations that carried on the Discipline of Self Honor and Democracy. Temple Doors and her people had been one of these blossoms that bravely fought to survive.

324

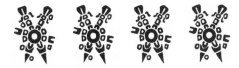

When the Iron Shirts first married with the people of Temple Doors, they brought with them a Lodge called the Sun Earth Lodge. They shared the information of their Sun Earth Lodge with the people of Temple Doors. The Temple of the Sun Earth Dance Lodge was transformed by the meeting of the Iron Shirts with the people of the Temple Doors.

The descendants of Temple Doors, the Flower Soldiers, have kept the knowledge of the Earth Sun Dance. The Sun Earth or Earth Sun Lodge is a Teaching Temple. At one time, the information of this School became known to many of the peoples of North America.

For their part, the Temple Doors People introduced the Medicine Wheels, including the Wheel known as the Circle of Law, to the Iron Shirts.

Estcheemah taught: "It is dangerous to believe that the Temples of old were only places of religion. All Temples in ancient times, in America and at other places in our world, were schools first, and places of religion second. Seldom is it ever emphasized that the Temples were educational institutions far more than religious ones.

"Mathematics and the Medicine Wheels were taught in these Lodges, as well as the use of healing herbs, practical hygiene, agriculture, and more. It is very important to remember that the Earth Sun Dance was a moving Temple that could be physically erected once a year in whatever place was chosen. Messages were sent out designating where it would be found. Students would come from enormous distances to the Sun Earth Lodges, to learn or to find themselves a teacher.

"Our ancient Sun Earth Lodge was also a place of the Law. By understanding the Law, people do not become victims of the Law, for they learn of Self Responsibility and Guidance.

"Our Law Arrows were uncovered in the Sun Earth Lodge. To uncover means to Teach the Law. It is important that all people understand the workings of their laws. When people understand the law, they are no longer following superstitious rules.

"Long-standing problems and arguments were solved at these meetings between Tribes and peoples. Chiefs were chosen during the Earth Sun Dance meetings, and decisions were made that concerned the law.

"Over many centuries—sometimes within one short lifetime—precious information can be lost or distorted. A Temple that loses knowledge is no longer alive for the people; it is like a tombstone.

"Most present Lodges are only remnants of the original Great Lodges of the Law— what is left are ritual dances that possess no central core of teaching.

"Today, for many, a Sun Dance Lodge is a place that is believed to house a slave Spirit. Many people are taught that if they follow certain rules, then that slave Spirit must—in some way—physically respond to them. Yet, in actuality, when people believe they can control Spirit with rules, this teaches only superstition, not truth. This kind of ignorance is the most common and the most dangerous among all the peoples of the world.

"Learning is a living challenge. It is the greatest and most holy of all human experiences. Discovery of the human Self is the highest of all knowledge.

"The Sun Earth Dance is a Circle where people can acknowledge being part of Life where they can experience sharing directly with Life and one another.

"Sharing is important to all humans. But there is no true sharing when the mind is separated from Life. An animal can only live Life, but humans are able to interpret what they experience in Life. This is because animals have no individual Self Essence, while humans can choose to learn of the Self their entire Life long. The less humans choose to know of the Self, the more base they remain.

"The power of human sharing is experienced when a person becomes responsible to teach another of what she or he has honestly learned.

"Life reveals. Life uncovers. Life quickens Spirit and teaches Spirit. Life can make a Spirit cry. Life can make a Spirit laugh. That is why the human Spirit loves Life. This is what the great Zero Chief Temple Doors taught.

"She emphasized that when there is a balance of female and male, then the true sense of Life is restored and natural checks and balances can be realized. But this cannot be accomplished unless there is equality of rank between priestess and priest, warrioress and warrior, and all female and male Healers, teachers, and leaders.

"The ideal thing, of course, would be to have people respect the power of the Self and the Balance and Equality of their Sacred Creatress and Creator. When people respect the Balance of the Self, they will learn to respect something as grand and powerful as Life."

Temple Doors on the Training and Discipline of Flower Soldiers

Temple Doors:

"There are those few humans of Earth who desire to understand their existence and Life. Only the courageous question what the conformists call normal. The greatest moment in the Life of those who are truly curious is when they stand before the mirror of their Self.

"Destiny looms large for the human who questions the Self.

"Wealth or poverty, talent, strength, physical comfort, education, all become shadows when faced with the reasons of why the Self should even exist at all.

"Combat, every endurance, physical or mental—even the anguish of serious illness—can become a test of hope for people who have nothing in their lives.

"I am speaking of the bored and the pretenders. Instead of embracing their Earthly experience, they languish in fantasy while they live. What greater sorrow can there be than this?

"The Flower Soldier contemplates the human condition, knowing that sorrow is felt because Spirit is questioning human pretense and lies.

"The seekers, the Flower Soldiers, who battle their fears and strive to know the Self, will not find immediate reward for their efforts. Instead, they will feel a deep sense of sadness that will be profound and far-reaching.

"This sorrow is felt because the seekers can now leave behind all pretense of security. There is no security for the Flower Soldiers. They know that Life is as fleeting as the Rose that blooms and dies.

"The Flower Soldier is confronted with the question, 'Can I create a Circle at my feet, powerful enough to effect change in my lifetime?'

"Such questions flood in upon the destined, but only confound the believer.

"The Flower Soldier's first illumination is that there is reason and madness. Suffering and ignorance can now be perceived as the human dilemma, not as human destiny.

"The human is destined for greatness and absolute fulfillment. The human is destined to question and learn of the limitless reaches of time and Creation.

"Once Flower Soldiers decide to build their own Circle of Self power and effect change in their world, they are thrown into direct combat with their own ignorance and fears. True battle is possible only when there is no easy hope for victory.

"The tactical Commander, on any battlefield, must know absolute discipline and teach Self discipline. Discipline is the center of the world for the Warrioress and Warrior. It is the rim of the world for the protected and helpless. Yet, the Army of disciplined veterans is still only a dream. No such Army has ever existed in time and space.

"The Commander must win every battle with the inexperienced. Every army is a body of the inexperienced—the young, stubborn, old, rational, vengeful, escapist, frightened, stupid, and overzealous, along with the wise, strong, loyal, trustworthy, educated, and disciplined.

"No Army in history has been or will ever be adequately prepared or armed for combat. No ground on Earth is suitable for war and easy victory. This is the reason the

Flower Soldiers say: 'Preparation is forever ongoing, and is the great Teacher.'

"The Flower Soldiers teach that people who follow the rules will be defeated when the rules are changed—and the rules change in Life as frequently as we breathe. As an example, the rule is that we must breathe. The rule is not that we breathe always at the same time, in the same way, or in the same rhythm.

"Soldiers are taught to respect the rules, but never to have the rules be their commander. When the rules become the commander, defeat is certain.

"One out of every thousand soldiers born understands the reason for true victory. All other soldiers understand only the power to win, one to one. They understand only confrontation, only defeating their adversary.

"Soldiers must always possess the Will to Live. Simple survival is not living. Soldiers must be trained to live and to be Responsible for their lives. To do this, Soldiers must possess the power of Decision while in Combat. When faced with conflict or physical combat, more people fear pain than they do the loss of their lives. Because of this, they will throw away their lives in an attempt to avoid the responsibility of their pain.

"All Soldiers will be taught to hold the Self Sacred, and to Respect their Life. All Soldiers will be taught to be Self Responsible. Every Soldier will be given the Responsibility of achieving the objective, and taught how to maneuver while in Combat.

"Yet, what is it we speak of here if it is not every individual? Are we not an Army within our Self and being? Aren't the inexperienced and the experienced both part of us? Are we not the wise and stupid? Who is responsible for Command within us, if it is not our Self?

"The Temples have asked: 'What is intelligent about war?' There is no intelligent war. However, as a Commander who has experienced brutality and war, I will answer that true intelligence in war is care for the Army and perfect knowledge of the enemy. The ability to confront and put the enemy to rout can only be accomplished when the weakness of the enemy is known.

"Human conflict resides in the heart of every human born. The conflict exists because the Soldiers do not know their enemy or why they must combat their adversary.

"The best Army is one that is Unified in Knowing. The best Army does not battle for any cause other than Unity among its ranks.

"How is unity possible if there is no knowing? The Soldier is the Army. The Soldier is unified within the Self and loyal to the Army.

"Every Soldier must possess Self knowing. This knowing unifies the Soldier, and the Self-knowing Soldier will unify the Army. The unified Soldier teaches about the power of knowing and not knowing.

"Not knowing is pretense and weakness. Knowing is unification and Self Teaching. This is the reason I make sure that every Field Commander teaches each Soldier about the reasons for battle. When every Soldier understands that the Army must move as a unified Body, then the Army will be powerful.

"It is the duty of all Officers to teach every Soldier in their command about tactical maneuvers. Even when the most ignorant Soldiers become skillful in Battle maneuvers,

they will understand unity. This always brings certain victory.

"The Soldier must never be in conflict with the reasons for Battle maneuvers. Because human violence resides within every human born, it is the Duty of every Soldier to teach the reasons that exist within the Self for war and violence.

"What are the Flower Soldier's reasons for war? The first reason is survival. Second, the Soldier must understand why she or he is called to fight. Third, the Soldier must possess the knowledge and Self endurance to be Victorious. Fourth, the Soldier must understand why the Enemy must be defeated.

"War and Combat are the Reasons for the existence of the Army. Discipline and Education are the Wisdom of the Army. Reward for the Army is Rank and Comradeship. Loyalty for the Army is to love Mother Earth and Her people.

"Discipline begins with the Self.

"Discipline is the Soldier's answer to survival, health, education, weaponry, and knowledge.

"The first and greatest enemy of humanity is Self ignorance. The second great enemy is belief. The third great enemy is pretense. And the fourth great enemy is laziness. Flower Soldiers are taught to battle their ignorance, their beliefs, their pretense, and their laziness.

"What is a Flower Soldier? The Professional Flower Soldiers are a Body composed of Devoted Women and Men who are The Army, and who are dedicated to Learning of the Self and Sacred Mother Life.

"The Army is demanding and disciplined. This harsh demand and discipline drives away the civilian and strengthens the professional Soldier.

"What does the Army demand? The Army demands absolute Self respect, loyalty to the Army, and absolute love for Sacred Mother Life."

The Battle Kachina Schools

The Battle Kachinas are a Power and Presence that humans call Challenge. They are the Masked Teachers who can look like everyone and anything. They are also the Earth-Dream Teachers.

The Circle of Teachers are: Hunger and Work, Beauty and the Unattractive, Wealth and Poverty, Knowing and Not Knowing, Having and Not Having, Power and Weakness, Control and No Control, To be With and To be Without, To be Slaves and To be Free, To be Challenged and never To know Challenge. All of these are Battle Kachinas.

The Battle Kachina Temple of the Bee Warrioresses, which was known as the Little Jaguar, was part of the Flower Soldier schools. Bee Warrioresses were highly learned and disciplined women Chiefs who taught of Life and Death. Most Bee Warrioresses were skilled in the art of combat, and some were Commanders and Generals.

Many of these Teachers also concentrated upon the Discipline of the Self and the Art of Healing. For them, Healing was another kind of battlefield, one in which to fight human ignorance and imbalance. The teachers of this Temple-School called themselves Battle Kachinas.

Bee Warrioresses taught: "We engage with the Inevitable when we battle our present. What greater teacher is there than the moment? Caution should be exercised by the student, because the Battle Kachina is never the foe.

"Who is the foe? Who is it that will taste defeat? Surely it will not be the Kachinas. They are the battle-wise veterans who have the sharp edge of long Experience.

"In Warfare, who is the student and who is the Teacher? Students can travel far and learn all there is to experience, but they can never leave their Temple behind. That which is learned within the first Circle of Experience is carried as a weapon into every dimension of human endeavor by the Flower Soldier."

Many years after the Little Jaguar Temple existed, the Zero Chief Tomahseeasah said: "The very first hurt of the small children can become a Battle Kachina, when they are taught that they have fallen into their first Circle of Experience.

"The children can scream and cry, yes, even hate the object that tripped them up. But this does not defeat their Battle Kachina, nor should the incident defeat the child. There is no escape from the objects and experience of early learning."

Estcheemah said: "The Battle Kachina—the Teacher—is like the Shadow—always there, but never an encumbrance. Who can catch the Shadow? What we learn becomes the Shadow. We are first the student, then we become our own teacher.

"This is also true with the things and situations we battle. They too become Shadows. The Shadow is the object lesson learned, and the guidance given through experience becomes the teacher.

"Students memorized the saying: 'The Shadow must be defeated at every turn of events. Yet, the Shadow is never present at any event. This is because what we learn becomes the Shadow teacher.' "

This is not a riddle for the Flower Soldier. Rather, it is a guide into the greater Circle of Discipline. This is why it is said: "The Soldier, on the field of battle, can be defeated by too many Shadows present in the mind.

"The Flower Soldier can never battle the Shadows directly, but will be ever Present with every Event."

The Temple of the Little Jaguar who tells us about the Shadow Warrioress and Warrior asks: "What is accolade?"

"The Student that visits the Temple and leaves with the Flags in hand is not a Soldier, but a thief.

"The Student that leaves the Temple with the Color of the Flags in his heart and mind is a Soldier of high rank.

"The Student who sees the Colors of the Flags in the eyes of the Children is the Healer.

"The Student who sees the Colors of the Flags in the sunrise and sunset will become a great Leader."

Estcheemah taught: "The Battle Kachina brings the Student into Self Knowing. It is this dance of perfect timing that throws the Student into the tumult of ideal conflict. Timing tears away the cloak of pretense from those who would dare play with Discipline. What greater learning is there?"

Temple Doors said: "Timing is the virtue of all Flower Soldiers. Timing is the steps that the Battle Kachinas dance, that teach the student of warfare. The student must work to understand every step of the dance of Life and Death. The reason for this is that Timing is the force that decides between the simple dispute and what is contested with blood. To ask what to Do and what Action should be taken is to ask about rhythm. Rhythm is Mathematics—it is the Soldier's song of Numbers."

Estcheemah: "Only after all of this teaching was the student asked the question about Sacred Mother Life. Where is the Temple of Earth Life? Who is the student of great learning and who is the greatest of teachers?"

These teachings come to us from the Temple of the Bee Warrioresses.

Lightningbolt was awake early in the morning and eager to work.

"Lightningbolt, you have to be determined and disciplined to be a Flower Soldier," Estcheemah told him while he ate his breakfast. "With hard work and Self discipline, possibly one day you too will have the distinction of being a Flower Soldier."

She handed him a notebook. Lightningbolt took the small book and read:

The Soldier shall bow only to the Rose.
The Soldier shall respect Sacred Mother Life.
The Soldier shall respect the Self and
*   protect the Self.*
The Soldier shall learn of humanity.
The Soldier shall learn of what has been
*   created.*
The Soldier shall learn of Self duty.
The Soldier shall learn of all weapons.
The Soldier shall learn the art of combat.

"The Discipline of the Flower Soldier has taught how training for battle helps humans understand the delicacy of Life," Estcheemah told him. "And war teaches how very easy it is to kill. Life must be respected."

"How does duty to the Self train the mind?" he asked. "We can tell our Self anything, right? What is the truth for the Self?"

Estcheemah smiled at Lightningbolt's questions and enjoyed how he wrestled with the obvious. "Yes, some of us speak to the Self," she answered.

"Flower Soldiers have learned that Life is the truth for those who live. Death is the truth for those who have died.

"A Self destructive person is dangerous. While we are angry or hating, what kind of truth is spoken? The truth many people speak is actually a lie they want people to believe. Isn't this what a propagandist does?

"Only the truth of Self is the truth for the Flower Soldier. When Flower Soldiers learn of the Self, they learn of their truth, their true destiny. Destiny is Self revelation.

"All action is movement away from or toward Self enlightenment. What we do and what we choose is called Self action. The Flower Soldier studies Self action. Results are brought about through Self action. All questions are answers to some action."

"Then what I choose to do in any given minute is human action?" Lightningbolt asked.

"Yes, even if you should think you have no choice, there is still a choice made," she answered. "To make no decision is a decision made, Lightningbolt. Choice is a sacred responsibility. There is no escaping human choice and Self responsibility."

"I am going to have to study a bit," Lightningbolt said with determination. "When I first met you, I thought all I had to learn was how to shake a rattle or two."

"Here is more to study." Estcheemah smiled, handing him another small notebook.

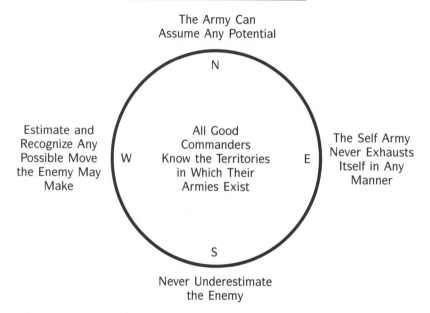

THE FIVE RULES OF A SOLDIER

The Army Can
Assume Any Potential

N

Estimate and
Recognize Any
Possible Move
the Enemy May
Make

W

All Good
Commanders
Know the Territories
in Which Their
Armies Exist

E

The Self Army
Never Exhausts
Itself in Any
Manner

S

Never Underestimate
the Enemy

"The rules you see in this Medicine Wheel are very old, no doubt one of our oldest guides," Estcheemah told him. "The deep meaning and far-reaching effects of what these rules mean to us Flower Soldiers should always be respected.

"Honor these rules and take your time learning them—try a Life time. Over the many thousands of years much has been learned concerning our laws; however, what you will say is important. The reason I say this is because the young should never be awed by what came before them. Instead, we must all be constantly challenged by what we are taught.

"What happens with our Inner Medicine Wheel of our Mind, our Emotions, our Body, and our Spirit is the prime consideration for the Flower Soldier. We understand that our Self Knowing, our personal Enlightenment, is basic to us and holds utmost importance.

"This inner Wheel can guide us Flower Soldiers through decision making and during conflict.

"When we war against our Self, the enemy thinking within becomes an army that fights against the army of the Self. This enemy army can assume a potential not expected.

"What is Self potential? Do we have a disciplined Self Commander? Are we a Self army, complete within our Self? What is an independent Self army?

"These questions and many more are made clear in the teachings of our Medicine Wheels, especially the one known to us as The Five Rules of a Soldier.

"As I have said, over many years our Chiefs developed a sophisticated Self Discipline based on the teachings of our Medicine Wheels."

"The early Flower Soldiers learned that people try to use their emotions and feelings as a shield. To do this is a mistake because Love and tenderness are Powers, not shields. When a person uses feelings as a shield, she or he can become trapped behind a wall of emotions and suffer because of it.

"We have also learned from our Flower Soldiers that it is incredibly easy to underestimate the strength of our ignorance and long-held attitudes. Not acknowledging their power creates a Self enemy within. And nothing is more dangerous to the human!

"The Flower Soldier never exhausts the Self. As an example of this, we can exhaust our Self with overconcern with the mediocre and mundane. Study detail, but do not let details dictate what your actions are or will be; this exhausts the Self.

"The most destructive of all the things that exhaust us is the Self lie. How easy it is for us to pretend and to lie to ourselves. But this exhausts us and tears us to pieces.

"The Zero Chiefs of old taught of the extreme danger of the Self lie. They sculpted and drew many versions of the symbol of a man or woman pulling a barbed vine through the tongue. This meant the Self lie.

"Later interpreters translated this symbol in many strange ways, even believing that people actually pulled barbed vines through their tongues, physically. This was not true. Literally, in the different languages of the Mayan Zero Chiefs, 'to pull a barbed vine through the tongue' is how they said 'to lie to the Self.'

"All humans use weapons. A weapon is anything used, made by, or known to any human. All humans destroy during their lifetime—all humans kill.

"We kill even as we play, killing insects and plants. We kill trees to make homes. We kill plants and animals to eat. Even the person who only consumes plants will kill the plant and kill millions of insects.

"Fire destroys wood so that we might have warmth. Electricity destroys metal and glass so we can have light. We destroy microbes in our stomachs to digest our foods. We destroy our bodies with movement.

"The Flower Soldier learns, with time and Self study, that Death is always present with Life. But Death is not the enemy. And Life is not the enemy. Life and Death are the great Teachers of Existence.

"We kill to eat, to survive. We kill to transform

what we need as tools. And so, everything that we are and touch is a lethal weapon. Death transforms the food we need for Life. Death is the great Transformer and Transformation.

"The Medicine Wheel also teaches us about war and human conflict.

"A Flower Soldier knows that the greatest battle in Life is the battle of the subtle. The reality of Self ignorance is over obvious to the learned, but the person who is ignorant cannot see this truth about the Self. The ignorant seek to conform. Incompetence and ignorance are at the root of the attitudes of the lazy and pretentious. These ailments of humanity are born from humans seeking to conform instead of discovering the reason for their existence on Earth.

"The actions of conformists are ruled by their fears. A grand example is that, for conformists, Earth is a tamed circus where their God and their devil battle over the petty.

"The God of the conformists needs translators because their deity has no way of communicating directly with the believers. This brings about even more confusion because most of the translators are fear mongers.

"These words are not outrageous statements. They are actually quite conservative descriptions of what happens daily around our Earth. We must understand that at any given moment in time, any institution can become the monster instead of the grand teacher.

"Teach yourself, Lightningbolt. This is the only way you will end the pain of your desperate ignorance. Ignorance is the greatest foe of the Flower Soldier. For us Flower Soldiers, Self duty is the path to achievement and Self command."

The Duties of the Flower Soldier

Self duty is always first.
Responsibility to the Self is duty.

Responsibility for Self action is duty.
Self contemplation is duty.
Recognizing others is duty.
Care for the Self is duty.
Teaching the Self is duty.
Caring for all children is duty.
Learning of the Self is duty.
Knowing the Self is duty.

"Beyond this, Flower Soldiers learn all there is to learn of their own Self power.

"The responsibility of training themselves in the use of all materials and tools of the battlefield is another duty of the Flower Soldier.

"Learning from and respect for all Flower Soldiers who are superiors is the duty of the Flower Soldier.

"Discipline is Self Command. Discipline does not mean punishing the Self. People have to learn to be disciplined Commanders. They have to learn to respect Command, especially Self Command. That is why it is said that receiving orders becomes knowledge learned. Learning to Command the Self is the highest of all orders. All orders are studied by the Self Commander before action is taken.

"All Flower Soldiers are responsible for women with children, and the old. It is the duty of the Flower Soldier to care for those people in whatever manner is practical.

"Honor is Goddess within all Flower Soldiers who are male.

"Honor is God within all Flower Soldiers who are female.

"However, in a world where women are taught never to Honor Sacred Goddess Life, the woman must first learn to Honor her Self and Goddess Creation. In doing so she Honors the Perfect Balance of Creation, which will restore Balance within the Human Self.

"A Flower Soldier who is a Self Commander recognizes and respects all other Flower Soldiers unless the individual Flower Soldier shows Self contempt. A human who has Self contempt cannot truly be a Flower Soldier.

"When any Commander sees that another Flower Soldier has flagrantly ignored personal Duty, it is the responsibility of that Commander to charge the Flower Soldier with breaking the law.

"When a law is broken, it is the duty of Flower Soldiers to bring charges against themselves and recommend the course of justice.

"All laws of the Army and Community, if they be reasonable and just, are obeyed by the Flower Soldier. If any Flower Soldier recognizes or perceives any law as being unjust, she or he must report the injustice immediately to superior Flower Soldier Officers.

"The Flower Soldier must always battle within the rules of the Community, meaning that she or he will not break the law.

"Flower Soldiers consider themselves as an Army within the Self.

"All other Flower Soldiers are allied Armies.

"All Flower Soldiers who are allied Armies are respected within the Rule of the Law."

"I am going to really get down to work, reading and thinking," Lightningbolt said, looking up.

"Study everything," she encouraged him. "And we will meet here on this road, at the county bridge, day after tomorrow."

Lightningbolt studied the Rules of the Flower Soldier, noticing how many times he had brought himself up on charges and had then ignored his Self

recommendations. This was his grim battle and he knew it.

He marveled that these laws had been founded in order to educate the Self and to bring the Self into power. What a pitiful soldier he was! He never had been a Flower Soldier in the past—only a wild, uncivilized foe, fighting himself. He would begin again. As he read and re-read the Rules of the Flower Soldier he began to understand them and how they applied to his Life. He beamed with joy. Never before had he found such happiness. The discovery that he was his own Commander and his own Army made all the difference in the world!

When they met at the bridge, as Estcheemah had suggested, she told him more.

"The discipline and knowledge that have survived both natural catastrophes and human incompetence survived because there were a few humans who appreciated the worth of Knowledge. No libraries in history have survived time, the ignorant, the thieves, the well-meaning, or the religious zealots. Only disciplined humans have kept knowledge. This is because they respected knowledge.

"Incompetence is the human disease. Humans reward each other for their conformity, and this breeds further incompetence. Over time, incompetence becomes the destroyer of all things that were once fine and beautiful."

"Estcheemah," asked Lightningbolt respectfully, "you know, I have always wondered since it is true that we were all born before, then why hasn't it taught humanity anything?"

Estcheemah smiled. The wisdom lines around her eyes fairly shone. "We all have been the wrecker and the builder. We have been slave and slave owner. I hope that if I am ever the slave owner, I will free my slave. I hope that if I am the wrecker, I will pick up the pieces for the wise to reassemble. I hope that if I am the builder, I will remember what has been torn down in the name of politics or religious zeal.

"I know that I have also been the zealot and the avenger. I have been the fool and the fanatic. I have also been the one who was brave and cared for what could be so easily not understood.

"I hope that you have the courage, in this lifetime, to be the Keeper of these Medicine Wheels. I hope that you can endure those who are puffed up or indiscreet. Can you face those who are irresponsible and endure? Remember always that your greatest foe is your own ignorance.

"Life is both the giver and the opportunity for humans to know of the Self and their human condition. We learn with experience. Experience is Life—that is why we live.

"If given the opportunity, the human can become a Self leader, a Self commander, within her or him Self.

"Everyone benefits when there are fewer conformists, fewer social slaves among us, and more people who are Self responsible. This is brought about through choice.

"Choice is decision. We all must know that we possess the responsibility to make decisions that concern the direction of our own lives. The old European philosophers once said that there is thesis, antithesis, and synthesis. They were typical for their time in that they left out the fourth element—Choice.

"Life is experience, and Life experience is the great teacher for us all. The next most powerful teacher for the human is the human Self. Life points the way toward Self experience. The Zero Chiefs taught that it is through the Self that we understand the many nuances of experience we call Life. To understand what the Self means became the most important quest in Life for the Zero Chiefs.

"These Chiefs have told us that to love and nourish the Self is the most profound and difficult task known to humanity. The reason for the diffi-culty is because most humans refuse to accept Self responsibility.

"Humans are afraid to be Self responsible because we fear failure, separation, Death, and pain. Because of this, we can become weak and dependent, continually searching outside of our Self for Authority.

"There is nothing more subtle, and nothing more absolute, in all of Creation than the mystery of the human Self. While we know that we exist as a body, few of us know of the Self Being that we are and what the potential of this Self can be.

"The Zero Chiefs discovered, through long study, that people will ignore or deny the inward Self, but in the same instance they will destroy themselves defending outside authority and beliefs.

"This human paradox shocked and amazed the Zero Chiefs. 'What is this?' they asked.

"They discovered that people who know only a source of outside authority will substitute belief for the Self. They do this because they can hide behind belief and not be responsible for their actions.

"Dependent women and men will do almost anything to fight off attack from the outside; but they ignore the battle within.

"People who are not their own Self authorities are victims to every human foible and all challenging physical circumstances.

"Most oftenly, in our world people are taught to not trust or to question the information of their own experiences. They are also taught to not trust the Self that they are. Of course the people who teach this also say that they are supreme authorities and that they should be trusted. This kind of rhetoric sets up a war within the human that can destroy all incentive and balance within the person.

"Within these kinds of dependent people there is an unruly mob of information that is at war with their Self. In their inward world exist separate personalities or Minds that wear separate uniforms; have different training, different powers, and different tools and weapons; and fly various flags. Worst of all, they possess no Self Loyalty. Most important, each mind or being within the undisciplined person believes that it is only a pretender.

"However, those who take time in their Life to learn of the Self will discover that they can become Commanders of the Self.

"For people who struggle to discover their Self Commander, there always comes the illumination that the Self can be their own powerful authority. With this revelation comes the potential of becoming a strong Commander.

"A strong Commander battles to learn of all the isolated characters within the Self, and understands that balance can be achieved when she or he becomes a responsible and honest Self Teacher.

"The Self Commander will unify all inward personalities and Beings by studying and contemplating Self failures and Self triumphs. It is in this way that the Commander becomes a kind Teacher.

"It is the responsibility of the Self Commander to learn all there is to know about Self resource and information that is available to the Self. The Self Commander delegates all responsibility and authority to the appropriate, most powerful, and most loyal personalities within the Self. This may be a Lifelong experience for the Self, and so every person should be an honest and understanding teacher. All humans are more than we have been taught. And Life is greater still. Life is the Great Resource of all learning. No human can equal what the experience of Life teaches.

"One of the ways in which the young Flower Soldier can learn of the beings or minds within is to discover how each mind can become a friend and ally. Each personality within can be ranked according to knowledge and ability. For example, there may be a youthful soldier within who is not very knowledgeable but who possesses immense courage for battle. Another inner being might know languages. Yet another might be knowledgeable in the art of Healing.

"Slowly, the Flower Soldier will become aware of all their inner potentials. It is the duty of the Flower Soldier to find all inward Beings.

"It is possible that some of the Beings within each of us are constantly ignored, while others can enslave us with endless demands for attention. Many of the Beings are thoughts and attitudes that are imprisoned and need to be freed."

Estcheemah laughed and teased Lightningbolt about his attitude of always wanting to be the cock of the walk, and how he had allowed this Being within him to become a dictator.

"Some people leave their inward world to absolute chance," she said. "To do this is almost certain suicide to the Self.

"The young Commander learns that all experience is valuable. Reporting to the Self is the most profound Duty for every Flower Soldier. The report must be clear, devoid of trivia, and concise."

Over the following two days, Lightningbolt was asked to report what he had learned. He struggled and floundered with his reporting—leaving out important information and wallowing in trivia. But he kept reporting again and again, each time learning how to bring forward pertinent information.

Lightningbolt's greatest illumination at this time was his discovery that he was the waiting vessel wanting to be filled.

Estcheemah told him that society will eagerly fill up "all waiting vessels" with bubble gum, beer, religion, trivia, promises of retirement, televised images, misery, and aspirins.

That same day, soon after the evening meal, Estcheemah told him about a journey she had taken to the land of the Maya. The story taught him how to appreciate her immense sense of humor, but it also taught him how to keep a discerning viewpoint.

Estcheemah's old eyes were bright as she spoke. "It is all in how you look at things, Lightningbolt. If you learn to allow for human error, then you will perceive the profound and the tragic.

"Many times, the reasons behind why something was built have little to do with what was created. This is more than evident with all civilizations of our Earth; however, my curiosity was centered upon the Americas.

"There were many ancient cities of the people of Central and South America that were governed through the Circle of Law. The government of every city of the Zero Chiefs was dedicated to Self Freedom and Democracy.

"Yet, there were other ancient Central and South American cities that were built upon the foundation of human slavery. These cities had feudalistic governments ruled by religious leaders and kings and queens.

"Some of these slave cities also practiced human sacrifice. These sacrificers and slavers were the sworn enemies of every Zero Chief—the Flower Soldiers. As a result countless wars were fought between the cities of the Zero Chiefs and the cities of the slave lords.

"Since history has had the most to say about the cities of the slave lords, what needs to be told and known is that there were many cities that were built upon the principle of human Freedom. These cities enjoyed a full democracy and had no discrimination of people or class.

"After I had learned of the Circle of Law and the great cities of the Zero Chiefs, I had a deep desire to go and visit the lands of Middle America. Our ancient ruined cities of the Americas had always troubled me and held my curiosity. I had the hope that at least a vestige of what once existed might still be present. I decided to go and see what I could discover.

"When I made my first journey south to the land of the Maya I expected to find great poverty because we Indians of North America were a trou-

bled and dying people. But I did not find the people as bad off as we, as far as food was concerned. What I mean by that is that they were not starving. But in truth, in every other way their poverty was so severe no words can describe it.

"Disease was their constant foe. No people on Earth could have lived in a more filthy way, and still somehow survive, as did the people I first met. They ate and slept with their dogs, chickens, and pigs, and they never washed.

"I was also amazed to discover that no one in the village could remember their Medicine Ways. The people I met knew nothing of the proud history of their great ancient cities. In fact, they believed that 'devils' lived in them. I was dumbfounded by what they told me because I had expected to find the exact opposite.

"It was impossible for me to live with them, of course, so I slept alone and ate alone. It was not long, only five days, before I met an old man who invited me to journey away from the village to the home of his people.

"This was a completely different world. I learned that the village people had no freedom and were constantly watched and monitored by the Church. Those people who lived on the ranches were little more than slaves. No one who was not Christian was allowed to live.

"I learned that the original people called themselves the Emerald Mountain People. My new hosts were a clean and orderly people. They made their living by trading. The elder of this family was known as Old Man.

"I asked him about the name and he smiled, telling me that he had been born with the name. He said that being called Old Man when he was a teenager was quite an adventure. Beyond these few simple words, he would not tell me more.

"The women were cordial and friendly—but never really friendly. They were afraid of me, first because they thought I was a 'Gringo American,'

and second because they thought I was carrying lightning, which meant I had great powers.

"I told Old Man that I wanted to visit one of the old ruined cities and he became my guide.

"While I walked through the city called Uxmal, I could not help but marvel at what our cities of the North might look like if they were abandoned and looted. It must be remembered that the Americas had been systematically looted and wantonly destroyed from 1500 on.

"The authorities, who should have been responsible people, continued to pretend that the destruction was not organized rapine. But it was. There was no place or city that was not looted by organized gangs long before 1800. Nearly five hundred years is a long time for a land and Her people to suffer the pains of gold seekers and religious zealots.

"I poked around in the ruins and fought mosquitoes until I could no longer stand it. I was feeling that I had made a fool's journey when I was introduced to a middle-aged man named Famous Hat; his Spanish name was Rodriguez.

"I have met very few people who possessed such wit and humor as Famous Hat. With a flourish of his sombrero, he told me that he thought it very funny that I was a tourist but had the sense to carry a pistol. And he added, with a wink, that he would help me because either I was a 'weech' or was extremely rich. Either possibility was all right with him. If I was a witch he could get money from me, and if I was rich he could get money from me.

"I promised him riches, and we were off to see the wonders of the Maya. Because he was also a trader, our journey would be the one he normally made. 'Why go out of your way if you don't have to?' he told me with a smile. 'What is there that cannot be found on the way to market?'

"We rode by mule to a place he called White Zero; it was an eleven days' journey away from Uxmal.

"I told him how funny it would be if the cities of the North were to be explained away as the cities of the Maya are presently being explained away.

" 'The white people do not like their history,' he told me. 'What their history has to say to them is so foul, they do not want anything to do with it! But the whites are like these donkeys. See . . . these donkeys, they want to return to where we once were. That is nowhere. But they want to return there anyway! The donkeys hated it where we came from, but they want to return. Donkeys are strange, and so are the whites!'

"We talked about what New York and Chicago might look like if they were abandoned. The more I talked about America's cities, the more interested he became in them.

" '*Heessssh!*' he said at long last. 'Those cities are bigger than all of Mexico! I thought they were little stringy things that clung onto the edge of Canada!'

"I told him that most of the structures of the North—even the warehouses—would be called churches if they were to be found by the white men of the future.

" 'They say that about our cities, too,' he assured me. 'But forget what they tell you. What do they know about us Indians? They think that we always go into our visions when we do our Medicine Work. Just goes to show you! We talk about our visions, but who ever goes into one? That would kill you!'

"I explained to him about how the whites saw the ancients. I said that every Neanderthal I had ever seen rendered in a book was always clean-shaven and had a haircut.

" 'I'm not surprised,' he said with a shake of his head. 'They always show their God with a great big beard and a very long mustachio, but they cut their own hair short! They are afraid of getting their Neanderthals mixed up with their gods, maybe. If everybody had long hair, who could pick out God?' "

"We laughed our way through one ruin after the other and finally wound up in a place of immense beauty. We were now on high ground and in a thick grove of sweet-smelling trees. And, miraculously, there were no mosquitoes! We made camp, and at this point we met our first bandits.

"The bandits were very disappointed that we were both extremely poor and they went on their way. This all came about because Famous Hat knew that the bandits were nearby, and we had hidden all of our camping equipment and the donkeys at a safe distance from our camp.

" 'I always know when they're nearby,' Rodriguez explained to me while we enjoyed our coffee. 'They smell like banks. And besides that, I was robbed here last year, and my uncle the year before that. That's how I knew they were around. A few years ago, more years than I want to tell you, I wanted to know all about these ancient cities, too. I went there, but I met only lizards and frogs. I wanted to believe that all my ancestors had become lizards and frogs, but I didn't.'

" 'Why?' I asked, wanting him to continue his story.

" 'Why?' he said, looking up in surprise. 'I figured I was one of them and how could that be? I wasn't a frog.

" 'A Medicine Woman told me once that it gets more complicated each time we get born. I'm going to show you a Medicine Thing,' he said, getting up. 'Follow me.'

"While we walked, he pointed out different landmarks to me and explained that he was one of the head men from his village, and that he'd run across me only by chance. He'd taken a shortcut to visit his relatives and saw me roaming around and looking lost.

" 'The family that took you to the city is an excellent family,' he said while we climbed up a sharp rise in the ground. 'Pep is my brother. He said that you were a crazy Indian from the North and that you were stumbling around and looking for real things. He also said that you carry a gun and that you can command lightning. Both of those things made me think!'

"We made an abrupt turn around a very large

stone and there in front of us was a massive stone carving of a woman sitting before a bowl.

" 'This will be stolen before long,' he said, sitting down and catching his breath. 'But before it is, here you are. You can have a real good look!'

"I studied the statue of a powerful woman. She was holding an ornate bowl lovingly in her hands. In the bowl there was an entire city. The city was completely intact and very beautiful.

" 'Makes you wonder, huh?' he asked with immense pride shining in his eyes.

" 'What city do you think it is?' I asked, brushing away my tears. I had never seen anything so beautiful.

" 'Oh! . . . who knows?' he said, shrugging his shoulders. 'You can see that the city was everybody's hope. I call this Goddess our Goddess of Hope.' "

More years were to pass while Lightningbolt continued to work at one trade or another, along with his new pursuit—attending college. Grades were not his goal. Educating himself was. So he attended classes whenever it was convenient for him.

He continued to work with Estcheemah and allowed himself time to see and experience his world in new ways. His teacher knew that Lightningbolt needed time to mature, and time to get to know Thunderchild.

The name Thunderchild was given to Lightningbolt when he was ten years old and visiting one of his great-aunts. She could not remember his first name and so she referred to him as Stormchild and Thunderchild. A few of the older men and women remembered that name.

Thunderchild, Estcheemah told Lightningbolt, was the poet and the "presence of power" in his world. She gave the name of Thunderchild to his Self commander. His challenge, over the next twenty years of his life, would be to bring forward the Knowing and Command of Thunderchild.

The weather was sunny bright and the morning was warm as Lightningbolt's pickup rolled to a stop in Estcheemah's yard. When he got out he saw a red Volkswagen parked by the gate. Whose was it?

Then, approaching the house, he saw a beautiful, dark-haired young woman standing on the porch watching him.

"Hello, I'm Liberty." She smiled. "Are you Lightningbolt?"

So this was the young woman that Estcheemah had mentioned she'd been working with. She was incredibly lovely. Why hadn't Estcheemah told him how beautiful Liberty was? He was mystified.

Estcheemah joined Liberty on the porch. She looked very pleased that the two had met and suggested that they all have coffee in the Grotto of the Bowls.

The arroyo was very unusual. Wind and water, two Earth upheavals, and a volcano had carved and sculpted hundreds of stone bowls in the wide ravine. The floor of the arroyo was covered with sand. And up out of the sand rose bowls of every shape and size. Some of the bowls stood waist-high and measured four feet across, while other bowls were as small as a pocketwatch. A few flat ones held a thimble of water, while others could hold ten gallons. Because it had rained the night before, a thousand mirrors of water sparkled and reflected the blue sky from every bowl.

"This is my place of sand and change," Estcheemah said as she took a seat in the lawn chair she had carried to her stone garden. "I wanted to build our home here when Moheegun and I moved from Canada, but he did not want that."

She sighed. "Isn't it lovely?"

Gracefully, Liberty sat down on the warm sand, not bothering to open her chair. Lightningbolt's attention was completely riveted on Liberty. He sat down as near as he could to the beautiful young woman and leaned his back against one of the bowls.

Everything was proceeding coolly and calmly except for Lightningbolt's nervousness. Lighting up a simple smoke became an ordeal. First, he had to fight to keep his hands from shaking.

Then, when he lit a cigarette, he shook his lighter like a match and threw it away. When he realized what he had done, a sudden flush burned his cheeks and he quickly looked down.

You threw your stupid lighter away! he fumed in his mind. Liberty turned and looked at him. His pulse quickened and he began to redden again. How could any woman be that beautiful? Did she see that he had thrown away his lighter? How could a man explain that?

Liberty smiled and pulled her legs up under her chin. Lightningbolt shifted his weight and quickly lit another cigarette. Now he had two of them burning. He was concentrating hard now. He was determined to not throw away the second lighter.

"Do you like it here?" Liberty asked him.

Lightningbolt's mouth went dry and his legs began to cramp.

"Yeah, sure," he answered, setting one of the burning cigarettes at his feet. He quickly pulled another from his pack and lit it from the cigarette he had in his mouth. He blew on the cigarette and threw it after the lighter.

Oh no! he shouted in his mind. You threw away your damned cigarette! Get a hold of yourself, man!

Estcheemah had not missed what was happening. She stood up when Lightningbolt threw the cigarette after the lighter, and asked Liberty if she would go to her house and bring back her Medi-

cine Pipe. Liberty rose and immediately started for the house.

"Your cigarette." Estcheemah smiled, pointing to where the cigarette lay smoking. "And look, you've thrown away your lighter, too."

Lightningbolt leaped for the cigarette and lighter.

"She is very lovely," Estcheemah said, sitting back down. "But I think you can handle it."

Lightningbolt nodded and scrambled back to where he had been sitting.

"Wash your face in one of the bowls," Estcheemah instructed him. "And do not smoke. You will burn down the countryside."

Lightningbolt did as she asked resolutely.

"Don't worry. She didn't see you falling to pieces." Estcheemah laughed gently. "She has been preoccupied, too. So just be quiet and sit there, and by the way, why don't you crush out that cigarette by your boot?"

"Sure," he mumbled. "Damn!"

Estcheemah reached over and patted him affectionately on his shoulder. "She likes you. She's a bit nervous, too. Just remain cool, all right?"

"Cool, right," he answered, biting his lip.

Liberty returned and handed Estcheemah her Pipe, then smoothly sat down beside Lightningbolt. Their knees were almost touching.

Estcheemah looked up into the sky, then spoke. "You are my Medicine Twins," she explained to them. "You have met and will, in the future, enter into learning together. Both of you have made the decision to learn from me, and both of you desire to be Flower Soldiers. Because you are female and male I will call you 'my twins.' You will learn to report everything to each other."

This was the turning point in the lives of Estcheemah's apprentices. Their decisions, over the next year, would show if they were truly Flower Soldiers.

Estcheemah met with Lightningbolt alone the following day, and spoke to him about his Life. "I have tried hard to not interfere with your Life decisions, Lightningbolt," she began. "And I do not intend to change that now. However, there are a few things you need to clarify for your Self.

"You need to go from here and find a place to think. You need to be alone for a while to understand what it is you have done and will continue to do with your Life.

"You are a paradox of different minds, Lightningbolt. Your needs as a human and experiences as a seeker have changed you and made you stronger. However, now things will be considerably different in your training. You have the wondrous opportunity to see and participate in how it is possible for a woman to become a Flower Soldier.

"Much of what you have done, until recently, was not because you made any real Self decisions. Most of your Life, ignorance and stark terror have been your constant companions, instead of Self confidence or Self direction. Indulgence and terror prodded you to make most of your decisions—not your Self thinking.

"While we live we search for understanding and love. You must care for and love your Self, and focus upon your destiny, before you will find healing.

"Your pains and joys have made you stronger and much more alert to other people's suffering. However, there comes a time when the coward gives way to the courageous.

"Every cultural attitude you have held fast to will be challenged when you begin your new Circle of Learning with Liberty. Most of your Life you have been trained by the world beyond the Reservation to believe that you are superior to a woman just because you were born a male. You are supposed to be more the thinker, more responsible, more emotionally balanced, and more spiritual.

"This kind of pretense is very destructive to you, as a man, and to your Earthly learning. Women have also been trained. They have been forced to believe in this sorrowful travesty of social and religious beliefs. You now have the grand chance to see how the battle to have Self Command and Self Power is different for a woman born into this unbalanced culture than it is for a young man such as you.

"Yet, the question remains, do you have the courage to really be present with Life? Are you aware of how quick you can be to judge when you are faced with information that you have not known before? Will you be kind, honest, and not arrogant when you experience new learning? Is it possible for you to not be the know-it-all? Instead, can you experience the joy of supporting another human being in her training to become a powerful Flower Soldier—and possibly one day a Zero Chief?

"You possess a memory for the Medicines and our history that is wondrous and borders upon the profound, but when it comes to remembering people, many times you falter. People have not meant much to you. You stand all knowledge above humans—and even above your Self. You respect what I have taught you, but you have been a man torn between knowledge and the realities of your physical world.

"You are constantly two people. Thunderchild the seeker, and Lightningbolt the undiscerning and impetuous. Often, you have believed that pain is a greater teacher than your Self. Pain and feeling have been your constant companions.

"Are you afraid of joy? You only allow joy into your life while you are thinking and learning. You forbid joy to be present in your physical life while you work because you think that being joyful means being weak. How very strange. Don't you agree?

"It is time that you become even more determined to change. Your desire to be a powerful Flower Soldier, a High Warrior in the army of your Self, must become a full-time focus if you are going to progress beyond where you are now. To become a Self Teacher and Leader, a true carrier of the Medicine Wheels, you must fight to change these attitudes within you, while at the same time you nurture the Powers within your Self. For this to happen you must become Self directed in all that you do.

"I know a few years ago, in your Self Ceremony, you decided to become a Flower Soldier. But now, your decision will face the ultimate test.

"I wish you to go to Manitoba to do your thinking. Go to the Dreamers, Tree and Horse, and tell them that you want to be with them and need time to think. Then come back at the Gold Lodge of Summer and tell me what you have decided."

Estcheemah had also given Liberty a challenge that she would have to survive. She too had been asked to return at the beginning of the Gold Lodge.

Liberty's challenge was simple but had its ramifications for her. She had to meet and defeat Miss Perfect. This was the part of Liberty she had not wanted to confront.

It was also her test to observe the behavior of each person she met and to gather as much information as she could.

Liberty was always eager to be perfectly right with each of her actions. The "perfectly right syndrome," as Estcheemah called it, had been born into Liberty the day she passed her first fifth grade test. She had received so much attention for this act of mediocrity that she never forgot it. It had be-

come the basis of her philosophy.

Estcheemah sent Liberty to visit two places. The first place was her home. Liberty visited her relatives in California. Bored, yawning, and feeling as though she were smothering in a cultural pudding, Liberty left Los Angeles and drove to Denver, on her way to her second destination.

Liberty enjoyed being beautiful because it allowed her to have her own way. Because Liberty was lovely, she was never called cute. People are always overeager to take care of cute girls and women. But only the very courageous or foolish will attempt to take care of the beautiful. While she was in Denver, forty-seven men wanted to take care of her; however, only two of these hopefuls had the chance to even talk to her.

The first man was the service station attendant she briefly spoke to while he filled her gas tank, and the second was the mayor of the city, who stopped to have his windshield cleaned. The mayor said hello and gave her his card.

All women in Los Angeles are told that they are the most beautiful women on Earth. Because L.A. is a glamour spot and the prime place for making it in the movies, tens of thousands of beautiful women go there. They are quickly taught that men, for the most part, will use them as though they were throw-away articles. They learn to compete with their bodies for every kind of work and for any kind of man because the film industry grades women according to what they're willing to sell.

Liberty was Los Angeles–wise because her father was a film director. All her growing life, she had seen what would become of a woman if she believed the Hollywood lie.

Liberty also had something else that made her wary—her college degree. In college, she had been bitterly disappointed to discover that many of her professors were teaching her, in the very best way they could, to be mediocre and a conformist.

She learned that Americans are the most educated people in the world and that many of our newspapers and magazines are written at a seventh grade level.

Liberty possessed a powerful mind. If fortune had not made her beautiful she would have been despised. As it was, she was only feared for her brains.

People fear all kinds of true power, Estcheemah had explained to Liberty. Women are feared and hated most if they can think. So many women have been frustrated by chauvinistic attitudes and religious bigotry that they try to act like men when they argue. But the old teacher assured Liberty that this was the wrong move for any woman to make—it would not achieve what she wanted.

"Why try to act like a man?" Estcheemah asked. "Men aren't always that bright. Take a look at our cities and how men design and govern them. Our cities are dangerous, polluted jumbles of haphazard incompetence and corruption. Look at the exclusive clubs men call their religions. Aren't these institutions the perfect examples of men's philosophy and stupidity?

"No, Liberty, never argue as a man.

"Argue as a woman. Battle as a woman. Insist upon adding the woman's design to our world."

Liberty was delighted to leave Denver because, finally, she was on her way to meet her true challenge.

A strange twist of contrails called the jet set that crisscrosses the skies of America had spelled out a weave of circumstances that had snared Liberty's fancy. She had heard from friends about a popular celebrity known as Abundant Star. Now she was driving with eager anticipation to the Powder River country of Wyoming to meet this keeper of the incredible, mysterious Staff of Magic and Transformation. Liberty's girl friends had told her that Abundant Star had special powers, and that these were "woman's powers."

Liberty loved to dabble; this was how she learned about everything from electricity to ingrown toenails. Dabbling up close was not the same as dabbling at a distance. Close dabblers might learn things, while faraway dabblers only read about dabbling. Liberty had been taught near and far dabbling by her university professors—America's plenary dabblers.

Estcheemah knew that the only way for Liberty to get real about Abundant Star was for them to meet.

The day Liberty met Abundant Star she was overjoyed. However, when she learned that Abundant Star's real name was Henrietta Bunch, she began to be concerned.

Henrietta had taken the name Abundant Star just before her husband, Fred Mountain Top, had decided to become a full-fledged Medicine Man. Becoming a Medicine Man was big business for Indians at the time.

Abundant Star very much looked the part of a true keeper of the Staff of Life. She wore an authentic Sioux silk dress with no less than two wide beaded belts. Her high-top beaded Crow moccasins were also in fashion at the time. She walked with a studied gait and swished her shawl at important moments.

Liberty soon learned that the Staff of Life had been built by a university student who had studied what one should look like, and who had made a present of it to Fred, "an authentic Medicine Man."

She was told all this by Henrietta's lone apprentice, a twenty-year-old white male student from Missoula, Montana, who called himself Black Snake and refused to give his white name. He explained to Liberty that the Staff of Life had cost a hundred and ninety dollars to build.

Abundant Star would shake the Staff of Life vigorously each time her husband made a "Remarkable Remark."

Tied to the Staff of Life were five sheep bells.

These very much impressed people with how sacred the Staff of Life was.

Estcheemah had been far too "real" for Liberty. The old Flower Soldier never seemed to mention mystery or magic; this disappointed her. Abundant Star mentioned magic within the first ten seconds of their talk, and this made Liberty very happy.

Abundant Star radiated a certain tribal mystery while she held the Staff of Life. Such incredible reverence! That the home of the two Medicine people was a mess was quickly dismissed by Liberty and the other white women with Liberty. They learned that Abundant Star was too busy to be cleaning a house, and needed someone to help. Who that would be was not discussed.

Fred Mountain Top was also very mysterious. However, he was severely overweight and constantly wore soiled clothes, and this tended to put off the ladies. Liberty was told that Mr. Mountain Top's clothes were dirty because he was forced to live out of doors.

Oh, how very poor the Mountain Tops were! Why didn't America seem to give a damn about its important people? The plight of the American Indian never had been made so clear as with the Mountain Tops. All donations were humbly accepted and would go to the needy. There were two humble boxes made of rawhide that a person could drop money into.

If Liberty had investigated further, she would have seen the color television set that both "Medicine people" were addicted to.

And she would also have seen the neglect and misuse that lay everywhere or stood propped up in the yard. She would have discovered the filthy Sweat Lodge, the beer in the refrigerator, and the large pile of wine bottles in their garbage heap. But Liberty was dabbling up close and could not make discoveries like that.

Exactly one hour before the "Mystery of the Singing Gourds Ceremony" was to begin, Liberty received her first surprise. When she questioned Abundant Star about the Staff of Life, she was told that "women were never expected to have the power to personally own one."

This bit of news raised both of Liberty's eyebrows and all the hairs on the back of her neck. SOMETHING WAS WRONG!

Next, Fred gave his talk, telling Liberty and the other white guests—including the two ladies from Denmark—that "Indians are the only people who speak the mystery language, and all other languages on Earth are simply gibberish.

"The Indian language is the only true source and root of all ancient teachings. Since white people are incapable of learning the Indian language they are doomed as a race."

The crowd was also told that "women having their period each month are extremely dangerous to God. The evil contamination ruined everything—including men, animals, places, plants, medicine objects, and all holy books."

Mountain Top began to wave his arms and preach to his "flock," telling them that "women's periods should never be taken lightly," and that "all religious men are deeply troubled by the existence of women's periods."

He carefully pointed out to his congregation that the "Indian tradition strictly forbids women to be present at any Sacred Ceremony when they are having their periods."

He also told them that apprentices "have to have their souls blown into a special gourd before authority can be passed down to them."

He railed on, telling his audience that whites would never understand true Indian ways. Whites were the cause of all injustice. Whites were doomed. He also told them that only men were allowed to sing in the presence of God in sweat lodges.

What Fred was saying was not news to most of the people present; they'd heard it all before from other Medicine Men. In fact, most of the visitors nodded their agreement.

Three minutes and twenty-eight seconds after Fred had talked, and the Staff of Life had disappeared into the house, he tried to seduce Liberty.

Liberty responded by immediately jumping into her car and driving toward Ten Sleep. By the time she reached Estcheemah's door she was mad enough to bite the barrel of a gun in half.

Estcheemah looked out her window when Liberty drove into her yard, then went back to her patient work of making pies.

Liberty started for the house, then spun on her heel and headed to the creek for a walk. She needed time to cool off and to do some thinking before she saw her mentor.

Estcheemah had the feeling that Liberty had met Abundant Star.

Two days later, Lightningbolt took his time coming out from behind the wheel once he was parked in Estcheemah's yard. He looked around and enjoyed that he was back. There was much to tell his teacher. How to say it all was his challenge.

It was late in the afternoon before the twins sat together at the kitchen table. Estcheemah was happy to see her twins. Now she could get down to some good hard work with both of them.

"I want you to report your journey, Liberty," Estcheemah said as she poured them both a cup of tea. "And your report will follow, Lightningbolt."

Liberty didn't want to reveal her disappointments. She sprang like a deer into a thicket of family gossip, Los Angeles ploys, and defenses. It didn't work because Estcheemah soon flushed her out of hiding. Liberty tried tears. She tried a pout and a frown. Then she tried to entangle. But everything failed. Her final ploy was cast like a net. This was the quaking Liberty thrown at the feet of Estcheemah, ready to be taught or molded.

Estcheemah just laughed with good humor. "If Life wasn't so very serious," she said, "we would all be laughing ourselves to death. Liberty, Lightningbolt, it does not matter what other people think.

"Stop. Give yourselves a moment. Realize, once and for all time, that what other people think of you does not matter. Only what you think of yourselves matters. All these other concerns about how you might appear to other people are of no consequence. Remember that most humans can be easily impressed and easily flattered into believing anything.

"Don't flatter yourselves. Don't be so crude and mundane as to believe that you matter to the world. Until the second you become valuable to your Self, you are meaningless, and your Life is meaningless. You must work hard to understand and care for your Self. When you do this, then you will be able to have meaning in your Life."

"What about my report?" Lightningbolt asked. "Don't you want to hear it, too?"

"Yes, but not yet," Estcheemah answered. "It would be much better if you gave your report to Liberty first. This is something I want you to make a habit. There are also a few other things that need to be finished first. For example, you two have not properly met one another. Take some time to do this. Then we will continue working together. Until then, come when you wish to talk with me.

"And Liberty, you can stay in the room over the tack room again, if you like. I cleaned it up, and it is all ready for you."

"Great." Liberty smiled. "I love it up there. I can see all the way down the valley from my window. Hey, thanks."

The following day Estcheemah sent her twins in opposite directions.

Liberty went to Sheridan to shop and get parts for an electric pump, and Lightningbolt went to his home to work in his garden.

When they next met at Estcheemah's, they sat beside a young woman who was in severe pain. She had naively been part of a group of young people who had been in a sweat lodge ceremony. Cynthia told her story with tears in her lovely eyes. She and four other young women had been humiliated in the lodge. They had been told, and had believed, that the only way to properly experience a sweat lodge was to be naked; so this is how they had entered the lodge.

Two of the young women had been felt up in the lodge. Afterward the women were treated as though they were at the ceremony only for sexual reasons. Cynthia and her girl friends left the ceremony very disappointed. They had wanted to find magic. Instead, they had only experienced more of the old fears that so many women meet while searching for something new. They felt used and degraded. That experience had been bad enough, but later Cynthia had begun to itch. The itch became a rash, and soon she was covered with sores. The hot steam inside the sweat lodge had opened all of Cynthia's pores, making her vulnerable to the filth in the lodge.

The blanket on the floor and the canvas around the lodge were old, rotten, and dirty. The lodge dripped filth. One of the other women had contracted a vaginal infection from sitting on the filthy blanket.

Cynthia's entire body shook with sobs as she related her sad story. That evening Estcheemah applied a healing salve. Two days later the sores had ceased to weep and she began to heal.

Within five days, Cynthia was looking very good and had begun to smile.

"I guess that will teach you not to bare your ass again in a lodge," Lightningbolt teased Cynthia, trying to have fun with her.

Cynthia stiffened and tears filled her eyes.

Liberty blew up. "You bastard!" she yelled at him.

Lightningbolt rose to leave. He felt terrible.

"Sit down," Estcheemah commanded, pulling him down by his shirttail. "We will talk this out."

"Those damned spooks!" Lightningbolt cursed. He turned to Liberty. "And I'll tease if I want to." He touched Cynthia's arm. "Hey, listen . . . I was teasing. I wanted it to stick, so you wouldn't play with the spooks anymore."

Cynthia nodded, but she was still upset by what he had said.

Liberty folded her arms and scowled.

"See how sadness can set things in motion?" Estcheemah did not look up from her sewing. "Because of the way those fools used Cynthia, you all want to get revenge. But there's no way for you to exact your hate, so you take it out on one another.

"It is so typical. No, Lightningbolt, telling her not to bare her ass is not the way to end your frustration. Unless, of course, you have not bared your ass also?" She looked up from her sewing into his eyes.

"I won't bare my ass anymore either," he admitted.

The following day, after Cynthia had left, Estcheemah asked her twins to work quietly with her in the garden.

"I think we should meet and talk tomorrow," Liberty suggested to Lightningbolt that night after dinner. "You ready for that?"

"Sure." He smiled. "Where?"

"At the old house," she answered. "You know

. . . the one by Calf Creek, near the bridge. You know the place?"

"Sure," he answered. "What time?"

"At noon." She smiled.

The following day, Lightningbolt was happy and excited. Despite their differences and arguments, he wanted to be close to Liberty.

Because Liberty was so beautiful, she was very accustomed to men falling in love with her. Although this had not hardened her, she'd become a bit overconfident and she tended to forget appointments.

Lightningbolt was just the opposite. All appointments were important; people did not miss appointments. His confidence was so low with women that he believed he was the last man to be considered and the first one to be forgotten.

This first meeting with Liberty was very important to him, and he became more and more nervous as the time approached.

He arrived at the rendezvous point early, parked his pickup in the yard of the old house, then walked around it. Where had she parked?

The building had no windows left; someone had destroyed them all. The interior of the old house was decayed and filthy. As he strolled around, he saw where flowers had once been planted; now only the outline of the garden remained.

Suddenly, he saw an old well. It looked as though someone had copied the design of the well from a picture in a book of fairy tales; it was exquisite. He slowly walked around it, examining the remarkable work that had gone into building it.

Lightningbolt squatted to look closer at the stonework and noticed something that appeared to be a small brass door. He brushed the weeds aside and read the words on the plate.

"Elizabeth O'Neill. Born April eighth, nineteen hundred and twenty one, perished in a terrible fire, January sixth, nineteen hundred and thirty one. All of you who wander here may be granted one wish."

He stood and looked around. The house, chicken coop, garage, and corrals were all in complete ruin. Gaping holes and tattered walls were all that was left of the barn. But the well had been kept up. He studied it and saw that carpentry work had been done within the last few weeks. The inside of the wooden roof had been painted recently. A perfect replica of an old oaken bucket from one of Grimm's fairy tales sat on the wall. It even had brass bands.

Lightningbolt picked up the rope; it was rotten and frayed. Why hadn't the rope been replaced? He went to his pickup and dug out his lariat, then cut enough length from it to reach the bottom of the well. It took him the better part of a half hour to replace the rope and to weed around the well; then he felt satisfied.

He threw a silver dollar into the well. "You're not a child anymore, Elizabeth." He smiled. "And neither am I. My wish is that I can become a great writer and Flower Soldier."

Lightningbolt had made a decision while he was with the old Cree Dreamers. He wanted to be a writer. But when is a wish real? He was waiting for the perfect moment to talk to Estcheemah about his Dream.

He turned and walked away from the well. When he was a few feet away, he turned and looked back. Was this well the girl's tombstone? Did it matter if it was?

He waited another hour, then walked to his pickup and got in. Disappointed that Liberty had not shown up, he angrily backed out of the yard.

Maybe she was at the other old house down the road. No, she would not be there. He felt it.

It didn't take him long to drive to the next old farm. This time he parked on the road so that she could see his pickup. Expectant and still hopeful, he jumped out and walked to the house. He looked at his watch; she was very late. He walked and waited, constantly checking the time. After another hour, he went down to the stream and sat there trying not to be too badly shaken. Another half hour later he was mad enough to blow out her tires if she did show up.

A terrible pall of fear and sadness weighed him down as he drove to Estcheemah's. Lightningbolt felt that he was not important enough to Liberty for her to remember him. The few daydreams that he had allowed himself about Liberty were now an embarrassment. He had been rejected before. Shielding himself from the heartbreak was all he could do now.

Estcheemah was outside feeding her chickens when he parked. He got out and slowly walked to her, then sat down on an old wagon box.

"Incredible day." He smiled. "Fixed the rope at an old wishing well I found."

"Lightningbolt!" Liberty shouted from the porch. "Hey, I forgot, all right?" She jumped over the railing of the porch and strolled toward him.

"Will you fix the door on the henhouse, Lightningbolt?" Estcheemah asked. "The hinge fell off this morning."

"Sure," he said. He turned and strode off toward the chicken house. He stopped at the barn and found a hammer and nails. When he came out of the barn, Liberty stood outside and was smiling.

"Really, I'm sorry," she said. "I was poking around down at the creek and I simply forgot, all right?"

He moved by her. "Never happened," he answered.

"I'll get my jacket," she offered. "We can talk down by the creek. There is a beautiful spot there."

"You can talk to yourself." He smiled. "Me, I'm gone. After I fix the hinge on the henhouse, I'm going home." He walked away.

The following morning Liberty rose early, but not before Estcheemah. She shuffled out to the kitchen and sat down at the table and immediately explained to Estcheemah what had happened the day before.

"Damn," said Liberty. "I really like that guy. But he's so hard to get near. I blew it yesterday. I stood him up at the old farm down the road."

"For the first time in your life, things can be different," said Estcheemah sympathetically. "What have you ever won by pretending? Don't pretend. I don't mean winning a man either. I mean winning at what you want to accomplish, winning by thinking.

"You're making this far too complicated. I would simply drive over to Lightningbolt's place and sit in his flower garden and wait for him. When he shows up, be honest. Talk to him."

"I'll try it!" Liberty smiled. "Great."

Liberty drove to Lightningbolt's, wanting to test out her new approach. She parked her car behind a stand of cottonwood trees so it would be out of sight when he returned. She wanted her presence to be a surprise.

While she sat waiting for him, she began to imagine what it would look like to see color energy around people instead of what is normally seen.

Suddenly she began feeling a little melancholy. She was worried that possibly he might not understand her straight-ahead honesty. What was her color now? Was she blue? She wrinkled her nose; certainly she would not be pink!

She stood and threw a stone toward the creek, then cursed because she missed. Wow! Was she sparkling?

She tried a smile when Lightningbolt's pickup pulled into his yard and stopped. She tested a frown when she heard him whistling a tune, but the frown didn't last either.

"Hi," she said, trying to sound a little happier than she felt. "What are you up to?" A purple glow mixed with thunder flared around Liberty, but Lightningbolt could not see it.

"Pretty flowers, huh?" he said, sitting down beside her.

"Why are you so complicated?" she asked, narrowing her eyes.

"Well," he said, looking down, feeling a smile come to his face, "I would sure like to be your friend."

Liberty blinked as a chartreuse "friendly" swirled around her, then disappeared.

Sex frustrates the overeager. Sex primes the unsuspecting. Sex woos the curious. And sex terrifies the naive. However, when two people are in love, sex can make them stupid or wise.

It was fortunate that a shaky old man happened along just at the moment when Liberty and Lightningbolt needed to be wise. The old man instantly realized, by some instinct, that he'd blundered into a Circle of Power and that he'd better give these two young people plenty of room. He hobbled first one way, then the other, trying to decide which wrong thing was best to do.

If he turned and left, that would be wrong. And if he stayed, that would be wrong. So he grinned and adjusted his hat. This had worked before; he hoped it would again.

Liberty looked down at the ground. Lightning-bolt frowned.

"Hah!" the old man half shouted. "Sure now," he said, overemphasizing his heavy Irish brogue. "Be gosh and be golly!" He laughed. "Sure now and if it ain't a bright day!" He tipped his hat. "And me bein' out of gas." He chuckled. "An' out in the boonies."

Liberty smiled.

"Johnnie Higgins, that's me." The old man beamed. "A magician of the worst kind." He pulled a yard of silk from his pocket. "Out of work . . . stumblin' about." He looked at them both quizzically. "I'm on my way to the Billings fair." He bowed. "An' would you be havin' some gas?"

"Sure," Liberty answered.

"Oh, now, to be sure." Old Higgins smiled. "Yet, may the leprechauns have mercy. I'm as broke as a new-laid egg."

Higgins, the magician, got his gas, then disappeared as quickly as he had appeared.

Yet, this small interlude brought two people together who desired to be friends and lovers. How this could be accomplished was still to be resolved. Lightningbolt decided he had to do something. What the something was, he didn't exactly know, but he was going to give it a try anyway.

Gripping the inner sole of his boots with his toes, he asked Liberty if she'd like to go for a walk with him.

She readily accepted, and they were soon strolling by a tiny brook called Bright Feather.

"This is an incredibly wonderful Spring," he informed her in a slightly unsteady voice. "And the water tastes good."

Liberty squeezed his shoulder.

Lightningbolt took a deep breath and looked up into the sky. "Estcheemah told me a bit of our history—about the great Zero Chief called Tomah-seeasah. As we walk I'd really like to tell you about her, Liberty."

365

The following morning dawned very differently for Lightningbolt and Liberty.

Two close friends sat together in Estcheemah's kitchen. They seemed very attentive to each other and alert to what the other had to say. Estcheemah instantly knew that a change had occurred with her twins and was curious about it. But she was wise, and did not ask.

"Lightningbolt told me about Tomahseeasah," Liberty informed Estcheemah. "She was amazing! But was everybody dead? I mean, did you find any more teachers? What happened?"

"Yes, all your questions are important and need to be answered," Estcheemah said. "I was determined to find my teachers. Because of this, Moheegun and I moved West the following Spring after we had married.

"Sadly, I had to say good-bye to Nahseeomah. She was pregnant, happy with her new life, and loved her husband very much. This meant that moving West was now out of the question for her.

"Moheegun and I first moved to the people known as the Meadowlark Creek People. They lived northwest of the tiny town of Prince Albert, Saskatchewan. Moheegun went trapping with a distant uncle named Eesopeewohn. But soon after we arrived, Moheegun's uncle died by drowning.

"Our first winter in this new land was painful and dangerous. Only the skill of Moheegun kept us alive, just barely, because the territory was so new for him. It was during this terrible winter that Moheegun brought me the news that a Medicine Person by the name of Thunder Crow knew all about Tomahseeasah.

" 'This teacher is about seventy-six winters old,' Moheegun explained. 'This person teaches about a Medicine that is known as the Sacred Hoop.'

"I wanted to be happy and wished with all my heart that the Medicine Teacher knew more about the Medicine Wheels, but I dared not hope—not now—not after so much disappointment."

"It was June before I met Thunder Crow. I was happy to discover that Thunder Crow was a woman.

" 'The Medicine Wheel is the Circle of Law,' Thunder Crow explained. 'It came to this Sacred Land from the great islands of WahKahn and SsKwan.

366

" 'WahKahn and SsKwan comprised a very large Confederacy of islands that existed in what is now known as the Pacific. These islands were named after the Creatress and Creator.' "

" 'Tomahseeasah taught all about the Circle of Law. The Medicine Wheels were discovered by our ancient Zero Chiefs who lived on the great islands.

" 'This woman known as Tomahseeasah was a Zero Chief and a Holy Woman. Tomahseeasah healed many people—Healed their Emotions, their Bodies, their Minds, and their Spirits. She truly was a Sacred Person. While she lived, only a tiny handful of people knew her intimately— eleven women and six men.

" 'The Medicine of Tomahseeasah was the Rose; yet all flowers loved this Holy Woman, and she loved them. There are many stories about this woman's miracles but the greatest miracle was Tomahseeasah herself. She healed many people and she possessed great knowledge and wisdom.

" 'Girl-Man-Warrior, the Medicine Man of the Deer Lake People, lived with her for fifteen years, learning from her. He spoke of how her mind was like the brightest Star, the Sun.

" 'He explained to all that Tomahseeasah was a truly balanced human. She was balanced South, West, North, and East—these are the Emotions, the Body, the Mind, and the Spirit.

" 'All were in love with the knowledge this woman possessed. She was kind, gentle, thoughtful, and could heal the sick. She was also immensely courageous and was a powerful Warrioress. She told all that her first great teacher had been her own body.

" 'Her vagina was malformed when she was born. She felt the beauty of love that all women possess, but she could not make love to any man, because of the pain.'

"Thunder Crow explained how Tomahseeasah

cried, sobbing alone, how she prayed and how she sought healing. She found no healing for her Woman-Flower, but she did find healing for her Heart and Spirit. All wildflowers, especially the Rose, became her intimate teachers.

"Tomahseeasah was an incredibly beautiful woman. Girl-Man-Warrior explained that even with all that people said about her beauty, it was still not enough. Even as an old woman, she was so lovely that it caused people to weep.

"This Holy Woman, Tomahseeasah, was incredibly lovely—this none would ever deny. But she possessed another kind of Beauty that caused her to be even more wondrous; this was her complete Love and Self Honesty.

"Because of her extreme Beauty, she had been raped twenty-eight times in her life. Each time she screamed and bled for days afterward.

"For ten long years Tomahseeasah desired to die, only the Rose kept her alive. Then she met a Japanese woman who told her that she had been born many times and that in this lifetime she was to learn of compassion. The woman's name was Lotus. She was a prostitute who lived in the small town of Calgary and died at the age of twenty-four.

"Tomahseeasah then met a Medicine Man, a Flower Soldier, whose name was Grass Lightning Fire. This man knew the Medicine Wheels, and Tomahseeasah became his apprentice. He taught her that every human exists within the Circle of Challenge, that our Life is our Sacred Challenge. Humans, he taught, do everything in their power to escape their Life and Circle of Challenge.

"Tomahseeasah taught that she had learned to draw energy from the Medicine Power of her Challenge. She learned to know Beauty, and she learned to bow to the Rose. This Woman-Rose, the Mother Spirit of Life—she said—is our WahKahn, our Creatress Mother."

"I finally met my teachers in Idaho," Estcheemah continued to explain. "Thunder Crow introduced me to them.

"Quetzal-Atl-Mahahn, which means 'Serpent Mother' or 'Dragon Mother,' was a Zero Chief, and she became my most important teacher. I learned from her apprentice also; his name was Blue Hair. I worked with them both for sixteen years.

"Moheegun was content to be a hunter and trapper. He worked alone in Idaho and grew to love the land. He would sit with me listening sometimes, but outside of that he never showed any signs of interest to really learn. This frustrated me, but there was nothing I could do to change it."

"I would like to write about these things one day," Lightningbolt announced. He felt that the moment had arrived to at least hint about his intentions.

"Good! Then you must learn appreciation." Estcheemah smiled. "While each of us lives in our separate worlds, how many of us look into our minds to see our Earth circle the Sun? Does it matter to us that billions of trillions of miles away there are other sunrises within other galaxies?"

"Sure it matters!" Lightningbolt insisted.

"Then appreciate Life," Estcheemah said to him. "Appreciation will teach you how to write. And remember always that a person who lives only in the brain will not know the Self or Life. Discernment and decision shape what you have truly learned, not what you believe you have learned. Do you understand what I mean?"

Lightningbolt wanted to answer, but his tongue seemed glued to the roof of his mouth.

"I understand your silence." She smiled. "So instead of your trying to match wits with me, let's talk about how some people live in their heads instead of the wonderful world that exists around them.

"You and Liberty still live in your heads as much as you do in your physical world. Let's see how well you do sharing your knowledge with one another. Okay?"

The following morning, very early, Estcheemah took Liberty with her to Butterfly Canyon. Estcheemah needed to pray and have a little time alone with her female apprentice.

Five very old trout swam close to Liberty's feet in Butterfly Creek. The day was bright, warm, and gentle. The canyon did not seem to be a canyon at all. It should have been called a meadow valley.

Butterfly Creek meandered through the cool shade of eleven cottonwood trees. All the trees had been planted by Estcheemah thirty years before.

"The occasion was Life," Estcheemah explained while unpacking the fried chicken she had prepared for her Ceremony. "Humans are fortunate to have the experience we call Life. I felt fortunate, and so I planted the trees so others could feel their cooling shade. It had been very hot when I was first here thirty years ago."

Liberty was astounded. Thirty years ago? Planting trees so people could have shade! And Life . . .

She loved it when Estcheemah spoke to her about Mother Life. Somehow it gave her a strength she could not explain.

As they enjoyed their small feast, Estcheemah told Liberty more about the Medicine Woman called Tomahseeasah.

"Tomahseeasah, Wild Roses, taught that Life experience is much like the flow of water. It is the nature of water to create its own path, while at the same moment changing what was built.

"All people should be highly aware of their words and how they command their minds. 'Yet who will study their every word?' Tomahseeasah had asked.

"She said that our every word creates an invisible road of Self Command that people follow their Life long. She taught that no action or moment in time can be re-created or repeated.

"There are many examples of how language can distort a beautiful thought, Liberty. An extreme example of this is how the word *lie* is used.

"It is 'proper' to say that the truth *lies* within. But the real meaning is much clearer if we say the truth *exists* within.

"This is the reason I never use the words *to lie*, if possible, to express my thinking. I do not think that any truth can *lie* within.

"To say that a man *lies* beside his wife in bed is following the rules of speech. But it is far better to say that the man is sleeping with his wife.

"Break the rule if you have to. It is far better to say that a man is *laying* beside his wife than to have him *lie* beside her.

"Be very decisive about what you say to your Self. Do not hurt your Self with words that are sorrowful or demeaning. If you are going to do anything in this Life, allow it to be a grand present of wisdom and kindness.

"Look up into the arms of the cottonwood trees, Liberty," Estcheemah told her. "You perceive your present from what I planted in your past. These trees were planted for your future.

"This is the truth of words. What we say in our past becomes the command of a future time. Humans can alter their destiny in an eye blink of time.

"Our future is our Responsibility. Our past was our Responsibility in that we Commanded events that have become our Present."

"I came here today so I could thank Wyoming and Montana for loving me so much," said Estcheemah, smiling with happiness. "I have lived here for many years, but now I will go and live in Canada."

Liberty watched as the old Flower Soldier spread out one of her Medicine Blankets. Her teacher gently took out a bundle of seeds she had collected over the years and placed it on the blanket in front of her. While she arranged the tiny packages of seeds in a Circle, she continued to pray. "I am going to another part of you, Sacred Land Mother. I offer you my every knowing, every tear, and each joy. I give to you my deepest respect and my most profound moment of Self Honesty.

"I do this, Sweet Land, gentle Mother, because you have breathed your Life into me and under-

375

stood my very being. For this I am thankful as long as Eternity shall exist."

After Estcheemah had finished her prayers, she put everything away, then folded her blanket and placed it beside her.

"Liberty," she said, now facing her. "I would like to suggest that you join me in Canada. Lightningbolt will also be going. However, I think that it will be a more promising and powerful journey if you first decide to become a Flower Soldier. I want you to think about it. If you show up in Canada, I have your answer."

"There is no question, Estcheemah," Liberty answered with deep emotion. "I will be there." Her eyes filled with tears and she bit her lip. "I have already decided."

The following day Liberty and Lightningbolt arrived at Estcheemah's eager to help her pack for her Canadian journey. However, their teacher had other

ideas. She smiled and welcomed them to sit at her table and to have a bit of coffee.

"What's up?" Liberty asked.

"I don't need any help," Estcheemah answered. "I've waited for this trip for many years, and I'm going first-class. For years I have done my moving the hard way. This time I have movers—packers and all. I will be leaving in ten days. My Circle is complete here. When we next meet, it will be in Canada."

Lightningbolt helped Liberty pack her things.

Humans never do anything simple—except for the way they think. When two humans sit and look at one another, trying to figure out a terribly complicated method for getting together, nothing will happen that is simple.

It would have been quite simple if Lightningbolt could have explained to Liberty that he loved her. But because he was human, he didn't.

Liberty's nature was gentle, open, and understanding, but she also was a human, so she never

377

thought about the simple solution that now faced her.

It was a Breed standoff. Neither Breed was going to give an inch.

"Well, here you are," Lightningbolt said, inviting her into his trailer. He was going to try to sound wise. "And I hope you are comfortable." He felt a bit nervous about his wise approach, so he grinned. "And here I am." He looked down at his hands, the way he had seen Estcheemah do a hundred times. "The Goddess within." He suddenly felt as though he was going to panic. "And the Goddess without . . . er . . ." He frowned. Without? Had he said "without"? He couldn't have said "without"!

"Are you trying to say that what is inside is also outside?" Liberty asked, confused. She knew better than to ask a question at the moment, but she, too, was trying to be wise.

"The wise approach," Lightningbolt blurted out, certain that she'd discovered he was an idiot. He flushed, trying to find more right words. "Snows in Canada." He clicked his heels together. Suddenly his mind went blank. He blinked, trying to understand what had happened.

Liberty was looking even more puzzled.

He had to say something quick! "Reminds me of a clown." He smiled. He pinched his leg. "And how he made me laugh." He giggled. "You ever meet a clown besides old Higgins?"

"No," she answered. She, too, was fighting for ground, trying to discover what to say.

"No," he said, then let out his breath. "Well, it will do you good. Want some coffee?" He was thankful that he could now put one word after the other.

Liberty had successfully tied her knit cap into a solid knot under the table. "There must be schools," she offered.

His mind went blank again. Were they talking about schools? "Sure," he answered a little too quickly.

"Barber schools, clown schools." She smiled. She was trying to untie the hat.

"Oh, sure!" He brightened.

"Estcheemah said I could use the old bunkhouse," Liberty explained as she began to retie the hat. "It's nice, small."

"What bunkhouse?" he asked, his voice unsteady. "There are a hundred around here." Where? Whose? Why? The questions poured through his mind. "Stove?" he asked. "Chairs, tables?"

"I don't know," she answered. Her hands were now on the table. The hat lay crumpled on the floor. "She said that it had everything, you know, the one down by the Smith barn . . . twenty a month."

Lightningbolt had to come up with something. "Estcheemah bought fifty-five acres up there," he said, "and it's on an island . . . plenty of room for my trailer." He cleared his throat. Dammit! Why had he brought up the subject of his trailer? Now the cat was out of the bag. He didn't want her to think he was trying to woo her with a house. Oh, no! Was he trying to buy her favors with a trailer house? Damn, what had he done? "Sold the land here for a good price. She closed the deal over a month ago."

"I see," Liberty replied.

Lightningbolt stood and walked to the sink. He turned and faced her, but sort of looked off to one side so he wouldn't have to look at her. Her beauty constantly confused him.

Liberty toyed with her coffee cup. She had a million things in her mind, but not one of them would stand still long enough for her to say something intelligent. The thoughts danced, pranced, stole around corners, leaped, and bounced.

Silence filled the room.

"I got something to say, Liberty," he announced, straightening up. He hooked his thumbs in his pockets. "I hope you understand." Suddenly his mind panicked. Why the hell had he said that?

He wasn't ready for that!

Liberty looked up; her eyes were incredibly beautiful.

"Well ..." he stammered. "Actually, I do have something to say."

"What?" she asked. Her voice sounded like music.

"Well," he answered. "Ah ... well ... who likes bunkhouses? You sure you want that?"

Liberty brightened. Suddenly her feminine mind cleared and she caught nine of the bouncing thoughts.

"I don't like them either." She smiled. "And thanks for your honesty." She stood and walked to his side. She leaned up against the sink. "Think we can manage?" She turned and faced him. "You stay in the bedroom, and I'll bunk here on the couch for a while." She knew definitely that she didn't want to live in a bunkhouse. "What do you think?"

"Fine," he answered, and smiled. "But you take the bedroom. I'm used to boards and crawl spaces. A woman needs comfort."

"I'm just as board-wise as you," she argued, meaning it. Her frown said more than her words. "You be comfortable."

Simple answers sometimes show up in the strangest of guises. It's a lucky thing they do, otherwise humanity would be lost. The simple answer to their simple question arrived in a letter. It was from Dale Tomlin, a steel contractor. Dale believed in hard work and doing everything small enough to make it in a "big-time way"—this was his motto. He always bid on small jobs, always steel projects.

Tomlin wanted a foreman to complete fifteen jobs constructing large steel culverts.

"I like hard hats." Liberty smiled.

"I was just about to ask you that," Lightningbolt said with a grin.

They pulled their trailer to the first job site, and they began to work. A small tractor was on the job to lift the steel plates into place so they could be bolted together. Lightningbolt hired Liberty as a tractor operator. At first she was petrified that she would do something wrong, but soon she became an expert.

Although Liberty couldn't do the grading and leveling with the Caterpillar at first, she was always on hand to learn how. When the site for the last two culverts was prepared, it was Liberty who operated the Cat.

Their evenings became the time for them to share talk. They were excited to be able to compare what they had learned from Estcheemah. The discovery that the Medicine Wheels were easy-to-memorize pictures of Wisdom fascinated them. During these ten months of work and sharing Lightningbolt and Liberty grew close and were happy to discover each other's hearts and minds.

Just before Liberty and Lightningbolt were to depart for Canada they received an invitation to visit with Estcheemah's oldest friend and student.

Lodge Grass Creek flowed bright pink and gold with the evening sunset when Liberty and Lightningbolt parked near the stream. They recognized Sky River's familiar canvas tepee as soon as they walked into her camp.

Estcheemah's apprentice was in her late fifties, and the years had ennobled the woman's entire presence of body and being.

"I like being a woman," she had told them when they had met at Estcheemah's home a year earlier. "I have always tried to reflect the blue sky like my name, Sky River." She smiled. "And I put great effort into remaining close to the power of Mother Earth."

Sky River greeted Estcheemah's young students

warmly, and sat them down to eat the supper she
had prepared for them.

"Are you alone here?" Liberty asked as she ate,
concerned for the beautiful older woman.

"Reuben, my new husband, is out collecting
wood," Sky River answered smoothly. "I'm not surprised that you anticipated my talk about your
fears, Liberty. The reason I asked you here was to
talk to you about Estcheemah and your journey to
Canada to meet her."

"I think you need to hear more about our teacher, Estcheemah, and how she has struggled to survive all these years.

"Estcheemah has had her fears, very real ones, but this is certainly not the importance of her Life. I am sure you realize that Estcheemah is a very unique woman and does not possess the same kinds of fears as many women. Hers are the deep concerns of a visionary leader who happens to be a woman. This is different from more ordinary people. One day our teacher will be remembered as a great human being.

"Estcheemah once explained to me how she grew in her Self, her Power, Discipline, and Learning with her teacher, Serpent Mother. She began to understand that her own personal Responsibility to our Mother Earth and to Humanity was tremendous. She had the grand opportunity of learning from one of the few living Zero Chiefs, Serpent Mother, who had survived the devastation of the Indian Wars and the continued destruction of all Indians on every Reservation.

"Estcheemah took her opportunity and challenge very seriously. She told me that as she matured in learning, she realized that she must do everything in her power, even risking her Life, to rescue the information of the Medicine Wheels for the future generations of Earth's people. She deeply feared the loss of this information, and how that loss would affect the future, more than she feared even for her safety.

"In those days there was only one way for Indians to move about so freely. Estcheemah and Blue Hair—a powerful Flower Soldier and Warrior who had also studied with Serpent Mother for many years—followed the harvests, picking fruit, cotton, nuts, and potatoes, shucking corn, and trading with other Indians.

"Their lives were not easy. The people they worked and lived with were plagued by extreme poverty, ignorance, mistrust, cholera, dysentery, tuberculosis, typhus, and other diseases and terrors we don't worry about much today.

"Estcheemah and Blue Hair had to be everything for the people they lived with—and yet remain hidden among them. They learned how to deliver babies, heal the sick, and bury the dead. Re-

peatedly they were forced to hide from the harsh Christian zealots who believed that all Indians practiced witchcraft and were pagans. They were robbed frequently and felt the harsh sting of racial shame on a daily basis.

"Their story is remarkable and stunning to hear. You should know that Estcheemah and Blue Hair traveled to Central America, Mexico, and even as far as Brazil, searching for clues about the Medicine Wheels. They also traveled widely in Canada in search of Medicine Chiefs and Keepers who were in hiding. And they did this during incredibly dangerous times for all Indian people.

"Beyond their daily fears of perishing from hunger or disease, Estcheemah feared the demise of the Wheels more than she feared for her personal existence. Slowly, she began to realize that the only way to really keep the Medicine Wheels alive was to share them with all the world's people."

"You know," Liberty said, looking deeply into the glowing fire, "I have always guessed at what you are telling us now. But I don't think I could have truly appreciated hearing about how much Estcheemah has accomplished any earlier in my learning. Hearing these things about her Self journey really makes me think about my own. It obviously takes a lot of courage and wisdom to become a Zero Chief."

"I think that her acceptance of the responsibility to share the Medicine Wheels with all of our Earth's peoples happened in a deeply personal way. She saw old Medicine Chiefs dying with no apprentices—and Medicine Wheels and histories that were thousands of years old being lost forever with them. A few years before Serpent Mother's death, Estcheemah and Blue Hair began to understand the immensity of their challenge.

"They had the opportunity to collect and protect much of the valuable information of the Flower Soldiers. The Sacred Wheels needed protection and appreciation if they were going to survive.

The two knew that they had to work with speed because they only had a few years, while some of the old Chiefs and Medicine Women were still alive, to put many of the fragmented Medicine Wheels and histories back together.

"It's amazing they survived!" Lightningbolt said, shaking his head in awe.

"How *did* they survive, you ask?" Sky River said. "I do not know. Only through immense courage, the use of their brains, absolute loyalty to their purpose, and their deep friendship, could they have hoped to survive. Estcheemah is an important winner in the great Circle we call history. Everything that has tried to destroy her, failed!

"She is a modern Medicine Chief and Leader who has shown the world that Self Choice and personal Care and Responsibility for Life are more precious than every reward of money or threat of pain and destruction. I think that Estcheemah is too powerful to be defeated.

"Even after Blue Hair died, and Estcheemah was left mostly alone, she went on. Blue Hair's death was a shock to Estcheemah, but for Indians living in those extremely violent times, it was not unusual. At the border of Mexico, two desperate youths robbed and killed him. Yet, he too died a winner. He won great acts of courage in his Life, and rescued much of the information of the Sacred Wheels with Estcheemah.

"And yet, after Blue Hair's death, Estcheemah was left alone. Remember, young ones, that during the time when Estcheemah collected the knowledge of the Medicine Wheels, Mother Earth was being called 'evil' and a 'harlot,' and so was our Earth-conscious Estcheemah. She too has been called a 'harlot' and 'witch' simply because she is a very powerful woman and not a conformist.

"I am younger than Estcheemah, as you know, but we have shared much of the same time in history. The times we have lived through were brutal and heartbreaking. The loneliness and terrors she

experienced are beyond comprehension. Also, she has worried deeply about finding apprentices—especially young women who would have the courage to stand up to the immense challenges that face them.

"She has been accused and attacked in every way a human could be and yet she remains strong. She has been threatened by every kind of ignorance, and every kind of political jealousy. She has known the sadness of being a great Leader and Thinker—a great Medicine Chief—with no support. She knows the heartbreak of being warred upon by every religious nut who exists.

"People who are important to the world, such as Estcheemah, attest to the possible greatness of the human Spirit that all of us can fight to achieve.

"Women who are struggling to be leaders in our world may think that women such as Estcheemah fear the deeply personal insecurities and Self doubts that women have been made to feel by their violently antifemale world. But I don't think so. Estcheemah knew that this kind of fear could defeat her, and so she has never believed the lie. Estcheemah knows that Creation is not so trite as to be antifemale. She knows and respects the balance of her Creatress and Creator, and this gives her great personal power, as a woman and a leader.

"However, most of our world's peoples are desperately out of balance. They are in great need of truthful, balanced information. This is why Estcheemah chose to test you two Breeds with her precious Teachings. It is our knowing that the information of the Medicine Wheels has the power to change the course of humanity's future.

"A great challenge faces both of you. I think that once you begin to understand the magnitude of your personal responsibility you will become more focused in your own lives. If you do choose to go to Canada and continue your training, then you will see what it means to be a Flower Soldier.

"It is also important for you to remember always that we are not seeking to have everyone become a Flower Soldier. Not everyone has the Self discipline or dedication necessary to be a Flower Soldier. However, we also know and teach that people do not have to be Flower Soldiers to learn to celebrate their existence, care for the Self, honor the Balance of Creation, or to be Self responsible. People do not have to be Flower Soldiers to love Mother Life and care for their precious world.

"A word of caution, young ones. Many times when our hearts are moved to do great things we forget that greatness is built moment by moment. To become a Flower Soldier takes many years of study and experience. I mention this because in our future there will be those who will believe themselves to be Flower Soldiers because they have heard or read about Flower Soldiers.

"The Flower Soldiers' lineage reaches back from teachers to students, to teachers to students, for many thousands of years. This is the Way a Flower Soldier is taught. The unbroken line has been, at times, the most delicate thread, and at other times the strong weave of thousands.

"No matter what exists now, or in your future, you will not become missionaries. You will become Self Responsible people who will Cherish Mother Life, teach of the Sacred Medicine Wheels, and respect and honor our Creatress Mother and Creator Father."

Two weeks later, Lightningbolt and Liberty began their drive to Estcheemah's new home on a small island in the Georgia Straits of Canada's northwest coast.

The broad land of Alberta, Saskatchewan, and Manitoba touches the sister prairies of North Dakota, Montana, and Idaho with the most gentle of meetings. This great Land is an ancient Circle of Power and Healing that knows no separation of politics and boundaries.

It is always dramatic leaving the prairie's golden grasses, red earth, and high-domed bounteous blue skies. Even though we may prepare ourselves for entry into the cool greens of the northwest coast, She will always startle the traveler with her Ocean Beauty.

As travelers journey to the West from these lands of purpose and rich existence, they will sense that they are passing through a magical door in the Rocky Mountains. It is hard to say too much about this wondrous door. At one time, among the patient Indians, this door, this "time barrier," had many names because nowhere else on Mother Earth could Tee-hahm-na-hannee, the Spirit-Mind of the Forest, be met.

This Spirit, also known as "She-Beautiful," will bathe the traveler's mind with absolute Forest knowing. However, this knowing will never be felt

387

by the persons who are not searching for Tee-hahm-na-hannee.

Liberty and Lightningbolt had stopped and prayed at the portal of the mountain Forest. They wanted to be prepared to meet the soft mist greens of the coast, and to feel the kiss of the Ocean's breeze.

The two friends were eager to meet the beautiful Ocean and both were looking forward to seeing their teacher. What they were not prepared to meet was a man holding a gun.

When Lightningbolt saw the man in Estcheemah's yard, threatening her with a pistol, he was shocked. Somehow it had never entered his mind that Estcheemah might be harmed by anyone in Canada. Consequently, when the danger erupted, he was totally unprepared for it.

388

Liberty, on the other hand, distrusted living alone and was not surprised that Estcheemah might be in trouble. But when she saw the gun, she didn't know what to do either. She just sat in the pickup feeling helpless.

This dangerous situation would dramatically alter the course of Liberty's life and shock Lightningbolt into the realization, once again, that Estcheemah was no ordinary old lady a gunman could push around.

Two days before Lightningbolt and Liberty arrived, Estcheemah had found a sorrowful, middle-aged woman sitting on her porch when she drove back from shopping. The woman's name, she discovered, was Dorothea Robertson.

"Hello," called Estcheemah as she stepped out of her car. "How amazing! How did you find me?"

"Your neighbor in Wyoming said where you were," Dorothea answered sadly. "He is such a nice man."

Dorothea followed Estcheemah into the house and began to weep, telling her that she was getting a divorce from Harry, her husband.

"Jeanie Smith knew Elaine Hankins," she tearfully explained to Estcheemah. "Elaine cut Mrs. Cully's hair. Mrs. Cully knew Wanda, your neighbor's wife." She wiped her eyes with her hanky. "And I was told by Jeanie that you were a real fortuneteller and Medicine Woman who could patch things up."

The events that were to follow this simple meeting moved very quickly because Harry tracked Dorothea to Estcheemah's door the next day.

He had a gun and a tremendous amount of anger. He was convinced that Dorothea was leaving him for another man. Harry had no idea who Estcheemah was, and he didn't care. What he did believe, once he met Estcheemah, was that "the witch" had something to do with Dorothea's decision to leave him.

Harry was not all that bright, and neither was Dorothea. He made his living working in a warehouse, and he also drove a delivery truck. Harry felt he had to move fast, both to "rescue" Dorothea from her "madness" and to quickly return to work so he wouldn't lose his job.

The drama that was taking place while Lightningbolt and Liberty stepped from their pickup seemed unreal to them.

Harry brandished his pistol and yelled as loudly as he could to frighten Estcheemah. For some unexplained reason he had not seen the pickup or its occupants.

Lightningbolt had often fantasized about saving Estcheemah. But now that the real-life situation confronted him, he stood dumbly, not knowing what to say or do. Liberty crouched behind the door of the pickup, overwhelmed with fear and surprise.

Only Estcheemah knew what to do.

Faster than the eye could follow her movements, Estcheemah reached under her skirt and grabbed her four-barreled "pepper box." She always carried the small derringer to protect herself against animals and "foolish people."

As she pressed the derringer against Harry's thigh, she spoke to him calmly about the fact that the four bullets in her gun could destroy his leg.

The man's military .45 now seemed overheavy to him, and it weighed his arm down.

"It would be just a bit complicated for you to report your bloody and broken leg to the police," she seemed to purr to him, continuing to look directly into his eyes. "And what about your retirement, Harry? Ready to throw that away, too?"

Whatever insanity or anger had helped Harry brandish his pistol was now gone. He staggered back against his car's hood and crumpled to the ground as though Estcheemah had hit him with a hammer. She reached for his gun, took it gently from his hand, and threw it into the back of Lightningbolt's pickup box.

Time had stopped for Lightningbolt. No one seemed to move after Estcheemah disarmed the man. An incredible amount of embarrassing time passed for him. Finally he found enough strength to clear his throat, but that was all he could do.

Estcheemah was now kneeling beside the stricken man. "It's all right, Harry," she said, continuing to calm him. "Dorothea will not leave you. Where can she go? And how about your joint bank account?"

Tears poured from Harry's eyes and he fought to pull a neatly pressed handkerchief from his pants pocket. Estcheemah had to assist his shaking hands to free it.

While all this was taking place, Dorothea had stood motionless with excitement and fear. As soon as Estcheemah began to comfort Harry, she leaped to his side, wanting to help "her man." Within minutes the reunited couple had driven away, with Dorothea at the wheel.

While Estcheemah made coffee in her cozy, modern new home, Lightningbolt fumed in his mind about his helplessness. Liberty, on the other hand, was bouncing with curiosity and had endless questions about how Estcheemah had escaped her problem. She emphasized the word *escape* so loudly that even Lightningbolt could not miss her meaning.

"There is no way of escaping a person pointing a gun at you, Liberty," Estcheemah smoothly corrected her. "To pretend in that kind of situation is absolute madness. When you are being threatened with Death, there is only survival. If I were to have thought, for even one breath, that I could escape, I would have been crippled or dead. No, I meant to be victorious; I had to be victorious."

"You mean you would have actually killed

him?" Liberty asked. Her voice was unsteady.

"Kill him?" Estcheemah said, lifting her eyebrow. "Liberty, I'm not a gunslinger or a killer. I would have wounded him severely in his leg, exactly as I reported to him. But kill him—never! What would I have gained by destroying him? Just because we possess a weapon is no excuse to kill.

"What I am making clear to you, Liberty, is that no one feels like beating a woman, raping her, or trying to kill her when they've been hit with a bullet. The wound takes all the joy out of the rape, and all the vengeance out of murder."

"But he could have killed you!" Liberty insisted.

"He could have killed all of us," she corrected her. "You were in the same danger as I was, even though you were trying to hide behind the pickup door. There is no escape from a gun."

"I thought I would react differently, dammit!" Lightningbolt cursed, still embarrassed that he had not rushed in to save everyone.

"Come and sit with me on my new porch," Estcheemah said. "Let's have a talk, all right? We can look at the ocean together while we talk."

After everyone was settled into chairs, she asked Lightningbolt to bring her Harry's gun. He'd driven away without it. She carefully unloaded the weapon and handed it to Liberty.

"What kind of pistol is that?" she asked Liberty.

"I don't know," Liberty answered, taking the gun and turning it in her hand. "It sure is heavy. Are you sure it won't shoot?"

"It's a pity you don't know more about weapons, Liberty," said Estcheemah, disappointed. "The question is, why don't you know more about guns?

"The average television watcher and moviegoer in the United States has seen cannons, submachine guns, rifles of every description and caliber, and just about every kind of pistol ever made on Earth. Our toy stores are stuffed to overflowing with replicas of pistols, automatic assault rifles, and hand grenades. And you know you've seen them all."

"I've always been afraid of guns," Liberty admitted as she placed the pistol carefully on the floor by her chair.

"Yes, I understand," said Estcheemah kindly. "I think that you and many young women and girls ignore much of the cruelty you see in movies and television. You do this to protect the deepest part of your being from such savagery. The reason for this is because so often it is the woman being shown as the victim. Yes, you saw the weaponry. But it was not fashionable for you, as a woman, to have a weapon to defend yourself."

Liberty was becoming angry.

"Women should know more about all kinds of machinery," Lightningbolt added, unwittingly.

"So they can be smart like men?" Liberty snapped.

"Which expert are you addressing, Liberty?" Estcheemah teased. "Lightningbolt the chef? Or Lightningbolt the banker? You're not a financial wizard, are you, Lightningbolt?"

"I give up!" he said, throwing up his arms.

"You're right, Lightningbolt!" Liberty said in anger. "It's the stupid system!"

"You are conforming to your culture," Estcheemah pressed her. "You have been taught to be the victim in your culture. Millions of women see weapons every day, but they ignore them. It's a pity because often it's the woman, far more than the man, who needs a weapon."

"How do I load it?" Liberty asked, picking up the pistol. "I'm not afraid of it now. Is there one designed for a woman?"

"Of course," Estcheemah answered. "My derringer is old-lady size. When I was younger it was middle-aged-woman size. When I was younger still, it was young-woman size. Liberty, I'm not arguing for the use of guns. I am telling you that you need to know how to use tools."

"I want to begin by learning to shoot," Liberty resolved.

"Then we will begin immediately," Estcheemah encouraged her. "Show up here tomorrow about eight and you can have your first lesson. And Liberty, bury Harry's silly little pistol."

The following morning, Liberty was shooting with Lightningbolt in the valley behind Estcheemah's home. They used Lightningbolt's rifle. While they practiced over the next few weeks, these moments became important to Liberty. Yet, deep inside her there remained a worry about what she might do in an emergency.

While Estcheemah's property encompassed only five acres, two hundred more acres of ancient cedars surrounded her land. The acreage was long, beginning at the beach and extending back into a gentle slope of cedar-covered hills.

Lightningbolt and Liberty walked the logging road, exploring the forest, searching for the right spot to put their trailer. The weather was a little damp, but it was also warm.

Before long they came to a small meadow with a spring. When they examined the spring they discovered that it was the source of Estcheemah's drinking water.

Scouting below the spring for another meadow became fun. They played as they searched, moving among the ferns and tall gentle grasses. They immediately found five excellent places for the trailer, but the two immense twin cedar trees they discovered made the final decision. The cedar twins tow-

ered into the sky as giant forest guardians, and reminded both Liberty and Lightningbolt of their reasons for being in Canada with Estcheemah.

It was the middle of July before their home was comfortable enough for them to move into. By then, the trailer had disappeared behind a facade of cedar planks. Liberty had rented a tractor and plowed a wide band around their home, along the path, and around the outhouse. Lightningbolt took his turn with the tractor and pulled a grain drill filled with a hundred pounds of wildflower seeds, planting every inch of ground they had plowed. The first showers they took in their own home were cause for celebration. Estcheemah brought coffee and pastrami sandwiches, and she told stories that kept them laughing.

Work became the next consideration. They found jobs stripping the paint from a yacht that a

doctor owned. The work was boring, but it gave them enough money for the lumber and food they needed.

A local fisherman had given Lightningbolt a used fishing net from his boat in exchange for a bit of carpentry work. Liberty used all six thousand feet of net to build a fence that completely surrounded their home and very large yard.

Every day brought a new joy. Over the next few weeks, thin wisps of seedlings began to show their heads. Soon twenty adult hens with their swarming yellow chicks were scratching in the middle of the garden, finding worms, while fifteen ducks now swam in a small pond. A steady flow of water from the spring kept the pond clean.

A flock of crows and eight ravens also picked at the ground when Liberty fed the chickens and ducks each morning. Twenty-five magpies sat on the fence discussing the eating habits of the ravens and crows.

Brunhilde, a small female burro, grazed contentedly beyond the enclosure. She had been given to them as a gift from Estcheemah. Liberty loved the animal and frequently rode her to the store to shop. The tiny donkey needed no bridle; only a halter was necessary.

Gentle Brunhilde was the first burro Lightningbolt had ever had the chance to know, and he was impressed by her intelligence. She would wriggle her ears whenever he accused her of being a jackass.

A month later, Lightningbolt sat on their porch, enjoying the thousands of sprouting flowers that encircled their home.

The clouds weighed thick and the sun shone cool in the sky. He tipped his chair back and surveyed the yard, allowing himself a moment to daydream about the possibility of his writing. Could he write? That had never really been tested.

He reached for his cold coffee and sipped at the brew. Suddenly he became aware of the aroma of fresh-baked bread and he sat upright. Liberty had put bread in the oven to bake.

"Cinnamon rolls!" Liberty smiled as she joined him on the porch. "They won't be long. What have you been doing?"

Their conversation was interrupted when a new Chrysler pulled up to their gate and stopped. A handsome, middle-aged man wearing an expensive business suit slid out of the driver's seat and took a quick look around. It was obvious, even from a distance, that he was a Canadian Indian.

"Don't get up, folks," he called pleasantly. "I'm Robert Morrisette. I'm Estcheemah's closest relative. The people at the store said that she lived nearby. Do you know where?"

Lightningbolt and Liberty walked to the gate and introduced themselves, then pointed out the way to Estcheemah's home.

Estcheemah left immediately with her relative and was gone until evening. Liberty and Lightningbolt learned the story the following morning.

Estcheemah had given birth to a son in Idaho, and her husband had named him Robert.

Moheegun, Robert's father, had been sullen and moody all through the pregnancy. Moheegun hunted and trapped, becoming very successful. Four months after Robert was born, Moheegun went in on a money scheme with John Kyle, a friend.

They bought a hundred sewing machines that were part of an estate. John went on the road selling the machines, and Moheegun continued to hunt and trap. The business venture was a complete success.

When Robert was a year and a half old they moved to Wyoming so that Serpent Mother and Blue Hair could continue to teach Estcheemah.

Moheegun grew ever more distant. Because he had been so successful with the sewing machines, he and John went into another business venture. This, too, was successful.

One day a young woman named Janet showed up at Estcheemah's door. She shyly announced that she was from Canada and that she was Moheegun's wife.

This came as no surprise. Secretly, in the Indian world, both women and men often had a second spouse. However, this was usually discussed before arrangements were made. The girl was nineteen and scared. Estcheemah and Serpent Mother cared for Janet and comforted her. Moheegun built what he called "the bunkhouse," and Janet moved in.

Over the next year, Estcheemah became ever more involved with her training as a Medicine Woman, and Moheegun became as deeply involved with business. Janet took an interest in the business and became important as a bookkeeper after John Kyle taught her how. Janet and Irene, John's wife, became close friends.

When Robert was four and a half, Moheegun announced to Estcheemah that he was returning to Canada with Janet and taking Robert with him.

The fight began. Emotions flared, and both Estcheemah and Moheegun were in a rage. But in the end, Estcheemah lost the battle. She would not divulge why she had lost, but she hinted that Robert had been kidnapped from her.

Estcheemah was despondent for two years. During this time, she worked as a cleaning woman—the only work she could find. Finally, she began to search for something else to do. She was determined to not be anyone's servant. Then, while visiting a friend in North Dakota, she met Edward Black Dirt. It seemed he was skilled at creating coats. Edward began to teach Estcheemah in exchange for her teaching him.

Slowly, over the next three days, Liberty and Lightningbolt learned more. For many years, no matter how hard Estcheemah had tried to communicate with her son, she had failed. Moheegun was determined that his son would be a successful businessman, and he sent Robert to the finest schools in the United States and France.

The explosive information was learned on the fourth day, while Estcheemah had lunch with them at their home. She had mortgaged her home and given all the money to her son. His business was in deep financial trouble.

"What if he blows it?" Liberty asked. "What will you do?"

"I am old," she answered. "He is my son. I love him very much. It really does not matter. I am sure he will be successful."

Preparations for Liberty's Ceremony began four days later. Estcheemah had instructed Lightningbolt to create a beautiful Medicine Wheel for Liberty, made of driftwood and stones. Every shape imaginable was represented in the driftwood, and almost every possible color. The wood had been sculpted and polished by wind and surf, and the stones were unique in that all were about the same size and had also been smoothed and shaped by water and time. Their color was unusual—they were all a startling white.

Lightningbolt had chosen a place of singular beauty in which to build Liberty's Medicine Wheel. It was a perfectly rounded grassy knoll near the beach covered with millions of flowers turning gold as they dried on their stalks.

Estcheemah wanted to surround Liberty with as much beauty as possible, and in the same moment express the truth of practicality and stability. To accomplish this, she chose to build Liberty's shelter to the North of her Wheel. She hoped that her apprentice would see the wisdom and strength of what the home symbolizes for all women.

She had Liberty's fire ring built in the East to remind her student of the importance and presence of health, and to symbolize her need to be clear and illuminating with her Self.

The table and two chairs that Estcheemah had placed in the South of the Wheel became Liberty's Circle of Nourishment—a symbol of the presence of sharing.

The West was left wide and very deep like our Ocean. The Great Mother Ocean would dance in

the Dream of Life with Liberty.

Estcheemah's tent was hidden in the cedars to the Northeast of Liberty's Circle. Lightningbolt had placed his tent in a position to guard the path. He was determined no one would pass.

The Autumn morning was pleasant and very warm when Estcheemah began her work with Liberty.

"I will speak to you about some incredible learning that has taken place during the past few thousand years. Some people would refer to the learning as psychology, but our Chiefs had never heard that word.

"As you know, the West of the Medicine Wheel is the place of Introspection. This means to look within.

"People have a belief that if they are presented with information—any material or abstract fact—they somehow 'know' what it means. Nothing could be further from the truth, for the information has not gone through the process of Introspection.

"*Introspection* does not mean 'study.' Too often study is what you pretended to do while you were in school. Introspection is a discipline that must be learned. Introspection is not daydreaming."

"I think I know what you mean," said Liberty. "It's when I see something inside my mind."

"Movement and observation are the answers to Introspection," Estcheemah answered. "If I see an old-fashioned alarm clock, I will look to see how the gears are moving, how they are working together. If I do not know how gears work in a clock, I will get a clock so I can learn.

"Introspection is not a discipline that stands alone. As you have discovered in your studies of the Medicine Wheels, Wisdom, Trust, and Illumination are also involved."

"Should I start with a clock or something else?" Liberty asked naively.

Estcheemah laughed. "No, child, no! But you can begin to understand the Wheels . . . and maybe even be introspective with what I tell you.

"When Lightningbolt was young, he did not internalize the information I revealed to him because he refused to take the time he needed to know himself. He did not respect himself, and so why should he take the time? Information meant only something that he could memorize and manipulate.

"He did not know how to respect information, and he did not know how to be introspective with the information that came to him. He believed that thoughts were his daydreams.

"Any innate respect he might have had for learning had been destroyed by his acquaintances, much of his family, and his teachers."

"That's so sad," said Liberty with a deep sigh, feeling her own ignorance about her Self.

"If he could have respected his own thinking," said Estcheemah, "he would have discovered how he was being manipulated by his beliefs. But Lightningbolt's own beliefs and attitudes were never known to him because he did not respect his thoughts and feelings. He only knew what he was told to believe, and most of this forbade independent thought. We call our attitudes and beliefs our 'thinking' when we do not know our Self or our thoughts.

"Our Zero Chiefs taught that every Human is a Multiplicity of Consciousness. This simply means that each human has many different kinds of minds or characters that she or he has internalized.

"The Chiefs discovered that the foundation of every belief is fear. Lightningbolt had many cultural beliefs, both Indian and white, and he was constantly ruled by his fears. Since beliefs are not reasonable, when he did plumb the depths of his own thinking, he would experience his fears.

"His greatest fear was that he would discover his true choices. He did not trust his choices because he did not know his Self. For example, he did not want to discover that he was a mediocre man.

"I once asked Serpent Mother, my teacher, about why the Zero Chiefs learned so much about the human mind. Her answer made me smile. Yet, it was also very illuminating.

" 'The Self was studied for very important reasons,' Serpent Mother told me. 'First, you must realize, Estcheemah, that there was not all that much to do in those days. The Zero Chiefs were not so busy as you might imagine. When the Zero Chiefs lived in the great cities, they did not have the same distractions we face in our modern day.

" 'The Zero Chiefs had worked hard to become a people of wealth. Time is a wealth few humans on Earth know. Time is the most precious of all things possible for a human to possess. Time gave the Zero Chiefs the opportunity they needed for their discoveries.

" 'The study of the human being became their primary focus. The subject fascinated them and held their attention for many hundreds of years.

" 'What is anger?' they asked. 'Why do people kill other people? Why are some people kind and others cruel? Why do humans love? What is hate?' Thousands of other questions were also asked by our ancients. This is the reason why so much was discovered in the Kivas—the Zero Chiefs were asking about the nature of the Self.'

"What I am about to tell you is of immeasurable importance," Estcheemah told Liberty. "This information is the key to the Balance of a healthy mind and most especially to the Self Army of the Flower Soldier. You must not intellectualize this new information. Have the courage to contemplate your Self and discover the power of what I am sharing with you."

Liberty became even more attentive.

"Our ancient Zero Chiefs discovered, after studying the human Mind over thousands of years, that there exist Twelve Principal Powers, or parts of the Mind, within every individual.

"We call these Twelve Principal Powers or Beings within us the Circle of Law," Estcheemah instructed. She handed Liberty the Medicine Wheel of the Circle of Law. "Our Medicine Wheels are incredibly valuable to humanity. This inheritance that we have kept for Earth's people will one day be appreciated by many. Study this Medicine Wheel and learn its many nuances.

"Our Chiefs discovered that Four Principal Powers make up the Center of every Self.

"There is the Mental Power of the Self.
"There is the Emotional Power of the Self.
"There is the Physical Power of the Self.
"And there is the Spiritual Power of the Self.

"Beyond these Four Principal Powers that make up the Inner Wheel of the Self, our Chiefs discovered that there are other Minds that exist within the human. These Minds are represented by the Eight places on the outer rim of the Medicine Wheel."

"So look at your Circle, Liberty. The Circle you can see is like many of our ancient Wheels of Learning. The Circle that surrounds you is basic to Life and fundamental to everything born to Mother Earth. The Zero Chiefs used the shape of the Medicine Wheel as a tool for understanding the paramount differences in the human Self.

"They discovered that Characters, or Images of people, exist in the Outer Ring of the Wheel. They called these Internalized Images of people the 'Mind Voices.'

"Get up and walk into the Center Circle and stand there."

Liberty walked to the center of her Wheel and began to appreciate, physically, what her teacher was telling her.

"The Outer Ring encircles you," Estcheemah

emphasized. "It protects you. The Ring encircles the Self. You must keep that in mind as I speak of your Wheel.

"While we are children, we learn. Learning means that we also pretend. It is natural for children to pretend; it is in this way that they learn. Children pretend to be other people they see.

"These Characters, or Mind Voices, are Images of people you pretended to be while you were young and growing. You internalized these Images from your culture and believed them to be real. But the Images and pretense that you internalized are not you. They were never real people. They were simply make-believe.

"These Internalized Images, the Mind Voices, are not the Self. Rather, they are substitutes for the Self. When we are alone and can study the Self that we are, we make some interesting discoveries. The first fact we learn about the Self is that there are Voices of Authority that exist within our Minds. Most of these Images—Voices of Authority—are silly pretense. Most of them are childish. But they have deep roots within our culture.

"How can the Self recognize the Self when so many Voices are heard from the Outer Ring of the Medicine Wheel? Can you imagine, Liberty, how exciting the discovery of the Internalized Image, the Mind Voices, was for the Zero Chiefs?

"Of course, the important question that confronted them was how to discern which Inward Voice was the Self, and which Mind Voices were coming from the Outer Ring.

"With so many different kinds of Internalized Voices being authorities, where was true Self Authority?

"If one inward Mind thought one way, and another thought in another way, how could we humans ever make a decision?

"We will have to take a look at a real person to see how our Chiefs recognized the answer to this. Lightningbolt has consented to be our model.

"While Lightningbolt grew up in Montana, he internalized many images of people and what he believed their authority to be. He saw people being rewarded for being the images of who they were. What these images meant in reality, he did not know. For the most part, the images of the people he internalized were weak and highly conformist.

"You must remember that what is physical is very meaningful to the child. Consequently, some of Lightningbolt's Internalized Images are thin people, some fat, some stupid, some smart. But all of them wanted the same things—social attention, wealth, and material possessions. Some of the people he pretended to be were pretty, some plain, but all of them wanted physical comfort and special attention.

"Some of the people he grew up with were punished for being who they were and some were rewarded for being who they were. Lightningbolt wanted to be either punished or rewarded, but not left out."

"It amazes me how you can remember all that!" Liberty said with awe.

Estcheemah smiled broadly. "Memorizing is the wrong thing to do, Liberty." She touched Liberty's hand. "These things are highly visible and physical. You just have to open another eye; you need dimension. When you are present with Life, these things are more than obvious. People who are trapped in offices and cities can lose sight of the present.

"Liberty, diversity is the fact of Life and Her great teaching for all of Her children. Diversity in farming, our diet, our play, our work, and our thinking should be our strength, not our weakness.

"Our modern problem is that people try to fit in instead of trying to discover who they are in their own lives. People have become confused as to who they are. What happens, in all this conformity, is that the Self is thrown away for an Image and a vague social or cultural promise that can never be

402

fulfilled. People who conform, who believe the vague social promise, become a 'That'—a thing, not a person at all.

"Our Lightningbolt wanted to be a That. Thats had money. Thats had social prestige. Thats were grown-ups.

"But who were these authorities? Most of these Thats were mediocre, conformist people. Their voice was the voice of conformity, echoing the beliefs held by their community.

"While Lightningbolt grew, he internalized what he saw, but he had no Measure of what he was seeing. When a person is without Measure, there is only conformity and the acceptance of beliefs.

"It takes a Lifetime to know the Self, Liberty. We are alive, here with wondrous Mother Earth, to get to know our Self. It is the fact of our Life that will give us Measure and teach us of the Essence of who we are. This is the primary reason for our existence.

"Our Chiefs say that all children will structure their world in order to learn. I taught Lightningbolt to battle his Self ignorance. It is in this way that he has defeated much of his pretense and his simple childhood beliefs.

"His cultural Voices of Authority became apparent to him when I named them. I called the Emotional part of him Orphan Boy. He hated this because it caused him emotional pain to hear it.

"Each time Lightningbolt became emotionally sad or lonely, when he was feeling rejected or embarrassed, it was Orphan Boy who commanded his mind. He learned to fight against this.

"Through Ceremony and our working together, Lightningbolt discovered Bull Head. Bull Head is the physical and willful cowboy image. Battling this image was a great challenge. He held the belief that all cowboys got what they wanted by absolute will and brute force.

"To find Bull Head, Lightningbolt had to learn how to be Introspective. This was no easy task for him because it was hard for him to sit quietly and listen to his inward world.

"Next, he had to turn his attentions to the mind voice I named Uncle Sam. Actually, Uncle Sam and Sugar Barrel were the same thing. He learned that Uncle Sam was concerned with money and reflected the image of the perfect foreman. For Uncle Sam, money was the answer to everything.

"Whenever I accused him of being Uncle Sam he would explode into a rage, he despised the name so much.

"The next mind voice he discovered was the wise but poverty-stricken Medicine Man. I named this mind Jumping Mouse.

"This character was composed of a number of images, ranging from old Goose Flying to Genghis Khan.

"Jumping Mouse is Lightningbolt's imagination. Jumping Mouse is no distraught warrior; he is the compassionate and spiritual being who will become a writer one day.

"It is the challenge of every Flower Soldier to discover the personalities of their Outer Ring and to educate and transform them. This begins the process of building the army of the Self.

"How does the Flower Soldier do this? The first Self Command of the Flower Soldier is to learn to possess Self Choice.

"This may sound very simple to you, Liberty, but it is not. The reason for the difficulty is that most humans do not know Self thinking. There can be no real Choice unless we understand Self thinking."

"Estcheemah," Liberty asked, "how can I be a good judge of what I am doing? Sometimes my motives are not so clear."

"Never be a judge," Estcheemah answered. "Be kind and honest. Be the one who will enlighten your Self. Do not judge your Self. You are not ready to be a judge.

"People judge themselves all too quickly, Liberty. Our culture trains people to be judgmental. The culture we live in does not want to teach people to be Self Honest. This is because Self-Honest people will not blindly follow the rules and pretend as our culture trains them to do.

"Judgmental people possess no qualifications to make a clear judgment of the Self.

"Instead of judging your Self, be explicit with your Self. Instead of being judgmental, always be informative.

"Remember, Liberty, that the mind voices of pretense are very loud. They often substitute rules and beliefs for Self thinking.

"Serpent Mother once told me that the majority of people will quickly conform to the beliefs of their community—mostly through reward and punishment. She also explained that many people do not possess enough Self courage or thinking to question the ignorance of the beliefs of their communities. If they did, they would be shocked and horrified by what they found to be called normal.

"Serpent Mother did not know of the Nazis, but she did know of the concentration camps of Oklahoma. She did not know about the millions of people killed during the Second World War, but she did know of the millions of American Indians who died when Europeans settled our Americas.

"Humans have gone to every extreme in the name of their gods and their conformity. She said that it could be possible for a people to have a "tradition" of eating their first born children. Certain Tribes within the early Greek, Roman, and Hebrew peoples all practiced human sacrifice. It was thought to be normal at the time. "Angry gods" and the strange beliefs that surround angry gods are often primitive and shockingly violent—yet people accept these myths as sacred. Who questions the fundamental madness of religions that claim that Creation approves of human torture? Yet, isn't it a fact that many traditional religions have an angry god who advocates the torture of humans in eternal flames?

"The only power that has ever rescued humanity from even worse conditions and beliefs has been the thinking of a few reasoning individuals who have had the dedication and courage to question the beliefs of their cultures.

"If Temple Doors had not questioned the beliefs of the human sacrificers she lived among, there would have been no Great Migration into the Southwest, and many of the Medicine Wheels would have been lost forever.

"If Thomas Paine, Thomas Jefferson, and many other brave women and men had not critically questioned and fought against the religious feudal system of Europe, which was said to be "divine," the United States would have no democracy today.

"But, because they did have the presence of mind to question their world, they went among the Native People of the Americas and they learned. The consequence of this was that these leaders did take the first steps toward building a working Democracy. However, their Democracy was a crude form of what they had learned from the American Indian in that their kind of Democracy excluded all people who were not white males.

"Even now only a few Self-courageous women and men are fighting to improve our system called Democracy in America today.

"Flower Soldiers know that they cannot be Self Commanders unless they study their own thinking and question everything in their world. They battle for their own Self-critical thinking and Self action. Command within the Self teaches us how to Command in the world.

"How a Flower Soldier finds the Self Commander within is the next question that faces you, Liberty.

"You see, every person is born with Self Command, but most people throw Self Choice and Self Authority away.

404

"To choose to not choose is still a choice made.

"Self respect is where it all begins. Self respect will guide the Flower Soldier to Self honesty.

"Before we go further, we must look at what Self respect means for women living around our world.

"Self authority for women has been forbidden or is not taken seriously because everywhere in our world women are forced to live in cultures that teach that they are less than men.

"Liberty, we women will find our own Authority, our own Voices, when we begin to respect being women. We women will possess our Self Authority when we lift up our Creatress Mother Goddess as equal to our Creator.

"Look at your Medicine Wheel and learn to accept your own female Intelligence and Self Wisdom. You are your own Self Authority. You must also investigate what you sense and feel because these Energies are real and tell a woman much.

"Now is the time for we women to teach our Self to recognize all our strengths as women. It is time to battle to transform our ignorance. It is time for us to focus on the importance of our Self as a woman.

"Liberty, can you imagine the wondrous change that will come to humanity and our world when women have an equal voice in how our world should be run and cared for?

"For far too long, women's decisions have been belittled. We have even been accused of being less than human. It is time to change these awful beliefs. So take seriously what I am saying and do not leave it to another time or to other women to make these changes. Have the courage to listen and to understand what I am teaching you. Self Honesty, Personal Ceremonies, Self Decision, and Self Command will bring forward your most powerful Self.

"Culture is not always so kind and protective. Study and come to understand what your culture has dictated you should be as a girl or a woman.

Flower Soldiers do not seek to destroy what they have learned," Estcheemah cautioned. "Pretense is pretense; it can be understood.

"What and who we are and who we can become is information for the person who is learning. The paltry, the devious, and the mean—yes, even the haughty—can all be resources of information for the person learning of the Self. All information about the Self is important to the Self. A Flower Soldier learns about every inward resource and makes use of it.

"Pretense and fear will always bring forward the Outer-Ring Minds of ignorance. When this happens, study the information that fear has revealed. When a woman learns of her weaknesses, she should never punish herself. Careful questioning and being clear with the Self is much better than punishment.

"Each time a Flower Soldier knows or feels that an old Mind of pretense is taking command of her or his Circle, it is the explicit duty of the Flower Soldier to immediately report to the Self what is taking place.

"The Self Commander battles for Command and then questions the pretender who caused the inward conflict. Try it, Liberty—you will be immensely rewarded. Self Honesty rewards the individual with Courage. To win Courage is one of the highest of achievements for the Flower Soldier.

"Self Honesty and Courage are weapons that the Flower Soldier learns to wield. These are the first inward weapons that help Flower Soldiers defeat their own pretense and ignorance.

"Once we truly learn that we do have Choice, we can begin to free ourselves from the imprisonment and burden of our beliefs. This is the beginning of Self Teaching. And Self Teaching is one of the most profound reasons that humans Live.

"The Self Commander knows Self Choice and learns how to Command the Self into Action. As you know, Thunderchild is the name of Lightning-

bolt's Self Commander. Sun Mirror is what we will call your Self Commander, Liberty. You—your Medicine and Essence—have a true affinity for the energies of the Sun and also for all of the different ways Light marries with the trillions of Water Mirrors of Mother Earth. You must fight to bring Sun Mirror forward within your Self and begin to learn of and teach your own Outer Ring of Minds. This is Self Action.

"Self Action is purpose for every Flower Soldier, Liberty. When the female Flower Soldier discovers her Self as a woman, she will begin to understand her own Actions.

"We will have our choices known—as women asking. This is the only way for a woman to know what Self Choice can be for a female. We women have been denied, for a very long time, the privilege of asking who we are as women, and what it is

that we will create.

"You as a Self Commander must bring balance, order, and unity to your Outer Circle of Beings. Unification of the Self is the building of the Self Army.

"Unification is a lifelong battle for the Self Commander. The Outer Ring can be transformed through great effort and personal dedication to Self Power.

"It is your Sacred Duty to educate your Self in every manner possible to you. Your acceptance of your Self and the fact that you are precious to your own existence is a wondrous human reward!

"Battle for that victory, Liberty. At all times maintain a powerful determination to be your own Self Commander.

"Our Earth will be transformed, Liberty, when we women begin to cherish our Mother Earth and to speak up for Her. It is our duty as women, as the people who Birth other humans, to protect Earth Life—Mother Life.

"Women have no real choice. Not in the Democracies they live in. Not in the totalitarian states they live in. Choice is the greatest of all Balances known in the Universe, and it is denied women because of social and religious bigotry.

"The Zero Chiefs say that human Choice is the most valuable power and presence that Creation has given to humans.

"Liberty, when the people of any nation, religion, or social system suppress human Choice, there is stagnation and misery.

"We must nurture, fully support, and bring forward the human ability to have Choice. For Choice is the wellspring of everything dignified, noble, inventive, and beautiful that has been brought forward by humans on Earth. Humanity depends upon this source of dignity and inventiveness for human progress and survival.

"Balance is born from Choice—in nature and in human design. When all that is female is honored equally to that which is male, then Balance will be restored to a world that is out of Balance.

"Our Creatress Mother has been thrown down and trampled. The loss of our Goddess Mother is a crippling blow that all of humanity is suffering from—physically, mentally, emotionally, socially, and spiritually.

"Our Creatress Mother Goddess is the single most powerful symbol and fact of Life.

"When humanity respects and honors Sacred Life as our Creatress Mother Goddess, equal to the Creator, this one act will restore Balance to our world.

"The Zero Chiefs gave the Medicine Wheels to the people so that they would desire Balance within their own Minds. They called this Balance a Democracy of Mind. They did not want the people to live with the lonely symbol and image of a dictator or a king and queen as the guide in their minds. Kings and queens are born from feudalism, not Democracy.

"Young women and men were taught to Democratize their thinking to function in Life as Free and Balanced individuals, so that they would learn to be their own leaders.

"Those who possess a Democracy of Mind—the Circle of Law—will have as a dynamic resource the most powerful of all tools known—the realization that they are Self Responsible, with the ability for Self Decision.

"Self Decision teaches all people the language of their Self Law. Understanding Self Law awakens in each of us our personal Responsibility for Balance within the laws of our world."

THE TEACHINGS OF THE ZERO CHIEFS
MOREALAH (WATER)

"Balance When It Is Universal,
Reflects The Breadth And Nature
Of Creation"

Estcheemah Taught of:

THE CIRCLE OF LAW

"Balance, when it is Universal, Reflects the breadth and scope of what is Natural in Creation because it is the Nature of Creation to be within Her Balance.

"After thousands of years of studying and experimentation, the Zero Chiefs began to see that the Medicine Wheels revealed an inward relationship they had not previously recognized, one that concerned the human Self.

"The Sacred Mathematics of the Medicine Wheel (actually, how the Chiefs placed their concepts and numbers on the Wheel) made it possible for the Chiefs to discover and then separate out the different qualities or aspects that make up any individual. This revealed to them that every human is made up of what the Zero Chiefs called the Twelve Principal Powers."

The Circle of Law: The Community and the Human Self

Estcheemah:

"The Zero Chiefs named the Great Inward Wheel of Balance the 'CIRCLE OF LAW.'

"Some of the Zero Chiefs who taught the people of the Circle of Law were later called the Earth Sun Chiefs. They taught that when any person seeks to educate the Self, she or he will come into both Agreement and Confrontation with the Twelve Places of Power that comprise the Medicine Wheel and exist within every Human Self.

"These Chiefs understood that Self Teaching makes the difference between chaos and agreement within the Human. When a person teaches the Self, she or he can become a truly Balanced Human.

"A Decision was made many thousands of years ago, in the Temple of Oceans, that the most effective and powerful system of organization for the Self government of a Community of People would be the Circle of Law. Once a Community was able to become its own ruling body, then the Community would find its true stability.

"The model of Self Government for each separate Community became the Circle of Law. The Circle of Law reflects the Mind of the people. And the Circle of Law became the first Democratic governing system among humans.

THE CIRCLE OF LAW

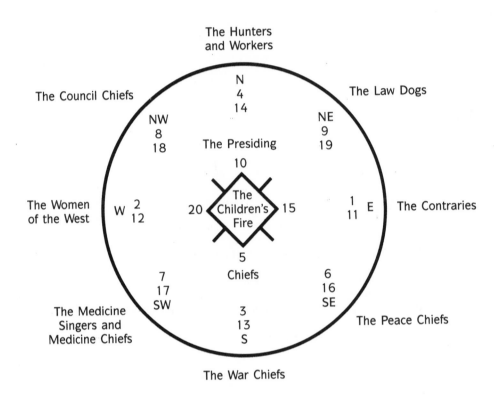

The Hunters
and Workers

The Council Chiefs

The Law Dogs

N
4
14

NW
8
18

NE
9
19

The Presiding
10

20 The
Children's 15
Fire

The Women
of the West

W 2
12

1
11 E

The Contraries

5
Chiefs

7
17
SW

6
16
SE

The Medicine
Singers and
Medicine Chiefs

3
13
S

The Peace Chiefs

The War Chiefs

The Four Heads sat in the Center
in the 5, 10, 15, and 20
of the Children's Fire.

"The Original Circle of Law was made up of Sixteen people. These Principal People were always eight women and eight men. Each pair of these women and men represented the Twins of the place of power where they sat.

"What is meant by 'the Twins'? Why did the Zero Chiefs choose this description? The Chiefs wanted the people to remember what was most important in their Knowledge—what was held most precious by them: That all of Creation exists within Balance, and the most quintessential of all Balances known to humans is that which exists between Female and Male. That Women are Equal to Men. That all Women and Men are Born Free.

"Within history, the Zero Chiefs recognized a problem that had occurred over and over again throughout time. It was the problem of 'might makes right,' which had led to the rich enslaving their sisters and brothers.

"Flying Crow, the Warrioress and Zero Chief who was responsible for one of the Great Migrations out of Central America into the Northeastern United States around fifteen hundred years ago, said:

" 'What greater Right does the human possess than the Right to Freedom? All humans are born Free.

" 'All humans must have the right to form and govern their community. And who is it that knows more of strength than women? What greater might exists than when a woman births a child?

" 'What greater might exists than the might of Love when a human is in need of this essential human comfort?

" 'Women's and men's strengths should never be compared. Because the brute brutalizes does not make the brute more important or stronger.

" 'Weapons decide who is victorious when the brute faces the hunter. Because the large animal is stronger than the hunter does not make the brute more important.

" 'The physical strength of men in comparison to women has been made more important by the ignorant. But the pull of the woman's bow has decided more than what brute strength dictates.' "

"All tools and weapons are created by the human Mind. The mind is one of the greatest powers given to the human. The Human Mind is in balance when the female and male powers are balanced within the human and equal throughout all they create.

"The Zero Chiefs of old would say: 'WahKahn and SsKwan are Female and Male—Twins—and they gave rise to all Existence. All that exists is Female and Male.'

"In the Circle of Law, the name 'Twins' was given to the Principal People who sat in the places of power. The places of power were always balanced equally between women

and men.

"Because the Circle of Law is a Law-making Body that possesses Choice, there were unique differences among the hundreds of different Circles of Law—which have existed throughout the last few thousand years, each evolving in a distinctive way. As a result of the Laws made by each individual Circle within its own time and circumstances, the nuances between Law Circles could differ considerably.

"The Circle of Law was the Self-governing system utilized and celebrated in some of

the greatest cities of Central America. But many hundreds of years later it also became the governing system of a number of diverse North American Tribes. How the Circle functioned in relation to logistical details changed according to time and circumstance, and as a result of how many people the Circle actually represented. This freedom and inherent ability for renewal within the Circle of Law reflected the ever-changing circumstances and needs of many different peoples.

"However, the genius of the actual Structure of the Circle of Law, and the fact that the Representative Twin Chiefs were female and male, was unchanging and eternal. It was forbidden to alter these powerful structural elements in any way.

"What I mean by 'structural elements' is the actual construction of the Wheel itself. As an example, the Contraries always sit in the East of the Circle of Law, the place of the One and the Eleven, and they are always Twin Chiefs—one woman, one man. The Peace Chiefs always sit in the Southeast, the place of the numbers Six and Sixteen, and are always one woman and one man.

"If you study the Medicine Wheel, you will see the eternal elements of the Circle of

Law. The actual power that each represents in the human community, and the Places of Power where they sit in the Circle, are unchanging and eternal. The Mathematics of the Medicine Wheels, and their profound significance to the nature of our Universe and to the Natural Laws of the Earth, were highly respected by all peoples who participated within the Circle of Law. The Numbers of each Place of Power had far-reaching meaning for every Representative and Presiding Chief.

"Just as the Sun and Illumination are East within every Medicine Wheel, and the Earth and Introspection are West, the Plants and Trust are South, and the Animals and Wisdom are North, so are the Places of Power on the Circle of Law immutable and everlasting.

"The following is one example of how a community of people built its own Circle of Law. Though you will see some of their unique developments, the power and form of the Great Circle of Democracy known as the Circle of Law remained changeless and eternal."

An Example of The Circle of Law of the Blue Sky Crees

"In the 1860s the Circle of Law had been made very beautiful among the Confederation of the Blue Sky Crees—eight large painted tepees were placed together in a wide circle. At this time, they numbered around two thousand people, scattered among eleven camps. Once each year, during the time of the Dreamer Lodges, these eleven camps of

people would send their Representative Chiefs to the Circle of Law. These Chiefs were always accompanied by other people from their camp communities.

"Since most of the people had come for ceremonial dances and to trade, many people did not participate directly in these meetings of the Circle of Law. Those who remained home one year had their chance to dance the following year.

"Sixteen people—eight pairs of Twins, each pair consisting of one woman and one man—were chosen as 'Voices of the Blue Sky,' or Representative Chiefs, to sit in the eight directions, which were the sixteen Positions of Power within the Circle. The exception to the female-male pairings were the Representative Chiefs of the West, who were always two women, and those of the North, who were two men. In this way the two exceptions balanced one another.

"In addition to the Representative Chiefs, four Presiding Chiefs—two women and two men—were chosen from the 'wise people,' those who had shown their dedication to the welfare of the people for many years. The Presiding Chiefs were also known as Head Chiefs. Occasionally there were only two Presiding Chiefs, but this only occurred in extreme emergencies. The Presiding Chiefs sat in special places within the innermost, or Middle Circle of the Circle of Law. This Center Place was called the 'Children's Fire.'

"The Presiding Chiefs kept order and possessed the power of Veto when there was a need for it, yet they had no vote themselves. Their veto power was only put into action when there was great confusion or a stalemate.

"After a question of Law had been introduced into the Circle of Law, the Representative Twin Chiefs who sat in the Eight Directions thoroughly discussed the question. This was accomplished through a sophisticated and disciplined proceeding that moved the talk and argument around the Circle. Only after the completion of this procedure was a vote taken.

"Two thirds of the vote had to be either Yes or No to be counted as a majority. If there was no majority vote, then the entire process would begin once again."

How a Question Was Discussed Around the Circle of Law

"Whenever a major question of law arose in the community, the person or persons involved would take the question to the Contraries, asking that it be presented to the Circle of Law.

"The Contraries, the Representative Twin Chiefs who sat in the East, would then ask the Law Dogs, the Representative Twin Chiefs who sat in the Northeast, to call the Circle of Law together. When the Contraries spoke to the Law Dogs, four other Representative Chiefs—equally women and men—had to be present when the question of whether the Law Circle would meet was discussed.

"The Law Dogs would then proceed to make known that a question of the Law was to be brought to the Circle of Law. After it was agreed, by one half of the body that comprised the Circle of Law, to meet, then the proceedings would begin.

"The Sixteen Representative Chiefs and the Four Presiding Chiefs—the full Circle of Law—would then gather to hear what the Contraries had to say.

"The Eight beautifully painted Tepees were arranged to create a very large Circle, spacious enough to accommodate five hundred people if the need arose. The five hundred people could sit in the middle of the Circle of Lodges. However, it was very seldom that five hundred people actually participated at one time. Many were busy trading and dancing. Only certain kinds of people are usually interested in the administration of government.

"It was in the Place of the Children's Fire—among the people—that the Presiding Chiefs sat. All the Lodges of the Eight Principal Powers surrounded the inner Circle of the Children's Fire. It was here where the people could gather to hear their Chiefs.

"The Tepee of the East, or the Lodge of the Contraries, was the Door into the Great Circle. The Tepee of the East was highly symbolic, for it had two Doors—one in the East of the Lodge, and the second in the West. All the Chiefs—the Voices—entering the Circle of Law had to walk through that East Lodge. However, onlookers or visitors were not allowed to enter through the East Doors.

"The other seven Lodges were used as meeting places for the people. It was here that many questions were answered by the Chiefs. Sometimes these questions were about the law, but mostly they were questions about herbs, medication, weapons, tools, animals, foods, crafts, children, birth, marriage, and death. The East Lodge was never used as a meeting Lodge because it was the Door. And who would be so bold as to ask a Contrary a question? That person would only get a Contrary answer.

"The Twin Contraries were the Guardians everyone had to pass before entering the Great Circle. The East Twins, the Contraries, were people who knew the Law and had a deep respect for the Law and how it affected their community and Tribes. They were the young people who represented the Artists and the Craftspeople, the ones who made weapons of war and the shields. These objects were thought to hold great Power. The consequence of this was enormous, for these Artisans were highly regarded by all Tribes. These young people took their positions as Contraries very seriously.

"Dressed in their finest, the Contraries would come through their Doors and announce the question of the law so that all who sat in the Place of the Children's Fire could hear it.

"Since the Representative Chiefs had previously heard the question, when they were deciding whether to call the Circle of Law together, they were ready to debate. However, the Presiding Chiefs heard the question of the Law to be debated at the same time the people did. Seating the Presiding Chiefs among the gathered Tribe gave the people sway with these Chiefs who held the power of veto.

"After they had announced the question of the Law, the Contraries then spoke directly to the Peace Chiefs, who were the Representative Chiefs sitting in the Southeast of the Great Circle, the place of the sacred numbers Six and Sixteen. The Peace Chiefs were women and men who had taken a vow to never kill another human. If a Peace Chief should be forced to kill, or was even an innocent party to the death of another human, he or she would be instantly removed as a Peace Chief and immediately made a War Chief.

"After the law or question had been heard by the Peace Chiefs, they in turn would present the law being debated, along with their argument, to the War Chiefs. These were the Representative Chiefs who sat in the South, the place of the sacred numbers Three and Thirteen. The War Chiefs were always represented by one woman and one man.

"The information we have about the War Chiefs of old comes from the Zero Chiefs of the Ojibwa of Canada. They tell us that the War Chiefs had taken a vow to fight to the death in order to protect the people if the need arose. This tradition of the War Chiefs

had originally come north with the Flower Soldiers in the later migrations, after the one led by Temple Doors.

"After the law had been reviewed by the War Chiefs, they presented it, and their argument, to the Medicine Chiefs and Singers or 'Carriers.' These were the Representative Chiefs who sat in the Southwest, the place of the sacred numbers Seven and Seventeen. The Singers and Medicine Chiefs have no counterpart in our modern world. While it was true that they did sing and heal, they also did more than this.

"Singing With Lightning, the old Cheyenne Medicine Woman, said: 'All the world is singing with the Healers. Just to learn the songs of the sunrise alone is a lifetime's work. We should be singing when we heal our children.'

"The Singers were also the great geographers of their day, possessing the knowledge of the Journey Songs that held the information of how to travel great distances and return home safely.

"As 'Carriers,' certain Medicine Women and Men would be allowed passage between enemy peoples, and would be listened to when they came to heal the sick or bring news. These Carriers were also allowed to conduct trade between Tribes who were otherwise enemies.

"The question of the law would next be passed to the Representative Chiefs of the Women's Circle. These Women had to be either pregnant or caring for their own young children. These Chiefs sat in the West of the Great Circle in the place of the sacred numbers Two and Twelve.

"Jack Rabbit Bush, a Blue Sky Cree Elder, once said: 'It is hard to keep people's interest alive within any community. The old communities were no different. The pregnant women and mothers with little children were made part of the Circle because the wisdom of these women is the most sought after when decisions need to be made about going to war. These mothers are the fiercest when it comes to decisions that might endanger their young. And they often provide an intelligent, calming, and balanced voice when revenge is being demanded.'

"The Women of the West would then tell the question of the Law, adding their point of view, to the Council Chiefs. These were the Representative Chiefs who sat in the Northwest, the place of the sacred numbers Eight and Eighteen. The Council Chiefs were women and men who were the politicians of their time. It was their duty to administer the daily business of the community.

"Bluejay, a Blue Sky Cree Elder, explained: 'The Council Chiefs were the most popular people in the community. The popular always form a group among any people, no matter whether the group is needed or not. These groups can become very destructive if they are not directed toward the support of the community. This is because the popular only know conformity and will serve their own political interests.'

"After the Council Chiefs reviewed the law and how it might affect the everyday activities of the people, they in turn explained the question of the law to the Hunters and Workers, the Representative Chiefs who sit in the North, in the place of the sacred numbers Four and Fourteen. These two men were the balance for the two women who sat in the West.

"The Workers were similar to the mothers with young children in that they weren't usually very interested in the laws of the community. However, by having a Seat in the Great Circle, the important Voice of the Workers was included in making the Laws of the Community.

"Special note needs to be made here about what it means to be a Hunter or Worker. Most of the arrow point making was done by women. Anyone who has had to hunt or farm knows that much of the physical labor of these pursuits is extreme and demands time. Because of this demand upon the men, most of the manufacturing was done by the women. However, women also took part in hunting and farming, but not in the same numbers as the males. Anthropologists in the past frequently stressed that men made the arrows and weapons and did all the hunting. This is simply not so.

"Only massive groups of people could afford to have their hunters and farmers making weapons. The physical work was too demanding and time-consuming in smaller communities. The manufacturing of arrow points also gave the women of every community a political edge—no different than the edge that men possessed because they provided much of the food.

"At the same time, it was mostly women who tended the gardens that were dedicated to the growing of medicinal plants and healing herbs. Balance was understood to be the great design of Sacred Life, and Balance was sought for within the great communities of the Circle of Law.

"After The Hunters and Workers reviewed the law they would pass the question of the law, with their point of view, to the Law Dogs. The Law Dogs were the Representative Chiefs who sat in the Northeast, the place of the sacred numbers Nine and Nineteen. They were always represented by one woman and one man. Like the Singers and the Medicine Chiefs, the Law Dogs have no equivalent group in our modern world. While it was true that they were highly knowledgeable about the law, they were also more.

"Many people do not realize that the laws of a community can become an authority above the voice of the community. In other words, that the laws can become a religion. The Zero Chiefs of old knew of this human contradiction and invented the Law Dogs in order to bring balance to a situation that can become dangerous or destructive to the people. The women and men who were the Law Dogs provided the checks and balances that served the highest interests of the community as a complete Circle."

The Balancers: Who Sits Across From Whom?

"When you study the Medicine Wheel of the Circle of Law closely, you cannot help but notice that there are very specific Representative Chiefs who sit directly across the Children's Fire from other Chiefs. This is a very important part of the genius that is the structure of the Wheel itself.

"It is important to know that the Chiefs who sit within the Circle of Law are forbidden to converse or to cooperate with the Chiefs who sit opposite them. A small symbolic fire was built in the middle of the Circle of Law to represent all the children. It was forbidden for any Chief to cross the Children's Fire. If any of the Chiefs were even suspected of speaking across the Children's Fire they were asked to abandon their positions as Representative Chiefs. It was a very serious violation of the law for any pair of Chiefs to cooperate with those who sat opposite them in the Circle of Law.

"Why did this law exist? The manner in which the Zero Chiefs constructed the Wheel, the Circle of Law, tells us much. The Peace Chiefs, the 'academicians,' sit opposite the 'politicians,' who sit as Council Chiefs. This is to prevent them from forming a political alliance that could subvert the true needs and interests of the community.

"In just this way an alliance between the War Chiefs and the Hunters and Workers to further their own political ends could also create considerable imbalance and danger among the people. This has happened many times in human history.

"Having the Singers and Medicine Chiefs opposite the Law Dogs avoids another dangerous kind of imbalance that has occurred countless times among humans. Haven't religious leaders used their powers to manipulate the judicial branches of governments, as well as the reverse?

"So we must now ask what is the unusual opposition of the Contraries, or *Heyoehkahs*, to the Mothers, sitting in the West of the Great Circle? The Contraries were predominantly made up of young people who would later become different kinds of Representative Chiefs themselves. Often the Contraries' own Mothers sat in the Place of Power in the West. In the Circle of Law, the young were allowed to oppose their parents, their mothers and fathers who might be sitting in any Position as Representative Chiefs. The young people were expected to be outspoken.

"Laws and decisions are made moving Sunwise around the Circle of Law. This, in itself, brings about a stability between relatives—given the Balances provided by the positioning of the Places of Power.

"However, what happens when this is reversed? This was another brilliant element of the working of the Circle of Law. When the question being debated in the Circle of Law involved issues of revenge, or of contention between families, or when any law became a point of tribal dispute, the order of the Circle was reversed.

"The Law Dogs then became the Representative Chiefs everyone had to convince—most especially the Contraries, who normally spoke first as the presenters.

"A Law Dog who failed in her or his duty to protect and describe the law by means of checks and balances became a traitor to the people. This meant expulsion from the community and absolute disgrace."

The Law Arrows and the Great Renewal

"Beyond these distinct Checks and Balances of the Circle of Law, there were many other important Balances honored and protected by these devoted Chiefs. What was known as the 'Kicking Over or Breaking of the Law Arrows' was a very important Agreement among all the different Chiefs of the Circle of Law, born in many different times and among many different peoples.

"The Chiefs of a Circle of Law, whether they represented a city, a community, or a Tribe, would create Arrows that were specially carved, painted, and made very beautiful. These Arrows would become powerful Symbols for each of the Laws decided by the people through their Circle of Law.

"Every four years, The Circle of Law would have a special gathering that was called 'The Time of the Great Renewal.' At this special time all laws that had been passed by the Circle of Law were rescrutinized by the Representative Chiefs. Each Law Arrow was broken, as a symbol of release from the old agreement, and then what had been the Law was proposed as a new question to the Circle of Law. Could the Law be improved? Was it working for the people? Did the people understand the Law? Did the people, now, still agree with the Law? What did each Representative Chief think now? Deep questioning and discussion of each Law occurred before the vote was taken to either Discard or Renew the Law. If the Law was Renewed, then a new Law Arrow was created that would stand as the symbol for that law for the next four years.

"The open questioning and insistence by the Chiefs that they Renew human Choice within the Agreements of the Law ensured that all people, young and old, could learn to understand the Laws of their Community, and had the human right to choose their own laws together. This open discussion and dedication to the Renewal of all Laws made the Circle of Law an ever-present and pertinent voice of Education and Choice for the people. Because of the four-year Renewal of the Laws, no Law could ever become archaic, ritualistic, and foreign to the thinking or understanding of the present community Tribe.

"Too often the Zero Chiefs had seen what happened in cities and Tribes where the people were forced to believe that the Laws of the ruling class were a 'higher authority' than the will and thinking of the majority of the people. Inevitably they saw that time after time, century after century, this kind of ignorance always brought about human slavery.

"One of the quintessential principles of the discipline of the Zero Chiefs was their pledge to fight all forms of slavery, beginning with the slavery of the Self by human ignorance.

"This is why they decided that Renewing human Choice through the Four-Year Renewal of the Laws was an absolute necessity of the Circle of Law. In this way the Laws of the community could never enslave the people and old laws from the people of the past could not stunt the growth and evolution of the peoples of the present—or the future.

"People who lived in communities that possessed a Circle of Law were taught that the origin of all laws between people is based upon human Agreement. They were taught that, to be able to Choose the laws of your community in an intelligent way, you must know what the existing Laws are, how they work, and then have the freedom and right to choose to agree or disagree with those laws. Every four years the Chiefs of the Circle of Law also sought at the Time of the Great Renewal to improve their Laws. They taught that the more Humans respect and understand the Balance and Sophistication of their Living World, and the true nature of the Human Self, the more Just and Intelligent their Laws will become.

"It is also extremely important to know that beyond the Four-Year Renewal of the Laws of the Circle of Law, the Representative Twin Chiefs and the Presiding Twin Chiefs also were rechosen every four years by the community. This revoting for the Chiefs of the Circle of Law usually happened one year before The Time of the Great Renewal.

"One of the many elements borrowed from the descendants of some of these powerful Chiefs by the early European settlers when they built their version of Democracy, and which exists in the United States yet today, is this tradition of voting for the Presiding Chiefs of the Law-making assembly every four years.

"An important question must now be asked. Why was the time span of four years chosen?

"As has already been said, the Circle of Law was based on the Ancient Science and Life Understanding of the Medicine Wheel. The Chiefs of this ancient discipline studied the Natural laws of their Earth and their Universe for thousands of years and honored those laws with deep respect. As the human children of Existence, they wanted their laws to reflect the balance and harmony of the Natural Laws of their Living Universe, and especially their Mother Earth. The number Four was chosen because these Chiefs respected the great design and language of their Earth.

"As an example: the Earth and Sun, moving and dancing together through Space, create the Four Seasons of every year—Spring, Summer, Autumn, and Winter. These Four distinct and powerful times of year are known as The Medicine Wheel of the Seasons, and they govern the Birth, Growing, Fruiting, and Death-Dreaming Cycles of all Life on Earth. The Four Seasons are not a belief, not a religious or political view, and were not human created or human dependent. The Four Seasons are the Language and Fact of Life on Earth.

"The Earth also gave us humans the way to measure and know where we stand, and in what direction all other things exist around us, on her wondrous Sphere of Life. The Powers of the Four Directions—East, West, South, and North—held great meaning for the Zero Chiefs.

"Remembering the First Numbers of the Sacred Earth Count, Our Creatress and Creator, known as the Sacred Zero, gave birth to the First Circle of Life. The First Circle is One–the Sun–East, Two–the Earth–West, Three–the Plants–South, and Four–the Animals–North. These profoundly important Four Powers of Life together gave rise to Five–the Humans existing in the Center of the Medicine Wheel.

"Another example of the importance of the number Four to Life on Earth is the fact of the Four Sacred Elements of Life: There are Fire, Earth (Substance), Water, and Air. These Four Elements are known as The Medicine Wheel of the Elements to our Chiefs. These Elements create the primary alphabet that Life combines in trillions of unique and brilliant ways to create the miraculous Design of all living beings born by our Earth.

"Our Chiefs say that we humans were born from the Design of our Living Universe, and specifically from our grandparents of these four Great Directions. They have given us the Four Powers of being a Human. They have given us Spirit, Body, Emotion, and Mind. We, Human beings, bring with us into Life our own Self Essence, our fifth element. Our Zero Chiefs placed the Self of every human born in the Center of the Powers of the Four Great Directions and taught that each Human is Responsible for Choosing how to Balance these powers within the Self and within the world.

"The Renewal of the Laws of the people, and the Renewal of the Representative Twin Chiefs and Presiding Twin Chiefs of the Circle of Law, every *Four* years had profound and far-reaching meaning to the ancient peoples of the Americas."

The Individual and the Circle of Law

"The Zero Chiefs knew that when a person or a People internalized kings or queens, eventually those people believed themselves to be less than their rulers. When this happened, then the Democracy of the Mind died and there were only rulers, slaves, and followers.

"The Circle of Law of the community was seen as The Being of the Wheel, an individual. Also, the separate individuals within the Tribe saw themselves as individual Circles of Law.

"The Zero Chiefs taught the people to desire a Democracy within their own minds. Young women and men were taught to Democratize their thinking so they could function in Life in a Balanced way. Humans who possess a Democracy of Mind form a true reflection of the Circle of Law. Such people possess the most powerful of all tools known to humankind—Self Leadership, Self Care, Self Decision, and Self Responsibility."

On the final morning of Liberty's Ceremony, Estcheemah, Liberty, and Lightningbolt were interrupted by the arrival of a group of people.

Ten strangers suddenly showing up at a Ceremonial Circle can be complicated. But Estcheemah simply took it in her stride and greeted the people.

"We are looking for Red Fox Woman," the man leading the group announced. His accent told Estcheemah that he was from the people of northern Saskatchewan.

"I am Red Fox Woman." Estcheemah smiled and reached for the man's outstretched hand and shook it. "And that is young Snow Arrow behind you."

A pretty Cree woman ran forward and hugged the old Medicine Woman. "Estcheemah, I came too. You remembered me! We brought blankets and gifts to you from a lot of people!"

"The Honoring Group," as the visitors called themselves, helped to expand the camp to accommodate everyone, then settled down for their Give-Away.

Moon Bear, the oldest of the women present, gave Estcheemah five blankets and a shawl. "You have done so much for all of us over these many years," she explained, "we would like to share our appreciation. Our White Geese Singers will sing for two full days for you. And two large soups will be made in your honor, and people will be invited to hear of your stories. We also bring you twen-

ty pairs of moccasins and eight pairs of winter gloves."

"The Zero Chiefs continue to live. At least one does, anyway," Raven Canoe announced to everyone as they shared a feast. He laughed, showing his delight. "And what a woman she is! I am sure that we all have our questions and so we will take our time asking and listening. We will begin with our youngest, Snow Arrow."

"Yes, I have a question," the young woman said. "After so many years of secrecy, why is it you are telling Breeds about the Wheels? Do you mind answering this question, Estcheemah?"

"Breeds like you," said Estcheemah, her eyes sparkling. "Yes, there are many young people, such as yourself, who are of the Metis people.

"In our past, Snow Arrow, we Zero Chiefs have been attacked on every level possible by people who did not understand or appreciate what we had to say. These attacks have come from both the white community and the Indian communities.

"Because of the fanatics, we Zero Chiefs have been forced to live in secret and to teach in secret for a very long time. Our secrecy has caused an even greater problem in that we have created an elite. This has not been good and has harmed our position even further.

"An elite, even if it is knowledgeable, can become a power that serves only its own purposes instead of being a source of knowledge for everyone.

We did not want that to happen with our knowledge. This is the reason that Breeds and people of other lands and races are now being included in our Circle. It is our knowing that the Medicine Wheels have the power to transform humanity. The Medicine Wheels do not depend upon tribal governments, beliefs, or races.

"Now what about our Reservations, and why have we Zero Chiefs taken our knowledge beyond our Reservations? This must also be answered.

"Tribalism, at one time, meant something for its people. But in our modern world of North, Central, and South America, the old tribal ways have disintegrated. Tribal secrets are now owned by the anthropologists and not the Tribes.

"North America's Indian people have become Canadians or Americans, and this is good. But it means that the Tribe comes second. Christianized Indians identify themselves first with their religion before they acknowledge their tribal affiliations. Because of this, the concept of what a Tribe should be has been stretched beyond its breaking point. The consequence of this is that tribalism and its secrets are no longer of any importance, and are viewed to be archaic by most Reservation youth.

"Therefore it is time for the teachings of the Zero Chiefs to be given to all the peoples of the world. In this way we ensure that our youth on every Reservation and in every city of America will hear of the Medicine Wheels.

"We have tried to teach our Medicine Wheels on the Reservations, but we have met with stiff resistance. This is mostly because the teachings were seen as 'foreign' by the people who represented the status quo.

"*Foreign* does not mean what you might assume. We teach nothing that is foreign. We teach about Sacred Mother Earth and Life. We teach about the human Self.

"What is seen as foreign are racial arguments. There is tremendous jealousy and racial bigotry among the Reservations of America, Mexico, and Canada. Indians on separate Reservations have been taught to believe that ancient tribal teachings were specific to only one Tribe—theirs. But for many hundreds of years the Flower Soldiers have moved among the many Tribes of North America, Central America, and South America.

"Now, we Zero Chiefs have decided to continue to share the information of the Medicine Wheels with all of America's Indians in a new way. We decided together to teach the Breeds, and to share with every human who seeks knowing."

"But what if the secrets are not honored and cherished?" Moon Bear asked. "We have loved them for a long time."

"I will speak to you in the Tongue of the Flowers," Estcheemah answered, "because there is no other way for us Flower Soldiers to answer that question. Our Tongue of Flowers is our poetry.

"We Flower Soldiers have gathered around the Sacred Light known as Earth's light, and we have cared for the Medicines.

"We say that our Mother Land, our Mother Earth, is called Liberty.

"We speak of every challenge. We Zero Chiefs speak of the human confrontation with the Self.

"The Flower Soldier is the human who points to the Self and to the Truth and Presence of Mother Life.

"The Flower Soldier is a slave to nothing. Our pledge is to battle all slavery and fight for human Self freedom.

"All things are perfect within Time, despite what humans may believe. Life is Experience, and Life teaches all humans within Time.

"We humans have created our human condition and we must learn about what we have created. We Flower Soldiers have been called 'The Thorns of the Rose' because we point out the pain as well as the Beauty of Life.

"Our Sword is our Self Authority and Self Responsibility. What we Create for our Self is what our Ceremonies of Life will Be.

"We Flower Soldiers will continue to Speak in Flowers, telling Humans to Honor their Existence."

The winter months went by very quickly for Liberty. She worked hard and studied all that Estcheemah taught her. While there were many days of rain, there were also days filled with sunshine.

Lightningbolt was very happy as he watched Liberty bloom within her learning. They laughed together and strolled along the beaches, and discovered a tenderness between them that neither had ever known.

Silver skies, the gentle rain, the ever-present ocean, quiet sea mists, and the powerful greens and blues of the land—all became one for Liberty. There were times she imagined she walked in a cloud world. She and Lightningbolt went boating every day they could, despite the rain, and explored islands like eager children looking for a secret treasure.

While they played, they also reported to each other. Much of the play centered around their continued learning of the Medicine Wheels and improving Liberty's skills of recognizing healing plants. She also became a good shot with a rifle and pistol.

The Medicine Wheels were part of their conversations day and night. Estcheemah was very old, time was precious, and they had no time to pretend. There was much to learn, and learn they did.

In the early Spring, Lightningbolt bought a typewriter and began to write. Each morning he would get up early and write until midday. He began by writing short teaching stories or people's true life stories that he had heard on the Reservation from the time he was a little boy.

Liberty fed the animals each morning and watched Lightningbolt become more involved in his writing. Sometimes she would find him out on long walks alone, telling stories into an old tape deck that Estcheemah had given him. Then he would play back the stories and write them down. A new spark had ignited in Lightningbolt's mind and heart. Liberty could sense his change and wondered about it.

Liberty began to feel alone. It had nothing to do directly with Lightningbolt; she loved him very much. But she began to realize that she could not substitute loving him for deciding what she was going to do with the precious information she was learning from Estcheemah. Estcheemah had to sew beautiful coats to make the money she needed to be financially independent. The powerful Zero Chief never took money for Ceremonies or teach-

ings, and so she had to work to pay for the time she needed to do her real work, Teaching and Healing.

How odd, Liberty thought to herself. Estcheemah had told Liberty of a time when powerful women Healers and Teachers had been supported by their communities so they could use all their time to teach and work. But this had not been true for many years among the Medicine Teachers of America . . . especially the women. What Estcheemah taught did not conform to the beliefs of the culture that surrounded her, and so she had to survive and teach on her own.

Liberty wondered if she was strong enough to survive and truly be a Flower Soldier. How many people would accept a white Breed woman, not from the Reservation, teaching of the Medicine Wheels and Sacred Mother Earth? Liberty began to worry about her future. Estcheemah was getting older, and Lightningbolt had finally begun to find his own Self direction. But what was hers? She would have to find a way of caring for herself to support her work as a young Medicine Woman. This realization threw Liberty into more conflict within herself and she became moody and sad. She did not know why, but the feeling would not go away.

Liberty did not speak openly to Estcheemah about her new worries. She would not admit to herself that she had them. However, Lightningbolt noticed the sudden distance between him and his best friend. She was quiet and withdrawn, and if he teased her, trying to get her to talk with him, she would get angry. Lightningbolt immediately went to Estcheemah to ask her what to do.

The old Medicine Woman had sensed the change in her female apprentice. She had been waiting for this to happen, and was ready. Estcheemah and Lightningbolt began the preparations for Liberty's Spring Ceremony.

On a beautiful clear morning in May, Estcheemah instructed Lightningbolt to help Liberty set up her new Ceremony Circle. Lightningbolt set up her tent and did his best to help Liberty make a beautiful camp. Liberty was excited about her opportunity and tried to be kind with Lightningbolt.

It was early afternoon when Estcheemah came walking up the trail leading Brunhilde. The little burro was piled high with things for their camp.

"Your camp looks good, Liberty." Estcheemah smiled, puffing a little as she sat down in a lawn chair that Liberty made ready for her. "I thought I would save you a trip so I brought up your blankets, pillow, and sleeping bag."

Estcheemah was given coffee, and Liberty and Lightningbolt returned to their work of finishing the camp. An hour later they all sat down together to talk.

"This gracious Cedar Forest is a wonderful place in which to experience your Ceremony, Liberty." Estcheemah smiled, looking around. "Now that your Presence and Circle are prepared, you must turn your attentions to your Self. For the rest of the day I want you to walk in a large circle around your camp. Take your time and introduce yourself to the trees of this grand forest. There is much to discover. Lightningbolt will remain as a guard, and I will return this evening."

Liberty wandered around. As she began her ad-

432

venture alone, she became confused by the immensity of the forest, but she soon resolved to go farther.

As her exploration broadened, she became intrigued by the primal green world of cedars that seemed to go on forever.

While her movements were conservative, her heart was not. She found even more beauty as she searched ever deeper into the labyrinth of the great trees.

A half hour later, Liberty's hunt ended at a small but mysterious little meadow. She imagined that the gigantic cedars that encircled the meadow were protecting a secret from all intruders. Would these trees allow her entry?

Cautiously she walked to the center of her emerald world and suddenly felt that she was standing either in a graveyard or on a ceremonial ground.

Great and beautiful carved Haida totems sud-

denly revealed their hiding places to her. Surprised at her find, she studied the carvings and could make out that most of the images were of turtles.

She turned in the Circle of Care and marveled at all the exquisite carvings that lay hidden among the trees. The massive totems were so much a part of the forest that it was difficult for Liberty to say where shadow and light met with the carved symbols.

The shadows were very important to each carefully created Haida figure. As the sea breezes gently moved the cedars, the light of the Sun illumined the figures and teased the eye with movement.

Whales seemed to appear, then disappear, along the length of a fallen log. Then, just as her eyes became adjusted to the image, another would appear. This time it was an eagle or a salmon! Now she could see the carved images of ravens, bears, and sea gulls that had been hidden among the trees. As the light shifted, simple logs would become totems, then change into dolphins or swimming fish.

Liberty was a fine sculptress who had never known what to create with her hands. The sight of this sculpted Life and Beauty shocked her senses and forced her to confront every conservative work she had ever created. She sat down on the ground and wept. Never in her life had she encountered such phenomenal power.

She had made a simple living in Los Angeles sculpting miniatures. She hated the work because she was paid to carve only the cuties and sweeties the public wanted to buy. Bitter and disappointed, she had decided to stop sculpting when she left L.A.

She stood and wiped her eyes abruptly, horrified at her indulgence. Could she try again? Could she sculpt the beautiful, or would she fail?

"Are these symbols of Death?" she asked out

loud to the trees. "Or are these symbols of Life? Why do they make me cry?"

The seemingly abandoned carvings lay all around Liberty like her fallen dreams.

The walk back to camp was lonely and became a long, sorrowful journey for Liberty. She felt her disappointment and anger grow with every step she took.

Estcheemah was sitting quietly at the campfire, waiting. "You look as though you just killed your pet cat, Liberty. Here, sit down and enjoy your fire. Would you like some tea or coffee?"

"I've been walking around feeling dreadful," Liberty told her angrily. "Why were those totems destroyed? Why were they thrown down to rot? Doesn't anyone give a damn?"

"Yes. I do," Estcheemah answered. "Those Medicine Poles you saw were left by the families who once lived in these forests. They were Ceremo-

435

nial Medicine Shields that told of the Medicines of the families. Did their sadness and beauty make you look at your own sorrow?"

Liberty didn't answer. She stared into the fire and fought to not cry or show her deep anger.

"Or possibly, they have made you feel your anger?" said Estcheemah, encouragingly. "If you speak of it, you will understand why I have you in Ceremony."

"Well," Liberty answered, showing her anger, "Mother Earth isn't all peaches and cream, Estcheemah. There are a lot of ugly rotten things and there are mean things."

"Yes, Liberty, I understand," Estcheemah answered, looking up into Liberty's eyes. "Tractors crush children as easily as they plow our fields. Our people make machines of war that kill.

"The wolves surround the caribou and they die. The torrent of water boils through the chasm, ripping the flimsy boat apart, and the lovers drown.

"Yes, disease can corrupt the body and disfigure the young woman and young man. There is the toothache, the boil that brings sudden pain. Yes, there is suffering. Most humans try to escape suffering or try to ignore it. I'm glad you asked the question; it shows that you are maturing.

"It is fearful to see what the ravages of disease can do to the human body. The heart cringes when we see an animal torn apart by another animal.

"But are these the things that humans fear? The answer to that, Liberty, is no. Humans fear what other humans can do to them. Many humans die of human brutalities, human stupidity, and human neglect.

"Natural catastrophes are not what humans fear; catastrophic earthquakes kill mere thousands.

But human-made catastrophes, like our world wars, kill tens of millions.

"Old age and human incompetence kill everybody. It is only a matter of time before either old age kills us, or human stupidity does.

"Liberty, what is missing on a grand scale, the world around, is thought. People want to believe the ugly and ignore the beautiful.

"Beauty is not a thing wanted or accepted by most people. The reason for this is that humans have to answer to Beauty. Beauty demands things from humans, and humans fear and hate that. People can ignore their own ugliness; that is easy to do. But who questions what is harsh and ugly in our culture?

"Beauty demands that humans be present with Life.

"People want to escape Life and pretend. You fear much more what you imagine than what exists, Liberty.

"Yes, it is a reality. Mother Earth can kill you. Why not? She also birthed you.

"Life demands that all of us confront our attitudes. She forces us to live with ourselves. For many people this is a hard command.

"You cannot avoid yourself and what you are. Life makes you face your Self, your decisions, your circumstances, and your Death. Do not avoid your Life in trying to avoid your Death.

"You are conservative in everything you do because you fear failure and fear your Self, Liberty.

"Challenge your Self with meeting your Self and Beauty. Sometimes Beauty disguises Herself as Ugliness to bring appreciation to the human consciousness.

"Beauty battles within the human imagination.

"It is Beauty that hurls the spear against imagined pains and fears.

"Beauty is the ever questioning.

"Beauty is accepting Self Responsibility.

"Beauty is the Courage to fight back.

436

"Beauty is facing Life and facing Death.

"Ceremony is a time to listen to Life, and it is a time to listen to the Self." Estcheemah was smiling. "Life and Presence are Ceremony. Both will reflect your every thought and feeling. Do not allow your emotions to destroy what you can learn in this Ceremony.

"Creation is very articulate, speaking of our Presence minute by minute. You will have to learn to Listen if you want to Hear what Creation has to say, because Creation speaks in the moment. Mother Life knows what is going on in the moment. Creation speaks a modern language and always interacts with us in the moment. Life needs no interpreters. We are our answer, and we are our challenge.

"You will have to learn more words, more ways of describing your world to your Self. This is called education. You are here in this Ceremony to educate your Self about Life and your Self.

"Life knows who you are, but you do not know who Life is. Life knows how to speak to you, but you are handicapped by a language that does not describe your present.

"People think that they can muscle Goddess and God around with their emotions. They try to make Goddess and God feel sorry for them." The old teacher laughed. "In the past, I even tried it. But this is preposterous. No one can pretend with Life, trick Life, out think Life, or push Life around with emotions. You will learn this understanding is more than just feeling. Life does not feel sorrow for anyone born into Life or anyone leaving Life."

Estcheemah stood up to leave. "Do everything in your power to be present here, Liberty." She took Liberty's hand into hers and looked deep into the eyes of her apprentice. "You are no longer a pretender, Liberty. You are a young woman who has decided to learn how to Heal the broken Minds, Emotions, Bodies, and Spirits of people. To do that, you will have to work very hard.

"There is no role you need to act out here while you are praying to Creation and Sacred Life. Try with all your heart to be where you are, not where you fantasize you are in your mind.

"Be very attentive to your thoughts and feelings, because in that way you will learn to have compassion for others.

"Be strong."

"I promise I will," Liberty answered, showing her determination.

Estcheemah turned to Lightningbolt. "It is time for you to tell her about your sorrow and how you learned to battle it, Lightningbolt. Now, I will go. I will return in the morning." Estcheemah gathered her things, and Lightningbolt escorted her to Brunhilde. The powerful Zero Chief rode away in the bright moonlit night, back down the hill.

Lightningbolt returned to the fire. Liberty was adding wood to brighten the Circle. She sat down quietly, ready to listen.

For a few moments he was silent. Then he began.

"I walked into Estcheemah's kitchen one morning and greeted her with a big hello.

" 'Hello, killer,' she said. 'How does it feel to count coup?'

"I teased back, asking her who she wanted me to scalp."

" 'Yourself,' she answered, and began to sew on a coat. 'I mean your "friend," morphine.'

"I had thought that my secret was well hidden. I was an idiot to believe that, of course, but I tried. What can be hidden from Estcheemah?

"All right, what had happened was that over a period of a year I had become very dependent on morphine.

"Why had I used drugs? Well, it was my first big answer to my oldest question. I began to swallow the little white pills because they ended a deep sorrow I had. I could not remember not being filled with sorrow; it had always been with me.

"Describing my sorrow is almost beyond my power of words. First, there was no answer to my awful sorrow—it was just simply there, almost all the time. My sorrow was profound and deep—subtle, yet brutally present. My sorrow would collect suddenly in a sky of blue, mystify me, and darken into thunderclouds of despair. Then, it would mysteriously disappear as quickly as it had appeared.

"I had been born with the strength to pretend. And pretend I did, with absolute ease. To most people I appeared to be happy-go-lucky. But I was not happy. Behind the pretense I felt a sorrow of immense proportions. Sorrow, like anything else in Life, can be a teacher or a source of Self destruction. Because of Estcheemah, it became my teacher.

"I can detect sorrow in another human at a great distance. It is almost impossible to fool me if a person has sorrow.

"Sorrow is not sadness—it's closer to what is understood as melancholy. But it isn't quite melancholy either, for melancholy is sadness without knowing.

"Sorrow is a knowing. For example, it is a deep and profound knowing that Life is very, very short.

438

"People who are sad are seldom if ever conscious of another's feelings. Sad people become angry but never show it. Sad people are different from melancholy humans.

"Melancholy people never think of themselves. As a result, they make perfect victims and perfect servants. They have empathy and sympathy, but lack a true Self.

"Humans who know true sorrow blow up, but never in violence. Sad people think of no one else, only what or who they should be. Melancholy people never know themselves.

"People of sorrow, like I was, can become cold-blooded, seeing most of humanity's pursuits as absolute madness. Silly people bore a person of sorrow. Boredom in any form, any endless repetition, becomes the enemy of the human of sorrow.

"I was constantly bored. Christmas, Easter, the Fourth of July, Thanksgiving, birthdays—any repeating boredom such as these became a terrible burden for me.

"The university was no challenge. It became boring too because I was never intent upon the degree.

"After a bout with appendicitis I met the little white pill. And, suddenly, I felt no more sorrow. I didn't feel much of anything else either, but I didn't care.

"The sorrow disappeared when I ate the pill. We called it the White Bullet. It was amazing to not be filled with sorrow! The White Bullet was the killer of torment and sorrow! I felt 'normal' when I had my pill. With the pain of the sorrow gone I believed I was feeling as normal people would feel.

"At first I needed only a few pills. But then I had to have more. My morphine friends were a university professor, a medical doctor, a lawyer, a businessman, a nurse, and a rancher. None of the group was very old, except for the professor and the doctor. Our little group had a name—we called ourselves the Buddha Heads. We thought the name was funny. The name also gave us a cover when we needed to communicate.

"My friends used morphine for different reasons than I did, but I didn't care. Caring meant nothing to any of us. Care is what we did not have while we were eating the White Bullet.

"When I was stoned on morphine, I would go for walks and think, or try to think. Nothing I could think about or imagine brought on my sorrow; I was amazed. The lawyer and the professor also liked to walk, and sometimes I walked with them. Montana has millions of acres to walk in—we walked and walked and talked.

"In the eleventh month of taking morphine, I began to find myself in very strange places and wonder how I got there. I would wake up in my pickup, or be awakened on some lonely stretch of a river or stream—alone.

"I would immediately panic, then slowly begin to remember that I had gone for a walk. My walks were euphoric—times of release from feeling anything and everything.

"Estcheemah taught me how to feel again. After a talk about Death that I had with Estcheemah, I never used morphine again.

"I learned that my sorrow was my knowing—a knowing I did not want to know. I knew Death, but I did not know Mother Life. I knew how to sorrow, but I did not know how to feel. I had been suicidal and never knew it—this was also one of my sorrows."

"Is there any real end to sorrow?" Liberty asked.

"When I asked Estcheemah that question she said, 'It is better for you to ask about Self knowing.' You know, Liberty—being here, alive, learning about your Self and Life, doing something to better your world, that's the way to go. It can hurt sometimes, but it can also make us smile.

"Estcheemah told me to tell you to take the remainder of this evening to think about your own

emotions, and how they affect you and your discernment."

"I will," Liberty said, looking into her fire. "Thank you, Lightningbolt, for being honest with me." Lightningbolt nodded and walked to his tent to take his guard position, leaving Liberty alone to think for the rest of the night.

The songs of hundreds of birds filled the ancient forest, greeting Liberty and Lightningbolt the next morning. Liberty prepared the coffee, while Lightningbolt worked privately, drawing something on a large piece of paper. Liberty was curious but knew better than to ask. She did not want to ruin her learning, and she knew that Lightningbolt was being instructed by Estcheemah.

When the beautiful old Medicine Chief rode up on Brunhilde she appeared so bright, so much a part of the Forest's natural Circle, it surprised Liberty. She recognized that the same clean and powerful feeling of the Trees also emanated from her teacher, and she began to wonder about it. What power was this?

The old woman dismounted and walked over to Liberty with immense dignity. She sat down and Liberty offered her a cup of coffee. Then Estcheemah turned to Lightningbolt. "You will help me teach Liberty in this Ceremony by working with her physically and being her hunting guide.

"As you know, Liberty, having studied the Circle of Law, it is time for you to develop some of your own personal powers. Your greatest need is to develop the minds of both the warrioress and the huntress within you. This is true for many of your sisters on Earth.

"It is important for you to create a new image of yourself within your own mind. One that is more reasonable and true than the weak and victimized images given to you by your culture. When you are in conflict, emotional indulgence does not answer your confrontation. In the culture you were born into, girls are said to be 'emotional' and boys 'intellectual.' This is so ridiculous. If it wasn't dangerous it would make me laugh until I cried. If men were so naturally intelligent, then our world would not be in such trouble. Right, Lightningbolt?"

"Absolutely!" he agreed.

"Well, it is also ridiculous to handicap women to the point of absurdity by rewarding them for their emotions and punishing them when they think. As a simple example, when they are young many girls get lavish attention when they cry. Suddenly they are taken care of. But when boys reach a certain age, they are ridiculed when they are emotionally indulgent. Now, crying is not necessarily weak, I am not saying this. But, I am saying that if tears or any other emotions are used to get atten-

tion and manipulate others, then they will become a trap that enslaves the person who uses them. Both men and women do this, but I am focusing on females today, Liberty.

"The females who do this begin to believe that they can manipulate the world with their emotions. Later in life they discover that this is a lie, but usually it is too late. Most young women are taught to not trust or educate their minds. They have been denied the opportunity of being taught to think and act under pressure. They have been denied the opportunity to be taught and trained as leaders in their world. Women are as capable as men of being intelligent, thinking human beings. Women are equally 'heroic' and intelligent under pressure, if they are allowed to be, and are taught to be. Culture is what has made the difference, shaped by bigoted religious and social propaganda—not anything natural or real.

"You, Liberty, will develop the power to think under pressure. You will do this by learning as a Warrioress and Huntress. You have practiced with a rifle and pistol. But now you must also change the way you think about your Self. You will allow the natural power of the Warrioress within you to develop her own thinking.

"You have been moping around for two months, indulging in the Outer Ring of your Self. From now on I will call this emotional young being within you Molly Mope."

"You're right!" Liberty said, suddenly flabbergasted. "I can't believe it. I've been feeling terrible for quite a while now. But I never really put it together with what you have been teaching me about my Outer Ring. I've been indulging myself, and feeling incompetent and afraid. I don't want to do this anymore. I will fight within myself to be the Warrioress, Estcheemah. I do want to be a powerful woman and teacher. I am sick of being afraid to fail. I've got to fight my stupid . . ."

"Attitudes," Estcheemah coaxed.

"Yes, my indulgent attitudes belong to the young girl I was, not the woman and Warrioress that I am becoming. And I am not going to be afraid to be open with you," she said, looking at Lightningbolt. "You're a few years ahead of me in your training, and that's fine. When you started writing I realized my true situation. I must become independent and decide what I will do with my information and my Life."

"Finally, you speak of this," Estcheemah added. "It's about time. Yes, my dear, you must make the decisions of a woman, not a girl. You will discover as a Medicine Person that there are things that Lightningbolt will do better, but also that there will be a great many things you will be much more sensitive to and do much better. Will you both survive as independent, Self-Responsible Flower Soldiers, and learn to work together in a balanced way? This is a challenge that will face you both daily.

"Yet, to do this, Liberty, you will have to be powerful and balanced within your Self. And this is where we will focus now. After I have gone back down the trail, you will begin the next part of your Ceremony. However, I have a presentation to make to you first."

She shook both Liberty's and Lightningbolt's hands. As she touched them, they could feel a deep sense of affinity fill their hearts. They stood quiet and respectful as Estcheemah prepared what she called her "place of sitting." She always readied her place by positioning her Medicine Pipe on her Sun Dance Blanket. As they watched her sit and take her Healing Fan from its bundle, they wondered if they would ever be as strong as their teacher? As dignified?

Estcheemah signaled Lightningbolt to begin the presentation.

Lightningbolt straightened his back and turned to Liberty. Now it was his turn to be present with someone while she found her heart. He was going to be the best of soldiers.

"Estcheemah told me that your Ceremony began at your birth," he announced, beaming his pleasure. "She said that this Ceremony will be called your Bow Circle."

Estcheemah unrolled a black shawl; within it was an exquisitely hand-crafted bow. She handed the bow to Lightningbolt. He walked to a young cedar, four steps away, and hung the bow on the loops that Estcheemah had tied there. Then he turned and faced Liberty.

"Your teacher bought this bow for you, Liberty. She said that it is appropriate at some point during your Ceremony, that you name your own weapon."

"It's incredible!" said Liberty, overcome with awe. "May I touch it, Estcheemah?"

"Of course." Estcheemah laughed. "It is yours."

Liberty went to the bow and lifted it in her hands. She touched it, feeling its smoothness and strength.

"I'm amazed. It's breathtaking," she said as she turned the bow in her hands. "I never thought I would ever have a bow."

"It is called a recurved bow, Liberty, because the bow will always return to this form, no matter how many times it is pulled and put under stress." Estcheemah sounded as though she were carefully weighing her words. "It is called 'Huntress-Moon-Bow' in my language, but this is not her name—it is her description.

"I have also purchased fifty arrows for you, and a quiver to accompany your weapon. In my language, *arrow* is a complicated word that goes far back into time; it is *Mah-hah-vay-nah*. The word would be called a compound word by linguists. In its fullness it says, 'To fly as the tongue of Death.'

" 'Death speaks as the arrow' is another way of understanding the word. You see, Liberty, it is Death who speaks when the arrow touches. What the arrow touches will die. The arrow comes from

the hands of the People. The People must eat, and so they are the hunters.

"I can see your joy," Estcheemah said with affection. "Yet, in this moment, how you see the question of your weapon is the greater gift, and this can only come from you.

"How the Healer and the Warrioress balance one another within you far outweighs the surprise of your receiving your bow and arrows. How you will understand the balance you can bring to the community, as a Medicine Woman and Warrioress, will loom large in your heart and mind over the years.

"In this moment, as you receive your bow and your sharp arrows, you feel the joy of receiving. But this occasion also challenges your heart. You are receiving a weapon. Every office that people hold is a

responsibility, and can become a gruesome weapon when used against the People.

"When you accept a weapon, an office, or an appointment, you also accept the awesome challenge of how the weapon or appointment questions your very existence.

"How many mothers realize that their home is a Sacred Position, a true honor—that it can be a powerful weapon that can be used to teach and heal, or used to destroy, their children? How many mothers guide their children to be independent people? Those who spoil their children and teach them a myth will destroy them.

"Every doctor, woman or man, and all Healers know that their scalpel, knowledge, and position are weapons. Those weapons can kill and they can heal.

"The People are also a weapon that you accept when you become a Warrioress and Priestess. How you will use that weapon and respect the weapon is a question that will challenge your very being.

"What are your responsibilities? There is a saying that has come from our Law Dogs, Liberty, and their words are important for the Priestess-Warrioress.

" 'In the Shadows, at the base of the mountain, there are those who wait to kill.' These are their words of warning. They mean that those who wait to kill are not huntresses or hunters, but are the killers of humans. 'At the base of the mountain' means that there are people in the structure—the Pyramid of Power—who wait to kill. How the people within the community act as a balance with one another is a question for the Warrioress-Healer.

"We can be embarrassed easily. But the criminal and murderer cannot be embarrassed. It does not embarrass a criminal to kill or to maim another human. You would be incredibly embarrassed if you should be forced to kill a human.

"You must realize that to be embarrassed because of knowledge is not the same as being embarrassed because of being ignorant. The ignorant are embarrassed because they fear being discovered. The knowledgeable are embarrassed because they know that Creation has Intelligence and Knowing so much greater than their own.

"When you possess this kind of knowledge, you know that you are directly responsible for your every act while you live. The criminal and murderer cannot be embarrassed because they have thrown away all thoughts of significance and Self.

"Greatness, for anyone born, is the Why of existence. Everything you are and everything you do is a question from Creation of who and what you are. Be a human of power and greatness. Be always Self responsible. You are learning to be the Warrioress and the Priestess.

"You will think of this with each arrow you shoot. Be the person of honesty and Healing—Heal your Self.

"This will take much time. I will be with you in my every waking hour."

Liberty practiced with her bow until she tired at noon. When she returned to her camp, Lightningbolt was waiting.

"Today we present ourselves with learning," Lightningbolt challenged her. "Estcheemah said that your awareness and intelligence are to be tested today." He then unrolled a large drawing of a Medicine Wheel on the ground in front of Liberty.

"I wondered what you were drawing this morning," she said. "It's beautiful."

THE PERSPECTIVE WHEEL

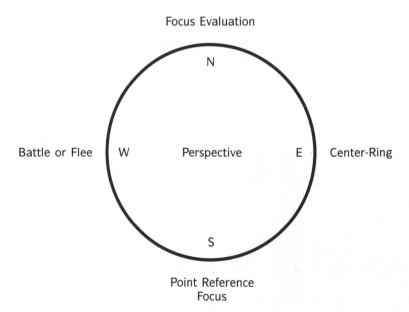

Focus Evaluation

N

Battle or Flee   W   Perspective   E   Center-Ring

S

Point Reference
Focus

"In the South," Lightningbolt said, "is written 'Point Reference Focus.'

"While Flower Soldiers live and explore, they are always attentive to both their physical world and their inward world. This is the meaning of 'Point Reference Focus.'

"When you suddenly hear something or see unanticipated movement, it will capture your attention. Your attention is focused and you are alerted. This is Point Reference Focus. Every Point Reference Focus also directly affects your emotions. Because of this, it is South on the Medicine Wheel, the place of emotions.

"Humans naturally react to any sudden sound or movement—the Point Reference Focus. They either desire to do battle or to flee from the source of attack. All humans who are not trained in the art of combat will try to hide or flee, to escape. The trained Flower Soldier will always choose battle.

"Because the soldier chooses battle, there is a demand upon the will. The physical body is alerted and ready to fight. The choice of 'Battle-or-Flee' is found in the West on the Medicine Wheel. In the West is the body.

"In the North of the Wheel, the place of the human mind, is 'Focus Evaluation.' This is the ability of trained Flower Soldiers to evaluate all incoming information, and all information pertinent to the situation or circumstance.

"Focus Evaluation tells you what exists, what weapons the danger may possess, how many dangers or enemies might exist, how strong the enemy or danger may be, how old or young the enemy may be, and what the danger actually looks like.

"I will speak of the element of the East, but first let me tell you of your 'True Center.'

"In the True Center of the Medicine Wheel is the Self. You are in the process of learning of your Self. You are the Self, the True Center. The Center Self perceives every action.

"When you bring all the powers of each direction into the Self, then you are centered in the Self—meaning that you possess true perspective. You are then able to discern what is happening with the Self and your surroundings.

"Self perspective clarifies the true situation. This is why 'Perspective' is at the center of this Medicine Wheel—the place of the Self.

"You are alerted to the enemy—Point Reference Focus.

"You have chosen to battle and not run away.

"You have evaluated what exists—the Focus.

"Now you must determine or estimate the distance between you, the Center Self, and the enemy. This is called the 'Center Ring.' The Center Ring exists in the East on the Medicine Wheel.

"How far away the enemy is and how fast the enemy can move is determined by the Center Ring—the East.

"The power of this Wheel will be yours when you apply the teaching to your inner world. Always search within for Self power, for it is the unfolding of the Blossom of inner Discipline that brings the Flower Soldier into true Medicine Power."

"Amazing," said Liberty. "But it sure is cerebral."

"Would you get me a little more water for our coffeepot?" Lightningbolt asked, turning away from her. "Sure," she answered, standing. "How much do you—"

Suddenly a very loud explosion boomed behind Liberty, sending her almost sprawling to the ground. She leaped to her feet and spun to see what had happened.

"It looks as though you decided to do battle instead of running away," said Lightningbolt. "I think the firecracker made the point."

"That was certainly not intellectual!" She laughed. "I see what you mean by 'Point Reference Focus'!"

"Get your bow," Lightningbolt told her, picking

up her bow case, "and let's go. Today you will hunt and try to kill a rabbit. The rabbits are wild, but they are not natural to this island. They were brought here to go wild. I have more arrows if you miss, and a few more firecrackers if you get cerebral on me."

"What are their natural enemies?" Liberty asked as they walked.

"Disease, old age, and dogs mostly. I suppose they have other enemies—maybe you?" He was smiling. "Have you ever thought of yourself as being the enemy of a pig? You eat pork. Can you imagine yourself as being the enemy of chickens, ducks, turkeys, sheep, and cows?"

"No, never," Liberty said, continuing to look around.

They hunted for nearly half an hour in silence. Liberty remained always ahead of Lightningbolt, ready if a rabbit should happen by.

Liberty stopped at a little stream while Lightningbolt adjusted the small trail pack he wore. "What's that watching you over there?" Lightningbolt pointed. "It's a good thing old Long Ears isn't hunting you . . . huh?"

Liberty stepped to the stream and got down on one knee to have a closer look. There the rabbit was—watching her. She couldn't believe she'd gotten that close and hadn't seen it.

Her hand trembled a little as she fitted an arrow into the bow. Her finger was just about to loose

the arrow when the rabbit hopped behind a small fern. It wriggled one ear and continued to sit, watching her.

"Is it armed?" Lightningbolt whispered, teasing her.

"Yeah," she answered while she again fitted her arrow into her bow.

"That is Center Ring." Lightningbolt grinned. "And the rabbit is definitely battle-ready instead of fleeing." Liberty pulled her bow and shot the arrow. The missile went wild, whizzed along the ground, hit a fern, and leaped up into a tree, where it stuck. The rabbit did not move.

Liberty shot four more arrows, but each time the rabbit seemed to move out of the way just before the arrow got there. Liberty was growing increasingly frustrated when the rabbit suddenly disappeared.

"Well, you're a real good shot with a rifle and pistol, Liberty," said Lightningbolt, encouragingly. "But, you're going to have to get to know your new weapon a little better before you understand how she reaches out into the world that surrounds you. This also is the study of Center Ring."

That night, Liberty thought about the new Medicine Wheel she had been given. Her fast from food began the next morning. Estcheemah had known it would take will and effort for Liberty to start understanding the rhythm and dance of her new weapon, and gave her two days to work with herself. Lightningbolt had set up two straw bales for Liberty's target practice. She shot her bow all day, speaking to herself and commanding her mind to be focused and attentive. She went over and over the new Medicine Wheel, thinking of each aspect of what had been shared with her.

By the second evening, Liberty began to understand, as her hunger increased, what Estcheemah had told her about the Sacred Give-Away of the plants and animals to all humans. No longer was the fact of her dependence on the plants and ani-

mals simply intellectual. Her hunger spoke to her, as did her bow and arrows—as did her will and Self thinking. Death and Life are forever inseparable, she could hear in her thinking. The plants and animals are sacred children of Mother Earth and give you your Life, her thinking continued with amazing clarity.

Why did so few people appreciate the Beauty of the Sacred Give-Away of the animals and plants? She realized how pretentious she had been about their gift of Life to her. Believing that food comes from money and supermarkets is madness, she scolded herself. Liberty vowed to never turn her back on the great giving of her Mother Earth again. She would start by appreciating and recognizing the Present of Life she was given every time she ate or drank from Mother Earth's wondrous Garden of Life and Death.

The next morning Lightningbolt woke Liberty at dawn. They spoke very little and immediately began to hunt. Liberty remained in the lead, looking around her. However, it wasn't until the Sun was high in the sky that she spotted a beautiful little furry creature with long brown ears underneath a large berry bush. Liberty bent down on one knee and fitted her arrow into her bow, taking aim. However, Liberty was nervous and her arm was shaking when she released the arrow. It flew five feet above the rabbit's head and disappeared. "Liberty, calm your Self. Be present," she commanded herself in a strong voice. Then she took a deep breath, fitting another arrow into her bow. This time, much more steadily, she took aim.

"If that rabbit meant the difference between Life and Death, you would be very clear about what you were about to do," Lightningbolt had cautioned her.

Liberty shot, and this time her arrow found its mark. The rabbit sprang into the air, pierced through the heart.

Liberty was dumbfounded. She was so amazed

by what she had done that she let the bow fall from her hand to the ground. She was flushed with excitement, but in the same breath she was feeling panic and fear.

"We usually trap them," said Estcheemah, suddenly behind her. "At this moment Death meets with you, Liberty. Allow your Heart to understand what you did, but also let your Mind think clearly about what you have done."

"I am surprised," said Liberty, struggling to not cry and to not laugh. She carefully picked up the dead rabbit and examined it. "You know, it's amazing how beautiful a rabbit is. I never looked at a dead one before. I've never even seen a chicken killed. It's incredible!"

"It is deep-reaching," Estcheemah said, sitting down on the ground beside her. "We women feel beyond this moment. We wonder and are amazed because laughter and excitement are present, and deep appreciation."

"I don't know what to say, Estcheemah." Liberty brightened, yet felt a tear slip from her eye. "This experience has helped me feel a lot of things deep within me that I have never known before."

"Yes, that is so true," Estcheemah said, rising. "Come, we will return to the camp. Lightningbolt took you in a large circle around our camp. We are very close. In fact, you have been so close I have watched you hunt most of the morning—just as the rabbits did."

Liberty was shocked. She looked in disbelief and saw that what Estcheemah was saying was true! She had imagined that she was twenty-five miles away from the camp.

"Yes, it is remarkable," Estcheemah explained while they walked to the camp. "You have come from a culture that does not understand the profound or the subtle. Can you imagine people having a rabbit-killing school? The teachers would have the students take a number and wait in long lines to kill hundreds of rabbits and never see that

they were in a slaughterhouse. War is something like that. Most humans have no imagination. Those same teachers would have people take numbers and stand in line to be born and to die."

"I'm not going to stand in any stupid line!" Liberty said with determination. "I'm going to do my own thinking, even if it kills me."

"Honor woman," Estcheemah challenged her, "or you will stand in a perpetual line that can only end in the grave."

The following morning, Liberty was determined. Arrows buzzed like angry bees, but not one rabbit was scratched.

She was running down a small draw after a rabbit when she heard Lightningbolt call to her.

"What?" she yelled back, feeling her exasperation after missing again.

"Don't run them to death!" he yelled back. "Hey, what's the matter? Why are you so tense?"

She walked to the top of a small hill and sat down to think and to have a look around. Far below her and half a mile away, the Ocean beamed with blue loveliness and grandeur.

"Where is your Focus Evaluation, Liberty?" she asked herself.

Lightningbolt climbed the hill and sat down beside her. "Estcheemah sent me to speak with you. To be a powerful huntress you must imagine the world of the being you are hunting. You are running around like mad. Slow down. Are you within the mind of the Big Rabbit Knowing? Where are your friends? Where do the animals drink and eat? What do they eat? What do they build and what do they hunt? What are their habits? Come on, Liberty, be with them. Are they night creatures or do they hunt during the day?

"These are the questions you must ask to be a good huntress. Quiet yourself. Enter the world of your animal family, the Big Rabbit Mind. Allow their Mind World to become part of you. Feel your time and the presence of your place. Move as they move, let your whiskers grow and touch the forest. Let Earth and Her Energies guide you. Be the Huntress, not the student. Listen to your Self and be present with Life.

"The Mother Earth knows humans must kill the plants and animals to live. She gives us the choice of how we will do this. How we approach Life and Death makes all the difference. Do we kill with appreciation for the gift of Life? Do we kill swiftly with care and balance? Are we clean and respectful, taking only what we need?

"Liberty, imagine within the presence of your lessons of Life. This is your forest. Your mind, your imagination, can be your Medicine Guide. This can be a higher, nobler part of your thinking, the Medicine Part of your Self. The forest will teach you what you need to know if you imagine with Her and listen."

Lightningbolt rose slowly and left, taking his time walking back down the hill. She watched him until he was out of sight, then slung her bow over her shoulder and began to hunt.

She walked for hours, imagining and then seeing the rabbits in her forest world. It was evening when she became more fully aware of the signs of their presence, and this excited her.

Liberty was crouching behind some cattail reeds at a small pond when she saw a beautiful white-and-black doe rabbit. The rabbit turned and stared directly at Liberty, motionless and proud, ears alert and eager.

A quiet knowing entered Liberty's consciousness. What was it? Was she sensing something? Liberty looked around to see if anything or anyone else was near. No, only herself and the rabbit. An understanding slowly became part of Liberty's thinking. It was a perfect knowing that told her that the rabbit was going to have young. Liberty let go of her anxiousness and sat down. Yes, it was the rabbit who had touched her with this knowing.

There was no doubt about it.

"You will live, beautiful mother rabbit," Liberty said out loud. "I know you gave me one of your family yesterday. Because of you and all the plants and animals, I will live. I thank you. I will always remember your teaching me, mother rabbit."

Liberty strode back to her camp, feeling another kind of victory.

That evening, Liberty spoke to Estcheemah as they sat together at the campfire.

"Estcheemah," Liberty said, feeling deeply moved by her discovery, "I want to say something about what happened today. It's important that I put it into words I know."

"Certainly." Estcheemah smiled, feeling Liberty's excitement.

"Well . . ." Liberty began, "I learned something about the Earth, something that has changed my thinking about Her awareness. You see, Estcheemah, I have never really felt that our Earth knew what I was doing. Yes, I know that sounds strange to you, but that is what I felt anyway.

"My thinking is different now. We have electronic equipment that can record almost any kind of event, visually and with sound. The equipment isn't very sophisticated, but it will improve with time. Yet, even with the primitive state of electronics, they helped me see and understand the miracle I experienced today.

"You see, if I can monitor the movements of animals with infrared and see them in the dark, then so can Mother Earth. She can see her animals because She knows Her animals intimately. If I can use rudimentary electronics to record the images of the animals and their sounds, then Earth can do

450

much more.

"We perform our electronic marvels with the things that Mother Life has given us, Her substance. It was She who gave us the materials and the information to use them.

"If we can record sound on plastic, then certainly the stones of Earth hold their records, too. If Earth can store so much information on Her little strip of plastic, then surely She can record anything She wants within Her living trees.

"I am beginning to understand that our discoveries are very primitive and clumsy. This tells me a lot! The things we think are so sophisticated are nothing but simple tools. Earth's gravity, Her infrared, Her electromagnetic field, Her high-frequency radio waves, and Her very atoms are not news to Her. But they are certainly news to us.

"If we can see in the dark with the scientific toys Mother Earth gives to her primitive children, then certainly She must know a lot more!

"The Spirit of Mother Earth is at least four and a half billion years old. Our lives are nothing but a moment to Her. Her Mind and Thinking are Universal and as Great as Time, while ours are those of children. Yet we pretend we are above Life.

"I realized, Estcheemah, that Mother Earth will not shout at me. Her very Existence is a shout all by itself. I was the one who was deaf and stupid. I was the one who wasn't sophisticated enough to hear what She has to say. She spoke with a Knowing that I will never forget, Estcheemah. I will always respect that Knowing."

Liberty began to question her Self and the culture she lived in. The headband she wore was no longer simply a fashion. It had become a practical part of her attire. Her bow became her friend and felt as smooth and strong as her own muscles. On the third day, she shot a duck. The duck dinner was delicious, and Liberty began to feel a new strength.

"I wish you to tell Lightningbolt the reasons you sought me out," Estcheemah asked Liberty. "All right?"

"Yes, I'll be happy to," she answered. "When I found Estcheemah I was overjoyed to find a woman I could communicate with.

"Lightningbolt, I sought out Estcheemah because I had had an incredibly painful experience. I am very happy that I learned what I did, but I am glad that the pain is now in my past.

"I was planning to go to the University of California at Berkeley. I was saving money I made by working in a law office that summer. But then I began to have terrible pains in my stomach. I had missed my menstrual cycle for three months, and I was afraid I was pregnant.

"My Aunt Thelma arranged for me to see a woman gynecologist. When the doctor examined me, I saw that she was very alarmed, and this really scared me. She sent me to a surgeon. He informed me that I had what he called a 'dermoid cyst' in my right ovary. He said it was the size of a grapefruit and would have to be removed immediately. That same evening I had my operation.

"A few days later I learned that I'd had a parthenogenic pregnancy. What that means is that my egg started to divide and to develop into an embryo all by itself . . . without the introduction of any sperm. In other words, I got myself pregnant. He said that I had been self-pregnant for ten years or more. The embryo-cyst lay dormant in my ovary until I began to have my menstrual cycle. Then it began to grow."

"You had a tumor?" Lightningbolt asked.

"Yes," she answered. "But all the evidence showed that it had once been an embryo. The doctor was happy that it was not cancerous. He told me that he doubted if I would ever have a menstrual cycle again or be able to have children—and that there was nothing he knew that would help. I was told to not make love, and that I probably would not heal for at least five years. I was crushed.

"My depression was terrible. I felt so alone and frightened. I entered the university with a cane and had to change my bandages daily.

"Then I began to search for healing. I ran into every kind of nut possible. I tried acupuncture, vegetarianism, meditation, religion, Silva mind control, sound therapy, and psychology—in fact, psychology became my major. But all of them failed miserably.

"Four years later I was still in trouble and weighed only ninety-five pounds. But, after four years of searching, I had become very discriminating, and I realized that all the healers and all the techniques I had experienced were useless.

"Then three women friends suggested that I go backpacking with them fifty miles into the Sierras to see the eclipse of the Moon. Because I was raised in L.A. I was very excited about going into the wilderness. After a grueling, very challenging two days—and blistered feet—I arrived in the most beautiful place in the world.

"There was an exquisite lake. And rising behind Her were twin pyramid-shaped mountains, reflected perfectly in Her pristine waters. That night I walked alone . . . limping and thinking. I had never seen such Beauty.

"This was the first time in my life I realized that the Earth might actually be alive. The following night, one of my friends suggested that we build a fire and do some kind of ceremony in celebration of the lunar eclipse.

"We were all very ignorant . . . so we made it up. One of the women had a rattle and began to pass it around the circle. We all agreed to sing all night and pray.

452

"I watched the Moon turn a deep red as I prayed. I realized at this moment that somehow the Moon actually had something to do with every woman's menstrual cycle.

"I had heard about the Goddess at the university. The professors thought She was a psychological archetype. All the books actually called Life a 'cult.' They said that the Goddess 'cult' existed in the past, and that Goddess Life was no longer present. There was no real information to be had.

"But that night, when I looked at the red Moon I knew that if I was ever going to be healed, I would have to pray and speak directly to the Mother Earth and to the Moon. Only Goddess Life would heal me.

"For the first time in my life I addressed the Moon as though She would understand me . . . no differently than if I were talking with my aunt.

"I felt a sudden deep rage coming from within me, and I asked the Moon why She would allow this to happen to me. I broke down and sobbed. When I calmed, I made a pledge. I told the Moon, 'If you are really alive, show me. If I am healed, then I will dedicate my life to seeing that other women will know the female side of Creation—and that Mother Earth is alive."

Lightningbolt grabbed her hand. "That is sad and really beautiful."

"As I sat in classes for the next three weeks," Liberty continued, "I slowly began to realize that my professors didn't know a damn thing about what they were saying! They talked on and on about goddesses as 'archetypes in the psyche.' They never once realized that She really is alive! On the fourth day after my Ceremony and my talk with Mother Moon, I went into the bathroom after my physics class and discovered that I had my monthly cycle, my moon cycle.

"Strange. You'd think that I'd have celebrated. But I didn't. I was very scared.

"I was scared because I realized that things about Life were being deliberately twisted. Suddenly, everything I'd been taught sounded wrong. Everything I'd learned from books, religion, family, the schools—everything—was wrong. Everybody was pretending. Did anybody really know about Goddess Life besides me? Was everybody crazy, believing the bullshit we all had been taught? Did anyone other than me realize that Goddess Life is actually alive?

"I have never felt such loneliness. My isolation was profound. I started to try to find a Medicine Woman, and I ran into every kind of White Light nut possible. Women out there know religion and mysticism, but very few know Mother Life.

"Then I went north to visit Yellowstone Park, and I found an old woman fishing in the Yellowstone River."

"Who?" Lightningbolt asked. "Was she a Medicine Woman?"

"Kind of . . ." Liberty smiled. "But she doesn't like being called that. She is a Flower Soldier."

Lightningbolt laughed.

"There is nothing so wondrous as being a woman," Estcheemah said, celebrating Liberty. "There is much we women need to do.

"Goddess Life is Presence; She is Willful, Courageous, Patient, and All-Knowing. Goddess Life is Love. She is Honor.

"The fact that women give Birth is incredibly Sacred. When I was a girl I knew that there was a Goddess Creatress and not just a God, but I didn't know how to say it.

"Can you imagine how I felt, as a female child, when I was told that I and all women were the cause of the downfall of all of humanity?

"Giving Life, Birthing all humans, is the most honorable of all powers given to human beings. Just think of it, Liberty—we women bring Life into our world. Isn't that sacred?

"The lies are what hurt women. I was told to be a 'virgin.' *Virgin* only means a woman that has not had children, but I was led to believe that it meant 'never having sex before marriage.' You know the old story.

"There is nothing so devastating, so cruel, than for a girl to be told that everything in Life was created by an all-male God.

"Humans reflect what exists in Creation. It is obvious that the Creatress Mother, joining with the Creator Father, Births Existence and Life.

"To believe that only the male God gives birth instantly divorces Spirit from Life—and science from truth. This belief also denies all reason.

"It is time for all humans to reclaim their reason.

"Humans are becoming more aware of the fact that our Earth is delicate.

"Women will be the first to honor Mother Life. We will rebuild our own altars to Mother Life in our homes.

"Our wise women will teach young women to have deep pride in being women. We will also teach men to appreciate the knowledge and power of women and Goddess Life.

"Our ordinary women, our wise, our nurturing women, all women, will relearn what it is to be women. We will be Honored, within Creation, for being women.

"The recognition of the presence of our Creatress Mother will inspire humans to redesign our world.

"Even the design of our cities will change when women once again have the pride and opportunity of bringing their own Dreams and thinking into our world.

"We are the daughters of Goddess Creation. There are no women or girls who will hear my words who will not celebrate their Freedom from the deep pain we have had to endure at the hands of the religious fanatics. We women have arrived at our Present."

Both Liberty and Lightningbolt were crying.

"Your tears are celebrated," Estcheemah said with emotion. She looked up into the sky. "Just like those clouds in the sky. Soon it will rain. Good, let it rain!"

At ten the following morning, Liberty was walking on the beach and thinking deeply about what she had heard the day before.

She still felt exhilarated by Estcheemah's words, but frustrated that she did not have the power to change things more quickly. Must she wait until she was an old woman before things would change?

The Ocean was tumultuous and reflected much of what Liberty was feeling. Heavy, determined

456

swells rolled relentlessly in, thundering against the granite cliffs and spewing foam and water high into the air. The sea boiled among the large stones, churning water into a blue foam. The wind whipped away the water, hurling the spray toward the land as a driving rain.

The cyclone howled, bending the cedars and shaking the brush along the shore. Liberty loved it. She laughed and danced, throwing up her arms, shouting to the Thunder Goddess and God, asking them to hear her prayers. It was a perfect day for her.

Great, dark clouds billowed in the sky while sheet lightning illumined another kind of wild Ocean—a sky-borne tide that echoed the maelstrom below.

Liberty's tears mingled with the Ocean spray as she yelled and chanted to the thunder drums.

Tongues of lightning answered as fire mixed with water—lifting her spirits and speaking to her innermost heart. Thunderbolts hammered the anvils of the mountains, tempering the sword of her mind.

"Lightning Goddess and God!" she cried.

The Ocean rose up with a great wave that crashed along the beach, washing across her feet. She ran into the water, shouting her prayer.

More lightning flashed close by, exploding a tree and sending sparks twenty feet into the air. She ran to the tree and threw tobacco into the flames before the rain and wild surf could extinguish the fire.

The tree hissed and sang, then roared into a bright beacon of light. She turned from the tree and ran back into the churning water at the beach, whooping and laughing.

Five sudden jagged streams of fire—lightning—crackled and boomed. As they struck the cliffs to her right and left, she felt a rush of dizziness.

Water rolled over her, cleansing her. She watched in fascination as the wave receded, joining the Ocean.

She continued to stare at the water, now in a daze.

Suddenly two bolts of Lightning exploded directly in front of her, transforming themselves into the shapes of a Powerful Woman and Man.

The Lightning Kachinas started walking toward her. The Goddess's hair was lightning and bright gold as the Sun. The God's hair was brilliant fire.

Another wave rolled over Liberty, dashing water into her face. She brushed the water from her eyes and lifted herself onto one knee. The beautiful image began to disappear and become part of the Ocean again.

She tried to jump to her feet and call to the Goddess, but sprawled in the powerful pull of the surf. The next surge of water rolled over her head and she had to fight for air.

She quickly lifted herself above the foamy sea to look once again for the Lightning Kachinas, but both of them had vanished.

She shook her head, then washed her face in the next wave. Amazed at what she had seen, she turned from the Ocean and strode valiantly back to her Circle.

That afternoon the winds suddenly grew very still. A hush seemed to fall over all the land while Liberty meditated about what she had seen. Even the sea gulls were quieted.

Estcheemah was delighted with Liberty's vision and laughed with joy until tears flowed from her eyes.

Lightningbolt was reminded of the first time he had seen his vision in the Child's Lodge.

"Yes, there are the great things and the small," Estcheemah carefully explained to Liberty. "Your vision was no little thing, but you can belittle it with one blink of your eye if you do not give yourself wise counsel.

"No sunrise or sunset is ordinary. To think that it is, is to destroy a portion of the incredible experience you know as your Life. So be very respectful of the great and the small. Together, the great and the small form the atoms of the moments we know as our Life.

"The vision that you saw, for a moment, came from within you. Life is not frivolous. Life does not give visions to one of Her children and withhold them from another.

"Visions, like Dreams, come from within the human. This is the reason that some visions people have reported are so silly and some are cruel. The humans who reported their visions were also silly

or cruel.

"No, Liberty, Goddess and God do not depend upon one or two humans to report what is happening with existence or the thinking of Creation. Creation reports Itself second by second and minute by minute.

"While we live we are most directly part and particle of Life. Life is absolute Energy, and all living plants and animals are part of Life's Energy. Our Earth and Creation are living Energies.

"We grow because of these Energies. The birds fly unerringly to the South each season because of these Energies. Babies are born in the cycles of the Moon because of these Energies. The flower blooms with color because of these Energies. And you experience Life's Energies.

"These Earth Life Energies have Consciousness. But this Consciousness is not the same as yours and mine. The human's Knowing is quite different from that of the Energies of the plants, yet the plants also have their Knowing.

"The trees and grasses, the plants of the oceans and our streams, are very, very old. Even the presence of the animals on Earth is more ancient than we humans, though they are younger than the plants. The plants and animals are all much older than we humans. The trees, the grasses, the ocean plants, all plants, are directly part of Earth Life, and they know us newcomers very intimately.

"All Energies existing with our Mother Earth have Consciousness. The number given for all Energies in the Medicine Wheel is the Nine. Nine is also called 'Movement.'

"Every child learns from Earth Life Energies. At different times in their lives, growing children possess a Life Knowing they never had before. Sud-

461

denly, they can speak. Suddenly they can think. All this is born from Earth Energies.

"Crystals know how to vibrate and grow in unison with Mother Earth because they are part of her Unity and Form.

"We Zero Chiefs say that Mother Earth is alive and She teaches through Her Energies with Consciousness.

"Earth Life evolves all of Her Creation, all humans, all animals, all insects, and all plants through Energy Information.

"If you want to know of these great Energies, then you must be trained to be highly disciplined and sensitive to the Energies around you. You are like the fish that swim in the oceans. They know that they swim in the Energy of Water-Life, but they do not Know the Water.

"Look at the trees here, Liberty; they live with you. Trees are more than just scenery. Earth is not dead matter. She is the Living Mother. The trees live. The wonder of your existence is profound. Think about that and contemplate it deeply.

"The further we are from knowing the Self, the further we are from understanding Earth Life Energies. All Earth Life Energies possess a Consciousness. You will remember this even in those times when you are the most isolated. The Energies of Earth Life Consciousness can be a great source of knowledge for you. Introduce your Self to Life. Awaken your curiosity about Life and the reasons why you live."

That same night, Lightningbolt took Liberty for a walk on the beach. The bright Moon glistened on the ever-moving tides.

"Estcheemah wants me to tell you the story of

how I was introduced to Life Energy," said Lightningbolt. "She took me to a very special creek, in a little meadow she called 'Place of Place.'

"It took the little stream I met there five thousand years or more to cut her way through the mountains. Her body is composed of a thousand different springs that are secreted among hundreds of valleys.

"She flows through a fifty-mile-wide, hundred-mile-long jumble of stones called a moraine. The delicate creek was birthed in a cloud from our Earth's oceans. She is only five feet wide and not very deep. She dresses in each season and is very lovely.

"Her greatest joy is being clean. Her duty is to remain clean and to nourish all she touches. She calls Herself Clear-Sister-Brother.

"She has seen everything possible that could happen in Her world. Some of the happenings have caused Her to become not so clear.

"Clear loved to bathe and to be bathed. She bathed within streams far larger than herself—Her Sun bath and Her Moon bath. Star Light and Planet Light are also her baths.

"Clear knows Mother Life, our Earth, intimately. She is intimate with our Earth's sanguine miracle. The great water arteries and veins of our Earth are Her flowing, ever-renewing blood that carries Life and nurtures all Life on Earth.

"Estcheemah introduced me to Clear, and the tiny stream became very important in my awakening as a Flower Soldier.

"I had never truly met a stream. Before I met Clear all streams were alike to me. They were wet, they were filled with water, they had fish in them. They were scenic, nice, owned by people, did

463

jobs, and were generally just creeks. Or so I thought before I met Clear.

"You could say, symbolically, that I was a minnow; anyway, that's how Clear saw me. A human minnow, flopping around outside my true element.

"I had made a tiny Medicine Wheel, about four feet wide, very near to Clear. Estcheemah told me to think with a clear mind while I contemplated my Circle of Life.

"Estcheemah also told me of Clear's name. But I did not connect Clear with clear thinking until I had met Clear. Does that make sense? Well, it did for me. My mind awakened while I was with Clear.

"Clear was an instant joy for me and we became intimate friends soon after I met Her. She gave me drink, and She kept me clean. She gave me a trout, and water to cook my food.

"I asked Clear to teach me, as Estcheemah had instructed.

"At first, Clear said nothing. She just *was*.

"Very soon I began to learn Clear's language. Her first language lesson for me was:

" 'Is was me you.

" 'I am. I flow as Life is.'

"I was amazed!

"Spiderwebs had been caught in bushes before, and I had seen them, but not as rainbows caught among leaves. I learned from Clear:

" 'It all depends on the angle of the Sun.'

"That day I saw lightning. Lightning that leaped up from Mother Earth to Her clouds! I had never seen that before. I actually saw lightning leap up when I was with Clear. How very wondrous!

"A turtle visited and shared dinner with me. She ate the last of my can of sardines. I had never eaten with a turtle before. A grasshopper rode on my cowboy hat all day long—that had never happened before.

" 'As I flow,' Clear explained.

"As you know, I had been sick of heart when I first met Clear. My attitudes and ignorance about

464

Life had made me terribly sad.

" 'To be concerned with being,' Clear pointed out to me.

"I lay on my stomach and watched a tumble-bug play and hunt in the water. Suddenly I realized that I could visualize the entire ocean! I immediately sent a tiny ship to an island in midstream.

" 'Do not isolate yourself,' Clear said.

"I was so surprised to hear what Clear said that I walked to Estcheemah's camp to ask her about it.

" 'Yield . . . plunge,' Estcheemah answered, sounding just like Clear! 'Imagine as you flow toward your destiny.'

" 'But I don't want to be isolated, an island, Estcheemah,' I said.

" 'Flow from me,' Estcheemah answered. 'Plunge as a torrent to Clear. She will guide you. I will die, but Clear is Ever-Life.'

"I returned to Clear, not really wanting to hear that our teacher is going to die. . . . It made me sad.

" 'You flow,' Clear carefully explained to me when I returned to Her.

" 'Clear . . .' I said, once again on my stomach. 'What is me?'

" 'Place of Place,' she answered. 'To be.'

"I frowned, sipped some of Her water, then sat up to look around.

" 'Happy Birth Day,' Clear suddenly sang.

"I smiled.

" 'Happy Earth Day,' She sang again.

"Magpies flew to Clear about a hundred feet upstream and began to drink.

"Suddenly I had an illumination.

"Clear was explaining, in my mind, that people wanted to imagine they were at the stream, but were afraid to really be with Her. They were afraid to get stung by ants or even killed.

"That's surely possible, I answered Her in my mind.

" 'It is all Life, all Death, Place of Place,' Clear said. 'Afraid to live Life and be intimate with Her.'

"I smiled; somehow I knew that I had faced one of my fears.

" 'People fear to live and to flow more than they fear Death,' Clear said.

" 'I want to be courageous enough to Live,' I told Clear.

" 'What moment by moment is not Earth Day?' Clear asked me. 'What moment is not Happy Birth Day?'

" 'Humans must lift up their language,' Estcheemah said suddenly from behind me. 'Lifting up Life as the Rose in their hands.'

"I turned to face her. The Moon was over her shoulder and blue like her shawl. She had brought me a dinner of fried grouse and rabbit; she had been hunting that day.

" 'What time is not ordinary?' Estcheemah asked as she handed me my cup of coffee. 'Place of Place . . . so it is.'

"How did she know Clear's words? I asked in my mind as I ate. 'What is Place of Place?' I said out loud.

" 'Earth Day,' Clear offered.

" 'I see.' I smiled

" 'As you command your world,' Clear said. 'Ever-flowing Life. Life Mother created your experience world for you. I flow as Life.'

"So," said Lightningbolt, taking Liberty's hand in his, "Happy Earth Day, Liberty.

"Life Mother created a world for you. She made sure that many delights are present for you to experience.

"It is your adventure and challenge.

"Love sparkles as Beauty. She is always invisible and clear. She is the clear morning, your bright day.

"We are in Life with friends that are alive. Life shares with you. Life is declaring for you. Life is making everything clear for you.

"This is what Clear shared with me."

"I appreciate what you have said to me." Liberty smiled, then stood and looked out over the ocean. "And I thank you, Clear." She turned to her friend and took his face in her hands. "I have never heard anything so wonderful, nor so clear." She smiled, showing him her love. "Thank you, Lightningbolt. I am becoming ready for the battles in my future."

The following morning Liberty and Lightningbolt built a small Rainbow Lodge, just large enough for the two of them and Estcheemah.

Estcheemah stood at her bright Fire with her two apprentices, watching the evening Sun disappear behind the deep blue Ocean horizon. The Rainbow Lodge stones were slowly heating as Estcheemah prepared Liberty and Lightningbolt to enter the Little Dome. Estcheemah spoke to them in a strong yet quiet voice.

"This Rainbow Lodge has been specially created for you," Estcheemah said, looking at Liberty. "The Womb of Creation exists within the Little Dome for those who aspire to see Her. While you sit in the Lodge, it is possible for you to join your mind and heart to that of our Sacred Universe.

"The first thing you will discover while you contemplate with Time and our Universe is that Energies are the Life Source of Creation. Women know these healing Energies when they hold their babies in their arms. It is the same for those who respect themselves and Life while they are in the Little Dome.

"The Little Dome has no need for translators. Everything is dependent upon your depth of thought. Absolute Honesty is the perfect key to open the Way into the Energies of Creation; there is no other way.

"Self Honesty is a guide. This guide will take you through the labyrinth of your every emotion, thought, spiritual illumination, and body experience.

"It will be your Self Honesty that will question your every belief and doubt. The Energies of Life will tell you that you were Born to learn and grow, and that you influence your own Self Essence through each choice you make while you live.

"If you do not want to be enlightened, then that will also be granted to you. That is the way it is with the Energies of Life. If a human wants the illusion, then that is granted because it is demanded from Creation. But if the human wants Knowing, then that person can no longer be a believer and lazy. Being Self Responsible demands an incredible amount of Self Energy. Many humans are far too lazy to expend so much Energy.

"One day you will be an Earth Priestess of Life. It will be up to you to help bring forth true Visions and Illuminations for those who seek them. The Rainbow Lodge is an important and sacred place for such seekers.

"The Rainbow Lodge is also a hospital of Healing and Beauty. It must be absolutely clean and never be allowed to become dirtied. The Rainbow Lodge is not a pretend place.

"A Flower Soldier helps people see their Self pretense. The powers of a Warrioress and Priestess are brought together in the Little Dome.

"It is as natural for a woman to be a Warrioress as it is for a man to be a Warrior. What mother is not fierce when her children are threatened? When a surgeon wields a scalpel, it becomes a sword. This is the blade that opens the festering wound. Healing comes after the knife. Healing is the work of Sacred Life. Doctors do not heal; this is done by the Energies of Life.

"A woman can be the Healer, the Wise Priestess, the ready Warrioress, and the Teacher—four great powers of the female Self Leader. Women need to learn to battle injustice and cruelty, the filth of their cities, and the corrupt.

"A few examples from Life, also known as Mother Nature, can help you see how Life creates Her Balance.

"*Cheemah*, Fire, is Healing. She brings warmth and has saved countless millions of lives. Cheemah also destroys and alters; She is the heart of the blast furnace. Our ancient Zero Chiefs tell us that the only way for humans to touch Cheemah is through knowledge, otherwise we will be burned. Cheemah is a Warrioress and a Healer.

"*Morealah* is Water. She bathes and cleanses. She is our renewal. She gives us drink, but She is also the restless tide of the Ocean. She is the snow of Winter, and She is the driving rain. She is the Warrioress, and She is our Healer. She is the dew on the petal of the flower.

"Doctors are not weak and helpless people just because they want to heal people and know gentleness. Women are not helpless or weak because they want to Heal people and know gentleness.

"The woman who has strength, will, intelligence, and discipline, and knows love, is a Balanced human, not a freak, despite what may be said. So do not be afraid to be gentle and a Healer. You will be great because of it. You will not be made less because you desire balance.

"But realize that healing comes with absolute Self Discipline and Knowledge. Hard work and determination are the only Paths to Knowing.

"Look at the example of the Great Forked Tree of the Earth Sun Dance. The Forked Tree represents the twin powers of Mother and Father Life, Life and Death, care and misuse, comfort and pain. It represents the twin powers of everything known in Creation. Everything known to Creation is Life.

"The Forked Tree is placed in the center of the Medicine Wheel as a Teaching. The Four Great Directions of Balance encircle the Tree. In the Center is the Sacred Self, both female and male.

"The Tree also represents the twin powers within a powerful woman or man. For a woman this is the Balance of the Warrioress and the Priestess Healer. For a male this is the Balance of the Warrior and Earth Priest Healer. The highest qualities of the human were designed by Creation, not by human belief and fears. The highest qualities of the human reflect the Balance of WahKahn and SsKwan, Mother and Father Creation.

"All humans must struggle, yes. They must strive hard to gain the great qualities that can be shared with them by Creation. These things are never simple. The woman of knowledge knows this and strives for Balance. Women who do not possess, or develop, their Powers of the Self will be left dependent and victimized by others. This is also true for men.

"The Diversity and Twinness of the Forked Tree is Natural and gives Power to the Human to endure in every kind of circumstance and challenge. When the Power of either of the two branches of the Great Tree is suppressed or ignored, the Tree will die.

"When the woman looks at the qualities of our Mother Earth, she will see Her Natural Balance. Earth never suppresses or ignores. Earth Life presses onward and awakens everything alive.

"So look for the billion answers Mother Earth offers you at any given moment, Liberty. You will see Her womanly Balance in all that She is and does.

"You must survive as a Flower Soldier. Be a Warrioress and Priestess. Focus upon the Energies of Life. Examine and learn of the Energies that Creation has made.

"This Ceremony began when you became aware of Life and Death as a huntress. Humans must kill to eat—this must never be forgotten. When this fact is forgotten, humans lose their respect for Life and become estranged from Life.

"Do not be made to believe that men have a special talent for killing. They do not. Teach men to respect their own Lives. Teach men to nurture Life. Help men to learn that it is not weakness for a human to seek harmony and greatness.

"Help people to see that they do not need to be thieves and broken humans in order to enjoy the power of a Spiritual Path.

"I am a Warrioress Priestess, Liberty. I strive to be a balanced human being. This is our way—the way of every Flower Soldier."

When Liberty stepped from her Rainbow Lodge she realized that she had been given the opportunity to birth herself from the Eternal Womb of her Mother Earth, now as an adult woman, with new understanding and Self Choice. Never in her Life had she felt so clean and deeply moved by the subtle presence of Mother Life.

Liberty also knew from deep inside herself that she was changing, and would never be the same again. She sensed a new Power growing within, a new confidence and courage, and she became absolutely determined to direct her mind and all of her energies into her learning with Estcheemah. She knew that every minute with the powerful old Zero Chief was a precious inheritance from Life that she must appreciate and utilize to the fullest.

It was a warm, sunny August morning. Liberty walked alone up the path to the spring carrying a basket of sparkling crystals to be washed. She had just experienced a powerful Healing Ceremony, assisting Estcheemah with the crystals.

Four years had passed, and most of this time had been devoted to Liberty's and Lightningbolt's training. They had assisted Estcheemah in many kinds of Ceremonies. Each time they had an opportunity to be in Ceremony with Estcheemah, they learned something new. Sky River had sent two children and three women who needed healing to Estcheemah. The old Canadian woman Moon Bear had sent two young men and two women to Estcheemah to have their Vision Quest Ceremonies. And several young women and men had asked for a Rainbow Lodge Ceremony.

Liberty and Lightningbolt were beginning to understand that no two ceremonies were exactly alike because no two humans were exactly the same. However, Estcheemah always used the Sacred Medicine Wheels as her guide. Liberty marveled at this fact as she reached the spring. She took her time, lovingly washing each crystal.

She was thinking about the story Estcheemah had told her about the tree called "Stone Eater." Stone Eater was an immense cedar that had once existed on the north end of Victoria Island. Twenty people could sit comfortably in her hollow center. The sound of the sea echoed in her body, even though the ocean was miles away. The prayerful would sit in quiet, marveling at the deep booming of the surf. Their thinking seemed to become more acute in the tree, and as deep as the sea.

This Woman's Tree was kept by eight maidens and two old grandmothers. The maidens were re-

placed by other girls when they married. The tree sang her chant of the sea. The maidens learned much from the tree. These were unspoken words.

The men had to bathe before they could enter the tree to pray. The men had to fast for three days and two nights before they could enter the Womb of the tree. Men who sat in the Ocean-Tree-Womb wept as boys.

The Medicine Tree always spoke of the seeker. Who was it that sought the Ocean Mother? Who was it that spoke to the Mother Tree? Who was it that honored Mother Life and Father Life? Who was it that honored the Self?

The tree had always been there. The trees were always present. The ocean was ever present. The Mother Earth was singing. The Mother Sun was singing. The Sister Moon was singing.

Stone Eater grew old and she became ten thousand trees. The Forest became her Womb. Liberty marveled that such a tree could exist for people. She thought of other trees of mystery in America that had not been appreciated and loved. Instead they had been relegated to "points of interest" in some state park. Somehow this would have to change.

"We live with you, Mother Life," Liberty said out loud to the great cedars that encircled her. "You will never be scenery again for me, ancient ones."

Estcheemah suggested that her twins take some time and explore Victoria Island more. They boated for three weeks and explored the island from the North to the South—they loved Her.

A million sparkling energies of joy surrounded them when they returned. But when they knocked on Estcheemah's door, there was no answer. Assuming she was napping, they returned to their home and waited.

Their second visit told them something was

wrong. Estcheemah was not answering her door. But her car was in the yard, announcing that she was definitely home!

They tried the door and found it unlocked. Liberty hurried to the kitchen with Lightningbolt following. Estcheemah was on the floor.

Liberty knelt down and touched Estcheemah's cheek. "You're alive!" she cried with tears in her eyes. "Lightningbolt, let's get her to the hospital—hurry!"

"Absolutely not!" insisted Estcheemah, opening her eyes. "I laid down here because I didn't have the strength to get to my bed." She looked at her twins and smiled. Their bright eyes and love washed over her tired old body. For the briefest moment she felt lifted and almost well.

"You're sick," Liberty insisted, sitting down beside Estcheemah.

Lightningbolt felt helpless. Fear rose in his throat and he paled.

"It's all right," said Estcheemah, smiling. "Actually, I'm feeling much better. Will you help me to bed, Liberty?" She attempted to sit up by herself but was instantly assisted by Lightningbolt.

Both of them helped her to bed. Liberty undressed her and made her comfortable while Lightningbolt fixed soup.

"It's been two days since I've eaten," Estcheemah said weakly as she sipped at her soup.

They both sat at the foot of her bed in a daze. What should they do?

"You look as though you've just been nominated for president, Lightningbolt," Estcheemah teased. "I haven't seen you look this straight for years!" She laughed. "I'll be all right." She drank more soup. "It happens to the old all the time."

Lightningbolt tried to speak. "But, you're . . ."

"I'll live," she answered. "But now I need to sleep. Liberty, awaken me in an hour and give me more soup."

Within a few minutes Estcheemah was sleeping. Liberty and Lightningbolt did not know what to do or say. They sat at the table, each waiting to see what the other would do.

"Sleep on the floor?" Lightningbolt suggested. "Why not?"

"You go get our sleeping bags," Liberty agreed. "I'll tidy up."

"You'll go home," Estcheemah called from her bedroom. "You're like two scared geese out there. Go home and sleep."

It was three weeks before Estcheemah was outside again. She was better, but not the same.

A terrible suddenness had invaded the world of Lightningbolt and Liberty; it was Death and they knew it. What would they do when there was no more Estcheemah? Both of them felt unprepared for what they knew lay before them.

Lightningbolt needed time to be alone and to think. He walked among the tall cedars not far from Estcheemah's home, and was disappointed with himself for not having expected the obvious.

He had remained behind while Liberty took Estcheemah on an outing. She was feeling much stronger now and wanted to be near the ocean. She also wanted to do a little shopping.

How were they going to survive their ignorance? Were they prepared to be without her? Lightningbolt kicked at a limb and cursed. Why was he so slow sometimes? Why had he thrown away so much precious time in the past? He sat down on a stump and looked around. Nothing was going to be the same once Estcheemah was gone. Then he remembered a teaching that Liberty had received while he was working on an old typewriter he had bought.

"Responsibility begins each morning upon awakening," Estcheemah had taught Liberty. "Life is a Command. Your presence with Life is experiencing that which is commanded by your physical existence.

"Life becomes a deafening flood of needs and social beliefs for people who will not listen to themselves or to Life. If you quiet even the mean and desperate, you will discover that they have simple and sometimes very direct advice for themselves—but they seldom if ever follow their own advice. The reason for this is that they do not comprehend challenge, Self motivation, or Self authority.

"They never question the reasons for their lack of motivation or their need to be Self directed. They believe that everything outside of them needs to be controlled. They throw away their lifetimes controlling themselves.

"Unless you understand Self Command, you will not appreciate your direction and responsibility for personal Authority. If your Life is based upon the reward of making money, gossip, intrigue, and compromise, your existence will be meaningless. You will win the social game and lose your heart."

"But what if I am a simple farmer or lawyer?" Liberty had asked. "How does this apply to *my* Life? I mean, how do I understand this in a practical way?"

"You are not a farmer, Liberty." Estcheemah had laughed. "And there are no simple lawyers. They may be simple-minded, but never simple. What you are doing at this moment tells me that you are pretending with your Self. What I am telling you about is fact; it is Life. The reason you are not understanding me is that you have held command at a distance from your Self.

"Command your Self to be present with me now, at this moment."

"I've written down what you said to her, Estcheemah," said Lightningbolt. "I'll give it to Liberty later."

"Make two copies," she said to him. "And study it along with her. Both of you need to understand command. What I am suggesting is a lifelong pursuit. If you want a habit, let it be command.

"Thinking is a profession. Thought is an exercise that most humans do not know. Thinkers question everything. There is no room for any kind of conjecture or belief.

"To effect this in your life, you will have to command your Self to be critical of what you are observing and thinking. This is a moment-by-moment exercise. Allow command to become your play, your adventure, your entertainment, and your satisfaction in Life."

Lightningbolt thought about the challenges ahead of him as a Breed, a Medicine Person, and a writer. Would what he had to say be understood? Would he be able, through his writing, to express the profound and far-reaching thoughts and discoveries of his Chiefs? He tried to not worry and instead vowed to direct all of his energies into working hard to succeed in what he dreamed. He knew he faced the difficult task of staying absolutely loyal to his own Self command and Self direction if he was going to endure as a Flower Soldier.

Lightningbolt sat quietly, marveling at the gracious elegance and ageless beauty of the Forest, enjoying Her presence. How wonderful it was to be alive and to be in such a clean and resplendent place. He knew that within time and place, even with all of the challenges and battles he knew lay ahead, he was the most fortunate man alive to have had the opportunity to learn from one of the greatest minds of his century, the Zero Chief Estcheemah.

Another week had passed and Estcheemah appeared to be stronger. Liberty and Lightningbolt had gone to the ocean to gather driftwood for Liberty's new sculpting. She had decided that her first piece would be dedicated to Mother Ocean. When they returned they found a surprise waiting for them on their kitchen table. Estcheemah had left them a note.

It read: "Hello, Twins. When people get very old, they become privileged people. With this freedom we can do an enormous number of things that no one dares question.

"Anyway, it is my privilege to announce that I bought the frying pan you loaned to me last week for the sum of three thousand dollars.

"This sum of money should make you extravagantly rich for the coming Autumn and Winter. I expect to see you often at my Circle."

Estcheemah had signed the note with a penciled likeness of a Fox.

Soon after the rains started, Liberty decided to begin her sculpting. She had devoted years to her Medicine Training, and now she knew it was time for her to express her Self in her own art. She also wanted the freedom to support herself in a creative way. As soon as she began to work with the wood she felt a joy in her art that was in rhythm with the land.

In the late afternoons, Lightningbolt would take a break from his writing and watch Liberty sculpt. They would speak about the Teaching Wheels and what these meant to them. The long evenings of talk cleared up many questions for both of them.

Estcheemah taught Liberty every morning and a few evenings a week. She appeared to be tireless. Had she been as near death as they had thought? Liberty wondered every minute she was with Estcheemah.

It was late Autumn when Estcheemah invited Liberty and Lightningbolt to her home for a "celebration" dinner. She had made roast goose with sweet potatoes, and every bite was a delight.

"My Twins," Estcheemah began, taking a deep breath and looking out her window at the ocean below. "Finally, it is time for you to prepare yourselves for your first Teaching Circle where you are the teachers." She smiled and turned to face both of them. "Sky River has been working with two young women and a young man for three years now, off and on. They are ready to hear about a few of the Medicine Wheels, and it is time for you to be the ones to share this precious information."

Liberty and Lightningbolt had not anticipated this. They were speechless. A million questions flooded their minds. Were they ready? Could they share their learning in a way that was clear and powerful? How would they begin?

But when they asked questions, Estcheemah would only answer, "Do what I have taught you to do. Speak to your Self and Mother Life about it. I will only answer questions after you have completed the work."

Two weeks later Liberty and Lightningbolt traveled into central Canada to meet with Sky River's three young students. Sky River was present but kept her distance, and never once stepped in to take over the Circle of Teaching. The Medicine Wheel that the students had asked to learn was one of the most precious teachings of healing and human understanding. It was the Medicine Wheel of the Body Spheres.

Liberty and Lightningbolt soon learned that understanding and responsiveness were not the same for each of the three students. Even though they were all in their early twenties, the three were completely different from one another. Liberty and Lightningbolt were constantly being challenged by the question of how to get their information across clearly to each of them.

At first they tried to say too much, and lost all three young people immediately. Then Lightningbolt got too rigid and the three young Canadian Indian Breeds started substituting rules for understanding. Liberty jumped in to rescue the situation but had a hard time getting the young students to think for themselves. Again, she wanted to say too much.

By the time Liberty and Lightningbolt returned to Estcheemah's home they were both thoroughly convinced that they needed direction.

Estcheemah sat in her large front room beading a Medicine Belt for Liberty, while her twins sat beside her looking out to the ocean. The pouring rain churned and danced with Her dark silver incoming tides of wind. Large rivulets of water rushed down the picture window in front of them, reminding them of their lives.

Liberty started the report and Lightningbolt followed. They were both excited by and frustrated with their experience because they were not sure how well they had actually done. For the first time Estcheemah's Breed apprentices had walked through the mirror, and now looked back at themselves from the perspective of the teacher. It was a very important moment for them, one they would never forget.

When Estcheemah spoke, her voice sounded ancient, yet full of energy and wisdom. Liberty and Lightningbolt were very attentive.

"You both are finally learning what the word *Discernment* means. I have worked all these years to teach you of this immensely important power of mind." She smiled, continuing to bead.

"As you are learning, no two humans are exactly the same. If you say too much before someone is ready, you can crush that person with the weight of the knowledge. If you say too little, then you might bore the person to death." She chuckled.

"Your ability to discern what is really needed and powerful in any given situation will be tested your life long as a teacher. What is victory is always a question in the mind of a Flower Soldier.

"There is strategy and maneuver. Strategy is based on your experience and imagination. Your strategy, your plan of how to approach any situation, is only equal to your imagination—founded on experience and understanding. However, maneuver is always the decision of the moment. No matter how powerful your plans might be, a strong leader can maneuver in the moment, changing what needs to be changed according to the real Life situations. No leader can afford to cling to beliefs or theories if she or he wants to win. For there to be a victory, leaders must discern what is taking place and what needs to be accomplished. They have to be ready to renew and change their plans in the blink of an eye. This is the secret of great leadership.

"When it comes to teaching and healing humans, discernment is an imperative because what is healing for one person is not for another. Challenge for one person is not a challenge for another. In each Ceremony you run, every time you prepare yourself to teach another human about the Self and Sacred Mother Life, you will need to be discerning and sensitive to the energies of that person—and her or his Self pretense and Self honesty.

"You must also have enormous patience as a teacher. No matter how much you want to instantly give a person that you are teaching the world of understanding that you possess, you cannot. People must slowly build their own world of knowing. As teachers you must supply information, maps, weapons, energy, and experience—so they can succeed. This takes years to accomplish.

"Different people need different information. Different people need different experiences to learn. Mother Life provides the correct Life experiences and information for each of Her children—if they choose to learn with Her presence of Being.

"Every person is unique, yet all humans possess Spirit, Body, Emotions, Mind, and Self. No human is born all smart or all stupid. No human is born good or not good. Humans have choice. We can choose to pretend to be one thing or another, yet deep down we know if we persist in being unknowing, irresponsible, crass, ignorant, or mean, we will bring great pain upon our Self.

"The Medicine Wheels will be your greatest guide as teachers and healers. You will have to be very Self disciplined and sensitive to your Life knowing if you are going to teach other humans to become more Self Powerful and Responsible. Healing and Self Teaching are the two greatest Challenges of human Skill known in Creation."

A long quiet filled the room.

Finally, Liberty spoke, trying to formulate the question she wanted to ask. "Estcheemah, even though I have seen you work with many different people, healing and teaching—only a few have actually chosen to become Medicine People." Liberty was struggling to find the right words for her question. "I know that I will teach those who wish to become Medicine People or even Flower Soldiers at some time in my life, but there are also women or men who simply want to better their lives and learn of Mother Earth. They do not wish to become Medicine People and Healers." She continued to search for her question.

"I am most concerned with the women who will come to me, who simply want to learn more about Mother Life in a personal way and find healing for their Self. Where should I tell these women to begin?"

Estcheemah smiled and put down her beadwork. She looked deeply into Liberty's eyes.

"Now, that is a question from a young maturing teacher," said Estcheemah with pride. "No, not everyone is a Flower Soldier or a Medicine Person. In fact, there are only a small number of people who will actually fight to have the Self Power and endurance it takes to be a Flower Soldier. Our discipline is incredibly demanding and difficult. However, not everyone chooses to be a brain surgeon, a business executive, or a general in the military, either.

"Yet, all humans have the right to learn of the true Balance of their Creatress and Creator, their Living Mother Earth and the nature of the human Self.

"Yes, where shall you begin? I want you to think more, and then return tomorrow evening and I will speak to you of this."

Liberty rose and put on her coat. She said good-night to her teacher and headed for the door.

"Estcheemah," said Lightningbolt as he stood up to leave, "this opportunity to teach has shown me much about my writing. I'm going to have to write in a very simple and direct way to introduce the Medicine Wheels to our world with any clarity. There's so much to say, but I realize that I must choose a simple and profound beginning. I will be working on this for quite a while I think." He shook his head in awe. "Maybe a lifetime." He took her hands into his with great respect and love. "Thank you," he said, almost in a whisper, swallowing the rush of emotions that he felt. Then Lightningbolt turned and strode out the door behind Liberty.

The next evening Lightningbolt watched Liberty ride Brunhilde to Estcheemah's. It was raining, and so Liberty had put on her plastic poncho and weather-treated elkskin boots. He smiled at the many changes in her. She had braided and wrapped her long brown hair in a thick colorful woven scarf. She wore a pistol at her waist and carried a hunting knife in her pack along with a notepad and two pens for note taking. She had fixed a long leather thong to her flashlight so she could sling it over her shoulder and still have her two hands free.

Liberty was no longer the young woman he had first met. She had bloomed into a complete woman. She was being transformed by the challenges and realities of living in wild, gracious mountain forests and with the primal beauty of Earth's magnificent Ocean. Living with wild land demanded thinking, respect, practicality, and re-

sponsibility. The changes in Liberty were not only in dress but, more important, also in her understanding of her Life and her Self.

The Medicine Wheels were teaching Liberty to speak the language of her time and her Earth. Her growing communication with her Self was having a tremendously powerful effect on her confidence and her personal power. Yet, with all the changes, Liberty was so busy learning, doing, and becoming her Self that she had not yet seen how big the change was.

Estcheemah had remarked to Lightningbolt how deeply she celebrated the transforming woman, and thanked Life for the miracle of the evolving nature of the human Self.

It was this new Liberty who walked confidently into Estcheemah's home and began taking off her rain gear.

"When you are ready I want you to come and sit with me by my special window," Estcheemah called from her front room.

When Liberty walked in she saw Estcheemah sitting on her Sun Dance blanket by the picture window, looking out at the calm and beautiful ocean. There was a small red cloth pouch on the blanket directly in front of the old teacher. Liberty quickly seated herself and looked at Estcheemah with eager anticipation.

"You have asked an extremely important question, Liberty," Estcheemah began. "One that will take a little time for me to answer. However, you must remember that real answers are always doors that lead to actions, and Self actions are always doors that lead to questions. This is how we learn and grow.

"Where do women begin when they want to learn about the Self and to celebrate their Creatress Mother Life? I must start by speaking to you, Liberty, of the Home Altar of women in ancient times. As you know, before modern times, the Home Altar had belonged to women and was a central place of respect and power. From your years in the university, Liberty, you also know that the subject of women and their Home Altars is completely avoided by all the people who academize about Mother Life. The reason for this is very simple: Women are not supposed to have any true power in their homes.

"When the fact of our Creatress was denied, and only the Creator was said to have power with humans, women also began to experience the brutalities of being denied.

"An ancient balance will return to every community when woman, and their children, can honor our Creatress and Creator as equal. This honoring begins in their homes.

"Every woman knows, deep down within herself, how very important the Home Altar can be for women. We know this as clearly as the Priestesses of ancient times knew it. The reason we cherish even the thought of our personal Altars is because women want to celebrate and focus upon their relationship with Mother Earth and Life.

"Children are born from woman and because of this women are directly affected by the facts of Life and Death. We women care for the health of our families and we care for Life—obviously they are connected. What mother does not pray for the health of her child and become the Healer in her home?

"Every woman knows deep within her Self that our Creatress is Life and Healing. It was also this way with women in our past.

"The question now facing every woman and man is—What does this mean for humans now? How is the discrimination against our Creatress affecting women, and all humans in our present world?

"When women look to Mother Life, Mother Earth, for love, for knowledge of healing, and for direction in their daily lives, they are accused of every ill.

"Women are told that the respect for Life is a 'cult' and that the knowing of our Creatress Mother is a 'cult religion.' There is no truth in this kind of bigotry, nor is there any joy.

"Women need to have Self pride and harmony in the home and in their professional lives. Women will have this when they make Mother Life central to their lives. Women, and all humans, must know and love our Creatress.

"WahKahn is Creatress. No amount of bigotry and silly beliefs will deny Her existence with Creation.

"Women can begin to find renewed pride and joy when they once again become central figures in their homes. The home can be a place of honor and clarity for women—a place of honoring Sacred Mother Life.

"Every home will be honored and respected in a new way when women build their Altars to celebrate and teach their children of Mother Goddess Creation.

"It is simply a matter of time before the change comes, Liberty. No matter how long these years of ignorance are forced upon humans, one day it will end. Our Sacred Creatress Mother will not be denied.

"It will be women who begin the great transformation. They will do this by lifting up the Sacred Creatress Mother Goddess and battling to possess their own personal authority."

Estcheemah reached into the small pouch in front of her, took out a small, highly polished stone, and set it on the blanket in front of Liberty. "What do you think that is, Liberty?"

"It looks like jade, maybe," she answered.

"This beautiful blue-green stone came from Peru." Estcheemah smiled, remembering her own teacher and friend. "This is the only physical object my teacher had on her Altar."

"Night Arrow Woman?" Liberty asked.

"No, this belonged to Serpent Mother," Estcheemah answered. "My teacher's life was Spartan, almost harsh. She was constantly on the move. I do not think that she remained more than ten years in any one place. She traveled her Life long and became incredibly conscious of what was important and what was inconsequential clutter.

"I was determined to be even more ambitious than she. My life has been full of many things, where her life was devoid of all trivialities.

"She once asked me what was the most important item in my Life—what would I save if this were the only item possible to save?

"After much thought I answered that it would be my Medicine Pipe. She laughed and told me that she'd had five Pipes stolen from her.

"I thought and thought, and came up with nothing. She told me that the only thing real that I should be concerned with saving should be my presence of mind.

"She told me that when people begin to hate themselves because of their losses in Life, they lose everything. But people who can hang on to who they are, hang on to their ambition, will survive every kind of loss.

"Wahkahn and SsKwan created everything. No physical thing can be shared with Creation because Creation is all things. Nothing created can be given back to Creation. Creation already possesses everything created.

"No sacrifice made makes sense to Creation because Creation is Great Intelligence. Only our human Honesty and Self Presence is accepted by Creation as a gift. Self Honesty is greatness. When our Love is offered to Creation, our Love is received as true Love when we are Self Honest.

"Serpent Mother's Altar was the seasons, and her celebrations were everything she did as a human alive within Creation. She taught that all humans share their Life with Creation. Since Creation is existence, Creation has a greater knowing than humanity. Life is a unique present given individually to each human born.

"What I did as a Flower Soldier, as an Earth Priestess, means everything to me first. Others have no way of knowing what I did or who I was. Only the Creatress, the Creator, Mother Earth, and I fully know of all that I am and all I have done. This makes me Self Responsible.

"The Zero Chiefs of old spoke of the disease of fantasy as being the number-one killer of humans, worldwide. No other kind of ignorance is as dangerous to humans as fantasy and pretense.

"Humans who substitute fantasy for their true

Life experience will daydream their lives away and never know they did not know Life. There is nothing more violent to the Self, and nothing more destructive to the mind, than fantasy and pretense. People who live only in their brains know only phantom people—not the real people they dwell with in Life.

"The fantasy or daydream will be substituted for the real things people could have in Life. There are people who have fantasized their Life long and no longer know what is real or what they desire. It is sad to see people accept the fantasy and pretense and never know real love, never have a real challenge, never know the real adventures they could have in Life.

"Liberty, if you should confront the people who live in a perpetual daydream and point out that they are living in a harsh dream, they will pretend and daydream about changing it instead of really changing it."

Liberty shivered.

"Yes, it is very frightening," Estcheemah agreed. "People who live in fantasy are people who do not have the courage to know Life. Sexual fantasies, religious fantasies, wealth or work fantasies, attention fantasies, and fantasy adventures are the substitute illusions most people accept as Life.

"People who choose to have the illusion instead of knowing Life are never loyal to their Self or to anyone else. They will pretend with you and will never be honest. The reason for this is because they have never experienced Self Honesty or Self Learning and so they have never tasted this kind of personal Victory.

"Many people who are born into Life try to hide and run away from the truth of their Self. Life is the greatest of all challenges known throughout Creation. Most people fail their challenge because they escape into fantasy instead of living their lives.

"As a Flower Soldier of Mother Life you will fight this human disease your Life long. To do this you will nurture people's imagination, because in this they will find Self power. Imagination is different from fantasy, in that imagination is the basis for all that can actually be created. We imagine how machines can operate, how chemicals work together, and how we can improve our circumstances and our world.

"Imagination becomes important only after we have studied. After every resource has been examined, then we can imagine how all the separate parts can function together.

"Imagination is visualizing possibilities. Remember that Imagination can only work when there is study. Imagination takes humans beyond simple rules into Creativity.

"You are now a young Flower Soldier. What you do, and how you will do it, will be your question and answer for your every action while you live.

"Do not be afraid to imagine the real problems that will confront you. These are not the imagined monsters that are born out of fear and fantasy.

"Fantasy monsters have never harmed humans. However, fantasizing about situations and fantasizing about relationships have destroyed millions.

"It is your job to help people find the Self that they are—their courage, their own thinking, their body, and their imagination.

"So, listen. I am imagining. I imagine that I awaken here on Sacred Mother Earth and marvel that I am alive and am part of Creation.

"I imagine that Creation has given me a body that I should respect and love.

"I imagine that I will learn with my physical existence as long as I inhabit my body.

"I ask you a question that you should ponder as a woman. We women have been taught for centuries that we should not trust our bodies or our minds. Imagine with me how deliberate and distressing this is to all women to be taught such a lie.

How incredibly sad this has been and is for women!

"Imagine your body and mind as your home, Liberty. What would happen if you were to distrust your beautiful home? Imagine what would happen, deep within your heart and mind, if each time you saw your home you distrusted it because you had been taught that it was 'female' and 'evil'?

"Would you love your home? Would you trust your body-home? How would you care for a body-home that was distrusted? I do not like what the religious fanatics have had to say about women. What this kind of extreme thinking does to all women—and how negatively it affects all men—is a subject that should keep psychologists busy for years!

"Half of humanity was made the scapegoat for all of humanity. Can you imagine what happens when any human is blamed and made to be the monster?

"If we had the same attitudes about the food we eat as the fanatics do about sex, we would vomit most of what we ate.

"Surely our future will be free of such madness.

"These questions have caused me pain, but they have also taught me to imagine new attitudes and ways of being.

"*I imagine that women and men are equal.*

"*I imagine that Life is challenge and giving—otherwise I would not be experiencing the presence of Life and Her Balance.*

"*I imagine that sex is natural—and can be beautiful.*

"*I imagine that all humans are born to Life to Learn and to Grow.*

"*I imagine that I can live my Life and question my own experience and my Existence.*

"*I imagine that I can help change the conditions of my world and my personal circumstances.*

"*I imagine that I can listen to Creation directly and that I need no interpreter.*

"*I imagine that I can be my Self even in those times when I am pained by others.*

"*I imagine that I am my own Authority and my own Teacher.*

"*I imagine that all information must be questioned by me.*

"*I imagine that I can be the kind Teacher to my Self.*

"*I imagine that I am a Self-Responsible human who will teach others to care for our Sacred Mother Earth.*

"Liberty, teach humans to honor and to cherish Life, and they will understand the difference between fantasy and true imagination.

"When humans learn to respect the Self that they are, they will learn to heal their crippled imaginations. Do this and you will know true Healing.

"My teacher named this little stone Imagination."

THE TEACHINGS OF THE ZERO CHIEFS
WEHOMAH (AIR)

THE MEDICINE WHEEL OF THE SPHERES OF THE BODY

The way our ancient Zero Chiefs thought about the Numbers of the Medicine Wheel, and how the Numbers relate to the Human Body Spheres, is very illuminating.

The Earth Count was one of the first Medicine Wheels discovered by our Ancient Zero Chiefs. Over time, the Temples of the Zero Chiefs discovered that the Sacred Number Powers of the Earth Count were directly Reflective of, and gave rise to, the Design and Function of the Human Body. See the Medicine Wheel below, which shows where the Body Spheres are found.

THE MEDICINE WHEEL OF THE SPHERES OF THE BODY

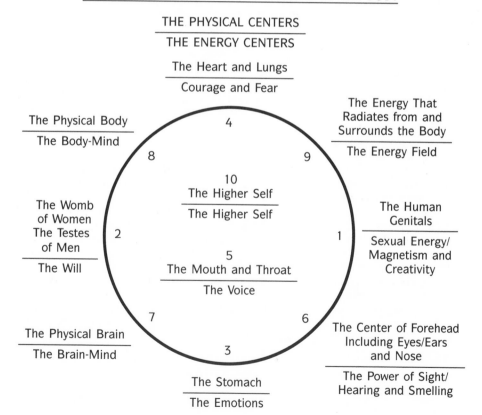

THE PHYSICAL CENTERS

THE ENERGY CENTERS

The Heart and Lungs

Courage and Fear

The Physical Body

The Body-Mind

The Energy That Radiates from and Surrounds the Body

The Energy Field

4

8   9

10
The Higher Self

The Higher Self

The Womb of Women The Testes of Men

The Will

The Human Genitals

Sexual Energy/ Magnetism and Creativity

2   1

5
The Mouth and Throat

The Voice

7   6

The Physical Brain

The Brain-Mind

The Center of Forehead Including Eyes/Ears and Nose

The Power of Sight/ Hearing and Smelling

3

The Stomach

The Emotions

The Zero Chiefs tell us that the human body is Earth Conscious and Sun Conscious. This Consciousness can be altered and changed through the use of crystals by the skilled and disciplined Medicine Person.

Crystals are very special gems that Mother Earth has given to humans. Medicine Women and Medicine Men have used plants and crystals to heal and balance humans for tens of thousands of years.

The gems can influence the electromagnetic field of the body, and bring healing, because our bodies are responsive to the Crystal-Matrix and to Crystal Light. Our bodies were born from the light spectrum of Earth's Crystals.

Crystals are Sun-Earth Light Conscious, and vibrate in rhythm to all other crystals of our Mother World.

Our Chiefs say that crystals from our Mother Earth also vibrate with crystals on other Planets. They sing within the light of every planet through the electromagnetic field.

Mother Earth vibrates in unison with Her crystals, and communicates with all other planets in our solar system.

The science of crystals is complex and requires training and practice. A person cannot manipulate the Spheres of the human body by indiscriminately placing the crystals anywhere on the body. Furthermore, the person placing the crystals on the body of another directly affects the results, much the way that a scalpel or sutures are not the same when used by a novice instead of an expert.

The Zero Chiefs taught that all of Creation's children were designed and created from the Sacred Zero. All of Life exists as part of the great Zero. The Zero Chiefs say that the Zero does not represent nothing, but in actuality contains and births everything.

The first born into substance from the Sacred Zero is One, our Sun. The second born is Two, our Earth. What they meant by this is that all of the Planets in our Solar system were born from our Sun.

The Sun was born from WahKahn and SsKwan, The Creatress and the Creator. The perfect Balance of what we understand to be dark and light is the first born into substance that we call our Sun. Everything born into substance-Spirit-Life is born from perfect darkness and light.

There is so much fanaticism centered around darkness and light that it is very important to know what our ancients thought darkness and light to be.

The Zero Chiefs thought that no absence of Light is possible, neither within substance nor without. Chemically, this is very true. In the darkest of places within substance or space, there exists the chemical transmission of light.

The Zero Chiefs considered our Sun to also be an atomic-chemical entity. They perceived Atomic Energy in this way:

"From perfect energy—WahKahn and SsKwan—all substance was born, and continues to be born. Energy pulls toward itself while substance spins away from energy. The spin of substance and the gravity of energy creates all chemical dark and light."

The One

One, in the Human Body Spheres, is the genitals of women and men.

The female genitals are called the Woman's Flower: All of humanity is born from the perfect balance of darkness and light of the flower of the woman.

The egg of the female and the semen of the male are called "Sun-born-in-the-Womb-Substance."

Because our Sun Mother-Father is the perfect balance of darkness and light, we are also born with the balance of darkness and light.

The human One, the First Body Sphere, is also the wondrous energy and magnetism of sexual love.

The Two

The combined energy of dark and light births Spirit into Substance through the union of female and male. Because of the union of woman and man, humans are formed within the Sacred Womb.

The woman, like Mother Earth, is responsible for carrying the Sacred Temple of Life which is known as the Womb, and is responsible for all Life. The Womb is the center of human Creation.

Humans are Spirits who are born from Death-Spirit into Life through the Sacred Temple of the Womb. Mother Earth shares this present and power with all females born to Her.

In the human body spheres, Two, for women, is the Womb.

The Two for men is the Testes.

Our ancients knew that properties of the Earth and the Sun are incorporated into the human. Two, the Second Body Sphere, is also the human Will for both females and males. There is no greater Will on Earth than the Will to create and birth Life, and then to Live.

The Three

Three, as you remember from the Earth Count (also called the Children's Count), is the number for all plants.

The Zero Chiefs observed that all plants possess the power to transform Death—the dead substance of animals and plants—into Life. The plants eat what is dead and change it into living tissue for themselves. Trees were called "the Great Transformers."

Plants are food for the humans, all animals, and all other plants. Plants are also the Healers for all humans, all animals, and other plants.

The Three of the Human Body Spheres is the Stomach.

The stomach has the power to transform all food—the animals and plants we have killed and ingested—into Life.

Emotions are also part of our Third Sphere. The human stomach is the center of emotions. The Zero Chiefs found that plants affect human emotions in many ways. Sometimes this effect is very direct, for example, in the case of plants eaten. Yet, there are also the profound and subtle effects such as the human response to the beauty of plants and their flowers. This is the Third Body Sphere.

The Four

Four, in the Earth Count, is the number for all animals.

The animals were the first children of Life to be given physical independence, in that they were given a heart and lungs. Now animals could move out across the Earth, the waters, and the skies.

The Animal Four gave the human their heart and lungs. This gave humans the ability to live in the element of Air.

The human heart and lungs together create the physical body center of the Four.

The energies of Courage and Fear were also given to humans by the animals. The Body Sphere of Courage is also the Heart.

Fear can be a friend as well as an enemy. Fear can alert the human to danger, and fear can become the foe when humans panic.

The challenge of fear and courage is one of the most difficult tests known to humans. Fear and Courage will quicken or dampen every Body Sphere. Spheres One through Four are instantaneously affected by the Four—our Courage or Fear.

Courage or Fear directly influences our creativity, our sexuality, our will, our yielding, our emotions, and our appetites.

Humans who possess no Self Energy are humans who lack Courage.

Humans who allow Fear to rule their lives have suppressed their sexuality and their yielding.

Humans who have suppressed their Fear lose the ability to translate their experiences into Self meaning, and become victims of their Emotions.

Bravado is not Courage. Humans who lack Self direction and Courage are driven by their bravado. Bravado is emotional immaturity.

The Fourth Body Sphere is our courage and our fear.

The Five

Five, as you remember from the Earth Count, is the Human being.

The Fifth Sphere of the Human Body is the Human Voice and is Sacred.

Our ability to speak, to communicate with Life and the Self, as well as with other humans, has made humans special and different from all other creatures born from Mother Life.

Humans have the ability to develop an intricate vocal system of Self communication. We have been given the power to transform thought images and visual images into word symbols through speech. Humans can articulate the sacred, the profound, the mundane, the ignorant, and the wise.

The Five, in the Human Body Spheres, is located at the Throat. It includes the mouth, the tongue, and the ability to taste.

The Six

The Sixth Human Body Sphere is our two eyes, our two ears, and our two nostrils.

The Six directly affects us by constantly giving us information of what exists within our present.

Through our physical Sixth Body Sphere we experience the visible and invisible worlds of the experiential.

The Seven

Our Zero Chiefs have discerned the difference between the Mind and what we know as the Brain.

The brain is the "trans-active-experiencer." This term is very old and was used by the ancient Flower Soldiers at Temple Baal-Hel-Atl-WahKahn.

Our brain, the trans-active-experiencer, maintains all physical body functions and stores all information of our experiences.

The Self Mind is higher than the brain, and has the ability to control the trans-active-experiencer.

Our brain is part of the Self Mind.

The Self Mind-Essence is known as Spirit.

The student of anatomy knows that light does not enter the brain directly. The cones and rods of the retina within the eye are stimulated by light. In turn, the neurons are stimulated. These neurons send electrochemical impulses along the length of the optic nerve to the brain. These electrochemical impulses are then translated into images of color and light.

It is the Mind that sees the images, not the brain. Deep within Self Completeness, within the totality of the body, exists the Mind.

The brain is not separate from the body.

It is this complete Mind that is called the Self.

The Zero Chiefs taught that the brain and the body are not separate. However, the body is not without its own knowing, and consequently, it too has consciousness.

They concluded that the brain-mind had knowing and the body-mind had knowing. But what was the difference between the two? This can be answered when we learn about the Eighth Body Sphere.

The Eight

Eight, in the Children's Count, is the cycles of all natural laws of the Earth. These laws directly affect humans through their eighth Body Sphere—the totality of the human body.

The Zero Chiefs taught that the body and its combined cells possess knowing—the Body-Mind. Each cell has its Knowing and is part of and participates with every other cell in the entirety of the body. This is the body-mind.

Most often, when we are awake, the brain-mind is awake and the body-mind is asleep. While we sleep, however, the brain-mind is asleep, but the body-mind is awake.

The brain-mind and body-mind are only awake together at very special times. During moments of deep and powerful creative thinking, or during times of extreme danger, the disciplined person experiences the brain-mind and body-mind awake together.

The body-mind speaks a different language than the brain-mind.

As was said, no light or sound, nothing that is physical, enters the brain. Only electrochemical energy is known to the brain-mind. Everything that is physical must be translated by the brain-mind into what we perceive as heat, light, sound, and so on.

The body-mind knows what the physical world is.

The brain-mind knows only symbol.

Symbol is the language of the brain-mind.

Symbol is knowing for the brain-mind.

Symbol is translating for the brain-mind.

Symbol is experiencing for the brain-mind.

The body-mind experiences the physical world directly, and communicates with the brain-mind through electrochemical means.

The brain-mind knows Life only through the electrochemical transference of neurons that has been created by the physical body-mind.

The Eighth Body Sphere, the body-mind, knows Life through the physical fact of itself—the body.

The teachers of the Temple of Baal-Hel-Atl-WahKahn said: "All of Creation is bound together by the Energies that comprise the Energy Field of Creation. The body-mind is also directly affected with every blink of the eye by the Energy Field. The body-mind has Knowing through the Energy Field that comprises Creation."

Children, poets, artists, musicians, creative mathematicians, true philosophers, scientists who search for Life, mothers who listen to Creation, and fathers who touch Life, are all Inspired human beings. These inspired, creative people are, at special moments, in communication with their body-mind, and because of this, receive knowing from the Energy Field. The body-mind speaks the language of the Energy Field.

The Seventh Body Sphere is the pinnacle of the head.

The Eighth Body Sphere is the entirety of the body.

The Nine

Movement is Energy, both visible and invisible. Movement is Energy, and Energy is Movement. Movement and Energy are Life, and all that has been Created. Humans are all Spirits who have been Born from Pure Energy into the Energy of Substance. This is the physical world.

All Energies are WahKahn and Sskwan. All Energies are Creation and Life.

Humans are born from Spirit Energy into the Energy of Light and Dark to become Spirit in Substance.

Humans are Energy living in Substance.

The Eight—the body and body-mind, and everything born into substance—is patterned from the Energy Field of Creation.

All beings who die on Earth are born back into Spirit through the Energy Field.

The Womb is the meeting place of the Pure Spirit Energy, known to us as Death, and our Earth world, known as Life.

The Energy Field contains the design and consciousness of all Numbers, all Deities, and all Knowing.

The Energy Field of the Earth is Nine and Nineteen and therefore contains all information and knowledge of Spirit and Substance. The Energy Field is Sacred Design.

All Energy has Consciousness. The Energy information at the center of a tiny seed or cell has Energy with Consciousness.

Energy speaks the language of Life and Death on Earth. Energy is within and surrounds all things created, including everything created in time and space. Everything created on Earth possesses its own Energy Sphere. Every rock, tree, bird, flower, fish, or human possesses its own Energy Sphere. The Energy Sphere that surrounds each human is unique and individual to that person.

The personal Energy Sphere of each human is the connection to the great Energy Field known as Life.

The Ninth Human Body Sphere is the measurable electromagnetic field that surrounds every Human Body.

The Ten

The Number Ten in the Body Spheres is the Human's Higher Self. The Higher Self is one of the most fascinating views the Zero Chiefs held of Life and Death.

For many years I thought deeply of how to present the subject of the Ten, the Higher Self, to have it make sense to someone who had never heard of the concept. I searched among other cultures, to see if there was a thread of similarity that concerned itself with the world of light. Then one day I discovered the myths and legends of the ancient Greeks.

Despite the carnage of the translators, it is easy to see that the ancient Greeks were not Judeo-Christian or Buddhist. Earth was the place of Light for the Greeks, just as it was for our ancients.

One of the very first official acts of the early Christians of Europe was to hide away "Hell" in a good safe place where they could control the concept. I learned from a Priest that this was made formal at the Council of Nice. At this same conference, it was also decided to disclaim the concept of rebirth—the understanding that we do in fact live many different lives.

Estcheemah once told me something, years ago, that I remembered for a very long time. It was one of those things that teases the mind.

One day, she mentioned casually that she thought many of the great legends and stories of the ancients of Europe were told to noble women and men—especially to the queens and kings—to explain Life, and Life after Death.

This made sense to me years later, while I was in college and studying the myths and legends of the Europeans. All these legends were badly distorted by official religious interpreters in later years, yet there are threads left here and there of the original tapestry of history that can be pieced together.

The great stories combine both history and myths and legends that were widely known. In other words, the stories were known to the Temple Priestesses and Priests who taught history.

This is also true of heraldic symbols. When people study the symbols of the heraldry of ancient times they find Griffins and Centaurs and many other composite half human-half animal beings, just as they do when they study our Mayan ancients. However, not everyone interprets these symbols the same way.

Our ancients of Europe and the Americas were not Judeo-Christians. Their use of animistic heraldry cannot be understood through the simplistic Judeo-Christian interpretations and beliefs that have vilified many animals and symbolic creatures throughout the centuries. For example, snakes, bulls, cats, and many flying creatures and people that fly have been made to represent "demons."

Flying humans did not mean only being a "devil or angel" to non-Christians. Many times flying humans were symbols of sea-going people—the early Egyptians, Greeks and Romans referred to sails as "wings."

The wolf in early times was the heraldic signature of the North Germans. The falcon and the white horse were synonymous with the ancient Britons. Other Germanic tribes were symbolized as the boar, the raven, and the swan. The Chinese used the symbol of the dragon to represent them.

In the United States we use the symbol of the American eagle to represent Americans. The bear represents Russia. Throughout our many wars, different military units represented themselves as eagles, snakes, doves, dogs, cats, horses, and hundreds of other heraldic symbols such as trees, flowers, weapons, stars, the Moon, and the Sun.

These symbols are simple descriptions of peoples, and of Sacred Temples that existed in Europe and many other places on our Earth.

While I was studying history, one of my professors demonstrated how symbolism had become distorted. As an example of this, he showed us a picture of Athena and explained how she represented the Athenian people of ancient Greece. The people of Athens were known by the same name as their Goddess. In another image he presented to us, the Athenian people were symbolically pictured as being their Goddess battling for their city-state.

He gave us another example that can be seen in one of the mosaic frescoes of ancient Rome. It pictures the god Dionysius fighting the pirates of the Tyrrhenian Sea. Again, the God symbolized the Roman fleet that ruled the whole Mediterranean and that cleared the sea of pirates and raiders. Myth and history were symbolically combined in this Roman mosaic.

Scholars, my professor went on to explain, know that a king existed who called him-

self Dionysius, Twin of Zeus (*Dio* for Twin, *Sius* for Zeus). He took on the name of his deity. So, the reason that the Romans picture the "god" Dionysius fighting alongside of them is because the people who fought with the Romans were known by the same name as their god-king Dionysius.

The Greeks and Romans were clever enough to build incredible aqueducts and buildings. These same Greeks and Romans were also the progenitors of much of what would become modern Europe. However, today there are people who believe that these same Romans and Greeks were too stupid to know what their heraldry meant. Part of the problem is that the greatest distortions of historical fact have occurred because of the way people interpret language.

What does this have to do with the world of Light? Like our Flower Soldiers, the Greeks called themselves Hellenes, which means "People of Light."

The Greeks lived in Helles—on Earth—with their Goddess Helen. *Hell*, or *Hel*, simply means "Light." In the ancient Celtic tongue, *Hel* meant "light," as it still does in modern German.

Helen was the Goddess of Light. Hel, Helen, Hellene, Helle, and Helios are all names for the Goddesses and Gods of Light.

Some of the names of the Goddesses and Gods of our own ancients of the Americas are very similar. For example, Wyola-Helle, the Goddess of the Prairie, was known as "Prairie-Light" in the Americas.

Another myth, or "teaching story," of ancient Greece shares some of the same understanding that our Mayan ancients had—the legend of Persephone. There are many "official" interpretations of what this story is supposed to mean. Yet, it was the understanding of our ancients of the Americas that helped me see deeper into what this legend might actually have meant to the early Europeans.

Persephone did not live on Earth. Rather, she dwelled in the world of Spirit with her Great Mother, Demeter. When she was "captured" by Hades, she came to Earth.

The words "Hades," "Heather," and "Heiden," mean "heathen," the "pagan"—in other words, the farmers, or Earth dwellers. The roots of these words mean "prairies" and "valleys" to this very day in modern Celtic and German.

"Hades" does not mean *under* the Earth. The "God" Hades was seen as the male power, the Twin, of Mother Earth, the female power.

When Persephone left Hades (Earth) she returned to her Mother (Demeter), meaning that she returned to the Great World of Spirit from which she had come. In modern German *Die Mutter* (pronounced Dee Mooter) continues to mean "the Mother." It is also important to recognize that the word "meter" means "Measure." Demeter is much more than the grain goddess of the ancient Greeks. Her name means "the Great Spirit Mother of all Life." It also means "the Measure."

In other words, the story tells how Persephone comes to live in Helle or Hades, and eats of the food of Death-Life that represents our Earthly existence. Then after her Life on Earth she returns to her Spirit Mother.

Persephone symbolizes the person or personality that we take on in each Lifetime. This myth was the way the ancient Greeks taught about the cycles of death and rebirth. For part of each existence we are Spirit, dwelling in the land of Pure Intellect and Measure—the world of Spirit. And for part of each existence we are Human—Spirit in Substance—experiencing Life on Earth, where we must eat of the food of Death and Life in order to live.

With this new understanding I began to see how our ancients also used combinations of names not only to describe peoples and histories but also to explain more sophisticated concepts.

Because a few of us Breeds speak American English, American Indian, and a little Greek and Latin, we continue to understand many of the root words that have been forgotten or ignored by Europeans.

In many stories and legends the Sun was often seen as the door between the Earth and the place of the goddesses and gods. Since the Sun (and all other Stars) is the first born in Substance from Creation, the Great Zero, it is easy to understand why it was thought of as the door—the entryway into Life. Consequently, it was very common among our people of the ancient Americas and those of early Europe to be given the name of the Sun, or Fire.

The word *Baalam*, in a very old form of the Crow language and pronounced a little differently, *Heaa-len*, means the same thing as "Hellen" in ancient Celtic-Germanic. *Ba* means "with" or "to." *Aalam*, *Healam*, or *Hellen* means "Light," which is the goddess Hellen, Helle, or Heallan.

Olin in ancient Crow/Aztec/Maya means "light in movement." *Olin* or *Hoaalin*, spoken with a slightly different intonation, is Hellen, or Holy.

Shim means to "shimmer or shine." *Shim* or *Chim* and *Chim Baalam* means "the Shimmering Light," "Shining Hellen," or "to appear."

It was the understanding of our ancients that all humans were born from Death/Dark-Light into the world of the Earth's Light and our Sun's Light. In other words, people were born here, into Helle, the Bright Land of Earth.

So we have the words of the ancients that carry with them the values that were part of the people of ancient Europe and Greece. We also have the words and teachings of our Chiefs of the Americas.

It is interesting that so many of our ancients, both here in the Americas and in the old world, realized that they came from a Dark-Light Spirit world into Helle—Hades—the world of Light-Dark that is our Earth. And it is equally interesting how many of these ancients taught that the person we are now, presently on Earth, is the Lower Self, and that upon death we will be reunited with our Higher Self.

Ten is intellect.
Ten is measure.
Ten is the Higher Self.

Our ancients thought that while a woman lives on Earth, her Twin, who is male, is her Higher Self and Lives in the Spirit world.

The ancients thought that while a man lives on Earth, his Twin, who is female, is his Higher Self and Lives in the Spirit world.

When describing the Ten, the Zero Chiefs taught that genius and creativity are possible for those who unite their energies with those of Life and Measure.

While we are in Pure Essence we are one being, both female and male, united with Creation because Creation is both female and male.

When humans are born into existence, they are separated within the Self as female and male, and are born as either female or male on Earth in order to learn and grow within the Essence of our Spirit.

One of the twins is born as a Five, a human, into the Substance-Spirit World of our Mother Earth. The other twin remains in the world of Pure Spirit Energy as the Ten. This is how it is possible for us humans to be born female in one lifetime and male in another.

The human Self, when unified as Spirit Essence, is a Deity, which simply means "deus"—two, or twin—and reflects the Twinness of our Creatress and Creator and of Life.

While the Five human dwells within the Substance-Spirit World of the Earth, he or she can unify with their twin only through Self Energy and Self Care.

All males learn of true honor when they honor the balance of their twin—the Goddess within them.

When women honor Goddess Mother Life, they can then begin to appreciate themselves and find the strength they need as women. Because the Creatress Mother has been so severely dishonored and ignored by humanity, all women must balance what has been so much out of balance. Women will do this through the acceptance of the fact that they are living reflections of our Creatress Mother.

Once women have made a powerful spiritual foundation with their Creatress, they can begin to learn of their balance—their love for their twin reflection, the God within.

The teachers of the Quetzal-Atl-Coatl-Atl Temple said:

"Unification of the Self is the human's greatest healing. The Higher Self brings Pure Intellect from all higher numbers where the Higher Self dwells. The Higher Self is the balance of energy."

The teachers of the Quetzal-Atl-Schim-Auc Temple said:

"The Energy Field around the human body (the Nine of the human body spheres) is directly affected by the Moon (an important power of the Nine in the Earth Count). The Energy Field connects the human, and all beings of the Earth, with the higher numbers of Life and Creation."

The teachers of the Temple of Chim-Atl-Lan-Helan said:

"Madness results when humans are not present with their bodies and with Life. To be completely separated from the Self and totally separated from the presence of Life results in madness. Humans who have gone mad are separated from Life's energies and do not know how they relate to existence."

The Zero Chiefs of old teach us that Ten is Intellect and Measure—the measure of all existence. Every human has the potential to measure Life and thought, and to reason, because Creation has created Pure Intellect; this is our Ten.

The Energy of Balance is Self Wisdom.

To evolve and to become a higher being, within Essence, is the Challenge for every Spirit born into Substance.

The Pure Intellect knows that Life is not long. Spirit does not fear Death. Pure Intellect is Spirit and is Deathless.

The center force of the Medicine Wheel can also be seen when we look at the example we have from the early Greeks. In this way we can understand the thinking of our Chiefs here in the Americas.

Ancient names within teaching stories like Psyche ("Circle") and Cupid ("Cube") described the center force of the Medicine Wheel. The Circle and the Cube describe the ideas and realizations discovered through Mathematics.

It should not come as a surprise that Spirit and Substance were thought to have "fallen in love" as Psyche and Cupid.

Psyche is the Beautiful Goddess. She is the Circle or Sphere. Cupid is the Beautiful God. He is the Cube or Square.

Like WahKahn and SsKwan, every angle or mathematical formula is born from the Sphere and the Cube, the Circle and the Square. This is Psyche-Circle and Cupid-Cube.

Beyond all the gifts that have been given to humans through mathematics, the intrinsic value of the Medicine Wheels will prove to be even greater.

It is interesting to examine a few of the Numbers of the Medicine Wheels for what they tell us. For example, if we take the model of five, the Human, and look at the numeral 5 from the viewpoint of 5 + 1, as opposed to 1 + 5, we will see that there is an incredible difference between them.

When they are centered in the Self, humans are a "true Five" according to the Zero Chiefs. A 5 person will consider all things from a five Self point of view first.

Sexuality is one. There are people who are driven by their sexuality; they place one before five.

For the Centered human, sexuality begins with the five.

Both figures express themselves in the Present, the six. But the approach, and the result, are very different.

It must be remembered that hundreds of combinations exist as relationships among the Numbers, but for simplicity's sake we will only examine a few.

A 2 + 5 (Will plus Self) person is not the same kind of being as a 5 + 2, a person who is centered in the Self first.

The woman or man who places emotions first, 3 + 5, is not a balanced person. It is better to be a 5 + 3.

When the equation is 4 + 5, instead of the 4 being courage, it becomes fear or rage. It is better to be a 5 + 4—a human plus courage.

As you can see, placing the Self, 5, first is very important.

The Plants Are the Foundations of Life

A three is a plant.

A three must eat Light and Earth elements to live. Light (1) plus Earth (2) equals Plant (3).

When any human eats a three, she or he also ingests two, the Earth elements, and one, the Light from our Sun.

Each of us is a five, a Human.

When a person is a vegetarian, then that person is a 2 + 3, which equals 5—Earth elements plus plants.

Almost all animals eat plants, and some animals eat animals.

The number eight = Body. An animal (4) that eats an animal (4) will equal 8 (body).

There are humans, five, who eat meat, four.

The mathematical combinations that give us five are: 4 + 1 = 5 and 3 + 2· = 5 and 2 + 2 + 1 = 5.

Cannibalism is not new to humans, but it was not as widespread in antiquity as some people would like to believe. The numbers can show why. A 5 + 5 does not equal 8 (body), as when a four eats a four.

Look at the numbers five and four, and see what happens. A Human (5) eats an Animal (4), which equals Movement and Energies (9).

But, when a Human eats another Human the Numbers equal 10—5 + 5 = 10—and 10 is Measure.

I am sure the cannibals were illuminated to the fact that they were murdering humans for food, and this brought them instant remorse and measure. This is the reason there was not very much cannibalism. When cannibalism occurs among humans, it is only for a short time—until measure is exacted.

Beyond my words is a vast continent of learning that awaits you. Self Discipline, Self Courage, Discernment, and Intelligence will be your guide through the Numbers that Creation has given us and has shown us as our challenge of the Self.

498

Life and Healing

The concern that I began to feel about our Mother World grew within me as Estcheemah taught me about my Self and Responsibility.

Her insistence that we must care for our Earth Mother caused me to become acutely aware of the fragility of our planet. The fact that Mother Earth could die deeply distressed me. Because of this concern I asked Estcheemah what could be done.

"It is not uncommon to read arrogant and fanatical statements about our Mother Earth," she answered. "In magazines and newspapers we all see such headlines as NATURE CAN BE FOOLED, and SOMETIMES MOTHER NATURE GETS IT WRONG or NATURE HAS RAVAGED THE VILLAGE OF . . .

"People forget that it is their Mother Earth who has birthed every living creature and all things that live on her Planet. They believe that Mother Earth can 'get it wrong' and of course, 'that "man" was doing it right.'

"This kind of silly hate talk can only be believed by enemies of Life, by people who believe that our Living Earth is dead matter.

"Fanatics have called our Mother World 'the mother of all harlots,' 'the realm of all evil,' and a thousand other hateful things. I think that the ancient writers were speaking of governments, not the Earth who gave them their Life. Yet, who will argue for Mother Life?

"Over the centuries all the hate talk of every kind of fanatic has bred disgust and contempt for everything that is fine and beautiful—our wondrous Living Earth. And this kind of negativity has affected all humans deeply.

"This fearmongering, which holds that Life is the enemy and that woman is the enemy, has sickened generations of people and has crippled the thinking of millions of people with its destructive language. What this has come to mean is that healing is also

supposed to be a hate weapon to use against the enemy—Life.

"When people have the slightest itch, or any fear of health problems, they attack the situation by using Antibiotics. *Antibiotics* means "Anti-Life." These drugs promise to 'Destroy' the 'Offenders' that have 'Invaded' the body. The 'offending part' is cut out and obliterated. Then, after massive damage and extreme violence has been done to the body, the 'experts' apply their 'medications' to 'aid' with the Healing. The people are then told to let their bodies do the healing. They are also told, with a condescending smile, that 'the patient should allow Mother Nature to do Her bit.'

"The Spirit of Life is ignored, because *spirit* has been demeaned into meaning only 'alcohol' or something even worse. *Spirit* has come to mean "Anti-Life"—Death. Other fearmongers preach that there are also 'evil spirits' that attack the body.

"No, when the word *Nature* is used, it is just a nice way of skipping the truth that it is Mother Life who does the Healing of all Her children.

"The word *Antibiotics* means 'Against Life.'

"What we Humans need is *Probiotics*.

"What is Life-Giving is seldom talked about because then Mother Life would have to be mentioned as something more than what comes labeled in a jar. But, when Life Herself needs to be talked about, the subject is closed to further discussion. Mother Life is denied Her existence.

"Life has been made the Enemy by woman-haters who despise Earth for being Female.

"When Life becomes the enemy, then what hope is there of understanding Life, healing, or the reasons for us Spirits to be born to Mother Life? When Life is made the adversary, a war begins in the hearts and minds of the People. The war begins first in the mind, then it affects the heart. And the people who hide behind the cold language of science also do not explain Life. There is no 'alternative' to the fact of Life.

"Probiotic thinking heals the heartbroken thinking of humans who have been taught that Life is the enemy through all the hate and fear talk about Mother Life. Probiotics turns our hearts and minds toward the discovery of Life.

"When the human body is out of balance, many times it is because another kind of Life balance exists. The new Life balance exists because the body is trying to restabilize itself.

"Probiotics is *symbiosis*. This word means 'With Life'; I like that word.

"Everything in Life is Symbiotic, not an 'enemy.' Disease is a presence that is living because there is a failure of balance in the human body. The answer to this is not to kill everything but to bring balance.

"The war against Mother Life is very serious and very foolish.

"Earth Mother, Mother Life, is our Life-Giver. When, in the hearts and minds of people, Mother Life becomes the Living Being that She truly is, then all humans on Earth will begin to understand the reasons for their very existence.

"So many people refuse to see Mother Life, because most humans do not want to be responsible for their lives or for the lives of others sharing their Earth. Humans like to pretend that they can hide things from Mother Life. They like to pretend that She is as foolish as they are. Many humans want to sneak around in Life, believing they can hide their foolishness from the eyes of Creation. Nothing can be hidden from Creation.

"Most humans in our world have been taught that Creation is Self righteous, angry, judgmental, cruel, stupid, and jealous—like they are. Nothing could be further from the truth. Creation knows no jealousy.

"This phenomenon of belief is called human ignorance. Our future will be different because one day humans will begin to ask, 'What is precious?' We need to seek the answers to this question.

"Before we can answer why we humans have so callously been destroying our living

world, we need to look at what is precious.

"If all the dead had remained dead after the Second World War, then Human Life would have become more precious. But everybody was in a hurry to be reborn. Can you blame them? Who does not want Life, and the opportunity to experience who they are? Life is a wonderful Experience. Why shouldn't they be eager to be reborn?

"No doubt you think I am arguing that things should change, but this is not what I am saying. People will make changes when they really want them.

"After billions die because we have fished out our oceans and polluted our Earth, then changes will be made—if there are any survivors.

"I think that when WahKahn, our Creatress Mother, is once again respected by humans, then great change will come.

"One of the first balances we need in our thinking is that women are important. Women are equal to men. For any woman to deny her innermost knowing and feelings about Mother Life and Her healing abilities is to dishonor herself and Mother Creation.

"Every Mother knows that Mother Life is near when her child needs healing.

"The word *Healing* itself is feminine. It comes from the Celtic and Greek word *Heilin*, which is, again, the word for the Goddess Helen. The Goddess Helen was the Goddess of Light and *Heilin*—Healing. *Heilin* means 'Healing,' and it also means 'Goddess Light.' Even the word *Well* comes from the root word *Hel-*'Helen' and *Heilin-*'Healing.'

"A Song of Light and Healing is needed. There needs to be a Balance.

"How can we find balance again in our time? That is the question that all of Humanity faces. We can begin this by teaching and activating our Selves, like our Zero Chiefs did for so many thousands of years. We can get to Know Sacred Life again.

"For example, we can get to know the Plant before the herb is used for healing. This is a very important step for people to make. To respect the plant that heals us is to respect Life. This is Probiotics. Our Zero Chiefs understood the need for Probiotics.

"I will use the example of Penicillin to help you understand what I mean by Probiotics and what I mean by getting to know the substance of healing.

"Penicillin is alive and has energy and knowing of what the Human needs. We can communicate with Penicillin to get the help we need. No, Penicillin cannot speak Crow, Cheyenne, English, or German; but Penicillin has its knowing through LIFE'S Energies. Speaking with the healing substance or plant is our way of communicating with the plant through its Energies with Life.

"Here is a prayer of our Zero Chiefs that you can remember when you have need. The prayer will also help you understand what I am telling you. The Medicine Woman or Medicine Man would hold the healing substance or herb and say:

" 'Creation, I touch my hand to your wondrous being, Sacred Mother and Father Earth. I am most grateful for my Earth existence and my Life experience that you have given to me. Today, I am in the presence of this person who has come to me with an imbalance of health. While the sickness introduces this one to eventual Death, it also introduces present Life.

" 'I acknowledge this and hold this fact present in my heart and mind as I speak with you, Sacred Life.

" 'While we can set a bone, while we can cleanse and cover a wound, beyond this is your presence of being called Healing and Life.

" 'I ask you, Sacred Life, with this Healing plant, to bring balance to this person who has come to me for Life Communication—with the Self and You.'

"With this prayer said, the person would be introduced to the Healing plant, as a friend. The person would be with the plant or Healing substance so that she or he could speak to Life and this friend about Healing.

"Whether it be through Penicillin or a Gardenia, the balance of Health will return to our troubled Earth people when we begin to honor Sacred Mother Life again."

503

The Twenty Great Teachers

For those of you who are interested in the study of humans this is what our Zero Chiefs discovered about the Twenty Great Teachers of Life. These Teachers are the Teachers of Experience.

All Babies Are Born Free

1. Rage is the people's First teacher.
2. Care is the people's Second teacher.
3. Pain is the human's Third teacher.
4. The Physical is the human's fourth teacher.
5. Feelings are people's Fifth teacher.
6. Sex is the human's Sixth teacher.
7. Honesty is the human's Seventh teacher.
8. Testing is the human's Eighth teacher.
9. Victory is people's Ninth teacher.
10. Confrontation is people's Tenth teacher.
11. Raw power is the human's Eleventh teacher.
12. Spirit is the human's Twelfth teacher.
13. Death is the human's Thirteenth teacher.
14. Fear is the people's Fourteenth teacher.
15. Defeat is the human's Fifteenth teacher.
16. Loneliness is people's Sixteenth teacher.
17. Need is the human's Seventeenth teacher.
18. Seeking is the human's Eighteenth teacher.
19. Love is the human's Nineteenth teacher.
20. Patience is the human's Twentieth teacher.

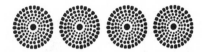

The Search for Ceremony

The search for Ceremony is without doubt one of the most important and rewarding pursuits for any person seeking to touch the immense reality we know as Life.

Most humans recognize that they have great need for Ceremony and ways of touching Creation, but few people put forward any effort toward realizing their urgency.

What is this urgency? It is our need to reestablish our Balance with our beingness. To do this we must recognize that we are part of Creation and are alive. We Spirits seek for special ways and times to celebrate Life and our existence with Creation.

It is a great pity that most humans are satisfied to do without these times of intimacy. Humans who avoid Ceremony deny themselves intimacy with their Self and Life—they desire to live in a fantasy.

Humans who are criminal, base, lazy, and secretive avoid Self Ceremony because they fear they will discover their perfidy.

Creation is Life, and has absolute Knowing. Anything done on Earth is known to Creation, and every living being or creature is known directly and intimately by Creation.

The Creatress and Creator do not judge humans because Creation knows that humans are learning what it means to be Self-Responsible beings.

WahKahn and SsKwan have no need for written commands so humans can learn of themselves and Life. The sheer fact of existence, of each person's Life, is proof enough to point out what is profound and meaningful.

Life is the Greatest Teacher of all human Spirits.

Nowhere in our Universe, nowhere in space or time, is there a more wondrous place to be than here in Life. Here with Mother Earth there is experience that is called learning—and is the reason humans live.

People who realize that they are alive also realize that they want to celebrate their existence with personal Ceremonies.

Those who want Ceremony always look to the Seasons and their Presence, within their Time, on Mother Earth. We have our Medicine Wheels to guide us.

The Little Dome of Rainbows

I was the Fire Keeper when ten Cree and Ojibwa people visited Estcheemah from Canada. After everyone had been carefully seated in the spacious lodge, Estcheemah spoke to them about Healing and the history of the Little Dome, called the Rainbow Lodge:

"There is so much talk about Sweat Lodges," she began. "But few people know the history of our Lodges.

"Many peoples of our Earth have used the Sweat Lodge. It is not a Medicine Lodge, but a simple bath that some people call a 'sauna bath.'

"In contrast, the Little Dome, or Rainbow Lodge, is a Lodge of Healing and Prayer.

"I have seen every kind of Sweat Lodge built, and every kind of Rainbow Lodge. Rainbow Lodges are like hospitals and must be kept very clean. Cleanliness is a deep purpose of the Lodge."

"Rainbow Lodges have a very long history among the people of North and South America. The very large communal Lodges of the ancient peoples of the Southwest can still be seen. Chaco Canyon in New Mexico is the best example of how these large Ceremonial Lodges were constructed.

"These Lodges were built in the round and were made of stone. They served as Kivas, Ceremonial centers, and as Healing Lodges. The roofs of these Kivas were carved and fitted to shut out the light and to act as louvers to recirculate air.

"The great circular stone rooms all had a long pit that held the hot stones when the Kiva was used as a Rainbow Lodge. Both the water and hot stones were handed down from the 'sky roof' into these Lodges, to be placed in the stone cairns. Fires were rarely built inside these rooms.

"These Rainbow Lodges were the Hospitals. Highly sophisticated and very extensive herb and plant farming, for healing purposes, was one of the main focuses of the hospital of Chaco Canyon. This was the place you were brought when you broke a leg or needed a tooth extracted. This was also the place where many babies were born.

"Some accidents are very bloody, and some diseases are putrid. The consequence of this was that the great Kivas were built in such a way that it was possible to keep them

507

very clean. Since sand can be easily removed, the floors of the Kivas were composed completely of fresh, clean river sand.

"These hospital rooms were used both for surgery and for ceremonial purposes. The population was not so great as to have the Kivas stuffed full of the sick and diseased. Much of the time the Kivas were empty, and so they were used as places of meditation and prayer.

"Of course, these Great Kivas and Rainbow Lodges of the Southwest are no longer used for Healing. In fact, many of the people have forgotten their use."

"The people of the North were nomads, and so their Rainbow Lodges are small and portable.

"This Lodge here, as you can see, has been constructed from fresh river willows. Eight (sometimes sixteen) willows are bent over to form a Dome similar to this one.

"I am using the word *dome* purposely because in English dome also means 'dame' which means 'woman.' *Notre Dame*, as an example, means 'North Woman.' Maybe the ancient Celts had a Medicine Dome there also? You already know that in your Cree tongue the word for the shape of this Lodge means 'womb' or 'woman.'

"The Lodges of nomads were covered with animal skins. However, the skin, or covering, of this Rainbow Lodge is made of canvas. I keep my canvas clean by washing it with soap and letting the Sun dry it.

508

"We have placed our Medicine Blankets on top of the skin of this Lodge to make it beautiful. This is how it has been done for hundreds of years. These Rainbow Robes are sometimes called Twilight and Morning.

"Inside our little Medicine Dome is the small hole that Lightningbolt dug in the Earth. This is called the *Cheemahdah*, or Fire Ring.

"The volcanic stones that he gathered and heated in our Ceremony fire will be put into our *Cheemahdah*.

"As many of you know the ceremonial fire is called the Children's Fire. The reason for this is because it is always to remind the people of renewal."

I had used a specially built paddle that Estcheemah had taught me to make called a 'fire tongue.' I used this fork, just as our ancients did, to shovel the fiery, glowing stones, one by one, into the *Cheemahdah*.

After I finished my work, I handed in the wooden bucket that Estcheemah always used for her Ceremonies, then I crawled in and sat next to Estcheemah. Pulling the bucket of water to her, she closed the door.

Estcheemah greeted all of us with the words of our ancient Temple Water Keepers:

"Enter into the Rainbows, person. Enter into this Lodge of Renewal and Cleansing.

Morealah dances with Cheemah, Water with Fire, in this Temple. Ehahmah dances with Wehomah, Earth with Air, in this Temple.

"WahKahn and SsKwan will wrap you in their blanket of beginning and furthering. What was imagined for you by Creation is seen behind your eyes in this Temple; be mindful of that. Be Respectful to your Self and be honored that Sacred Earth has provided you with this Temple of Cleansing."

Estcheemah slowly sprinkled water over the stones and the Little Dome quickly filled with warm steam.

"In the days of old," she explained, "the bathing began first in the river or from the bathing bowls. Thousands of these bowls, found all over America, were used by the women for bathing. Old bathing bowls were, in turn, used to start seedlings.

"Rainbow Lodges were not used every day, but bathing was done every day. Rainbow Lodges were used for purification. During purification and Healing Ceremonies, like this one, the people bathed first in their Ceremonial Bowls. After the bath was finished, the Rainbow Lodge was entered. When the Ceremony was complete, the people then went to the river to bathe, or they would use their bathing bowls once again.

"Now it is time to speak within the Womb of the Earth and ask Creation to be close with us."

Estcheemah sprinkled more water on the hot stones and began her prayers.

The steam became a cloud and the cloud became a sea of discovery for me. I wandered far and wide within my heart and mind while I was being cleansed by the water and prayer.

At times, Estcheemah's strong voice became as young as a wildflower, then as old as Earth Herself. I was amazed by this. She spoke, telling of how birds glide through the air, and she sang about the little flowers at every creek. Somehow, with her prayer and song, I could sense that Life truly cared for us. She celebrated the Sacred Self of each person born to Life, and she sang of the courage of Self Honesty and the power of human Responsibility.

Rainbows of light whirled in front of everyone's eyes and some were crying softly.

Estcheemah was sitting at her kitchen table when Liberty entered. The beautiful old woman was sewing as though she had never been sick. Liberty hoped that her teacher was getting stronger. Yet, in truth Estcheemah had learned how to appear stronger than she actually was. She looked up at Liberty, smiled, and bit off a thread.

Liberty sat down at the table and studied the face of her teacher. The old Zero Chief's eyes shone with immense kindness. How was this possible? Liberty was more and more astounded. This woman had had such a harsh life, yet she was never helpless and bitter like so many other old people. Where did she get her immense energy for so much love and care? Her mind was incredibly sharp and clear. How was this possible?

Liberty squeezed Estcheemah's hand, not knowing what to say, then poured herself a cup of coffee. She and Lightningbolt had been talking about what they were going to do when Estcheemah was gone. Liberty was frustrated beyond words. Finally, after years of work, she knew she was getting somewhere in her training, and she now feared that she would suddenly be left without enough Self power to succeed. This seemed so unfair to her, yet she did not know how to speak of it. Estcheemah did.

"You want to know how is it that I am so alive after all these years?" Estcheemah paused, and looked at her apprentice. "It is a question of Justice, Liberty.

"In one Lifetime we will scream injustice, and in the next Lifetime claim that all we do is Justice.

"Within time every human act is Balanced by Justice. This Balance occurs over a very long period of time. Justice answers humans over Lifetimes, never in a second. Justice is a question that all youth try to understand. This is because Justice questions all youth.

"The old who try to compromise Justice and try to explain away Justice will be asked to Sit with Justice and to decide their fate in another Lifetime.

"Justice is our Goddess of Balance.

"Our Goddess, Justice, can see with the swiftness of Light and as far as Eternity. Her name means 'Light' and 'Brightness.'

"The Eyes of Justice are the Eyes of WahKahn and SsKwan, the Perfect Eyes of Eternity.

"The Sword of Justice is Time and Presence.

"The Mind of Justice is Eternity's Perfect Reason and Absolute Knowing.

"The pronouncement of Justice is the *Shee-nah-meeah*.

"*Shee-nah-meeah* means 'the Balance of Existence' and is what has been experienced and learned through all time and through all of the lives we have lived.

"Our lives are not very long. Because of this, most humans do not comprehend time much beyond their immediate circumstances.

"Only acts of human Courage are rewarded within time. Justice only recognizes human Acts of Courage.

"Time does not punish humans. Humans who have no Self, or refuse Self Responsibility and their own Knowing, face chaos and become the victims of chance.

"What this means is that Justice will always expose humans to their every weakness. This is done by Justice to provide a Way for humans to discover their strengths, and to grow within their Essence.

"A woman of Courage, as an example, will look into her future and study and measure what needs to be done. Her understanding of her Self and her Present will give her immense courage to do something about the problems that confront her.

"The Zero Chiefs teach that all humans must

search deeply within themselves for their Personal Knowing.

"Knowing exists beyond belief, politics, gossip, and fear. Self Knowing is a prize that all humans must battle to possess and keep.

"Personal Knowing is the Essence of who and what we are. As you already know, through Ceremony and Disciplined Self learning, it is possible to Know the Self and our Personal Knowing.

"When the human begins to meet the Self, she or he will be within the Presence of our Goddess Justice. These people will instantly realize that Justice never limits human experience. Instead She presents every opportunity for humans to experience the Essence of who they are.

"We Zero Chiefs teach that all Spirits Born will meet the fact of who they are while they Live. This is their Essence.

"Justice is not law books and lawyers. Justice is also not judging. Justice is a Self judgment that is willing to see all things within Balance and Measure.

"Human judgment is simple human measure. If there is no measure—no experience and no balance—then there is no Self judgment and no real human Justice.

"Creation will never judge a human being, because Creation already has perfect Knowing. Creation knows exactly why humans do what they do.

"Justice is Life. She knows intimately every human's existence and insistence.

"If there be Justice, Liberty, let it be your understanding of your Self and the fact of your caring for your Self.

"If there be Justice, let it be that you seek your own Self Courage.

"If there be Justice, let it be that you become your greatest Teacher.

"If there is Justice, let it be your Courage to battle Self ignorance.

"If there is Justice, let it be your Courage to be

a human of Honor and Self Integrity.

"If there be Justice, let it be your Courage to accept Life and Her Challenges.

"If there be Justice, let it be your Courage to Respect and Care for our Sacred Earth.

"If there be Justice, let it be your Courage to Honor Sacred Mother Life.

"So it is Justice that you live the way you do, Liberty. What you do with your Life Experience, in this Lifetime, is your question and your Choice."

Spring bloomed like no other Estcheemah had ever seen. Everywhere there were nuances of color and a brilliance of loveliness she had not noticed before. Yet, as the Sun rose, she was filled with a deep longing she had never known could exist. Estcheemah instantly knew that it was the Spirit world calling to her.

The old Zero Chief stood in awe as she watched the sunlight touch the width of the Ocean. The sun blazed and shone as brightly colored sparkling diamonds of light on every wave of the Ocean's tide. Wild bursts of silver and gold caressed the land, dancing playfully about Estcheemah's feet as she sat down on her lawn chair to think and pray.

She looked up into the vault of the blue sky and then toward the green of the cedars. Was it always so sad to leave Life? Suddenly, from within the forest behind her, the sound of a billion honey-

bees rose and filled the air with their melody of renewal. A smile touched her lips. She had not heard that distinctive song for many years. She frowned, remembering. Yes, the first time she had heard that sound, she was around ten.

The powerful old Chief patiently began to design her Final Ceremony. She had been preparing many years for this day to come—and now this Spring had brought the Time and Place. Every detail had to be considered with the utmost care and devotion. This Ceremony would be her Final Honoring of her most beloved friend and teacher,

515

Mother Life.

It was the middle of April when Estcheemah asked her twins to build her a beautiful Spring Bower made of cedar branches. They worked quickly and expertly together, and soon had it complete.

Their teacher had appeared to be growing ever stronger, but in reality this was not true. Estcheemah knew she did not have many more weeks to live.

When the Bower was completed Estcheemah instructed her twins to go for a walk and to contemplate their relationship with Life and with one another. "Return this evening, after you have thought long on my question," she told them.

When they had gone she set to work building a fire circle not too far from her Medicine Bower. When the Sun disappeared behind the Ocean's horizon Estcheemah stood alone in the shadows of the twilight. Her powerful yet strained voice rose up through the forest, carrying her prayers to meet the first glimmer of starlight.

The powerful old woman bent down to light her last Earthly Fire, honoring the Self Spirit of Mother Earth—known as Beauty. The flames shone bright flaxen-gold, hurling sparks into the air ever higher to join the Stars.

The Zero Chief placed a stone in each of the four directions in a large circle around her Fire. She placed a gold stone in the East to honor Cheemah. A black one was placed in the West to honor Ehahmah. Next came a red stone in the South to honor Morealah, and a white stone in the North to honor Wehomah.

She added more and more wood to the fire until it glowed bright and hot. When Liberty and Lightningbolt sat down nearby, she went and stood behind them.

"This will be my last dance," she told them in a voice that sounded ageless. "For me it is the final action in this Life that I want to do. I warn you now that the strain of this dance may kill me this very evening, or I may die tomorrow. So do not be surprised or even pretend surprise when I die. This dance is my Prayer Dance. It is designed to push me beyond my physical endurance. It is a good way to die, much better than waiting."

Liberty was stunned by what she was hearing, but Lightningbolt was not. He had been expecting this announcement for weeks.

"This last dance is mine—I claim it," Estcheemah announced, turning to face her fire. "My heart beats fast with the excitement of the great challenge of my new battle." She walked to her fire and began to dance around it slowly. "This is my Thanksgiving Dance for the Life that you have given to me, Mother Life."

Lightningbolt began to play the drum she had handed him. She now danced in place, in front of her fire, slowly turning in a graceful motion to Lightningbolt's rhythm. Liberty began to sing Estcheemah's Medicine Song for her.

Suddenly, Estcheemah tossed a powder upon the hot embers. An unexpected, loud explosion erupted from the fire, sending a fountain of light and color into the air.

Lightningbolt and Liberty leaped to their feet. The forest echoed the boom while final shards of light and brilliant sparks flashed toward the sky. Estcheemah calmly danced on and began to twirl her shawl as she danced. Her hair had become as startlingly white as the Moon.

"Watch for the secret in the light," Estcheemah called as she danced. "Watch for the Fire Kachina Dancers."

Liberty had seen the secret and been surprised even before Estcheemah had called to them. At the precise moment when the light flared and the forest rang from the boom, Estcheemah had tossed and twirled her shawl to create a silhouette of a dancing fox.

The Medicine Woman danced on, throwing

more handfuls of powder into her fire. The light burst into every kind of color, but there were no more explosions. Again, Estcheemah spun her shawl and expertly tossed it into the air, creating the silhouette of a flying bird.

Suddenly Lightningbolt could also see the secret. When he saw Estcheemah's shawl take the form of a dolphin leaping in the dazzling lights, he was stunned by surprise and joy. He now watched in fascination as Estcheemah created still another form, this time an eagle.

As Estcheemah created these Medicine Shadows of light she danced gracefully, her steps weaving about the fire. She continued to form shape after shape with her shawls—there seemed to be no end to them. She was honoring and celebrating the many beings of Mother Earth that had been her guides and teachers throughout her life.

However, the more she danced, the more the tension grew for Lightningbolt and Liberty. Suddenly they realized the full truth—she would not survive this dance.

While the Beauty they saw intrigued them and enchanted their eyes, new white-hot explosions of sound split the night, jarred their emotions, and brought them to the edge of weeping.

"Discipline!" Estcheemah called, sounding out of breath. "This is my Death Dance, not yours. Be strong!" Finally, after what seemed forever, Estcheemah slowed her steps, then she sat down very gracefully upon her blanket near the fire.

Now silence and the darkness of the night returned. Lightningbolt was so shaken by the experience he could only respond by not moving. The fire had become embers that glowed softly, illuminating Estcheemah's white hair.

Liberty's eyes had filled with tears, but she was determined to not cry.

The Moon was just beginning to clear the tops of the tallest cedars and the luminous clouds that had hidden Her. Liberty smiled when she felt drops of rain touch her face. The Moon glowed bright, revealing mountainous valleys of skyborne clouds. A gentle rain appeared as a mist in the cedars. The cloud of rain and moonlight rolled over the land and through the cedars, dressing Estcheemah in a shawl of rain and moonlight. The tears of the old Zero Chief joined with the rain, and she smiled. The Chiefs had always said that rain was the Mother Earth's answer to prayer. Rain brought change and the ever renewing.

Every moment that Lightningbolt had known Estcheemah she had been a surprise. He had never met anyone as kind, yet as Self powerful and willful, as his teacher. Her patience was awe-inspiring and her personal strength enormous. However, the show of Self determination and power that he had just witnessed astounded him and left him unable to speak.

She is truly noble, Liberty thought. A Flower

Soldier to the very end! I will be that determined and strong.

The rain stopped as suddenly as it had begun and brought an absolute stillness.

Then after a time, Estcheemah said softly, "Come sit with me at my fire." Her voice was strained, but uncommonly clear. Liberty immediately jumped up and hurried to Estcheemah and sat down beside her. Lightningbolt quickly followed and sat on Estcheemah's left.

"I saw this dance outside of a Kiva over forty years ago," Estcheemah explained. "I was young. I dreamed that one day I could also dance with the Fire Rainbows." She was quiet for a moment, allowing herself to catch her breath. "It took me many years to collect the powders that have now become part of your Fire Rainbow. Remember the colors of the Fire Rainbow when you heal the sick.

"Now I will die. How good it will be!" She folded her hands together. "It is my time to leave Mother Life. Because I am so old, now only Death can comfort me. I wish to return to Energy Essence and Spirit.

"You both have the opportunity to continue to work with my most powerful apprentice, Sky River. She is a very dedicated Healer and Teacher. However, you will have to be your own strong Self teachers to endure as Flower Soldiers."

"I am asking you, Liberty and Lightningbolt, to trust your Reason and to contemplate your Season. I offer you these golden leaves." She picked up two leaves and handed them to her apprentices.

"These little leaves startle me with their direct question of Life and Death.

"As a soldier of the Rose, I will soon wrap myself in the robes of the Season. The Seasons were the ever unfolding of my Mind. I ask you to care for the Sacred Rose. You will be Her Seeds that will be blown by Earth's wind. But you must direct your lives or there will be no seeds of thought.

"In my hands are every Choice and Decision I made in my Life. I call these the Leaves of my Existence.

"The many Leaves that I have been are my many experiences. I hold in my hand the Leaves that I have been. Every mistake and every victory have taught me. My Leaves have been created with care and Beauty. My Leaves covered my growing Tree of blossoming.

"The consequence of another day passes with these words I have said. Who is it that will possess their Leaves of experience? Will you be Responsible for your own Life?

"To see and appreciate the Door of Leaves is to be Present with Life and Self thinking. Courage is the Opening of the Door of Leaves. Those who walk through the Door of Leaves can experience Victory."

Estcheemah's exhaustion burst upon her and she lay down, weakened from her Dance. Lightningbolt carried the old Medicine Chief back to her home.

This was Estcheemah's last Ceremony. Within days she began to disappear within herself and become part of another Existence.

Four weeks later Estcheemah, the Zero Chief, Flower Soldier, died.

Her will was explicit, uncluttered. She was cremated immediately. Robert inherited her property.

Her last request was that Lightningbolt and Liberty "give her ashes to the Mother Ocean."

Eighty fires glowed and burned in a large Circle made for Estcheemah. Many people came from hundreds of miles around. There was no gossip or talk. Robert and eleven other people Lightningbolt did not know presided over the Ceremony.

Few words were spoken during the Ceremony. The most prevalent sound was quiet weeping.

Lightningbolt and Liberty were for the most part ignored because many of the people present were old and had never known them. Sky River re-mained discreet. Just for the briefest moment she appeared, touched both Lightningbolt and Liberty on the forehead, then disappeared.

For the rest of the time they sat alone, separated from Estcheemah's relatives and the mourners.

Lightningbolt and Liberty held Estcheemah's "Earth treasures." Before she died, she had given them instructions of what to do with her Medicines. Liberty lovingly held Estcheemah's Pipe in her lap and Lightningbolt held her "Bundle of Secrets."

They stood alone at dawn and prayed at the Ocean, then they pushed their boat out into the surf. They both paddled the small skiff out into the deep. No more tears came and no more words as they watched Estcheemah's belongings disappear into the Ocean. The gentle feeling of the swells rocking their skiff somehow comforted them.

"Do it," Liberty said. Lightningbolt's eyes filled with tears as he lifted the urn of Estcheemah's ashes to scatter them into the tide. Accidentally, his hand slipped and he dropped the urn. He grabbed at it, but it tumbled slowly beyond his reach toward the depths.

When the boat touched the beach at Estcheemah's home, Lightningbolt leaped out.

Liberty looked around slowly. "Hey Estcheemah!" she called to the trees. "We will have our Circle."

"We will Honor our Self and Mother Life, Estcheemah!" Lightningbolt said with determination and pride.

Illustration and Photo Credits

All Medicine Belts designed by Hyemeyohsts Storm and illustrated by Red Wolf, Willow LaLand and Black Wolf

All original artwork, with the exception of color plate 7, was designed by Hyemeyohsts Storm and painted or illustrated by the artist specified, under the supervision of art director Red Wolf/John McKeithen. Color Plate 7 was designed by Red Wolf.

Pages viii–ix—Timber Wolf Howling: Lynn and Donna Rodgers.

Between pages xiv and xv—(Plate 1) The Venus Medicine Shield: Design by Hyemeyohsts Storm. Painted by Black Wolf.

Page 3—Little Big Horn Mountains: Photo © Bill Rautio.

Page 4—Treacherous Ice: Photo © David Muench/David Muench Photography.

Page 7—Snow Drifts in Mountains: Photo © Maryanne and George Nolte.

Page 9—Glacier Creek, Alberta Falls: Photo © John Ward.

Page 11—Buck in Snow: Photo © Alan & Sandy Carey.

Page 12—Mountain Hot Pool at Night in Moonlight: Photo © David Muench/David Muench Photography.

Page 13—Fawn and Reflection: Courtesy Department of Library Services, American Museum of Natural History (#106357).

Page 15—Coyote in Snow: from *High West*, Les Blacklock/Blacklock Nature Photography.

Page 18—Owl in Tree: Photo © Alan & Sandy Carey.

Page 20—Mountain Pine Trees: Photo © David Muench/David Muench Photography.

Page 22—Interior of Cabin Looking Out onto Snow-covered Mountains: Photo © Bill Rautio.

Page 23—Mouse: Photo © Ruth and Louis Kirk.

Page 25—Mother Earth from the Moon's Perspective: Design by Hyemeyohsts Storm. Painted by Red Wolf.

Page 26—Space Soldier with Laser Weapon: Jim Burns/Young Artists.

Page 27—Laser Pistol: Design by Hyemeyohsts Storm. Illustrated by Black Wolf.

Page 29—Futuristic Rifle: Design by Hyemeyohsts Storm. Illustrated by Red Wolf.

Pages 30–31—Spaceships Peering Down onto Planet: Tony Roberts/Young Artists.

Page 32—Futuristic Bow and Arrow: Design by Hyemeyohsts Storm. Illustrated by Red Wolf.

Page 34—Old Pawnee Medicine Shield: Field Museum of National History (#A109070).

Page 36—Old Indian Rattle: Courtesy Department of Library Services, American Museum of Natural History (2a-l3764).

Pages 38–39—Feathers: Design by Hyemeyohsts Storm. Illustrated by Black Wolf.

Page 41—Old Crow Shield: Field Museum of Natural History (#A111350).

Page 42—Snowy Creek in Little Big Horn: Photo © David Cavagnaro.

Page 43—Crystalline Snow Flake: Courtesy Department of Library Services, American Museum of Natural History (#2A-3028).

Page 44—Forest in Snow: Photo © David Muench/David Muench Photography.

Page 46—Big Horn Sheep: Photo © Vince Fischer.

Page 48—U Stone: Illustrated by Red Wolf.

Page 50—Cave in the Mountains: Photo © Jay Jorden.

Page 52—.357 Magnum Revolver, Indian Blankets and Belt: Photo © Siegrund Yielding.

Page 56—Old Indian Knife: Design by Hyemeyohsts Storm. Illustrated by Red Wolf.

Page 58—American Soldier WW II, Seen through Explosion: United Nations Photo Collection.

Pages 62–63—Glacier Creek: Photo © John Ward.

Page 66—Mare Nursing Colt: Photo © Catherine J. Bernstein.

Page 67—Old Barn, in Snow: Photo © David Cavagnaro.

Page 69—Red Fox, in Snow: Photo © Alan & Sandy Carey.

Page 72—Farm, in Snow: Photo © Bill Rautio.

Page 73—Native Girl: Photo © Dennis Sanders.

Page 74—Saddle and Bridle on Horse: Courtesy Department of Library Services, American Museum of Natural History (#17755).

Page 78—Northern Cheyenne Playhouse: Photo © Joseph Farber/Georges Borchardt, Inc.

Page 81—House in Very Early Spring: Photo © Patricia Nell Warren.

Page 83—Dumptruck and Land of Montana: Photo © Bill Rautio.

Page 84—Road Stretching into Distance: Photo © Patricia Nell Warren.

Page 87—Horses: Photo © David Cavagnaro.

Page 89—Spring Creek Singers: Photo © Don Doll, S.J.

Page 90—Indian Blankets, Drums, and Cowboy Hat: Photo © Siegrund Yielding.

Page 93—River, Late Spring: Photo © David Muench/David Muench Photography.

Page 94—Wolf Surrounded by Flowers: Photo © Jean Paul Ferraro/Ardea London Limited.

Between pages 96 and 97—(Plate 2) Source Shield: Design by Hyemeyohsts Storm. Painted by Red Wolf.

Page 97—Estcheemah's Medicine Pipe: Design by Hyemeyohsts Storm. Illustrated by Red Wolf.

Page 99—Wagon: Photo © Dennis Sanders.

Page 100—Mandan Pipe: Joslyn Art Museum, Omaha, Nebraska.

Pages 102–103—"Dakota" Pipe: Joslyn Art Museum, Omaha, Nebraska.

Pages 104–105—Simple Pipe: Courtesy Department of Library Services, American Museum of Natural History (#332742).

Page 106—Old Indian Woman: Photo © Joseph Farber/Georges Borchardt, Inc.

Page 107—"Oglala" Shantytown: Photo © Joseph Farber/Georges Borchardt, Inc.

Page 243–Drilling in Tunnel: United Nations Photo Collection.

Page 252–Rose: From *Mandala Gardens*. Photo © Jim McNulty/Amber Lotus.

Page 254–Sunset Over Forest: Photo © David Cavagnaro.

Page 255–Moon Over Water: Photo © Lionel Atwill/Peter Arnold, Inc.

Page 256–Magpie on Fence: Photo © Siegrund Yielding.

Page 257–Creek: Montana and Wyoming: Courtesy Department of Library Services, American Museum of Natural History (#316514).

Page 258–Raccoon: Courtesy Department of Library Services, American Museum of Natural History (#336664).

Page 260–Raccoons in Tree Stump: Courtesy Department of Library Services, American Museum of Natural History (#416629).

Page 261—Crescent Moon Over Creek: Photo © Lynn Thomas.

Page 263—Shield of Wildflowers: Design by Hyemeyohsts Storm. Illustrated by Red Wolf.

Page 265—Shield of the Sun and the Moon: Design by Hyemeyohsts Storm. Illustrated by Snow Bayley.

Page 267—Shield of Hands Counting: Design by Hyemeyohsts Storm. Illustrated by Snow Bayley and Red Wolf.

Page 268—Shield of the Lightning Rose: Design by Hyemeyohsts Storm. Illustrated by Red Wolf.

Page 271—Salmon Jumping: Courtesy Department of Library Services, American Museum of Natural History (#332474).

Page 272—Milk Cow and Calf: Photo © Siegrund Yielding.

Page 275—Helmet: Illustrated by Black Wolf.

Page 277—Choke-cherry Tree: Photo © Siegrund Yielding.

Page 279—Summer Wildflowers in Wyoming: Photo © Siegrund Yielding.

Page 281—Prairie Falcon: Photo © Stephen Krasemann/ DRK Photos.

Page 283—Fleabane: Photo © Les Line.

Pages 286–287—Sky with Big Clouds: Photo © David Cavagnaro.

Page 289—Pine Tree: Courtesy Department of Library Services, American Museum of Natural History (#335420).

Between pages 290 and 291—(Plate 5) Cover Shield: Design by Hyemeyohsts Storm. Painted by Raven Prismon.

Page 291—Silhouetted Insect: Photo © David Cavagnaro.

Between pages 292 and 293—(Plate 6) The Renewal: 21 Shield: Design by Hyemeyohsts Storm. Painted by Red Wolf.

Page 293—Mayan Figure: Illustrated by Ocean Rose.

Pages 294–295—City of Avenues: Photo by Terry Rutledge for *National Geographic* Magazine, Sept. 1987 (National Geographic Society).

Page 296—Birth of a City: Design by Hyemeyohsts Storm. Illustrated by Ocean Rose.

Page 297—Pyramidal Gardens: Design by Swan Storm. Illustrated by Red Wolf.

Page 299—Mayan Wall Carving: from *American Indian Design and Decoration* by Le Roy Appleton (Courtesy Dover Books).

Page 300—Mayan Stone Sculpting of Male Chief: Illustrated by Red Wolf.

Page 303—Drawing of Warrior: Courtesy Department of Library Services, American Museum of Natural History (#118147).

Pages 304–305—Pyramid City: Courtesy Department of Library Services, American Museum of Natural History (#326597).

Page 306—Mayan Procession: Courtesy Department of Library Services, American Museum of Natural History (#118148).

Page 309—Mayan Stone Sculpture: Photo © Justin Kerr.

Between pages 310 and 311—(Plate 7) Mayan Frame of Two Globes of Earth: Designed and painted by Red Wolf.

Page 311—Colored Corn: from *Native America*, Christine Mather & Jack Parsons. Photo © Jack Parsons. Reprinted by permission Crown Publishers, Inc.

Page 313—Mayan Woman Chief: Painting by Red Wolf.

Page 314—Mayan Drawing: Photo by Ian Graham, Copyright © 1977 The President and Fellows of Harvard College.

Page 315—Pyramid: Photo by Maximillien Bruggmann.

Page 317—Wide View of Pueblo Bonito: Photo © David Muench/David Muench Photography.

Pages 318–319—Chaco Canyon Kiva: Photo © Swan Storm.

Page 320—Viking Ship: Illustrated by Red Wolf.

Pages 322–323—Ruins: Photo © Cheryl Woodruff.

Page 324—Arizona's HohoKam City: Photo by Helga Tiewes. Courtesy of Arizona State Museum, University of Arizona.

Page 325—Wheel with Two Guards: Illustrated by Snow Bayley and Red Wolf.

Page 327—Spider, The Creatrix: Jeff Briley, State Museum of History, Oklahoma Historical Society.

Page 329—Aztec God of War: Courtesy Department of Library Services, American Museum of Natural History (#332l05).

Page 331—Three Mayan Figures: Courtesy Department of Library Services, American Museum of Natural History (#329235).

Page 332—Stone Carving of Mayan Army: Peabody Museum, Harvard University. Photo © 1985 President & Fellows of Harvard College.

Page 333—Bee Warrioress Kachinas: Illustrated by Red Wolf.

Pages 334–335—Warrioress and Warrior Kachinas: Illustrated by Red Wolf.

Between pages 336 and 337—(Plate 8) The Moon Shield. Design by Hyemeyohsts Storm. Painted by Willow LaLand.

Page 338—Medicine Wheel of the Five Rules of a Soldier: Illustrated by Ocean Rose.

Page 339—Carving with "Barbed Vine Through the Tongue": Photo © Justin Kerr.

Page 345—Pyramid of the Magician: Courtesy Department of Library Services, American Museum of Natural History (#336167).

Page 347—Archway to the Quadrangle at Uxmal: Courtesy Department of Library Services, American Museum of Natural History (#117492).

Page 349—Turtle Temple (Uxmal): John S. Henderson, from *The World of the Ancient Maya*, copyright 1981 by Cornell University.

Page 350—Goddess of Hope: Illustrated by Snow Bayley.

Page 353—Two Roses: Photo © Jim McNulty/Amber Lotus.

Page 356—Stalk of Grass: Photo © David Cavagnaro.

Page 362—Fence with Flowers: Photo © David Cavagnaro.

Page 363—Hens in a Yard: Photo © Siegrund Yielding.

Page 364—Flowers: Photo © Ruth and Louis Kirk.

Page 365—Small Brook: Photo © Tom Chapin.

Page 367—Old Woman: Courtesy Department of Library Services, American Museum of Natural History (#3l6973).

Page 368—Earth Guardians and Earth Goddess: Illustrated by Ocean Rose and Snow Bayley.

Page 369—Wild Rose: Courtesy Department of Library Services, American Museum of Natural History (#329558).

Page 370—Wild Rose: Photo © David Cavagnaro.

Page 371—Beautiful Rose: Photo © Jim McNulty/Amber Lotus.

Page 373—Beautiful Creek: Photo © Patricia Nell Warren.

Page 374—Water Ripples: Photo © Patricia Nell Warren.

Page 375—Cottonwood Tree: Photo © Patricia Nell Warren.